Expert Performance Indexing in Azure SQL and SQL Server 2022

Toward Faster Results and Lower Maintenance Both on Premises and in the Cloud

Fourth Edition

Edward Pollack
Jason Strate

Apress®

Expert Performance Indexing in Azure SQL and SQL Server 2022: Toward Faster Results and Lower Maintenance Both on Premises and in the Cloud

Edward Pollack
Albany, NY, USA

Jason Strate
Hugo, MN, USA

ISBN-13 (pbk): 978-1-4842-9214-3
https://doi.org/10.1007/978-1-4842-9215-0

ISBN-13 (electronic): 978-1-4842-9215-0

Managing Director, Apress Media LLC: Welmoed Spahr
Acquisitions Editor: Jonathan Gennick
Development Editor: Laura Berendson
Coordinating Editor: Jill Balzano

Cover image designed by Freepik (www.freepik.com)

Distributed to the book trade worldwide by Springer Science+Business Media LLC, 1 New York Plaza, Suite 4600, New York, NY 10004. Phone 1-800-SPRINGER, fax (201) 348-4505, e-mail orders-ny@springer-sbm. com, or visit www.springeronline.com. Apress Media, LLC is a California LLC and the sole member (owner) is Springer Science + Business Media Finance Inc (SSBM Finance Inc). SSBM Finance Inc is a **Delaware** corporation.

For information on translations, please e-mail booktranslations@springernature.com; for reprint, paperback, or audio rights, please e-mail bookpermissions@springernature.com.

Apress titles may be purchased in bulk for academic, corporate, or promotional use. eBook versions and licenses are also available for most titles. For more information, reference our Print and eBook Bulk Sales web page at http://www.apress.com/bulk-sales.

Any source code or other supplementary material referenced by the author in this book is available to readers on GitHub (https://github.com/Apress). For more detailed information, please visit http://www. apress.com/source-code.

Printed on acid-free paper

To my wonderful family: Theresa, Nolan, and Oliver.
Without you, there would be no me.

Table of Contents

About the Authors

Edward Pollack is a Microsoft Data Platform MVP with decades of experience in data, software development, and systems. He has spoken at many events in the SQL Server and data communities; has organized his own SQL Saturday events in Albany, NY, and elsewhere; and supports groups that provide free technical training, such as CanCode Communities. Ed has authored many articles, as well as two Apress books—*Dynamic SQL: Applications, Performance, and Security in Microsoft SQL Server* and *Analytics Optimization with Columnstore Indexes in Microsoft SQL Server: Optimizing OLAP Workloads*—and a chapter in *Expert T-SQL Window Functions in SQL Server*. His first patent was issued in 2021, focused on the compression of geographical data for use by analytic systems.

In his free time, Ed enjoys video games, sci-fi and fantasy, traveling, and baking. He lives in the sometimes-frozen icescape of Albany, NY, with his wife, Theresa, and sons, Nolan and Oliver, and a mountain of (his) video game plushies that help break the fall when tripping on (their) toys.

Jason Strate is a database architect and administrator with more than 15 years of experience. He has been a recipient of Microsoft's Most Valuable Professional designation for SQL Server since July 2009. His experience includes design and implementation of both OLTP and OLAP solutions, as well as assessment and implementation of SQL Server environments for best practices, performance, and high-availability solutions. He is a SQL Server MCITP and participated in the development of Microsoft Certification exams for SQL Server 2008.

Jason is actively involved with his local PASS chapter (SQL Server User Group) and serves as its director of program development. He worked with the board to organize the PASSMN SQL Summit 2009 for the local community. He enjoys helping others in the SQL Server community and does this by presenting at technical conferences and user group meetings. Most recently, he has presented at the SSWUG Virtual Conferences, TechFuse, numerous SQL Saturdays, and PASSMN user group meetings.

Jason is a contributing author for the Microsoft white paper "Empowering Enterprise Solutions with SQL Server 2008 Enterprise Edition." He is an active blogger with a focus on SQL Server and related technologies.

About the Technical Reviewer

Mark Adams has been a senior Oracle database administrator for 26 years. He also has 8 years of concurrent experience as a SQL Server database administrator. His expertise in Oracle Internals has spawned his interest in SQL Server Internals. He earned a bachelor's degree in computer science from Youngstown State University. You can contact Mark at markadamsoracleandsqlserver.wordpress.com.

Acknowledgments

A huge shout-out to the long list of organizers, speakers, colleagues, and volunteers who have supported and advised me over the years and provided opportunities to grow personally and professionally.

Thank you for providing chances to write, speak, and share my perspectives and knowledge when I was young and still stumbling through this world. Those first (and second… and third…) chances are invaluable!

To all of you who helped me arrive at where I am today (you know who you are), thank you!

Introduction

Indexing is a part of database development that is always relevant. Even as technology improves and more automated processes are developed to assist in performance tuning and management, understanding effective indexing will always be a key skill as data and queries grow in size and complexity.

What Is This Book About?

This book discusses indexing from all angles, both entry-level and advanced, describing how indexes can be used to improve performance against many types of data in SQL Server. A full understanding of indexing allows database professionals and developers to architect efficient data structures and write efficient code. This directly leads to faster queries, less usage of computing resources, and ultimately a savings of both time and money.

Expert Performance Indexing in Azure SQL and SQL Server 2022 is structured into three sections overall:

- *Chapters 1-3*: Fundamentals of indexing and index structures

- *Chapters 4-9*: Introduction to indexing different types of data

- *Chapters 9-17*: Effective strategies for creating, maintaining, and fine-tuning indexes

The purpose of this book is to provide enough information that database professionals at any level can become familiar with the indexing features provided by SQL Server 2022 and be able to use those features to improve database performance. Each chapter discusses a single critical component of indexing in SQL Server, providing enough high-level information to be able to quickly make changes to tackle common data challenges.

In addition, advanced features are discussed, allowing for a fuller understanding of how indexes are stored and used in SQL Server. This enables the ability to manage performance against larger and more complex data including columnstore indexes, memory-optimized data, and spatial data.

CHAPTER 1

Index Fundamentals

The goal of this book is to help improve SQL database performance through the use of indexes. To accomplish this, the purpose and use of indexes will be introduced. This will lead to a discussion of how data is stored in indexes, focusing on clustered, non-clustered, and columnstore indexes. We will also explore heaps. Indexing is a key component in any database, whether it is stored on premises or in Azure (or another cloud service).

This chapter provides the building blocks for understanding the logical design of indexes.

Why Build Indexes?

The most important asset any business owns is its data. Databases exist to store that data, and a key piece in providing data is delivering it efficiently. Being able to access data quickly improves the value that the business gains from it. The way to ensure speedy access to data is through the use of effective indexing.

Indexes apply order to data, and that order allows data to be efficiently sorted, filtered, and aggregated. This reduces the time and computing resources required to perform these operations.

The alternative to indexed data is a scenario where it is stored in unordered heaps. A heap is just a table without an index. Without order, SQL Server must scan the entire table to return any data from it. With larger tables, this process is prohibitively expensive. For example, to return one row from an unindexed table that is 1 TB in size would require reading the entire terabyte of data to find the single row that was queried for.

To illustrate this, consider an analogy that is often used to describe indexes—a library. Libraries contain many shelves of books. In a library, the most common task that is performed is finding a book. Most visitors want either a specific book or one that is related to a very limited topic.

1

E. Pollack and J. Strate, *Expert Performance Indexing in Azure SQL and SQL Server 2022*, https://doi.org/10.1007/978-1-4842-9215-0_1

A library with no system for ordering books would be useless to most visitors. The idea of searching through tens of thousands of books by hand one at a time would constitute an absurd amount of work. Libraries use the Dewey Decimal Classification system to organize books by topic and type, using a detailed set of numbers to label them. For example, books about science would be found in the range of 500–599. Mathematics books are limited to the range 510–519, and geometry would be found specifically in 516.

This classification system acts as an index for the library, allowing a visitor looking for a good book on geometry to be able to locate it quickly and efficiently. There is no need to wander around the library looking for books about geometry and no need to read through irrelevant books to find them. The index exists on subject and aligns with the most common search patterns for visitors at a library.

What happens when a search is made for a specific author, rather than a topic? What if there is a need to locate books about Edgar F. Codd? An educated guess could be made that these books would be in a section related to databases or computing. The only way to know for certain, though, would be to manually search through a whole lot of books to eventually find the correct ones.

Libraries solve this using a card catalog or computer. These systems allow for books to be searched by other criteria, such as author, publish date, language, or title. In the preceding example, a search could be made for a book containing a title with the words "Edgar Codd" in it. This is far more efficient than searching through stacks of books on science, mathematics, and computing while hoping for success. This system provides secondary indexes, in addition to the Dewey Decimal System, thus allowing visitors to search for books using a variety of different criteria.

These systems are far more efficient than the alternative of wandering around the library, scanning through endless books. Alternatively, a small enough library does not require a card catalog, the Dewey Decimal System, or a computer. A Little Free Library may contain 10 or 20 books. In this case, scanning the titles of each book takes very little time and is more efficient than trying to use a complex system to organize them.

This analogy is intended to introduce the concept of indexing without an immediate dive into database structures. As indexing is discussed in more detail, the library example will be referenced as a way to anchor the more technical details in this book to a simpler example rooted in everyday life.

Major Index Types

There are a variety of ways to describe indexes and their function. To simplify a discussion of indexes, they will be divided into three categories that will be discussed in this section. Heaps and clustered indexes describe how data in the underlying table structure is stored. Non-clustered indexes are secondary indexes built on top of heaps or clustered indexes that organize data by other columns and then reference the clustered index (or heap) to retrieve additional information. The following provides a brief description of each index type and its significance.

Heap Tables

As mentioned in the library analogy, in a Little Free Library, the books available change often; usually there are only one or two short shelves of books. In these cases, the owner doesn't spend time organizing the books under the Dewey Decimal System. Instead, the books are placed on the shelves as they are acquired. In this case, there is no order to how the books are stored in the library. By default, this is how SQL Server stores data in tables. With no explicit system of order defined, data is stored in an unordered structure called a *heap*.

In a heap, the first row added is the first record in the table, the second row is the second record in the table, the third row is the third record in the table, and so on. A heap is a table with no explicit order defined on its data.

When a table is created without any clustered index, its storage structure is called a *heap*. Rows are inserted into the table in the order in which they are added. Rows are read by scanning all rows in the table in order to find the ones that are needed to satisfy a query.

A clustered index may be added to a table to enforce a data order and remove its status as a heap. Memory-optimized tables are not stored as heaps and are discussed in more detail in Chapter 8.

Note   Many people do not consider heaps to be indexes. In the context of this discussion, they will be treated as indexes since they assist in determining where data is located and how it will be accessed by queries.

Clustered Indexes

In the library analogy, the Dewey Decimal System was used to assign a number to all books in the library. This number allowed books to be sorted and determined where a book was located in the library. The subject of the book, not when it is added, determines the location of the book. This system defines how books are physically stored in the library and is the primary method of searching for books. In a table, the index that provides this functionality is called a *clustered index*.

In a clustered index, one or more columns are selected as the *key columns* for the index. Key columns are used to sort and determine where to store data in the table. Whereas a library places books on the shelves based on their Dewey Decimal number, a clustered index determines the location of rows in a table based on the order of the key columns of the index.

The columns used as the key columns for a clustered index are selected based on the most frequently used method for accessing the records in the table. In a table with states and provinces, the most common method of finding a row in the table would likely be through its abbreviation. In that scenario, using the state/province abbreviation as the key column for the clustered index would be a sensible choice. Oftentimes, the primary key columns in a table will also serve as the clustered index key columns. This is not required, and occasionally there are reasons to have different columns used for the primary key and clustered index.

As with heaps, clustered indexes determine where data is stored in a table. In a clustered index, the non-key columns are stored alongside the key columns. This equates to the clustered index determining the layout of the table itself.

Because it defines the fundamental organization of a table, there may only be a single clustered index on any table at one time.

Non-clustered Indexes

In the library analogy, the Dewey Decimal System was the clustered index that defined order within the bookshelves based on the subject of each book. Despite the usefulness of that system, visitors often want to search for books using other criteria, such as author, title, or age level. If the book's subject matter is not known, then the Dewey Decimal System provides no help in locating it.

- Libraries solve this problem with computers and card catalogs. These provide a place where books can be cross-referenced using other common details, such as author or title. These solutions are analogous to non-clustered indexes within a database.

Note   Because heaps provide no data order, non-clustered indexes are generally created against clustered indexes and not on top of heaps.

Non-clustered indexes are secondary indexes that are created on top of an existing clustered index (or heap). In a non-clustered index, columns are selected and sorted based on their values. These columns contain a reference to the heap or clustered index location of the data they reference. This is similar to how a card catalog works in a library. The order of books on the shelves is static, but additional shortcuts are created so that they can be quickly located using other search criteria.

For example, a table containing states and provinces that is ordered by the state name may also contain their country, language, or other details. There are many legitimate reasons to search this table based on those other criteria, and a non-clustered index allows a lengthy territory list to be searched quickly based on other details besides the state abbreviation or name.

Unlike clustered indexes and heaps, a table may contain many non-clustered indexes. While there can technically be as many as 999 non-clustered indexes defined on a table, it would be challenging to concoct a practical example of a table with hundreds of indexes on it. Multiple non-clustered indexes allow data to be searched in multiple ways, in addition to the clustered index. While a table can contain many indexes, each one should service a legitimate use case. Indexes require storage and maintenance, and therefore creating too many can be an unnecessary burden on SQL Server.

Other Index Types

Within the realm of clustered indexes, non-clustered indexes, and heaps are a wide variety of index types, each of which assists in searching for different types of data. The library card catalog example thus far focused on the experience of a visitor searching for a book, but there are many other scenarios that would require different organizational structures in order to resolve.

Consider the following library information requests:

- Report on counts of books by subject across all libraries.

- Search for specific text across all books in a library.

- Map out the geographic origin of all books in a library.

While quite useful, a card catalog would not be capable of solving these problems. The same is true in SQL Server, and therefore a variety of indexes exist to solve different data access needs. The following are brief overviews of different index types. Later chapters in this book will provide details on their function and use.

Columnstore Indexes

The details associated with a library book, whether stored in a card catalog or a computer, are all stored together. A single entry contains everything you ever wanted to know about a book. This is effective when the goal is to find a single book or a small set of books.

When trying to understand books at a higher level, this system stops being efficient. For example, consider a librarian who would like to count how many books exist in a library per subject. Looking up books one at a time would be slow. Even an automated process would be sluggish as it would need to sort through all data on all books in order to retrieve their subjects and increment the overall counts.

Solving this challenge would require an alternate way of storing data that maintains a list of subjects that contains some basic statistics and links to all books within each subject. This solution is analogous to columnstore indexes, which create a structure that organizes data by column, rather than by row.

In a columnstore index, rows are grouped together and each column's data compressed and stored separately. In a structure like this, queries that require data for few columns across many rows can perform efficiently as there is no longer a need to read all details of each row. Columnstore indexes exist as a solution to analytic data requests and assist in reporting, analytics, and data science.

For the remainder of this book, indexes will be classified as rowstore or columnstore, when applicable. Rowstore indexes store all details of a row together sequentially. Rowstore indexes are ideal for transactional data processing, as is typically seen in the day-to-day use of software applications. Columnstore indexes are built for analytic data processing, which is typically seen in data warehouses, reporting, and projects involving data science and machine learning.

The benefit of this type of index is that only the columns and rows required for a query need to be read. In data warehousing scenarios, often less than 15 percent of the columns in an index are needed for the results of a query.[1]

Columnstore indexes may be clustered or non-clustered. Clustered columnstore indexes are unordered and include every column in the table. In this case, the columnstore index becomes the fundamental storage structure for a table. Non-clustered columnstore indexes target specific columns in a table and will allow for analytics to occur over any columns in that index. They are ordered by the underlying order of the clustered rowstore index.

Columnstore indexes tend to compress very effectively. This is because values for a single column will be far more repetitive than values across many different columns. Therefore, columnstore compression will generally see compression ratios that are far greater than standard row or page compression. Consuming less storage means that less memory is required when executing queries, ultimately leading to faster results.

Because of their structure, columnstore indexes provide significant value for data warehousing and other analytic solutions. Columnstore indexes will be discussed in greater detail later in this book.

JSON and XML Indexes

Consider a need to search the table of contents for all books in a library. A table of contents provides a hierarchical view of a book. There are chapters that outline the main sections for the book, followed by subchapter headings that provide additional details for each chapter. This relationship model is similar to how XML documents are designed; there are nodes and a relationship between them that defines the structure of that information.

As with the card catalog analogy earlier, it would not be efficient to look through every book in the library to find those that contain chapters about Edgar Codd. Similarly, finding chapters written by Edgar Codd or that include information about him would be a difficult task without some better way to accomplish it.

One method of solving this problem would be to make a list of every book in the library and for each one a list all of its chapters. Within each chapter entry could be tags or keywords related to its contents. This provides the same benefit that a card catalog

---

[1]www.red-gate.com/simple-talk/wp-content/uploads/2013/07/Columnstore-Indexes-for-Fast-DW-QP-SQL-Server-11.pdf

provides, but for some less standard and less structured information. It doesn't matter how many chapters a book has or how many subjects are contained within each; this chapter list would list as many or as few as exist in each book.

In a database, this is what *XML indexes* and indexing JavaScript Object Notation (JSON) can accomplish.

For every node in an XML document, an entry is made in the XML index. This information is persisted in internal tables that SQL Server can use to determine whether the XML document contains the data that is being queried. Similarly with JSON, the values to index are materialized with an index on a calculated column.

Creating and maintaining XML indexes can be quite costly. Every time the index is updated, it needs to shred all the nodes of the XML document into the XML index. The larger the XML document is, the more costly this process will be. However, if data in an XML column will be queried often, the cost of creating and maintaining an XML index will be offset by removing the need to shred all the XML documents at runtime.

Spatial Indexes

Every library has maps. Some maps cover the oceans; others are for continents, countries, states, or cities. Many different kinds of maps can be found in a library, of which there could be multiple types that target the same area. There are two basic challenges that exist with all maps:

- Which maps overlap or include the same locations or information in each?

- Which books are published at or take place in a given location?

Retrieving all maps that contain the city of Minneapolis or retrieving a list of all books that were published within 25 miles of Minneapolis would be difficult questions to answer without a system built to assist with them.

Databases traditionally are not built to answer questions like these. Tables represent entities, and different entities can be related using joins, but ultimately these relationships are one-dimensional in nature. In the physical world, data often exists in more than one dimension. Maps are two-dimensional, and buildings and floor plans are three-dimensional. To solve this problem, SQL Server provides the capabilities for *spatial indexes*.

Spatial indexes dissect the spatial information that is provided into a four-level representation of the data. This representation allows SQL Server to plot out the spatial information, both geometry and geography. This data structure can then be used to determine where rows overlap and the proximity of one point to another point.

There are a few restrictions that exist with spatial indexes. The main one is that spatial indexes must be created on tables that have primary keys. Without a primary key, the spatial index creation will not succeed. Additionally, when creating spatial indexes, they are restricted from using parallel processing; and only a single spatial index can be built on a table at a time, which impacts the speed in which they can be created. Also, spatial indexes cannot be used on indexed views. These and other restrictions are covered in Chapter 7.

Similar to XML indexes, spatial indexes have up-front and maintenance costs associated with their sizes. The benefit is that when spatial data needs to be queried, the value of the spatial index can be quickly realized. As with all indexes, their primary purpose is to speed up reading data, whereas the cost is in creating and maintaining the index. Spatial indexes will be discussed in more depth in Chapter 7.

Hash and Range Indexes

As books come into the library, sometimes the frequency in which they are returned exceeds the rate in which they are placed back into the stacks. It takes time to sort the books and put them where they go. At these times, a librarian is often there keeping track of what is returned. For these books, the librarian can often remember which books are where in the queue of returned books and get the book you want without the use of the card catalog. This is in essence what memory-optimized tables do with hash and range indexes. The only difference is that with hash and range indexes, millions of rows, or books, can be kept in memory without needing to rely on disk-based structures to support them.

A hash index allows a memory-optimized table to provide precise point lookups of data within the table. Using the library analogy, the index (a.k.a. the librarian) can remember exactly where the book is in the table and index each time it is needed.

Alternatively, a range index provides memory-optimized tables with the capability to efficiently identify ranges of items. For instance, if the index, or librarian, needed all the books returned between 8:00 a.m. and 12:00 p.m., the index would be able to scan across the rows efficiently instead of accessing rows one by one.

Hash and range indexes are only allowed on memory-optimized tables. The reference to remembering where the books are is really what is different about hash and range indexes over other index types. Between disk and memory, the structure of a clustered index is relatively unchanged. With hash and range indexes, the structure is designed specifically for fast memory access and leverages disk solely to support transactional consistency and the ability to rebuild the index in memory when the database is brought online.

Full-Text Search

The last scenario to consider is the idea of finding specific terms within books. Card catalogs do a great job of providing basic book information such as author, title, or subject. The subject of a book isn't the only keyword you may want to use to search for books, though. At the back of many books are keyword indexes to help you find other subjects within a book. When this book is completed, there will be an index, and it will provide the ability to look up a keyword and identify which pages it appears on, if it is in the book at all.

Consider a library in which every book has a keyword index. If all of those keywords were added to their own card catalog, then a visitor would be able to find every book in the library that contains a specific keyword. In addition, they would know exactly where in each book the keyword is referenced. This is a broad overview of what a full-text index is and how it works, with the fundamental difference that a full-text index in SQL Server will index and search most words, whereas an index in a book will only index a smaller set of keywords that are most relevant to the reader.

Index Variations

The discussion thus far has covered different types of indexes and how they can help in searching through different types of data. There are a variety of ways in which indexes can be created, and each provides slightly different functionality. Some not only index data but allow for business rules to be directly enforced on the underlying data while potentially improving index performance.

Primary Key

In the library analogy, Dewey Decimal numbers were a valuable way to organize books by subject, allowing for books on a specific topic to be quickly and efficiently found. Dewey Decimal numbers are not unique to a book, though, and many books may share the same number. The Dewey Decimal number may be viewed as a clustered index for books in a library. Similarly, titles, authors, publication date, and other details are all repeated across many books.

To meaningfully manage a library, there must be some unique number that identifies each book and is never repeated. In a library, books are uniquely identified by their ISBN (International Standard Book Number) such that no two books share the same ISBN.

In a database, the primary key uniquely identifies a row in the table. No two rows in a table are allowed to have the same primary key value. Typically, a primary key will be created on a single column, though it can be composed of multiple columns when the need arises.

Because a primary key is a unique value explicitly defined for every row in a table, it cannot be NULL. In addition, a table may only have a single primary key defined on it at a time. To maintain uniqueness, a primary key must be built alongside an index, which may be clustered or non-clustered. Primary keys are typically built on a table's clustered index, though rare use cases may necessitate separate columns for the primary key and clustered index. More information on this is included in Chapter 11.

Unique Index

There may be more than a single column or set of columns that can be used to uniquely identify a row in a table. When the need arises to define multiple ways to uniquely identify rows, unique indexes may be used.

A unique index is a separate entity from a primary key and may be defined as either clustered or non-clustered. A table may contain multiple unique indexes, though it may still only have one clustered index and one primary key.

Similar to the primary key, a unique index is constrained so that values may not be repeated within the index. It provides a mechanism to uniquely identify rows in a table and can be created across a single column or multiple columns.

One notable difference between a primary key and a unique index is that NULL is allowed in a unique index, whereas a primary key must be defined on NOT NULL columns. A NULL value is considered a discrete value and therefore may not be repeated in the same way that non-NULL values may not be repeated.

Included Columns

Suppose there was a need to find all books in a library written by Douglas Adams and how many pages are in each book. The simplest solution is to look up each book in the card catalog one by one, locate each book, and check how many pages are in it. While simple, this is tedious and relies on a heavily manual process to get results.

An ideal solution would be to either include the page count in the card catalog or have a separate list of books with page counts included. Either would provide a solution whereby page counts could be quickly retrieved without having to actually locate any of the books. When it comes to indexing, including information outside of the indexed columns is done through *included columns*.

When a non-clustered index is built, there is an option to add included columns into the index. These columns are stored as unsorted data alongside the key columns in the index. Included columns cannot include any columns that have already been used in the initial sorted column list of the index.

In terms of querying, included columns allow users to look up information outside the sorted columns. If everything they need for the query is found in the key and included columns, the query does not need to access the table's heap or clustered index to return query results. Similar to the card catalog example, included columns can significantly improve the performance of a query when a similar column list is requested each time.

Partitioned Indexes

Books that include a lot of data can get fairly large. Consider a dictionary or the complete works of William Shakespeare. These are exceptionally large books that would be impractical to publish in a single volume. A 20,000-page book is simply too large to physically publish. In addition, the ability for a person to read (or even simply reference) a book that large would be quite challenging. Books can get large enough that the idea of containing them in a single volume just isn't practical. The best example of this is an encyclopedia.

It is rare that an encyclopedia is contained in a single book. The size of the book and the width of the binding would be beyond the ability of anyone to manage. Also, the time it takes to find all the subjects in the encyclopedia that start with the letter *S* is greatly improved because you can go directly to the S volume instead of paging through an enormous book to find where they start.

This problem isn't limited to books. Tables and their indexes can get to a point where their size makes it difficult to continue to maintain them using a reasonable amount of time and resources. Similarly, if the table has millions or billions of rows, being able to scan across limited portions of the table vs. the entire table can provide significant performance improvements. To solve this problem on a table, indexes can be partitioned.

Partitioning can occur on both clustered and non-clustered indexes. It allows an index to be split along the values supplied by a function. By doing this, the data in the index is physically separated into multiple partitions, while the index itself is still a single logical object.

Filtered Indexes

By default, non-clustered indexes contain one record in them for every row in the table for which the index is associated. In most cases, this is ideal and provides the index an opportunity to assist in selectivity for any value in the column. For the purposes of this discussion, selectivity is a measure of how many rows in a table meet a given filter criteria.

There are situations when including all records in a table in an index is less than ideal. For instance, the set of values most often queried may represent a small number of rows in a table. In this case, limiting the rows in the index will reduce the amount of work a query needs to perform, resulting in an improvement in the performance of the query. Another could be where the selectivity of a value is low compared with the number of rows in the table. This could be an active status or shipped Boolean values; indexing on these values wouldn't drastically improve performance, but filtering to just those records would provide a significant opportunity for query improvement.

To assist in these scenarios, non-clustered indexes can be filtered to reduce the number of records they contain. When the index is built, it can be defined to include or exclude records based on a simple comparison that reduces the size of the index.

Besides the performance improvements outlined, there are other benefits to using filtered indexes. The first improvement is reduced storage cost. Since filtered indexes have fewer rows in them (because of the filtering), there will be less data in the index, which requires less storage space. Less storage usage also means that less memory is consumed when the index is read into memory. Another benefit is reduced maintenance cost. Smaller indexes require less time and resources to reorganize and rebuild.

Compression and Indexing

Today's libraries have a lot of books in them. As the number of books increases, there is a point where it becomes more difficult to manage the library with the existing staff and resources. Because of this, there are a number of ways that libraries find to store books, or the information within them, to allow better management without increasing the resources required to maintain the library. As an example, books can be stored electronically. This reduces the space consumed by physical books in the library while allowing for a streamlined checkout/return process.

Similarly, indexes can reach the point of becoming difficult to manage when they become too large. Also, the time required to access the records can increase beyond acceptable levels. There are two types of compression available in SQL Server: row-level and page-level compression.

With *row-level compression*, an index compresses each record at the row level. When row-level compression is enabled, a number of changes are made to each record. The metadata for the row is stored in an alternative format that decreases the amount of information stored in each column. The main changes to the records are numerical data changes from fixed to variable length and blank spaces at the end of fixed-length string data types that are not stored. Another change is that null or zero values do not require any space to be stored. This incurs some overhead to manage the compressed data. Therefore, blindly applying row-level compression to tables is not an optimal decision, and care must be taken to target rows that will compress well.

Page-level compression applies compression across all rows stored on a page, instead of compressing each row individually. When page-level compression is enabled, similarities between string values in columns are identified and compressed. This will be discussed in detail in Chapter 13.

With both row-level and page-level compressions, there are some important details to consider. Compressing a record takes additional CPU time. Although the row will take up less storage and memory (when read), the CPU is the primary resource used to manage the compression task before it can be stored. Depending on the content of the table that is to be compressed, the effectiveness of that compression will vary.

Index Data Definition Language

Similar to the richness in types and variations of indexes available in SQL Server, there is also a rich data definition language (DDL) that surrounds building indexes. In this section, the DDL for building indexes will be examined. First, the CREATE statement and its options will be discussed and paired with the concepts discussed previously in this chapter.

For the sake of brevity, the backward compatibility features of the index DDL will not be explored. The details of which syntax is available in each version of SQL Server are thoroughly documented in Microsoft's Create Index documentation. This book is written using syntax compatible with SQL Server 2022. While most of the Transact-SQL (T-SQL) included will work in any modern version of SQL Server, there is value in verifying and testing those details before attempting to release new code to a production environment.

More specific indexing implementations, such as XML, spatial, and full-text indexes, will be explored in later chapters of this book.

Creating an Index

Before an index can exist within your database, it must first be created. This is accomplished with the CREATE INDEX syntax shown in Listing 1-1. As the syntax illustrates, most of the index types and variations previously discussed are available through the basic syntax.

Listing 1-1. CREATE INDEX Syntax

```
CREATE [ UNIQUE ] [ CLUSTERED | NONCLUSTERED ] INDEX index_name
    ON <object> ( column [ ASC | DESC ] [ ,...n ] )
    [ INCLUDE ( column_name [ ,...n ] ) ]
    [ WHERE <filter_predicate> ]
    [ WITH ( <relational_index_option> [ ,...n ] ) ]
```

```
    [ ON { partition_scheme_name ( column_name )
        | filegroup_name
        | default
        }
    ]
    [ FILESTREAM_ON { filestream_filegroup_name | partition_scheme_name |
    "NULL" } ]
[ ; ]
```

The choice between CLUSTERED and NONCLUSTERED indexing determines whether an index will be built as one of those two basic types. Excluding either of these types will default the index to non-clustered.

The UNIQUE keyword determines if index values must be unique or not. Including it within the CREATE INDEX syntax will make the index unique. The syntax for creating an index as a primary key will be included later in this chapter.

The <object> option determines the base object over which the index will be built. The syntax allows for indexes to be created on either tables or views. The specification of the object can include the database name and schema name, if needed.

After specifying the object for the index, the sorted columns of an index are listed in the order by which they will be sorted and used by the index. These columns are referred to as the *key columns*. Each column can appear in the index only a single time. By default, the columns will be sorted in the index in ascending order, but descending order can be specified if needed. An index can include up to 32 columns as part of the index key with a total size not to exceed 1,700 bytes. Prior to SQL Server 2016, it was limited to 16 columns and 900 bytes.

As an option, included columns can be specified on any non-clustered index, which are added after the key columns for the index. Included columns are not sorted; therefore, a sort order cannot be specified when adding included columns to an index. Between the key and non-key columns, there can be up to 1,023 columns in an index. The size restriction on the key columns does not affect included columns.

If an index will be filtered, the filter definition is specified next. The filtering criteria are added to an index using a WHERE clause. The WHERE clause can use any of the following comparisons: IS , IS NOT , = , <> , != , > , >= , !> , < , <= , and !<. A filtered index cannot use comparisons against a computed column, a user-defined type (UDT) column, a spatial data type column, or a HierarchyID data type column.

Many options are available when creating an index. In Listing 1-1, there is a segment for adding index options, noted by the tag `<relational_index_option>`. These index options control how indexes are created and how they will function in a variety of scenarios. Listing 1-2 provides the DDL for the options available for CREATE INDEX.

Listing 1-2. CREATE INDEX Options

```
PAD_INDEX = { ON | OFF }
 | FILLFACTOR = fillfactor
 | SORT_IN_TEMPDB = { ON | OFF }
 | IGNORE_DUP_KEY = { ON | OFF }
 | STATISTICS_NORECOMPUTE = { ON | OFF }
 | STATISTICS_INCREMENTAL = { ON | OFF }
 | DROP_EXISTING = { ON | OFF }
 | ONLINE = { ON | OFF }
 | RESUMABLE = {ON | OF }
 | MAX_DURATION = <time> [MINUTES]
 | ALLOW_ROW_LOCKS = { ON | OFF }
 | ALLOW_PAGE_LOCKS = { ON | OFF }
 | MAXDOP = max_degree_of_parallelism
 | DATA_COMPRESSION = { NONE | ROW | PAGE}
   [ ON PARTITIONS ( { <partition_number_expression> | <range> }
   [ , ...n ] ) ]
```

Each of the options allows for different levels of control on the index creation process. Options with defaults indicate the default option by underlining it. It is worthwhile to use the default options when working with indexes unless there is a specific use case that necessitates altering them. Table 1-1 lists the options available for CREATE INDEX. In later chapters, examples will be provided along with strategies for applying them. Further information on the CREATE INDEX syntax and examples of its use can be found in SQL Docs for SQL Server.

Table 1-1. *CREATE INDEX Syntax Options*

Option Name	Description
FILLFACTOR	Defines the amount of empty space to leave in each data page of an index when it is created. This is applied only at the time an index is created or rebuilt.
PAD_INDEX	Specifies whether the FILLFACTOR for the index should be applied to the nonleaf data pages for the index. The PAD_INDEX option is used when data manipulation language (DML) operations that lead to excessive nonleaf-level page splitting need to be mitigated.
SORT_IN_TEMPDB	Determines whether to store temporary results from building the index in the tempdb database. This option will increase the amount of space required.
IGNORE_DUP_KEY	Changes the behavior when duplicate keys are encountered when performing inserts into a table. When enabled, rows violating the key constraint will fail. When the default behavior is disabled, the entire insert will fail.
STATISTICS_NORECOMPUTE	Specifies whether any statistics related to the index should be recreated when the index is created.
STATISTICS_INCREMENTAL	Specifies whether statistics collected for the index should be created on the index as a whole or per partition.
DROP_EXISTING	Determines the behavior when an index of the same name on the table already exists. By default, when OFF, the index creation will fail. When set to ON, the index creation will replace the existing index.
ONLINE	Determines whether a table and its indexes are available for queries and data modification during index operations. When enabled, locking is minimized, and an intent shared is the primary lock held during index creation. When disabled, the locking will prevent data modifications to the index and underlying table for the duration of the operation. ONLINE is an Enterprise Edition–only feature until SQL Server 2016 Service Pack 1.

(continued)

Table 1-1. (*continued*)

Option Name	Description
RESUMABLE	Identifies whether an indexing operation will be resumable. New as of SQL Server 2019.
MAX_DURATION	Determines the maximum number of minutes for a resumable indexing operation to execute until pausing. New as of SQL Server 2019.
ALLOW_ROW_LOCKS	Determines whether row locks are allowed on an index. By default, they are allowed.
ALLOW_PAGE_LOCKS	Determines whether page locks are allowed on an index. By default, they are allowed.
MAXDOP	Overrides the server-level maximum degree of parallelism during the index operation. The setting determines the maximum number of processors that an index can utilize during an index operation.
DATA_COMPRESSION	Determines the type of data compression to use on the index. By default, no compression is enabled. With this, either the page- or row-level compression type may be specified.

To demonstrate the CREATE INDEX syntax, an index will be built on the table *Sales.SalesOrderDetail* in *AdventureWorks2017*. The key column for the index is *ProductID* with the columns *OrderQty* and *UnitPrice* included as non-key columns. Additionally, the index will be PAGE compressed. The code in Listing 1-3 builds this index.

Listing 1-3. CREATE INDEX Example

```
USE AdventureWorks2017;
GO

CREATE INDEX IX_Sales_SalesOrderDetail_ProductID
ON Sales.SalesOrderDetail (ProductID)
INCLUDE (OrderQty, UnitPrice)
WITH (DATA_COMPRESSION = PAGE);
```

Altering an Index

After an index has been created, there will sometimes be a need to modify the index.
Altering an index is the way in which an index rebuild or reorganization can be executed
as part of ongoing index maintenance. In addition, altering an index allows for some
index options to be adjusted, such as the compression type.

To modify an index, the ALTER INDEX syntax is used. Listing 1-4 shows the basic
syntax for altering an index.

Listing 1-4. ALTER INDEX Syntax

```
ALTER INDEX { index_name | ALL }
 ON <object>
 { REBUILD
   [ [PARTITION = ALL] [ WITH ( <rebuild_index_option> [ ,...n ] ) ]
   | [ PARTITION = partition_number [ WITH ( <single_partition_rebuild_
   index_option> [ ,...n ] ) ] ] ]
 | DISABLE
 | REORGANIZE
       [ PARTITION = partition_number ]
       [ WITH ( LOB_COMPACTION = { ON | OFF } ) ]
 | SET ( <set_index_option> [ ,...n ] )
 | RESUME [WITH (<resumable_index_options>,[...n])]
 | PAUSE
 | ABORT
   } [ ; ]
```

When using the ALTER INDEX syntax for index maintenance, there are two options
in the syntax that can be used. These options are REBUILD and REORGANIZE. The REBUILD
option recreates the index using the existing index structure and options. It can also be
used to enable a disabled index. The REORGANIZE option re-sorts the leaf-level pages of
an index. This is similar to reshuffling the cards in a deck to get them back in sequential
order. Both of these options will be discussed more thoroughly in Chapter 11.

Additionally, the ALTER INDEX syntax can be used to disable an index. This is
accomplished through the DISABLE option under the ALTER INDEX syntax. A disabled
index will not be used or made available by the database engine. After an index is
disabled, it can be reenabled only by altering the index again with the REBUILD option.

Beyond those functions, many of the index options available through the CREATE INDEX syntax are also available with the ALTER INDEX syntax. The ALTER INDEX syntax can be used to modify the compression of an index. It can also be used to change the fill factor or the pad index setting. Depending on the needs of a given index, this syntax can be used to change any of the available options, though there are some limitations with how the options are used. When REBUILD ALL partitions is used on an index, all of the same options that were available with the CREATE INDEX syntax can be modified, as shown in Listing 1-5. However, when a single partition is targeted with a REBUILD operation, the list of options available is greatly reduced, as shown in Listing 1-6. This is because some index properties are universal and apply to an entire index, whereas others can be defined on a partition-by-partition basis.

Listing 1-5. ALTER INDEX Rebuild Options

```
PAD_INDEX = { ON | OFF }
 | FILLFACTOR = fillfactor
 | SORT_IN_TEMPDB = { ON | OFF }
 | IGNORE_DUP_KEY = { ON | OFF }
 | STATISTICS_NORECOMPUTE = { ON | OFF }
 | STATISTICS_INCREMENTAL = { ON | OFF }
 | ONLINE = { ON [ ( <low_priority_lock_wait> ) ] | OFF }
 | RESUMABLE = { ON | OFF }
 | MAX_DURATION = <time> [MINUTES}
 | ALLOW_ROW_LOCKS = { ON | OFF }
 | ALLOW_PAGE_LOCKS = { ON | OFF }
 | MAXDOP = max_degree_of_parallelism
| DATA_COMPRESSION = { NONE | ROW | PAGE }
    [ ON PARTITIONS ( {<partition_number> [ TO <partition_number>] }
    [ , ...n ] ) ]
```

Listing 1-6. ALTER INDEX Single-Partition Rebuild Options

```
SORT_IN_TEMPDB = { ON | OFF }
 | MAXDOP = max_degree_of_parallelism
 | RESUMABLE = { ON | OFF }
```

```
| MAX_DURATION = <time> [MINUTES}
| DATA_COMPRESSION = { NONE | ROW | PAGE } }
| ONLINE = { ON [ ( <low_priority_lock_wait> ) ] | OFF }
```

For REORGANIZE, the options for ALTER INDEX are limited to LOB_COMPACTION, shown in Listing 1-7. When LOB_COMPACTION is set to ON, the reorganization will attempt to compact large object (LOB) pages, allowing space within the index associated with these pages to be reduced and released. Without this option, the reorganization will not release these pages.

Listing 1-7. ALTER INDEX Reorganize Options

```
LOB_COMPACTION = { ON | OFF }
```

Like the CREATE INDEX syntax, starting with SQL Server 2019, it is possible to resume ALTER INDEX statements. Listing 1-8 shows that for the ALTER INDEX syntax, the options available are similar to CREATE INDEX with the exception of the inclusion of the low-priority lock wait.

Listing 1-8. ALTER INDEX Resumable Options

```
MAXDOP = max_degree_of_parallelism
 | MAX_DURATION =<time> [MINUTES]
 | <low_priority_lock_wait>
```

The low-priority lock wait provides the ALTER INDEX syntax with the ability to predefine how it will behave when blocked by a SCH-M lock, shown in Listing 1-9. This is supported on REBUILD, REORGANIZE, and resumable options. This option allows the ALTER INDEX to terminate its own or other transactions that are blocking the ALTER INDEX operation after a set amount of time. This can be useful when there is a queue of ALTER INDEX statements waiting to execute and one of them gets held up by another transaction.

Listing 1-9. ALTER INDEX Low-Priority Lock Wait Options

```
WAIT_AT_LOW_PRIORITY ( MAX_DURATION = <time> [ MINUTES ] ,
 ABORT_AFTER_WAIT = { NONE | SELF | BLOCKERS } )
```

There is one type of index modification that is not possible with the ALTER INDEX syntax. When altering an index, the key and included columns cannot be changed. If there is a need to change the key or included columns in an index, then a new index needs to be created and the old one dropped.

As an example of the ALTER INDEX syntax, the index built in the last section will be disabled. Using the script in Listing 1-10, the index is disabled. While disabled, the index exists solely as metadata, without the underlying data structure. For more information on the ALTER INDEX syntax and examples of its use, it can be searched for in SQL Docs.

Listing 1-10. ALTER INDEX Example

```
USE AdventureWorks2017;
GO

ALTER INDEX IX_Sales_SalesOrderDetail_ProductID
ON Sales.SalesOrderDetail
DISABLE;
```

Dropping an Index

There will be times when an index is no longer needed. This may be due to changing usage patterns of the database, or perhaps the index is similar enough to another index that maintaining both is not necessary.

To *drop*, or remove, an index, the DROP INDEX syntax may be used. This syntax includes the name of the index and the table/view that the index is built against. Listing 1-11 shows the syntax for dropping an index. Starting with SQL Server 2016, the DROP INDEX syntax supports the IF EXISTS clause, allowing indexes to be dropped without first verifying that they exist.

Listing 1-11. DROP INDEX Syntax

```
DROP INDEX [ IF EXISTS ]
      index_name ON <object>
   [ WITH ( <drop_clustered_index_option> [ ,...n ] ) ]
```

Besides dropping an index, there are additional options that can be added, if needed. These options primarily apply to dropping clustered indexes. Listing 1-12 details the options available for use with a DROP INDEX operation.

Listing 1-12. DROP INDEX Options

```
  MAXDOP = max_degree_of_parallelism
  | ONLINE = { ON | OFF }
| MOVE TO { partition_scheme_name ( column_name )
          | filegroup_name
          | "default"
          }
[ FILESTREAM_ON { partition_scheme_name
          | filestream_filegroup_name
          | "default" } ]
```

When a clustered index is dropped, the base structure of the table will change from a clustered index to a heap. When built, a clustered index defines where the data for a table is stored. When changing from a clustered index to a heap, the target location of the new heap structure must be specified. If the location is anywhere other than the default filegroup, it will need to be specified. The location for the heap can be a single filegroup or defined by a partitioning scheme. This information is set through the MOVE TO option. Along with the data location, the FILESTREAM location may also be adjusted using these options.

The performance impact of the drop index operation may be something that needs to be considered. Because of this, there are options in the DROP INDEX syntax to specify the maximum number of processors to utilize along with whether the operation should be completed online. Both of these options function similarly to those in the CREATE INDEX syntax.

To remove the index used in the last two sections, we can use the code in Listing 1-13 to drop the index. More information on the DROP INDEX syntax and examples of its use can be found in Microsoft's online docs.

Listing 1-13. DROP INDEX Example

```
USE AdventureWorks2017;
GO
DROP INDEX IX_Sales_SalesOrderDetail_ProductID ON Sales.SalesOrderDetail;
```

Index Metadata

Before delving into indexing strategies, it is important to understand the index-related information available in SQL Server. All details of an index and how it was built are stored in system views. All user and system databases contain these catalog views, and only indexes that are unique to each database in which they are queried will be returned.

These views are incredibly useful and provide a detailed accounting of index metadata that is not as conveniently available elsewhere.

sys.indexes

The sys.indexes catalog view provides information on each index in a database. For every table, index, or table-valued function, there is one row within the catalog view. This provides a full accounting of all indexes in a database.

The information in sys.indexes is extensive and can answer many basic questions about an index including its type, options, filter, and more. This metadata can indicate if an index is clustered or non-clustered, its fill factor, filter definition, if it is unique, and so on.

sys.index_columns

The sys.index_columns catalog view lists the columns included in each index. For each key and included column that is a part of an index, there is one row in this catalog view. The sequence of key columns is provided in addition to the sort order of each column. This view can be used to locate duplicate indexes or determine if an index functionally overlaps another index.

sys.index_resumable_operations

The sys.index_resumable_operations catalog view lists the execution status for resumable index rebuilds. For each index rebuild that is paused or currently executing, there is a record in this catalog view. The view describes the DDL for the resumable index rebuild operation and provides a state to identify if it is running or paused.

sys.xml_indexes

The catalog view sys.xml_indexes is similar to sys.indexes. This catalog view returns one row per XML index in a database. The chief difference with this catalog view is that it also provides some information that is unique to XML indexes. The view includes information on whether the XML index is a primary or secondary XML index. If the XML index is a secondary XML index, the view includes a type for the secondary index.

sys.selective_xml_index_paths

The sys.selective_xml_index_paths catalog view is a subset of the indexes in sys.indexes, which contains only selective XML indexes. For each selective XML created for an XPath, there is one entry in this catalog view. Selective XML indexes allow for an XML index to be created over a subset of an XML document and can save significant space and improve query performance when accessing XML data. This is discussed in detail in Chapter 6.

sys.selective_xml_index_namespaces

The sys.selective_xml_index_namespaces catalog view identifies the namespace associated with selective XML indexes. For each namespace associated with an XML index, there is an entry in this catalog view identifying the namespace and indicating if it is the default.

sys.spatial_indexes

The sys.spatial_indexes catalog view is also similar to sys.indexes. This catalog view returns one row for every spatial index in a database. The main difference with this catalog view is that it provides additional information specific to spatial indexes. The view includes information on whether the spatial index is a geometric or geographic index.

sys.spatial_index_tessellations

The sys.spatial_index_tessellations catalog view augments the sys.spatial_indexes catalog view and provides details on the bounding boxes and grids associated with a spatial index.

sys.column_store_dictionaries

The sys.column_store_dictionaries catalog view supports columnstore indexes. This catalog view returns one row for each dictionary used in a columnstore index. A column may have more than one dictionary defined on it, depending on its data profile and the partitioning details of the table. This metadata describes the structure and type of dictionary built for the column.

sys.column_store_segments

The sys.column_store_segments catalog view supports columnstore indexes by returning at least one row for every column in a columnstore index. Columns can have multiple segments of approximately 1 million rows each. The rows in this catalog view describe the contents of each segment (e.g., whether the segment has null values and what the minimum and maximum data IDs are for the segment).

sys.column_store_row_groups

The sys.column_store_row_groups catalog view supports columnstore segments by returning a row per columnstore rowgroup. This includes details such as the number of rows in a rowgroup, its state, and physical location in the database.

sys.hash_indexes

The sys.hash_indexes catalog view is similar to sys.indexes, but pertains exclusively to hash indexes on memory-optimized tables. This view removes a few columns that are not relevant and adds the column *bucket_count*. This added column returns the number of buckets created for each hash index. For hash indexes, buckets refer to the memory locations created to store values in the index. The relationship between buckets and indexed values is detailed in Chapter 8.

sys.fulltext_catalogs

The sys.fulltext_catalogs catalog view contains one row for every full-text catalog in a database.

sys.fulltext_indexes

The sys.fulltext_indexes catalog view contains one row for every full-text index in a database. The view describes the full-text catalog that the index is a part of and provides details on the state of the index and how it is being updated.

sys.fulltext_index_columns

The sys.fulltext_index_columns catalog view supports sys.fulltext_indexes. It contains one row for every column associated with a full-text index.

Summary

This chapter presented a number of fundamentals related to indexes. The various types of indexes available within SQL Server were presented. From heaps to non-clustered to spatial indexes, each index was introduced and related to the library Dewey Decimal System as a real-world analogy to indexing. This example helped illustrate how each of the index types interacted with the others and the scenarios where one index can provide value over another.

Data definition language was provided for creating, altering, and dropping indexes. DDL has a rich set of options that can be used to finely tune how an index is structured to help improve its performance within a database.

This chapter also included information on the metadata contained within catalog views that document indexes within SQL Server. Each catalog view provides information on the structure and makeup of an index. This information can assist in researching and understanding how tables are indexed and facilitate improvements based on common query and maintenance patterns.

The details in this chapter provide the framework for what will be discussed later in this book. This information provides a starting point from which indexing can be more deeply discussed. The remainder of this book will build on this framework, allowing for effective indexing strategies to be architected and implemented to improve query and application performance.

CHAPTER 2

Index Storage Fundamentals

Where the previous chapter discussed the logical design and syntax of indexes, this one will focus on the physical implementation of indexes. Understanding how indexes are stored and interact with SQL Server and the storage engine is key to better understanding the benefits of indexes and how to make more effective use of them.

This discussion will start with the basics of data storage in SQL Server, including data pages, their format, and how they are managed. This information will then be extended into the basic structure of different index types and how each is implemented in SQL Server.

Storage Basics

A number of structures are used to store and organize data within databases. This chapter will focus on those that directly relate to tables and indexes. This discussion will begin with pages and extents and then delve deeper into the different types of pages available in SQL Server and how they relate back to indexes.

Pages

The basic storage unit for data in SQL Server is the page. Pages are used to store everything from the rows in tables to the structures used to map out indexes at their lowest levels.

When space is allocated to database data files, the space is divided into pages. During allocation, each page is created to use 8 KB (8,192 bytes) of space, and pages are numbered starting at 0, incrementing by 1 for every page allocated. When SQL

© Edward Pollack and Jason Strate 2023
E. Pollack and J. Strate, *Expert Performance Indexing in Azure SQL and SQL Server 2022*,
https://doi.org/10.1007/978-1-4842-9215-0_2

Server interacts with the database files, the smallest unit in which an input/output (I/O) operation can occur is at the page level. When using STATISTICS IO, for example, the counts for reads and writes are measured in pages.

There are three primary components to a page: the page header, its records, and the offset array, as shown in Figure 2-1. All pages begin with the page header. The header is 96 bytes and contains metadata about the page, such as the page number, its owning object, and the type of page. If rows will be stored on the pages, such as with data and index pages, the end of the page will contain an offset array. The offset array is 36 bytes and provides pointers to the location of the start of rows on the page. Between these two areas are 8,060 bytes where records and other page data are stored.

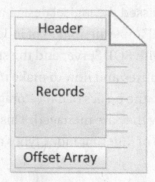

Figure 2-1. *Page structure*

If the page includes an offset array, it begins at the end of the page. As rows are added to a page, each one is added to the first open position in the records area of the page. Next, the starting location of the page is stored in the last available position in the offset array. For every row added, the data for the row is stored further away from the start of the page, and the offset is stored further away from the end of the page, as shown in Figure 2-2. Reading from the end of the page backward, the offset can be used to identify the starting position of every row, sometimes referred to as a *slot*, on the page.

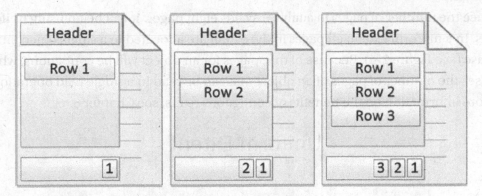

Figure 2-2. *Row placement and offset array*

While the basics of pages are the same, there are different ways in which pages are used. These uses include storing data pages, index structures, and large objects. Details of each of these use cases and how they interact with a SQL Server database will be discussed later in this chapter.

Extents

Moving up from the *page*, the next basic structure for data storage is the *extent*. An extent is a group of eight physically contiguous pages in a data file. All pages must belong to an extent, and extents cannot have fewer or more than eight pages. There are two types of extents used by SQL Server databases: *mixed extents* and *uniform* extents.

A mixed extent contains pages that are allocated to multiple objects. For example, when a table is first created and there are fewer than eight pages allocated, it will be built as a mixed extent. The table will use mixed extents as long as the total size of the table is less than eight pages, as shown in Figure 2-3. By using mixed extents, databases can reduce the amount of space allocated to small tables.

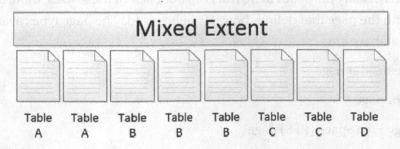

Figure 2-3. *Mixed extent*

Once the number of pages in a table exceeds eight pages, it will begin using uniform extents. In a uniform extent, all pages in the extent are allocated to a single object in the database (see Figure 2-4). Because of this, pages for an object will be contiguous, which increases the number of pages of an object that can be read in a single read operation. For more information on the benefits of contiguous reads, see Chapter 6.

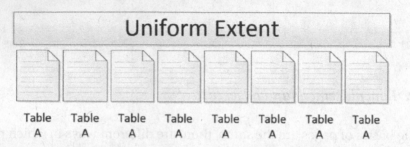

Figure 2-4. *Uniform extent*

Since SQL Server 2016, the use of uniform extents has become default behavior for all extent allocations in all databases. The behavior can be modified using the MIXED_ PAGE_ALLOCATION database option, which will default the allocations to use mixed extents. With SQL Server 2014 and earlier versions, this behavior was reversed and defaulted to allocating mixed extents. This behavior could be modified in those versions using trace flag 1118, which would instruct SQL Server to use uniform extents, as is the current default behavior. The key to these configuration considerations is that SQL Server defaults to using uniform extents, which mitigates a significant amount of page allocation contention issues.

Page Types

A page can serve many purposes in SQL Server. For each of these uses, there is a type associated with the page that defines how it is being used. The page types available in a SQL Server database are

- File header page

- Boot page

- Page Free Space (PFS) page

- Global Allocation Map (GAM) page

- Shared Global Allocation Map (SGAM) page

- Differential Changed Map (DIFF) page

- Minimally Logged (ML) page

- Index Allocation Map (IAM) page

- Data page

- Index page

- Large object (text and image) page

The next few sections will expand on the types of pages and explain how they are used. While not all of the page types deal directly with indexing, each will be defined and explained to help provide an overall understanding of data storage. With every database, there are similarities in the way pages are laid out. For instance, in the first file of every database, the pages are laid out as shown in Figure 2-5. There are more page types available than the figure indicates, but as the examinations of each page type will show, only those in the first few pages are fixed. Many of the others appear in patterns that are dictated by the data in the database.

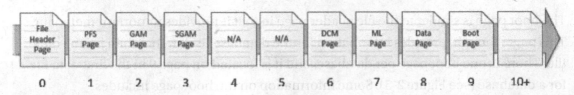

Figure 2-5. *Data file pages*

Note   Database log files do not use the page architecture. Page structures apply only to database data files. A discussion of log file architecture is outside the scope of this book.

File Header Page

The first page in any database data file is the file header page, shown in Figure 2-5. Since this is the first page of a data file, it is numbered 0. The file header page contains metadata about the database file that includes

- File ID

- Filegroup ID

- Current size of the file

- Max file size

- Sector size

- LSN information

There are a variety of other details stored on the file header page that will not be discussed further as they are out of scope for a discussion of indexing.

Boot Page

The boot page is similar to the file header page in that it provides important metadata. This page, though, provides information for the database itself rather than for the data file. There is one boot page per database, and it is located on page 9 in the first data file for a database (see Figure 2-5). Some information on the boot page includes

- Database version

- Create date

- Database name

- Database ID

- Compatibility level

One important attribute on the boot page is the attribute `dbi_dbccLastKnownGood`. This attribute provides the date that the last known `DBCC CHECKDB` completed successfully. While database maintenance isn't within the scope of this book, regular consistency checks of a database are critical to ensuring high availability.

Page Free Space Page

To track whether pages have space available for inserting rows, each data file contains Page Free Space (PFS) pages. These pages, which are the second page of the data file (see Figure 2-5) and located every 8,088 pages after that, track the amount of free space in the database. Each byte on the PFS page represents one subsequent page in the data file and provides basic allocation information regarding the page. This includes the approximate amount of free space on the page.

When the database engine needs to store LOB data or data for heaps, it must locate the next available page and determine how full the currently allocated pages are. This functionality is provided by PFS pages. Within each byte are flags that identify the current amount of space that is being used. Bits 0–2 determine whether the page is in one of the following free space states:

- Page is empty.

- 1–50 percent full.

- 51–80 percent full.

- 81–95 percent full.

- 96–100 percent full.

Along with free space, PFS pages also contain bits to identify several other types of information for a page. For example, bit 3 determines whether there are ghost records on a page. Bit 4 identifies whether a page is part of the index allocation map, described later in this chapter. Bit 5 indicates whether the page is part of a mixed extent. Bit 6 identifies whether a page has been allocated.

Through the additional bits, SQL Server can determine how a page is currently being used at a high level. This includes whether the page is currently allocated. If it is not, is it available for LOB or heap data? If it is allocated, then the PFS page provides details as described earlier in this section.

Finally, when the ghost cleanup process runs, it does not need to check every page in a database for records to clean up. Instead, the PFS page can be checked, and only those pages with ghost records need to be managed.

Note   The indexes themselves handle free space and page allocation for non-LOB data and indexes. The allocation of pages for these structures is determined by the definition of the structure.

Global Allocation Map Page

Similar to the PFS page is the Global Allocation Map (GAM) page. This page determines whether an extent has been designated for use as a uniform extent and whether the extent is free and available for allocation.

Each GAM page provides a map of all subsequent extents in its GAM interval. A GAM interval consists of the 64,000 extents (4 GB) following the GAM page. Each bit on the GAM page represents one extent following the GAM page. The first GAM page is located on page 2 of the database file (see Figure 2-5).

To determine whether an extent has been allocated as a uniform extent, SQL Server checks the bit on the GAM page that represents the extent. If the extent is allocated, then the bit is set to 0; otherwise, it is set to 1, and the extent is free and available for other purposes.

Shared Global Allocation Map Page

Nearly identically to the GAM page is the Shared Global Allocation Map (SGAM) page. The primary difference between the pages is that the SGAM page determines whether an extent is allocated as a mixed extent. Like the GAM page, the SGAM page is also used to determine whether pages are available for allocation.

Each SGAM page provides a map of all subsequent extents in each SGAM interval. An SGAM interval consists of the 64,000 extents, or 4 GB, that follow the SGAM page. Each bit on the SGAM page represents one extent following the SGAM page. The first SGAM page is located on page 3, after the GAM page of the database file (see Figure 2-5).

The SGAM pages determine when an extent has been allocated for use as a mixed extent. If the extent is allocated for this purpose and has a free page, the bit is set to 1. When it is set to 0, either the extent is not used as a mixed extent, or it is a mixed extent with all pages in use.

Differential Changed Map Page

The next page is the Differential Changed Map (DCM) page. This page is used to determine whether an extent in a GAM interval has changed. When an extent changes, a bit value is changed from 0 to 1. These bits are stored in a bitmap row on the DCM page with each bit representing an extent.

DCM pages are used to track which extents have changed between full database backups. Whenever a full database backup occurs, all the bits on the DCM page are reset to 0. The bit then changes back to 1 when a change occurs within the associated extent.

The primary use for DCM pages is to provide a list of extents that have been modified for differential backups. This is far more efficient than checking every page or extent in the database to see whether it has changed. Instead, the DCM pages provide the list of extents to back up.

The first DCM page is located at page 6 of the data file. Subsequent DCM pages occur for each GAM interval in the data file.

Minimally Logged Page

Following the DCM page is the Minimally Logged (ML) page, formerly known as the Bulk Changed Map page. The ML page is used to indicate when an extent in a GAM interval has been modified by a minimally logged operation. Any extent that is affected by a minimally logged operation will have its bit value set to 1, and those that have not will be set to 0. The bits are stored in a bitmap row on the ML page with each bit representing an extent in the GAM interval.

As the former name of ML pages (Bulk Changed Map) implies, these pages are used in conjunction with the BULK_LOGGED recovery model. When the database uses this recovery model, the ML page is used to identify extents that were modified with a minimally logged operation since the last transaction log backup. When the transaction log backup completes, the bits on the ML page are reset to 0.

The first ML page is located at page 7 of the data file. Subsequent ML pages occur for each GAM interval in the data file.

Note that while there are other ways to accomplish minimally logged operations in SQL Server (such as BCP or bulk columnstore index inserts), the Minimally Logged page only tracks those associated with the *bulk_logged* recovery model.

Index Allocation Map Page

Most of the pages discussed so far provide information about whether there is data on the pages they cover. In addition to understanding if a page is open and available, SQL Server needs to know whether the information on a page is associated to a specific table or index. The pages that provide this information are the Index Allocation Map (IAM) pages.

Every table or index first starts with an IAM page. This page indicates which extents within a GAM interval are associated with the table or index. If a table or index crosses more than one GAM interval, there will be more than one IAM page for the table or index.

There are four types of pages that an IAM page associates with a table or index. These are data, index, large object, and small-large object pages. A bitmap row is used on the IAM page to associate a page to a table or index.

Also located on the IAM page is an IAM header row. The IAM header provides the sequence number of IAM pages for a table or index, the starting page for the GAM interval that the IAM page is associated with, and a single-page allocation array. This is used when less than an extent has been allocated to a table or index.

The IAM page provides a map through which all the pages of a table or index come together. This page is used when all extents for a table or index need to be located.

Data Page

Data pages are the most prevalent type of pages in any database and are used to store the data in a database's tables. Except for LOB data types, all data for a record is located on data pages. LOB data types are stored on large object pages, discussed later in this section.

Index Page

Similar to data pages are index pages. These pages provide information on the structure of indexes and where data pages are located. For clustered indexes, the index pages build a hierarchy of pages that are used to navigate the clustered index's binary tree structure. For non-clustered indexes, index pages perform the same function but are also used to store the key values that comprise the index.

To build the hierarchy of pages within an index, the data contained in an index page provides a mapping of key values and page addresses. The key value is the key value from the index that the first sorted row on the child table contains, and the page address identifies where this is found.

Index pages are constructed similarly to other page types in that they have a page header that contains all the standard information, such as page type, allocation unit, partition ID, and allocation status. The row offset array contains pointers to where the index data rows are located on the page. The index data rows contain two pieces of information: the key value and a page address.

Index pages provide a map of how all data pages in an index are linked together, and therefore play an outsize role in understanding data storage in SQL Server.

Large Object Page

The limit for data on a single page is 8 KB. The maximum size, though, for some data types can be as high as 2 GB. Therefore, for these data types, another storage mechanism is required to store them: the large object page type.

The data types that can utilize LOB pages include text, ntext, image, nvarchar(max), varchar(max), varbinary(max), and xml. When the data for one of these data types is stored on a data page, the LOB page will be used if the size of the row exceeds 8 KB. In these cases, the column will contain references to the LOB pages required for the data and store them on LOB pages instead (see Figure 2-6).

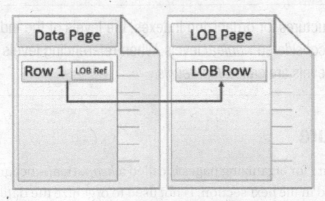

Figure 2-6. *Data page link to the LOB page*

> **Note**   SQL Server 2022 includes System Page Latch Concurrency Enhancements that allow for concurrent GAM and SGAM updates, which will greatly reduce contention in scenarios when workloads generate heavy updates to GAM or SGAM pages.

Organizing Pages

So far, the low-level components that make up the internals for indexing have been reviewed. While the low-level structures that comprise indexing internals are important, their context is only meaningful when applied to the organization and storage of data within a database.

The organizational structures in SQL Server are

- Heap

- B-tree

- Columnstore

These structures map to specific index types that will be discussed later in this chapter. In this section, the ways to organize pages will be examined in order to build that understanding.

> **Note**   In the structures for organizing indexes, the levels of the index that contain index pages are considered *nonleaf* levels. When referencing levels that contain data pages, the levels are called *leaf levels*.

Heap Structure

The default structure for organizing pages is called a *heap*. Heaps occur when a B-tree structure, discussed in the next section, is not used to organize the data pages in a table. Conceptually, a heap can be envisioned to be a pile of data pages in no particular order, as shown in Figure 2-7. In this example, the only way to retrieve all of the "Madison" records is to check each page to see whether "Madison" is on the page.

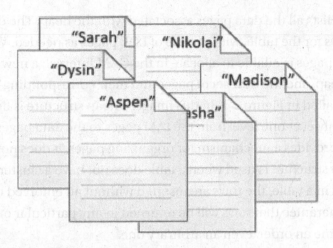

Figure 2-7. *Heap pile example*

From an internals perspective, though, heaps are more than a pile of pages. While unsorted, heaps have a few key components that organize the pages for easy access. All heaps start with an IAM page, shown in Figure 2-8. IAM pages map out which extents and single-page allocations within a GAM interval are associated with an index. For a heap, the IAM page is the only mechanism for associating data pages and extents to a heap. The heap structure does not enforce any sort of ordering on the pages that are associated with the heap. The first page available in a heap is the first page found in the database file for the heap.

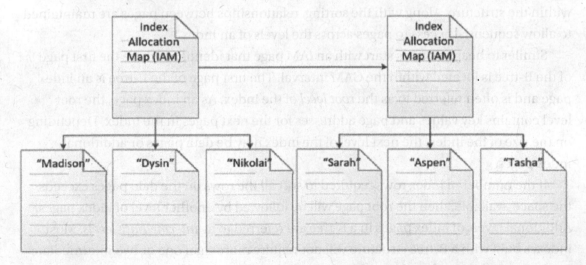

Figure 2-8. *Heap structure*

The IAM page lists all the data pages associated with the heap. The data pages for the heap store the rows for the table, with the use of LOB pages as needed. When the IAM page has no more pages available to allocate in the GAM interval, a new IAM page is allocated to the heap, and the next set of pages and their corresponding rows are added to the heap, as detailed in Figure 2-1. In this image, a heap structure is flat. From top to bottom, there is only ever one level from the IAM pages to the data pages of the structure.

While a heap provides a mechanism for organizing pages, it does not relate to an index type. A heap structure is used when a table does not have a clustered index. When a heap stores rows in a table, the rows are inserted without an enforced order. Therefore, a heap does not guarantee that rows will be returned in any particular order, and code should never assume an order, even an arbitrary one.

B-Tree Structure

The second available structure that can be used for indexing is the *B-tree*. The B-tree is often referred to as a balanced or binary tree, though its creators never formally provided an authoritative meaning for the "B" in B-tree. This is the most commonly used structure for organizing indexes in SQL Server and is used by both clustered and non-clustered indexes.

In a B-tree, pages are organized in a hierarchical tree structure, as shown in Figure 2-9. Within the structure, pages are sorted to optimize searches for information within the structure. Along with the sorting, relationships between pages are maintained to allow sequential access to pages across the levels of an index.

Similar to heaps, B-trees start with an IAM page that identifies where the first page of the B-tree is located within the GAM interval. The first page of the B-tree is an index page and is often referred to as the *root level* of the index. As an index page, the root level contains key values and page addresses for the next pages in the index. Depending on the size of the index, the next level of the index may be data pages or additional index pages.

If the number of index rows required to sort all the rows on the data pages exceeds the space available, then the root page will be followed by another level of index pages. Additional levels of index pages in a B-tree are referred to as *intermediate levels*. Most indexes built with a B-tree structure will not require more than one or two intermediate levels. Even with a wide indexing key, millions to billions of rows can be sorted with just a few levels.

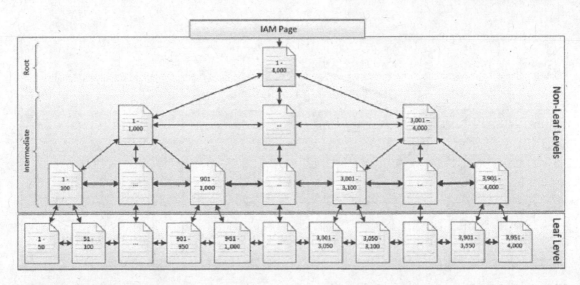

Figure 2-9. *B-tree structure*

The next level of pages below the root and intermediate levels of the indexes, referred to as the *nonleaf levels*, is the *leaf level* (see Figure 2-9). The leaf level contains all data pages for an index. The data pages are where the key values and the non-key values for the row are stored. Non-key values are not stored on the index pages.

Another differentiator between heaps and B-trees is the ability within the index levels to perform sequential page reads. Pages contain links to the previous and next pages within their page header. With index and data pages, these properties are populated and can be used to traverse the B-tree to find the next requested row from the B-tree without returning to the root level of the index and traversing the B-tree repeatedly. To illustrate this, consider a situation where rows are requested with key values between 925 and 3,025 from the index shown in Figure 2-9. Through a B-tree, this operation can be done by traversing the B-tree down to key value 925, shown in Figure 2-10. After that, all rows through key value 3,025 can be retrieved by accessing the pages after the first page in order, finishing the operation when the last key value is encountered.

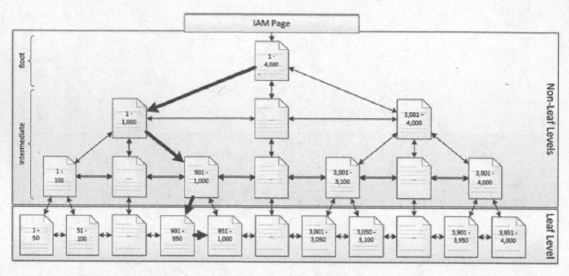

Figure 2-10. *B-tree sequential read*

One option available for tables and indexes is the ability to partition these structures. Partitioning changes the physical implementation of the index and how the index and data pages are organized. From the perspective of the B-tree structure, each partition of an index has its own B-tree. If a table is partitioned into three different partitions, there will then be three B-tree structures for the index.

Columnstore Structure

Columnstore structures are used exclusively by clustered and non-clustered columnstore index types. The columnstore structure diverges from the traditional method of storing and indexing data from a rowwise to a column-wise format. This means that instead of storing values for each column in a row sequentially, column data is grouped together and stored independently from the data for other columns in a table. For instance, in the example in Figure 2-11, instead of four rows stored one after another on a page, three column "groups" are stored.

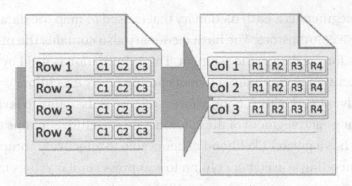

Figure 2-11. *Row-wise vs. column-wise storage*

The physical implementation of the columnstore structure does not introduce any new page types, relying solely on existing page types. A columnstore begins with an IAM page, shown in Figure 2-12. From the IAM page are LOB pages that contain the columnstore information. For each column stored in the columnstore, there are one or more segments. Segments contain up to about 1 million rows worth of data for the columns that they represent. An LOB page can contain one or more segments, and the segments can span multiple LOB pages.

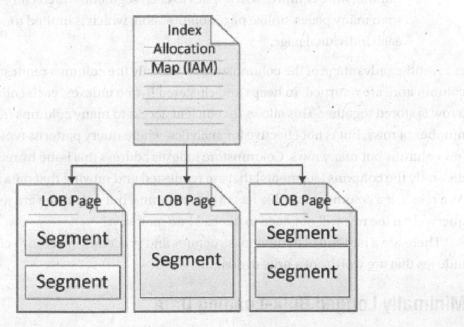

Figure 2-12. *Columnstore structure*

Within each segment is a hash dictionary that is used to map the data that comprises the segment of the columnstore. The hash dictionary also contains the minimum and maximum values for the data in the segment. This information is used by SQL Server during query execution to eliminate segments during query execution.

One of the advantages of the columnstore structure is its ability to leverage compression. Since each segment of the columnstore structure contains the same type of data, SQL Server has a greater likelihood of being able to effectively compress that data.

Dictionary encoding is used per column to compress similar values into a dictionary and then index references to the dictionary. Within each segment, rows are reordered (a.k.a. optimized via Vertipaq optimization). Finally, classic compression algorithms similar to page compression are used to reduce the size of repeated data patterns.

There are several significant differences between row/page compression and columnstore compression:

1. While row and page compressions are optional for rowstore tables, columnstore index compression is required for all columnstore indexes.

2. Columnstore compression applies to each segment, which can span many pages, unlike page compression, which is limited to each individual page.

Another advantage of the columnstore is that only the columns requested from the columnstore are returned. In heaps and clustered B-tree indexes, each column value for a row is stored together. This allows for efficient access to many columns from a small number of rows, but is not effective for analytics, where query patterns typically request few columns but many rows. Columnstore indexes address this issue by reading from disk only the columns (segments) that are requested and moving that data into memory. As a result, if a columnstore table has twenty columns, but only three are required for a query, then the rest will not need to be read into memory.

There are a handful of additional structures and processes specific to columnstore indexes that are worthy of a brief overview.

Minimally Logged Bulk-Loading Data

When more than 102,400 rows are inserted into a columnstore index in a single insert operation, a minimally logged bulk load process will be used to insert the rows more efficiently than a standard insert operation would. This greatly reduces the compute needed for write operations. Bulk-loading is ideal for OLAP tables given that writes are typically comprised of infrequent (but large) data load processes.

While bulk-loading removes the ability to fully examine the detail of an insert operation, it allows for inserts to execute more quickly and have significantly less impact on the transaction log when used. Consequently, because transaction log growth is smaller, transaction log backups are also smaller.

The Deltastore

Writing to a columnstore index is expensive as each change requires decompressing segments, writing changes, and then recompressing those segments. When bulk-loading is not possible, write operations will be made to delta rowgroups within the deltastore. These are clustered B-trees that are ideal for small trickle inserts or update operations. When data is read from a columnstore index, the contents of the deltastore will be read alongside compressed segments, returning results seamlessly to SQL Server.

An asynchronous system process called the tuple-mover will periodically merge rows from the deltastore into compressed segments. While this process is automatic and requires no user intervention, index maintenance may be used to influence its behavior.

The Delete Bitmap

For the same reasons that the deltastore is needed to allow for efficient insert operations, a mechanism must also be available to ensure that delete operations do not cause unneeded waits, locking, or resource consumption.

When data is deleted from a columnstore index, it is flagged as deleted in a clustered B-tree structure called the delete bitmap. This soft-deleted data remains in the columnstore index until index maintenance assists in cleaning it up.

When data is read from a columnstore index that contains deleted rows, the delete bitmap is used to identify and exclude them from the result set.

Index Characteristics

The first part of this chapter discussed the physical structures that are used to store indexes. Here, a clear line between the types of indexes available and these structures was not defined. In this section, the main index types for SQL Server will be discussed, along with the indexing structures that they use. For each, the requirements and restrictions associated with the indexes will be provided.

Heap

The first index type to discuss is the heap. A heap is not actually a type of index. It is instead the result of the lack of a clustered index on a table. A heap will, as the name implies, use the heap structure for organizing pages in a table.

There is only a single requirement for creating a table with a heap: a clustered index can't already be created on the table. If there is a clustered index, then a heap will not be used. Heaps and clustered indexes are mutually exclusive. Provided there is not a clustered index, there can be only a single heap on a table. The heap is used to store the data pages for the index, and this is done only once.

The primary concern when using heaps is that the data in the heap is not ordered. There is no column that determines the sort order for the data on its pages. The result of this is that, without other supporting non-clustered indexes, queries will always be forced to scan the information in the table.

Clustered Index

The second index type is the clustered index. Clustered indexes utilize a B-tree for storing data. For all practical purposes, a clustered index is the opposite of a heap. When a clustered index is built on a table, the heap is replaced with a B-tree structure, organizing the pages according to the key columns of the clustered index. The B-tree for a clustered index includes data pages with all data for the rows in the table.

Clustered indexes have a few restrictions when considering the columns for the index. The first restriction is that the total length for the key columns cannot exceed 900 bytes. Second, the clustering key in a clustered index should be unique. If columns in a clustering key are not unique, SQL Server will add a hidden uniquifier column to the row when it is stored. The uniquifier is a 4-byte numeric value that is added to nonunique clustering keys to enforce uniqueness. The uniquifier size is not considered part of the 900-byte limit. While a clustered index key does not need to be unique, it will benefit from uniqueness in being able to forgo the resources required by the added uniquifier.

There can be only a single clustered index per table. Since the clustered index is stored in the order of the clustering key and the data in the row is stored with the key, there can't be an alternative sort on top of the table in some other order. When building a clustered index on an existing table with a heap, be sure to have enough space available for a second copy of the data. Until the build of the index is complete, both copies of the data will exist.

As will be discussed in later chapters, it is often preferable to create clustered indexes on all tables. This preference is not an absolute, and there are rare situations when clustered indexes are not appropriate. While research is required to determine which structure is best, choosing to use a clustered index by default (instead of a heap) will be correct in nearly all use cases. Those scenarios where a heap is preferable are exceptions and should be handled on a case-by-case basis.

Non-clustered Index

Non-clustered indexes are similar to clustered indexes. They use the B-tree structure for storing data. The key columns are limited to 1,700 bytes for SQL Server 2016 and later and 900 bytes for all previous SQL Server versions.

Beyond the similarities to clustered indexes, there are some differences. First, there can be more than one non-clustered index on a table. There can be up to 999 non-clustered indexes on a table, each with no more than 16 columns. While the limit for non-clustered indexes is quite large, it is generally a best practice to only create indexes as needed and not to maintain unused or underused indexes as they consume memory and storage resources. In addition, write operations take longer as the number of indexes on a table increases as a write operation cannot complete until all indexes have been updated.

Instead of having a leaf level where data is stored in the B-tree, non-clustered indexes have page references to the locations in either the heap or clustered index on the table where the data is located. The process needed to retrieve columns from the clustered index that are not located within the non-clustered index is called a key lookup.

Columnstore Index

Columnstore indexes use the columnstore structure, as the name implies, and can be either clustered or non-clustered.

Some restrictions need to be considered with both types of columnstore indexes. The first is that not all data types are available to be used in columnstore indexes. The restricted data type list has shrunk in size as new versions of SQL Server are released. The following list outlines which data types are not allowed in clustered columnstore indexes, by version:

All versions (through SQL Server 2022): ntext, text, image, rowversion, timestamp, sql_variant, hierarchyid, spatial, XML

SQL Server 2016 and earlier: nvarchar(max), varchar(max), varbinary(max)

SQL Server 2012: uniqueidentifier

Note that non-clustered columnstore indexes allow the same data types with only one important exception: varchar(max), nvarchar(max), and varbinary(max) are not allowed in any version of SQL Server.

Columnstore indexes are limited to 1,024 columns. This means that a columnstore index cannot be created on a table with more than 1,024 columns. Due to columnstore indexes not enforcing data order, they cannot be unique or ordered or contain included columns. There can only be one columnstore index per table. This limitation is not problematic as clustered columnstore indexes automatically include all columns and non-clustered columnstore indexes may contain as many (or few) columns as are needed to satisfy their use case.

For tables that contain many years' worth of data, partitioning can be a valuable way to allow for old data to be easily moved out of the table via partition switching or partition truncation.

When using columnstore indexes, there are some features within SQL Server that they cannot be combined with. Since columnstore uses its own compression technology, it cannot be combined with row or page compression. Replication and filestream may also not be used with columnstore indexes. Computed columns are not allowed in columnstore indexes prior to SQL Server 2017. In SQL Server 2017 and later, a clustered columnstore index can contain non-persisted computed columns only. Persisted computed columns are not allowed on columnstore indexes, and computed columns are not permitted in non-clustered columnstore indexes.

Lastly, SQL Server 2014 introduced writable clustered columnstore indexes. Non-clustered columnstore indexes were still read-only in this version. As a result, there were a variety of restrictions that were specific to SQL Server 2014 that are worth listing, in case this version is used:

- Change tracking cannot be combined with columnstore indexes.

- Change data capture cannot be combined with columnstore indexes. SQL Server 2016 and later allow it with non-clustered columnstore indexes only.

- A clustered columnstore index is not accessible in a readable secondary in an AlwaysOn Availability Group.

- Multiple Active Result Sets (MARS).

- Non-clustered columnstore indexes cannot be created on views.

Note that these restrictions only apply to SQL Server 2014.

Summary

In this chapter, the components that are used as the building blocks for indexes were discussed in detail. This provides the foundation necessary to create indexes with predictable behavior.

This discussion included a detailed look at the different types of pages that SQL Server uses to store data in the database and how these pages are arranged together into extents. The structures used for organizing pages into logical storage were detailed as well as the basics for how each index type is organized in SQL Server.

CHAPTER 3

Examining Index Contents

With an understanding of how indexes are stored at the physical and logical levels, a deeper view of index storage can be gained by more closely viewing the details and contents of an index.

This deep dive will cross into a set of commands that are rarely used as part of day-to-day work and therefore will provide content that is both challenging and interesting to learn and test.

Warning   The tools used in this section are undocumented and unsupported. They do not appear in Books Online, and their functionality can change without notice. These tools have been around for a long time, and there are many blog posts that describe their behavior. When using older versions of SQL Server, it is important to understand these tools, since some dynamic management functions (DMFs) may not be available. Always test these tools on nonproduction data first and be sure to back up important data prior to testing.

Examining Pages

The first part of the previous chapter outlined the types of pages found in SQL Server databases. In addition, the structures available for organizing and managing the relationship between pages within databases have been reviewed. In the next section, dynamic management functions and DBCC commands will be used to examine pages in a database. For current versions of SQL Server, DMFs can be used, but on older releases, DBCC commands will need to be used instead.

© Edward Pollack and Jason Strate 2023
E. Pollack and J. Strate, *Expert Performance Indexing in Azure SQL and SQL Server 2022*,
https://doi.org/10.1007/978-1-4842-9215-0_3

By using these tools, a foundation will be built that will allow for a more in-depth look at the behaviors of indexes in this chapter and throughout the rest of the book. Also, this will provide the tools to explore indexes in extensive detail in any database.

Dynamic Management Functions

There are two dynamic management functions that will be used to examine the pages within a SQL Server database. These are

- sys.dm_db_database_page_allocations
- sys.dm_db_page_info

sys.dm_db_database_page_allocations

The DMF sys.dm_db_database_page_allocations provides information on page allocations within a database. The function can be used to investigate indexes and their associated pages. It can also be used to identify how extents have been allocated and whether the extents being used are mixed or uniform.

The DMF provides data similar to DBCC EXTENTINFO and DBCC IND, which are described later. An advantage of using the DMF is that the results can be filtered and merged with other DMFs. Additionally, it provides details on all pages allocated to an index, even those without data in them. One restriction of the output is that it only returns pages associated with data allocation, such as the data, index, and IAM pages.

Listing 3-1 shows the syntax for using sys.dm_db_database_page_allocations. The execution requires five parameters, which are defined in Table 3-1.

Listing 3-1. sys.dm_db_database_page_allocations Syntax

```
SELECT * FROM sys.dm_db_database_page_allocations ({database_id},
{TableId | NULL}, {IndexId | NULL}, { PartitionId | NULL },
{DETAILED | LIMITED})
```

Table 3-1. *Parameters for sys.dm_db_database_page_allocations*

Parameter	Description
@DatabaseId	Database from which to return the page listing for tables and indexes. The parameter is required and accepts the use of the DB_ID() function.
@TableId	Object_id for the table from which to return the page listing. The parameter is required and accepts the use of the OBJECT_ID() function. NULL can also be used to return all tables.
@IndexId	Index_id from the table that the page list is from. The parameter is required and accepts the use of NULL to return information for all indexes.
@PartitionId	ID of the partition that the page list is returning. The parameter is required and accepts the use of NULL to return information for all indexes.
@Mode	Defines the mode for returning data. The options are DETAILED and LIMITED. With LIMITED, only page metadata is returned, such as page allocation and relationship information. Using the DETAILED mode, additional information is provided such as page type and interpage relationship chains.

When executing sys.dm_db_database_page_allocations, results include the columns defined in Table 3-2. For every page allocation, there will be one row in the results.

Table 3-2. *Columns for sys.dm_db_database_page_allocations*

DMF Column	Description
database_id	ID of the database
object_id	Object ID for the table or view
index_id	ID for the index
partition_id	Partition number for the index
rowset_id	Partition ID for the index
allocation_unit_id	ID of the allocation unit
allocation_unit_type	Type of allocation unit

(*continued*)

Table 3-2. (*continued*)

DMF Column	Description
allocation_unit_type_desc	Description of the allocation unit
extent_file_id	File ID of the extent
extent_page_id	Page ID for the extent
allocated_page_iam_file_id	File ID for the Index Allocation Map page associated with the page
allocated_page_iam_page_id	Page ID for the Index Allocation Map page associated with the page
allocated_page_file_id	File ID of the allocated page
allocated_page_page_id	Page ID for the allocated page
is_allocated	Indicates whether a page is allocated
is_iam_page	Indicates whether a page is the Index Allocation Map page
is_mixed_page_allocation	Indicates whether a page is allocated to a mixed extent
page_free_space_percent	Percentage of space free on the page
page_type	Page type ID for the allocated page
page_type_desc	Description of the page type
page_level	Level of the page in the B-tree index
next_page_file_id	File ID for the next page
next_page_page_id	Page ID for the next page
previous_page_file_id	File ID for the previous page
previous_page_page_id	Page ID for the previous page
is_page_compressed	Indicates whether the page is compressed
has_ghost_records	Indicates whether the page has ghost records

With this DMF, there are several use cases that can be investigated that will help demonstrate leveraging sys.dm_db_database_page_allocations. To begin, a database, a table, and a small amount of data will be created, as shown in Listing 3-2.

Listing 3-2. Script for Creating dbo.IndexInternalsOne with 12 Rows

```
USE master;
GO
CREATE DATABASE Chapter2Internals;
GO
USE Chapter2Internals;
GO
CREATE TABLE dbo.IndexInternalsOne
(
    RowID INT IDENTITY(1, 1),
    FillerData CHAR(8000)
);
GO
INSERT INTO dbo.IndexInternalsOne
DEFAULT VALUES;
GO 12
```

After creating the table, the script will be used in Listing 3-3 to illustrate how SQL Server stores the rows in the table and how they can be examined with sys.dm_db_ database_page_allocations. As Figure 3-1 shows, there is one Index Allocation Map page allocated to the table, which is within a mixed page allocation. This means that multiple indexes can use that extent to allocate these pages. There are eight pages allocated to the first data page extent of the index starting at page 312 and another four pages allocated from an extent starting at page 320. Additionally, there are four pages allocated but not assigned a page type on the extent at page 320. There is an index allocation map and extents with data pages allocated to that map.

Listing 3-3. Extent Allocation with sys.dm_db_database_page_allocations

```
SELECT DPA.extent_file_id,
       DPA.extent_page_id,
       DPA.page_type_desc,
       DPA.allocation_unit_type_desc,
       DPA.is_iam_page,
       DPA.is_mixed_page_allocation,
       COUNT(*) AS page_count
```

```
FROM sys.dm_db_database_page_allocations(DB_ID(), OBJECT_ID('dbo.
IndexInternalsOne'), NULL, NULL, 'DETAILED') DPA
GROUP BY DPA.extent_file_id,
        DPA.extent_page_id,
        DPA.page_type_desc,
        DPA.allocation_unit_type_desc,
        DPA.is_iam_page,
        DPA.is_mixed_page_allocation
ORDER BY DPA.extent_page_id,
        DPA.page_type_desc;
```

	extent_file_id	extent_page_id	page_type_desc	allocation_unit_type_desc	is_iam_page	is_mixed_page_allocation	page_count
1	1	344	IAM_PAGE	IN_ROW_DATA	1	1	1
2	1	352	DATA_PAGE	IN_ROW_DATA	0	0	8
3	1	376	NULL	IN_ROW_DATA	0	0	4
4	1	376	DATA_PAGE	IN_ROW_DATA	0	0	4

Figure 3-1. *Extent allocation results for dbo.IndexInternalsOne*

Index Allocation Map pages are always part of a mixed extent since the allocation determines the index mapping for multiple tables. To demonstrate, the script in Listing 3-4 can be run, which creates a second table that includes a clustered index via a primary key. Reviewing the results in Figure 3-2, the six rows were added to an extent that starts at page 328, bypassing the four pages that were allocated but not used in the previous table. The Index Allocation Map page belongs to the same extent as that of dbo.IndexInternalsOne, which starts at page 232, showing that this extent is indeed mixed. Additionally, an index page is allocated to the table to support the B-tree structure of the clustered index.

Listing 3-4. Script for Creating dbo.IndexInternalsTwo with 12 Rows

```
USE Chapter2Internals;
GO
CREATE TABLE dbo.IndexInternalsTwo
(
    RowID INT IDENTITY(1, 1) PRIMARY KEY,
```

```
    FillerData CHAR(8000)
);
GO
INSERT INTO dbo.IndexInternalsTwo
DEFAULT VALUES;
GO 6
SELECT DPA.extent_file_id,
       DPA.extent_page_id,
       DPA.page_type_desc,
       DPA.allocation_unit_type_desc,
       DPA.is_iam_page,
       DPA.is_mixed_page_allocation,
       COUNT(*) AS page_count
FROM sys.dm_db_database_page_allocations(DB_ID(), OBJECT_ID('dbo.
IndexInternalsTwo'), NULL, NULL, 'DETAILED') DPA
GROUP BY DPA.extent_file_id,
         DPA.extent_page_id,
         DPA.page_type_desc,
         DPA.allocation_unit_type_desc,
         DPA.is_iam_page,
         DPA.is_mixed_page_allocation
ORDER BY DPA.extent_page_id,
         DPA.page_type_desc;
```

	extent_file_id	extent_page_id	page_type_desc	allocation_unit_type_desc	is_iam_page	is_mixed_page_allocation	page_count
1	1	232	IAM_PAGE	IN_ROW_DATA	1	1	1
2	1	328	NULL	IN_ROW_DATA	0	0	1
3	1	328	DATA_PAGE	IN_ROW_DATA	0	0	6
4	1	328	INDEX_PAGE	IN_ROW_DATA	0	0	1

Figure 3-2. *Extent allocation results for dbo.IndexInternalsTwo*

Beyond extent-level details, this DMF can be used to investigate indexes at the page level to understand all pages allocated to the table and how they relate to other pages in an index. Using the script in Listing 3-5, it can be seen that the extent starting on page 232 includes the allocated pages 235 and 236 for the index allocation maps, as shown in Figure 3-3. The extent starting at page 312 includes pages 312, 313, and so on, which is similar to the extent starting at page 328, which includes pages 328, 329, and so on. Add to this the ability to see per page its level within the B-tree and the connections between pages, verifying the ability to move up and down the index and from page to page via the data pages.

Listing 3-5. Script for Reviewing All Allocated Pages

```
USE Chapter2Internals;
GO
SELECT DPA.page_type_desc,
       DPA.allocation_unit_type_desc,
       DPA.object_id,
       DPA.index_id,
       DPA.extent_page_id,
       DPA.allocated_page_iam_page_id,
       DPA.allocated_page_page_id,
       DPA.page_level,
       DPA.next_page_page_id,
       DPA.previous_page_page_id
FROM sys.dm_db_database_page_allocations(DB_ID(), OBJECT_ID('dbo.
IndexInternalsTwo'), NULL, NULL, 'DETAILED') DPA
```

	page_type_desc	allocation_unit_type_desc	object_id	index_id	extent_page_id	allocated_page_iam_page_id	allocated_page_page_id	page_level	next_page_page_id	previous_page_page_id
1	IAM_PAGE	IN_ROW_DATA	597577167	1	232	NULL	236	0	NULL	NULL
2	DATA_PAGE	IN_ROW_DATA	597577167	1	328	236	328	0	330	NULL
3	INDEX_PAGE	IN_ROW_DATA	597577167	1	328	236	329	1	NULL	NULL
4	DATA_PAGE	IN_ROW_DATA	597577167	1	328	236	330	0	331	328
5	DATA_PAGE	IN_ROW_DATA	597577167	1	328	236	331	0	332	330
6	DATA_PAGE	IN_ROW_DATA	597577167	1	328	236	332	0	333	331
7	DATA_PAGE	IN_ROW_DATA	597577167	1	328	236	333	0	334	332
8	DATA_PAGE	IN_ROW_DATA	597577167	1	328	236	334	0	NULL	333
9	NULL	IN_ROW_DATA	597577167	1	328	236	335	NULL	NULL	NULL

Figure 3-3. *Extent allocation results for reviewing all allocated pages*

sys.dm_db_page_info

Another dynamic management function that helps understand how indexes operate is sys.dm_db_page_info. This DMF is documented and supported by Microsoft, unlike sys.dm_db_database_page_allocations. It provides page header row information for database pages. This information includes number of slots, free bytes, minimally logged status, ghost records, and page linking details.

Listing 3-6 shows the syntax for using sys.dm_db_page_info. The execution requires four parameters, which are defined in Table 3-3. Note that while the parameters allow NULL, the function will return an error if any are set to NULL.

Listing 3-6. sys.dm_db_page_info Syntax

```
SELECT * FROM sys.dm_db_database_page_allocations ({database_id},
{FileId}, {PageId}, {DETAILED | LIMITED})
```

Table 3-3. *Parameters for sys.dm_db_page_info*

Parameter	Description
@DatabaseId	Database to return page header information from.
@FileId	File Id for the page that will be returned.
@PageId	Page id for the page that will be returned.
@Mode	Defines the mode for returning data. The options are DETAILED and LIMITED. With LIMITED, only page metadata is returned. Under the DETAILED mode, page descriptive columns will be populated.

When returning data from sys.dm_db_page_info, results include the columns defined in Table 3-4. For every page requested, there will be one row of header information in the results.

Table 3-4. *Columns for sys.dm_db_page_info*

Column Name	Description
database_id	ID of the database
file_id	ID of the data file
page_id	ID of the page
page_header_version	Version of the page header
page_type	ID for the page type
page_type_desc	Text description of the page type
page_type_flag_bits	Type flag bits in the page header

(continued)

Table 3-4. (*continued*)

Column Name	Description
page_type_flag_bits_desc	Description of type flag bits in the page header
page_flag_bits	Flag bits in the page header
page_flag_bits_desc	Text description of flag bits in the page header
page_lsn	Log sequence number associated with last page modification
page_level	Level of the page in the index
object_id	ID of the object associated with the page
index_id	ID of the index
partition_id	ID of the partition
alloc_unit_id	ID of the allocation unit
is_encrypted	Indicates whether a page is encrypted
has_checksum	Indicates whether a page has a checksum value
checksum	Checksum value for a page
is_iam_page	Indicates whether a page is the Index Allocation Map page
is_mixed_extent	Indicates whether a page is part of a mixed extent
has_ghost_records	Indicates whether the page has ghost records.
has_version_records	Indicates whether the page has version records
has_persisted_version_records	Indicates whether the page has persisted version records
pfs_page_id	Page ID of the PFS page associated with this page
pfs_is_allocated	Indicates whether the PFS page has allocated this page
pfs_alloc_percent	Allocation percentage as indicated by the PFS page
pfs_status	Bit value for the PFS status
pfs_status_desc	Text description of the PFS status
gam_page_id	Page ID of the GAM page associated with this page
gam_status	ID value indicating the GAM status of this page
gam_status_desc	Text description of the GAM status of this page

(*continued*)

Table 3-4. (*continued*)

Column Name	Description
sgam_page_id	Page ID of the SGAM page associated with this page
sgam_status	ID value indicating the SGAM status of this page
sgam_status_desc	Text description of the SGAM status of this page
diff_map_page_id	Page ID of the differential map page associated with this page
diff_status	ID value indicating the differential map status of this page
diff_status_desc	Text description of the differential map status of this page
ml_map_page_id	Page ID of the Minimally Logged page associated with this page
ml_status	ID value indicating the Minimally Logged page status of this page
ml_status_desc	Text description of the Minimally Logged page status of this page
prev_page_file_id	File ID for the previous page
prev_page_page_id	Page ID for the previous page
next_page_file_id	File ID for the next page
next_page_page_id	Page ID for the next page
fixed_length	Unknown
slot_count	Total number of used and unused slots
ghost_rec_count	Number of records marked as ghost on the page
free_bytes	Number of free bytes on the page
free_bytes_offset	Offset of free space at the end of the data area
reserved_bytes	Number of reserved bytes on the page
reserved_bytes_by_xdes_id	Space contributed by m_xdesID to m_reservedCnt
xdes_id	Latest transaction contributed by m_reserved

This header information is quite extensive and can be used to identify how pages are interrelated between different structures, such as PFS pages, or use it to inspect pages to verify checksum, number of slots, or free space. The code in Listing 3-7 retrieves all page allocations for the two previously created tables, including page header information for all of the assigned pages.

Listing 3-7. Query Using sys.dm_db_page_info

```
USE Chapter2Internals;
GO
SELECT T.name,
       DPA.page_type_desc,
       DPI.page_id,
       DPI.pfs_page_id,
       DPI.gam_page_id,
       DPI.sgam_page_id,
       DPI.diff_map_page_id,
       DPI.ml_map_page_id,
       DPI.prev_page_page_id,
       DPI.next_page_page_id,
       DPI.fixed_length,
       DPI.slot_count,
       DPI.free_bytes
FROM sys.dm_db_database_page_allocations(DB_ID(), NULL, NULL, NULL,
'DETAILED') DPA
    INNER JOIN sys.tables T ON T.object_id = DPA.object_id
    CROSS APPLY sys.dm_db_page_info(DPA.database_id, DPA.allocated_page_
file_id, DPA.allocated_page_page_id, DEFAULT) DPI;
```

Once executed, results will be returned that are similar to those in Figure 3-4. The results show the same previous and next page connections for dbo.IndexInternalsTwo, but no page IDs listed for dbo.IndexInternalsOne. Additionally, the PFS, GAM, SGAM, DIFF, and ML pages are identified for both tables, which are the same since the database is smaller than the threshold required for having multiples of these page types. Also shown are the number of slots, length, and free bytes per page. Of note is page 329, which is the index page for dbo.IndexInternalsTwo, that has six slots, one for each page that the index page manages in the clustered index.

	name	page_type_desc	page_id	pfs_page_id	gam_page_id	sgam_page_id	diff_map_page_id	ml_map_page_id	prev_page_page_id	next_page_page_id	fixed_length	slot_count	free_bytes
1	IndexInternalsOne	IAM_PAGE	235	1	2	3	6	7	0	0	90	2	6
2	IndexInternalsOne	DATA_PAGE	312	1	2	3	6	7	0	0	8008	1	83
3	IndexInternalsOne	DATA_PAGE	313	1	2	3	6	7	0	0	8008	1	83
4	IndexInternalsOne	DATA_PAGE	314	1	2	3	6	7	0	0	8008	1	83
5	IndexInternalsOne	DATA_PAGE	315	1	2	3	6	7	0	0	8008	1	83
6	IndexInternalsOne	DATA_PAGE	316	1	2	3	6	7	0	0	8008	1	83
7	IndexInternalsOne	DATA_PAGE	317	1	2	3	6	7	0	0	8008	1	83
8	IndexInternalsOne	DATA_PAGE	318	1	2	3	6	7	0	0	8008	1	83
9	IndexInternalsOne	DATA_PAGE	319	1	2	3	6	7	0	0	8008	1	83
10	IndexInternalsOne	DATA_PAGE	320	1	2	3	6	7	0	0	8008	1	83
11	IndexInternalsOne	DATA_PAGE	321	1	2	3	6	7	0	0	8008	1	83
12	IndexInternalsOne	DATA_PAGE	322	1	2	3	6	7	0	0	8008	1	83
13	IndexInternalsOne	DATA_PAGE	323	1	2	3	6	7	0	0	8008	1	83
14	IndexInternalsOne	NULL	324	NULL	NULL	NULL	NULL	NULL	NULL	NULL	NULL	NULL	NULL
15	IndexInternalsOne	NULL	325	NULL	NULL	NULL	NULL	NULL	NULL	NULL	NULL	NULL	NULL
16	IndexInternalsOne	NULL	326	NULL	NULL	NULL	NULL	NULL	NULL	NULL	NULL	NULL	NULL
17	IndexInternalsOne	NULL	327	NULL	NULL	NULL	NULL	NULL	NULL	NULL	NULL	NULL	NULL
18	IndexInternalsTwo	IAM_PAGE	236	1	2	3	6	7	0	0	90	2	6
19	IndexInternalsTwo	DATA_PAGE	328	1	2	3	6	7	0	330	8008	1	83
20	IndexInternalsTwo	INDEX_PAGE	329	1	2	3	6	7	0	11	11	6	8018
21	IndexInternalsTwo	DATA_PAGE	330	1	2	3	6	7	328	331	8008	1	83
22	IndexInternalsTwo	DATA_PAGE	331	1	2	3	6	7	330	332	8008	1	83
23	IndexInternalsTwo	DATA_PAGE	332	1	2	3	6	7	331	333	8008	1	83
24	IndexInternalsTwo	DATA_PAGE	333	1	2	3	6	7	332	334	8008	1	83
25	IndexInternalsTwo	DATA_PAGE	334	1	2	3	6	7	333	0	8008	1	83
26	IndexInternalsTwo	NULL	335	NULL	NULL	NULL	NULL	NULL	NULL	NULL	NULL	NULL	NULL

Figure 3-4. *Page header results from sys.dm_db_page_info*

DBCC Commands

While exploration of data structures can be done with dynamic management functions, there will be some scenarios where further research will be desired. To accomplish this in SQL Server, the following DBCC commands can be used:

- DBCC EXTENTINFO
- DBCC IND
- DBCC PAGE

DBCC EXTENTINFO

Like sys.dm_db_database_page_allocations, DBCC EXTENTINFO provides information about extent allocations that occur within a database. This identifies how extents have been allocated and whether the extents being used are mixed or uniform. Listing 3-8 shows the syntax for using DBCC EXTENTINFO. When using the command, there are four parameters that can be populated, which are defined in Table 3-5.

Listing 3-8. DBCC EXTENTINFO Syntax

```
DBCC EXTENTINFO ( {database_name | database_id | 0}
    , {table_name | table_object_id}, { index_name | index_id | -1}
    , { partition_id | 0}
```

Table 3-5. *DBCC EXTENTINFO Parameters*

Parameter	Description
database_name | database_id	Specifies either the database name or the database ID where the page will be retrieved. This defaults to the current database if this parameter is not provided or if zero is used for its value.
table_name | table_object_id	Specifies which table to return in the output by providing either the table name or the object_ID for the table. If no value is provided, the output will include results for all tables.
index_name | index_id	Specifies which index to return in the output by providing either the index name or the index_ID. If −1 or no value is provided, then the output will include results for all indexes on the table.
partition_id	Specifies which partition of the index to return in the output by providing the partition number. If 0 or no value is provided, then the output will include results for all partitions on the index.

When executing DBCC EXTENTINFO, a dataset is returned that includes the columns defined in Table 3-6. For every extent allocation, there will be one row in the results. Since extents are comprised of eight pages, there can be as many as eight allocations for an extent when there are single-page allocations, such as when mixed extents are used. When uniform extents are used, there will be only one extent allocation and one row returned for the extent.

Table 3-6. *DBCC EXTENTINFO Output Columns*

Parameter	Description
file_id	File number for where the page is located.
page_id	Page number for the page.
pg_alloc	Number of pages allocated from the extent to the object.
ext_size	Size of the extent.
object_id	Object ID for the table.
index_id	Index ID associated with the heap or index.
partition_number	Partition number for the heap or index.
partition_id	Partition ID for the heap or index.
iam_chain_type	The type of IAM chain the extent is used for. Values can be in-row data, LOB data, and overflow data.
pfs_bytes	Bytes array that identifies the amount of free space, whether there are ghost records, whether the page is an IAM page, whether it is allocated, and whether it is part of a mixed extent.

To demonstrate how this command works, an example will be provided that illustrates how extents are allocated. In the example, shown in Listing 3-9, dbo. IndexInternalsOne will be reused from the last section.

Listing 3-9. DBCC EXTENTINFO dbo.IndexInternalsOne

```
USE Chapter2Internals
GO
DBCC EXTENTINFO(0, IndexInternalsOne, -1)
```

The results for the DBCC command, shown in Figure 3-5, show that there are 13 total pages allocated to the table. The items of interest in these results are the pg_alloc and ext_size columns. In the first row, the pages allocated are nine, accounting for the Index Allocation Map page and the eight pages for the extent. In the second row, there are 4 pages allocated, which is the balance of the 12 records inserted into the table. Both rows should have 8 for the extent size, since uniform extents are allocated.

	file_id	page_id	pg_alloc	ext_size	object_id	index_id	partition_number	partition_id	iam_chain_type	pfs_bytes
1	1	312	9	8	581577110	0	1	72057594043170816	In-row data	0x4444444444444444
2	1	320	4	8	581577110	0	1	72057594043170816	In-row data	0x4444444400000000

Figure 3-5. *DBCC EXTENTINFO for pages in dbo.IndexInternalsOne*

In SQL Server versions prior to SQL Server 2016, the behavior will be quite different since it will leverage single-page allocations for each transaction until the first extent is filled. This behavior change is due to the behavior of trace flag 1118 becoming default behavior for SQL Server.

Though DBCC EXTENTINFO doesn't provide as much detail as `sys.dm_db_database_page_allocations`, it can be useful for identifying extents assigned to a table, especially when using SQL Server versions prior to SQL Server 2012.

DBCC IND

The next command that can be used to investigate indexes and their associated pages is `DBCC IND`. This command returns a list of all pages associated with the requested object, which can be scoped to the database, table, or index level, similar to `sys.dm_db_database_page_allocations`. Listing 3-10 shows the syntax for using `DBCC IND`. When using this command, there are three parameters that can be populated, each of which is described in Table 3-7.

Listing 3-10. DBCC IND Syntax

```
DBCC IND ( {'dbname' | dbid}, {'table_name' | table_object_id},
           {'index_name' | index_id | -1})
```

Table 3-7. *DBCC IND Parameters*

Parameter	Description
database_name | database_id	Specifies either the database name or the database ID where the page list will be retrieved. This defaults to the current database if this parameter is not provided or if zero is used for its value.
table_name | table_object_id	Specifies which table to return in the output by providing either the table name or the object_ID for the table. If no value is provided, the output will include results for all tables.
index_name | index_id	Specifies which index to return in the output by providing either the index name or the index_ID. If −1 or no value is provided, the output will include results for all indexes on the table.

For every page that is allocated to the requested objects, DBCC IND returns one row per page in the resulting dataset; the columns are defined in Table 38. Unlike DBCC EXTENTINFO, DBCC IND does explicitly return the IAM page in the results.

Table 3-8. *DBCC IND Output Columns*

Column	Description
PageFID	File number where the page is located.
PagePID	Page number for the page.
IAMFID	File ID where the IAM page is located.
IAMPID	Page ID for the page in the data file.
ObjectID	Object ID for the associated table.
IndexID	Index ID associated with the heap or index.
PartitionNumber	Partition number for the heap or index.
PartitionID	Partition ID for the heap or index.
iam_chain_type	The type of IAM chain the extent is used for. Values can be in-row data, LOB data, and overflow data.
PageType	Number identifying the page type. These are listed in Table 3-9.

(continued)

Table 3-8. (*continued*)

Column	Description
IndexLevel	Level at which the page exists in the page organizational structure. The levels are organized from 0 to N, where 0 is the lowest level of the index and N is the index root.
NextPageFID	File number where the next page at the index level is located.
NextPagePID	Page number for the next page at the index level.
PrevPageFID	File number where the previous page at the index level is located.
PrevPagePID	Page number for the previous page at the index level.

Within the results from DBCC IND is the PageType column that returns the type of page, which can include data, index, GAM, or any other of the page types discussed in the previous chapter. Table 3-9 shows a full list of the different page types and their corresponding ID values.

Table 3-9. *Page Type Mappings*

Page Type	Description
1	Data page
2	Index page
3	Large object page
4	Large object page
8	Global Allocation Map page
9	Shared Global Allocation Map page
10	Index Allocation Map page
11	Page Free Space page
13	Boot page
15	File header page
16	Differential Changed Map page
17	Minimally Logged page

The primary benefit of using DBCC IND is that it provides a list of all pages for a table or index with their locations in the database. This can be used to help investigate how indexes behave and where pages are located. Several examples will be provided that illustrate how this data can be obtained and used.

For the first example, the tables created in the last section will be revisited, examining the output for each of these, comparing it with the DBCC EXTENTINFO output. This code example includes DBCC IND commands for IndexInternalsOne and IndexInternalsTwo, as shown in Listing 3-11. The database ID passed in is 0 for the current database, and the index ID is set to –1 to return pages for all indexes.

Listing 3-11. DBCC IND Example

```
USE Chapter2Internals;
GO
DBCC IND (0, 'IndexInternalsOne',-1);
```

In the DBCC EXTENTINFO example, there were two extent allocations for the table IndexInternalsOne, as shown in Figure 3-5. These results show 13 pages allocated to the table. The DBCC IND results, shown in Figure 3-6, detail all pages that were part of two extent allocations.

In these results, there is a single IAM page and 12 data pages allocated to the table. Where DBCC EXTENTINFO provided page 312 as the start of the extent allocation, containing nine pages, it was not possible to identify where the IAM page was based on that limited information. It was in another extent that the results did not list, and the results for DBCC IND identify it as being on page 235. The benefit of using DBCC IND for listing the pages of an index is that exact page numbers are provided without the need for any guesswork. Also note that the index level in the results returns as level 0 with no intermediate levels. Heap structures are flat, and therefore the pages are in no particular order.

	PageFID	PagePID	IAMFID	IAMPID	ObjectID	IndexID	PartitionNumber	PartitionID	iam_chain_type	PageType	IndexLevel	NextPageFID	NextPagePID	PrevPageFID	PrevPagePID
1	1	235	NULL	NULL	581577110	0	1	72057594043170816	In-row data	10	NULL	0	0	0	0
2	1	312	1	235	581577110	0	1	72057594043170816	In-row data	1	0	0	0	0	0
3	1	313	1	235	581577110	0	1	72057594043170816	In-row data	1	0	0	0	0	0
4	1	314	1	235	581577110	0	1	72057594043170816	In-row data	1	0	0	0	0	0
5	1	315	1	235	581577110	0	1	72057594043170816	In-row data	1	0	0	0	0	0
6	1	316	1	235	581577110	0	1	72057594043170816	In-row data	1	0	0	0	0	0
7	1	317	1	235	581577110	0	1	72057594043170816	In-row data	1	0	0	0	0	0
8	1	318	1	235	581577110	0	1	72057594043170816	In-row data	1	0	0	0	0	0
9	1	319	1	235	581577110	0	1	72057594043170816	In-row data	1	0	0	0	0	0
10	1	320	1	235	581577110	0	1	72057594043170816	In-row data	1	0	0	0	0	0
11	1	321	1	235	581577110	0	1	72057594043170816	In-row data	1	0	0	0	0	0
12	1	322	1	235	581577110	0	1	72057594043170816	In-row data	1	0	0	0	0	0
13	1	323	1	235	581577110	0	1	72057594043170816	In-row data	1	0	0	0	0	0

Figure 3-6. *DBCC IND for dbo.IndexInternalsOne*

The tables in the previous example were organized in a heap structure. For the next example, the output from DBCC IND will be examined for a table with a clustered index. In Listing 3-12, the table dbo.IndexInternalsThree is created with a clustered index on the RowID column. Four rows are then inserted, after which DBCC IND is used.

Listing 3-12. DBCC IND Clustered Index Example

```
USE Chapter2Internals
GO
CREATE TABLE dbo.IndexInternalsThree
      (
      RowID INT IDENTITY(1,1)
      ,FillerData CHAR(8000)
      ,CONSTRAINT PK_IndexInternalsThree  PRIMARY KEY CLUSTERED (RowID)
      )
GO
INSERT INTO dbo.IndexInternalsThree DEFAULT VALUES
GO 4
DBCC IND (0, 'IndexInternalsThree',-1)
```

Figure 3-7 shows the results from this example. Note the change in how IndexLevel is returned as compared with the previous example (in Figure 3-6).

	PageFID	PagePID	IAMFID	IAMPID	ObjectID	IndexID	PartitionNumber	PartitionID	iam_chain_type	PageType	IndexLevel	NextPageFID	NextPagePID	PrevPageFID	PrevPagePID
1	1	237	NULL	NULL	629577281	1	1	72057594043301888	In-row data	10	NULL	0	0	0	0
2	1	360	1	237	629577281	1	1	72057594043301888	In-row data	1	0	1	362	0	0
3	1	361	1	237	629577281	1	1	72057594043301888	In-row data	2	1	0	0	0	0
4	1	362	1	237	629577281	1	1	72057594043301888	In-row data	1	0	1	363	1	360
5	1	363	1	237	629577281	1	1	72057594043301888	In-row data	1	0	1	364	1	362
6	1	364	1	237	629577281	1	1	72057594043301888	In-row data	1	0	0	0	1	363

Figure 3-7. *DBCC IND for dbo.IndexInternalsThree*

Here, the third row in the result set has an IndexLevel of 1 and a PageType of 2, which is an index page. With these results, there is enough information to rebuild the B-tree structure for the index, as shown in Figure 3-8. The B-tree starts with the IAM page, which is page number 1:237. This page is linked to page 1:361, which is an index page at index level 1. Following that, pages 1:360, 1:362, 1:363, and 1:364 are at index level 0 and doubly linked to each other.

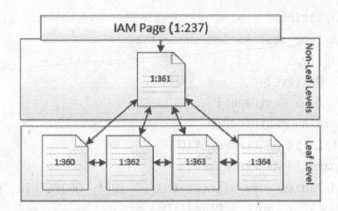

Figure 3-8. *DBCC IND for dbo.IndexInternalsThree*

In both examples, DBCC IND was used to investigate the pages associated with a heap or a clustered index. This DBCC command provides the information on all pages of the table or index, including the IAM page. These pages include the page numbers to identify where they are in the data file. The relationships between the pages are also included, such as the next and previous page numbers that are used to navigate to adjacent pages in a B-tree.

sys.dm_db_database_page_allocations can provide this same information (and more). To demonstrate this, Listing 3-13 shows how to get DBCC IND information from sys.dm_db_database_page_allocations. If the outputs are compared, it can be noted that they are nearly identical, with only a few scenarios where NULL and 0 are returned differently. Given the choice of tools, the DMF should be used preferentially over the DBCC command.

Listing 3-13. DBCC IND Output from sys.dm_db_database_page_allocations

```
USE Chapter2Internals;
GO
SELECT
allocated_page_file_id AS PageFID
,allocated_page_page_id AS PagePID
,allocated_page_iam_file_id AS IAMFID
,allocated_page_iam_page_id AS IAMPID
,object_id AS ObjectID
,index_id AS IndexID
,partition_id AS PartitionNumber
```

```
,rowset_id AS PartitionID
,allocation_unit_type_desc AS iam_chain_type
,page_type AS PageType
,page_level AS IndexLevel
,next_page_file_id AS NextPageFID
,next_page_page_id AS NextPagePID
,previous_page_file_id AS PrevPageFID
,previous_page_page_id AS PrevPagePID
FROM sys.dm_db_database_page_allocations(DB_ID(), OBJECT_ID('dbo.
IndexInternalsTwo'), 1, NULL, 'DETAILED')
WHERE is_allocated = 1;
GO
DBCC IND (0,'dbo.IndexInternalsTwo',1)
```

DBCC PAGE

The last command available for examining pages is DBCC PAGE. While the other two commands provide information about the pages and their relationship with tables and indexes, the output from DBCC PAGE provides the actual contents of a page. Listing 3-14 shows the syntax for using DBCC PAGE.

Listing 3-14. DBCC PAGE Syntax

```
DBCC PAGE ( { database_name | database_id | 0}, file_number, page_number
          [,print_option ={0|1|2|3} ])
```

The DBCC PAGE command accepts a number of parameters. Through these parameters, it is able to determine the database and specific page requested, which is then returned in the result set in the requested format. Table 3-10 details the parameters for DBCC PAGE.

Table 3-10. *DBCC PAGE Parameters*

Parameter	Description
database_name | database_id	Specifies either the database name or the database ID where the page will be retrieved. This defaults to the current database if this parameter is not provided or if zero is used for its value.
file_number	Specifies the file number for the data file in the database from where the page will be retrieved.
page_number	Specifies the page number in the database file that will be retrieved.
print_option	Specifies how the output should be returned. There are four print options available: *0—page header only*: Returns only page header information. *1—hex rows*: Returns the page header information, all the rows on the page, and the offset array. In this output, each row is returned individually. *2—hex data*: Returns the page header information, all the rows on the page, and the offset array. Unlike option 1, the output shows all the rows as a single block of data. *3—data rows*: Returns the page header information, all the rows on the page, and the offset array. This option differs from the other options in that the data in the columns for the row is translated as listed with their column names. This parameter is optional, and 0 is used as the default when no option is selected.

Note   By default, the DBCC PAGE command outputs its messages to the SQL Server event log. In most situations, this is not the ideal output mechanism. Trace flag 3604 allows you to modify this behavior. By utilizing this trace flag, the output from the DBCC statements returns to the Messages tab in SQL Server Management Studio (SSMS).

Through DBCC PAGE and its print options, everything that is on a page can be retrieved. What is the value in delving into the detailed contents of pages? Looking at an index or data page can provide an understanding of unexpected index behavior (such as poor performance). Insight can be gained into how the data within rows is structured, such as why rows may be larger than expected. The size of rows does have an important impact on how indexes behave as when a row gets larger, the number of pages required to store the index increases. More pages for an index will result in the need for more memory to cache it, ultimately leading to higher resource consumption and longer query wait times. A larger index size may alter the decisions the query optimizer makes, ultimately changing the execution plan and performance of a query that uses it.

Another reason to use DBCC PAGE is to observe what happens to a data page when various operations occur. As the examples later in this chapter will illustrate, DBCC PAGE can be used to uncover what happens during page splits and forwarded record operations.

To help demonstrate how to use DBCC PAGE, a few demonstrations will be shown with each of the print options. These demos will be based on the code in Listing 3-15, which uses sys.dm_db_database_page_allocations to identify page numbers for the examples. For each example, an illustration will be provided of some of the ways that results can differ between page types. While the page numbers in each database may differ slightly, the demos are based on an IAM page of 238, index page of 377, and data pages of 376 and 378, as shown in Figure 3-9.

Listing 3-15. DBCC IND Query for DBCC PAGE Examples

```
USE [Chapter2Internals];
GO
CREATE TABLE dbo.IndexInternalsFour (
    RowID INT IDENTITY(1, 1) NOT NULL,
    FillerData VARCHAR(2000) NULL,
    CONSTRAINT PK_IndexInternalsFour
        PRIMARY KEY CLUSTERED ([RowID] ASC));

INSERT INTO dbo.IndexInternalsFour (FillerData)
VALUES (REPLICATE(1, 2000)),
(REPLICATE(2, 2000)), (REPLICATE(3, 2000)),
(REPLICATE(4, 2000)), (REPLICATE(5, 25));

SELECT allocated_page_file_id AS PageFID,
       allocated_page_page_id AS PagePID,
       allocated_page_iam_file_id AS IAMFID,
       allocated_page_iam_page_id AS IAMPID,
```

```
        index_id AS IndexID,
        allocation_unit_type_desc AS iam_chain_type,
        page_type_desc,
        page_level AS IndexLevel,
        next_page_file_id AS NextPageFID,
        next_page_page_id AS NextPagePID,
        previous_page_file_id AS PrevPageFID,
        previous_page_page_id AS PrevPagePID
FROM sys.dm_db_database_page_allocations(DB_ID(), OBJECT_ID('dbo.
IndexInternalsFour'), 1, NULL, 'DETAILED')
WHERE is_allocated = 1;
```

	PageFID	PagePID	IAMFID	IAMPID	IndexID	iam_chain_type	page_type_desc	IndexLevel	NextPageFID	NextPagePID	PrevPageFID	PrevPagePID
1	1	238	NULL	NULL	1	IN_ROW_DATA	IAM_PAGE	0	NULL	NULL	NULL	NULL
2	1	376	1	238	1	IN_ROW_DATA	DATA_PAGE	0	1	378	NULL	NULL
3	1	377	1	238	1	IN_ROW_DATA	INDEX_PAGE	1	NULL	NULL	NULL	NULL
4	1	378	1	238	1	IN_ROW_DATA	DATA_PAGE	0	NULL	NULL	1	376

Figure 3-9. *Page allocations for dbo.IndexInternalsFour*

Page Header–Only Print Option

The first print option available for DBCC PAGE returns only the page header where print_
option equals 0 (the default). The page header is returned with all DBCC PAGE requests;
using this option limits the results to the page header exclusively. Two sections are
returned as part of the page header.

The first section returned is the buffer information. The buffer provides information
on where the page is currently located in memory in SQL Server. To read a page, the page
must first be read from disk and written to memory. This section provides the address
that could be used to find the current memory location of the page.

The second section is the page header itself. The page header contains attributes that
describe the page and its contents. Not all attributes are currently in use by SQL Server,
but there are many that are worth further discussion. These key attributes are detailed in
Table 3-11.

Table 3-11. *Page Header Key Attribute Definitions*

Attribute	Definition
m_pageId	File ID and page number for the page.
m_type	The type of page returned; see the page type list in Table 3-9.
Metadata: AllocUnitId	Allocation unit ID that maps from the catalog view sys.allocation_units.
Metadata: PartitionId	Partition ID for the table or index. This maps to partition_ID in the catalog view sys.partitions.
Metadata: ObjectId	Object ID for the table. This maps to the object_ID in the catalog view sys.tables.
Metadata: IndexId	Index ID for the table or index. This maps to the index_ID in the catalog view sys.indexes.
m_prevPage	Previous page in the index structure. This is used in B-tree indexes to allow reading sequential pages along index levels.
m_nextPage	Next page in the index structure. This is used in B-tree indexes to allow reading sequential pages along index levels.
m_slotCnt	Number of slots, or rows, on the page.
Allocation Status	Lists the locations of the GAM, SGAM, PFS, DIFF (or DCM), and ML (or BCM) pages for the page requested. It also includes the status for each from those metadata pages.

To demonstrate the use of DBCC PAGE for the page header–only option, the code in Listing 3-16 can be used. The results should be similar to those in Figure 3-10. In this scenario, the page number is provided at the top of the page, indicating that it is page 1:377. The m_type is 2, which means it is an index page. The m_slotCnt shows that there are two rows on the page. Referring to Figure 3-10, the row count would correlate to the two index records needed to map data pages 1:376 and 1:378 to the index. Finally, the allocation statuses show that the page is allocated on the GAM page, it is 0 percent full (per PFS page), and the page has been changed since the last full backup (per the DCM page).

Listing 3-16. DBCC PAGE with the Page Header–Only Print Option

```
DBCC TRACEON(3604)
DBCC PAGE(0,1,377,0)
```

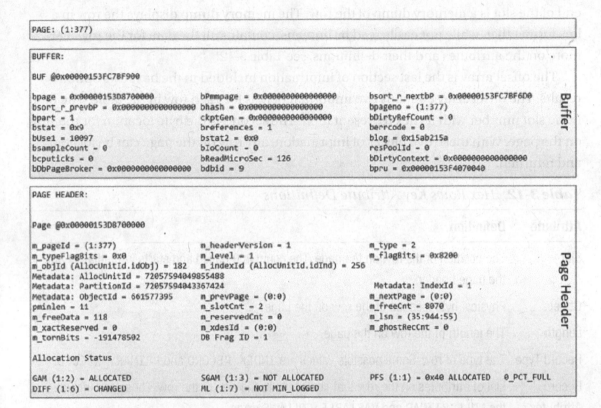

Figure 3-10. *DBCC PAGE output for the page header-only print option*

The page header–only option shows that there is a lot of useful information in the page header. It provides enough information to envision how this page relates to the other pages in the index and the extent it occupies. This information is similar to sys.dm_db_page_info, but generally speaking, DBCC PAGE provides more information than the DMF.

Hex Rows Print Option

The next print option available for DBCC PAGE is the hex rows print option, where print_option equals 1. This expands on the previous option by adding into the output an entry for every slot on the page and the offset array that describes the location of each slot on the page.

The data section of the page repeats for every row that is on the page and contains all metadata and the data associated with that row. For the metadata, the row includes the slot number, page offset, record type, and record attributes. This information helps define the row and what contributes to the row size (besides the size of the data). At the end of the slot is a memory dump of the row. The memory dump displays the row in a hex format that, while not easily read by humans, contains all the data for the row. For more on the attributes and their definitions, see Table 3-12.

The offset array is the last section of information included in the hex rows option results. The offset array contains two important details for each row in the table. The first is the slot number with its hex representation. The second is the byte location for the slot on the page. With these two pieces of information, any row on the page can be located and returned.

Table 3-12. *Hex Rows Key Attribute Definitions*

Attribute	Definition
Slot	The position of the row on the page. The count is 0 based and starts immediately after the page header.
Offset	Physical byte location of the row on the page.
Length	The length of the row on the page.
Record Type	The type of row. Some possible values are INDEX_RECORD and PRIMARY_RECORD.
Record Attributes	List of attributes on the row that contribute to the size of the row. These can include the NULL_BITMAP and VARIABLE_COLUMNS array.
Record Size	Size of the row on the page.
Memory Dump	The memory location for the data on the page. For the hex rows option, it is limited to the information in that slot. The memory address is provided, and afterward a hex dump of the data is stored in the slot.

For the hex rows example, the index page (1:279) investigated in the previous section will be further reviewed. This time, the hex rows print option will be used, which is when a print_option of 1 is set in DBCC PAGE, as shown in Listing 3-17.

The results for the DBCC PAGE command will be lengthier than the previous execution since they include the row data with the page header. To focus on the new information, the buffer and page header results have been excluded in the sample output in Figure 3-11. In the data section, there are two slots shown, slot 0 and slot 1. These slots map to the two index rows on the page, which can be verified through the record type of INDEX_RECORD for each of the rows. The hex data for the rows contains the page and range information for the index record, but that isn't translated with this print option. The last section contains the offset table with the slot information for both rows in the table. Note that the offset ends with 0 and counts up from the bottom. The rows start after the header incrementing up, while the offset array starts at the end of the page incrementing backward. In this manner, new rows can be added to the table without reorganizing the page.

Listing 3-17. DBCC PAGE with the Hex Rows Print Option

```
DBCC TRACEON(3604)
DBCC PAGE(0,1,377,1)
```

```
PAGE: (1:377)

BUFFER:
...

PAGE HEADER:
...

DATA:

Slot 0, Offset 0x60, Length 11, DumpStyle BYTE
Record Type = INDEX_RECORD          Record Attributes =                Record Size = 11
Memory Dump @0x0000003BCD3F8060
0000000000000000:   064edfce 3b780100 000100                           .N▮;x.....

Slot 1, Offset 0x6b, Length 11, DumpStyle BYTE
Record Type = INDEX_RECORD          Record Attributes =                Record Size = 11
Memory Dump @0x0000003BCD3F806B
0000000000000000:   06050000 007a0100 000100                           .....z.....

OFFSET TABLE:
Row - Offset
1 (0x1) - 107 (0x6b)
0 (0x0) - 96 (0x60)
```

Figure 3-11. *DBCC PAGE output for the hex rows print option*

The hex rows print option includes the page header information but expands on it to provide insight into the actual rows on the page. This information can prove valuable when attempting to understand a row's size on the page and why it may be larger than expected.

Hex Data Print Option

The third print option available for DBCC PAGE is the hex data print option, where print_ option equals 2. This print option, like the previous one, starts with the output from the page header–only print option and adds to it. The information added through this option includes the hex output of the data section of the page and the offset array. With the data section, the detail is output unformatted—just as it appears on the actual page. The output in this format can be useful when there is a need to see the page in its raw form.

To demonstrate the hex data print option, the script in Listing 3-18 will be used. In it, the DBCC PAGE command is used to retrieve the page from dbo.IndexInternalsFour that contains the last row. This row contains 25 fives in the FillerData column.

Listing 3-18. DBCC PAGE with the Hex Data Print Option

```
USE Chapter2Internals
GO
DBCC TRACEON(3604)
DBCC PAGE(0,1,377,2)
```

In the results, shown in Figure 3-12, the output contains a large block of characters in the data section. The block contains three components. On the far left is page address information, such as 0x0000003BCEBF8000. The page address identifies where on the page the information is located. The middle section contains the hex data that is contained in that section of the page. The right side of the character block contains the character representation of the hex data. For the most part, this data is not legible, except when it comes to character data being stored from character data types, such as char and nchar.

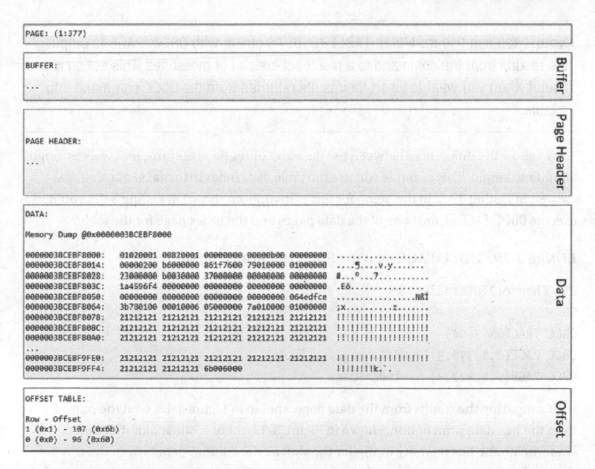

Figure 3-12. *DBCC PAGE output for the hex data print option*

Initially, the hex data print option may seem less useful than the other print options, and, in many situations, that will be the case. The true value in this print option is that DBCC PAGE does not try to interpret the page for you. It displays the page as is. With the other print options, the output will sometimes be reordered to conform to expected slot orders; an example of this is demonstrated in Chapter 10.

Row Data Print Option

The last print option available for DBCC PAGE is the row data print option, where print_option equals 3. The output from this print option can change depending on the type of page that is being requested. The basic information returned for most pages is identical to that returned from the hex rows print option: the data split per row in the hex format. The output varies, though, between data pages and index pages. For these page types, this print option provides some extremely useful information about the page.

Note   You can use the WITH TABLERESULTS option with DBCC PAGE to output the results from the command to a result set instead of messages. This option is useful when you want to insert the results returned from the DBCC command into a table.

To show the differences between the data and index page outputs, let's walk through another example. This example will use the table dbo.IndexInternalsFour that was created in Listing 3-15. In the demo for this print option, shown in Listing 3-19, you'll execute DBCC PAGE against one of the data pages and the index page for the table.

Listing 3-19. DBCC PAGE with the Row Data Print Option

```
USE Chapter2Internals
GO
DBCC TRACEON(3604)
DBCC PAGE(0,1,378,3) -- Data page
DBCC PAGE(0,1,377,3) -- Index page
```

Comparing the results from the data page, shown in Figure 3-13, with the output from the hex data print option, shown in Figure 3-12, there is one major difference. Underneath the hex memory dump for the slot, all the column details from the row are decoded and presented in a legible format. It starts with slot 0 column 1, which contains the RowID column, which it shows to have a value of 5. The next column, column 2, is the FillerData column, which contains 25 fives. For each of these columns, the physical length is noted along with the offset of the value within the row. The last value provided in the data section of the page is the KeyHashValue. This value isn't stored on the page. Instead, it is a hash value that was created when the page was placed in memory based on the keys on the page. This value is shown in tools that are used by SQL Server to report information about pages back to the end user. It may be familiar to anyone who has seen this value while investigating deadlocks.

```
PAGE: (1:378)

BUFFER:

...

PAGE HEADER:

...

Slot 0 Offset 0x60 Length 40
Record Type = PRIMARY_RECORD          Record Attributes =   NULL_BITMAP VARIABLE_COLUMNS
Record Size = 40
Memory Dump @0x0000003BCC7F8060

0000000000000000:    30000800 05000000 02000001 00280035 35353535   0............(.55555
0000000000000014:    35353535 35353535 35353535 35353535 35353535   5555555555555555555

Slot 0 Column 1 Offset 0x4 Length 4 Length (physical) 4
RowID = 5

Slot 0 Column 2 Offset 0xf Length 25 Length (physical) 25
FillerData = 5555555555555555555555555

Slot 0 Offset 0x0 Length 0 Length (physical) 0
KeyHashValue = (59855d342c69)
```

Figure 3-13. *DBCC PAGE output for the row data print option for a data page*

With the index page, there is not a change in the message output from other page types. Instead, the difference is the result set. Instead of solely providing a message output, a table is also returned. The table includes one row for every index row on the page. Reviewing the output for the index page, shown in Figure 3-14, there are two rows returned. The first row indicates that page 1:376 is the child page to the index page. It also shows that the key value for the index is RowID, which is NULL for the first index row. This indicates that this is the start of the index and no values are limiting the first ones on the child page. The second row maps to page 1:378 with a key value of 5. In this case, the key value indicates that the first row on the child page has a RowID of 5. Since the key value can change from index to index, the results from the DBCC PAGE command with these options will change as well. For every index variation, the output will return the relevant values for the index.

	FileId	PageId	Row	Level	ChildFileId	ChildPageId	RowID (key)	KeyHashValue	Row Size
1	1	377	0	1	1	376	NULL	NULL	11
2	1	377	1	1	1	378	5	NULL	11

Figure 3-14. *DBCC PAGE output for the row data print option for an index page*

The row data print option is one of the most useful options for the DBCC PAGE command. For data pages, it provides total insight into the data stored on the page, how much space it takes up, and its position. This provides a direct line into understanding why only certain rows may be fitting on the page and why, for instance, a page split may have occurred. The result set from the index page output is equally as useful. The ability to map the index rows to pages and return the key values can provide insight into how the index is organized and how the pages are laid out.

Summary

In this chapter, tools were provided that allow the details of how index data is stored to be viewed directly in SQL Server. Despite being minimally documented tools, DBCC PAGE and DBCC IND allow for a vast amount of knowledge to be gleaned from indexes that would otherwise be challenging to obtain.

Used with caution, these tools are a valuable asset to an administrator or architect looking to gain intimate knowledge of index structures and their storage.

CHAPTER 4

Fragmentation

A discussion of index internals must also address the impact of fragmentation on storage and performance. This chapter provides an overview of fragmentation, its impact on data storage, and how it can harm performance.

Page Fragmentation

SQL Server stores information in the database on 8 KB pages. In general, rows in tables are limited to that size; if they are smaller than 8 KB, SQL Server stores more than one row per page. One of the challenges with storing more than a single row per page is handling situations where the total size of all rows on a page exceeds 8 KB of space. In these situations, SQL Server must change how the rows on a page are stored. Depending on how the pages are organized, there are two ways in which SQL Server will handle the situations: forwarded records and page splits.

Note   This discussion does not consider two situations where single records can be larger than a page. These other situations are row overflow and large objects. With row overflow, SQL Server will allow a single record on a page to exceed the 8 KB in certain situations. Also, when large object values exceed the 8 KB size, they utilize LOB pages instead of data pages. These do not have a direct impact on the page fragmentation discussed in this section.

© Edward Pollack and Jason Strate 2023
E. Pollack and J. Strate, *Expert Performance Indexing in Azure SQL and SQL Server 2022*,
https://doi.org/10.1007/978-1-4842-9215-0_4

Forwarded Records

The first method for managing records when they exceed the size of a data page is through forwarded records. This applies only when the heap structure is used. With forwarded records, when a row is updated and no longer fits on the data page, SQL Server will move that record to a new data page in the heap and add pointers between the two locations. The first pointer identifies the page on which the record now exists, often called the *forwarded record pointer*. The second is on the new page, pointing back to the original page on which the forwarded record existed; it's called the *back pointer*.

The following is a logical example of how forwarding operates. Consider a page, numbered 100, that exists on a table using a heap (see Figure 4-1). This page has four rows on it, and each row is approximately 2 KB in size, totaling 8 KB in space used. If the second row is updated to now consume 2.5 KB, it will no longer fit on the page. SQL Server selects another page in the heap or allocates a new page (if needed), the page numbered 101 in this case. The second row is then written to that page, and the pointer to the new page replaces the row on page 100.

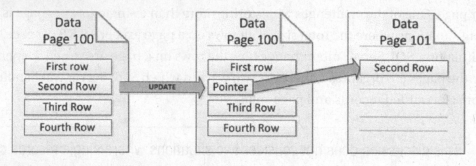

Figure 4-1. Forwarded record process diagram

The next consideration is to examine how records are forwarded on a table. For example, create a table named dbo.HeapForwardedRecords, as shown in Listing 4-1. To represent the rows from this logical example, sys.objects will be used to add 24 rows to dbo.HeapForwardedRecords. Each of these rows has a RowID to identify it and 2,000 characters, resulting in four rows per page in the table. sys.dm_db_index_physical_ stats can be used to verify (see Figure 4-2) that there are six pages in the table with a total of 24 rows.

Listing 4-1. Forwarded Record Scenario

```
USE AdventureWorks2017
GO
CREATE TABLE dbo.HeapForwardedRecords
(
  RowId INT IDENTITY(1,1)
  ,FillerData VARCHAR(2500)
);
INSERT INTO dbo.HeapForwardedRecords (FillerData)
SELECT TOP 24 REPLICATE('X',2000)
FROM sys.objects;
DECLARE @ObjectID INT = OBJECT_ID('dbo.HeapForwardedRecords');
SELECT object_id, index_type_desc, page_count, record_count, forwarded_
record_count
FROM sys.dm_db_index_physical_stats (DB_ID(), @ObjectID, NULL, NULL,
'DETAILED');
```

	object_id	index_type_desc	page_count	record_count	forwarded_record_count
1	660197402	HEAP	6	24	0

Figure 4-2. *Physical state of dbo.HeapForwardedRecords before forwarding records are introduced*

The next step in this demonstration is to create forwarded records in the table. To do this, every other row in the table will be updated to expand the values of FillerData from 2,000 to 2,500 characters, shown in Listing 4-2. As a result, two of the rows will be too large to fit in the space remaining on the pages where they are located. Instead of 8 KB of data, there will be about 9 KB being written to the 8 KB page.

Because of this, SQL Server will need to move records off the page to complete the updates. Since moving one of the rows off the page will leave enough room for the second row, only one record will be forwarded. The output from sys.dm_db_index_physical_stats (see Figure 4-3) verifies that this is the case. The page count increases to nine, and six records are logged as being forwarded. One item of particular interest is the record count. While the number of rows in the table did not increase, there are now six additional records in the table. This is because the original record for the row is still in its original position with a pointer to another record elsewhere that contains the data for the row.

Listing 4-2. Script to Cause Forwarded Records

```
USE AdventureWorks2017
GO
UPDATE dbo.HeapForwardedRecords
SET FillerData = REPLICATE('X',2500)
WHERE RowId % 2 = 0;
DECLARE @ObjectID INT = OBJECT_ID('dbo.HeapForwardedRecords');
SELECT object_id, index_type_desc, page_count, record_count, forwarded_
record_count
FROM sys.dm_db_index_physical_stats (DB_ID(), @ObjectID, NULL, NULL,
'DETAILED');
```

	object_id	index_type_desc	page_count	record_count	forwarded_record_count
1	660197402	HEAP	9	30	6

Figure 4-3. *Physical state of dbo.HeapForwardedRecords after forwarding records*

The challenge with forwarded records is that they cause rows in the table to be referenced in two locations, resulting in an increase in the amount of I/O required when retrieving data from and writing data to the table. The larger the table and the more forwarded records that exist, the more likely that forwarded records can have a negative impact on performance.

Page Splits

The second approach for handling pages where the size of the rows on the page exceeds the size of the page is to perform a page split. A page split is used on any index that is implemented under the B-tree index structure, which includes clustered and non-clustered indexes. With page splits, if a row is updated to a size that will no longer fit on the data page on which it currently exists, SQL Server will take half of the rows on the page and place them on a new page. Then SQL Server will attempt to write the data for the row to the page again. If the data will then fit on the page, the page will be written. If not, then the process will be repeated until it fits on the page.

To explain how page splits operate, an update operation that results in a page split will be explored. Similar to the previous section, consider a table with a page numbered 100 (see Figure 4-4). There are four rows stored on page 100, and each is approximately 2 KB in size. Suppose that one of the rows, such as the second row, is updated to 2.5 KB in size. The data for the page will be 8.5 KB, which exceeds the available space, which causes a page split to occur. To split the page, a new page is allocated, numbered 101, and half of the rows on the page (the third and fourth rows) are written to the new page. At this point, the second row can be written to the page since there is now 4 KB of open space on the page.

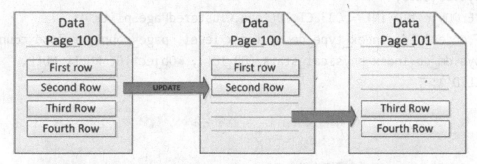

Figure 4-4. *Page split process diagram*

The following is an example of how page splits occur on a table, walking through a scenario in which page splits are forced to occur on a table. To start the example, the table dbo.ClusteredPageSplits will be created, as provided in Listing 4-3. Into this table 24 rows will be inserted that are each about 2 KB in length. This will result in four rows per page and six data pages allocated to the table. Consider the information on index level 0, which is the leaf level. Since the table is using a B-tree, through the clustered index, there will be an additional page that is used for the index tree structure. On index level 1, there are six records, which reference the six pages in the index. This information can be confirmed in Figure 4-5.

Listing 4-3. Page Split Scenario

```
USE AdventureWorks2017
GO
CREATE TABLE dbo.ClusteredPageSplits
(
  RowId INT IDENTITY(1,1)
  ,FillerData VARCHAR(2500)
  ,CONSTRAINT PK_ClusteredPageSplits PRIMARY KEY CLUSTERED (RowId)
);
INSERT INTO dbo.ClusteredPageSplits (FillerData)
SELECT TOP 24 REPLICATE('X',2000)
FROM sys.objects;
DECLARE @ObjectID INT = OBJECT_ID('dbo.ClusteredPageSplits');
SELECT object_id, index_type_desc, index_level, page_count, record_count
FROM sys.dm_db_index_physical_stats (DB_ID(), @ObjectID, NULL, NULL,
'DETAILED');
```

	object_id	index_type_desc	index_level	page_count	record_count
1	676197459	CLUSTERED INDEX	0	6	24
2	676197459	CLUSTERED INDEX	1	1	6

Figure 4-5. *Physical state of dbo.ClusteredPageSplits before page splits*

Causing page splits on the table can be accomplished by updating some of the records to exceed the size of the page. This will be done by issuing an UPDATE statement that increases the FillerData column in every other row from 2,000 to 2,500 characters in length, using the script in Listing 4-4. The resulting rows on each page will be 9 KB in size, which, like the previous example, exceeds the available page size, thus causing SQL Server to use page splits to free up space on the page.

Investigating the results (Figure 4-6) after the page splits have occurred shows the effect of the page splits on the table. For starters, instead of 6 pages at the leaf level of the index, there are 12 pages at index level 0. As mentioned, when a page split occurs, the page is split in half, and a new page is added. Since all data pages were updated in the table, all of the pages were split, resulting in a doubling in the number of pages at the leaf level. The only change at index level 0 was the addition of six pages to reference the new pages in the index.

Listing 4-4. Script to Cause Page Splits

```
USE AdventureWorks2017
GO

UPDATE dbo.ClusteredPageSplits
    SET FillerData = REPLICATE('X',2500)
WHERE RowId % 2 = 0;
USE AdventureWorks2017

GO

UPDATE dbo.ClusteredPageSplits
    SET FillerData = REPLICATE('X',2500)
WHERE RowId % 2 = 0;

DECLARE @ObjectID INT = OBJECT_ID('dbo.ClusteredPageSplits');

SELECT object_id, index_type_desc, index_level, page_count, record_count
FROM sys.dm_db_index_physical_stats (DB_ID(), @ObjectID, NULL, NULL,
'DETAILED');
```

	object_id	index_type_desc	index_level	page_count	record_count
1	676197459	CLUSTERED INDEX	0	12	24
2	676197459	CLUSTERED INDEX	1	1	12

Figure 4-6. *Physical state of after page splits*

There are two distinctions between page splits and forwarded records worthy of discussion. First, when the page splits occurred, the number of records on the data pages did not increase. A page split moves the location of records to make room for the ones within the logical index ordering. The second is that page splits do not increase the record count. Since page splits have made room for the records, there is no need for additional records to point to where data is stored.

Page splits can lead to performance problems similar to forwarded records. These performance issues occur both when the page split is occurring and afterward. During the page splits, the page that is being split needs to be locked exclusively while the records are split between two pages. This results in contention when someone needs to access a row other than the one being updated when the page split happens. After the page is split, the physical order of the data pages in the index will typically not be in their logical order within the index. This hampers SQL Server's ability to perform contiguous reads, decreasing the amount of data that can be read in single operations. In addition, the more pages that need to be read into memory for a query to execute, the slower the query will perform compared with the same results using fewer pages.

Summary

In this chapter, fragmentation was introduced, demonstrated, and described in detail. With an understanding of the impact of fragmentation on index storage and performance, the question of resolving fragmentation can be addressed in Chapter 11. Here, a more in-depth approach will be provided for identifying and resolving index fragmentation.

CHAPTER 5

Index Metadata and Statistics

With an understanding of the logical and physical fundamentals of indexes, the metadata that describes how indexes function can be discussed. These statistics provide insight into how SQL Server manages and uses indexes. It also provides the information needed to determine why an index may or may not be selected and how it is behaving. This chapter will provide a deeper understanding about where and how this information is collected. Some additional DBCC commands and dynamic management objects (DMOs) that are provided by SQL Server will be presented, as well as how that information is generated and can be used.

There are four domains of information that the statistics in this chapter will cover. The first domain is column-level statistics. This provides the query optimizer with information on the population of data within a column and, thus, an index. The next is index usage statistics. Information here provides insight into whether and how an index is being used. The third is operational statistics, which provides details about how an index has been used. The last domain of information is physical statistics, which provides insight into the physical characteristics of the index and how it is distributed within the database.

Additionally, in this chapter, the metadata and statistics that are available for columnstore indexes will be reviewed, as well as the information that is collected. This information provides an understanding of what is being stored in columnstore indexes and how that might impact the performance of queries against those indexes.

© Edward Pollack and Jason Strate 2023
E. Pollack and J. Strate, *Expert Performance Indexing in Azure SQL and SQL Server 2022*,
https://doi.org/10.1007/978-1-4842-9215-0_5

Column-Level Statistics

Column-level statistics are one of the most important areas within SQL Server when it comes to indexes. These statistics provide information on how values are distributed across the key column(s) of an index. SQL Server uses this to determine the anticipated frequency and distribution of values within an index; this is referred to as *cardinality*.

Through cardinality, the query optimizer develops a set of cost-based execution plans to find the best execution plan for executing the submitted request. If the statistics for an index are incorrect or no longer represent the data in the index, then the plan that is created will be less likely to be optimal. It is important to understand and be able to interact with statistics to be certain that indexes in an environment not only exist but also provide their expected benefits.

Note   Often, when indexes are rebuilt to "fix" performance issues, the fragmentation is usually not the cause of or direct solution to the issue. When rebuilt, indexes receive new statistics, and execution plans related to those indexes need to be recompiled, either of which is the likely cause of the performance issue vs. any index fragmentation.

There are many ways to interact with statistics within SQL Server. Some of the most common mechanisms will be reviewed in the sections that follow. For each of these methods, there will be a discussion of what they are, what they provide, and the value in using each method.

DBCC SHOW_STATISTICS

The first and likely most familiar way to interact with statistics is through the DBCC command SHOW_STATISTICS. This command will return the statistics for the requested database object, either a table or an indexed view. The information returned is a statistics object that includes three different components: the header, the histogram, and the density vector. Each provides SQL Server with an understanding of the data available in the index.

Returning the statistics object can be done with the DBCC syntax in Listing 5-1. This syntax accepts the name of the table or indexed view for the statistics, and then the target is returned. The target is either the name of the index or the column-level statistics that were created.

Listing 5-1. DBCC SHOW_STATISTICS Syntax

```
DBCC SHOW_STATISTICS ( table_or_indexed_view_name , target )
[ WITH [ < options > ]
```

There are four options that can be included with the DBCC command: NO_INFOMSGS, STAT_HEADER, DENSITY_VECTOR, and HISTOGRAM. Any or all of these options can be included in a comma-separated list.

The option NO_INFOMSGS suppresses all informational messages when the DBCC command is executed. These are error messages generated with severity from 0 to 10, with 10 being the highest severity. In most cases, since these error messages are informational, they are not of value when using this DBCC statement.

The options STAT_HEADER, DENSITY_VECTOR, and HISTOGRAM limit the output from the DBCC command. If one or more of the options are included, then only the statistics components for the items included will be returned. If none of these is selected, then all components are included. There is the STATS_STREAM option that will not be discussed as it is deprecated and may not be included in future releases of SQL Server.

With this DBCC command defined, its statistics components can be discussed in further detail. Each will be defined, and then an example of their contents from the AdventureWorks2017 database will be explored. Listing 5-2 provides the results needed for this review.

Listing 5-2. DBCC SHOW_STATISTICS for an Index on the Sales. SalesOrderDetail Table

```
USE AdventureWorks2017
GO
DBCC SHOW_STATISTICS ( 'Sales.SalesOrderDetail'
, PK_SalesOrderDetail_SalesOrderID_SalesOrderDetailID )
```

Stats Header

The stats header is the metadata portion of the statistics object. These columns, listed in Table 5-1, are primarily informational. They provide the number of rows that were considered when building the statistics and how those rows were selected through filtering. Table 5-1 also includes information on when the statistics were last updated, which can be useful when investigating potential issues with statistics quality.

Table 5-1. *Stats Header Columns from DBCC SHOW_STATISTICS*

Column Name	Description
Name	Name of the statistics object. For index statistics, this is the same name as the index.
Updated	Date and time that the statistics were last updated.
Rows	Total number of rows in the table or indexed view when the statistics were last updated. For filtered statistics or indexes, the count pertains to the number of rows that matched the filter criteria.
Rows Sampled	Count of rows sampled for statistics calculations. Histogram and density values are estimates when the Rows Sampled value is less than the value in Rows.
Steps	Number of steps in the histogram. Each step spans a range of column values followed by an upper-bound column value. The histogram steps are defined on the first key column in the statistics. The maximum number of steps is 200.
Density	Calculated as 1/*distinct values* for all values in the first key column of the statistics object, excluding the histogram boundary values. As of SQL Server 2008, this value is no longer used by the query optimizer, but is provided for information purposes and backward compatibility.
Average Key Length	Average number of bytes per value for all key columns in the statistics object.
String Index	Indicates whether the statistics object contains string summary statistics to improve the cardinality estimates for query predicates that use the LIKE operator.
Filter Expression	When populated, this is the predicate for the subset of table rows included in the statistics object.
Unfiltered Rows	Total number of rows in the table before applying the filter expression. If Filter Expression is NULL, Unfiltered Rows is equal to Rows.
Persisted Sample Percent	Added in SQL Server 2016, shows the sample percentage to use for updates to the statistics. If zero, then there is no sample percentage set for the statistics.

Reviewing the stats header information for PK_SalesOrderDetail_SalesOrderID_SalesOrderDetailID on Sales.SalesOrderDetail, shown in Figure 5-1, there are a number of items of interest. Since the Rows and Rows Sampled values are the same, these statistics are not based on estimates. The statistics were last updated on October 27, 2017 (though this value will likely differ in another copy of this database). There are 163 steps, out of a possible maximum of 200 steps, in the statistics histogram. The number of steps is equal to ranges. In this case, 163 steps mean there are 163 ranges of values, each with an upper bound provided in the statistics. The upper-bound value defines the maximum value within the range. If step 1 had an upper-bound value of 42, then step 1 would cover values 0–42. The next step would then start with 43 and include values up through its upper bound. Note the lack of a filter expression and unfiltered rows; neither the index nor statistics are filtering out rows. Lastly, the Persisted Sample Percent is set to 0, which means all rows were sampled for the statistics, which can be confirmed by comparing Rows with Rows Sampled.

Name	Updated	Rows	Rows Sampled	Steps	Density	Average key length	String Index	Filter Expression	Unfiltered Rows	Persisted Sample Percent
1 PK_SalesOrderDetail_SalesOrderID_SalesOrderDeta...	Oct 27 2017 2:33PM	121317	121317	163	0.2703436	8	NO	NULL	121317	0

Figure 5-1. *Stats header for an index on the Sales.SalesOrderDetail table*

Density Vector

The next component of the statistics object is the density vector. The density vector describes the columns within a statistics object. There is a row for each key value in the statistics or index object. For instance, if there are two columns in an index named SaleOrderID and SalesOrderDetailID, there will be two rows in the density vector. The density vector will have a row for SaleOrderID and a row for SaleOrderID and SalesOrderDetailID, shown in Figure 5-2. There are three pieces of information available for the density vector: the density, average length, and columns included in the vector (column names detailed in Table 5-2).

	All density	Average Length	Columns
1	3.178134E-05	4	SalesOrderID
2	8.242868E-06	8	SalesOrderID, SalesOrderDetailID

Figure 5-2. *Sample of the density vector for an index on the Sales. SalesOrderDetail table*

The value of the density vector is that it helps the query optimizer adjust cardinality for multiple column statistics objects. As discussed in the next section, the ranges within the histogram are based solely on the first column of the statistics object, and the density provides an adjustment between when single- or multicolumn queries are executed. While the focus for updating statistics is often on changes in the histogram, the density vector provides a valuable means to adjust ranges in the histogram to adjust for differences in the distribution of data beyond the first column of the index.

Table 5-2. *Density Vector Columns from DBCC SHOW_STATISTICS*

Column Name	Description
All Density	Returns the density for each prefix of columns in the statistics object, one row per density. The density is calculated as 1/*distinct column values*. The closer the density is to 1, the more uniform the values are in the columns.
Average Length	Average length, in bytes, to store the column values for each level of the density vector.
Columns	Names of columns in each density vector level.

Histogram

The last component of the DBCC SHOW_STATISTICS output is the histogram. The histogram provides the details of the statistics object that the query optimizer uses to determine cardinality. When building the histogram, SQL Server calculates a number of aggregates that are based on either a statistics sample or all the rows in the table or view. The aggregates measure the frequency in which values occur and group the values into no more than 200 *steps*. For each of these steps, a distribution of the statistics columns is computed that includes the number of rows in the step, the upper bound of the step, the number of rows matching the upper bound, the distinct rows in the step, and the average number of duplicate values in the step. Table 5-3 lists the columns that match these aggregates. With this information, the query optimizer is able to estimate the number of rows returned for ranges of values in an index, thus allowing it to calculate a cost associated with retrieving the row.

Table 5-3. *Histogram Columns from DBCC SHOW_STATISTICS*

Column Name	Description
RANGE_HI_KEY	Upper-bound column value for a histogram step. This column value is also called a *key value*.
RANGE_ROWS	Estimated number of rows whose column value falls within a histogram step, excluding the upper bound.
EQ_ROWS	Estimated number of rows whose column value equals the upper bound of the histogram step.
DISTINCT_RANGE_ROWS	Estimated number of rows with a distinct column value within a histogram step, excluding the upper bound.
AVG_RANGE_ROWS	Average number of rows with duplicate column values within a histogram step, excluding the upper bound (RANGE_ROWS/DISTINCT_RANGE_ROWS for DISTINCT_RANGE_ROWS > 0).

There are 163 steps in the histogram for this example. Figure 5-3, which includes a number of rows from the histogram, shows how a few of the steps in Sales. SalesOrderDetail are aggregated. The second item in Figure 5-3 shows a RANGE_HI_KEY value of 43692, which means that all SalesOrderID values between 43660 and 43692 are included in these estimates. There are 282 rows in this series, based on the RANGE_ROWS value, with 32 distinct rows in the series. Translating these numbers to the SalesOrderDetail table, there are 32 distinct SalesOrderID values with 282 SalesOrderDetailID items between them. Lastly, there are 28 SalesOrderDetailID items for SalesOrderID 43692.

	RANGE_HI_KEY	RANGE_ROWS	EQ_ROWS	DISTINCT_RANGE_ROWS	AVG_RANGE_ROWS
1	43659	0	12	0	1
2	43692	282	28	32	8.8125
3	43898	716	28	205	3.492683
4	44079	403	27	180	2.238889
5	44288	766	34	208	3.682692
6	44488	570	27	199	2.864322
7	44538	614	35	49	12.53061
8	44570	370	32	31	11.93548
9	44758	409	27	187	2.187166
10	44801	504	26	42	12

Figure 5-3. Sample of the histogram for an index on the Sales. SalesOrderDetail table

The value in the AVG_RANGE_ROWS column is quite important and can be the cause of performance problems when statistics are out of date. It states how many rows can be expected when any one value or range of values from the index are retrieved. To check the accuracy of the range average, execute the queries in Listing 5-3, which will aggregate some of the values in the second step. After it is complete, the results (as seen in Figure 5-4) will show that the averages closely match the average range rows value of 8.8125.

Listing 5-3. Query to Check AVG_RANGE_ROWS Estimate

```
USE AdventureWorks2017
GO

SELECT (COUNT(*)*1.)/COUNT(DISTINCT SalesOrderID) AS AverageRows
FROM Sales.SalesOrderDetail
WHERE SalesOrderID BETWEEN 43672 AND 43677;

SELECT (COUNT(*)*1.)/COUNT(DISTINCT SalesOrderID) AS AverageRows
FROM Sales.SalesOrderDetail
WHERE SalesOrderID BETWEEN 43675 AND 43677;

SELECT (COUNT(*)*1.)/COUNT(DISTINCT SalesOrderID) AS AverageRows
FROM Sales.SalesOrderDetail
WHERE SalesOrderID BETWEEN 43675 AND 43680;
```

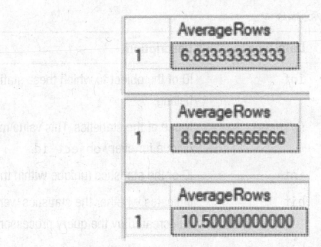

Figure 5-4. *Results of AVG_RANGE_ROWS estimate validation*

This histogram is a valuable tool to use when the statistics of an index are in question. If there is a need to determine why a query is not performing as well as expected or why a query plan is estimating rows inaccurately, the histogram can be used to validate these behaviors and results.

Catalog Views

Using DBCC SHOW_STATISTICS provides the most detailed information on query optimization statistics. It does, however, rely on the user knowing that the statistics exist. While by default, each index will have statistics created for it, column-level statistics require an alternative method for discovering them. This is accomplished through two catalog views: sys.stats and sys.stats_columns.

sys.stats

The catalog view sys.stats returns one row for every statistics object that exists within a database, regardless of whether statistics were created based on an index or column. Table 5-4 provides details on the columns in sys.stats.

Table 5-4. *Columns for sys.stats*

Column Name	Data Type	Description
object_id	int	ID of the object to which these statistics belong.
name	sysname	Name of the statistics. This value must be unique for every object_id.
stats_id	int	ID of the statistics (unique within the object).
auto_created	bit	Indicates whether the statistics were autocreated by the query processor.
user_created	bit	Indicates whether the statistics were explicitly created by a user.
no_recompute	bit	Indicates whether the statistics were created with the NORECOMPUTE option.
has_filter	bit	Indicates whether the statistics are aggregated based on a filter or subset of rows.
filter_definition	nvarchar(max)	Expression for the subset of rows included in filtered statistics.
is_temporary	bit	Indicates whether the statistics are temporary. Added in SQL Server 2012.
is_incremental	bit	Indicates whether the statistics are incremental. Added in SQL Server 2014.
has_persisted_sample	bit	Indicates whether the statistics have a persisted sample rate. Added in SQL Server 2019.
stats_generation_method	int	Flag identifying the generation method for the statistics. Added in SQL Server 2019.
stats_generattion_method_desc	varchar(80)	Text description identifying the generation method for the statistics. Added in SQL Server 2019.

sys.stats_columns

As a companion to sys.stats, the catalog view `sys.stats_columns` provides one row for every column within a statistics object. Table 5-5 lists the columns in `sys.stats_columns`.

Table 5-5. *Columns for sys.stats_columns*

Column Name	Data Type	Description
object_id	int	ID of the object of which this column is part
stats_id	int	ID of the statistics of which this column is part
stats_column_id	int	1-based ordinal within a set of stats columns
column_id	int	ID of the column from `sys.columns`

STATS_DATE

An important consideration when reviewing the accuracy of statistics is whether the statistics are out of date. A frequent method for determining whether statistics are out of date is through the STATS_DATE function. This function provides the date of the most recent update to statistics. The syntax for the function, shown in Listing 5-4, accepts an object_id and stats_id. In the case of indexes, the stats_id is the same value as the index_id.

Listing 5-4. STATS_DATE Syntax

```
STATS_DATE ( object_id , stats_id )
```

While the STATS_DATE function is routinely used to identify out-of-date statistics, that approach isn't effective for this task. The date that statistics were last updated does not necessarily reflect anything about the rate at which data has changed. A table that hasn't had an update in years with stats that are months old won't have out-of-date statistics, while a table with constant inserts, updates, and deletes with stats that were updated the previous day could have statistics that no longer represent the values in the index. While the function can be useful as a catchall for indexes whose statistics change slowly, it should be used with caution due to the example just given.

sys.dm_db_stats_properties

A better method for identifying the rate of change in statistics, which provides a qualifier that is reflective of the data, is the sys.dm_db_stats_properties DMO. The DMO, introduced in SQL Server 2008, provides the details on the number of rows that have changed since the statistics were last updated. The syntax for sys.dm_db_stats_properties, shown in Listing 5-5, accepts an object_id and stats_id. As with STATS_DATE, stats_id is the same value as the index_id. Table 5-6 lists the columns in sys.dm_db_stats_properties.

Listing 5-5. Syntax for sys.dm_db_stats_properties

```
sys.dm_db_stats_properties (object_id, stats_id)
```

Table 5-6. *Columns for sys.dm_db_stats_properties*

Column Name	Data Type	Description
object_id	int	ID of the object in question.
stats_id	int	ID of the statistics. For indexes, the ID matches the index ID.
last_updated	datetime2(7)	Date and time that the statistics were last updated.
rows	bigint	Total number of rows in the table or indexed view when the statistics were last updated. For filtered statistics or indexes, the count pertains to the number of rows that matched the filter criteria.
rows_sampled	bigint	Total number of rows sampled for statistics calculations. Histogram and density values are estimates when the rows_sampled value is less than the value in rows.
steps	int	Number of steps in the histogram. Each step spans a range of column values followed by an upper-bound column value. The histogram steps are defined on the first key column in the statistics. The maximum number of steps is 200.

(continued)

Table 5-6. *(continued)*

Column Name	Data Type	Description
unfiltered_ rows	bigint	Total number of rows in the table before applying the filter expression. If Filter Expression is NULL, unfiltered_rows is equal to rows.
modification_ counter	bigint	Count of the total number of inserted, deleted, or updated rows since the last time statistics were updated for the table.
persisted_ sample_percent	Float	A sample percentage used for statistics updates that do not explicitly specify one. A value of zero means there is no persisted sample percentage for this statistic. Added in SQL Server 2016.

Since sys.dm_db_stats_properties provides the opportunity for a better understanding of whether statistics are out of date, its output can show how changes to values in a table affect the modification_counter column. To do this, the table dbo. SalesOrderHeaderStats will be created with some indexes, as shown in with Listing 5-6. To investigate modification_counter, the query in Listing 5-7 will be used to see changes in the column. Figure 5-5 shows that there are 20,000 rows in the table with a current modification_counter value of 0 for each index and statistic listed.

Listing 5-6. Prepare a Table for sys.dm_db_stats_properties Review

```
USE AdventureWorks2017
GO

DROP TABLE IF EXISTS dbo.SalesOrderHeaderStats;

SELECT SalesOrderID
,OrderDate
,SalesOrderNumber
INTO dbo.SalesOrderHeaderStats
FROM Sales.SalesOrderHeader
WHERE SalesOrderID <= 63658
```

```
CREATE CLUSTERED INDEX CIX_SalesOrderHeaderStats
    ON dbo.SalesOrderHeaderStats(SalesOrderID)
CREATE INDEX CIX_SalesOrderHeaderStats_OrderDate
    ON dbo.SalesOrderHeaderStats(OrderDate)
CREATE INDEX CIX_SalesOrderHeaderStats_SalesOrderNumber
    ON dbo.SalesOrderHeaderStats(SalesOrderNumber)
```

Listing 5-7. sys.dm_db_stats_properties Query for dbo.SalesOrderHeaderStats

```
USE AdventureWorks2017
GO

SELECT
    OBJECT_SCHEMA_NAME(s.object_id)
    +'.'+OBJECT_NAME(s.object_id) AS object_name
    ,s.name as statistics_name
    ,x.last_updated
    ,x.rows
    ,x.rows_sampled
    ,x.steps
    ,x.unfiltered_rows
    ,x.modification_counter
FROM sys.stats s
    CROSS APPLY sys.dm_db_stats_properties(s.object_id, s.stats_id) x
WHERE s.object_id = OBJECT_ID('dbo.SalesOrderHeaderStats')
```

	object_name	statistics_name	last_updated	rows	rows_sampled	steps	unfiltered_rows	modification_counter
1	dbo.SalesOrderHeaderStats	CIX_SalesOrderHeaderStats	2019-06-09 15:07:49.1800000	20000	20000	3	20000	0
2	dbo.SalesOrderHeaderStats	CIX_SalesOrderHeaderStats_OrderDate	2019-06-09 15:07:49.2866667	20000	20000	199	20000	0
3	dbo.SalesOrderHeaderStats	CIX_SalesOrderHeaderStats_SalesOrderNumber	2019-06-09 15:07:49.3166667	20000	20000	157	20000	0

Figure 5-5. *Query results for sys.dm_db_stats_properties on dbo.*
SalesOrderHeaderStats

With a table to work with, changes can be made to the data in the table and the impact of those changes observed in statistics. For the examples, five different queries will be used, provided in Listing 5-8. The first updates the OrderDate column resulting in 40 rows changed. The second query updates 50 rows where the SalesOrderNumber is set to its current value. The third query updates the SalesOrderNumber column again but reverses the value for the same 50 rows. The fourth query inserts 11,465 records into the table. The final query deletes the first 20,000 records from the table. Between each of these queries, execute the code in Listing 5-7; doing so will provide statistics detail, as shown in the output in Figure 5-6.

Listing 5-8. Sample DML Queries on dbo.SalesOrderHeaderStats

```
USE AdventureWorks2017
GO

UPDATE dbo.SalesOrderHeaderStats
set OrderDate = GETDATE()
WHERE SalesOrderID % 500 = 1

--execute code in Listing 5-7

UPDATE dbo.SalesOrderHeaderStats
SET SalesOrderNumber = SalesOrderNumber
WHERE SalesOrderID % 400 = 1

--execute code in Listing 5-7

UPDATE dbo.SalesOrderHeaderStats
SET SalesOrderNumber = REVERSE(SalesOrderNumber)
WHERE SalesOrderID % 400 = 1

--execute code in Listing 5-7

SET IDENTITY_INSERT dbo.SalesOrderHeaderStats ON
INSERT INTO dbo.SalesOrderHeaderStats (SalesOrderID
,OrderDate
,SalesOrderNumber)
SELECT SalesOrderID
,OrderDate
,SalesOrderNumber
FROM Sales.SalesOrderHeader
WHERE SalesOrderID > 63658
SET IDENTITY_INSERT dbo.SalesOrderHeaderStats OFF
```

```
--execute code in Listing 5-7

DELETE FROM dbo.SalesOrderHeaderStats
WHERE SalesOrderID <= 63658

--execute code in Listing 5-7
```

Figure 5-6. *Query results for sys.dm_db_stats_properties for sample queries on dbo.SalesOrderHeaderStats*

Reviewing the results in Figure 5-6 provides some interesting insight into how the modification_counter column is populated. Any insert, update, or delete is considered a single change for the index and statistics. Looking at the results for query 1, the 40 rows changed the result in modification_counter for CIX_SalesOrderHeaderStats_ OrderDate to increase to 40. Similarly, when SalesOrderNumber was changed in queries 2 and 3, each query resulted in an increase of 50 to modification_counter, whether the value changed or not. Increasing the number of records caused all three indexes to increase the modification_counter value by 11,465, which coincides with the number of records inserted. Finally, in the query 5 results, 20,000 records were deleted. Interestingly enough, in the results for the last query, the statistics from CIX_SalesOrderHeaderStats were updated to better reflect the changes in values in the index.

While sys.dm_db_stats_properties doesn't provide a list of all distinct records in a table and the impact that might have on statistics, it does provide details that identify the volume of change on an index and the statistics that support it. When trying to determine whether an index has statistics that may be out of date, this DMO is extremely useful.

sys.dm_db_stats_histogram

While getting the histogram for statistics can be done with DBCC SHOW_STATISTICS, SQL Server 2016 introduced the DMO function sys.dm_db_stats_histogram. This function returns output similar to the DBCC command with the added benefit that it can be joined with other DMOs to increase the usability of the data. The syntax for the function, shown in Listing 5-9, accepts an `object_id` and `stats_id` with the columns listed in Table 5-7 returned in the output.

Listing 5-9. Syntax for sys.dm_db_stats_histogram

```
sys.dm_db_stats_histogram (object_id, stats_id)
```

Table 5-7. *Columns for sys.dm_db_stats_histogram*

Column Name	Data Type	Description
object_id	int	ID of the underlying object that the stats belong to.
stats_id	int	ID of the statistics. For indexes, the ID matches the index ID.
step_number	int	Number of steps in the histogram. Max value is 200.
range_high_key	sql_variant	Upper-bound column value for a histogram step. The column value is also called a *key value*.
range_rows	real	Estimated number of rows whose column value falls within a histogram step, excluding the upper bound.
equal_rows	real	Estimated number of rows whose column value equals the upper bound of the histogram step.
distinct_range_rows	bigint	Estimated number of rows with a distinct column value within a histogram step, excluding the upper bound.
average_range_rows	real	Average number of rows with duplicate column values in the histogram step, excluding the upper bound (`range_rows`/`distinct_range_rows for distinct_range_rows > 0`).

If sys.stats is combined with sys.dm_db_stats_histogram, as is done in Listing 5-10, a histogram for all statistics on Sales.SalesOrderDetail can be retrieved. This provides information on all steps and their range values. Scroll through the results, shown in Figure 5-7, to rows 163 and 164 to see where the range_high_key value changes from numeric to character data with the change between the statistics and steps.

Listing 5-10. sys.dm_db_stats_histogram Query for Sales.SalesOrderDetail

```
USE AdventureWorks2017;
GO
SELECT h.object_id,
       h.stats_id,
       h.step_number,
       h.range_high_key,
       h.range_rows,
       h.equal_rows,
       h.distinct_range_rows,
       h.average_range_rows
FROM sys.stats s
    CROSS APPLY sys.dm_db_stats_histogram(s.object_id, s.stats_id) h
WHERE s.object_id = OBJECT_ID('Sales.SalesOrderDetail');
```

	object_id	stats_id	step_number	range_high_key	range_rows	equal_rows	distinct_range_rows	average_range_rows
161	1810105489	1	161	74648	640	5	298	2.147651
162	1810105489	1	162	74869	511	7	220	2.322727
163	1810105489	1	163	75123	591	3	253	2.335968
164	1810105489	2	1	27520246-6C...	0	1	0	1
165	1810105489	2	2	B0AB9011-08...	966	1	966	1
166	1810105489	2	3	8E575E65-59...	2559	1	2559	1

Figure 5-7. *Query results for sys.dm_db_stats_histogram on Sales. SalesOrderDetail*

This new function is an excellent tool to view and inspect histograms. For example, if there were multiple indexes and statistics on a column, a query could be written that includes just those statistics and filter the range_high_key to only include the steps that match the records needed. At that point, the average_range_rows are available and provide an understanding of why SQL Server may have chosen one index over another.

sys.dm_db_incremental_stats_properties

With incremental index maintenance, which is discussed in Chapter 9, statistics need to be able to support incremental updates and the metadata needed to describe them. As a companion to sys.dm_db_stats_properties, the function sys.dm_db_incremental_stats_properties provides visibility to the stats properties of incremental statistics and indexes. The syntax for sys.dm_db_incremental_stats_properties, shown in Listing 5-11, includes the same parameters as the other functions: object_id and stats_id. The columns returned are identical to those in Table 5-6, except this function includes a partition_number column that provides the partition for the incremental statistics.

Listing 5-11. Syntax for sys.dm_db_incremental_stats_properties

```
sys.dm_db_incremental_stats_properties (object_id, stats_id)
```

Statistics DDL

This section has primarily focused on discussing index-level statistics. These statistics are automatically created when an index is created and then dropped when the index is dropped. Statistics can also be created on non-indexed columns and can provide significant value. When manually creating or dropping statistics on unindexed columns, there are two DDL statements that can be used to accomplish this: CREATE and DROP STATISTICS. Since they are outside the scope of this book, they will not be discussed. The third DDL statement, UPDATE STATISTICS, applies to all statistics including index-level statistics. Since UPDATE STATISTICS is primarily tied to index maintenance, it is discussed in Chapter 9.

Column-Level Statistics Summary

Query optimization statistics are a vital piece of indexing. They provide the information that the query optimizer requires in order to build cost-based query plans. Through this process, SQL Server can identify high-quality plans through their calculated costs. In this section, statistics and how they are stored were reviewed, as well as the tools needed to fully understand their details and their relationship to indexes.

Note that all missing index dynamic management objects are reset when the SQL Server service is restarted. Therefore, this data must be sampled regularly in order for it to be most useful. This is especially true on SQL Servers that restart regularly for routine maintenance.

Index Usage Statistics

The next domain of information to discuss are index usage stats. These statistics are accumulated through the DMO `sys.dm_db_index_usage_stats`, which returns counts of different types of index operations and when those operations were last performed. This provides an understanding of how frequently an index is being used and how recent that usage is.

`sys.dm_db_index_usage_stats` is a dynamic management view (DMV). Because of this, it does not require any parameters. It can be joined to other tables or views through any of the JOIN operators. Indexes appear within the DMV after they have been used for the first time or since the reset of the statistics.

Note   Along with restarting the SQL Server service, closing or detaching a database will reset all the statistics for an index that have been accumulated in `sys.dm_db_index_usage_stats`.

Within the DMV `sys.dm_db_index_usage_stats`, three types of data are provided: header columns, user statistics, and system statistics. In the next few sections, each will be explored to gain an understanding of what information they hold and how it can be used.

Header Columns

The header columns for the DMV provide referential information that can be used to determine for which index the statistics were accumulated. Table 5-8 lists the columns that are part of this. These columns are primarily used to join the DMV to system catalog views and other DMOs.

Table 5-8. *Header Columns in sys.dm_db_index_usage_stats*

Column Name	Data Type	Description
database_id	smallint	ID of the database in which the table or view is defined
object_id	int	ID of the table or view in which the index is defined
index_id	int	ID of the index

One of the first things that can be done with sys.dm_db_index_usage_stats is to check to see whether an index has been used since the last time the statistics in the DMV were reset. Similar to the T-SQL statement in Listing 5-12, the header columns can provide a list of indexes that have not been used. If using the AdventureWorks2017 database, the results will look similar to those in Figure 5-8. In these results, indexes that have not been used are returned.

Listing 5-12. Query for Header Columns in sys.dm_db_index_usage_stats

```
USE AdventureWorks2017
GO

SELECT TOP 10 OBJECT_NAME(i.object_id) AS table_name
      ,i.name AS index_name
      ,ius.database_id
      ,ius.object_id
      ,ius.index_id
FROM sys.indexes i
      LEFT JOIN sys.dm_db_index_usage_stats ius
            ON i.object_id = ius.object_id
            AND i.index_id = ius.index_id
            AND ius.database_id = DB_ID()
WHERE ius.index_id IS NULL
AND OBJECTPROPERTY(i.object_id, 'IsUserTable') = 1
ORDER BY table_name, index_name
```

	table_name	index_name	database_id	object_id	index_id
1	Address	AK_Address_rowguid	NULL	NULL	NULL
2	Address	IX_Address_AddressLine1_AddressLine2_City_StatePr...	NULL	NULL	NULL
3	Address	IX_Address_StateProvinceID	NULL	NULL	NULL
4	Address	PK_Address_AddressID	NULL	NULL	NULL
5	AddressType	AK_AddressType_Name	NULL	NULL	NULL
6	AddressType	AK_AddressType_rowguid	NULL	NULL	NULL
7	AddressType	PK_AddressType_AddressTypeID	NULL	NULL	NULL
8	AWBuildVersion	PK_AWBuildVersion_SystemInformationID	NULL	NULL	NULL
9	BillOfMaterials	AK_BillOfMaterials_ProductAssemblyID_ComponentID...	NULL	NULL	NULL
10	BillOfMaterials	IX_BillOfMaterials_UnitMeasureCode	NULL	NULL	NULL

Figure 5-8. sys.dm_db_index_usage_stats header columns query results

This type of information can be useful for managing the indexes in a database. It is an excellent resource to quickly identify the indexes that have not been used in a while. This strategy of index management is discussed further in later chapters.

User Columns

The next set of columns in the DMV sys.dm_db_index_usage_stats are the user columns. The user columns provide insight into how indexes are being used within query plans. The columns are listed in Table 5-9 and include statistics on how many times (and the most recent time) each operation occurred.

Table 5-9. User Columns in sys.dm_db_index_usage_stats

Column Name	Data Type	Description
user_seeks	bigint	Aggregate count of seeks by user queries
user_scans	bigint	Aggregate count of scans by user queries
user_lookups	bigint	Aggregate count of bookmark/key lookups by user queries
user_updates	bigint	Aggregate count of updates by user queries
last_user_seek	datetime	Date and time of last user seek
last_user_scan	datetime	Date and time of last user scan
last_user_lookup	datetime	Date and time of last user lookup
last_user_update	datetime	Date and time of last user update

sys.dm_db_index_usage_stats monitors four types of index operations. These are represented through the columns user_seeks, user_scans, user_lookups, and user_updates.

The first of the index usage columns is user_seeks. The operations for this column occur whenever a query executes and returns a single row or range of rows for which it has a direct access path. For instance, if a query executes and retrieves all the sales details for a single order or a small range of orders, similar to the queries in Listing 5-13, the query plan for these would use a seek operation (see Figure 5-9).

Listing 5-13. Index Seek Queries

```
USE AdventureWorks2017
GO

SELECT * FROM Sales.SalesOrderDetail
WHERE SalesOrderID = 43659;

SELECT * FROM Sales.SalesOrderDetail
WHERE SalesOrderID BETWEEN 43659 AND 44659;
```

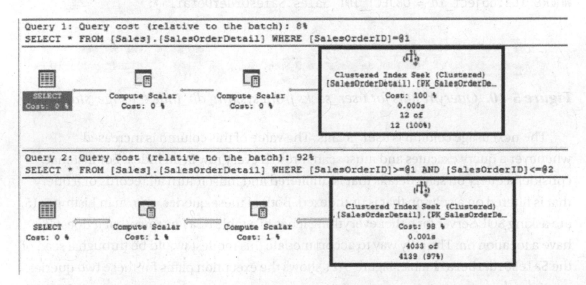

Figure 5-9. *Query plans for seek queries*

After running the queries from Listing 5-13, the DMV sys.dm_db_index_usage_stats will be counted into the user_seeks column. Listing 5-14 provides a query to investigate this. The results in Figure 5-10 show that the value in the user_seeks column is 5, which matches the count of operations from Listing 5-13. Based on this, two queries were executed using the index, and both were able to use the index to go directly to the rows that were requested.

Listing 5-14. Query for user_seeks from sys.dm_db_index_usage_stats

```
USE AdventureWorks2017
GO
SELECT TOP 10
    OBJECT_NAME(i.object_id) AS table_name
    ,i.name AS index_name
    ,ius.user_seeks
    ,ius.last_user_seek
FROM sys.indexes i
    INNER JOIN sys.dm_db_index_usage_stats ius
              ON i.object_id = ius.object_id
              AND i.index_id = ius.index_id
              AND ius.database_id = DB_ID()
WHERE ius.object_id = OBJECT_ID('Sales.SalesOrderDetail');
```

	table_name	index_name	user_seeks	last_user_seek
1	SalesOrderDetail	PK_SalesOrderDetail_SalesOrderID_SalesOrderDet...	5	2019-08-26 18:10:00.700

Figure 5-10. *Query results for user_seeks from sys.dm_db_index_usage_stats*

The next usage column is user_scans. The value of this column is increased whenever a query executes and must scan through every row in an index. For instance, consider a query on sales details that is unfiltered and must return all records or a query that is filtered on a column that is unindexed. Both of these queries, shown in Listing 5-15, are asking SQL Server for either everything it has in a table or a few rows that it doesn't have a location on. The only way to accommodate this request would be through a scan of the SalesOrderDetail table. Figure 5-11 shows the execution plans for these two queries.

Listing 5-15. Index Scan Queries

```
USE AdventureWorks2017
GO

SELECT * FROM  Sales.SalesOrderDetail;

SELECT * FROM  Sales.SalesOrderDetail
WHERE CarrierTrackingNumber = '4911-403C-98';
```

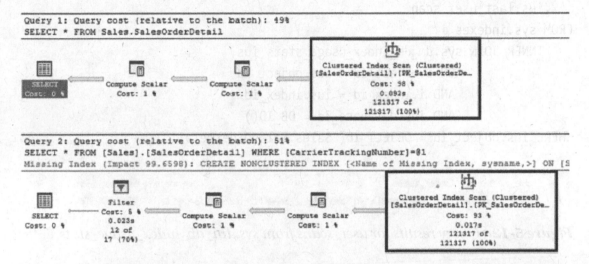

Figure 5-11. *Query plans for scan queries from sys.dm_db_index_usage_stats*

When index scans occur, they can be seen in sys.dm_db_index_usage_stats. The query in Listing 5-16 provides details from the DMV showing a count of scans. Since there were two scans, one for each of the two queries, the results in Figure 5-12 show that there have been two operations under user_scans. This information can be useful when trying to troubleshoot situations where there are large numbers of scans on a table. By looking at these details, it is possible to find the indexes with high scans and then research why queries using those indexes are choosing scans, rather than seeks.

Listing 5-16. Query for user_scans from sys.dm_db_index_usage_stats

```
USE AdventureWorks2017
GO

SELECT TOP 10
    OBJECT_NAME(i.object_id) AS table_name
    ,i.name AS index_name
    ,ius.user_scans
    ,ius.last_user_scan
FROM sys.indexes i
    INNER JOIN sys.dm_db_index_usage_stats ius
              ON i.object_id = ius.object_id
              AND i.index_id = ius.index_id
              AND ius.database_id = DB_ID()
WHERE ius.object_id = OBJECT_ID('Sales.SalesOrderDetail');
```

	table_name	index_name	user_scans	last_user_scan
1	SalesOrderDetail	PK_SalesOrderDetail_SalesOrderID_SalesOrderDet...	2	2019-06-09 19:38:49.773

Figure 5-12. *Query results for user_scans from sys.dm_db_index_usage_stats*

The third column in the DMV is user_lookups. User lookups occur when a seek on a non-clustered index occurs, but the index does not have all of the required columns in it to satisfy the query. When this happens, the query must look up the columns from the clustered index. An example would be a query against the SalesOrderDetail table that is returning the ProductID and CarrierTrackingNumber columns, which is filtered on ProductID; Listing 5-17 shows this query. Figure 5-13 shows the query plan, which includes a seek on the non-clustered index and a key lookup on the clustered index.

Listing 5-17. Index Lookup Query

```
USE AdventureWorks2017
GO

SELECT ProductID, CarrierTrackingNumber
FROM Sales.SalesOrderDetail
WHERE ProductID = 778
GO
```

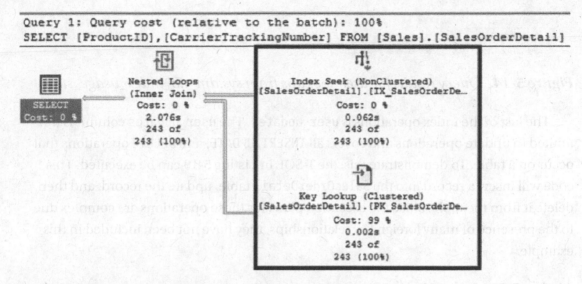

```
Query 1: Query cost (relative to the batch): 100%
SELECT [ProductID],[CarrierTrackingNumber] FROM [Sales].[SalesOrderDetail]
```

Figure 5-13. *Query plans for seek and key lookup*

In sys.dm_db_index_usage_stats, there will be a tally of one for both user_seeks and user_lookups. To see these values, use Listing 5-18, which will return the results in Figure 5-14. Patterns between these columns can help with determining proper clustered index keys or identifying when to modify indexes to avoid key lookups. Key lookups are not necessarily problematic, but can be a performance bottleneck if overused and left unchecked. Effective management of key lookups will be further discussed later in this book.

Listing 5-18. Query for user_lookups from sys.dm_db_index_usage_stats

```
SELECT TOP 10
    OBJECT_NAME(i.object_id) AS table_name
    ,i.name AS index_name
    ,ius.user_seeks
    ,ius.user_lookups
    ,ius.last_user_lookup
FROM sys.indexes i
    INNER JOIN sys.dm_db_index_usage_stats ius
            ON i.object_id = ius.object_id
            AND i.index_id = ius.index_id
            AND ius.database_id = DB_ID()
WHERE ius.object_id = OBJECT_ID('Sales.SalesOrderDetail');
```

	table_name	index_name	user_seeks	user_lookups	last_user_lookup
1	SalesOrderDetail	PK_SalesOrderDetail_SalesOrderID_SalesOrderDet...	5	1	2019-08-26 19:45:26.037
2	SalesOrderDetail	IX_SalesOrderDetail_ProductID	1	0	NULL

Figure 5-14. *Query results for user_lookups from sys.dm_db_index_usage_stats*

The last of the index operations is user_updates. The user_updates column is not limited to update operations and covers all INSERT, UPDATE, and DELETE operations that occur on a table. To demonstrate this, the T-SQL in Listing 5-19 can be executed. This code will insert a record into the SalesOrderDetail table, update the record, and then delete it from the table. Since the execution plans for these operations are complex due to the presence of many foreign key relationships, they have not been included in this example.

Listing 5-19. Index Update Queries

```
USE AdventureWorks2017
GO

INSERT INTO Sales.SalesOrderDetail
(SalesOrderID, CarrierTrackingNumber, OrderQty, ProductID, SpecialOfferID,
UnitPrice, UnitPriceDiscount, ModifiedDate)
SELECT SalesOrderID, CarrierTrackingNumber, OrderQty, ProductID,
SpecialOfferID, UnitPrice, UnitPriceDiscount, GETDATE() AS ModifiedDate
FROM Sales.SalesOrderDetail
WHERE SalesOrderDetailID = 1;

UPDATE Sales.SalesOrderDetail
SET CarrierTrackingNumber = '999-99-9999'
WHERE ModifiedDate > DATEADD(d, -1, GETDATE());

DELETE FROM Sales.SalesOrderDetail
WHERE ModifiedDate > DATEADD(d, -1, GETDATE());
```

At the completion of the execution of the code listing, there were three operations that occurred on the table. For each of these operations, sys.dm_db_index_usage_stats accumulated one tick in the user_updates column. Execute the code in Listing 5-20 to see the activity that occurred on the index. The results will be similar to those in Figure 5-15. Besides the changes made to the clustered index for SalesOrderDetail, updates made to the non-clustered indexes are also included. Being able to see the full effect of an insert, update, or delete on a table can help provide a better understanding of all I/O that occurs when write operations are executed.

Listing 5-20. Query for user_updates from sys.dm_db_index_usage_stats

```
USE AdventureWorks2017
GO
SELECT TOP 10
    OBJECT_NAME(i.object_id) AS table_name
    ,i.name AS index_name
    ,ius.user_updates
    ,ius.last_user_update
FROM sys.indexes i
    INNER JOIN sys.dm_db_index_usage_stats ius
            ON i.object_id = ius.object_id
            AND i.index_id = ius.index_id
            AND ius.database_id = DB_ID()
WHERE ius.object_id = OBJECT_ID('Sales.SalesOrderDetail');
```

	table_name	index_name	user_updates	last_user_update
1	SalesOrderDetail	AK_SalesOrderDetail_rowguid	2	2019-08-26 19:45:26.770
2	SalesOrderDetail	PK_SalesOrderDetail_SalesOrderID_SalesOrderDet...	3	2019-08-26 19:45:26.770
3	SalesOrderDetail	IX_SalesOrderDetail_ProductID	2	2019-08-26 19:45:26.770

Figure 5-15. *Query results for user_updates from sys.dm_db_index_usage_stats*

System Columns

The last set of columns in sys.dm_db_index_usage_stats are the system columns. System columns return the same general information as the user columns, except that they only include activity related to background processes. Whenever a non-user process triggers within SQL Server, such as an automatic statistics update, that activity will be tracked through these columns. Table 5-10 lists the system columns.

Table 5-10. *System Columns in sys.dm_db_index_usage_stats*

Column Name	Data Type	Description
system_seeks	bigint	Number of seeks by system queries
system_scans	bigint	Number of scans by system queries
system_lookups	bigint	Number of lookups by system queries
system_updates	bigint	Number of updates by system queries
last_system_seek	datetime	Time of last system seek
last_system_scan	datetime	Time of last system scan
last_system_lookup	datetime	Time of last system lookup
last_system_update	datetime	Time of last system update

For most common usage, these columns can be ignored. It is valuable, though, to understand how they are aggregated. To see an example, execute the code in Listing 5-21, which may run for up to 1 minute. This will change a majority of the rows in the SalesOrderDetail table. Since more than 20 percent of the rows have changed, an automatic statistics update will be triggered. The statistics update is not directly related to user activity and is instead a background (a.k.a. system) process.

Listing 5-21. Update for Sales.SalesOrderDetail

```
USE AdventureWorks2017
GO

UPDATE Sales.SalesOrderDetail
SET UnitPriceDiscount = 0.01
WHERE UnitPriceDiscount = 0.00;
```

After the update has completed, run the T-SQL statements in Listing 5-22. This will return results from sys.stats and the system columns from sys.dm_db_index_usage_stats, shown in Figure 5-16. Within these is the system_scans column that shows three system scans have occurred on Sales.SalesOrderDetail. These related to statistics updates, one of which occurred on the UnitPriceDiscount column. Looking at the times when the statistics were created shows the updates on CarrierTrackingNumber, then SalesOrderDetailId, ModifiedDate, and finally UnitPriceDiscount.

Listing 5-22. Query for System Columns in sys.dm_db_index_usage_stats

```
USE AdventureWorks2017
GO

SELECT S.object_id,
       S.name,
       S.auto_created,
       STATS_DATE(S.object_id, S.stats_id),
       X.stats_column_names
FROM sys.stats S
    CROSS APPLY
(
    SELECT STRING_AGG(C.name, ',') AS stats_column_names
    FROM sys.stats_columns SC
        INNER JOIN sys.columns C
            ON C.object_id = SC.object_id
                AND C.column_id = SC.column_id
    WHERE S.object_id = SC.object_id
        AND S.stats_id = SC.stats_id
) X
WHERE S.object_id = OBJECT_ID('Sales.SalesOrderDetail');
SELECT OBJECT_NAME(i.object_id) AS table_name
    ,i.name AS index_name
    ,ius.system_seeks
    ,ius.system_scans
    ,ius.system_lookups
    ,ius.system_updates
    ,ius.last_system_seek
    ,ius.last_system_scan
    ,ius.last_system_lookup
    ,ius.last_system_update
FROM sys.indexes i
    INNER JOIN sys.dm_db_index_usage_stats ius
```

125

```
              ON i.object_id = ius.object_id
              AND i.index_id = ius.index_id
              AND ius.database_id = DB_ID()
WHERE ius.object_id = OBJECT_ID('Sales.SalesOrderDetail');
```

	object_id	name	auto_created	(No column name)	stats_column_names
1	1810105489	FK_SalesOrderDetail_SalesOrderID_SalesOrderDet...	0	2017-10-27 14:33:07.540	SalesOrderID,SalesOrderDetailID
2	1810105489	AK_SalesOrderDetail_rowguid	0	2017-10-27 14:33:08.960	rowguid
3	1810105489	IX_SalesOrderDetail_ProductID	0	2017-10-27 14:33:09.097	ProductID
4	1810105489	_WA_Sys_00000006_6BE40491	1	2017-10-27 14:33:14.420	SpecialOfferID
5	1810105489	_WA_Sys_00000003_6BE40491	1	2019-08-26 13:44:53.120	CarrierTrackingNumber
6	1810105489	_WA_Sys_00000002_6BE40491	1	2019-08-26 19:45:26.347	SalesOrderDetailID
7	1810105489	_WA_Sys_0000000B_6BE40491	1	2019-08-26 19:45:26.413	ModifiedDate
8	1810105489	_WA_Sys_00000008_6BE40491	1	2019-08-26 19:49:53.133	UnitPriceDiscount

	table_name	index_name	system_seeks	system_scans	system_lookups	system_updates	last_system_seek	last_system_scan	last_system_lookup	last_system_update
1	SalesOrderDetail	AK_SalesOrderDetail_rowguid	0	0	0	0	NULL	NULL	NULL	NULL
2	SalesOrderDetail	FK_SalesOrderDetail_SalesOrderID_SalesOrderDet...	0	3	0	0	NULL	2019-08-26 19:49:53.017	NULL	NULL
3	SalesOrderDetail	IX_SalesOrderDetail_ProductID	0	1	0	0	NULL	2019-08-26 19:45:26.277	NULL	NULL

Figure 5-16. *sys.stats and sys.dm_db_index_usage_stats system columns query results*

From a usefulness perspective, these columns are not typically significant with respect to a user application, but do allow for a fuller picture of index usage across all SQL Server functions.

Index Usage Stats Summary

In this section, the statistics found in DMV sys.dm_db_index_usage_stats were discussed. This DMV provides extremely useful statistics about how and if indexes are being used in a database. By monitoring these statistics over the long run, it is possible to understand which indexes are providing the most value. Strategies for using these columns to improve indexing performance will be discussed in Chapter 9.

Index Operational Statistics

The third area of statistics to consider are index operational stats. These statistics are presented to users through the DMO sys.dm_db_index_operational_stats. From a high level, this DMO provides detailed information on I/O, locking, latching, and access methods that occur on indexes. Through this information, indexes that may be encountering performance issues can be identified. Once identified, it is possible to learn what is causing those performance issues. This section provides an understanding of the statistics provided in the DMO and how to investigate indexes using these statistics.

Unlike sys.dm_db_index_usage_stats, sys.dm_db_index_operational_stats is a dynamic management function (DMF). Because of this, it requires parameters to be supplied when it is used. Table 5-11 details the parameters for this DMF.

Table 5-11. *Parameters for sys.dm_db_index_operational_stats*

Parameter Name	Data Type	Description
database_id	smallint	ID of the database where the indexes reside. Providing the value 0, NULL, or DEFAULT will return index information for all databases. The function DB_ID can be used in this parameter.
object_id	int	Object ID of the table or view for which information should be returned. Providing the value 0, NULL, or DEFAULT will return index details for all tables or views in the database.
index_id	int	Index ID of the index for which information should be returned. Providing the value -1, NULL, or DEFAULT will return details for all indexes on the table or view.
partition_number	int	Partition number for which index information should be returned. Providing the value 0, NULL, or DEFAULT will return details for all partitions.

Through the parameters, statistics on indexes can be as widely or narrowly focused as necessary. This flexibility is useful since sys.dm_db_index_operational_stats does not allow the use of the CROSS APPLY or OUTER APPLY operator. When passing the parameters into the DMF, the syntax for doing so is defined in Listing 5-23.

Listing 5-23. Index Operational Stats Syntax

```
sys.dm_db_index_operational_stats (
    { database_id | NULL | 0 | DEFAULT }
    , { object_id | NULL | 0 | DEFAULT }
    , { index_id | 0 | NULL | -1 | DEFAULT }
    , { partition_number | NULL | 0 | DEFAULT }
)
```

> **Note**   The DMF `sys.dm_db_index_operational stats` can accept the use
> of the Transact-SQL functions `DB_ID()` and `OBJECT_ID()`. These functions can
> be used for the parameters `database_id` and `object_id`, respectively.

Header Columns

For every row that is returned through the DMF, there will be a `database_id`, `object_id`, `index_id`, and `partition_number`. These columns are defined further in Table 5-12. As is implied through the `partition_number`, the granularity of the results for this DMF is at the partition level. For nonpartitioned indexes, the partition number will be 1.

Table 5-12.   *Header Columns in sys.dm_db_index_operational_stats*

Column Name	Data Type	Description
database_id	smallint	ID of the database on which the table or view is defined
object_id	int	ID of the table or view on which the index is defined
index_id	int	ID of the index
partition_number	int	1-based partition number within the index or heap
hobt_id	bigint	ID used to identify the heap or B-tree (hobt) associated with an index partition. New as of SQL Server 2016

The header columns provide the basis for understanding which indexes the statistics apply to. This will help provide perspective regarding the information that is returned. Also, they can be used to join to catalog views, such as `sys.indexes`, to provide the names of the indexes.

The useful information in this DMF comes in the rest of the columns returned by the function. The information that can be returned provides insight into DML activity, the page allocation cycle, data access patterns, index contention, and disk activity. In the following sections, each column returned by the DMF will be reviewed, as well as how they provide insight into index usage.

DML Activity

Understanding DML activity on an index is an ideal place to begin analysis of index usage statistics. Table 5-13 lists the columns that represent this activity. They provide a count of the number of rows that are affected by DML operations. The statistics that follow are similar to those in sys.dm_db_index_usage_stats, but with a few differences in perspective that will be discussed next.

Table 5-13. *DML Activity Columns in sys.dm_db_index_operational_stats*

Column Name	Data Type	Description
leaf_insert_count	bigint	Cumulative count of leaf-level rows inserted.
leaf_delete_count	bigint	Cumulative count of leaf-level rows deleted.
leaf_update_count	bigint	Cumulative count of leaf-level rows updated.
leaf_ghost_count	bigint	Cumulative count of leaf-level rows that are marked to be deleted but not yet removed.
nonleaf_insert_count	bigint	Cumulative count of inserts above the leaf level. For heaps, this value will always be 0.
nonleaf_delete_count	bigint	Cumulative count of deletes above the leaf level. For heaps, this value will always be 0.
nonleaf_update_count	bigint	Cumulative count of updates above the leaf level. For heaps, this value will always be 0.

Within sys.dm_db_index_operational_stats, there are two areas where DML activity can be tracked: the leaf and nonleaf levels. For more information on DML activity on leaf and nonleaf pages, see Chapter 4.

The difference between these two types of data changes is important to identifying whether index changes occurred directly via DML activity or as the result of internal indexing changes. Nonleaf-level DML activity happens when leaf-level activity results in a change in how the index is structured and is not something that can be directly influenced with an INSERT, UPDATE, or DELETE statement.

Both leaf-level and nonleaf-level DML activities are broken apart into statistics based on the type of DML operation that has occurred. As previously indicated, DML activity monitors INSERT, UPDATE, and DELETE activities. For each of these operations, there is a column in sys.dm_db_index_operational_stats. Additionally, there is a column that counts records that have been ghosted off the leaf-level DML activity.

During DELETE operations, rows affected by the statement are deleted in a two-phase operation. Initially, the records are marked for deletion. When this occurs, the records are referred to as being *ghosted*; the rows in this state are counted in leaf_ghost_count. At regular intervals, a cleanup thread within SQL Server will go through and perform the actual delete operation on rows marked as ghosted. At that point, the records will be counted in the leaf_delete_count. This process improves the performance of delete operations since the actual delete of a row happens after the transaction is committed. In the event of transaction rollback, the ghost flag on a row is all that needs to revert rather than an attempt to recreate the row in the table. This activity occurs only at the leaf level; nonleaf pages are deleted whenever all the rows associated with the pages have been deleted or otherwise removed.

While this activity on the DMF is similar to that found in sys.dm_db_index_usage_stats, there are some stark differences. The first is that the information in sys.dm_db_index_operational_stats is more granular than that in sys.dm_db_index_usage_stats. Operational stats report down to the leaf and nonleaf levels, whereas usage stats do not. Along with the granularity is the difference in how the counts are tabulated. Usage stats count one for every plan that performs the operation on the index, regardless of how many rows are affected. Operational stats differ in that the count increments for every row that has the DML operation performed. To summarize, usage stats aggregate when the index is used, and operational stats aggregate based on how much of the index is used.

The code in Listing 5-24 illustrates how operational stats are tabulated. In the listing, 79 rows are added to the table dbo.Karaoke. Then 44 rows are deleted from the table. This is followed by 35 rows being updated in the table. The last query returns operational stats based on the DML activity. Figure 5-17 shows the results of the final query.

Listing 5-24. DML Activity Script

```
USE AdventureWorks2017
GO

IF OBJECT_ID('dbo.Karaoke') IS NOT NULL
  DROP TABLE dbo.Karaoke;
```

```
CREATE TABLE dbo.Karaoke
(
 KaraokeID INT
,Duet BIT
,CONSTRAINT PK_Karaoke_KaraokeID PRIMARY KEY CLUSTERED (KaraokeID)
);
INSERT INTO dbo.Karaoke
    SELECT ROW_NUMBER() OVER (ORDER BY t.object_id)
        ,t.object_id % 2
    FROM sys.tables t;
DELETE FROM dbo.Karaoke
WHERE  Duet = 0;

UPDATE dbo.Karaoke
SET    Duet = 0
WHERE  Duet = 1;

SELECT OBJECT_SCHEMA_NAME(ios.object_id) + '.' + OBJECT_NAME(ios.object_id)
AS table_name
    ,i.name AS index_name
    ,ios.leaf_insert_count
    ,ios.leaf_update_count
    ,ios.leaf_delete_count
    ,ios.leaf_ghost_count
FROM sys.dm_db_index_operational_stats(DB_ID(),NULL,NULL,NULL) ios
    INNER JOIN sys.indexes i
       ON i.object_id = ios.object_id
          AND i.index_id = ios.index_id
WHERE ios.object_id = OBJECT_ID('dbo.Karaoke')
ORDER BY ios.range_scan_count DESC;
```

	table_name	index_name	leaf_insert_count	leaf_update_count	leaf_delete_count	leaf_ghost_count
1	dbo.Karaoke	PK_Karaoke_KaraokeID	79	35	0	44

Figure 5-17. *DML activity query results (results may vary on your system)*

The value in looking at DML activity in an index is to help understand what is happening to the data in an index in detail. For example, if a non-clustered index is being updated often, it may be beneficial to look at the columns in the index to determine whether the volatility of the columns matches the benefit of the index. It is good to review indexes with high amounts of DML activity and consider whether the activity matches the understanding of the database platform. An index that is written often and rarely (or never) read is a good candidate to consider for removal.

SELECT Activity

After DML activity, the next area of information that can be evaluated is the information on SELECT activity. The SELECT activity columns, shown in Table 5-14, identify the type of physical operation that was used when queries were executed. There are three types of access that SQL Server collects information on: range scans, singleton lookups, and forwarded records.

Table 5-14. *Access Pattern Columns in sys.dm_db_index_operational_stats*

Column Name	Data Type	Description
range_scan_count	bigint	Cumulative count of range and table scans on the index or heap.
singleton_lookup_count	bigint	Cumulative count of single row retrievals from the index or heap.
forwarded_fetch_count	bigint	Count of rows that were fetched through a forwarding record.

Range Scan

Range scans occur whenever a range of rows or a table scan is used to access data. When considering a range of rows, it can be anywhere from 1 to 1,000 or more rows. The number of rows in the range is not material in how SQL Server accesses the data. With table scans, the number of rows is also not important, but it is assumed that it includes all records in the index. In sys.dm_db_index_operational_stats, these values are stored in the column range_scan_count.

To see this information collected in range_scan_count, execute the code in Listings 5-13 and 5-15 from the previous section. Before doing this, take the AdventureWorks2017 database offline and then bring it back online. This will reset the statistics returned from the DMOs. In these two code samples, four queries will be executed. The first two will result in index seeks in the query plan, shown in Figure 5-9. The second two queries result in index scans, as shown in the execution plans in Figure 5-11. Running the code in Listing 5-25 will show, as displayed in Figure 5-18, that all four queries used a range scan to retrieve the data from the table.

Listing 5-25. Query for range_scan_count from sys.dm_db_index_ operational_stats

```
USE AdventureWorks2017
GO
SELECT OBJECT_NAME(ios.object_id) AS table_name
    ,i.name AS index_name
    ,ios.range_scan_count
FROM sys.dm_db_index_operational_stats(DB_ID(),OBJECT_ID('Sales.
SalesOrderDetail'),NULL,NULL) ios
    INNER JOIN sys.indexes i
        ON i.object_id = ios.object_id
            AND i.index_id = ios.index_id
ORDER BY ios.range_scan_count DESC;
```

	table_name	index_name	range_scan_count
1	SalesOrderDetail	PK_SalesOrderDetail_SalesOrderID_SalesOrderDet...	4

Figure 5-18. *Query results for range_scan_count*

Singleton Lookup

The next statistics column collected on SELECT activity is singleton_lookup_count. Values in this column are increased whenever the key lookup, formerly bookmark lookup, is used. In general terms, this is the same type of information as collected in the column user_lookups in sys.dm_db_index_usage_stats. There is a significant difference, though, between user_lookups and singleton_lookup_count. When a key lookup is used, `user_lookups` will increment by one to indicate that the index operation has been used. With `singleton_lookup_count`, every row that uses the key lookup operation will be counted in this column.

For example, running the code in Listing 5-17 will result in a key lookup. This can be validated by examining the execution plan, shown in Figure 5-13. The statistics from this were discussed previously and are shown in Figure 5-19. The new information to look at can be investigated by running the T-SQL statement in Listing 5-26. This shows a value of 243 in `singleton_lookup_count`. This is an important distinction for this column. Rather than knowing that key lookups have occurred, this statistic provides information on the size of lookup operations. Consider scenarios where the ratio of singleton lookups to range scans was high. This may indicate that there are other indexing alternatives to consider.

Listing 5-26. Query for singleton_lookup_count from sys.dm_db_index_operational_stats

```
USE AdventureWorks2017
GO
SELECT OBJECT_NAME(ios.object_id) AS table_name
    ,i.name AS index_name
    ,ios.singleton_lookup_count
FROM sys.dm_db_index_operational_stats(DB_ID(),OBJECT_ID('Sales.
SalesOrderDetail'),NULL,NULL) ios
    INNER JOIN sys.indexes i
        ON i.object_id = ios.object_id
        AND i.index_id = ios.index_id
ORDER BY ios. singleton_lookup_count DESC;
```

	table_name	index_name	row_lock_count	row_lock_wait_count	row_lock_wait_in_ms
1	SalesOrderDetail	IX_SalesOrderDetail_ProductID	44	0	0
2	SalesOrderDetail	PK_SalesOrderDetail_SalesOrderID_SalesOrderDet...	0	0	0
3	SalesOrderDetail	AK_SalesOrderDetail_rowguid	0	0	0

Figure 5-19. *Query results for singleton_lookup_count*

Forwarded Fetch

The last column of statistics collected on SELECT activity is forwarded_fetch_count. Forwarded records occur in heaps when a row increases in size and can no longer fit on the page where it currently resides. The column forwarded_fetch_count increases by one each time a record forward operation occurs.

To demonstrate, the code in Listing 5-27 builds a table with a heap and populates it with values. An UPDATE statement then increases the size of every third row. The size of the new row will exceed the available space on the page, resulting in a forwarded record.

Listing 5-27. T-SQL Script for Forwarded Records

```
USE AdventureWorks2017
GO

CREATE TABLE dbo.ForwardedRecords
    (
    ID INT IDENTITY(1,1)
    ,VALUE VARCHAR(8000)
    );
INSERT INTO dbo.ForwardedRecords (VALUE)
SELECT REPLICATE(type, 500)
FROM sys.objects;
UPDATE dbo.ForwardedRecords
SET VALUE = REPLICATE(VALUE, 16)
WHERE ID%3 = 1;
```

Once the script is completed, the sys.dm_db_index_operational_stats script in Listing 5-28 can be used to view the number of times that forwarded records have been fetched. In this case, the 222 records that were forwarded translated to a forwarded_fetch_count of 222, as shown in Figure 5-20. This column is useful when looking into the performance counter Forwarded Records/sec. Reviewing this column will help identify which heap is leading to the counter activity, providing a focus on the table to investigate.

Listing 5-28. Query for forwarded_fetch_count from sys.dm_db_index_operational_stats

```
 USE AdventureWorks2017
GO
SELECT OBJECT_NAME(ios.object_id) AS table_name
       ,i.name AS index_name
       ,ios.forwarded_fetch_count
FROM sys.dm_db_index_operational_stats(DB_ID(),OBJECT_ID('dbo.
ForwardedRecords'),NULL,NULL) ios
       INNER JOIN sys.indexes i
           ON i.object_id = ios.object_id
              AND i.index_id = ios.index_id
ORDER BY ios.forwarded_fetch_count DESC
```

	table_name	index_name	forwarded_fetch_count
1	ForwardedRecords	NULL	222

Figure 5-20. *Query result for forwarded_fetch_count*

Locking Contention

As data is read or written within SQL Server databases, it is locked to provide consistency as other operations may attempt to use it. At times, locking for one user can interfere with another user's requests. sys.dm_db_index_operational_stats provides columns that detail the counts of locks and time spent waiting for locks to resolve. Table 5-15 lists three groups of columns that relate to three types of locks that are tracked in sys.dm_db_index_operational_stats to provide insight into locking contention: row locks, page locks, and index lock promotion.

Table 5-15. *Index Contention Columns in sys.dm_db_index_operational_stats*

Column Name	Data Type	Description
row_lock_count	bigint	Cumulative number of row locks requested
row_lock_wait_count	bigint	Cumulative number of times the database engine waited on a row lock
row_lock_wait_in_ms	bigint	Total number of milliseconds the database engine waited on a row lock
page_lock_count	bigint	Cumulative number of page locks requested
page_lock_wait_count	bigint	Cumulative number of times the database engine waited on a page lock
page_lock_wait_in_ms	bigint	Total number of milliseconds the database engine waited on a page lock
index_lock_promotion_attempt_count	bigint	Cumulative number of times the database engine tried to escalate locks
index_lock_promotion_count	bigint	Cumulative number of times the database engine escalated locks

Row Lock

The first set of columns consists of the row lock columns. These columns include row_lock_count, row_lock_wait_count, and row_lock_wait_in_ms. Through these columns, the number of locks that occur on a row can be measured, as well as whether there was contention when acquiring the row lock. Row lock contention can often be observed by its effect on transaction performance through blocking and deadlocking.

To demonstrate how this information is collected, execute the code in Listing 5-29. In this script, rows from the Sales.SalesOrderDetail table are retrieved based on ProductID. In the AdventureWorks2017 database, the query retrieves 44 rows.

Listing 5-29. T-SQL Script to Generate Row Locks

```
USE AdventureWorks2017
GO

ALTER INDEX ALL ON Sales.SalesOrderDetail REBUILD;

SELECT SalesOrderID
    ,SalesOrderDetailID
    ,CarrierTrackingNumber
    ,OrderQty
FROM Sales.SalesOrderDetail
WHERE ProductID = 710;
```

To observe the row locks that were acquired by the query, use the row lock columns in the query provided in Listing 5-30. In these results, for each row that was returned by the query against Sales.SalesOrderDetail, there is one lock included in the results of sys.dm_db_index_operational_stats, shown in Figure 5-21. As a result, there were a total of 44 row locks placed on the index IX_SalesOrderDetail_ProductID.

Note that there is no information returned for the row_lock_wait_count and row_lock_wait_in_ms columns. This is because the script was not blocked by any other query. Had the query in Listing 5-29 been blocked by another transaction, then the values in these columns would have been adjusted to reflect that blocking.

Listing 5-30. Query for Row Locks in sys.dm_db_index_operational_stats

```
USE AdventureWorks2017
GO

SELECT OBJECT_NAME(ios.object_id) AS table_name
    ,i.name AS index_name
    ,ios.row_lock_count
    ,ios.row_lock_wait_count
    ,ios.row_lock_wait_in_ms
FROM sys.dm_db_index_operational_stats(DB_ID(),OBJECT_ID('Sales.
SalesOrderDetail'),NULL,NULL) ios
    INNER JOIN sys.indexes i
```

```
            ON i.object_id = ios.object_id
              AND i.index_id = ios.index_id
ORDER BY ios.range_scan_count DESC;
```

	table_name	index_name	page_lock_count	page_lock_wait_count	page_lock_wait_in_ms
1	SalesOrderDetail	IX_SalesOrderDetail_ProductID	2	0	0
2	SalesOrderDetail	PK_SalesOrderDetail_SalesOrderID_SalesOrderDet...	44	0	0
3	SalesOrderDetail	AK_SalesOrderDetail_rowguid	0	0	0

Figure 5-21. *Query results for row locks*

Page Lock

The next set of columns are the page lock columns. The columns in this group have similar characteristics to the row lock columns, with the exception that they are scoped at the page level instead of the row level. For every page that relates to an accessed row, a page lock is acquired. These columns are page_lock_count, page_lock_wait_count, and page_lock_wait_in_ms. When monitoring for locking contention on an index, it is important to look at both page and row levels to identify whether the contention is on the individual rows being accessed or different rows accessed on the same page.

To review the differences, continue with the query from Listing 5-29 and retrieve the page lock statistics that were collected in sys.dm_db_index_operational_stats for the query. This information is available using the script in Listing 5-31. The results are a bit different than those for the row locks. For the page locks, see Figure 5-22; there are only two page locks on the index IX_SalesOrderDetail_ProductID. In addition, there are 44 page locks on PK_SalesOrderDetail_SalesOrderID_SalesOrderDetailID, which did not encounter any row locks.

Listing 5-31. Query for Page Locks in sys.dm_db_index_operational_stats

```
USE AdventureWorks2017
GO

SELECT OBJECT_NAME(ios.object_id) AS table_name
      ,i.name AS index_name
      ,ios.page_lock_count
      ,ios.page_lock_wait_count
      ,ios.page_lock_wait_in_ms
```

```
FROM sys.dm_db_index_operational_stats(DB_ID(),OBJECT_ID('Sales.
SalesOrderDetail'),NULL,NULL) ios
        INNER JOIN sys.indexes i
            ON i.object_id = ios.object_id
                AND i.index_id = ios.index_id
ORDER BY ios.range_scan_count DESC;
```

	table_name	index_name	index_lock_promotion_attempt_count	index_lock_promotion_count
1	SalesOrderDetail	PK_SalesOrderDetail_SalesOrderID_SalesOrderDet...	5	0
2	SalesOrderDetail	IX_SalesOrderDetail_ProductID	4	1
3	SalesOrderDetail	AK_SalesOrderDetail_rowguid	0	0

***Figure 5-22.** Query results for page locks*

The statistics for the locking behavior may not make sense initially, until considering the activity that occurred when the query (from Listing 5-29) executed. When the query executed, it utilized an index seek and a key lookup (see the execution plan in Figure 5-23). The index seek on IX_SalesOrderDetail_ProductID accounts for the 2 page locks and the 44 row locks. There were 44 rows that matched the predicate for the query, and they spanned 2 pages. The 44 page locks on PK_SalesOrderDetail_SalesOrderID_SalesOrderDetailID are the result of the key lookup operations that occurred for all rows from IX_SalesOrderDetail_ProductID. Together, the row and page lock columns help describe the activity that occurred.

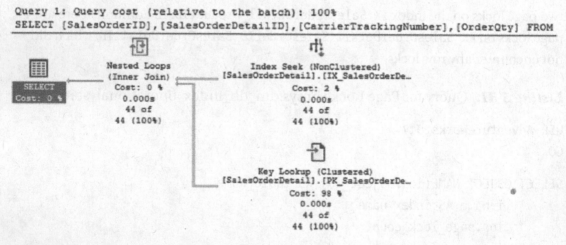

***Figure 5-23.** Execution plan for SELECT query*

While row and page locking are useful for identifying when contention exists, there is one aspect of locking that it does not provide: the types of locks that are being placed. The locks could be shared locks, or they could be exclusive locks. The lock wait count provides scope around the frequency of incompatible locks on the tables and the duration of those locks, though the details of the locks themselves are not identified.

Lock Escalation

The last piece with locking contention to discuss is the amount of lock escalation that is occurring in the database. When the number of locks acquired for a transaction exceeds the locking threshold on a SQL Server instance, the locks will escalate to the next higher level of locking. This escalation can happen at the page, partition, and table levels. There are a number of reasons for escalating locks on a database. One is that locks require memory, so the more locks there are, the more memory is required and the more resources are needed to manage locks. Another reason is that many individual low-level locks open the opportunity for blocking to escalate into deadlocking. For these reasons, lock escalations are important to consider with regard to object contention.

To help provide an understanding of lock escalation, a demo query from earlier will be modified slightly. Instead of selecting 44 rows, all rows where ProductID is less than or equal to 712 (see Listing 5-32) will be updated. The update will change ProductID to its current value, therefore not actually changing any data values, but still incurring update operations.

Listing 5-32. T-SQL Script to Generate Lock Promotion

```
USE AdventureWorks2017
GO

UPDATE Sales.SalesOrderDetail
SET ProductID = ProductID
WHERE ProductID <= 712
```

The script in Listing 5-33 can be used to review the statistics in sys.dm_db_index_ operational_stats to see whether there were any lock escalations. As the output from the script shows (Figure 5-24), the column index_lock_promotion_attempt_count recorded four events for PK_SalesOrderDetail_SalesOrderID_SalesOrderDetailID and IX_SalesOrderDetail_ProductID. Therefore, there were four opportunities for lock escalation that were triggered. The column index_lock_promotion_count shows that there was one lock escalation on IX_SalesOrderDetail_ProductID. For the two indexes, there were four instances when SQL Server considered whether a lock escalation was appropriate for the query. At the fourth check on IX_SalesOrderDetail_ProductID, SQL Server determined that a lock escalation was needed, and the lock was escalated.

Listing 5-33. Query for Lock Escalation in sys.dm_db_index_operational_stats

```
USE AdventureWorks2017
GO

SELECT OBJECT_NAME(ios.object_id) AS table_name
      ,i.name AS index_name
      ,ios.index_lock_promotion_attempt_count
      ,ios.index_lock_promotion_count
FROM sys.dm_db_index_operational_stats(DB_ID(),OBJECT_ID('Sales.
SalesOrderDetail'),NULL,NULL) ios
      INNER JOIN sys.indexes i
          ON i.object_id = ios.object_id
             AND i.index_id = ios.index_id
ORDER BY ios.range_scan_count DESC;
```

	table_name	index_name	index_lock_promotion_attempt_count	index_lock_promotion_count
1	SalesOrderDetail	PK_SalesOrderDetail_SalesOrderID_SalesOrderDet...	5	0
2	SalesOrderDetail	IX_SalesOrderDetail_ProductID	4	1
3	SalesOrderDetail	AK_SalesOrderDetail_rowguid	0	0

Figure 5-24. *Query results for lock escalation*

Monitoring lock escalation goes hand in hand with monitoring row and page locks. When row and page lock contention increases, either through increased frequency or through duration of lock waits, evaluating lock escalation can help identify the number of times SQL Server considered escalating locks and when those locks have been escalated. In some scenarios where tables are improperly indexed, locks can escalate more frequently and lead to increased blocking and deadlocking.

Latch Contention

In addition to locking, latch contention can also occur in indexes. Latches are short, lightweight data synchronization controls. From a high level, latches allow for isolation on memory objects while activities are executing. One example of a latch is when data is transferred from disk to memory. If there are disk bottlenecks while this occurs, latch waits will accumulate while the disk transfer completes. The value in this information is that when latch waits are occurring, the columns (shown in Table 5-16) provide a mechanism to track the waits down to specific indexes, thus allowing for focus on where indexes are stored as part of their management.

Table 5-16. *Latch Activity Columns in sys.dm_db_index_operational_stats*

Column Name	Data Type	Description
page_latch_wait_ count	bigint	Cumulative number of times the database engine waited because of latch contention.
page_latch_wait_in_ ms	bigint	Cumulative number of milliseconds the database engine waited because of latch contention.
page_io_latch_wait_ count	bigint	Cumulative number of times the database engine waited on an I/O page latch.
page_io_latch_wait_ in_ms	bigint	Cumulative number of milliseconds the database engine waited on a page I/O latch.
tree_page_latch_ wait_count	bigint	Subset of page_latch_wait_count that includes only the upper-level B-tree pages. This is always 0 for a heap.
tree_page_latch_ wait_in_ms	bigint	Subset of page_latch_wait_in_ms that includes only the upper-level B-tree pages. This is always 0 for a heap.
tree_page_io_latch_ wait_count	bigint	Subset of page_io_latch_wait_count that includes only the upper-level B-tree pages. This is always 0 for a heap.
tree_page_io_latch_ wait_in_ms	bigint	Subset of page_io_latch_wait_in_ms that includes only the upper-level B-tree pages. This is always 0 for a heap.

Page I/O Latch

Two sets of latch-related data are collected with respect to page I/O latches: page-level latching and tree page latching. Page-level latching occurs when data pages at the leaf levels of an index (the data pages) need to be retrieved. This differs from tree page latching, which happens at all the other levels of the index. Both of these statistics are measures of the number of latches created while moving data into the buffer and any time related to delays. Whenever time is accumulated in `page_io_latch_wait_in_ms` or `tree_page_io_latch_wait_in_ms`, it correlates with increases in wait times for the `PAGEIOLATCH_*` wait types.

To better understand how page I/O latches occur and the statistics can be collected, an example will be reviewed that will cause these waits to occur. In this demonstration, all data will be returned from `Sales.SalesOrderDetail`, `Sales.SalesOrderHeader`, and `Production.Product` via the script in Listing 5-34. Before executing the script, the buffer cache will be cleared to force SQL Server to retrieve the data for these pages from disk. Be sure to use this script only on a nonproduction server where clearing the buffer cache will not impact other processes.

Listing 5-34. T-SQL Script to Generate Page I/O Latch

```
USE AdventureWorks2017
GO

DBCC DROPCLEANBUFFERS
GO

SELECT *
FROM Sales.SalesOrderDetail sod
INNER JOIN Sales.SalesOrderHeader soh ON sod.SalesOrderID = soh.
SalesOrderID
INNER JOIN Production.Product p ON sod.ProductID = p.ProductID;
```

When the query completes, a number of page I/O latches will have occurred while copying the pages for the tables and indexes into the buffer cache. To review the page I/O latches, query against `sys.dm_db_index_operational_stats` on the page I/O latch columns using the script in Listing 5-35. The results, shown in Figure 5-25, indicate that there were page I/O latch waits on all three of the tables in the example query, including a whole 1 millisecond incurred on `Sales.SalesOrderHeader`. The results here are highly dependent on the underlying storage. Therefore, these numbers will vary greatly depending on the storage infrastructure used by this database, but should be consistent when retested against the same hardware.

Listing 5-35. Query for Page I/O Latch Statistics in sys.dm_db_index_operational_stats

```
USE AdventureWorks2017
GO
SELECT OBJECT_SCHEMA_NAME(ios.object_id) + '.' + OBJECT_NAME(ios.object_id)
as table_name
    ,i.name as index_name
    ,page_io_latch_wait_count
    ,page_io_latch_wait_in_ms
    ,CAST(1. * page_io_latch_wait_in_ms
      / NULLIF(page_io_latch_wait_count ,0) AS decimal(12,2)) AS page_io_
avg_lock_wait_ms
FROM sys.dm_db_index_operational_stats (DB_ID(), NULL, NULL, NULL) ios
INNER JOIN sys.indexes i ON i.object_id = ios.object_id AND i.index_id =
ios.index_id
WHERE i.object_id = OBJECT_ID('Sales.SalesOrderHeader')
OR i.object_id = OBJECT_ID('Sales.SalesOrderDetail')
OR i.object_id = OBJECT_ID('Production.Product')
ORDER BY 5 DESC;
```

	table_name	index_name	page_io_latch_wait_count	page_io_latch_wait_in_ms	page_io_avg_lock_wait_ms
1	Sales.SalesOrderHeader	IX_SalesOrderHeader_SalesPersonID	1	1	1.00
2	Sales.SalesOrderHeader	PK_SalesOrderHeader_SalesOrderID	77	60	0.78
3	Sales.SalesOrderDetail	PK_SalesOrderDetail_SalesOrderID_SalesOrderDet...	1	0	0.00
4	Production.Product	PK_Product_ProductID	4	0	0.00
5	Sales.SalesOrderHeader	IX_SalesOrderHeader_CustomerID	1	0	0.00
6	Sales.SalesOrderDetail	AK_SalesOrderDetail_rowguid	0	0	NULL
7	Sales.SalesOrderDetail	IX_SalesOrderDetail_ProductID	0	0	NULL
8	Production.Product	AK_Product_ProductNumber	0	0	NULL
9	Production.Product	AK_Product_Name	0	0	NULL
10	Production.Product	AK_Product_rowguid	0	0	NULL
11	Sales.SalesOrderHeader	AK_SalesOrderHeader_rowguid	0	0	NULL
12	Sales.SalesOrderHeader	AK_SalesOrderHeader_SalesOrderNumber	0	0	NULL

Figure 5-25. *Query results for page I/O latch*

Page Latch

The other kind of latching related to indexes that can occur in databases is page latching. Page latching covers any latching that occurs on non-data pages. Page latches include allocation of GAM and SGAM pages and DBCC and backup activities. As pages are allocated by different resources, contention can occur, and monitoring page latches can uncover this activity.

With regard to an index, one common scenario in which page latches can occur is when a "hotspot" develops on an index because of frequent inserts or page allocations. To demonstrate this scenario, the table dbo.PageLatchDemo will be created in Listing 536. Next, using a preferred load generator tool, execute five sessions of the code in Listing 5-37. To generate the load for this example, five query windows in SQL Server Management Studio run a copy of the load query. Through this example, hundreds of rows will be inserted quickly into the same series of pages, and numerous page allocations will be made. Since these inserts will be so close, a "hotspot" will be created, which will lead to page latch contention.

Listing 5-36. T-SQL Script to Generate Page Latch Scenario

```
USE AdventureWorks2017
GO

IF OBJECT_ID('dbo.PageLatchDemo') IS NOT NULL
        DROP TABLE dbo.PageLatchDemo;
CREATE TABLE dbo.PageLatchDemo
(
PageLatchDemoID INT IDENTITY (1,1)
,FillerData  bit
,CONSTRAINT PK_PageLatchDemo_PageLatchDemoID PRIMARY KEY
CLUSTERED  (PageLatchDemoID)
);
```

Listing 5-37. T-SQL Script to Generate Page Latch Load

```
USE AdventureWorks2017
GO
INSERT INTO dbo.PageLatchDemo
 (FillerData)
```

```
SELECT  t.object_id % 2
FROM sys.tables t;
GO 5000
```

To verify that the page latch contention did occur, use the script provided in Listing 5-38. The results, provided in Figure 5-26, show that there were numerous page latches and delays associated with them. In this example, the delay per page latch was over 20 milliseconds. In more critical situations, these values will be much higher and will help identify when an index is interfering with accessing or writing data to a table.

Listing 5-38. Query for Page Latch Statistics in sys.dm_db_index_ operational_stat

```
USE AdventureWorks2017
GO
SELECT OBJECT_SCHEMA_NAME(ios.object_id) + '.' + OBJECT_NAME(ios.object_id)
as table_name
,i.name as index_name
,page_latch_wait_count
,page_latch_wait_in_ms
,CAST(100. * page_latch_wait_in_ms
        / NULLIF(page_latch_wait_count ,0) AS decimal(12,2)) AS page_avg_
lock_wait_ms
FROM sys.dm_db_index_operational_stats (DB_ID(), NULL, NULL, NULL) ios
INNER JOIN sys.indexes i ON i.object_id = ios.object_id AND i.index_id =
ios.index_id
WHERE i.object_id = OBJECT_ID('dbo.PageLatchDemo');
```

	table_name	index_name	page_latch_wait_count	page_latch_wait_in_ms	page_avg_lock_wait_ms
1	dbo.PageLatchDemo	PK_PageLatchDemo_PageLatchDemoID	489858	105096	21.45

Figure 5-26. Query results for page latch

Note   Page I/O and page latch contentions are highly hardware-dependent. Results for the demonstration queries in this section will not identically match the results shown.

Page Allocation Cycle

As a result of the DML activity, leaf and nonleaf pages are allocated or deallocated from indexes from time to time. Monitoring page allocations is an important part of monitoring an index (see Table 5-17 for options). Through this monitoring, it is possible to get a handle on how an index is "breathing" between maintenance windows. This activity is the relationship between pages allocated to indexes through inserts and page splits and then the removal (or merging) of pages through deletes. By monitoring this activity, indexes can be better maintained by understanding when it may be useful to adjust the index FILLFACTOR value.

Table 5-17. *Page Allocation Cycle Columns in sys.dm_db_index_operational_stats*

Column Name	Data Type	Description
leaf_allocation_count	bigint	Cumulative count of leaf-level page allocations in the index or heap
nonleaf_allocation_count	bigint	Cumulative count of page allocations caused by page splits above the leaf level
leaf_page_merge_count	bigint	Cumulative count of page merges at the leaf level
nonleaf_page_merge_count	bigint	Cumulative count of page merges above the leaf level

As an example of how page allocation occurs on a table, execute the script in Listing 5-39. In this script, the table dbo.AllocationCycle is created. Afterward, 100,000 rows are inserted into the table. Since this is a new table, there is no contention on page allocations, and data is added in an orderly fashion. At this point, pages have been allocated to the table, and the allocations relate specifically to these inserts. This script will run for a minute or more. Ensure that Include Actual Execution Plan is not enabled when this is executed as this will greatly slow down execution by generating significant amounts of visual plan information.

Listing 5-39. T-SQL Script to Generate Page Allocations

```
USE AdventureWorks2017;
GO
SET NOCOUNT ON
```

```
DROP TABLE IF EXISTS dbo.AllocationCycle;
CREATE TABLE dbo.AllocationCycle (
    ID INT IDENTITY,
    FillerData VARCHAR(1000),
    CreateDate DATETIME,
    CONSTRAINT PK_AllocationCycle PRIMARY KEY CLUSTERED (ID)
);
GO
INSERT INTO dbo.AllocationCycle (FillerData, CreateDate)
VALUES (NEWID(), GETDATE());
GO 100000
```

To verify the allocations, the leaf and nonleaf allocation columns `leaf_allocation_count` and `nonleaf_allocation_count` from `sys.dm_db_index_operational_stats` can be checked. The script in Listing 5-40 shows that there are 758 allocations at the leaf level and 3 at the nonleaf level (see Figure 5-27). This is an important detail to consider when using these columns: a portion of the pages allocated can be insert-related.

Listing 5-40. Query for Page Allocation Statistics in sys.dm_db_index_operational_stats

```
USE AdventureWorks2017
GO
SELECT OBJECT_SCHEMA_NAME(ios.object_id) + '.' + OBJECT_NAME(ios.object_id)
as table_name
  ,i.name as index_name
  ,ios.leaf_allocation_count
  ,ios.nonleaf_allocation_count
  ,ios.leaf_page_merge_count
  ,ios.nonleaf_page_merge_count
FROM sys.dm_db_index_operational_stats(DB_ID(), OBJECT_ID('dbo.
AllocationCycle'), NULL,NULL) ios
  INNER JOIN sys.indexes i ON i.object_id = ios.object_id AND i.index_id =
ios.index_id;
```

	table_name	index_name	leaf_allocation_count	nonleaf_allocation_count	leaf_page_merge_count	nonleaf_page_merge_count
1	dbo.AllocationCycle	PK_AllocationCycle	758	3	0	0

Figure 5-27. *Query results for insert page allocations statistics in*
sys.dm_db_index_operational_stats

Note   After SQL Server 2014, the behavior for these columns changed so that for bulk inserts, only a single page is recorded for the leaf_allocation_count.

With this foundation of index metadata, the discussion can continue with using page allocations to monitor for page splits and to identify where modifications to the fill factor can be useful. To demonstrate this, page splits will be generated on the dbo. AllocationCycle table. The script in Listing 5-41 can be used to accomplish this. This script increases the length of the FillerData column on every third row to 1,000 characters.

Listing 5-41. T-SQL Script to Increase Page Allocations

```
USE AdventureWorks2017;
GO

UPDATE  dbo.AllocationCycle
SET     FillerData = REPLICATE('x',1000)
WHERE   ID % 3 = 1;
```

Once the data is modified, the results from executing the sys.dm_db_index_ operational_stats query in Listing 5-40 change drastically. With the size of the rows expanding, the number of pages allocated jumps up to 9,849 with a total of 35 nonleaf pages (Figure 5-28). Since the order of the rows hasn't changed, this activity is related to page splits from expanding the sizes of the rows. By monitoring these statistics, indexes affected by this pattern of activity can be identified.

	table_name	index_name	leaf_allocation_count	nonleaf_allocation_count	leaf_page_merge_count	nonleaf_page_merge_count
1	dbo.AllocationCycle	PK_AllocationCycle	9849	35	0	0

Figure 5-28. *Query results for update page allocations*

Compression

There are two columns in sys.dm_db_index_operational_stats that are used for monitoring compression. These columns, listed in Table 5-18, count the number of attempts that have been made at compressing a page and then the number of successful attempts in doing so. The primary value in these columns is providing feedback on PAGE-level compression. Failures can lead to decisions to remove compression because it is usually not practical to have compression enabled when there is a high rate of compression failures.

Table 5-18. *Compression Columns in sys.dm_db_index_operational_stats*

Column Name	Data Type	Description
page_compression_ attempt_count	bigint	Number of pages that were evaluated for PAGE-level compression for specific partitions of a table, index, or indexed view. Includes pages that were not compressed because significant savings could not be achieved.
page_compression_ success_count	bigint	Number of data pages that were compressed by using PAGE-level compression for specific partitions of a table, index, or indexed view.

Page compression can fail when the cost to compress the data exceeds the value in uncompressing that data later. This is typically found in data that has low patterns of repeating data, such as images. When image data is compressed, it often does not receive sufficient benefit from the compression, and SQL Server will not store the page as a compressed page. To demonstrate this, execute the code in Listing 5-42, which creates a table with page compression enabled and inserts a number of images into it.

Listing 5-42. T-SQL Script to Create a Table with Page Compression

```
USE AdventureWorks2017
GO
IF OBJECT_ID('dbo.PageCompression') IS NOT NULL
        DROP TABLE dbo.PageCompression;
CREATE TABLE dbo.PageCompression(
        ProductPhotoID int NOT NULL,
```

```
      ThumbNailPhoto varbinary(max) NULL,
      LargePhoto varbinary(max) NULL,
   CONSTRAINT PK_PageCompression PRIMARY KEY CLUSTERED (ProductPhotoID))
   WITH (DATA_COMPRESSION = PAGE);
INSERT INTO dbo.PageCompression
SELECT ProductPhotoID
   ,ThumbNailPhoto
   ,LargePhoto
FROM Production.ProductPhoto;
```

The insert into the table doesn't fail, but are all the pages compressed? To find out, execute the script in Listing 5-43; it returns the page_compression_attempt_count and page_compression_success_count columns. The results in Figure 5-29 show that 7 pages were successfully compressed, but 46 pages failed to compress. With this ratio of successes to failures for page compression, it is easy to see that the value of page compression on the clustered index of dbo.PageCompression is low.

Listing 5-43. Query for Page Compression Attempts in sys.dm_db_index_operational_stats

```
USE AdventureWorks2017
GO
SELECT OBJECT_SCHEMA_NAME(ios.object_id) + '.' + OBJECT_NAME(ios.object_id)
as table_name
,i.name as index_name
,page_compression_attempt_count
,page_compression_success_count
FROM sys.dm_db_index_operational_stats (DB_ID(), OBJECT_ID('dbo.
PageCompression'), NULL, NULL) ios
   INNER JOIN sys.indexes i ON i.object_id = ios.object_id AND i.index_id
= ios.index_id;
```

	table_name	index_name	page_compression_attempt_count	page_compression_success_count
1	dbo.PageCompression	PK_PageCompression	46	7

Figure 5-29. *Query results for compression*

LOB Access

The next group of columns in `sys.dm_db_index_operational_stats` pertains to large objects (LOBs). They provide information on the number of pages fetched and their size. There are also columns that measure the amount of LOB data that is pushed off and pulled into rows. Table 5-19 lists all these columns and others in this group.

Table 5-19. *LOB Access Columns in sys.dm_db_index_operational_stats*

Column Name	Data Type	Description
lob_fetch_in_ pages	bigint	Cumulative count of LOB pages retrieved from the LOB_ DATA allocation unit. These pages contain data that is stored in columns of type text, ntext, image, varchar(max), nvarchar(max), varbinary(max), and xml.
lob_fetch_in_ bytes	bigint	Cumulative count of LOB data bytes retrieved.
lob_orphan_ create_count	bigint	Cumulative count of orphan LOB values created for bulk operations.
lob_orphan_ insert_count	bigint	Cumulative count of orphan LOB values inserted during bulk operations.
row_overflow_ fetch_in_pages	bigint	Cumulative count of row-overflow data pages retrieved from the ROW_OVERFLOW_DATA allocation unit.
row_overflow_ fetch_in_bytes	bigint	Cumulative count of row-overflow data bytes retrieved.
column_value_ push_off_row_ count	bigint	Cumulative count of column values for LOB data and row-overflow data that is pushed off-row to make an inserted or updated row fit within a page.
column_value_ pull_in_row_ count	bigint	Cumulative count of column values for LOB data and row-overflow data that is pulled in-row. This occurs when an update operation frees up space in a record and provides an opportunity to pull in one or more off-row values from the LOB_DATA or ROW_OVERFLOW_DATA allocation unit to the IN_ROW_DATA allocation unit.

The LOB access columns are useful in determining the volume of large object activity and when data may be moving from large object to in-row-overflow storage. This is relevant when there are performance issues related to retrieving or updating LOB data. For example, the column `lob_fetch_in_bytes` measures the bytes from LOB columns retrieved by SQL Server for the index.

The script in Listing 5-44 can be used to demonstrate LOB activity. This does not represent all possible activity, but it covers the basics. At the start of the script, the table `dbo.LOBAccess` is created with the column `LOBValue`, which uses a large object data type. The first operation against the table inserts ten rows that are narrow enough that the `LOBValue` values can be stored on the data page with the rows. The second operation increases the size of the `LOBValue` column, forcing it to expand outside the 8 KB max for a data row. The final operation retrieves all rows from the table.

Listing 5-44. T-SQL Script to Create a Table with LOB Data

```
USE AdventureWorks2017

GO

IF OBJECT_ID('dbo.LOBAccess') IS NOT NULL
    DROP TABLE dbo.LOBAccess;
CREATE TABLE dbo.LOBAccess
  (
  ID INT IDENTITY(1,1) PRIMARY KEY CLUSTERED
  ,LOBValue VARCHAR(MAX)
  ,FillerData CHAR(2000) DEFAULT(REPLICATE('X',2000))
  ,FillerDate DATETIME DEFAULT(GETDATE())
  );
INSERT INTO dbo.LOBAccess (LOBValue)
SELECT TOP 10 'Short Value'
FROM Production.ProductPhoto;

UPDATE dbo.LOBAccess
SET LOBValue = REPLICATE('Long Value',8000);

SELECT * FROM dbo.LOBAccess;
```

Using the LOB access columns listed in Table 5-19, the results can be observed with the script in Listing 5-45. As the output in Figure 5-30 shows, the column column_value_push_off_row_count tracked ten row operations on the index where the row moved in-row data off into large object storage. The operation coincided with the update that increased the length of the rows. The other two statistics that were accumulated, lob_fetch_in_pages and lob_fetch_in_bytes, detail the number of pages and the size of the data retrieved via the SELECT statement. As these statistics illustrate, the LOB access columns provide granular tracking of LOB activity.

Listing 5-45. Query for LOB Access in sys.dm_db_index_operational_stats

```
USE AdventureWorks2017
GO

SELECT OBJECT_SCHEMA_NAME(ios.object_id) + '.' + OBJECT_NAME(ios.object_id)
as table_name
    ,i.name as index_name
    ,lob_fetch_in_pages
    ,lob_fetch_in_bytes
    ,lob_orphan_create_count
    ,lob_orphan_insert_count
    ,row_overflow_fetch_in_pages
    ,row_overflow_fetch_in_bytes
    ,column_value_push_off_row_count
    ,column_value_pull_in_row_count
FROM sys.dm_db_index_operational_stats (DB_ID(), OBJECT_ID('dbo.
LOBAccess'), NULL, NULL) ios
INNER JOIN sys.indexes i ON i.object_id = ios.object_id AND i.index_id =
ios.index_id;
```

table_name	index_name	lob_fetch_in_pages	lob_fetch_in_bytes	lob_orphan_create_	lob_orphan_insert_	row_overflow_fetch_	row_overflow_fetch_	column_value_push_	column_value_pull_
1	dbo.LOBAccess	PK__LOBAccess__3214EC274858D0A59	30	80000	0	0	0	0	10	0

Figure 5-30. *Query results for LOB access*

Row Version

The last group of columns in sys.dm_db_index_operational_stats report on version counts within indexes due to snapshot isolation columns. These columns were introduced in SQL Server 2019. While this book won't demonstrate their use within snapshot isolation levels, they are included here for completeness.

Table 5-20. Row Version Columns in sys.dm_db_index_operational_stats

Column Name	Data Type	Description
version_generated_inrow	bigint	Number of in-row version records retained by snapshot isolation transaction.
version_generated_offrow	bigint	Number of off-row version records retained by snapshot isolation transaction.
ghost_version_inrow	bigint	Number of in-row ghost version records retained by snapshot isolation transaction.
ghost_version_offrow	bigint	Number of off-row ghost version records retained by snapshot isolation transaction.
insert_over_ghost_version_inrow	bigint	Number of in-row inserts over ghost version records retained by snapshot isolation transaction.
insert_over_ghost_version_offrow	bigint	Number of off-row inserts over ghost version records retained by snapshot isolation transaction.

Index Operational Stats Summary

This section discussed the statistics available in the DMO sys.dm_db_index_operational_stats. While it is not a DMO that is widely used, it does provide extensive low-level detail regarding indexes that can be leveraged to dig more deeply into index behavior. From the columns on DML and SELECT activity to locking contention to compression, the columns in this DMO provide a wealth of information.

Index Physical Statistics

The last area of statistics that SQL Server collects are index physical stats. These statistics report information about the current structure of the index along with the physical effect of insert, update, and delete operations on indexes. These statistics are collected in the DMO sys.dm_db_index_physical_stats.

Like sys.dm_db_index_operational_stats, sys.dm_db_index_physical_stats is a dynamic management function. To use the DMF, parameters need to be supplied when it is used. Listing 5-46 details the parameters for this DMF.

Listing 5-46. Parameters for sys.dm_db_index_physical_stats

```
sys.dm_db_index_physical_stats (
    { database_id | NULL | 0 | DEFAULT }
  , { object_id | NULL | 0 | DEFAULT }
  , { index_id | NULL | 0 | -1 | DEFAULT }
  , { partition_number | NULL | 0 | DEFAULT }
  , { mode | NULL | DEFAULT }
)
```

The mode parameter for sys.dm_db_index_physical_stats accepts one of five values: DEFAULT, NULL, LIMITED, SAMPLED, or DETAILED. DEFAULT, NULL, and LIMITED are in effect the same value and will be described together. Table 5-21 lists the parameter values.

Note   The DMF sys.dm_db_index_physical_stats can accept the use of the Transact-SQL functions DB_ID() and OBJECT_ID(). These functions can be used for the parameters database_id and object_id, respectively.

Table 5-21. *Values for the mode parameter in sys.dm_db_index_physical_stats*

Value Name	Description
LIMITED	The fastest mode that scans the smallest number of pages. For an index, only the parent-level pages of the B-tree are scanned. In a heap, only the associated PFS and IAM pages are examined.
SAMPLED	This mode returns statistics based on a 1 percent sample of all the pages in the index or heap. If the index or heap has fewer than 10,000 pages, DETAILED mode is used instead of SAMPLED.
DETAILED	This mode scans all pages, both leaf and nonleaf, of an index and returns all statistics.

When executed, there are three areas of information that are reported from the DMF: header columns, row statistics, and fragmentation statistics. One word of caution: This DMF gathers the information that it reports as it is executed. If a system is heavily used, this DMF can interfere with production workloads.

Header Columns

The first set of columns returned from sys.dm_db_index_physical_stats are the header columns. These columns provide metadata and descriptive information around the types of information that are included in that row of the results. The header columns are listed in Table 5-22. The most important information to pay attention to when looking at the header columns are the alloc_unit_type_desc and index_level. These two columns provide information on what type of data is being reported on and where in the index the statistics are originating from.

Table 5-22. *Header Columns for sys.dm_db_index_physical_stats*

Column Name	Data Type	Description
database_id	smallint	Database ID of the table or view
object_id	int	Object ID of the table or view that the index is on
index_id	int	Index ID of an index
partition_number	int	1-based partition number within the owning object: a table, view, or index
index_type_desc	nvarchar(60)	Description of the index type
hobt_id	bigint	Heap or B-tree ID of the index or partition
alloc_unit_type_desc	nvarchar(60)	Description of the allocation unit type
index_depth	tinyint	Number of index levels
index_level	tinyint	Current level of the index

Row Statistics

The second group of columns in `sys.dm_db_index_physical_stats` are the row statistics columns. These columns provide details about the rows contained in the index, shown in Table 5-23.

Table 5-23. *Row Statistics Columns for sys.dm_db_index_physical_stats*

Column Name	Data Type	Description
page_count	bigint	Total number of index or data pages
record_count	bigint	Total number of records
ghost_record_count	bigint	Number of ghost records ready for removal by the ghost cleanup task in the allocation unit
version_ghost_record_count	bigint	Number of ghost records retained by an outstanding snapshot isolation transaction in an allocation unit

(continued)

159

Table 5-23. (*continued*)

Column Name	Data Type	Description
min_record_size_in_bytes	int	Minimum record size in bytes
max_record_size_in_bytes	int	Maximum record size in bytes
avg_record_size_in_bytes	float	Average record size in bytes
forwarded_record_count	bigint	Number of records in a heap that have forward pointers to another data location
compressed_page_count	bigint	The number of compressed pages

The first items of interest are the columns ghost_record_count and version_ghost_record_count. These columns provide a breakdown of the ghost_record_count found in sys.dm_db_index_operational_stats.

The next column to check is forwarded_record_count. This column provides an accounting to the number of forwarded records in a heap. This was also referenced in sys.dm_db_index_operational_stats with the forwarded_fetch_count column. In that DMF, the count provides the number of times that forwarded records were accessed. In sys.dm_db_index_physical_stats, the count refers to the number of forwarded records that exist within the table.

The last column to look at is compressed_page_count. The compressed page count provides a count of all the pages in an index that have been compressed. This helps provide a measure of value in having pages compressed by PAGE-level compression.

Fragmentation Statistics

The last group of statistics in the DMF are the fragmentation statistics. By far, fragmentation details are why most people make use of sys.dm_db_index_physical_stats. Fragmentation occurs in indexes when rows are inserted or modified in an index where the row no longer fits on the page where the index should be placed. When this happens, the page is split to move half of the data on one page onto another. Since there typically is not a contiguous page available after the page that has been split, it gets moved to an available free page. This results in gaps in an index where pages are expected to be continuous, preventing SQL Server from completing sequential reads while reading an index on disk.

There are four columns, shown in Table 5-24, that provide the information needed to analyze the state of fragmentation within an index. Each of these helps provide a view on the extent of the fragmentation and assists in determining how to mitigate the fragmentation.

Table 5-24. *Fragmentation Statistics Columns for sys.dm_db_index_physical_stats*

Column Name	Data Type	Description
avg_fragmentation_in_percent	float	Logical fragmentation for indexes or extent fragmentation for heaps in the IN_ROW_DATA allocation unit
fragment_count	bigint	Number of fragments in the leaf level of an IN_ROW_DATA allocation unit
avg_fragment_size_in_pages	float	Average number of pages in one fragment in the leaf level of an IN_ROW_DATA allocation unit
avg_page_space_used_in_percent	float	Average percentage of available data storage space used in all pages

The first fragment column is avg_fragmentation_in_percent. This column provides a fragmentation percentage for the index. As fragmentation increases, SQL Server will likely see an increase in the amount of physical I/Os required to retrieve data from an index. Using this column, a process can be built that mitigates fragmentation by rebuilding or reorganizing indexes. An index that is very fragmented (30 percent or more) may benefit from a rebuild, whereas an index that is less fragmented may benefit from reorganization. It is important to consider the purpose and usage of a table when designing index maintenance processes as there is no rule that can be blindly applied to all indexes. This will be further discussed in Chapter 9.

The next column, fragment_count, provides a count of all the fragments in an index. For each fragment created in an index, this column will summarize a count of those pages.

The third column is `avg_fragment_size_in_pages`. This column represents the average number of pages that are in each fragment. The higher this value is and the closer it is to `page_count`, the less I/O that SQL Server requires to read the data.

The last column is `avg_page_space_used_in_percent`. This column provides the amount of space available on pages. An index with little DML activity should be as close to 100 percent as possible. If there are no updates expected on an index, the goal should be to have the index as compacted as possible.

Index Physical Stats Summary

The primary purpose in looking at `sys.dm_db_index_physical_stats` is to help guide index maintenance. Through this DMF, statistics at each level of an index can be analyzed. Using this, the appropriate amount of maintenance for each level of an index can be identified. Whether the need is to defragment the index, modify the fill factor, or pad the index, the information in `sys.dm_db_index_physical_stats` can help guide this activity.

Columnstore Statistics

Columnstore indexes use a structure quite different from the typical B-tree or heap (also known as a rowstore). Because of this, there are some differences in the statistics collected for these indexes that relate to the underlying architecture and how it is accessed. To provide visibility to these different aspects, there are two DMOs that focus on the physical and operational statistics for columnstore statistics.

Columnstore Physical Stats

The first set of metadata to consider are the physical statistics being collected on columnstore indexes. This information can be accessed through the DMO sys.dm_db_column_store_row_group_physical_stats. This DMO has a row per rowgroup within a columnstore index. If a table is partitioned, then there will be a row per rowgroup per partition.

Header Columns

Since there is a row per rowgroup, each row will include object_id, index_id, partition_number, row_group_id, and delta_store_hobt_id. These columns are defined further in Table 5-25. Like other indexes, the partition_number validates that columnstore indexes can be partitioned. For nonpartitioned columnstore indexes, the partition number will be 1.

Table 5-25. *Header Columns in sys.dm_db_column_store_row_group_physical_stats*

Column Name	Data Type	Description
object_id	int	ID of the table or view on which the index is defined.
index_id	int	ID of the index.
partition_number	int	1-based partition number within the index or heap.
row_group_id	bigint	ID of the rowgroup.
delta_store_hobt_id	bigint	hobt_id of the rowgroup deltastore. If NULL, there is not an associated deltastore for the rowgroup.

Statistics Columns

The statistics columns for sys.dm_db_column_store_row_group_physical_stats provide extensive metadata for a columnstore index that can assist in understanding how its structure has been built. The statistics, defined in Table 5-26, provide insight necessary for managing a columnstore index. For example, total_rows and deleted_rows can be used to determine the portion of a rowgroup that is still active. In some cases, aggressive modifications on a rowgroup could leave empty rowgroups within tables. When rowgroups are smaller than 2^{20} rows, the state, trim reason, and transition to compressed information can help identify how rowgroups are being compressed. For example, if there are a large number of small rowgroups that are being closed due to BULKLOAD, it may be worthwhile to rebuild those rowgroups or make modification to the load process to try and insert more rows per insert operation.

Table 5-26. *Stats Columns in sys.dm_db_column_store_row_group_physical_stats*

Column Name	Data Type	Description
state	tinyint	ID number associated with state_desc.
state_desc	nvarchar(60)	Description of the rowgroup state, which can be INVISIBLE, OPEN, CLOSED, COMPRESSED, or TOMBSTONE.
total_rows	bigint	Full count of rows in the rowgroup including any row that has been marked deleted.
deleted_rows	bigint	Number of rows in the rowgroup marked for deletion.
size_in_bytes	bigint	Size of the rowgroup in bytes.
trim_reason	tinyint	ID number associated with the trim_reason_desc.
trim_reason_desc	nvarchar(60)	Description of why a COMPRESSED rowgroup has less than the million-row maximum of rows, which can be NO_TRIM, BULKLOAD, ROERG, DICTIONARY SIZE, MEMORY LIMITATION, RESIDUAL ROW GROUP, STATS MISMATCH, or SPILLOVER.
transition_to_ compressed_state	tinyint	ID number associated with the transition_to_ compressed_state_desc.
transition_to_ compressed_ state_desc	nvarchar(60)	Description of how the rowgroup transitions from a deltastore to a rowgroup, which includes NOT APPLICABLE, INDEX BUILD, TUPLE MOVER, REORG NORMAL, REORG FORCED, BULKLOAD, or MERGE.
has_vertipaq_ optimization	bit	Boolean identifying whether Vertipaq optimization was used during compression. This feature greatly improves the efficiency of columnstore compression.
generation	bigint	Rowgroup generation associated with this rowgroup.
created_time	datetime2	Clock time for when this rowgroup was created.
closed_time	datetime2	Clock time for when this rowgroup was closed.

Columnstore Operational Stats

Columnstore index operational statistics are provided by the DMO sys.dm_db_column_store_row_group_operational_stats. This DMO also returns one row per rowgroup within a columnstore index. If the table is partitioned, then a row per rowgroup per partition will be returned.

Header Columns

The header columns for sys.dm_db_column_store_row_group_operational_stats are similar to those of the columnstore physical stats DMO. The exception is that there are no references to the deltastore. This DMO returns the columns object_id, index_id, partition_number, and row_group_id. These columns are defined in Table 5-27.

Table 5-27. *Header Columns in sys.dm_db_column_store_row_group_ operational_stats*

Column Name	Data Type	Description
object_id	int	ID of the table or view on which the index is defined
index_id	int	ID of the index
partition_number	int	1-based partition number within the index or heap
row_group_id	bigint	ID of the rowgroup

Statistics Columns

In these columns, defined in Table 5-28, there are details about the number of scans for the rowgroup, the number of times the delete bitmap was scanned, and the number of times the partition for the columnstore was scanned. These details identify how frequently each rowgroup is accessed when compared with the rest of the index, as well as how often the delete bitmap is consulted, painting a picture of how data is written to each rowgroup.

Additionally, locks and blocking transactions that negatively impact the accessibility of the rowgroup can be measured, providing insight into when there are potential I/O or transactional bottlenecks that need to be addressed.

Table 5-28. *Stats Columns in sys.dm_db_column_store_row_group_operational_stats*

Column Name	Data Type	Description
scan_count	int	Number of scans through the rowgroup since the last SQL restart.
delete_buffer_scan_count	int	Number of times the delete buffer was used to determine deleted rows in this rowgroup. This includes accessing the in-memory hashtable and the underlying B-tree.
index_scan_count	int	Number of times the columnstore index partition was scanned. This is the same for all rowgroups in the partition.
rowgroup_lock_count	bigint	Cumulative count of lock requests for this rowgroup since the last SQL restart.
rowgroup_lock_wait_count	bigint	Cumulative number of times the database engine waited on this rowgroup lock since the last SQL restart.
rowgroup_lock_wait_in_ms	bigint	Cumulative number of milliseconds the database engine waited on this rowgroup lock since the last SQL restart.

Summary

This chapter provided an extensive look at the statistical information available in SQL Server that relates to indexes. This information provides a window into what will be an extensive journey into indexing in SQL Server. In upcoming chapters, this information will be leveraged by looking at the statistics that have been captured and using them to improve all aspects of index creation, usage, and maintenance.

CHAPTER 6

XML Indexes

The past couple chapters focused on indexing what is commonly referred to as *structured data*, where there is a common schema and organization around the data and its storage. In this chapter and the next few chapters, the indexing focus shifts to unstructured and semistructured data. With both structured and unstructured data, the task of indexing is to gain optimal efficiency for retrieving and manipulating it, but the data types that represent these types of data have differences in how they are stored in the database. These differences dictate how and why indexing is implemented as well as how the indexes are used by the query optimizer.

SQL Server has a specialized data type for storing the most common type of unstructured and semistructured data, XML. This chapter explores the types of indexes offered by SQL Server for optimizing XML data. The chapter will also show the impact of those indexes on the types of queries that can be written against XML data using XQuery and the impact on the choices made by the optimizer.

XML Data

Extensible Markup Language (XML) was developed during the 1990s and adopted as a standard by the World Wide Web Consortium in February 1998. XML data has been stored in databases for years, but until SQL Server 2005, it did not have a dedicated data type or access methods. When introduced, the XML data type extended the capabilities of SQL Server to appropriately manage this different data structure. With the acceptance of XML, the use and size of the total XML content within SQL Server databases grew. The growth was spurred by the advantages that XML offered application developers.

167

© Edward Pollack and Jason Strate 2023
E. Pollack and J. Strate, *Expert Performance Indexing in Azure SQL and SQL Server 2022*,
https://doi.org/10.1007/978-1-4842-9215-0_6

Benefits

The introduction of the XML data type allowed for the full capability of XML storage inside a SQL Server database. This included the ability to retrieve XML contents based on queries written against the XML itself. The strongest support that XML offers developers is that it is both text based and, nominally, self-documenting. Being text based means that XML is easily passed from one application to another, regardless of underlying operating system or programming language. The self-documenting nature of XML means that it is not necessary to have a structure defined in the same way as columns and tables are defined within a database. Instead, the elements and properties of the XML will describe what they are. XML is referred to as *semistructured* because there is generally a template defining an expected structure in order to help validate that any given set of XML is well-formed.

Indexing XML can be beneficial when processing extensive XML using SQL Server. The largest benefit for XML indexes will be in situations where there are large amounts of XML stored but there is a need to only retrieve a small subset of that data. In these scenarios, XML indexes can ensure that a small portion of XML data can be read quickly, rather than needing to slowly scan a document in its entirety.

Cautions

Although the XML data type sounds like a perfect fit for every instance of XML, some considerations should be evaluated when designing a column in SQL Server that will be storing XML. One of the most critical is that XML content should be well-formed. This ensures that the XML data type and features provided to utilize the data most efficiently are used to their full advantage. XML columns are stored as binary large objects, more commonly known as BLOBs. This storage means that runtime querying of this content is resource-intensive and slow in most cases. With any task that involves data retrieval, efficiency of that retrieval will be of concern. In SQL Server, indexing is paramount to how efficient or inefficient this can be. A complete lack of indexing or too many indexes will affect any data manipulation task. The XML data type is no exception to this guidance. XML indexing is unique compared with the other indexing methods in SQL Server.

XML Indexes

XML indexes fall into two main categories: primary/secondary and selective XML indexes. The main difference between these index types is how much of the XML data is included within the index. For primary/secondary indexes, all paths, nodes, and values are included in the index. This works well when it is unknown what portions of the XML will be most accessed. Alternatively, if only a limited portion of the XML will be accessed, then a selective XML index can provide better performance since the volume of data indexed is reduced. The next two sections will fully explore these categories of XML indexes.

Primary/Secondary XML Indexes

As the name implies, there are two types of indexes that fall under primary/secondary XML indexes: primary and secondary indexes. These two index types provide an indexing relationship within the XML documents similar to the relationship between clustered and non-clustered indexes. When implementing XML indexes, some basic rules apply to each:

- Only one primary XML index can exist on a column, though multiple primary XML indexes can exist on a table.

- Primary XML indexes cannot exist without a clustered index on the primary key of the table that the XML column is in. This clustered index is required for partitioning the table, and the XML index can use the same partitioning scheme and functioning.

- Primary XML indexes include all paths, tags, and values of the XML content.

- A secondary XML index cannot exist without a primary XML index.

- A secondary XML index extends the primary index including paths, values, and properties.

To demonstrate primary/secondary XML indexes, the table [Sales].[Store] within the AdventureWorks2017 database will be used. This table has an existing primary XML index on [Demographics] that will need to be dropped using the code in Listing 6-1.

Listing 6-1. Drop the Existing Primary XML Index on [Sales].[Store]

```
USE AdventureWorks2017;
GO
DROP INDEX IF EXISTS [PXML_Store_Demographics] ON [Sales].[Store]
```

It is useful to first benchmark the cost to execute an example query against this table. In the query in Listing 6-2, [Sales].[Store] will be queried for the stores with annual sales equal to $1,500,000. For a query returning less than 200 records, the cost is 12.751, shown in Figure 6-1, which is quite expensive. This is due to the XML Reader with XPath filter, which had to shred the entire XML document for all rows to find the requested records, which is a slow and resource-intensive process.

Listing 6-2. Query on [Sales].[Store] for AnnualSales

```
 USE AdventureWorks2017;
GO
WITH XMLNAMESPACES
(DEFAULT 'http://schemas.microsoft.com/sqlserver/2004/07/adventure-works/
StoreSurvey')
SELECT BusinessEntityID, Name, Demographics
FROM [Sales].[Store]
WHERE Demographics.exist('/StoreSurvey/AnnualSales[.=1500000]') = 1;
```

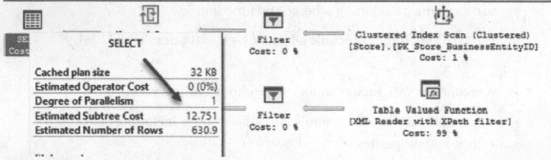

Figure 6-1. *XML query cost with no XML indexes*

Note   This chapter will use comparisons of estimated subtree cost vs. logical reads to demonstrate the value of XML indexes. While most analysis in this book focuses on reducing I/O through the use of indexes, parsing XML is generally a computationally expensive operation, hence a focus on query cost. Statistics time can also be used to roughly compare CPU measurements.

This query approach is costly, yet efficient with a small amount of data in the table. However, in real life, tables can become quite large, surpassing the point where scanning through multiple XML documents is efficient. For example, imagine a point-of-sale system that stores receipt information in XML documents for each sale. With this amount of data volume, performance would begin to suffer quickly.

Primary XML Index

Now that we know the cost of our example query without any XML indexes, let's look at what happens when we add a primary XML index. Using the CREATE INDEX code in Listing 6-3, create the primary XML index. More information on the syntax is in Chapter 1. This will create a primary XML index on the Demographics column.

Listing 6-3. Primary XML Index on [Sales].[Store]

```
USE AdventureWorks2017;
GO
CREATE PRIMARY XML INDEX [PXML_Store_Demographics] ON [Sales].[Store]
([Demographics])
```

When the primary XML index is created, all paths, tags, and nodes are indexed. For each of these items, a record is created in the XML index that contains that item, information on how that item appears in the XML document, and which row in the table is associated with the item. This is important because XML indexes will often dramatically increase the storage footprint of the underlying table. To demonstrate, run the code in Listing 6-4 to view the number of records and pages for each index. As the results in Figure 6-2 show, the number of records in the primary XML index greatly exceeds the number of records in the table by a factor of 13.

Listing 6-4. Primary XML Index details on [Sales].[Store]

```
USE AdventureWorks2017;
GO
SELECT [i].[name]
     ,[i].[index_id]
     ,[IPS].[index_level]
     ,[IPS].[index_type_desc]
     ,[IPS].[fragment_count]
     ,[IPS].[avg_page_space_used_in_percent]
     ,[IPS].[record_count]
     ,[IPS].[page_count]
FROM [sys].[dm_db_index_physical_stats](DB_ID(N'AdventureWorks2017'),
OBJECT_ID(N'Sales.Store'), NULL, NULL, 'DETAILED') AS [IPS]
    INNER JOIN [sys].[indexes] AS [i]
        ON [i].[object_id] = [IPS].[object_id]
            AND [i].[index_id] = [IPS].[index_id]
WHERE [IPS].[index_type_desc] <> 'NONCLUSTERED INDEX'
ORDER BY [i].[index_id]
        ,[IPS].[index_level];
```

	name	index_id	index_level	index_type_desc	fragment_count	avg_page_space_used_in_percent	record_count	page_count
1	PK_Store_BusinessEntityID	1	0	CLUSTERED INDEX	4	91.9024586113117	701	101
2	PK_Store_BusinessEntityID	1	1	CLUSTERED INDEX	1	16.1971830985915	101	1
3	PXML_Store_Demographics	256000	0	PRIMARY XML INDEX	6	98.4627996046454	9113	64
4	PXML_Store_Demographics	256000	1	PRIMARY XML INDEX	1	15.0976031628367	64	1

Figure 6-2. *Physical stats after creating the primary XML index*

With the primary XML index in place, the code from Listing 6-2 can be executed to demonstrate performance of the new index. Reviewing the execution plan, it becomes clear that the execution plan takes on an extremely different pattern, as shown in Figure 6-3. Instead of an estimated subtree cost of over 12, it has been reduced to 0.1535, and the XML Reader with XPath filter is replaced by a clustered index scan of the primary XML index. Under the covers, the query is still scanning the table, but it is doing so with much less effort. With larger tables, this indexing change will dramatically decrease the duration of the query.

```
Query 1: Query cost (relative to the batch): 100%
WITH XMLNAMESPACES(DEFAULT 'http://schemas.microsoft.com/sqlserver/2004/07/adven
```

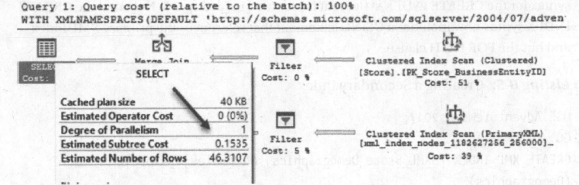

Figure 6-3. *XML query cost with a primary XML index*

The optimizer can make choices that are more evenly balanced using the primary XML index. The `clustered index scan` of the `Sales.Store` table is as high an estimated cost as the `clustered index seek` against the recently created XML index. This shift in where the work is occurring within the query engine will result in improved performance.

Caution   When a primary XML index is dropped, all secondary XML indexes will be dropped as they are dependent on the primary index. No warning will be given for this action.

Secondary XML Index

Secondary XML indexes provide the ability to further improve querying XML data. With secondary XML indexes, a choice will be made between the PATH, VALUE, and PROPERTY types when building the index. These options determine which elements from the primary XML index will be included in the secondary XML index and provide performance improvements based on the types of queries that are often run against XML documents. For example, if more queries are accessing property elements, then the PROPERTY type for the secondary XML index would be beneficial.

Returning to the example query in Listing 6-2, the existing function call is using both a path and value. Since this query is first searching for a path to check a value and other paths are not being accessed, a secondary XML index will be created using PATH. The syntax for the CREATE INDEX statement is provided in Listing 6-5. Note that the CREATE INDEX syntax now includes a USING statement that references the primary XML index and has the FOR PATH clause.

Listing 6-5. Creating a Secondary Index

```
USE AdventureWorks2017;
GO
CREATE XML INDEX [SXML_Store_Demographics] ON [Sales].[Store]
(Demographics)
USING XML INDEX [PXML_Store_Demographics]
FOR PATH;
```

Once the secondary XML index has been created, the example query from Listing 6-2 will be tested again to see how the execution plan changes. As shown in Figure 6-4, the execution plan is dramatically improved. The estimated subtree cost has been reduced by about half from 0.1535 to 0.0888, and the clustered index scan on the primary XML index is replaced with an index seek on the secondary XML index. Now the highest-cost item on the query is the clustered index scan on the table's clustered index. Using a secondary XML index has nearly removed the expense associated with accessing XML data.

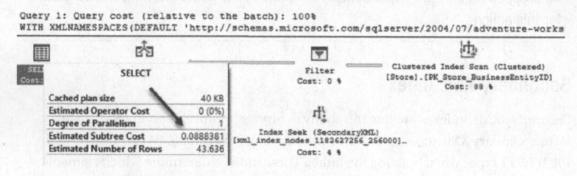

Figure 6-4. *XML query cost with a secondary XML index*

Note that a secondary XML index may sometimes be nearly as large as the primary XML index. This is demonstrated by running the code in Listing 6-4, which shows in Figure 6-5 that the same number of records are present in the primary and secondary XML indexes. In this case, this is to be expected since all of the data in the XML documents are values at XML paths. The advantage of the secondary XML index in this case is an ordering based on those paths that allows the XML indexes to be more selective.

	name	index_id	index_level	index_type_desc	fragment_count	avg_page_space_used_in_percent	record_count	page_count
1	PK_Store_BusinessEntityID	1	0	CLUSTERED INDEX	4	91.902458611317	701	101
2	PK_Store_BusinessEntityID	1	1	CLUSTERED INDEX	1	16.1971830985915	101	1
3	PXML_Store_Demographics	256000	0	PRIMARY XML INDEX	6	98.4627996046454	9113	64
4	PXML_Store_Demographics	256000	1	PRIMARY XML INDEX	1	15.0976031628367	64	1
5	SXML_Store_Demographics	256001	0	XML INDEX	4	97.7339510748703	9113	41
6	SXML_Store_Demographics	256001	0	XML INDEX	NULL	0	0	1
7	SXML_Store_Demographics	256001	1	XML INDEX	1	23.400049419323	41	1

Figure 6-5. *Physical stats after creating the secondary XML index*

Although `sys.dm_db_index_physical_stats` is beneficial for finding information needed to maintain all indexes, including XML indexes, there is a system view specifically for XML indexing: `sys.xml_indexes`. This view shows all options that have been applied to an XML index. Information returned by the view can be useful in further maintaining an index by knowing the type and other options set. This view is inherited from `sys.indexes` and also returns the columns provided in `sys.indexes`. Shown in Figure 6-6, the following additional columns exist:

- *using_xml_index_id*: The parent index for a secondary index. As discussed, secondary indexes require a primary index to exist before creation. This column will be NULL for primary XML indexes and used only for secondary indexes.

- *secondary_type*: A flag specifying the type on which a secondary index is based. Each secondary index is based on a specific type (V = VALUE, P = PATH, R = PROPERTY). For primary XML indexes, this column is NULL.

- *secondary_type_desc*: A description of the secondary index type. The values for the description map to those described in the secondary_ type column.

	name	index_id	type_desc	using_xml_index_id	secondary_type	secondary_type_desc	xml_index_type	xml_index_type_description	path_id
1	PXML_Store_Demographics	256000	XML	NULL	NULL	NULL	0	PRIMARY_XML	NULL
2	SXML_Store_Demographics	256001	XML	256000	P	PATH	1	SECONDARY_XML	NULL

Figure 6-6. *Results from sys.xml_indexes query*

It is important to consider the storage impact of primary and secondary XML indexes as the more data that is in the table and the more often that data is modified, the more of an impact these indexes will have on write operations. The performance improvement of using a secondary XML index needs to be weighed against the time taken to maintain it to decide whether (or not) to create the index. Strive to strike a balance between hardware resources, storage, index usefulness, number of indexes created, and number of times an index may realistically be needed when building primary and secondary XML indexes.

Selective XML Indexes

Introduced in SQL Server 2012, selective XML indexes address a significant problem with primary/secondary XML indexes. XML documents can be extremely large. Applying an index to the entire document has major performance implications for both creating and maintaining the index over time. Also, these excessively large indexes can add to the storage woes that are a frequent problem within organizations. When an index becomes large, it may not function as well as it did when it was smaller. For these reasons, the selective XML index was introduced.

Selective XML indexes allow an index to be created over a subset of the XML document. This makes for smaller, more nimble indexes that are targeted to specific paths within the XML. When the index is created, the document is parsed, and the XML is shredded. The shredded values are then stored in standard relational storage within the database. In addition to the selective XML index, secondary indexes can be added based on the nodes within the path that defines the selective XML index.

Selective XML indexes can achieve significant performance benefits over standard XML indexes when only a subset of elements is typically needed. However, if queries against XML columns are mostly ad hoc that may request any elements from within an XML document, then a standard XML index is likely to be more useful. Similarly, an XML document with a large number of node paths may benefit more from a standard XML index rather than a selective XML index.

To create a selective XML index, the following criteria must be followed:

- The table must have a clustered index that is defined on the primary key.

- The primary key size is limited to 128 bytes.

- The clustered index key columns are limited to 15 when used with a selective XML index.

The selective XML index will not be used for `query()` or `modify()` methods within XQuery statements. It will support `exist()`, `value()`, and `nodes()`. If `query()` and `modify()` are used together, it will only assist in a node lookup.

The script in Listing 6-6 creates a path within a selective XML index. Since only annual sales are being accessed in the document, the selective XML index can be limited to only that XML path.

Listing 6-6. Script for Creating a Selective XML Index

```
USE AdventureWorks2017;
GO
CREATE SELECTIVE XML INDEX [SEL_XML_Store_Demographics_AnnualSales]
ON [Sales].[Store] (Demographics)
WITH XMLNAMESPACES
(DEFAULT 'http://schemas.microsoft.com/sqlserver/2004/07/adventure-works/
StoreSurvey')
FOR (AnnualSales = '/StoreSurvey/AnnualSales');
```

After creating the selective XML index, the example query from Listing 6-2 will be revisited to see the impact on the execution plan. As shown in Figure 6-7, the estimated subtree cost is comparable to having the secondary XML index in place, but it's slightly more expensive with the selective XML index. To understand why SQL Server made this choice, the code in Listing 6-4 can be executed to see the storage footprint. As Figure 6-8 shows, the selective XML index is substantially smaller than the secondary XML index. Instead of potentially accessing 41 pages and 9,113 records, the selective XML index is limited to 701 records across 5 pages, which justifies the extra cost for the clustered index scan on the selective XML index.

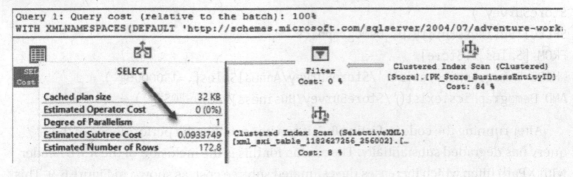

Figure 6-7. *XML query cost with the selective XML index*

	name	index_id	index_level	index_type_desc	fragment_count	avg_page_space_used_in_percent	record_count	page_count
1	PK_Store_BusinessEntityID	1	0	CLUSTERED INDEX	4	91.902458611317	701	101
2	PK_Store_BusinessEntityID	1	1	CLUSTERED INDEX	1	16.1971830985915	101	1
3	PXML_Store_Demographics	256000	0	PRIMARY XML INDEX	6	98.4627996046454	9113	64
4	PXML_Store_Demographics	256000	1	PRIMARY XML INDEX	1	15.0976031628367	64	1
5	SXML_Store_Demographics	256001	0	XML INDEX	4	97.7339510748703	9113	41
6	SXML_Store_Demographics	256001	0	XML INDEX	NULL	0	0	1
7	SXML_Store_Demographics	256001	1	XML INDEX	1	23.400049419323	41	1
8	SEL_XML_Store_Demographics_AnnualSales	256002	0	XML INDEX	1	90.0469483568075	701	5
9	SEL_XML_Store_Demographics_AnnualSales	256002	1	XML INDEX	1	1.21077341240425	5	1

Figure 6-8. *Physical stats after creating the selective XML index*

While this provides a much improved opportunity for XML indexing, there is an important restriction that should be considered. If queries evolve over time to the point where the selective XML index doesn't cover them, then performance will degrade. This differs from typical clustered and non-clustered indexes that index the entire contents of each value within a column, rather than a selective portion of each value.

To demonstrate this scenario, another XML element will be added to the query to filter on BusinessType. Exist() will be added to the WHERE clause, as shown in Listing 6-7, while also dropping the previously created primary/secondary XML indexes to prevent them from interfering with the output. Generally speaking, when selective XML indexes are used, primary/secondary XML indexes would not also be used.

Listing 6-7. Query on [Sales].[Store] for AnnualSales and BusinessType

```
USE AdventureWorks2017;
GO
DROP INDEX IF EXISTS [SXML_Store_Demographics] ON [Sales].[Store];
DROP INDEX IF EXISTS [PXML_Store_Demographics] ON [Sales].[Store];
WITH XMLNAMESPACES
(DEFAULT 'http://schemas.microsoft.com/sqlserver/2004/07/adventure-works/
StoreSurvey')
SELECT BusinessEntityID, Demographics
FROM [Sales].[Store]
WHERE Demographics.exist('/StoreSurvey/AnnualSales[.=1500000]') = 1
AND Demographics.exist('/StoreSurvey/BusinessType[.="OS"]') = 1
```

After running the code in Listing 6-7, it can be seen that the performance of the query has degraded substantially. The reason for this is the inclusion of the XML Reader with XPath filter, which increases the estimated subtree cost, as shown in Figure 6-9. This does not perform as poorly as the initial execution of this query, because the selective

XML index is still assisting with reducing the number of records where the entire XML document needs to be scanned with the function. But it is a degradation, and with large tables, this could cause a significant performance challenge.

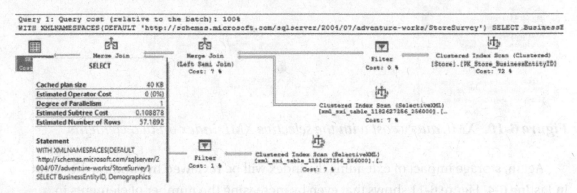

Figure 6-9. *XML query cost with the selective XML index and XML element not included*

Fortunately, selective XML indexes provide flexibility to tune for issues such as this one. Specifically, the FOR clause, shown in Listing 6-8, can be extended to include multiple XML nodes and paths. In this scenario, BusinessType is added to the index. As expected, and shown in Figure 6-10, the change in the index improves the performance of the query by dropping the estimated subtree cost to 0.108. This is the direct result of the addition of a second clustered index scan operation on the selective XML index.

Listing 6-8. Script for Creating a Selective XML Index

```
USE AdventureWorks2017;
GO
DROP INDEX IF EXISTS [SEL_XML_Store_Demographics_AnnualSales] ON [Sales].
[Store];
CREATE SELECTIVE XML INDEX [SEL_XML_Store_Demographics_
AnnualSalesBusinessType]
ON [Sales].[Store] (Demographics)
WITH XMLNAMESPACES
(DEFAULT 'http://schemas.microsoft.com/sqlserver/2004/07/adventure-works/
StoreSurvey')
FOR (AnnualSales = '/StoreSurvey/AnnualSales',
BusinessType = '/StoreSurvey/BusinessType');
```

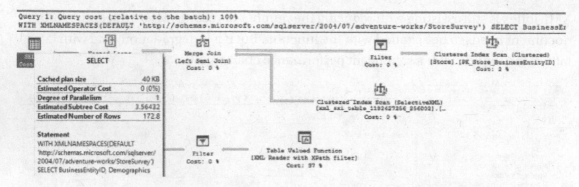

Figure 6-10. *XML query cost with the selective XML index on two elements*

Again, storage impact of extending the index will be reviewed by running the script in Listing 6-4. Figure 6-11 shows that even by increasing the number of elements in the index, the storage footprint of the index has not been changed significantly. It's 701 records across 6, instead of 5, pages.

	name	index_id	index_level	index_type_desc	fragment_count	avg_page_space_used_in_percent	record_count	page_count
1	PK_Store_BusinessEntityID	1	0	CLUSTERED INDEX	4	91.902458611317	701	101
2	PK_Store_BusinessEntityID	1	1	CLUSTERED INDEX	1	16.1971830985915	101	1
3	SEL_XML_Store_Demographics_AnnualSalesBusinessType	256000	0	XML INDEX	1	95.2433901655547	701	6
4	SEL_XML_Store_Demographics_AnnualSalesBusinessType	256000	1	XML INDEX	1	1.45787002718063	6	1

Figure 6-11. *Physical stats after creating the selective XML index on two elements*

While selective XML indexes are a more complex way to optimize reads against XML documents, the learning curve to get started is not significant. Selective XML indexes support more sophisticated XQuery than the examples provided in this chapter, allowing for more precision in exactly which segments of an XML document will be indexed.

Summary

This chapter covered the need to be able to search and index the unstructured and semistructured data that can be stored within SQL Server. XML indexes provide developers and database administrators with the options to improve the performance of searches through XML documents. This benefits queries both by filtering data and by retrieving it for display. Selective XML indexes offer the opportunity to get a more granular and detailed approach to XML indexing. XML indexes can require nontrivial amounts of storage; therefore, the space needed to accommodate them should be planned up front accordingly.

CHAPTER 7

Spatial Indexing

Spatial data types advance the storage capabilities of SQL Server, allowing data that defines shape and location information. Before these enhancements, spatial data was often stored as string or numeric values without implicit meaning within the database. This required cumbersome conversions and calculations to resolve the information into meaningful insights.

As part of spatial data support, SQL Server introduced the GEOMETRY and GEOGRAPHY data types. These types support planar and geodetic data, respectively. Planar data includes lines, points, and polygons on a 2D plane, while geodetic data includes similar data, but defined on a geodetic ellipsoid. Geodetic data describes data points that are identified on a map of Earth. These two data types can be described like this: GEOMETRY is a flat representation of the shape described, and GEOGRAPHY encompasses a rounded global representation.

Spatial data indexes are unique in how they are created and interpreted. Each index is composed of a set of grids. These grids consist of a set of cells, laid out similarly to a square spreadsheet. The grids can be up to 16 × 16 and as small as 4 × 4. The cells within the grid contain the values that define the objects that define the spatial data being stored. There is a distinct difference between the GEOGRAPHY and GEOMETRY data types in this type of indexing. The GEOMETRY data type requires a bounding box, which is a limit on the size of the area defined by the index. The GEOGRAPHY data type does not have a bounding box since it's bound by the size of the planet.

This chapter will explore spatial indexes, their behaviors, and their use within queries to enhance the performance of spatial data.

181

© Edward Pollack and Jason Strate 2023
E. Pollack and J. Strate, *Expert Performance Indexing in Azure SQL and SQL Server 2022*,
https://doi.org/10.1007/978-1-4842-9215-0_7

How Spatial Data Is Indexed

The grids that make up a spatial index are nested within each other. At the top layer, known as level 1, there can be, for example, a 4 × 4 grid. Each cell within that level 1 grid then contains another grid, consisting of the number of cells defined for that level, in this example 4 × 4. This second grid defines level 2. The cells in level 2 each have a grid that defines level 3, and the cells there contain another grid, level 4. Figure 7-1 shows how a GEOMETRY index consists of these four levels. The index is then made up of these four grids, each one being composed of a series of cells. This layering and grid hierarchy, called *decomposing*, is created when the index is created.

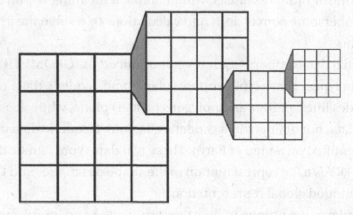

***Figure 7-1.** Grid storage representation of the GEOMETRY index storage and cells*

As many as 4 billion cells are possible, as shown in Figure 7-1. This is important when creating the index and determining what density to use at creation. Each layer, or level, can have a specified density. There are three levels of density (low = 4 × 4, medium = 8 × 8, and high = 16 × 16). If the density is omitted at the time an index is created, the default is medium. Manipulating the density is most commonly useful for tuning the storage space of the index. All layers may not be required at a high density. Save space by not using more density than is needed.

This background is necessary because the actual storage of the information from within these grids is the same B-tree format used to store standard indexes. Their definitions within storage and the retrieval of those definitions are radically different within spatial indexes than they are within standard indexes. To convert this information into a B-tree format, additional processing on top of the grid is necessary.

The next step in the indexing process that SQL Server performs is tessellation. *Tessellation* is the process that places or fits the objects into the grid hierarchy starting at layer 1. This process may require only the first layer of the grid but can require all four depending on the objects involved. Tessellation is essentially taking all data from the spatial column and placing it onto the grids in cells while retaining each cell that is touched. The index then knows exactly how to find the cells in each grid when a request is evaluated, using the B-tree.

Having the cells in a grid storage and tessellation process, however, does not fully work in theory as there are openings for the cells to be misused or not used efficiently based on the extreme number of touched cells to retain. With the GEOMETRY data type and indexes created on it, the bounding box is required because SQL Server needs a finite space. Creating such a box is done by using the coordinates xmin, xmax and ymin, ymax. The result can be visualized as a square having the x-coordinate and y-coordinate of the lower-left corner and the x-coordinate and y-coordinate of the upper-right corner. What is most critical when determining the bounding box with an index on a GEOMETRY data type is to ensure that all objects fall within the bounding box. This decision needs to also not make the bounding box excessively large, with lots and lots of empty cells. Therefore, there is a balancing act that results where a bounding box needs to be big enough for any data contained within, but not so large that excessive space is wasted. An index will be effective only for the objects or shapes within the bounding box. Not containing objects within a bounding box could severely impact the performance of spatial queries.

To retain the ability to use an index efficiently in the tessellation process, rules are applied. These rules are as follows:

> *Covering rule*: The covering rule is the most basic rule applied in tessellation. This is in no way related to the term *covering index*. The rule states that any cell that is completely covered is not recorded individually for that object. Covered cells are counted for the object. Not storing the details of covered cells saves processing time and data storage space.

> *Cells-per-object rule*: The cells-per-object rule is a more in-depth rule that applies a limit to the number of cells that can be counted for a specific object. In Figure 7-2, the circle shown covers 2 cells in level 1 and 12 in level 2. The circle is tessellated to the second layer because of a cells-per-object default of 16. If the circle did cover more than 16 cells at level 2, tessellation would not continue

through to level 2. Since the object would cover far more than 16 cells at level 3, tessellation stops here. Tuning the cells per object can enhance the accuracy of an index. Tuning this value based on the data stored can be very effective. Given the importance of the cells-per-object rule, the setting is exposed in a dynamic management view, `sys.spatial_index_tessellations`. This setting will be reviewed later in this chapter.

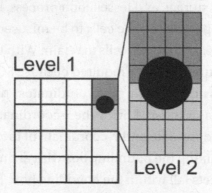

Figure 7-2. *Visual representation of an object and how many cells the object covers within the grid layers*

Deepest cell rule: The last rule of the tessellation process is the deepest cell rule. Each layer of grids and the cells within them are referenced in each deeper layer. In Figure 7-2, cells defined in level 2 are the only ones needed to completely refer to any other levels, in this case level 1. This rule is built into the optimizer's processing of how to retrieve data from the index.

With the GEOGRAPHY type, there is the added challenge of projecting the form in a flattened representation through the tessellation process. This process first divides the GEOGRAPHY grid into two hemispheres. Each hemisphere is projected onto the facets of a quadrilateral pyramid and flattened, and then the two are joined into a non-Euclidean plane. Once this process is complete, the plane is decomposed into the aforementioned grid hierarchy.

Creating Spatial Indexes

The Create Spatial Index statement has most of the same options of a normal clustered or non-clustered index. However, there are specific options that are required for this index type, as listed in Table 7-1.

Table 7-1. *Spatial Index Options*

Option Name	Description
USING	The USING clause specifies the spatial data type. This will be GEOMETRY_GRID or GEOGRAPHY_GRID and is required.
WITH GEOMETRY_GRID, GEOGRAPHY_GRID	The WITH options include the setting of the tessellation schema for either the GEOMETRY_GRID or the GEOGRAPHY_GRID based on the column data type.
BOUNDING_BOX	The BOUNDING_BOX is used in the GEOMETRY data type to define the bounding box of the cells. This option does not have defaults and must be specified when creating indexes on the GEOMETRY data type. The CREATE SPATIAL INDEX IDX_CITY_GEOM (in Listing 7-2) shows the syntax for this option. Setting the BOUNDING_BOX is done by setting the xmin and ymin and xmax and ymax coordinates, like so: BOUNDING_BOX = (XMIN = xmin, YMIN = ymin, XMAX = xmax, YMAX = ymax).
GRIDS	The GRIDS option is used for altering the density of each grid layer. All layer defaults are medium density but can be altered to low or high to further tune spatial indexes and density settings.

Take the CREATE TABLE statement in Listing 7-1 as an example.

Listing 7-1. CREATE TABLE with a GEOMETRY Data Type

```
USE AdventureWorks2017
GO
CREATE TABLE CITY_MAPS (
    ID BIGINT PRIMARY KEY
            IDENTITY(1, 1),
    CITYNAME NVARCHAR(150),      CITY_GEOM GEOMETRY
    );
GO
```

This table will consist of the primary key, the city name, and then a GEOMETRY column that holds map data for the city itself. The city's density may affect tuning the cells-per-object rule in tessellation as well as the density of each layer in the grid hierarchy.

To index the CITY_GEOM column, the CREATE statement in Listing 7-2 would be used with a grid layer density of LOW for the first two layers and then MEDIUM and HIGH for the third and fourth layers. This density change allows for tuning the object in the index and the covering cells as the layers go deeper in the grid. The cells-per-object setting is 24 maximum cells an object can cover. The bounding box coordinates are also set.

Listing 7-2. Definition of a Spatial Index on a GEOMETRY Column

```
USE AdventureWorks2017
GO

CREATE SPATIAL INDEX IDX_CITY_GEOM
ON CITY_MAPS (CITY_GEOM)
USING GEOMETRY_GRID
WITH (
BOUNDING_BOX = ( xmin=-50, ymin=-50, xmax=500, ymax=500 ),
GRIDS = (LOW, LOW, MEDIUM, HIGH),
CELLS_PER_OBJECT = 24,
PAD_INDEX  = ON );
```

To utilize and test the index created, the estimated and actual execution plans will need to be reviewed to determine whether the index has been used. In the case of spatial data, reviewing the actual results that a query will yield is also beneficial. SQL Server Management Studio has a built-in spatial data viewer that can be used for reviewing spatial data.

Listing 7-3 creates a table that can benefit from spatial indexing. The table is created to store ZIP codes and other data from the US Census Bureau. This table will be created in the AdventureWorks2017 database.

Listing 7-3. Creating a Table to Hold GEOMETRY-Related Data

```
USE AdventureWorks2017
GO
CREATE TABLE dbo.tl_2021_us_county (
    STATEFP CHAR(2) NULL,
    COUNTYFP CHAR(3) NULL,
    COUNTYNS CHAR(8) NULL,
    GEOID CHAR(5) NULL,
    NAME CHAR(100) NULL,
    NAMELSAD CHAR(100) NULL,
    LSAD CHAR(2) NULL,
    CLASSFP CHAR(2) NULL,
    MTFCC CHAR(5) NULL,
    CSAFP CHAR(3) NULL,
    CBSAFP CHAR(5) NULL,
    METDIVFP CHAR(5) NULL,
    FUNCSTAT CHAR(1) NULL,
    ALAND FLOAT NULL,
    AWATER FLOAT NULL,
    INTPTLAT CHAR(11) NULL,
    INTPTLON CHAR(12) NULL,
    GEOM GEOMETRY NULL
);
```

The GEOM column will store the GEOMETRY data. This column will be used to query the data from SQL Server Management Studio to show the imaging that can be done from other applications.

Note   For the examples in this chapter, a shape file and the tool OGR2OGR are required. The shape file will come from TIGER/Line Shapefile, 2021, nation, US, Current County and Equivalent National Shapefile available at `www2.census.gov/geo/tiger/TIGER2021/COUNTY/tl_2021_us_county.zip`. OGR2OGR is available in OSGeo4W from `http://download.osgeo.org/osgeo4w/osgeo4w-setup-v2.exe`. When installing the application, only install the GDAL package. After installation, run the PowerShell command [Environment]::SetEnvironmentVariable("GDAL_DATA", "C:\OSGeo4W64\share\gdal", "Machine") to set an environment variable. Finally, from the directory where the geography files were extracted to, run the command C:\OSGeo4W64\bin\ogr2ogr -f "MSSQLSpatial" MSSQL:"server=localhost;database=AdventureWorks2017;trusted_connection=yes;" -nln "tl_2021_us_county" -a_srs "ESPG:4269" -lco "GEOM_TYPE=geography" -lco "GEOM_NAME=geog4269" "tl_2021_us_county.shp" -s_srs EPSG:4269 -t_srs EPSG:26713.

Reviewing the actual data from a query of a GEOMETRY data type column is not useful in the normal grid and tabular result set from within SSMS. To take advantage of the spatial data features, using the Spatial Results tab in SSMS is much more effective. Given the table from Listing 7-3, a SELECT on the column GEOM can be executed, and the results of the SELECT statement will automatically generate the Spatial Results tab. For example, the query in Listing 7-4 will result in an image generated of the state of Washington, coding each county area in a different color.

Listing 7-4. Initial Query for Pulling Back Spatial Data

```
USE AdventureWorks2017
GO
SELECT  *
FROM    dbo.tl_2021_us_county AS tuc
WHERE   tuc.STATEFP = '41';
```

Click the Spatial Results tab in the result window of SSMS to reveal the image generated by the query. The results should look similar to the image in Figure 7-3.

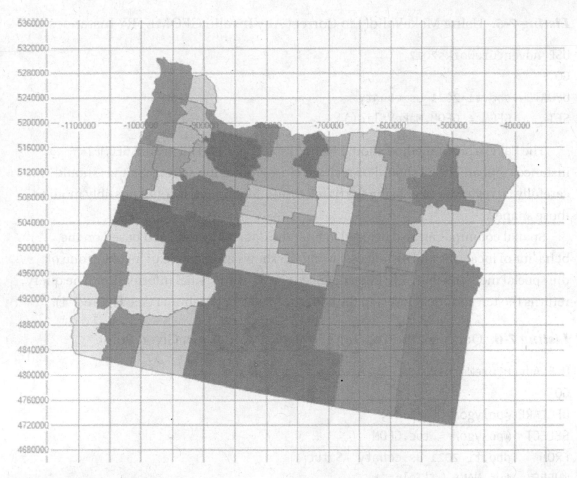

Figure 7-3. *Output from a spatial query against county data*

The query in Listing 7-4 used a standard column, STATEFP, to filter the information so that only counties within a particular state were viewed at one time. Before using this data, though, it is a good idea to ensure that only good shapes reside within the GEOM column. It is possible to have improper data stored, so cleaning the data may be required. To do this, the method MakeValid() can be used to modify any GEOMETRY instances, making them valid. According to the documentation from Microsoft, using the function can cause shapes to "shift slightly," but the extent to which it may affect the shapes under your control is unclear. Executing Listing 7-5 will result in an update to any invalid GEOMETRY instances in the GEOM column.

Listing 7-5. Using MakeValid() to Correct Any Invalid GEOMETRY Instances

```
USE AdventureWorks2017
GO
UPDATE   dbo.tl_2021_us_county
SET      GEOM = GEOM.MakeValid();
```

The MakeValid() method should be used sparingly, and all invalid GEOMETRY instances that are found should be reviewed in a production setting. Shapes should carefully be reviewed after using the MakeValid() function as it could possibly modify those shapes.

Spatial columns can also be used to filter the data being returned based on the behavior of locations and distances. Listing 7-6 shows an example of invoking one of the special methods that have been defined to work with spatial information. The query returns the ten counties closest to the county of Tulsa in Oklahoma (see Figure 7-4).

Listing 7-6. Query for the Top Ten Closest ZIP Codes to a Given Point

```
USE AdventureWorks2017
GO
DECLARE @polygon GEOMETRY;
SELECT   @polygon = tuc.GEOM
FROM     dbo.tl_2021_us_county AS tuc
WHERE    tuc.NAME = 'Tulsa';

SELECT TOP 10
         tuc.GEOM,
         tuc.GEOM.STDistance(@polygon),
         tuc.NAME
FROM     dbo.tl_2021_us_county AS tuc
WHERE    tuc.GEOM.STDistance(@polygon) IS NOT NULL
         AND tuc.GEOM.STDistance(@polygon) < 1
ORDER BY tuc.GEOM.STDistance(@polygon);
```

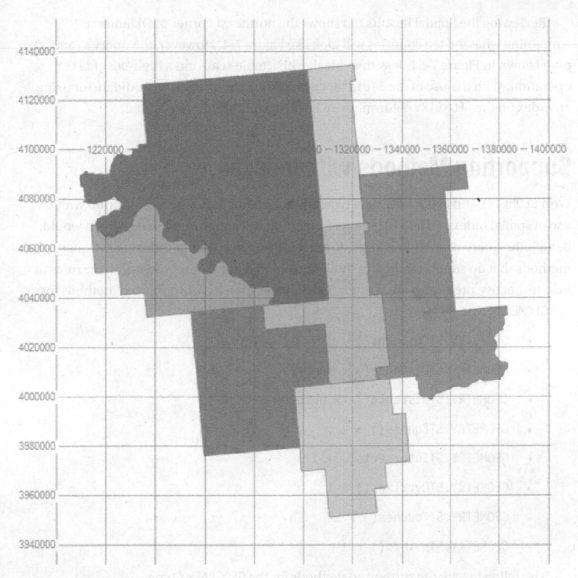

Figure 7-4. *Narrowing the results of the ZIP code data using STDistance()*

The query from Listing 7-6 creates the execution plan shown in Figure 7-5.

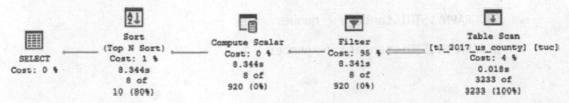

Figure 7-5. *Execution plan generated from STDistance() without indexing*

191

Reviewing the Spatial Results tab shows the northeast corner of Oklahoma containing what the ten counties will look like Figure 7-4. However, the query's execution plan shown in Figure 7-5 is less than ideal, with a table scan and a high-cost `filter` operation. With the use of the `STDistance` predicate, the query is a candidate for using an index on the `GEOMETRY` column, so an index can and should be added.

Supporting Methods with Indexes

With `GEOMETRY` and `GEOGRAPHY` data types, only certain methods are supported with the use of spatial indexes. The `STDistance()` method will support indexing, which would benefit the query shown in Listing 7-6. Before diving deeply into indexing the query, the methods that do support indexing should be pointed out. These methods have rules in how respective predicates are written. The following is a list of supported methods for the `GEOMETRY` type:

- `GEOMETRY.STContains() = 1`
- `GEOMETRY.STDistance() < number`
- `GEOMETRY.STDistance() <= number`
- `GEOMETRY.STEquals() = 1`
- `GEOMETRY.STIntersects() = 1`
- `GEOMETRY.STOverlaps() = 1`
- `GEOMETRY.STTouches() = 1`
- `GEOMETRY.STWithin() = 1`

The following are the supported methods for the `GEOGRAPHY` type:

- `GEOGRAPHY.STIntersects() = 1`
- `GEOGRAPHY.STEquals() = 1`
- `GEOGRAPHY.STDistance() < number`
- `GEOGRAPHY.STDistance() <= number`

For both GEOMETRY and GEOGRAPHY, to return any result that is not null, the first parameter and the second parameter must have the same spatial reference identifier (SRID), which is a spatial reference system based on a specific ellipsoid used to flatten or round the earth.

Recall that the query used in Figure 7-6 to return the counties around Tulsa uses the STDistance() method in the expression STDistance(@polygon) < 1. Based on the methods supported and analyzing the options and CREATE syntax for spatial indexing, the INDEX CREATE statement shown in Listing 7-7 can be used in an attempt to optimize the query.

Listing 7-7. CREATE Statement for a Spatial Index

```
USE AdventureWorks2017
GO
CREATE SPATIAL INDEX IDX_COUNTY_GEOM ON dbo.tl_2021_us_county
(
GEOM
) USING  GEOMETRY_GRID
WITH (
BOUNDING_BOX =(-91.513079, -87.496494, 36.970298, 36.970298),
GRIDS =(LEVEL_1 = LOW,LEVEL_2 = MEDIUM,LEVEL_3 = MEDIUM,LEVEL_4 = HIGH),
CELLS_PER_OBJECT = 16,
PAD_INDEX  = OFF, SORT_IN_TEMPDB = OFF, DROP_EXISTING = OFF,
ALLOW_ROW_LOCKS  = ON, ALLOW_PAGE_LOCKS  = ON) ON [PRIMARY];
GO
```

Executing the query in Listing 7-7 results in a much different execution plan, shown in Figure 7-6. It results in a shorter duration when executing and returning the results, plus spatial results. The largest difference in the execution plan is the use of the index IDX_COUNTY_GEOM.

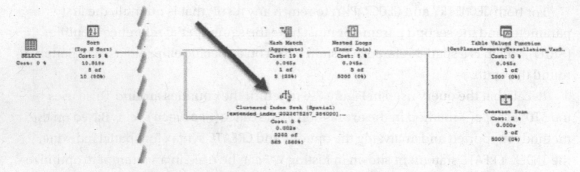

Figure 7-6. *Optimized details of a tuned execution plan using spatial data*

There is an overall improvement via a more optimal execution plan from the creation of the spatial index. The index and execution plan are good, but validating the actual improvement by checking the duration in execution time should not be skipped. By capturing the execution time using Extended Events, an overall review of the execution of the statement can be retrieved. In the case of the query that searches for the counties near Tulsa, the results with the index in place return 500 milliseconds. Dropping the index and executing the same query returns 1,500 milliseconds for total execution time. This test is extremely basic, but it is a solid foundation upon which to build a strategy for indexing existing spatial data to improve overall performance.

Understanding Statistics, Properties, and Information

Indexes in general have many data management views and functions that make their administration easier and more efficient than manual metrics gathering. With spatial indexes, there are additional catalog views that are included that assist in the unique settings and administration of them. In addition to these views, there are also built-in stored procedures that can be invoked to get information about spatial indexes.

The Views

There are two catalog views relevant to spatial indexes: sys.spatial_indexes and sys.spatial_index_tessellations. The sys.spatial_indexes view provides the type and tessellation scheme as well as basic information about each spatial index. The spatial_index_type column returned by sys.spatial_indexes returns a 1 for

GEOMETRY indexes and a 2 for GEOGRAPHY indexes. Listing 7-8 is an example query against the view, and Figure 7-7 shows the results.

Listing 7-8. Query to Retrieve Metadata About Spatial Indexes

```
USE AdventureWorks2017
GO
SELECT  name,
        type_desc,
        spatial_index_type,
        spatial_index_type_desc,
        tessellation_scheme
FROM    sys.spatial_indexes;
```

	name	type_desc	spatial_index_type	spatial_index_type_desc	tessellation_scheme
1	IDX_COUNTY_GEOM	SPATIAL	1	GEOMETRY	GEOMETRY_GRID

Figure 7-7. *Querying sys.spatial_indexes and results showing the IDX_WIZIP_GEOM index*

`sys.spatial_index_tessellations` can now be queried to see the parameters of the index and the tessellation scheme. Listing 7-9 is the query, and Figure 7-8 shows the results.

Listing 7-9. Query to Retrieve Information About Tessellation

```
USE AdventureWorks2017
GO
SELECT  tessellation_scheme,
        bounding_box_xmax,
        bounding_box_xmin,
        bounding_box_ymax,
        bounding_box_ymin,
        level_1_grid_desc,
        level_2_grid_desc,
        level_3_grid_desc,
        level_4_grid_desc,
        cells_per_object
FROM    sys.spatial_index_tessellations;
```

	tessellation_scheme	bounding_box_xmax	bounding_box_xmin	bounding_box_ymax	bounding_box_ymin	level_1_grid_		_4_grid_desc	cells_per_object
1	GEOMETRY_GRID	36.970298	-91.513079	36.970298'	-87.496494	LOW			16

Figure 7-8. *Querying sys.spatial_index_tessellations and partial results*

Both of these catalog views can be joined on `object_id` to become extremely useful for tuning and maintenance tasks. At times, it may prove effective to manipulate and recreate indexes as needed when the spatial data dictates a relevant need.

Stored Procedures

In addition to the catalog views, four stored procedures have been provided internally for further analysis of spatial indexes. These stored procedures return a complete listing of properties that are set on the indexes. The four procedures and their parameters are as follows:

```
sp_help_spatial_GEOMETRY_index [ @tabname =] 'tabname'
    [ , [ @indexname = ] 'indexname' ]
    [ , [ @verboseoutput = ] 'verboseoutput'
    [ , [ @query_sample = ] 'query_sample']
sp_help_spatial_GEOMETRY_index_xml [ @tabname =] 'tabname'
    [ , [ @indexname = ] 'indexname' ]
    [ , [ @verboseoutput = ]'{ 0 | 1 }]
    [ , [ @query_sample = ] 'query_sample' ]
    [ ,.[ @xml_output = ] 'xml_output' ]
sp_help_spatial_GEOGRAPHY_index [ @tabname =] 'tabname'
[ , [ @indexname = ] 'indexname' ]
[ , [ @verboseoutput = ] 'verboseoutput' ]
[ , [ @query_sample = ] 'query_sample' ]
sp_help_spatial_GEOGRAPHY_index_xml [@tabname = 'tabname'
[ , [ @indexname = ] 'indexname' ]
[ , [ @verboseoutput = ] 'verboseoutput' ]
[ , [ @query_sample = ] 'query_sample' ]
[ ,.[ @xml_output = ] 'xml_output' ]
```

Listing 7-10 shows how to execute these stored procedures. The example returns information about the GEOMETRY index IDX_COUNTY_GEOM created earlier in Listing 7-7. Figure 7-9 shows the results.

Listing 7-10. Investigating the Geometry Index

```
USE AdventureWorks2017
GO
DECLARE @Sample GEOMETRY
  = 'POLYGON((-90.0 -180.0, -90.0 180.0, 90.0 180.0, 90.0 -180.0,
-90.0 -180.0))';
EXEC sp_help_spatial_GEOMETRY_index 'dbo.tl_2017_us_county',
'IDX_COUNTY_GEOM', 0, @Sample;
```

	propname	propvalue
1	Total_Number_Of_ObjectCells_In_Level0_For_QuerySa...	1
2	Total_Number_Of_ObjectCells_In_Level0_In_Index	3233
3	Total_Number_Of_ObjectCells_In_Level1_For_QuerySa...	16
4	Total_Number_Of_Interior_ObjectCells_In_Level1_For_...	12
5	Total_Number_Of_Intersecting_ObjectCells_In_Level1_...	4
6	Total_Number_Of_Border_ObjectCells_In_Level0_For_...	1
7	Total_Number_Of_Border_ObjectCells_In_Level0_In_In...	3233
8	Number_Of_Rows_Selected_By_Primary_Filter	3233
9	Number_Of_Rows_Selected_By_Internal_Filter	0
10	Number_Of_Times_Secondary_Filter_Is_Called	3233
11	Number_Of_Rows_Output	0
12	Percentage_Of_Rows_NotSelected_By_Primary_Filter	0
13	Percentage_Of_Primary_Filter_Rows_Selected_By_Inte...	0
14	Internal_Filter_Efficiency	0.0
15	Primary_Filter_Efficiency	0

Figure 7-9. *sp_help_spatial_GEOMETRY_index example and results (results may vary)*

This information can be useful for adjusting the index to make it function better. These details are similar to the statistics that are available for standard indexes. Included are how many objects are available in each of the levels of the index. In addition, data is returned that matches the provided query sample. Seeing that a particular number of intersecting objects match the query sample shows whether a given object will be returned by the index. The percentage of objects in the index that are not returned from the query sample can also be retrieved by comparing the objects in the index to the ones that match. All of this helps understand how well the index is meeting spatial query requirements.

Tuning Spatial Indexes

As seen in Listing 7-7, when a spatial index is created, various options are available. Manipulating these options allows the behavior of a spatial index to be adjusted. Some experimentation will be necessary to arrive at the right set of options for the optimal behavior of an index. A combination of the execution plan and query performance metrics can help in arriving at an effective set of options.

For a GEOMETRY column, a bounding box can be added to the index. This limits the area that the index covers, which can allow an index to be created that can help satisfy certain query criteria better than a more generic index. For example, if the bounding box is changed and the index recreated, as shown in Listing 7-11, there is about a 10 percent reduction in execution time.

Listing 7-11. Adjusting the Bounding Box of the Spatial Index

```
USE AdventureWorks2017
GO
CREATE SPATIAL INDEX IDX_COUNTY_GEOM ON dbo.tl_2017_us_county
(
GEOM
)USING  GEOMETRY_GRID
WITH (
BOUNDING_BOX =(-96.9, -95.3, 36.4, 36.6),
GRIDS =(LEVEL_1 = LOW,LEVEL_2 = MEDIUM,LEVEL_3 = MEDIUM,LEVEL_4 = HIGH),
CELLS_PER_OBJECT = 16,
PAD_INDEX  = OFF, SORT_IN_TEMPDB = OFF, DROP_EXISTING = ON,
ALLOW_ROW_LOCKS  = ON, ALLOW_PAGE_LOCKS  = ON) ON [PRIMARY];
GO
```

By changing the bounding box, some objects are excluded from the index. Depending on the data and parameters used in the index, performance may not improve with more items filtered out from the index. Due to this complexity with spatial indexes, it is important to test and verify that the desired performance improvements are achieved as an index is adjusted and tested. Making changes to improve the queries for one set of counties may lead to poor performance for other counties in the United States. Therefore, there may not always be a simple solution available that can be implemented without some additional tweaking and validation.

Another adjustment that can be made is to change the grids of the index. The choice made in the examples so far is a standard choice if unsure of how the data is distributed and of how many matches it is likely to get from any one query. If a given query has a higher percentage of inclusive results, a different distribution on the grids can result in higher speed. It's largely a question of experimentation. But, just as with the bounding box, changing the grid distribution for one dataset could hurt another. Rigorous testing is required to ensure that a special index is optimal for common data profiles.

Using the same example, if the level 1 grid were to be adjusted into a HIGH detailed grid, there would be a 10 percent reduction in performance, making the query run slower. Changing it to MEDIUM neither benefited nor hurt the execution time. In this case, adjusting the grid levels in any combination didn't result in a significant improvement in speed, but having the HIGH level of detail on either level 1 or level 2 of the grid would negatively impact performance. With this experiment complete, it would be reasonable to choose to leave the default grids alone in this instance.

Restrictions on Spatial Indexes

Spatial indexes provide some unique features, as well as a set of restrictions. The following is a comprehensive list of restrictions for spatial indexing:

- Spatial indexes require an existing clustered index.

- A spatial index can be created only on a column of type GEOMETRY or GEOGRAPHY.

- Spatial indexes can be defined only on a table that has a primary key. The maximum number of primary key columns on the table is 15.

- The maximum size of index key records is 895 bytes. Larger sizes raise an error.

- The use of the Database Engine Tuning Advisor (DTA) is not supported.

- An online rebuild of a spatial index cannot be performed. Spatial index rebuilds are offline operations that leave the index unavailable while being rebuilt. If a rebuild is required, perform it at an off-hours time when the index is unlikely to be needed.

- Spatial indexes cannot be specified on indexed views.

- Only up to 249 spatial indexes can be created on any of the spatial columns in a supported table. Creating more than one spatial index on the same spatial column can be useful, for example, to index different tessellation parameters in a single column.

- An index build of spatial data cannot use available process parallelism.

Summary

Indexing spatial data is a complicated form of data storage and manipulation. This chapter covered the key components of how spatial data is processed and stored to help in managing and reviewing an implementation of the spatial data types in databases.

Spatial indexes provide the ability to quickly determine whether points lie within regions or whether regions overlap other regions. Instead of having to fully render each spatial artifact, spatial indexes allow queries to quickly calculate the results of the spatial function. A key to ensuring optimal performance is to examine the execution plan and validate that the spatial index is being used and that query duration is acceptable.

CHAPTER 8

Indexing Memory-Optimized Tables

The past few chapters have focused on indexing specialized data types in SQL Server. Memory-optimized tables are also available that allow schema and/or data to be persisted in memory, rather than on storage. Introduced in SQL Server 2014, these tables reside fully within memory while SQL Server is running, relying on disk-based structures to allow for schema/data to be persisted as needed.

With memory-optimized tables being primarily memory based, this has a significant impact on the traditional structures of a table and its indexes. In this chapter, memory-optimized tables will be reviewed, focusing on the differences between these tables and the more familiar disk-based tables. In addition, guidance will be provided as to how to create the ideal indexes on memory-optimized tables.

Note Depending on the source and SQL Server version, memory-optimized tables are also referred to as in-memory OLTP and Hekaton. This book will use the term *memory-optimized tables* as it aligns to the terminology used in Microsoft Books Online.

Memory-Optimized Tables Overview

Before diving into the indexing options for memory-optimized tables, it is important to review the basics of memory-optimized tables. A memory-optimized table is a table type introduced in SQL Server 2014. Unlike traditional tables and their indexes, memory-optimized tables reside entirely in memory. They are supported through disk structures but are not reliant on them for transactional processing. This differs from traditional tables, where the table is based on disk storage and typically only a portion of the table and its indexes reside in the buffer pool at any given time.

The value provided by memory-optimized tables are the performance gains provided for highly transactional workloads. By managing the entire table in memory, transactions do not need to wait for data to be written to the buffer pool. In addition, memory-optimized tables eliminate locking and latching, which improves OLTP workloads by eliminating the classic contention experienced by traditional tables.

The implementation of memory-optimized tables results in a few changes to the way in which tables are architected in SQL Server. Since the tables are now memory-resident, they are structured in a manner that is optimal for accessing the data in memory vs. retrieving a subset of the data from disk. For this reason, memory-optimized tables use hash and range indexes instead of B-trees for storing data. In addition, the tables do not need to read data from disk to the buffer pool like a traditional table, removing the need for latching between disk and memory structures.

To create memory-optimized tables in a database, there are prerequisites that need to be prepared within a database. To begin, a filegroup dedicated to memory-optimized data needs to be added to the database with a file to support memory-optimized tables. Additionally, the database should have the property MEMORY_OPTIMIZED_ELEVATE_TO_SNAPSHOT enabled. This property ensures that transactions against memory-optimized tables are executed under SNAPSHOT isolation. In Listing 8-1, the database MemOptIndexing is prepared using these settings.

Listing 8-1. Preparing a Database for Memory-Optimized Tables

```
USE master
GO

IF EXISTS(SELECT * FROM sys.databases WHERE name = 'MemOptIndexing')
DROP DATABASE MemOptIndexing
GO

CREATE DATABASE MemOptIndexing
GO

ALTER DATABASE MemOptIndexing
ADD FILEGROUP memoryOptimizedFG CONTAINS MEMORY_OPTIMIZED_DATA
--This file location may change in your environment
```

```
ALTER DATABASE MemOptIndexing
ADD FILE (name='memoryOptimizedData',
filename= 'C:\Program Files\Microsoft SQL Server\MSSQL15.MSSQLSERVER\MSSQL\
DATA\memoryOptimizedData')
    TO FILEGROUP memoryOptimizedFG

ALTER DATABASE MemOptIndexing SET MEMORY_OPTIMIZED_ELEVATE_TO_SNAPSHOT=ON
GO
```

Note   The file location for the filestream indicated in Listing 8-1 may need to change to fit a given environment.

The code in Listing 8-2 shows how to create a memory-optimized table. In this code example, the table dbo.SalesOrderHeader is created. There are two items of note in the table schema. First, the option that creates the table as a memory-optimized table is the MEMORY_OPTIMIZED=ON option. The second is the inclusion of a NONCLUSTERED HASH index on the table to index the data within memory. Other than those items, the table is much like any other table created in SQL Server.

Listing 8-2. Create a Memory-Optimized Table

```
USE MemOptIndexing
GO
IF OBJECT_ID('dbo.SalesOrderHeader') IS NOT NULL
    DROP TABLE dbo.SalesOrderHeader
CREATE TABLE dbo.SalesOrderHeader(
    SalesOrderID int NOT NULL,
    OrderDate datetime,
    DueDate datetime,
    ShipDate datetime,
    [Status] tinyint,
    CONSTRAINT IX_SalesOrderHeader_Hash PRIMARY KEY
        NONCLUSTERED HASH (SalesOrderID)
        WITH (BUCKET_COUNT = 35000))
    WITH (MEMORY_OPTIMIZED = ON)
IF  OBJECT_ID('tempdb..#tempHeader') IS NOT NULL
```

```
    DROP TABLE #tempHeader
SELECT SalesOrderID
    ,OrderDate
    ,DueDate
    ,ShipDate
    ,[Status]
INTO #tempHeader
FROM AdventureWorks2017.sales.SalesOrderHeader
INSERT INTO dbo.SalesOrderHeader
SELECT SalesOrderID
    ,OrderDate
    ,DueDate
    ,ShipDate
    ,[Status]
FROM #tempHeader
SET STATISTICS IO ON
SET STATISTICS TIME ON
PRINT 'Memory Optimized Table'
SELECT *
FROM dbo.SalesOrderHeader
ORDER BY SalesOrderID
PRINT 'Traditional Table'
SELECT *
FROM AdventureWorks2017.sales.SalesOrderHeader
ORDER BY SalesOrderID

SET STATISTICS IO OFF
SET STATISTICS TIME OFF
```

The additional code in Listing 8-2 inserts data into MemOptIndexing.dbo.
SalesOrderHeader and queries that same data. To demonstrate the impact of querying
data in a memory-optimized table, a similar query against AdventureWorks2017.sales.
SalesOrderHeader is included. Examining the results, shown in Listing 8-3, provides a
few insights into memory-optimized tables. There is no I/O impact from the memory-
optimized table. While the AdventureWorks2017.sales.SalesOrderHeader query
requires 689 reads, there are no reads for MemOptIndexing.dbo.SalesOrderHeader.

In addition, the amount of CPU time for MemOptIndexing.dbo.SalesOrderHeader is much lower, at 16 ms, than the CPU time for the query against AdventureWorks2017. sales.SalesOrderHeader, which is 78 ms.

Listing 8-3. Output from Creating and Querying a Memory-Optimized Table

```
(31465 row(s) affected)

(31465 row(s) affected)
Memory Optimized Table

 SQL Server Execution Times:
   CPU time = 0 ms,  elapsed time = 0 ms.
SQL Server parse and compile time:
   CPU time = 0 ms, elapsed time = 0 ms.

(31465 row(s) affected)
 SQL Server Execution Times:
   CPU time = 16 ms,  elapsed time = 310 ms.
Traditional Table

 SQL Server Execution Times:
   CPU time = 0 ms,  elapsed time = 0 ms.
(31465 row(s) affected)
Table 'SalesOrderHeader'. Scan count 1, logical reads 689, physical reads
0, read-ahead reads 0, lob logical reads 0, lob physical reads 0, lob read-
ahead reads 0.

 SQL Server Execution Times:
   CPU time = 78 ms,  elapsed time = 785 ms.

 SQL Server Execution Times:
   CPU time = 0 ms,  elapsed time = 0 ms.
```

While there are many more details of memory-optimized tables that can be discussed, this overview is intended to provide some of the most basic aspects. The rest of this chapter will examine indexing of memory-optimized tables. While memory-optimized tables are completely in memory, indexes are still required. Being in-memory doesn't prevent the need to find specific data or filter result sets. Indexes provide the mechanism for providing a path to data, regardless of where it resides.

To support indexing of memory-optimized tables, SQL Server supports two indexing options. These are hash and range indexes. Each memory-optimized table can support up to eight indexes. If a primary key is defined, this will be supported by one of the two index types and be one of the allowed indexes. If there is no primary key defined, the table must be created with at least one index. Additionally, memory-optimized tables do not allow indexing changes after creation. Therefore, all indexes need to be defined up front for a memory-optimized table when it is created.

The remainder of this chapter will focus on the hash and range indexes with considerations for how and when to build each of them against memory-optimized tables.

Note   Index operations for memory-optimized tables are non-logged activities since they occur only within memory and have no impact on the state of the data stored in the table.

Hash Indexes

One type of index that can be used for memory-optimized data is the hash index. Hash indexes separate the data in the table into a fixed number of buckets. Rows inserted into the table then use a hash function to assign rows to available buckets. These buckets provide the ability for queries to return specific rows based on the point lookup operations. Hash indexes are designed for query workloads where individual rows from a table need to be retrieved.

When creating hash indexes, the number of buckets to create is a function of the number of expected values for the indexed column(s). If a column or set of columns has a higher cardinality, a larger bucket count would be required. Ideally, the bucket count would be exactly equal to the number of distinct values for the indexed column(s). In reality, the number will be higher to allow for some amount of future growth.

This is an important part of creating and tuning hash indexes on memory-optimized tables. As the number of rows in each bucket increases, the time required to retrieve data increases due to hash collisions.

Optimal hash indexes need to have enough buckets to account for future growth (and avoid hash collisions) while not having too many buckets (and wasting space).

To demonstrate the impact of bucket size, Listing 8-4 creates two memory-optimized tables. Both tables have 1,000,000 rows in them, with the first table having 1,000 buckets and the second having 1,000,000 buckets. With this configuration, there will be approximately 1,000 rows per bucket for the first table and 1 row per bucket in the second table. Since an identity column is being indexed, each row will have a unique value for SalesOrderID.

Listing 8-4. Create Memory-Optimized Tables with Hash Indexes

```
USE MemOptIndexing
GO
IF OBJECT_ID('dbo.SalesOrderHeader_low') IS NOT NULL
    DROP TABLE dbo.SalesOrderHeader_low

CREATE TABLE dbo.SalesOrderHeader_low(
    SalesOrderID int NOT NULL
    ,Column1 uniqueidentifier
    ,CONSTRAINT IX_SalesOrderHeader_Hash_low PRIMARY KEY
        NONCLUSTERED HASH (SalesOrderID)
        WITH (BUCKET_COUNT = 1000))
    WITH (MEMORY_OPTIMIZED = ON);

WITH L1(z) AS (SELECT 0 UNION ALL SELECT 0)
, L2(z) AS (SELECT 0 FROM L1 a CROSS JOIN L1 b)
, L3(z) AS (SELECT 0 FROM L2 a CROSS JOIN L2 b)
, L4(z) AS (SELECT 0 FROM L3 a CROSS JOIN L3 b)
, L5(z) AS (SELECT 0 FROM L4 a CROSS JOIN L4 b)
, L6(z) AS (SELECT TOP 1000000 0 FROM L5 a CROSS JOIN L5 b)
INSERT INTO dbo.SalesOrderHeader_low
SELECT ROW_NUMBER() OVER (ORDER BY z) AS RowID, NEWID()
FROM L6;
GO
IF OBJECT_ID('dbo.SalesOrderHeader_high') IS NOT NULL
    DROP TABLE dbo.SalesOrderHeader_high
CREATE TABLE dbo.SalesOrderHeader_high(
    SalesOrderID int NOT NULL
    ,Column1 uniqueidentifier
```

```
    ,CONSTRAINT IX_SalesOrderHeader_hash_high PRIMARY KEY
        NONCLUSTERED HASH (SalesOrderID)
        WITH (BUCKET_COUNT = 1000000))
    WITH (MEMORY_OPTIMIZED = ON);
WITH L1(z) AS (SELECT 0 UNION ALL SELECT 0)
, L2(z) AS (SELECT 0 FROM L1 a CROSS JOIN L1 b)
, L3(z) AS (SELECT 0 FROM L2 a CROSS JOIN L2 b)
, L4(z) AS (SELECT 0 FROM L3 a CROSS JOIN L3 b)
, L5(z) AS (SELECT 0 FROM L4 a CROSS JOIN L4 b)
, L6(z) AS (SELECT TOP 1000000 0 FROM L5 a CROSS JOIN L5 b)
INSERT INTO dbo.SalesOrderHeader_high
SELECT ROW_NUMBER() OVER (ORDER BY z) AS RowID, NEWID()
FROM L6;
```

Warning   The code in Listing 8-4 may take up to 5 minutes to execute.

Prior to executing the next section of code for this demo, create an Extended Events session based on the Query Detail Tracking template. The session should be created with the default configuration and then launched to the Extended Events live data viewer. Add the columns session_id, statement, writes, physical_reads, logical_reads, duration, and cpu_time to the live viewer window. Lastly, filter the session_id in the output by the session_id values from Listings 8-5 and 8-6 and the event name sql_statement_completed.

When the query is executed against both tables to return the same row, as shown in Listing 8-5, slightly different performance can be observed between the two. In this sample, the execution time for the first query was 359 μs vs. 48 μs, as shown in Figure 8-1. While this difference is small in total duration, the difference between them is significant. In solutions where memory-optimized tables will be used to retrieve results, this kind of performance difference can be important, especially when queries are executed frequently.

Listing 8-5. Querying Memory-Optimized Tables with Hash Indexes—Single Row

```
USE MemOptIndexing
GO

SET STATISTICS TIME ON

PRINT 'Memory Optimized Table with 1000 buckets'
SELECT *
FROM dbo.SalesOrderHeader_low
WHERE SalesOrderID = 42
ORDER BY SalesOrderID

PRINT 'Memory Optimized Table with 1,000,000 buckets'
SELECT *
FROM dbo.SalesOrderHeader_high
WHERE SalesOrderID = 42
ORDER BY SalesOrderID
SET STATISTICS TIME OFF
```

name	timestamp	session_id	statement	writes	physical_reads	logical_reads	duration	cpu_time
sql_statement_completed	2019-07-21 23:11:24.0109838	88	SELECT @@SPID	0	0	0	22	0
sql_statement_completed	2019-07-21 23:11:24.0195896	88	USE MemOptIndexing	0	0	0	379	0
sql_statement_completed	2019-07-21 23:11:24.0227290	88	SET STATISTICS TIME ON	0	0	0	38	0
sql_statement_completed	2019-07-21 23:11:24.0227445	88	PRINT 'Memory Optimized Table with 1000 buckets'	0	0	0	7	0
sql_statement_completed	2019-07-21 23:11:24.0231525	88	SELECT * FROM dbo.SalesOrderHeader_low WHERE	0	0	0	359	0
sql_statement_completed	2019-07-21 23:11:24.0231590	88	PRINT 'Memory Optimized Table with 1,000,000 buckets'	0	0	0	2	0
sql_statement_completed	2019-07-21 23:11:24.0232204	88	SELECT * FROM dbo.SalesOrderHeader_high WHERE	0	0	0	48	0
sql_statement_completed	2019-07-21 23:11:24.0232235	88	SET STATISTICS TIME OFF	0	0	0	0	0

Figure 8-1. *Duration for memory-optimized table queries with hash indexes—single row*

It's important not to interpret the results of the last script to indicate that a 1:1 ratio of buckets to values is the best practice. If another set of queries is run that retrieves more than a single row, such as rows 42–420 being returned as shown in Listing 8-6, then the performance profile changes. In this case, the performance advantage shifts to buckets with more values. The results now are 86,973 µs for the query on the first table vs. 101,127 µs for the second table's query, as shown in Figure 8-2.

Listing 8-6. Query Memory-Optimized Tables with Hash Indexes—Multiple Rows

```
USE MemOptIndexing
GO

SET STATISTICS TIME ON

PRINT 'Memory Optimized Table with 1000 buckets'
SELECT *
FROM dbo.SalesOrderHeader_low
WHERE SalesOrderID BETWEEN 42 AND 420
ORDER BY SalesOrderID

PRINT 'Memory Optimized Table with 1,000,000 buckets'
SELECT *
FROM dbo.SalesOrderHeader_high
WHERE SalesOrderID BETWEEN 42 AND 420
ORDER BY SalesOrderID

SET STATISTICS TIME OFF
```

name	timestamp	session_id	statement	writes	physical_reads	logical_reads	duration	cpu_time
sql_statement_completed	2019-07-21 23:16:36.8736000	88	SELECT @@SPID	0	0	0	0	0
sql_statement_completed	2019-07-21 23:16:36.8963304	88	USE MemOptIndexing	0	0	0	43	0
sql_statement_completed	2019-07-21 23:16:36.9075833	88	SET STATISTICS TIME ON	0	0	0	2	0
sql_statement_completed	2019-07-21 23:16:36.9075957	88	PRINT 'Memory Optimized Table with 1000 buckets'	0	0	0	6	0
sql_statement_completed	2019-07-21 23:16:36.9546255	88	SELECT * FROM dbo.SalesOrderHeader_low WHERE				86975	135000
sql_statement_completed	2019-07-21 23:16:36.9546395	88	PRINT 'Memory Optimized Table with 1,000,000 buckets'	0	0	0	4	0
sql_statement_completed	2019-07-21 23:16:37.0957947	88	SELECT * FROM dbo.SalesOrderHeader_high WHERE				101127	110000
sql_statement_completed	2019-07-21 23:16:37.0958075	88	SET STATISTICS TIME OFF	0	0	0	2	0

Figure 8-2. *Duration for memory-optimized table queries with hash indexes—multiple rows*

When working with hash indexes, it is important to understand how SQL Server is using the buckets in the hash. One important thing to note is that just because there are enough buckets for each value to have its own bucket, that doesn't mean each value will get its own bucket. To review the statistics for hash indexes created in this chapter, run the query in Listing 8-7 that accesses the DMV sys.dm_db_xtp_hash_index_stats. This DMV provides information on the number of buckets and how those buckets are populated.

Listing 8-7. Query to Review Hash Index Statistics

```
USE MemOptIndexing
GO

SELECT OBJECT_NAME(hs.object_id) AS object_name
,i.name as index_name
,hs.total_bucket_count
,hs.empty_bucket_count
,FLOOR((CAST(empty_bucket_count as float)/total_bucket_count) * 100) AS
empty_bucket_percent
,hs.avg_chain_length
,hs.max_chain_length
FROM sys.dm_db_xtp_hash_index_stats AS hs
INNER JOIN sys.indexes AS i ON hs.object_id=i.object_id AND
hs.index_id=i.index_id
```

Reviewing the results of Listing 8-7, provided in Figure 8-3, reveals a few key metrics. The first index with 1,000 buckets specified (SalesOrderHeader_low) actually has 1,024 buckets for the index. This is because buckets are created in allocations that align to a power of two. This is the same reason there are 1,048,576 buckets for the 1,000,000-bucket index on SalesOrderHeader_high. The next notable property is the number of empty buckets in the hash index on SalesOrderHeader_high. With 1,000,000 rows and more than a million buckets, there are still 37 percent of the buckets that are empty. This happens because with the deterministic hashing function, some hashed values are repeated within the range of values before all the buckets are utilized. This is something to consider when building hash indexes, especially when aiming to have a 1:1 ratio of buckets to rows.

	object_name	index_name	total_bucket_count	empty_bucket_count	empty_bucket_percent	avg_chain_length	max_chain_length
1	SalesOrderHeader_low	IX_SalesOrderHeader_Hash_low	1024	0	0	976	1035
2	SalesOrderHeader	IX_SalesOrderHeader_Hash	65536	40674	62	1	7
3	SalesOrderHeader_high	IX_SalesOrderHeader_hash_high	1048576	398369	37	1	8

Figure 8-3. *Output from the hash bucket statistics query*

> **Note**   Query performance details were captured using an Extended Events session based on the Query Detail Tracking template with a filter for the session that included the demonstration queries. More information on building sessions can be found here: `https://docs.microsoft.com/en-us/sql/relational-databases/extended-events/quick-start-extended-events-in-sql-server?view=sql-server-ver16`.

Hash indexes on memory-optimized tables are the ideal indexing choice when queries will retrieve individual or small numbers of values from an index at any given time. When building the tables and hash indexes, focus on setting the number of buckets to a size that presents a reasonable ratio of values to buckets with consideration for the number of values that will be retrieved through typical queries.

Range Indexes

The second type of index that is supported for memory-optimized tables is the range index. Range indexes are used to support range and ordered scans of data. They leverage a variation of a B-tree, which Microsoft calls a Bw-tree. The key difference between these two structures is the reference between the nodes in the Bw-tree, which refers to memory locations vs. physical page location. When determining whether to include a range index on a memory-optimized table, the primary consideration will be whether a range of values will be scanned or ORDER BY statements will need to be supported.

> **Note**   You can find more information on Bw-trees at `http://research.microsoft.com/pubs/178758/bw-tree-icde2013-final.pdf`.

To create a range index on a memory-optimized table, the index is declared within the schema of the table by indicating a NONCLUSTERED index with the key values. As shown in Listing 8-8, the index IX_SalesOrderHeader is a range index on the SalesOrderID column. Unlike hash indexes, there are no other attributes to consider. Therefore, bucket counts are not relevant for range indexes.

Listing 8-8. Create a Table with a Range Index

```
USE MemOptIndexing
GO
IF OBJECT_ID('dbo.SalesOrderHeader_high_range') IS NOT NULL
    DROP TABLE dbo.SalesOrderHeader_high_range
CREATE TABLE dbo.SalesOrderHeader_high_range(
    SalesOrderID int NOT NULL
    ,Column1 uniqueidentifier
    ,CONSTRAINT IX_SalesOrderHeader_hash_high_range PRIMARY KEY
        NONCLUSTERED HASH (SalesOrderID)
        WITH (BUCKET_COUNT = 1000000)
    ,INDEX IX_SalesOrderHeader NONCLUSTERED (SalesOrderID)
    )
    WITH (MEMORY_OPTIMIZED = ON);

WITH L1(z) AS (SELECT 0 UNION ALL SELECT 0)
, L2(z) AS (SELECT 0 FROM L1 a CROSS JOIN L1 b)
, L3(z) AS (SELECT 0 FROM L2 a CROSS JOIN L2 b)
, L4(z) AS (SELECT 0 FROM L3 a CROSS JOIN L3 b)
, L5(z) AS (SELECT 0 FROM L4 a CROSS JOIN L4 b)
, L6(z) AS (SELECT TOP 1000000 0 FROM L5 a CROSS JOIN L5 b)
INSERT INTO dbo.SalesOrderHeader_high_range
SELECT ROW_NUMBER() OVER (ORDER BY z) AS RowID, NEWID()
FROM L6;
```

To demonstrate the value of the range index on memory-optimized tables, the table created in Listing 8-8 will be used with queries that will leverage range scans. Consider Listing 8-9, which queries the new table (dbo.SalesOrderHeader_high_range) and the table previously created with a hash index (dbo.SalesOrderHeader_high). By executing a query against both tables for the rows with SalesOrderID between 100 and 10,000, a significant difference in the execution time can be observed. The query against a hash index runs in 216 ms (see Figure 8-4), while the query against a range index runs in 97 ms. In this scenario, range indexes provide a substantial performance improvement.

Listing 8-9. Query Memory-Optimized Tables with a Range Scan

```
USE MemOptIndexing
GO
SET STATISTICS TIME ON
SELECT *
FROM dbo.SalesOrderHeader_high
WHERE SalesOrderID BETWEEN 100 AND 10000
ORDER BY SalesOrderID
SELECT *
FROM dbo.SalesOrderHeader_high_range
WHERE SalesOrderID BETWEEN 100 AND 10000
ORDER BY SalesOrderID
SET STATISTICS TIME OFF
```

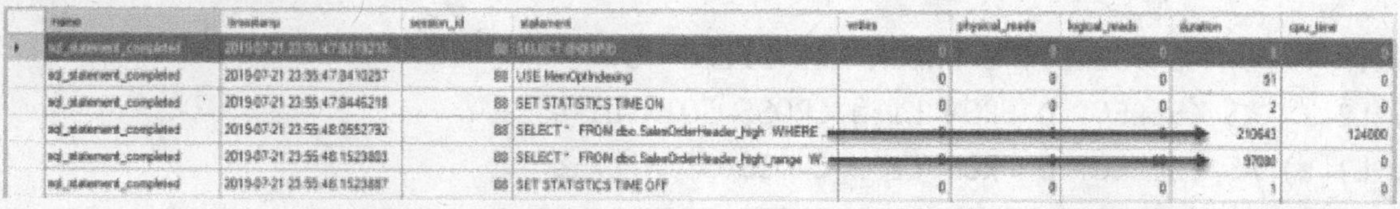

Figure 8-4. *Duration for memory-optimized table queries with a range scan*

In a similar fashion, ORDER BY statements are also greatly improved when range indexes on memory-optimized tables are available. Using the code in Listing 8-10, two queries are executed against the same tables from the previous demonstration. In this scenario, using the output in Figure 8-5 shows that the range scan took 462 µs compared with the 240,733 µs that the hash index required. This illustrates a substantial performance improvement through the use of the range index.

Listing 8-10. Query Memory-Optimized Tables with an ORDER BY Statement

```
USE MemOptIndexing
GO

SET STATISTICS TIME ON
SELECT TOP 100 *
FROM dbo.SalesOrderHeader_high
ORDER BY SalesOrderID
```

```
SELECT TOP 100 *
FROM dbo.SalesOrderHeader_high_range
ORDER BY SalesOrderID

SET STATISTICS TIME OFF
```

Figure 8-5. *Duration for memory-optimized table queries with TOP clause and ORDER BY*

Similar to hash indexes, range indexes provide a valuable performance improvement opportunity when creating memory-optimized tables. The need to perform range scans and order results is common in many applications. These operations are greatly improved by the use of range indexes.

Summary

This chapter looked at the types of indexes available for memory-optimized tables. These options, which include hash and range indexes, are the power behind the ability for memory-optimized tables to provide the incredible performance that they deliver. As demonstrated, each index type aligns to different querying patterns. It is important to understand those patterns to build the optimal indexes for memory-optimized tables and the workloads that they support.

CHAPTER 9

Full-Text Indexing

SQL Server supports mechanisms that allow you to store large amounts of unstructured text information. Since SQL Server 2008, one of those mechanisms has been the MAX length used with variable-length character data types VARCHAR and NVARCHAR. This means you can store up to 2 GB worth of character information within a single column. While SQL Server can store this information, the 1,700-byte limit for non-clustered indexes and 900-byte limit on clustered indexes make indexing through traditional means a challenge. Fortunately, SQL Server offers another indexing mechanism for searching within these large data types: full-text indexing.

Full-Text Indexing

Full-text indexing is another indexing feature in SQL Server that falls outside of the normal indexing methods and objects. This chapter will briefly describe full-text search (FTS) architecture, storage, and indexing for optimal performance.

Full-text search (FTS) allows large amounts of text-based content to be stored and efficiently searched. This content can include many different formats, such as Word document (.docx) files. This storage is in BLOB (binary large object) columns instead of plain-text data. The ability to store and search content of an unstructured nature provides a number of technical opportunities in a database management system.

Document retention is one such opportunity as it allows documents to be stored for vast lengths of time at a much lower cost. The search abilities allow for querying this content for a wide variety of needs. Imagine a shipping company that generates thousands of shipping documents from a template created in plain text. Those documents constitute a massive initiative for retention purposes to ensure shipments can be tracked for later needs. Storage warehouse rooms cost money to maintain. When the task of researching a specific shipment arises, the hours taken for that task are significant unless it can be automated.

© Edward Pollack and Jason Strate 2023
E. Pollack and J. Strate, *Expert Performance Indexing in Azure SQL and SQL Server 2022*,
https://doi.org/10.1007/978-1-4842-9215-0_9

If this shipping company is using the FTS feature and an indexing structure, then documents are scanned with systems that read the text into a system that later inserts it into a SQL Server database. This allows for full-text search of specific account numbers, shipping invoices, and any distinct text in the documents needed for later review. An index just like a book index can be created, making it even quicker to find specific documents. Going further, FTS lets specific content be found within the documents themselves. If a request is made to find all shipping documents that were sent by a specific freight company on a specific trailer, the FTS capabilities allow the information to be retrieved in a fraction of the time as compared with a manual process or an unindexed text search.

Creating a Full-Text Example

Now that the concept of FTS has been introduced, indexing strategy can be discussed. Full-text indexes are the backbone of searching and querying unstructured text data. This data can be a number of data types including char, varchar, nchar, nvarchar, xml, and varbinary. While it is possible to use text, ntext, and image, it's best to avoid their use as they are deprecated in SQL Server. The data types varchar, nvarchar, and varbinary provide equivalent types, respectively.

For the remainder of this section on full-text indexing, the contents of the white paper "Optimizing Your Query Plans with the SQL Server 2014 Cardinality Estimator" by Joseph Sack have been inserted into the sample table using the script in Listing 9-1. The document will be used to demonstrate full-text indexing and can be found in Books Online or downloaded from http://bit.ly/1II5UfU and placed in the directory c:\ temp. Additionally, the full-text catalog feature needs to be installed to successfully run the code in this chapter. Full-text catalog is not a feature that is installed by default, so it may need to be installed first.

Note   For all versions of SQL Server, to build a full-text index on Microsoft Office documents, the Filter Pack IFilters must be installed. Download and install Microsoft Office Filter Packs from https://support.microsoft.com/en-us/ help/945934/how-to-register-microsoft-filter-pack-ifilters- with-sql-server. Be sure to follow the additional steps to run sp_fulltext_ service and restart the SQL Server instance.

Creating a Full-Text Catalog

Using AdventureWorks2017, a table will be prepared that will be used for full-text searching. Using the varbinary(max) data type allows the import of most document types and images. In Listing 9-1, the CREATE TABLE and INSERT statements prepare the objects needed to create a full-text search index.

Listing 9-1. CREATE TABLE and INSERT Statements Used with Full-Text Search

```
USE AdventureWorks2017
GO
DROP TABLE IF EXISTS dbo.SQLServerDocuments;
CREATE TABLE dbo.SQLServerDocuments (
    SQLServerDocumentsID INT IDENTITY(1, 1),
    DocType VARCHAR(6),
    DOC VARBINARY(MAX),
    CONSTRAINT PK_SQLServerDocuments PRIMARY KEY CLUSTERED
        (SQLServerDocumentsID)
);
GO
DECLARE @worddoc VARBINARY(MAX);
SELECT  @worddoc = CAST(bulkcolumn AS VARBINARY(MAX))
FROM    OPENROWSET(BULK 'c:\temp\Optimizing Your Query Plans with the SQL
Server 2014 Cardinality Estimator.docx', SINGLE_BLOB) AS x;
INSERT  INTO dbo.SQLServerDocuments
        (DocType, DOC)
VALUES  ('docx', @worddoc);
GO
```

When creating an FTS index, a full-text catalog must first be created. Since SQL Server 2008, the catalog is contained in the database as a definition. The catalog itself is a virtual object and greatly enhances performance by eliminating I/O bottlenecks. A catalog contains all of the properties that are searchable.

The catalog is the link to the full-text index. Before getting started, let's review the syntax for CREATE FULLTEXT CATALOG, which is shown in Listing 9-2.

Listing 9-2. The CREATE FULLTEXT CATALOG Syntax

```
USE AdventureWorks2017
GO
CREATE FULLTEXT CATALOG <catalog name>
WITH <catalog specific options>
AS DEFAULT
AUTHORIZATION <the owners name - ownership>
ACCENT_SENSITIVITY = <ON|OFF>;
```

The first option that should be considered in the creation of a catalog is the AS DEFAULT setting. Commonly, full-text indexes are created without thought of the catalog to which they should be applied. If the catalog is omitted during index creation, the catalog that has been set as the default will be used.

Authorization and accent sensitivity are specific in the CREATE command. When omitting the authorization option, ownership will fall under dbo. This is the same for most objects in SQL Server when ownership is not declared. It is recommended that ownership is assigned for managing security and grouping objects under the proper areas. When specifying a user for ownership, a username must be specified that matches one of the following:

- The name of the user running the statement

- The name of a user that the user executing the command has impersonate permissions for

- The database owner or system administrator

Accent sensitivity dictates whether the catalog will be accent sensitive or insensitive. For example, with accent insensitive, the words "piñata" and "pinata" will be treated as the same words. Be sure to research whether accent sensitivity should be on or off prior to the creation of the catalog. If this option is changed, the full-text indexes on the catalog must be rebuilt.

For creating a full-text catalog on the white paper, execute the statement in Listing 9-3. For this catalog, the default options will be used for the syntax, which sets accent sensitivity to the collation of the table.

Listing 9-3. Creating a New Full-Text Catalog

```
USE AdventureWorks2017
GO
CREATE FULLTEXT CATALOG WhitePaperCatalog AS DEFAULT;
```

Creating a Full-Text Index

With the catalog created and the decision made for how to handle catalogs, accent sensitivity, and ownership, consideration can be made as to how to configure and create the full-text index. The most critical of these decisions is the requirement of a key index.

Syntax

The syntax in Listing 9-4 is used to create the full-text index. Table 9-1 describes the different options available.

Listing 9-4. CREATE FULLTEXT INDEX Syntax

```
USE AdventureWorks2017
GO
CREATE FULLTEXT INDEX ON <table name>
(<column name>)
KEY INDEX <index name [must be specified]>
ON <catalog filegroup>
WITH <index options>
CHANGE_TRACKING = <Manual | Auto | Off
STOPLIST = <default system or specified StopList name>;
```

In most other CREATE INDEX statements, the basic syntax and options are alike with slight modifications. With FTS index creation, there is a completely different set of options and considerations. The initial CREATE FULLTEXT INDEX is the same as any CREATE INDEX, with the given table required and then the column to index. After this, the other options are not typical to normal index creation.

221

Table 9-1. *Full-Text Index Options*

Option Name	Description
TYPE COLUMN	Specifies the name of the column that holds the document type for documents loaded in BLOB types, such as `.doc`, `.pdf`, and `.xls`. This option is used only for `varbinary`, `varbinary(max)`, and `image` data types. If this option is specified on any other data type, the `CREATE FULLTEXT INDEX` statement will throw an error.
LANGUAGE	Alters the default language that is used for the index with the following variations and options: • The language can be specified as string, integer, or hexadecimal. • If a language is specified, the language is used when a query is run using the index. • When a language is specified as a string value, the `syslanguages` system table must correspond to the language. • If a double-byte value is used, it is converted to hexadecimal at creation time. • Word breakers and stemmers for the specific language must be enabled, or a SQL Server error will be generated. • Non-BLOB and non-XML columns containing multiple languages should follow the 0 × 0 neutral language setting. • For BLOB and XML types, language types in the documents themselves will be used. For example, a Word document with a language type of Russian or LCID 1049 will force the same setting in the index. Use `sys.fulltext_languages` to review all the language types and LCID codings available.
KEY INDEX	Every full-text index requires an adjoining unique, single-key, non-null column to be designated. Specify the column in the same table using this option.
FULLTEXT_CATALOG_NAME	If the full-text index is not to be created using the default catalog, specify the catalog name using this option.

(continued)

Table 9-1. *(continued)*

Option Name	Description
CHANGE_TRACKING	Determines how and when an index is populated. Options are MANUAL, AUTO, and OFF [NO_POPULATION]. The MANUAL setting requires ALTER FULLTEXT INDEX ... START UPDATE POPULATION to be executed before the index is populated. The AUTO setting populates the index at creation time and automatically updates based on changes that are made ongoing. This is the default setting if CHANGE_TRACKING is omitted in the CREATE statement. The OFF [NO_POPULATION] setting is used to completely turn population off for the index, and SQL Server will not retain a list of changes. The index is populated upon creation one time unless the NO_POPULATION is specified.
STOPLIST	Specifies a StopList that will prevent certain words from being indexed. OFF, SYSTEM, and a custom StopList are available options. The OFF setting will not use a StopList and will have more overhead on performance of population of the index. The SYSTEM is the default StopList already created. A user-created StopList is a StopList that was created and can be used in association with a given full-text index.
SEARCH PROPERTY LIST·	Specifies the search property list to associate with the full-text index. Property lists allow greater control of full-text search by allowing differentiation of search between properties of a document, such as title or tags.

Key Indexes

Choosing the key index can be a straightforward choice given the restrictions of the key index being a unique, single-key, and non-nullable column. A primary key will commonly work well for this, like the primary key shown in Listing 9-1 on the dbo. SQLServerDocuments table. However, consideration should be given to the size of the key. Ideally, a 6-byte key is recommended and documented as optimal to reduce overhead on I/O and CPU resource consumption. Recall that one of the restrictions of the unique key is that it cannot exceed 900 bytes. If this maximum restriction is met, then population will fail. Resolving the problem could force a new index and alteration of the table itself to occur. This could create costly downtime for tables that are in high-use situations.

Population

Change tracking in full-text indexing should be weighed heavily when creating full-text indexes. The default setting of AUTO may have overhead that can affect the performance negatively if the contents of the column being indexed change frequently. For example, a system that is storing shipping invoices that never change and are inserted only once a month would likely not benefit from AUTO being set. A MANUAL population could be run at a given time by using the SQL Server Agent based on the loading of the contents in the table. Although not common, some systems are static and loaded only one time. This would be an ideal situation for using the OFF setting, with the initial population being performed only at that time.

The last option for population is incremental population. Incremental population is the same concept as an incremental update to data. As changes to data are made, they are tracked. Think of merge replication as a comparison. Merge replication retains changes by the use of triggers and insert/update/delete tracking rows into merge system tables. At a given point in time, a DBA can set a synchronization schedule to process those changes and replicate them to the subscribers. This is the same way incremental population functions. By using a `timestamp` column in the table, the changes are tracked. Only those that are found needing a change are processed. This does mean the requirement for a timestamp column on the table must be met in order to perform incremental populations. For data that has an extreme amount of change, this may not be ideal. However, for data that changes randomly and seldomly, incremental population may be ideal.

StopLists

StopLists are extremely useful in managing what not to populate. This can improve the population performance by bypassing what are known as *noise words*. As an example, consider the sentence "A dog chewed through the fiber going to the SAN causing the disaster recovery plans to be used for the SQL Server instance." In this sentence, the most useful words that should be indexed are *fiber*, *SAN*, *disaster*, *recovery*, and *SQL* or *Server*. *A*, *the*, *to*, and *be* would not be ideal. These are considered noise words and are not part of the population process. People rarely search for prepositions, adverbs, or other words that are used to connect ideas, rather than constitute the ideas themselves.

The use of a StopList can be extremely helpful in the overall population performance and parsing of full-text indexed content. Use of the StopList can be specific to languages as well. For example, *la* in French would be specified over *the* in English.

To create a custom StopList, use the `CREATE FULLTEXT STOPLIST` statement as shown in Listing 9-5. The system default StopList can be used to pre-generate all noise words already identified as such. For the white paper example, the name of the StopList would be `WhitePaperStopList`.

Listing 9-5. Creating a Full-Text StopList

```
USE AdventureWorks2017
GO
CREATE FULLTEXT STOPLIST WhitePaperStopList FROM SYSTEM STOPLIST;
```

To view the StopList, use the system views `sys.fulltext_stoplists` and `sys.fulltext_stopwords`. The `sys.fulltext_stoplists` view will hold metadata related to the StopLists that are created on the SQL Server instance. Determine the `stoplist_id` to join to `sys.fulltext_stopwords` to show a complete listing of the words. Alone, this StopList is no better than the system default StopList. To add words to the StopList, use the `ALTER FULLTEXT STOPLIST` statement as shown in Listing 9-6, which removes *Downtime* as a word to be indexed.

Listing 9-6. Modifying a Full-Text StopList

```
USE AdventureWorks2017
GO
ALTER FULLTEXT STOPLIST WhitePaperStopList ADD 'Downtime' LANGUAGE 1033;
```

To review the StopList words, run the query shown in Listing 9-7.

Listing 9-7. Using sys.fulltext_stoplists to Review StopList Words

```
USE AdventureWorks2017
GO
SELECT  lists.stoplist_id,
        lists.name,
        words.stopword
FROM    sys.fulltext_stoplists AS lists
INNER JOIN    sys.fulltext_stopwords AS words
```

```
        ON lists.stoplist_id = words.stoplist_id
WHERE   words.language = 'English'
ORDER BY lists.name;
```

The query results are shown in Figure 9-1; the word *Downtime* has been successfully added.

	stoplist_id	name	stopword
13	5	WhitePaperStopList	B
14	5	WhitePaperStopList	C
15	5	WhitePaperStopList	D
16	5	WhitePaperStopList	Downtime

Figure 9-1. *Query results of a StopList*

With the catalog, StopList, and key index availability defined in the table created in Listing 9-1, a full-text index can be created on the DOC column on the table. To create a full-text index, use the CREATE FULLTEXT INDEX statement (see Listing 9-8).

Listing 9-8. CREATE FULLTEXT INDEX Statement

```
USE AdventureWorks2017
GO
CREATE FULLTEXT INDEX ON dbo.SQLServerDocuments
(
DOC
TYPE COLUMN DocType
)
KEY INDEX PK_SQLServerDocuments
ON WhitePaperCatalog
WITH STOPLIST = WhitePaperStopList;
```

Once the index is created, population will immediately begin since there was no option added for CHANGE_TRACKING. Monitoring the status of the catalog will be discussed later in this chapter. It might take a while to load depending on the size of the document as the default AUTO setting takes effect. To query the content of the SQLServerDocuments table and DOC column, a CONTAINS statement can be run to return a specific word. Listing 9-9 shows an example of such a statement.

Listing 9-9. Using CONTAINS to Query for a Specific Word

```
USE AdventureWorks2017
GO
SELECT  ssd.DOC,
        ssd.DocType
FROM    dbo.SQLServerDocuments AS ssd
WHERE   CONTAINS (ssd.DOC, 'statistic');
```

Figure 9-2 shows the execution plan from the query.

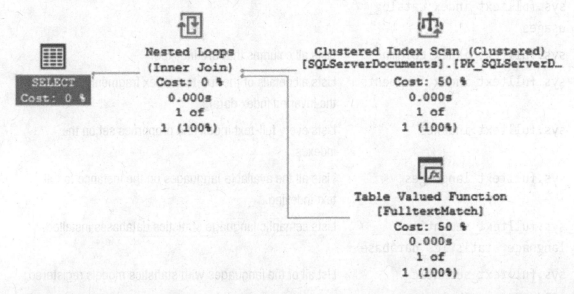

Figure 9-2. *Execution plan of CONTAINS and FTS index usage*

By searching by means of CONTAINS(ssd.DOC,'statistic'), the execution plan in Figure 9-2 shows the operation on FulltextMatch. It also returns the white paper with a document type of .docx as a match for this word search.

Full-Text Search Index Catalog Views and Properties

SQL Server provides a wealth of information about indexes in general. Performance, configurations, usage, and storage can be found within catalog views. As with other index objects, full-text indexes require the same attention and detail to maintenance and options to ensure they consistently improve performance rather than hinder it.

Table 9-2 describes the catalog views available to full-text search.

Table 9-2. *Full-Text Catalog Views*

Catalog View Name	Description
sys.fulltext_catalogs	Lists all full-text catalogs and high-level properties.
sys.fulltext_document_types	Returns a complete list of document types that are available for indexing. Each of these document types will be registered on the instance of SQL Server.
sys.fulltext_index_catalog_usages	
sys.fulltext_index_columns	Lists all columns that are indexed.
sys.fulltext_index_fragments	Lists all details of the full-text index fragments (storage of the inverted index data).
sys.fulltext_indexes	Lists every full-text index and properties set on the indexes.
sys.fulltext_languages	Lists all the available languages on the instance to full-text indexing.
sys.fulltext_semantic_language_statistics_database	Lists semantic language statistics databases installed.
sys.fulltext_semantic_languages	List all of the languages with statistics models registered.
sys.fulltext_stoplists	Lists every StopList created.
sys.fulltext_stopwords	Lists all StopWords in the database.
sys.fulltext_system_stopwords	Lists the preloaded system StopWords.

For informational purposes, while reviewing catalogs, properties, and status results for population, invoke the FULLTEXTCATALOGPROPERTY function, as shown in Listing 9-10.

Listing 9-10. Querying Properties from a Full-Text Index

```
USE AdventureWorks2017
GO
FULLTEXTCATALOGPROPERTY ('catalog_name' ,'property')
```

The information returned will provide a wealth of detail on the state of the catalog, including population status. The `catalog_name` parameter will accept any full-text catalog, and then a listing of properties can be utilized to return the specific information needed. Table 9-3 lists the properties that can be passed into the function.

Table 9-3. *Full-Text Catalog Properties*

Property Name	Description
AccentSensitivity	Catalog's current accent sensitivity setting. This returns 0, which means insensitive, or 1, which means sensitive.
IndexSize	Logical size in megabytes of the catalog.
ItemCount	The total items that have been indexed in the catalog.
LogSize	Backward capability property. This returns 0.
MergeStatus	Returns 1 if a master merge is in progress; otherwise, it returns 0.
PopulateCompletionAge	The elapsed time since index population, in seconds, measured since 01/01/1990 00:00:00. This will return 0 if population has not run yet.
PopulateStatus	PopulateStatus can return ten different values: *0*: Idle. *1*: Full population in progress. *2*: Paused. *3*: The population has been throttled. *4*: The population is recovering. *5*: The status is shut down. *6*: Incremental population is currently in progress. *7*: The status is currently building an index. *8*: The disk is full. *9*: Change tracking.
UniqueKeyCount	Number of individual full-text index keys in the catalog.
ImportStatus	Returns 0 when the full-text catalog is not being imported and 1 when it is being imported.

For example, to show the population status of the `WhitePaperCatalog` catalog used earlier, the statement in Listing 9-11 can be used. The result should be 0 for idle, since the index only has the single document and no other queries are running against it.

Listing 9-11. FULLTEXTCATALOGPROPERTY to Return Population Status of a Catalog

```
USE AdventureWorks2017
GO
SELECT FULLTEXTCATALOGPROPERTY('WhitePaperCatalog','PopulateStatus');
```

Catalogs and the referencing indexes can be reviewed by querying sys.fulltext_index_catalog_usages. This catalog view returns all the indexes that have been referenced from it, as shown in Listing 9-12.

Listing 9-12. Utilizing sys.fulltext_index_catalog_usages

```
USE AdventureWorks2017
GO
SELECT  OBJECT_NAME(ficu.object_id) [Object Name],
        ficu.index_id,
        ficu.fulltext_catalog_id
FROM    sys.fulltext_index_catalog_usages AS ficu;
```

Figure 9-3 displays the results, which show SQLServerDocuments is using a catalog associated with itself, while JobCandidate, ProductReview, and Document are using a shared full-text catalog. It is important to note that a single catalog can be used across multiple tables.

	Object Name	index_id	fulltext_catalog_id
1	JobCandidate	1	5
2	ProductReview	1	5
3	Document	1	5
4	SQLServerDocuments	1	8

Figure 9-3. *Results from sys.fulltext_index_catalog_usages*

For detailed information on all catalogs and settings currently applied to them, query sys.fulltext_catalogs. This catalog view is helpful in determining the default catalog and property status indicators, such as is_importing that shows whether the catalog is in the process of being imported.

For a detailed review of the full-text indexes in the database, the view `sys.fulltext_indexes` can be used along with other catalog views to create a more meaningful result set. Important information from this catalog view consists of the full-text catalog name and properties; change tracking property, crawl type, and state; and the StopList set to be used.

The query in Listing 9-13 returns a result set of all indexes including catalog and StopList information for the index.

Listing 9-13. Using All the Catalog Views for Full-Text Index Information

```
USE AdventureWorks2017
GO
SELECT  idx.is_enabled,

        idx.change_tracking_state,

        idx.crawl_type_desc,

        idx.crawl_end_date [Last Crawl],

        cat.name,

        CASE WHEN cat.is_accent_sensitivity_on = 0 THEN 'Accent InSensitive'

            WHEN cat.is_accent_sensitivity_on = 1 THEN 'Accent Sensitive'
        END [Accent Sensitivity],
        lists.name,
        lists.modify_date [Last Modified Date of StopList]
FROM    sys.fulltext_indexes idx
INNER JOIN sys.fulltext_catalogs cat
        ON idx.fulltext_catalog_id = cat.fulltext_catalog_id
INNER JOIN sys.fulltext_stoplists lists
        ON idx.stoplist_id = lists.stoplist_id;
```

Figure 9-4 shows the results of the catalog view query. This can be extremely useful when tuning full-text catalogs. For instance, if the index is out of date, details as to when it was last updated or crawled can be returned. Or if a full-text index has been tuned to remove noise by adding to the StopList, knowing when that change occurred in relation to the last crawl can help identify why performance did not improve.

	is_enabled	change_tracking_state	crawl_type_desc	Last Crawl	name	Accent Sensitivity	name	Last Modified Date of StopList
1	1	A	UPDATE_CRAWL	2019-05-01 22:49:37.933	WhitePaperCatalog	Accent Sensitive	WhitePaperStopList	2019-05-01 22:24:43.213

Figure 9-4. *Query results for full-text index information*

Summary

This chapter outlined how to create and query a full-text index. The need to be able to filter and query on large documents and free-form text is just as important as being able to use traditional structured indexes. With full-text indexing, not only can the contents of a column be examined, but also the contents of a file within a column, allowing applications to better identify documents and other artifacts that match contextually with the requests being submitted.

Indexing Myths and Best Practices

In the past few chapters, indexes have been introduced along with how they are structured. In the upcoming chapters, strategies will be discussed to build indexes and ensure that they behave as expected. In this chapter, some common myths will be dispelled while a foundation is built for creating effective indexes.

Myths result in an unnecessary burden when attempting to build an index. Knowing the myths associated with indexes can prevent the use of counterproductive indexing strategies. The following are the indexing myths discussed in this chapter:

- Databases don't need indexes.

- Primary keys are always clustered.

- Online index operations don't block.

- Any column can be filtered in multicolumn indexes.

- Clustered indexes store records in physical order.

- Indexes always output in the same order.

- Fill factor is applied to indexes during inserts.

- Deleting from heaps results in unrecoverable space.

- Every table should be a heap, or every table should have a clustered index.

© Edward Pollack and Jason Strate 2023
E. Pollack and J. Strate, *Expert Performance Indexing in Azure SQL and SQL Server 2022*,
https://doi.org/10.1007/978-1-4842-9215-0_10

When reviewing myths, it is worthwhile to take a look at best practices. Best practices may seem like myths in many ways as they are commonly held beliefs. The difference is that best practices stand up to scrutiny and are useful recommendations when building indexes. This chapter will examine the following best practices:

- Index based on a current workload.

- Use clustered indexes on primary keys by default.

- Properly target database-level fill factors.

- Properly target index-level fill factors.

- Index unique and foreign key columns if used for filtering.

- Balance index count.

Index Myths

One of the problems that are encountered when building databases and indexes is dealing with myths. Indexing myths originate from many different places. Some come from previous versions of SQL Server and its tools, features, or limitations. Others come from the advice of others, based on conditions in a specific database or scenario that are not universally applicable.

The trouble with indexing myths is that they cloud the water of indexing strategies. In situations where an index can be built to resolve a serious performance issue, a myth can sometimes prevent the correct approach from being considered. Throughout the next few sections, a number of myths will be discussed regarding indexing, with enough detail to effectively dispel them.

Myth 1: Databases Do Not Need Indexes

Usually, in an application that is being developed, one or more databases are created to store data for the application. In many development processes, the focus is on adding new features with the expectation that "performance will work itself out." An unfortunate result is that there are many databases that get developed and deployed without indexes being built because of the belief that they aren't needed.

Along with this, there are database developers who believe their databases are somehow unique from other databases. The following are some reasons that are heard from time to time:

- "It's a small database that won't get much data."

- "It's just a proof of concept and won't be around for long."

- "It's not an important application, so performance isn't critical."

- "The whole database already fits into memory; indexes will just make it require more memory."

- "I am going to use this database only for inserting data; I will never look at the results."

Each of these reasons is easy to break down. In today's world of big data, even databases that are expected to be small can start growing quickly as they are adopted. Besides that, small in terms of database size is relative and will be defined differently by everyone. One developer may believe 1 GB is small, whereas another could view 1 TB as small based on their prior experiences. Any proof of concept or unimportant database and application would not have been created if there wasn't a need or someone wasn't interested in expending resources for its features. Those same people likely expect that the features they asked for will perform as expected. Lastly, fitting a database into memory doesn't mean it will be fast. As was previously discussed, indexes provide alternative access paths for data, with the aim of decreasing the number of pages required to access the data. Without these alternative routes, data access will likely require reading and maintaining every page of a table in memory.

These reasons may not be the exact ones heard by any given developer, but they will likely be similar. The general idea surrounding this myth is that indexes do not help the database perform better. One of the strongest ways to break apart this excuse is by demonstrating the benefits of indexing against a given scenario.

To demonstrate, consider the T-SQL in Listing 10-1. This code sample creates the table MythOne. Next is a query similar to one in almost any application. In the output from the query, in Listing 10-2, the query is shown as generating 1,496 reads.

Listing 10-1. Table with No Index

```
USE AdventureWorks2017;
GO

SELECT * INTO MythOne
FROM Sales.SalesOrderDetail;
GO

SET STATISTICS IO ON
SET NOCOUNT ON
GO

SELECT SalesOrderID, SalesOrderDetailID, CarrierTrackingNumber, OrderQty,
ProductID, SpecialOfferID, UnitPrice, UnitPriceDiscount, LineTotal
FROM MythOne
WHERE CarrierTrackingNumber = '4911-403C-98';
GO

SET STATISTICS IO OFF
GO
```

Listing 10-2. I/O Statistics for the Table with No Index

```
Table 'MythOne'. Scan count 1, logical reads 1496, physical reads 0, read-
ahead reads 0,
lob logical reads 0, lob physical reads 0, lob read-ahead reads 0.
```

It could be argued that 1,496 isn't a lot of input/output (I/O). This might be true given the size of some databases and the amount of data in today's world. But the I/O of a query shouldn't be compared to the performance of the rest of the world; it needs to be compared to its potential I/O, the needs of the application, and the platform on which it is deployed.

Improving the query from the previous demonstration is as simple as adding an index on the table on the `CarrierTrackingNumber` column. To see the effect of adding an index to MythOne, execute the code in Listing 10-3. With the index created, the reads for the query were reduced from 1,496 to 15 reads, shown in Listing 10-4. With just a single index, the I/O for the query was reduced by nearly two orders of magnitude. An index in this situation provides a significant amount of value.

Listing 10-3. Adding an Index to MythOne

```
USE AdventureWorks2017;
GO

CREATE INDEX IX_CarrierTrackingNumber ON MythOne (CarrierTrackingNumber)
GO

SET STATISTICS IO ON
SET NOCOUNT ON
GO

SELECT SalesOrderID, SalesOrderDetailID, CarrierTrackingNumber, OrderQty,
ProductID, SpecialOfferID, UnitPrice, UnitPriceDiscount, LineTotal
FROM MythOne
WHERE CarrierTrackingNumber = '4911-403C-98';
GO

SET STATISTICS IO OFF
GO
```

Listing 10-4. I/O Statistics for the Table with an Index

```
Table 'MythOne'. Scan count 1, logical reads 15 physical reads 0, read-
ahead reads 0, lob logical reads 0, lob physical reads 0, lob read-ahead
reads 0.
```

These examples have shown that indexes provide a tangible benefit. If a situation is encountered where there is angst for building indexes on a database, try to break down the real reason for the pushback and provide an example similar to the one in this section. In Chapter 13, strategies will be discussed that can be used to determine what indexes to create in a database.

Myth 2: Primary Keys Are Always Clustered

The next myth that is quite prevalent is the idea that primary keys are always clustered. While this is true in many cases, it cannot be assumed that all primary keys are also clustered indexes. Earlier in this book, it was discussed how a table can have only a single clustered index on it. If a primary key is created after the clustered index is built, then the primary key is likely to be created as a non-clustered index.

To illustrate the indexing behavior of primary keys, a script will be used that includes building two tables. The first table, named dbo.MythTwo1, will be built first; then a primary key will be created on the RowID column. For the second table named dbo.MythTwo2, the script will create it and build a clustered index before creating the primary key. The code for this is in Listing 10-5.

Listing 10-5. Two Ways to Create Primary Keys

```
USE AdventureWorks2017;
GO

CREATE TABLE dbo.MythTwo1
    (
    RowID int NOT NULL
    ,Column1 nvarchar(128)
    ,Column2 nvarchar(128)
    );
ALTER TABLE dbo.MythTwo1
ADD CONSTRAINT PK_MythTwo1 PRIMARY KEY (RowID);
GO
CREATE TABLE dbo.MythTwo2
    (
    RowID int NOT NULL
    ,Column1 nvarchar(128)
    ,Column2 nvarchar(128)
    );
CREATE CLUSTERED INDEX CL_MythTwo2 ON dbo.MythTwo2 (RowID);

ALTER TABLE dbo.MythTwo2
ADD CONSTRAINT PK_MythTwo2 PRIMARY KEY (RowID);
GO

SELECT OBJECT_NAME(object_id) AS table_name
    ,name
    ,index_id
    ,type
```

```
    ,type_desc
    ,is_unique
    ,is_primary_key
FROM sys.indexes
WHERE object_id IN (OBJECT_ID('dbo.MythTwo1'),OBJECT_ID('dbo.MythTwo2'));
```

After running the code segment, the final query will return results like those shown in Figure 10-1. This figure shows that PK_MythTwo1, which is the primary key on the first table, was created as a clustered index. Then on the second table, PK_MythTwo2 was created as a non-clustered index.

	table_name	name	index_id	type	type_desc	is_unique	is_primary_key
1	MythTwo1	PK_MythTwo1	1	1	CLUSTERED	1	1
2	MythTwo2	CL_MythTwo2	1	1	CLUSTERED	0	0
3	MythTwo2	PK_MythTwo2	2	2	NONCLUSTERED	1	1

Figure 10-1. *Primary key sys.indexes output*

The behavior discussed in this section is important to remember when building primary keys and clustered indexes. If there are situations where they need to be separated, the primary key will need to be defined after the clustered index or as a NONCLUSTERED index.

Whereas a primary key defines a source of truth for uniqueness on a table, the clustered index provides a logical sort order for storage purposes. Understanding each use case allows for effective indexing in scenarios when the clustered index and primary key may not be on the same columns.

Myth 3: Online Index Operations Don't Block

One of the advantages of SQL Server Enterprise Edition is the ability to build indexes online. During an online index build, the table on which the index is being created will still be available for queries and data modifications. This feature is extremely useful when a database needs to be accessed and maintenance windows are short or nonexistent.

A common myth with online index rebuilds is that they don't cause any blocking. Like any myth, this one is false. When using an online index operation, there is an intent shared lock held on the table for the main portion of the build. At the finish, either a shared lock (for a non-clustered index) or a schema modification lock (for a clustered index) is held for a short time while the operation swaps in the updated index. This differs from an offline index build where the shared or schema modification lock is held for the duration of the index build.

To see this behavior in action, a table will be created, and Extended Events will be used to monitor the locks that are applied to the table while creating indexes with and without the ONLINE option. To start this demo, execute the code in Listing 10-6. This script creates the table dbo.MythThree and populates it with 10 million records. The last item it returns is the object_id for the table, which is needed for the subsequent parts of the demo. For this example, the object_id for dbo.MythThree is 624721278.

Note   The demos for this myth all require SQL Server Enterprise or Developer Edition.

Listing 10-6. MythThree Table Create Script

```
USE AdventureWorks2017
GO

CREATE TABLE dbo.MythThree
  (
  RowID int NOT NULL
  ,Column1 uniqueidentifier
  );
WITH L1(z) AS (SELECT 0 UNION ALL SELECT 0)
, L2(z) AS (SELECT 0 FROM L1 a CROSS JOIN L1 b)
, L3(z) AS (SELECT 0 FROM L2 a CROSS JOIN L2 b)
, L4(z) AS (SELECT 0 FROM L3 a CROSS JOIN L3 b)
, L5(z) AS (SELECT 0 FROM L4 a CROSS JOIN L4 b)
, L6(z) AS (SELECT TOP 10000000 0 FROM L5 a CROSS JOIN L5 b)
INSERT INTO dbo.MythThree
SELECT ROW_NUMBER() OVER (ORDER BY z) AS RowID, NEWID()
FROM L6;
GO

SELECT OBJECT_ID('dbo.MythThree')
GO
```

To monitor those events in this scenario, Extended Events will be used to capture the `lock_acquired` and `lock_released` events fired during index creation. Open sessions in SSMS for the code in Listings 10-7 and 10-8. Before running, update the `session_id` from Listing 10-8 for the `session_id` in Listing 10-7; for this scenario, the `session_id` is 42. Apply the same update with the `object_id`. After the Extended Events session is running, the live view can be used to monitor the locks as they occur.

Listing 10-7. Extended Events Session for Lock Acquired and Released

```
USE AdventureWorks2017;
GO

IF EXISTS(SELECT * FROM sys.server_event_sessions WHERE name =
'MythThreeXevents')
    DROP EVENT SESSION [MythThreeXevents] ON SERVER
GO
CREATE EVENT SESSION [MythThreeXevents] ON SERVER
ADD EVENT sqlserver.lock_acquired(SET collect_database_name=(1)
  ACTION(sqlserver.sql_text)
  WHERE [sqlserver].[session_id]=(42) AND [object_id]=(624721278)),
ADD EVENT sqlserver.lock_released(
  ACTION(sqlserver.sql_text)
  WHERE [sqlserver].[session_id]=(42) AND [object_id]=(624721278))
ADD TARGET package0.ring_buffer
GO
ALTER EVENT SESSION [MythThreeXevents] ON SERVER STATE = START
GO
```

In the example from Listing 10-8, two indexes are created, one built ONLINE and the other with the default option (offline). To see what locks are acquired and released, observe the locking behavior in the live viewer. By default, only the name and timestamp appear in the live viewer. The live viewer allows for customizing the columns that are displayed. In Figure 10-2, the columns `object_id`, `mode`, `resource_type`, and `sql_text` have been added to the defaults `name` and `timestamp`. To add additional columns, right-click a column header and select "Choose columns."

Listing 10-8. Online Index Operations on Non-clustered Index Creation

```
USE AdventureWorks2017
GO

CREATE INDEX IX_MythThree_ONLINE ON MythThree (Column1) WITH (ONLINE = ON);
GO

CREATE INDEX IX_MythThree ON MythThree (Column1);
GO
```

When the index is created with the ONLINE option, note that in Figure 10-2 SCH_S (Schema_Shared) and S (Shared) locks are acquired and released within milliseconds of each other. Because these locks are acquired and released throughout the index creation process, other transactions can continue to occur against the table. The SCH_S locks ensure that the schema of the table does not change, while the S locks pages from inserts, updates, and deletes. Because these locks are acquired for very short amounts of time, they allow the table to be available throughout the index creation process.

Note   If you do not see any results from the Extended Events session, it's likely due to a mismatch between the object_id for MythThree and the object_id traced through the Extended Events session.

---

object_id	name	mode	timestamp	sql_text
624721278	lock_acquired	SCH_S	2019-07-28 22:44:20.9149557	CREATE INDEX IX_MythThree_ONLINE ON MythThree (Column1) WITH (ONLINE = ON);
624721278	lock_released	SCH_S	2019-07-28 22:44:20.9151786	CREATE INDEX IX_MythThree_ONLINE ON MythThree (Column1) WITH (ONLINE = ON);
624721278	lock_acquired	IS	2019-07-28 22:44:20.9152222	CREATE INDEX IX_MythThree_ONLINE ON MythThree (Column1) WITH (ONLINE = ON);
624721278	lock_acquired	IS	2019-07-28 22:44:20.9152328	CREATE INDEX IX_MythThree_ONLINE ON MythThree (Column1) WITH (ONLINE = ON);
624721278	lock_acquired	SCH_S	2019-07-28 22:44:20.9152778	CREATE INDEX IX_MythThree_ONLINE ON MythThree (Column1) WITH (ONLINE = ON);
624721278	lock_acquired	S	2019-07-28 22:44:20.9371600	CREATE INDEX IX_MythThree_ONLINE ON MythThree (Column1) WITH (ONLINE = ON);
624721278	lock_acquired	SCH_S	2019-07-28 22:44:22.2173570	CREATE INDEX IX_MythThree_ONLINE ON MythThree (Column1) WITH (ONLINE = ON);
624721278	lock_released	S	2019-07-28 22:44:22.2176549	CREATE INDEX IX_MythThree_ONLINE ON MythThree (Column1) WITH (ONLINE = ON);
624721278	lock_acquired	SCH_S	2019-07-28 22:44:22.2187790	CREATE INDEX IX_MythThree_ONLINE ON MythThree (Column1) WITH (ONLINE = ON);

Figure 10-2. *Index creation with the ONLINE option*

With the default index creation, which does not use the ONLINE option, the S locks are held for the entirety of the index build. Shown in Figure 10-3, the S lock is taken before the SCH_S lock and isn't released until after the index is built. The result is that the index is unavailable during the index build.

object_id	name	mode	timestamp	sql_text
624721278	lock_acquired	SCH_S	2019-07-28 22:45:15.2028196	CREATE INDEX IX_MythThree ON MythThree (Column1);
624721278	lock_released	SCH_S	2019-07-28 22:45:15.2378991	CREATE INDEX IX_MythThree ON MythThree (Column1);
624721278	lock_acquired	S	2019-07-28 22:45:15.2496446	CREATE INDEX IX_MythThree ON MythThree (Column1);
624721278	lock_acquired	S	2019-07-28 22:45:15.2591628	CREATE INDEX IX_MythThree ON MythThree (Column1);
624721278	lock_acquired	SCH_S	2019-07-28 22:45:15.2670049	CREATE INDEX IX_MythThree ON MythThree (Column1);
624721278	lock_released	SCH_S	2019-07-28 22:45:24.4915553	CREATE INDEX IX_MythThree ON MythThree (Column1);
624721278	lock_released	S	2019-07-28 22:45:24.4915625	CREATE INDEX IX_MythThree ON MythThree (Column1);

Figure 10-3. *Index creation without the ONLINE option*

Myth 4: Any Column Can Be Filtered in Multicolumn Indexes

The next common myth with indexes is that regardless of the position of a column in an index, the index can use that column in an ordered search to filter data within the table. As with the other myths discussed so far in this chapter, this one is also incorrect. An index does not need to use all columns in an index. It does, however, need to start with the leftmost column in an index when performing an ordered search and use the columns from left to right, in their order, within the index. This is why the order of the columns in an index is critically important.

To demonstrate this myth, a few examples will be presented, as shown in Listing 10-9. In the script, a table is created based on Sales.SalesOrderHeader with a primary key on SalesOrderID. To test the myth of searching all columns through multicolumn indexes, an index with the columns OrderDate, DueDate, and ShipDate is created.

Listing 10-9. Multicolumn Index Myth

```
USE AdventureWorks2017
GO
IF OBJECT_ID('dbo.MythFour') IS NOT NULL
    DROP TABLE dbo.MythFour
GO

SELECT SalesOrderID, OrderDate, DueDate, ShipDate
INTO dbo.MythFour
FROM Sales.SalesOrderHeader;
GO
```

```
ALTER TABLE dbo.MythFour
ADD CONSTRAINT PK_MythFour PRIMARY KEY CLUSTERED (SalesOrderID);
GO
CREATE NONCLUSTERED INDEX IX_MythFour ON dbo.MythFour (OrderDate, DueDate,
ShipDate);
GO
```

With the test objects in place, the next behavior to observe is that of the queries against the table that could potentially use the non-clustered index. First, a query that uses the leftmost column in the index will be tested. Listing 10-10 gives the code for this. As shown in Figure 10-4, by filtering on the leftmost column, the query uses a seek operation on IX_MythFour.

Listing 10-10. Query Filtering on the Leftmost Column in the Index

```
USE AdventureWorks2017
GO
SELECT OrderDate FROM dbo.MythFour
WHERE OrderDate = '2011-07-17 00:00:00.000'
```

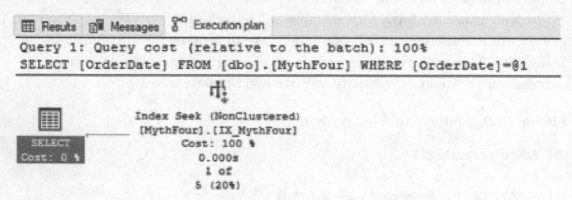

Figure 10-4. *Execution plan when filtering on the leftmost column in an index*

Next, consider what happens when filtering from other index key columns. In Listing 10-11, the query filters the results on the rightmost column of the index. The execution plan for this query, shown in Figure 10-5, uses a scan operation on IX_MythFour. Instead of being able to go directly to the records that match the OrderDate, the query needs to check all records to determine which match the filter. While the index is used, it isn't able to filter the rows based on the sort within the index.

Listing 10-11. Query Filtering on the Rightmost Column in the Index

```
USE AdventureWorks2017
GO
SELECT ShipDate FROM dbo.MythFour
WHERE ShipDate = '2011-07-17 00:00:00.000'
```

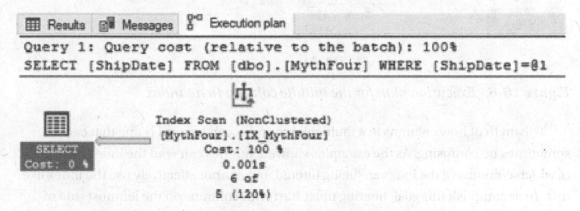

Figure 10-5. *Execution plan when filtering on the rightmost column in an index*

These examples have shown that the leftmost column can be used for filtering and that filtering on the rightmost column can use the index but cannot use it optimally with a seek operation. The last validation is to check the behavior of columns in an index that are neither on the left nor right side. In Listing 10-12, a query is included that uses the middle column in the index IX_MythFour. As with the previous example, the execution plan for the middle column query, shown in Figure 10-6, uses the index but also uses a scan operation. The query is able to use the index, but because it was unable to apply an ordered filter to the index, it could not be applied in an optimal fashion.

Listing 10-12. Query Using the Middle Column in the Index

```
USE AdventureWorks2017
GO
SELECT DueDate FROM dbo.MythFour
WHERE DueDate = '2011-07-17 00:00:00.000'
```

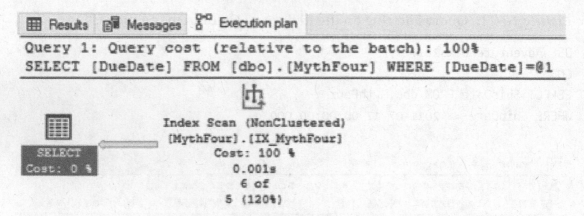

Figure 10-6. *Execution plan for the middle column in an index*

The myth of how columns in a multicolumn index can be used is one that can sometimes be confusing. As the examples showed, queries can read the index regardless of which columns of the index are being filtered, but cannot effectively use the index like this. To accomplish this goal, filtering must start with columns on the leftmost side of the index. When that isn't the typical use case, either reorder the columns of the index or create additional indexes if their use is critical to database performance.

Myth 5: Clustered Indexes Store Records in Physical Order

One of the more pervasive myths commonly held is the idea that a clustered index stores the records in a table in their physical order when on disk. This myth seems to be primarily driven by confusion between what is stored on a page and where records are stored on those pages. As discussed in Chapter 2, there is a difference between data pages and records. A demonstration will be provided that dispels this myth.

To begin this example, execute the code in Listing 10-13. This code will create a table named dbo.MythFive. Then, it will add three records to the table. The last part of the script will output, using sys.dm_db_database_page_allocations, the page location for the table. In this example, the page with the records inserted into dbo.MythFive is page 59624, as shown in Figure 10-7.

Note   The dynamic management function `sys.dm_db_database_page_allocations` is a replacement for DBCC IND. This function, introduced in SQL Server 2012, provides an improved interface to examining page allocations for objects in a database over its DBCC predecessor.

Listing 10-13. Create and Populate the MythFive Table

```
USE AdventureWorks2017
GO

IF OBJECT_ID('dbo.MythFive') IS NOT NULL
    DROP TABLE dbo.MythFive
CREATE TABLE dbo.MythFive
(
RowID int PRIMARY KEY CLUSTERED
,TestValue varchar(20) NOT NULL
);
GO

INSERT INTO dbo.MythFive (RowID, TestValue) VALUES (1, 'FirstRecordAdded');
INSERT INTO dbo.MythFive (RowID, TestValue) VALUES (3,
'SecondRecordAdded');
INSERT INTO dbo.MythFive (RowID, TestValue) VALUES (2, 'ThirdRecordAdded');
GO

SELECT database_id, object_id, index_id, extent_page_id, allocated_page_
page_id, page_type_desc
FROM sys.dm_db_database_page_allocations(DB_ID(), OBJECT_ID('dbo.
MythFive'), 1, NULL, 'DETAILED')
WHERE page_type_desc IS NOT NULL
GO
```

	database_id	object_id	index_id	extent_page_id	allocated_page_page_id	page_type_desc
1	8	2071678428	1	59616	59620	IAM_PAGE
2	8	2071678428	1	59624	59624	DATA_PAGE

Figure 10-7. *sys.dm_db_database_page_allocations output*

The evidence to dispel this myth can be uncovered with the DBCC PAGE command. To do this, use the PagePID identified in Listing 10-13 with page_type_desc of DATA_ PAGE. Since there is only a single data page for this table, that is where the data will be located. (For more information on DBCC commands, see Chapter 2.)

For this example, Listing 10-14 shows the T-SQL required to directly look at the data in the table. This command outputs a lot of information that includes some header information that isn't useful in this example. The portion that is needed is at the end, with the memory dump of the page, as shown in Figure 10-8. In the memory dump, records are shown in the order in which they are placed on the page. As the dump shows from reading the far-right column, the records are in the order in which they are added to the table, not the order that they will appear in the clustered index.

Listing 10-14. Viewing Data in the MythFive Table

```
DBCC TRACEON (3604);
GO

DBCC PAGE (AdventureWorks2017, 1, 59624, 2);
GO
```

```
Memory Dump @0x000000C8721F8000

000000C8721F8000:   01010000 00000001 00000000 00000800 00000000   ..................
000000C8721F8014:   00000300 44020000 3c1fbe00 e8e80000 01000000   ....D...<.¾.èè......
000000C8721F8028:   6d000000 72460000 02000000 00000000 00000000   m...rF..............
000000C8721F803C:   00000000 01000000 00000000 00000000 00000000   ..................
000000C8721F8050:   00000000 00000000 00000000 00000000 30000800   ................0...
000000C8721F8064:   01000000 02000001 001f0046 69727374 5265636f   ..........FirstReco
000000C8721F8078:   72644164 64656430 00080003 00000002 00000100   rdAdded0............
000000C8721F808C:   20005365 636f6e64 5265636f 72644164 64656430   .SecondRecordAdded0
000000C8721F80A0:   00080002 00000002 00000100 1f005468 69726452   ..............ThirdR
000000C8721F80B4:   65636f72 64416464 65640000 21212121 21212121   ecordAdded..!!!!!!!!
000000C8721F80C8:   21212121 21212121 21212121 21212121 21212121   !!!!!!!!!!!!!!!!!!!!
000000C8721F80DC:   21212121 21212121 21212121 21212121 21212121   !!!!!!!!!!!!!!!!!!!!
```

Figure 10-8. *Page contents portion of DBCC PAGE output*

Based on this evidence, it is easy to discern that clustered indexes do not store records in the physical order of the index. If this example were expanded, it would become evident that that the pages are in physical order, but the rows on the pages are not.

Myth 6: Indexes Always Output Rows in the Same Order

One of the more common myths that pertain to indexes is that they guarantee the output order of results from queries. This is not correct, and worse, it provides an invalid rationale toward writing inaccurate queries. As previously described in this book, the purpose of indexes is to provide an efficient access path to data. That purpose does not guarantee the order in which the data will be returned. The trouble with this myth is that, oftentimes, SQL Server will appear to maintain order when queries are executed under similar conditions, but when those conditions change, the execution plans change, and the results are returned in the order that the data is processed vs. the order that the end user might expect.

To explore this myth, it is necessary to look at how conditions can change on a query that is using a clustered index. In Listing 10-15, there is a single query, executed twice, for the Sales.SalesOrderHeader and Sales.SalesOrderDetail tables that is performing a simple aggregation. This is something that might appear in many types of queries in SQL Server.

Listing 10-15. Unordered Results with a Clustered Index

```
USE AdventureWorks2017
GO

SELECT soh.SalesOrderID, COUNT(*) AS DetailRows
FROM Sales.SalesOrderHeader soh
    INNER JOIN Sales.SalesOrderDetail sod ON soh.SalesOrderID = sod.
    SalesOrderID
    GROUP BY soh.SalesOrderID;
GO

DBCC FREEPROCCACHE
DBCC SETCPUWEIGHT(1000)
GO
SELECT soh.SalesOrderID, COUNT(*) AS DetailRows
FROM Sales.SalesOrderHeader soh
    INNER JOIN Sales.SalesOrderDetail sod ON soh.SalesOrderID = sod.
    SalesOrderID
    GROUP BY soh.SalesOrderID;
GO
```

```
DBCC FREEPROCCACHE
DBCC SETCPUWEIGHT(1)
GO
```

The conditions in which the two queries are executed vary a bit. The first query is running under the standard SQL Server cost model and generates an execution that performs a pair of index scans and a stream aggregation to return the results, shown in Figure 10-9. The results from the query, provided in Figure 10-10, provide support that SQL Server will return data in the desired output, provided that the SaleOrderID column is the column that the user wants sorted.

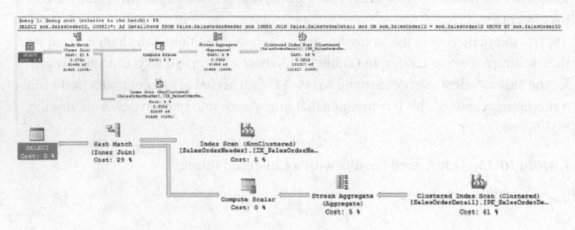

Figure 10-9. *Default aggregation execution plan*

	SalesOrderID	DetailRows
1	43697	1
2	43698	1
3	43699	1
4	43700	1
5	43701	1
6	43702	1
7	43703	1
8	43704	1
9	43705	1
10	43706	1

Figure 10-10. *Results from the default aggregation execution plan*

But what happens if the conditions on the SQL Server change, but the desired business rules do not? The second query executed in Listing 10-15 is the same query, but with a change in conditions. For this example, the DBCC command SETCPUWEIGHT is leveraged to change the cost of the execution plan. That change in cost results in the use of the parallel execution plan, shown in Figure 10-11. A side effect of the parallel plan is a change in the order in which the results of the query are returned, shown in Figure 10-12. While the results appear to still be ordered and the logic of the query hasn't changed, the first records returned are different. This occurs because one of the parallel threads returned its results faster than the others.

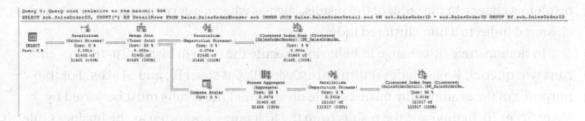

Figure 10-11. *Aggregation execution plan with parallelism*

	SalesOrderID	DetailRows
1	43659	12
2	43660	2
3	43661	15
4	43666	6
5	43667	4
6	43668	29
7	43669	1
8	43674	1
9	43675	9
10	43676	5

Figure 10-12. *Aggregation execution plan with parallelism results*

> **Warning**   Do not use DBCC SETCPUWEIGHT in production code to control parallelism or for any other reason. This DBCC command is strictly available to control environmental variables within SQL Server to test and validate execution plans.

The second condition to consider is when business rules change for a query. For instance, maybe a set of results wasn't originally filtered, but after a change to the application, the query may change to using a different set of indexes. This can also result in a change in the order of the results, such as when a query changes from using a clustered index to a non-clustered index.

To demonstrate this change in behavior, execute the code in Listing 10-16. This code runs two queries. Both queries return SalesOrderID, CustomerID, and Status. For the purposes of the example, the business rule dictates that the results must be sorted by SalesOrderID. In this case, the results from the first query are sorted as the business rule states, shown at the top of Figure 10-13. But in the second query, when the logic changes to request fewer rows by adding a filter, the results are no longer ordered, shown at the bottom of Figure 10-13. The cause of the change comes from a change in the indexes that SQL Server is using to execute the query. The change in indexes drives the results to be processed, as well as how they are ordered, in the way those indexes sort the data.

Listing 10-16.   Unordered Results with a Non-clustered Index

```
USE AdventureWorks2017
GO

SELECT SalesOrderID, CustomerID, Status
FROM Sales.SalesOrderHeader soh
GO

SELECT SalesOrderID, CustomerID, Status
FROM Sales.SalesOrderHeader soh
WHERE CustomerID IN (11020, 11021, 11022)
GO
```

	SalesOrderID	CustomerID	Status
1	43659	29825	5
2	43660	29672	5
3	43661	29734	5
4	43662	29994	5
5	43663	29565	5
6	43664	29898	5
7	43665	29580	5
8	43666	30052	5
9	43667	29974	5
10	43668	29614	5

	SalesOrderID	CustomerID	Status
1	51193	11020	5
2	51610	11021	5
3	51556	11022	5

Figure 10-13. *Query results demonstrating effect of filtering on order*

In these examples, a handful of scenarios were reviewed in which different SQL Server conditions can change how results are returned for a query. While an index might provide results from the query in the order desired this time, there is no guarantee that this will not change. It is important to not rely on indexes to enforce ordering. If order is required for a result set, always use the ORDER BY clause to ensure that the correct order is applied to a given result set.

Myth 7: Fill Factor Is Applied to Indexes During Inserts

When the fill factor is set on an index, it is applied to the index when the index is built, rebuilt, or reorganized. Unfortunately, with this myth, it is often believed that the fill factor is applied as records are inserted into a table. In this section, this myth will be investigated to see that it is not correct.

To begin pulling this myth apart, its premise will be directly tested. In the myth, the thought is that if a fill factor has been specified when rows are added to a table, the fill factor is used during the inserts. To dispel this portion of the myth, execute the code in Listing 10-17. In this script, the table dbo.MythSeven is created with a clustered index that has a 50 percent fill factor. That means that 50 percent of every page in the index should be left empty. With the table built, records will be inserted into the table. Finally, the average amount of space available on each page will be checked using the sys.dm_db_index_physical_stats DMV. Looking at the results of the script, as shown in Figure 10-14, the index is using 95 percent of every page vs. the 50 percent that was specified in the creation of the clustered index.

Listing 10-17. Create and Populate the MythSeven Table

```
USE AdventureWorks2017
GO

IF OBJECT_ID('dbo.MythSeven') IS NOT NULL
    DROP TABLE dbo.MythSeven;
GO

CREATE TABLE dbo.MythSeven
  (
  RowID int NOT NULL
  ,Column1 varchar(500)
  );
GO

ALTER TABLE dbo.MythSeven ADD CONSTRAINT
    PK_MythSeven PRIMARY KEY CLUSTERED (RowID) WITH(FILLFACTOR = 50);
GO

WITH L1(z) AS (SELECT 0 UNION ALL SELECT 0)
, L2(z) AS (SELECT 0 FROM L1 a CROSS JOIN L1 b)
, L3(z) AS (SELECT 0 FROM L2 a CROSS JOIN L2 b)
, L4(z) AS (SELECT 0 FROM L3 a CROSS JOIN L3 b)
, L5(z) AS (SELECT 0 FROM L4 a CROSS JOIN L4 b)
, L6(z) AS (SELECT TOP 1000 0 FROM L5 a CROSS JOIN L5 b)
INSERT INTO dbo.MythSeven
```

```
SELECT ROW_NUMBER() OVER (ORDER BY z) AS RowID, REPLICATE('X', 500)
FROM L6;
GO

SELECT object_id, index_id, avg_page_space_used_in_percent
FROM sys.dm_db_index_physical_stats(DB_ID(),OBJECT_ID('dbo.MythSeven'),NULL
,NULL,'DETAILED')
WHERE index_level = 0;
```

	object_id	index_id	avg_page_space_used_in_percent
1	7367216677	1	95.3103286384976

Figure 10-14. *Fill factor myth on inserts*

Sometimes when this myth is dispelled, the belief is reversed, and it is believed that the fill factor is broken or doesn't work. This is also incorrect. The fill factor isn't applied to indexes during data modifications. It is applied when the index is rebuilt, reorganized, or created. To demonstrate this, the clustered index on dbo.MythSeven can be rebuilt with the script included in Listing 10-18.

Listing 10-18. Rebuild the Clustered Index on the MythSeven Table

```
USE AdventureWorks2017
GO

ALTER INDEX PK_MythSeven ON dbo.MythSeven REBUILD

SELECT object_id, index_id, avg_page_space_used_in_percent
FROM sys.dm_db_index_physical_stats(DB_ID(),OBJECT_ID('dbo.MythSeven'),NULL
,NULL,'DETAILED')
WHERE index_level = 0
```

After the clustered index is rebuilt, the index will have the specified fill factor, or at least close to the value specified, as shown in Figure 10-15. The average space used on the table, after the rebuild, changed from 95 to 51 percent. This change is in alignment with the fill factor that was specified for the index.

	object_id	index_id	avg_page_space_used_in_percent
1	736721677	1	51.0748702742772

Figure 10-15. *Fill factor myth after index rebuild*

When it comes to the fill factor, there are a number of myths surrounding the index property. The key to understanding the fill factor is to remember when and how it is applied. It is not a property enforced on an index as it is used. It is, instead, a property used to distribute data within an index when it is created or rebuilt.

Myth 8: Deleting from Heaps Results in Unrecoverable Space

Heaps are an interesting structure in SQL Server. In Chapter 2, they were briefly reviewed as being less of an index and more a collection of pages for storing data. One of the index maintenance tasks that will be a part of the next chapter is recovering space from heap tables. As will be more deeply discussed in that chapter, when rows are deleted from a heap, the pages associated with those rows are not removed. This is generally referred to as *bloat* within the heap.

An interesting side effect of the concept of heap bloat is the myth that bloat never gets reused. The space stays in the heap and is not recoverable until the heap is rebuilt. Fortunately, for both heaps and database administrators, this is not the case. When data is removed from a heap, the space that the data previously held is made available for future inserts into the table.

To demonstrate how this works, a table will be built using the code in Listing 10-19. This demonstration creates a heap named MythEight and inserts 400 records, which results in 100 pages of data. This page count can be validated with the page_count column in the first result set in Figure 10-16. The next part of the script deletes every other row that was inserted into the heap. Generally, this should leave each page with half as many rows as it had previously, shown in the second result set in Figure 10-16. The last part of the script inserts 200 rows into the MythEight table, returning the row count to 400 records and reusing the previously used pages that had data removed from them. There is a slight growth in the page count from the last result set in Figure 10-16, but most of the new rows fit into the space already allocated.

Listing 10-19. Reusing Allocated Space from the MythEight Heap

```
USE AdventureWorks2017
GO

IF OBJECT_ID('dbo.MythEight') IS NOT NULL
    DROP TABLE dbo.MythEight;
CREATE TABLE dbo.MythEight
(
    RowId INT IDENTITY(1,1)
    ,FillerData VARCHAR(2500)
);

INSERT INTO dbo.MythEight (FillerData)
SELECT TOP 400 REPLICATE('X',2000)
FROM sys.objects;

SELECT OBJECT_NAME(object_id), index_type_desc, page_count, record_count,
forwarded_record_count
FROM sys.dm_db_index_physical_stats (DB_ID(), OBJECT_ID('dbo.MythEight'),
NULL, NULL, 'DETAILED');

DELETE FROM dbo.MythEight
WHERE RowId % 2 = 0;

SELECT OBJECT_NAME(object_id), index_type_desc, page_count, record_count,
forwarded_record_count
FROM sys.dm_db_index_physical_stats (DB_ID(), OBJECT_ID('dbo.MythEight'),
NULL, NULL, 'DETAILED');

INSERT INTO dbo.MythEight (FillerData)
SELECT TOP 200 REPLICATE('X',2000)
FROM sys.objects;

SELECT OBJECT_NAME(object_id), index_type_desc, page_count, record_count,
forwarded_record_count
FROM sys.dm_db_index_physical_stats (DB_ID(), OBJECT_ID('dbo.MythEight'),
NULL, NULL, 'DETAILED');
```

	(No column name)	index_type_desc	page_count	record_count	forwarded_record_count
1	MythEight	HEAP	100	400	0

	(No column name)	index_type_desc	page_count	record_count	forwarded_record_count
1	MythEight	HEAP	100	200	0

	(No column name)	index_type_desc	page_count	record_count	forwarded_record_count
1	MythEight	HEAP	111	400	0

Figure 10-16. *Heap reuse query results*

As the demonstration for this myth shows, space in a heap that previously held data is released for use by the table. For heaps that have large amounts of data being written to the table, there is not a significant need to monitor for page reuse, and the myth can be considered inaccurate. With heaps that have a lot of data deleted without the intention to replace it, then the space may be recovered with ALTER TABLE ... REBUILD. The syntax and impact of this statement are discussed in the next chapter.

Myth 9: Every Table Should Have a Heap/Clustered Index

The last myth to consider is twofold. On the one hand, some people will recommend that all tables should be built as heaps. On the other hand, others will recommend creating clustered indexes on all tables. The trouble is that this viewpoint will exclude considering the benefits that each of the structures can offer on a table. The viewpoint makes a religious-styled argument for or against ways to store data in databases without any consideration for the actual data that is being stored and how it will be used.

Some of the arguments against the use of clustered indexes are as follows:

- Fragmentation negatively impacts performance through additional I/O.

- The modification of a single record can impact multiple records in the clustered index when a page split is triggered.

- Excessive key lookups will negatively impact performance through additional I/O.

Naturally, there are common arguments against using heaps:

- Excessive forwarded records negatively impact performance through additional I/O.

- Removing forwarded records requires a rebuild of the entire table.

- Non-clustered indexes are required for efficient filtered data access.

- Heaps don't automatically release pages when data is removed.

The negative impacts associated with either clustered indexes or heaps aren't the only things to consider when deciding between one and the other. Each has circumstances where one will outperform the other.

For instance, clustered indexes perform best in the following circumstances:

- The table has a unique, ever-increasing key column.

- Ranges of data in a table will be accessed via queries.

- Records in the table will be inserted and deleted at a high rate.

On the other hand, heaps are ideal for some of the following situations:

- Data in the table will be used only for a limited amount of time where index creation time exceeds query time on the data.

- Key values will change frequently, which in turn would change the position of the record in an index.

- Copious numbers of records are being inserted into a staging table.

- The primary key is a non-ascending value, such as a unique identifier.

Although this section doesn't include a demonstration of why this myth is false, it is important to remember that both heaps and clustered indexes are available and should be used appropriately. Knowing which type of index to choose is a matter of testing, not a matter of doctrine.

A good resource to consider for those in the "cluster everything camp" is the Fast Track Data Warehouse Architecture white paper (`https://msdn.microsoft.com/en-us/library/hh918452.aspx`). The white paper addresses some significant performance improvements that can be found with heaps and also the point at which these improvements dissipate. The white paper helps show how changes in I/O system technologies, with flash and cache-based devices, can change patterns and practices regarding heaps and clustered indexes. This helps promote the idea of validating myths and best practices from time to time. Note that the preceding article was written for SQL Server 2012 and highlights how best practices evolve over time.

Index Best Practices

Similar to myths are the indexing best practices. A best practice should be considered the default recommendation that can be applied when there isn't enough information available to validate proceeding in another direction. Best practices are not the only option and are a place to start from when working with any technology.

When using best practices provided by someone else, such as those appearing in this chapter, it is important to validate them against your data workloads first. Always take them with a grain of salt. Best practices can be trusted to provide worthwhile guidance, but details may need to be considered when choosing and fine-tuning a solution. Exceptions will always exist. While solutions should never be architected based on exceptions, understanding that exceptions will occasionally appear allows for a balance between accepting best practices and building data structures to handle unusual use cases.

Given the preceding precautions, there are several best practices that can be considered when working with indexes. This section will review these best practices and discuss what they are and what they mean.

Index to the Current Workload

The most important aspect of indexing your databases is to index based on the current workload against that database. Consider reads, writes, availability, and contention when evaluating the variables that define a workload. Focus first on current database usage and then on future growth. Past usage can provide helpful guidance, but do not assume that future performance will always mimic past performance.

The indexing that is built for today will likely not be the indexing that will be needed in databases in the future. For this reason, the first best practice is to regularly review, analyze, and implement changes to the indexes in your environment. Realize that regardless of how similar two databases are, if the data in the databases and users are not the same, then the indexing for the two databases may need to be different. A detailed analysis of monitoring and index usage patterns can be found in Chapters 15 and 16.

Use Clustered Indexes on Primary Keys by Default

A reliable best practice is to use clustered indexes on primary keys by default. This may seem to run contrary to the ninth myth presented in this chapter. Myth 9 discussed whether to choose clustered indexes or heaps as a matter of doctrine. Whether the database was built with one or the other, the myth would have you believe that if your table design doesn't match the myth, it should be changed regardless of the situation. This best practice recommends using clustered indexes on primary keys as a starting point.

By clustering the primary key of a table by default, there is an increased likelihood that the indexing choice will be appropriate for the table. As stated earlier in this chapter, clustered indexes control how the data in a table is logically stored. Primary keys are often built on a column that utilizes the identity property that increments as each new record is added to the table. Those primary keys that are not identity columns are often set on columns that are numeric, increasing, and predictable. Choosing a clustered index for the primary key will provide the most efficient method to access this type of data.

If a table with a clustered primary key is providing suboptimal performance, then perform a more detailed review of the table to determine why this is the case. It may be an exception to the rule, or it may be indicative of another problem, such as the following:

- The workload could benefit from a non-clustered index.

- The table stores analytic data and could benefit from a columnstore index, instead of rowstore.

- Statistics are stale.

Specify Fill Factors

The fill factor controls the amount of free space left on the data pages of an index after an index is built or defragmented. This free space is made available to allow for records on the page to expand, reducing the risk that the change in record size may result in a page split. This is an extremely useful property of indexes to use for index maintenance. Modifying the fill factor can mitigate the risk of fragmentation. A more thorough discussion of fill factor is presented in Chapter 8. For the purposes of this best practice, the primary concern is with the ability to set the fill factor at the database and index levels as needed.

Database-Level Fill Factor

One of the database properties in SQL Server is the option to set a default fill factor for indexes. This setting is a SQL Server–wide setting and can be altered in the properties of SQL Server on the Database Properties page. By default, this value is set to zero, which equates to 100. Do not modify the default fill factor to anything other than 0 or 100, which has the same impact. Doing so will change the fill factor for every index in the database to the new value. This will add the specified amount of free space to all indexes the next time indexes are created, rebuilt, or reorganized.

On the surface, this may seem like a good idea, but this will blindly increase the size of all indexes by the specified amount. The increased size of the indexes will require more I/O to perform the same work as before the change. In addition, storage space will be consumed as indexes are rebuilt. For many indexes, making this change would result in a needless waste of resources.

Index-Level Fill Factor

At the index level, the fill factor should be modified for indexes that are frequently becoming heavily fragmented. Decreasing the fill factor will increase the amount of free space in the index and provide additional space to compensate for the changes in record length leading to fragmentation. Managing the fill factor at the index level is appropriate since it provides the ability to tune the index precisely to the needs of the database.

Some experimentation may be needed to become confident adjusting the fill factor on indexes, but with time a direct correlation can be drawn between adjusting the fill factor and less frequent fragmentation.

Index Foreign Key Columns

When a foreign key is created on a table, the foreign key column in the table should be indexed. This is necessary to assist the foreign key in determining which records in the parent table are constrained to each record in the referenced table. This is important when changes are being made against the referenced table. The changes in the referenced table may need to check all the rows that match the record in the parent table. If an index does not exist, then a scan of the column will occur. On a large parent table, this could result in a significant amount of I/O and potentially some concurrency issues.

An example of this issue would be state and address tables. There would likely be thousands or millions of records in the address table and maybe a hundred records in the state table. The address table would include a column that is referenced by the state table. Consider whether one of the records in the state table needed to be deleted. If there wasn't an index on the foreign key column in the address table, then how would the address table identify the rows that would be affected by deleting the state record? Without an index, SQL Server would have to check every record in the address table. If the column is indexed, SQL Server would be able to perform a range scan across the records that match to the value being deleted from the state table.

By indexing your foreign key columns, performance issues, such as the one described in this section, can be avoided. The best practice with foreign keys is to index their columns. If in the future it is determined that an index on a foreign key column is not needed by an application, it can be removed with confidence. Chapter 13 includes more details on this best practice and a code example.

Balance Index Count

Indexes are extremely useful for improving performance when accessing information in specific rows. Indexes are not without costs, though. The costs of having indexes go beyond just space within a database. When building an index, consider each of the following:

- How frequently will rows be inserted or deleted?

- How frequently will the key columns be updated?

- How often will the index be used?

- What processes does the index support?

- How many other indexes are on the table?

These are just some of the first considerations that need to be accounted for when building indexes. After the index is built, how much time will be spent updating and maintaining the index? Will the index be modified more frequently than it is used to return results for queries? How many columns are in the table, and are there more indexes than columns?

The trouble with balancing the index count on a table is that there is no precise number that can be recommended. An index improves query performance for queries that can use that index, but consumes resources, including

- Storage space in the data file (MDF or NDF)
- Backup size (maintaining backups of the index)
- Write speeds, maintaining the data in the index

Indexes can sometimes introduce contention if a workload happens to write to different indexes at one time in such a way that locking or blocking is introduced. To summarize in the simplest way possible, indexes improve query read speeds while slowing down write operations.

The number of indexes that it makes sense to have on a table is a per-table decision. Too few indexes may result in excessive scans of the clustered index or heap to return results from common queries. The table should not have too many indexes, where more time is being spent maintaining the indexes than returning results. While there is no golden rule to how many indexes a table should have, there is value in using caution if the count of indexes on a table increases past ten.

Equally important is being able to separate between indexes that serve frequent or critical queries and those that are rarely used. A table scan once a month may be preferable to an index that is maintained all day every day. Alternatively, if that single monthly query is a critical financial report, then that specialized index may be 100 percent worth the cost.

Summary

This chapter looked at some myths surrounding indexes as well as some best practices. For both areas, some commonly held beliefs were investigated and were presented with details around each of them.

With these myths, ideas that are generally believed about indexes were shown to be untrue. These myths covered clustered indexes, the fill factor, the column makeup of indexes, and more. The key to how to view anything that is believed about indexes that may be a myth is to take it upon yourself to test it.

Best practices were also defined and discussed. The best practices provided in the chapter should be the basis upon which indexes can be built. When unsure of how to index a table or workload, start by adhering to best practices. If adjustments are required in the future, then deviating from best practices is a reasonable response to change.

CHAPTER 11

Index Maintenance

Like anything in life, indexes require maintenance. Over time, the performance benefits of indexes can wane or, through data modifications, their sizes and the underlying statistics can drift and bloat. To prevent these issues, indexes must be maintained. Doing so will help ensure that a database will remain a lean, mean query-running machine!

With regard to maintenance, there are five areas to consider:

- Index fragmentation
- Heap bloat and forwarding
- Columnstore fragmentation
- Statistics
- In-memory statistics

Each plays a key role in maintaining a properly indexed and well-performing database.

This chapter explores all of these areas. This discussion will include issues that arise from not maintaining indexes as well as a review of strategies for implementing an index maintenance process. To illustrate how fragmentation occurs, there will be a number of simple demos. The statistics conversation will expand on the items discussed in Chapter 3 and lay out how to update statistics to keep them accurate.

Index Fragmentation

The first maintenance issue that can lead to a degradation of index performance is index fragmentation. Fragmentation occurs when the pages in an index are no longer physically sequential.

© Edward Pollack and Jason Strate 2023
E. Pollack and J. Strate, *Expert Performance Indexing in Azure SQL and SQL Server 2022*,
https://doi.org/10.1007/978-1-4842-9215-0_11

While index fragmentation generated a much greater concern in previous versions of SQL Server and with older storage systems, it is still something to be concerned with in SQL Server. The main challenge that arises with fragmentation is an increase in the amount of space required to store the index due to pages being split and left half-empty. This excess space impacts the amount of space the database consumes on disk, in memory, and through the CPU as it processes the data.

There are a few events in SQL Server that can lead to index fragmentation:

- INSERT operations

- UPDATE operations

- DELETE operations

- DBCC SHRINKDATABASE operations

Except for selecting data from the database, any write operation can potentially lead to fragmentation. Unless a database is read-only, fragmentation is a relevant concern that needs to be addressed before it becomes an issue.

Fragmentation Operations

The best way to understand fragmentation is to see it in action. In Chapter 3, the information returned by the dynamic management object (DMO) sys.dm_index_physical_stats was reviewed. In this section, a number of fragmentation-causing scripts will be reviewed, and the DMO will be used to investigate the amount of fragmentation that has occurred.

Fragmentation occurs when physical pages within an index are not sequential. When an insert occurs and the new row is not placed at the end of the pages for the index, the new row will be placed on a page that already has other rows on it. If there is not enough room on the page for the new row, then the page will split, leading to fragmentation of the index. Fragmentation is the physical result of page splits in the index.

Insert Operations

The first operation that can lead to index fragmentation is an INSERT operation. This is not usually considered the most likely operation to result in fragmentation, but there are database design patterns that can lead to fragmentation. There are two areas in which INSERT operations can lead to fragmentation: clustered and non-clustered indexes.

The most common pattern for designing clustered indexes is to place the index on a single column with a value that is ever-increasing. This is often done using a numeric data type and the IDENTITY property or an ever-increasing numeric key. When this pattern is followed, the chances of fragmentation occurring during inserts are relatively rare. Unfortunately, this isn't the only clustered index pattern that exists, and some others can lead to considerable fragmentation. For example, using unordered business keys or uniqueidentifier data types can often cause fragmentation.

Clustered indexes that use uniqueidentifier data type values often use the NEWID() function to generate a random, unique value to serve as the clustering key. This value is unique but not ever-increasing. The most recent value generated may or may not be after the previous value. Because of this, when a new row is inserted into the clustered index, it is most likely to be placed between a number of other rows already in the index. If there is not enough room in the index, fragmentation will occur.

To demonstrate fragmentation caused by the use of a uniqueidentifier as a clustered index, execute the code in Listing 11-1. This code creates a table named dbo. UsingUniqueidentifier. It is populated with rows from sys.columns, and then a clustered index is added. At this point, all pages in the index are physically sequential. Run the code in Listing 11-2 to view the results shown in Figure 11-1; these results show that the average fragmentation for the index is 0.00 percent.

Listing 11-1. Populate a Uniqueidentifier Table

```
USE AdventureWorks2017
GO
IF OBJECT_ID('dbo.UsingUniqueidentifier') IS NOT NULL
    DROP TABLE dbo.UsingUniqueidentifier;
CREATE TABLE dbo.UsingUniqueidentifier
(
RowID uniqueidentifier CONSTRAINT DF_GUIDValue DEFAULT NEWID()
,Name sysname
,JunkValue varchar(2000)
);
INSERT INTO dbo.UsingUniqueidentifier (Name, JunkValue)
SELECT name, REPLICATE('X', 2000)
FROM sys.columns
CREATE CLUSTERED INDEX CLUS_UsingUniqueidentifier ON dbo.UsingUnique
identifier(RowID);
```

Listing 11-2. View INSERT Index Fragmentation

```
USE AdventureWorks2017
GO
SELECT index_type_desc
  ,index_depth
  ,index_level
  ,page_count
  ,record_count
  ,CAST(avg_fragmentation_in_percent as DECIMAL(6,2)) as avg_frag_
in_percent
  ,fragment_count AS frag_count
  ,avg_fragment_size_in_pages AS avg_frag_size_in_pages
  ,CAST(avg_page_space_used_in_percent as DECIMAL(6,2)) as avg_page_space_
used_in_percent
FROM sys.dm_db_index_physical_stats(DB_ID(),OBJECT_ID('dbo.UsingUnique
identifier'),NULL,NULL,'DETAILED')
```

	index_type_desc	index_depth	index_level	page_count	record_count	avg_frag_in_percent	frag_count	avg_frag_size_in_pages	avg_page_space_used_in_percent
1	CLUSTERED INDEX	3	0	665	1994	0.00	4	166.25	76.03
2	CLUSTERED INDEX	3	1	3	665	0.00	3	1	76.66
3	CLUSTERED INDEX	3	2	1	3	0.00	1	1	1.01

Figure 11-1. *Starting fragmentation results (results may vary)*

With the table built with a clustered index based on a uniqueidentifier column, an INSERT can be made into the table to see the effect that it has on the index. To demonstrate, insert all the rows in sys.objects into dbo.UsingUniqueidentifier using the code in Listing 11-3. After the insert, the fragmentation of the index can be reviewed in the results, using the T-SQL in Listing 11-2. The results should be similar to those shown in Figure 11-2, which shows fragmentation in the clustered index at over 70 percent at index level 0 after adding 689 rows to the table.

Listing 11-3. INSERT into the Uniqueidentifier Table

```
USE AdventureWorks2017
GO

INSERT INTO dbo.UsingUniqueidentifier (Name, JunkValue)
SELECT name, REPLICATE('X', 2000)
FROM sys.objects
```

As this code sample demonstrated, clustered indexes that are based on values that are not ever-increasing result in fragmentation. The best example of this type of behavior is through the use of `uniqueidentifiers`. This can also happen when the clustering key is a computed value or based on an unordered business key. When looking at business keys, if a random purchase order is assigned to an order, then that value will likely behave similar to a `uniqueidentifier` data type value.

	index_type_desc	index_depth	index_level	page_count	record_count	avg_frag_in_percent	frag_count	avg_frag_size_in_pages	avg_page_space_used_in_percent
1	CLUSTERED INDEX	3	0	1191	2683	70.28	846	1.40780141843972	57.35
2	CLUSTERED INDEX	3	1	5	1191	80.00	5	1	82.38
3	CLUSTERED INDEX	3	2	1	5	0.00	1	1	1.70

Figure 11-2. *Post-INSERT fragmentation results (percentage results may vary)*

The other way in which INSERT operations can affect fragmentation is on the non-clustered indexes. While the clustered index values may be ever-increasing values, the values for the columns in the non-clustered index won't necessarily have that same quality. A good example of this is when indexing the name of a product in a non-clustered index. The next record inserted into the table may start with the letter *M* and will need to be placed near the middle of the non-clustered index. If there isn't room at that location, a page split will occur, and fragmentation will result.

To demonstrate this behavior, add a non-clustered index to the table dbo. UsingUniqueidentifier that was used in the previous demonstrations. Listing 11-4 shows the schema for the new index. Before inserting more records to see the effect of inserting into a non-clustered index, run Listing 11-2 again. The results will be similar to those in Figure 11-3.

Listing 11-4. Create a Non-clustered Index

```
USE AdventureWorks2017
GO

CREATE NONCLUSTERED INDEX IX_Name ON dbo.UsingUniqueidentifier(Name)
INCLUDE (JunkValue);
```

	index_type_desc	index_depth	index_level	page_count	record_count	avg_frag_in_percent	frag_count	avg_frag_size_in_pages	avg_page_space_used_in_percent
1	CLUSTERED INDEX	3	0	1191	2683	70.28	846	1.40780141843972	57.35
2	CLUSTERED INDEX	3	1	5	1191	80.00	5	1	82.38
3	CLUSTERED INDEX	3	2	1	5	0.00	1	1	1.70
4	NONCLUSTERED INDEX	3	0	895	2683	0.00	2	447.5	76.22
5	NONCLUSTERED INDEX	3	1	7	895	0.00	2	3.5	96.36
6	NONCLUSTERED INDEX	3	2	1	7	0.00	1	1	4.20

Figure 11-3. *Non-clustered index fragmentation results*

At this point, more rows need to be inserted into dbo.UsingUniqueidentifier. Execute the T-SQL in Listing 11-3 again to insert more records into the table and then use Listing 11-2 to view the state of fragmentation in the non-clustered index. With this complete, the non-clustered index is now more than 40 percent fragmented, as shown in Figure 11-4.

	index_type_desc	index_depth	index_level	page_count	record_count	avg_frag_in_percent	frag_count	avg_frag_size_in_pages	avg_page_space_used_in_percent
1	CLUSTERED INDEX	3	0	1566	3372	85.76	1353	1.15742793791574	54.95
2	CLUSTERED INDEX	3	1	9	1566	88.89	7	1.28571428571429	60.17
3	CLUSTERED INDEX	3	2	1	9	0.00	1	1	3.09
4	NONCLUSTERED INDEX	3	0	1354	3372	43.13	592	2.28716216216216	63.47
5	NONCLUSTERED INDEX	3	1	18	1354	83.33	4	4.5	63.53
6	NONCLUSTERED INDEX	3	2	1	18	0.00	1	1	15.96

Figure 11-4. *Non-clustered post-INSERT fragmentation results*

Whenever INSERT operations are performed, there is always a possibility fragmentation can occur. This will happen on both clustered and non-clustered indexes. Choosing ever-increasing key columns for clustered indexes will reduce the impact from insert-related fragmentation.

Update Operations

Another operation that can lead to fragmentation is an UPDATE operation. There are two main ways in which an UPDATE operation will result in fragmentation. First, the data in the record no longer fits on the page on which it currently resides. Second, the key value for the index changes, and the index location for the new key value is not on the same page or doesn't fit on the page where the record is destined. In both scenarios, the page splits, and fragmentation occurs.

To demonstrate how these situations lead to fragmentation, consider how increasing the size of a record in an update can lead to fragmentation. For this, a new table will be created, and a number of records will be inserted into it. Then a clustered index will be added to the table. The code for this is in Listing 11-5. Using the script from Listing 11-6, it can be seen that there is no fragmentation on the clustered index, as the results in Figure 11-5 show. One thing to pay attention to with these fragmentation results is that the average page space used is almost 90 percent. Because of this, any significant growth in record size will likely fill the available space on the pages.

Listing 11-5. Create a Table for UPDATE Operations

```
USE AdventureWorks2017
GO
IF OBJECT_ID('dbo.UpdateOperations') IS NOT NULL
    DROP TABLE dbo.UpdateOperations;
CREATE TABLE dbo.UpdateOperations
(
RowID int IDENTITY(1,1)
,Name sysname
,JunkValue varchar(2000)
);
INSERT INTO dbo.UpdateOperations (Name, JunkValue)
SELECT name, REPLICATE('X', 1000)
FROM sys.columns
CREATE CLUSTERED INDEX CLUS_UsingUniqueidentifier ON
dbo.UpdateOperations(RowID);
```

Listing 11-6. View UPDATE Index Fragmentation

```
USE AdventureWorks2017
GO

SELECT index_type_desc
    ,index_depth
    ,index_level
    ,page_count
    ,record_count
```

271

```
    ,CAST(avg_fragmentation_in_percent as DECIMAL(6,2)) as
    avg_fragmentation_in_percent
    ,fragment_count
    ,avg_fragment_size_in_pages
    ,CAST(avg_page_space_used_in_percent as DECIMAL(6,2)) as
    avg_page_space_used_in_percent
FROM sys.dm_db_index_physical_stats(DB_ID(),OBJECT_ID('dbo.UpdateOperations
'),NULL,NULL,'DETAILED');
```

	index_type_desc	index_depth	index_level	page_count	record_count	avg_fragmentation_in_percent	fragment_count	avg_fragment_size_in_pages	avg_page_space_used_in_percent
1	CLUSTERED INDEX	2	0	206	1997	0.35	4	71.5	89.77
2	CLUSTERED INDEX	2	1	206	0.00		1	1	45.91

Figure 11-5. *Initial UPDATE fragmentation results*

Now increase the size of some of the rows in the index. To accomplish this, execute the code in Listing 11-7. This code will update the JunkValue column for every five rows from a 1,000-character value to a 2,000-character value. Using Listing 11-6 to view current index fragmentation, it can be seen that, through the results in Figure 11-6, the clustered index is now more than 99 percent fragmented and the average page space used has dropped to about 50 percent. As this code demonstrates, when a row increases in size during an UPDATE operation, the potential exists for significant fragmentation.

Listing 11-7. UPDATE Operation resulting in fragmentation

```
USE AdventureWorks2017
GO
UPDATE dbo.UpdateOperations
SET JunkValue = REPLICATE('X', 2000)
WHERE RowID % 5 = 1
```

	index_type_desc	index_depth	index_level	page_count	record_count	avg_fragmentation_in_percent	fragment_count	avg_fragment_size_in_pages	avg_page_space_used_in_percent
1	CLUSTERED INDEX	2	0	571	1997	99.65	571	1	53.61
2	CLUSTERED INDEX	2	1	571	0.00		1	1	91.69

Figure 11-6. *UPDATE fragmentation results after record length increase*

The second way in which an index can incur fragmentation is by changing the key values for the index. When the key values for an index change, the record may need to change its position in the index. For example, if an index is built on the name of the product, then changing the name from Acme Mop to XYZ Mop will change where the product name will be placed in the sorting for the index. Changing the location of the record in the index may place the record on a different page, and if there is not sufficient space on the new page, then a page split and fragmentation will occur.

To demonstrate this concept, execute Listing 11-8 and then use Listing 11-6 to obtain the results shown in Figure 11-7. For the new non-clustered index, there is currently no fragmentation.

Note   If key values for a clustered index change often, that may indicate that the key values selected for the clustered index are inappropriate.

Listing 11-8. Create a Non-clustered Index for UPDATE Operations

```
USE AdventureWorks2017
GO

CREATE NONCLUSTERED INDEX IX_Name ON dbo.UpdateOperations(Name) INCLUDE
(JunkValue);
```

	index_type_desc	index_depth	index_level	page_count	record_count	avg_fragmentation_in_percent	fragment_count	avg_fragment_size_in_pages	avg_page_space_used_in_percent
1	CLUSTERED INDEX	2	0	571	1997	99.65	571	1	53.61
2	CLUSTERED INDEX	2	1	1	571	0.00	1	1	91.69
3	NONCLUSTERED INDEX	3	0	351	1997	0.00	3	117	87.01
4	NONCLUSTERED INDEX	3	1	2	351	0.00	1	2	80.81
5	NONCLUSTERED INDEX	3	2	1	2	0.00	1	1	0.57

Figure 11-7. *UPDATE fragmentation results after adding a non-clustered index*

At this point, some key values need to be modified. Using Listing 11-9, perform UPDATE activity on the table and update one out of every nine rows. To simulate changing the key values, the UPDATE statement reverses the characters in the column. This small amount of activity is enough to cause a significant amount of fragmentation. As the results in Figure 11-8 illustrate, the non-clustered index went from no fragmentation to more than 30 percent fragmentation.

One thing to note is that the fragmentation on the clustered index did not change with these updates. Not all updates will result in fragmentation. Only those updates that move data around because of space being unavailable on the pages where the records are currently stored will result in fragmentation.

Listing 11-9. UPDATE Operation to Change Index Key Values

```
USE AdventureWorks2017
GO

UPDATE dbo.UpdateOperations
SET Name = REVERSE(Name)
WHERE RowID % 9 = 1
```

	index_type_desc	index_depth	index_level	page_count	record_count	avg_fragmentation_in_percent	fragment_count	avg_fragment_size_in_pages	avg_page_space_used_in_percent
1	CLUSTERED INDEX	2	0	571	1997	99.65	571	1	53.61
2	CLUSTERED INDEX	2	1	1	571	0.00	1	1	91.69
3	NONCLUSTERED INDEX	3	0	438	1997	29.45	135	3.24444444444444	69.72
4	NONCLUSTERED INDEX	3	1	3	438	66.67	2	1.5	66.96
5	NONCLUSTERED INDEX	3	2	1	3	0.00	1	1	1.27

Figure 11-8. *UPDATE fragmentation results after changing index key values*

Delete Operations

The third type of operation that can cause fragmentation is the DELETE operation. Deletes are a bit different in nature in that they create fragmentation within a database. Instead of relocating pages because of page splits, a delete can lead to pages being removed from an index. Gaps will then appear in the physical sequence of pages for the index. Since the pages are no longer physically sequential, they are considered fragmented. This is significant since once the pages are deallocated from the index, they can be reallocated to other indexes, comprising a more traditional form of fragmentation.

To demonstrate this type of behavior, create a table, populate it with a number of records, and then add a clustered index. Listing 11-10 shows the script for these tasks. Run the script followed by the script from Listing 11-11 to get the current fragmentation for the clustered index. The results should match those in Figure 11-9. The average fragmentation (as a percent column (avg_fragmentation_in_percent)) shows that there is no fragmentation currently in the index.

Listing 11-10. Creating a Table for DELETE Operation

```
USE AdventureWorks2017
GO
IF OBJECT_ID('dbo.DeleteOperations') IS NOT NULL
    DROP TABLE dbo.DeleteOperations;
CREATE TABLE dbo.DeleteOperations
(
RowID int IDENTITY(1,1)
,Name sysname
,JunkValue varchar(2000)
);
INSERT INTO dbo.DeleteOperations (Name, JunkValue)
SELECT name, REPLICATE('X', 1000)
FROM sys.columns
CREATE CLUSTERED INDEX CLUS_UsingUniqueidentifier ON dbo.
DeleteOperations(RowID);
```

Listing 11-11. View DELETE Index Fragmentation

```
USE AdventureWorks2017
GO
SELECT index_type_desc
    ,index_depth
    ,index_level
    ,page_count
    ,record_count
    ,CAST(avg_fragmentation_in_percent as DECIMAL(6,2)) as
    avg_fragmentation_in_percent
    ,fragment_count
    ,avg_fragment_size_in_pages
    ,CAST(avg_page_space_used_in_percent as DECIMAL(6,2)) as
    avg_page_space_used_in_percent
FROM sys.dm_db_index_physical_stats(DB_ID(),OBJECT_ID('dbo.DeleteOperations'),
NULL,NULL,'DETAILED')
```

	index_type_desc	index_depth	index_level	page_count	record_count	avg_fragmentation_in_percent	fragment_count	avg_fragment_size_in_pages	avg_page_space_used_in_percent
1	CLUSTERED INDEX	2	0	286	2000	0.00	3	96.3333333333333	89.91
2	CLUSTERED INDEX	2	1	1	286	0.00	1	1	45.91

Figure 11-9. *Fragmentation results before DELETE operation*

To demonstrate fragmentation caused by DELETE operations, every other 50 records in the table will be deleted using the code in Listing 11-12. As before, Listing 11-11 will be used to view the state of fragmentation in the index. The results, shown in Figure 11-10, indicate that the DELETE operation resulted in about 13 percent fragmentation. With DELETE operations, the rate at which fragmentation usually occurs is not too fast. Also, since the fragmentation is not the result of page splits, the order of the pages does not become physically out of order. Instead, there are gaps in the contiguous pages. However, pages left empty could be reused in future INSERT and UPDATE transactions, which could result in the pages being physically out of order.

Listing 11-12. Performing DELETE Operation

```
USE AdventureWorks2017
GO
DELETE dbo.DeleteOperations
WHERE RowID % 100 BETWEEN 1 AND 50
```

	index_type_desc	index_depth	index_level	page_count	record_count	avg_fragmentation_in_percent	fragment_count	avg_fragment_size_in_pages	avg_page_space_used_in_percent
1	CLUSTERED INDEX	2	0	161	1000	12.42	22	7.31818181818182	79.97
2	CLUSTERED INDEX	2	1	1	161	0.00	1	1	25.83

Figure 11-10. *Fragmentation results after DELETE*

Note that fragmentation resulting from delete operations may not appear immediately after a DELETE operation is executed. When records are to be deleted, they are first marked for deletion before the record itself is actually deleted. While it is marked for deletion, the record is considered to be a ghost record. During this stage, the record is logically deleted but is physically still present in the index. At a future point, after the transaction has been committed and a CHECKPOINT has completed, the ghost cleanup process will physically remove the row. At this time, the fragmentation will become visible in the index.

Shrink Operations

The last type of operation that can lead to fragmentation is when databases are shrunk. Databases can be shrunk using either DBCC SHRINKDATABASE or DBCC SHRINKFILE. These operations can be used to shrink the size of a database or its files. When they are used, the pages at the end of a data file are relocated toward the beginning of the data file. For their intended purpose, shrink operations can be effective tools.

Unfortunately, these shrink operations do not consider the nature of the data pages that are being moved. To the shrink operation, a data page is a data page. The priority of the operation is that pages at the end of the data file find a place at the beginning of the data file. As discussed, when the pages of an index are not physically stored in order, the index is considered fragmented.

To demonstrate the fragmentation damage that a shrink operation can cause, a database will be created and a shrink performed on it. The code for this appears in Listing 11-13. In this example, there are two tables: FirstTable and SecondTable. Some records will be inserted into each table. The inserts will alternate back and forth with three inserts into FirstTable and two inserts into SecondTable. Through these inserts, there will be alternating bands of pages allocated to the two tables. Next, SecondTable will be dropped, which will result in unallocated data pages between each of the bands of pages for FirstTable. Using Listing 11-14 will show that a small amount of fragmentation exists on FirstTable, shown in Figure 11-11.

Listing 11-13. Shrink Operation Database Preparation

```
USE master
GO
IF EXISTS (SELECT * FROM sys.databases WHERE name = 'Fragmentation')
DROP DATABASE Fragmentation
GO

CREATE DATABASE Fragmentation
GO

Use Fragmentation
GO

IF OBJECT_ID('dbo.FirstTable') IS NOT NULL
    DROP TABLE dbo.FirstTable;
```

```
CREATE TABLE dbo.FirstTable
(
RowID int IDENTITY(1,1)
,Name sysname
,JunkValue varchar(2000)
,CONSTRAINT PK_FirstTable PRIMARY KEY CLUSTERED (RowID)
);

INSERT INTO dbo.FirstTable (Name, JunkValue)
SELECT TOP 750 name, REPLICATE('X', 2000)
FROM sys.columns

IF OBJECT_ID('dbo.SecondTable') IS NOT NULL
    DROP TABLE dbo.SecondTable;
CREATE TABLE dbo.SecondTable
(
RowID int IDENTITY(1,1)
,Name sysname
,JunkValue varchar(2000)
,CONSTRAINT PK_SecondTable PRIMARY KEY CLUSTERED (RowID)
);

INSERT INTO dbo.SecondTable (Name, JunkValue)
SELECT TOP 750 name, REPLICATE('X', 2000)
FROM sys.columns
GO

INSERT INTO dbo.FirstTable (Name, JunkValue)
SELECT TOP 750 name, REPLICATE('X', 2000)
FROM sys.columns
GO

INSERT INTO dbo.SecondTable (Name, JunkValue)
SELECT TOP 750 name, REPLICATE('X', 2000)
FROM sys.columns
GO
```

```
INSERT INTO dbo.FirstTable (Name, JunkValue)
SELECT TOP 750 name, REPLICATE('X', 2000)
FROM sys.columns
GO

IF OBJECT_ID('dbo.SecondTable') IS NOT NULL
    DROP TABLE dbo.SecondTable;
GO
```

Listing 11-14. View Index Fragmentation from Shrink

```
Use Fragmentation
GO

SELECT index_type_desc
    ,index_depth
    ,index_level
    ,page_count
    ,record_count
    ,CAST(avg_fragmentation_in_percent as DECIMAL(6,2)) as
    avg_fragmentation_in_percent
    ,fragment_count
    ,avg_fragment_size_in_pages
    ,CAST(avg_page_space_used_in_percent as DECIMAL(6,2)) as
    avg_page_space_used_in_percent
FROM sys.dm_db_index_physical_stats(DB_ID(),OBJECT_ID('dbo.FirstTable'),
NULL,NULL,'DETAILED')
```

index_type_desc	index_depth	index_level	page_count	record_count	avg_fragmentation_in_percent	fragment_count	avg_fragment_size_in_pages	avg_page_space_used_in_percent
1	CLUSTERED INDEX	3	0	750	2250	2.27	21	35.7142857142857	75.38
2	CLUSTERED INDEX	3	1	2	750	0.00	2	1	60.21
3	CLUSTERED INDEX	3	2	1	2	0.00	1	1	0.30

Figure 11-11. *Fragmentation of FirstTable after inserts*

With the database prepared, the next step is to shrink the database. The purpose of this is to recover the space that had been allocated to SecondTable and trim down the size of the database to only what is needed. To perform the shrink operation, use the code in Listing 11-15. When the SHRINKDATABASE operation completes, Figure 11-12 will

279

show that running the code from Listing 11-14 causes the fragmentation for the index to increase from just over 2 percent to more than 35 percent. This is a significant change in fragmentation on a database with just a single table. Consider the effect of a shrink operation on a database with dozens, hundreds, or thousands of indexes.

Listing 11-15. Shrink Operation

```
DBCC SHRINKDATABASE (Fragmentation)
```

	index_type_desc	index_depth	index_level	page_count	record_count	avg_fragmentation_in_percent	fragment_count	avg_fragment_size_in_pages	avg_page_space_used_in_percent
1	CLUSTERED INDEX	3	0	750	2250	35.47	269	2.78810408921933	75.38
2	CLUSTERED INDEX	3	1	2	750	0.00	2	1	60.21
3	CLUSTERED INDEX	3	2	1	2	0.00	1	1	0.30

Figure 11-12. *Fragmentation of FirstTable after shrink operation*

This has been a simple example of the damage in terms of fragmentation that a shrink operation can have on an index. As was evident even with this example, the shrink operation led to a significant amount of fragmentation. Most SQL Server database administrators will agree that shrink operations should be an extremely rare operation on any database. Some database administrators are also of the opinion that this operation should never be used on any database for any reason. The guideline that is most often recommended is to be extremely cautious when database shrink operations are performed. The most dangerous pattern to adopt is a cycle of shrinking a database to recover space, causing fragmentation, and then expanding the database through defragmenting the indexes. This constitutes a waste of time and resources that could be better spent on real performance and maintenance issues.

Another important note on shrink operations is that most busy production tables will grow over time. If this is the case, then shrinking the database only provides temporary relief against inevitable future growth. Because of this, shrink operations should be reserved for scenarios when the amount of space recouped is far more significant than any fragmentation that may result from it.

Fragmentation Variants

Traditionally, when index fragmentation is discussed, the primary focus is on fragmentation within the clustered or non-clustered index. This is not the only consideration to keep in mind when evaluating index fragmentation. It is also valuable to consider whether the table or index has bloat, forwarding, or segmentation, each of which is a variation on the idea of index fragmentation. In this section, these other two areas in which fragmentation-type maintenance can be required on tables will be reviewed:

- Heap bloat and forwarding

- Columnstore fragmentation

Heap Bloat and Forwarding

As discussed in Chapter 3, heaps are collections of unordered pages in which data for a table is stored. As new rows are added to the table, the heap grows as new pages are allocated. Insert and update operations can cause changes to heaps that can require maintenance on the table.

To begin, bloating within a heap will be reviewed. For heaps, bloating occurs when records are deleted from the heap without being reused for new records. As discussed in Chapter 10, this is not a matter of records going to new pages but an overall decline in the number of records in the table. The pages will be reused, but when they are not, the pages remain allocated, and this can have an impact on performance.

To demonstrate this activity, the script in Listing 11-16 will be used. This script starts with a heap table that has 400 records inserted into it. Next, half of the records are deleted, leaving 200 in the table. As shown in Figure 11-13, the record count for the table reflects these changes, but in both cases the DMV results show that there are 100 pages associated with the table. This is because pages are not removed from a heap unless maintenance activities force this to occur. Through the ALTER TABLE statement on dbo.HeapTable with the REBUILD option, the table is rebuilt, and the excess pages are flushed.

Listing 11-16. Impact of Deletes on Heap Page Allocations

```
USE AdventureWorks2017
GO

IF OBJECT_ID('dbo.HeapTable') IS NOT NULL
    DROP TABLE dbo.HeapTable;
CREATE TABLE dbo.HeapTable
(
    RowId INT IDENTITY(1,1)
    ,FillerData VARCHAR(2500)
);
INSERT INTO dbo.HeapTable (FillerData)
```

```
SELECT TOP 400 REPLICATE('X',2000)
FROM sys.objects;

SELECT OBJECT_NAME(object_id), index_type_desc, page_count, record_count,
forwarded_record_count
FROM sys.dm_db_index_physical_stats (DB_ID(),OBJECT_ID('dbo.HeapTable'),
NULL,NULL,'DETAILED');

SET STATISTICS IO ON;
SELECT COUNT(*) FROM dbo.HeapTable;
SET STATISTICS IO OFF;

DELETE FROM dbo.HeapTable
WHERE RowId % 2 = 0;

SELECT OBJECT_NAME(object_id), index_type_desc, page_count, record_count,
forwarded_record_count
FROM sys.dm_db_index_physical_stats (DB_ID(),OBJECT_ID('dbo.HeapTable'),
NULL,NULL,'DETAILED');

SET STATISTICS IO ON;
SELECT COUNT(*) FROM dbo.HeapTable;
SET STATISTICS IO OFF;

ALTER TABLE dbo.HeapTable REBUILD;

SELECT OBJECT_NAME(object_id), index_type_desc, page_count, record_count,
forwarded_record_count
FROM sys.dm_db_index_physical_stats (DB_ID(),OBJECT_ID('dbo.HeapTable'),
NULL,NULL,'DETAILED');

SET STATISTICS IO ON;
SELECT COUNT(*) FROM dbo.HeapTable;
SET STATISTICS IO OFF;
```

	(No column name)	index_type_desc	page_count	record_count	forwarded_record_count
1	HeapTable	HEAP	100	400	0

	(No column name)
1	400

	(No column name)	index_type_desc	page_count	record_count	forwarded_record_count
1	HeapTable	HEAP	100	200	0

	(No column name)
1	200

	(No column name)	index_type_desc	page_count	record_count	forwarded_record_count
1	HeapTable	HEAP	50	200	0

	(No column name)
1	200

Figure 11-13. *Results from deleting from a heap*

To help emphasize that the pages are still in the table, Figure 11-14 shows the pages that are read when counting all rows in the table, further demonstrating that there are 100 pages being accessed. When considering the impact on performance for heaps after a delete, an excessive number of pages in a heap compared with the amount of data will increase the amount of effort required by SQL Server to execute queries against it. In the case of this demonstration, the COUNT(*) queries process twice the amount of data that is required.

```
Table 'HeapTable'. Scan count 1, logical reads 100, physical reads 0, read-ahead reads 0, lob logical reads 0,
Table 'HeapTable'. Scan count 1, logical reads 100, physical reads 0, read-ahead reads 0, lob logical reads 0,
Table 'HeapTable'. Scan count 1, logical reads 50, physical reads 0, read-ahead reads 0, lob logical reads 0,
```

Figure 11-14. *I/O impact from deletes on a heap*

The other area of consideration for the maintenance of heaps is the volume of forwarded records in the table. Forwarded records, discussed in Chapter 3, are records within a heap that no longer fit in the original location in which they were added to the heap. To accommodate the change in the size of the record, the record is stored on another page, and the previous record location includes a pointer to the new location.

The impact of this change is an increase in the number of pages in the heap, because new pages are added for existing records, and it takes an additional I/O operation to go from the first page to the forwarded page when looking up a record. While this may not appear to be a significant problem, in aggregate the accumulated impact of forwarded records increases the amount of I/O for a system and adds to latency in query execution.

To demonstrate the impact of forwarded records on queries, execute the code in Listing 11-17. This script creates a table with a heap, runs a number of queries, updates the records to cause forwarding of heap records to occur, and then completes by re-executing the previous set of queries.

Listing 11-17. Forwarded Record Impact on Query Performance

```
USE AdventureWorks2017
GO
SET NOCOUNT ON

IF OBJECT_ID('dbo.ForwardedRecords') IS NOT NULL
    DROP TABLE dbo.ForwardedRecords;

CREATE TABLE dbo.ForwardedRecords
    (
    ID INT IDENTITY(1,1)
    ,VALUE VARCHAR(8000)
    );

CREATE NONCLUSTERED INDEX IX_ForwardedRecords_ID ON
dbo.ForwardedRecords(ID);

INSERT INTO dbo.ForwardedRecords (VALUE)
SELECT REPLICATE(type, 500)
FROM sys.objects;

SET STATISTICS IO ON
PRINT '*** No forwarded records'
SELECT * FROM dbo.ForwardedRecords;

SELECT * FROM dbo.ForwardedRecords
WHERE ID = 40;

SELECT * FROM dbo.ForwardedRecords
WHERE ID BETWEEN 40 AND 60;
SET STATISTICS IO OFF
```

```
UPDATE dbo.ForwardedRecords
SET VALUE =REPLICATE(VALUE, 16)
WHERE ID%3 = 1;

SET STATISTICS IO ON
PRINT '*** With forwarded records'
SELECT * FROM dbo.ForwardedRecords;

SELECT * FROM dbo.ForwardedRecords
WHERE ID = 40;

SELECT * FROM dbo.ForwardedRecords
WHERE ID BETWEEN 40 AND 60;
SET STATISTICS IO OFF
```

There are three queries from Listing 11-17 that are included to demonstrate the impact of forwarded records on heaps:

- SELECT *: To demonstrate the impact of an index scan

- SELECT *with equality predicate*: To demonstrate the impact on a singleton lookup

- SELECT *with inequality predicate*: To demonstrate the impact on a range lookup

For the SELECT * query, before the forwarded records are in the heap, the query executes with 99 reads, as shown in Figure 11-15. After the forwarded records are introduced, the reads increase to 561. This increase is because of the new pages added to the heap to accommodate the increases in the row sizes. With the second query, the singleton lookup grows from three reads to four reads, which represents the additional read required to go from the original location for the record to the forwarding location. In the last query, the range query with the lookup executes with 23 reads, but after the forwarded records are added to the table, the reads jump to 30 reads.

```
*** No forwarded records
Table 'ForwardedRecords'. Scan count 1, logical reads 99, physical reads 0,
Table 'ForwardedRecords'. Scan count 1, logical reads 3, physical reads 0,
Table 'ForwardedRecords'. Scan count 1, logical reads 23, physical reads 0,
*** With forwarded records
Table 'ForwardedRecords'. Scan count 1, logical reads 561, physical reads 0
Table 'ForwardedRecords'. Scan count 1, logical reads 4, physical reads 0,
Table 'ForwardedRecords'. Scan count 1, logical reads 30, physical reads 0,
```

Figure 11-15. *I/O statistics for forwarded record queries*

The overall effect of the forwarded records is an increase in reads. While the increase may not be significant on a per-query basis, over time the impact adds up. Scans of heaps with forwarded records access more pages, and lookups require an extra I/O. Reducing the impact of forwarded records in heaps is an important part of maintaining indexes and optimizing performance.

Columnstore Fragmentation

Columnstore indexes operate very differently from standard rowstore indexes (clustered, non-clustered, and heaps). An interesting component of columnstore indexes is the read-only nature of segments. As discussed in Chapter 2, small inserts into a columnstore index will be processed by the deltastore and later asynchronously merged into compressed rowgroups. In addition, deletes are processed as soft deletes. Rows are flagged as deleted, but not immediately removed, resulting in segments that contain data that is no longer part of the table.

To demonstrate each of these concepts, execute the code in Listing 11-18 to prepare a table with a clustered columnstore index. After the table is built, the two sets of rows are inserted. The first set contains 1,000 rows, and the index is reorganized to force the rowgroup to compress to columnstore format. The second set contains 105,000 rows, which is more than the 102,400 threshold that automatically inserts rows directly into compressed rowgroups. Figure 11-16 shows that the inserted records are compressed directly into columnstore format.

Note   Depending on your environment, the script in Listing 11-18 may take a while to run.

Listing 11-18. Prepare a Columnstore Table

```
USE ContosoRetailDW
GO
IF OBJECT_ID('dbo.FactOnlineSalesCI') IS NOT NULL
    DROP TABLE dbo.FactOnlineSalesCI
CREATE TABLE dbo.FactOnlineSalesCI(
    [OnlineSalesKey] [int] NOT NULL,
    [DateKey] [datetime] NOT NULL,
    [StoreKey] [int] NOT NULL,
    [ProductKey] [int] NOT NULL,
    [PromotionKey] [int] NOT NULL,
    [CurrencyKey] [int] NOT NULL,
    [CustomerKey] [int] NOT NULL,
    [SalesOrderNumber] [nvarchar](20) NOT NULL,
    [SalesOrderLineNumber] [int] NULL,
    [SalesQuantity] [int] NOT NULL,
    [SalesAmount] [money] NOT NULL,
    [ReturnQuantity] [int] NOT NULL,
    [ReturnAmount] [money] NULL,
    [DiscountQuantity] [int] NULL,
    [DiscountAmount] [money] NULL,
    [TotalCost] [money] NOT NULL,
    [UnitCost] [money] NULL,
    [UnitPrice] [money] NULL,
    [ETLLoadID] [int] NULL,
    [LoadDate] [datetime] NULL,
    [UpdateDate] [datetime] NULL
)
INSERT INTO dbo.FactOnlineSalesCI
SELECT *
FROM dbo.FactOnlineSales
CREATE CLUSTERED COLUMNSTORE INDEX FactOnlineSalesCI_CCI ON
dbo.FactOnlineSalesCI
```

```
DECLARE @we int= 1

WHILE @we <= 5
BEGIN
    INSERT INTO dbo.FactOnlineSalesCI
    SELECT TOP 1000 *
    FROM dbo.FactOnlineSales
    ALTER INDEX ALL ON dbo.FactOnlineSalesCI REORGANIZE
        WITH (COMPRESS_ALL_ROW_GROUPS =ON)
    SET @we += 1
END

WHILE @we <= 10
BEGIN
    INSERT INTO dbo.FactOnlineSalesCI
    SELECT TOP 105000 *
    FROM dbo.FactOnlineSales
    SET @we += 1
END

SELECT*
FROM sys.column_store_row_groups
WHERE object_id=OBJECT_ID('dbo.FactOnlineSalesCI')
ORDER BY row_group_id DESC
```

	object_id	index_id	partition_number	row_group_id	delta_store_hobt_id	state	state_description	total_rows	deleted_rows	size_in_bytes
1	366624349	1	1	33	NULL	3	COMPRESSED	105000	0	1425752
2	366624349	1	1	32	NULL	3	COMPRESSED	105000	0	1425752
3	366624349	1	1	31	NULL	3	COMPRESSED	105000	0	1425752
4	366624349	1	1	30	NULL	3	COMPRESSED	105000	0	1425752
5	366624349	1	1	29	NULL	3	COMPRESSED	105000	0	1425752
6	366624349	1	1	28	NULL	3	COMPRESSED	48696	0	516640
7	366624349	1	1	27	NULL	3	COMPRESSED	1000	0	21144
8	366624349	1	1	26	72057594051100672	4	TOMBSTONE	1000	NULL	188416
9	366624349	1	1	25	NULL	4	TOMBSTONE	47696	0	0
10	366624349	1	1	24	NULL	4	TOMBSTONE	1000	0	0

Figure 11-16. *Columnstore rowgroup result set*

The piece that is interesting at this point is that the rowgroups created are much smaller than the max size for a rowgroup (about 1 million rows). Since they are smaller, there may be an opportunity to optimize the number of pages that they use by increasing the

number of records per rowgroup. This can be done by rebuilding the columnstore index.
To illustrate the value in rebuilding columnstore indexes, execute the code in Listing 11-19.
This shows that the logical reads before the rebuild are 83,423 over two scan operations and
then drop to 833 logical reads after the rebuild, shown in Figure 11-17. This is a massive
drop in pages accessed. When considering the effect of this type of maintenance over large
fact tables using columnstore indexes, these types of excessive allocations of pages will
greatly impact performance. Additionally, comparing Figures 11-16 and 11-18, the table
also has far fewer rowgroups, from 34 to 14 after the columnstore index rebuild.

Listing 11-19. Impact of Inserts on a Columnstore Table

```
USE ContosoRetailDW
GO

SET STATISTICS IO ON
SELECT DateKey,COUNT(*)
FROM dbo.FactOnlineSalesCI
GROUP BY DateKey

ALTER INDEX ALL ON dbo.FactOnlineSalesCI REBUILD

SELECT DateKey,COUNT(*)
FROM dbo.FactOnlineSalesCI
GROUP BY DateKey

SET STATISTICS IO OFF

SELECT *
FROM sys.column_store_row_groups
WHERE object_id = OBJECT_ID('dbo.FactOnlineSalesCI')
ORDER BY row_group_id DESC
```

Figure 11-17. *I/O statistics for columnstore table inserts*

	object_id	index_id	partition_number	row_group_id	delta_store_hobt_id	state	state_description	total_rows	deleted_rows	size_in_bytes
1	366624349	1	1	13	NULL	3	COMPRESSED	710	0	14552
2	366624349	1	1	12	NULL	3	COMPRESSED	573986	0	7236192
3	366624349	1	1	11	NULL	3	COMPRESSED	1048576	0	12770312
4	366624349	1	1	10	NULL	3	COMPRESSED	1048576	0	12597528
5	366624349	1	1	9	NULL	3	COMPRESSED	1048576	0	12710856
6	366624349	1	1	8	NULL	3	COMPRESSED	1048576	0	12640272
7	366624349	1	1	7	NULL	3	COMPRESSED	1048576	0	11976416
8	366624349	1	1	6	NULL	3	COMPRESSED	1048576	0	12349392
9	366624349	1	1	5	NULL	3	COMPRESSED	1048576	0	11560104
10	366624349	1	1	4	NULL	3	COMPRESSED	1048576	0	11566808

Figure 11-18. *Rowgroup statistics after columnstore index rebuild*

The next type of fragmentation that occurs with columnstore indexes is through delete operations. While this is called *fragmentation*, when deletes occur on columnstore indexes, the rows are not removed from the indexes. Instead, they are flagged as deleted and continue to consume space within rowgroups. Because of this, pages allocated to a clustered columnstore index that have all their records deleted will still be active within the index.

To illustrate the impact of soft-deleted rows in a columnstore index, the script in Listing 11-20 will be used to delete the 2007 data from the table. Another statement will then rebuild the columnstore index. Between these operations, an aggregate query will be executed to provide an analytic operation to gauge the impact of deletes on the I/O of queries.

Listing 11-20. Delete Operations on a Clustered Columnstore Index

```
USE ContosoRetailDW
GO

SET STATISTICS IO ON

SELECT DateKey,COUNT(*)
FROM dbo.FactOnlineSalesCI
GROUP BY DateKey

DELETE FROM dbo.FactOnlineSalesCI
WHERE DateKey <'2008-01-01'

SELECT DateKey,COUNT(*)
FROM dbo.FactOnlineSalesCI
GROUP BY DateKey

ALTER INDEX ALL ON dbo.FactOnlineSalesCI REBUILD
```

```
SELECT DateKey,COUNT(*)
FROM dbo.FactOnlineSalesCI
GROUP BY DateKey

SET STATISTICS IO OFF
```

After running these queries and rebuilding the index, the resulting performance numbers will be shown to be quite significant. Executing the first query results in 659 logical reads for the aggregate query, as shown in Figure 11-19. Deleting a year of data results in the aggregate query requiring 79,982 logical reads, which is an increase from the original query with 365 fewer rows returned. This is because of the pages required to manage the deleted rows. After rebuilding, the I/O drops to just 444 logical reads.

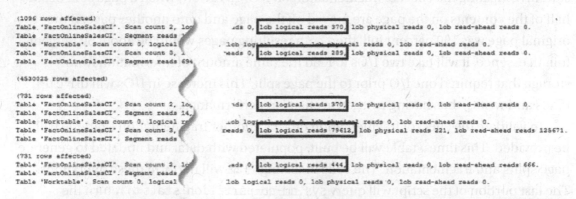

Figure 11-19. *Statistics I/O results for delete operation demonstration*

Through the addition of new rows and the deletion of existing rows, there are reasons to consider the maintenance requirements of columnstore indexes. The issues that affect these indexes are not the same as those of traditional clustered indexes, but they are significant, nonetheless.

Fragmentation Issues

These demonstrations have shown a number of ways in which indexes can become fragmented, but there hasn't been a discussion about why this is important. There are a couple important reasons fragmentation within indexes can be a problem:

- Index I/O
- Contiguous reads

As the fragmentation of an index increases, each of these two areas affects the index's ability to perform well. In some worst-case scenarios, the level of fragmentation can be so severe that the query optimizer will stop using the index in query plans.

Index I/O

I/O is an area of SQL Server where it is easy to have performance bottlenecks. Likewise, there are a multitude of solutions to help mitigate these bottlenecks. From the perspective of this chapter, the primary focus will be on the effect of fragmentation on I/O.

Since page splits are often the cause of fragmentation, they provide a good place to start investigating the effect of fragmentation on I/O. To review, when a page split occurs, half of the contents on the page are moved off the page and onto another page. If the original page was 100 percent full, then both resulting pages would be about 50 percent full. In essence, it will take two I/Os to read the same amount of information from storage that required one I/O prior to the page split. This increase in I/Os will drive up reads and writes, thus having a negative effect on performance.

To validate the effect of fragmentation on I/O, another fragmentation example will be provided. This time a table will be built, populated with data, and updated to generate page splits and fragmentation. The code in Listing 1122 will perform these operations. The last portion of the script will query sys.dm_db_partition_stats to return the number of pages that have been reserved for the index. Execute the fragmentation script from Listing 11-21. This will show that the index at this point is more than 99 percent fragmented. The results from Listing 11-21 shows that the index is using 209 pages. See Figure 11-20 for the results.

Listing 11-21. View Index Fragmentation for the I/O Example

```
SELECT index_type_desc
    ,index_depth
    ,index_level
    ,page_count
    ,record_count
    ,CAST(avg_fragmentation_in_percent as DECIMAL(6,2)) as
    avg_fragmentation_in_percent
    ,fragment_count
    ,avg_fragment_size_in_pages
```

```
    ,CAST(avg_page_space_used_in_percent as DECIMAL(6,2)) as
    avg_page_space_used_in_percent
FROM sys.dm_db_index_physical_stats(DB_ID(),OBJECT_ID('dbo.IndexIO'),NULL,
NULL,'DETAILED')
```

Listing 11-22. Script to Build the Index I/O Example

```
USE AdventureWorks2017
GO
IF OBJECT_ID('dbo.IndexIO') IS NOT NULL
    DROP TABLE dbo.IndexIO;

CREATE TABLE dbo.IndexIO
(
RowID int IDENTITY(1,1)
,Name sysname
,JunkValue varchar(2000)
);

INSERT INTO dbo.IndexIO (Name, JunkValue)
SELECT name, REPLICATE('X', 1000)
FROM sys.columns

CREATE CLUSTERED INDEX CLUS_IndexIO ON dbo.IndexIO(RowID);
UPDATE dbo.IndexIO
SET JunkValue = REPLICATE('X', 2000)
WHERE RowID % 5 = 1

SELECT we.name, ps.in_row_reserved_page_count
FROM sys.indexes we
INNER JOIN sys.dm_db_partition_stats ps ON we.object_id = ps.object_id AND
we.index_id = ps.index_id
WHERE we.name = 'CLUS_IndexIO'
```

	name	in_row_reserved_page_count
1	CLUS_IndexIO	585

Figure 11-20. *Fragmentation of CLUS_IndexIO*

Would removing the fragmentation from the index have a noticeable impact on the number of pages in the index? As this demo will demonstrate, reducing fragmentation does have an impact.

The next step in this demonstration is to remove the fragmentation from the index. To accomplish this, execute the ALTER INDEX statement in Listing 11-23, which eliminates the fragmentation. In the rest of the chapter, the mechanics of removing fragmentation from an index will be discussed. The effect of this command is that all the fragmentation has been removed from the index. Figure 11-21 shows the results from Listing 11-23. They show that the number of pages that the index is using dropped from 585 to 417. The effect of removing the fragmentation is an impressive reduction of almost 30 percent in pages in the index.

Listing 11-23. Script to Rebuild an Index to Remove Fragmentation

```
USE AdventureWorks2017
GO

ALTER INDEX CLUS_IndexIO ON dbo.IndexIO REBUILD

SELECT we.name, ps.in_row_reserved_page_count
FROM sys.indexes we
INNER JOIN sys.dm_db_partition_stats ps ON we.object_id = ps.object_id AND
we.index_id = ps.index_id
WHERE we.name = 'CLUS_IndexIO'
```

	name	in_row_reserved_page_count
1	CLUS_IndexIO	417

Figure 11-21. *Page count resulting from rebuild operations*

This proves that fragmentation can influence the number of pages in an index. More pages in an index result in the need to read more pages to get the data that is needed by a query. Reducing the count of pages can help with allowing SQL Server databases to process more data in the same number of reads, hence improving the speed at which they read the same information across fewer pages.

Contiguous Reads

The other negative effect that fragmentation can have on performance relates to contiguous reads. Within SQL Server, contiguous reads affect its ability to utilize read-ahead operations. Read-ahead allows SQL Server to request pages into memory that are expected to be used. Rather than waiting for an I/O request to be generated for the page, SQL Server can read large blocks of pages into memory with the expectation that the data pages will be used by the query in the future.

As previously discussed, fragmentation within an index occurs because of breaks in the continuity of physical data pages in an index. Each time there is a break in the physical pages, I/O operations must change the place in which data is being read from SQL Server. This is how fragmentation creates a hindrance in contiguous reads.

Defragmentation Options

SQL Server offers a number of ways in which fragmentation can be removed or mitigated within an index. Each of the methods has pros and cons associated with using it. In this section, these options will be reviewed alongside the reasons for using each one.

Index Rebuild

The first method for removing fragmentation from an index is to rebuild the index. Rebuilding an index builds a new contiguous copy of the index. When the new index is complete, the existing one is dropped. Index rebuild operations are accomplished through either a CREATE INDEX or ALTER INDEX statement. Typically, indexes with more than 30 percent fragmentation are considered good candidates for index rebuilds. Note that 30 percent and lower levels of fragmentation in most databases will not show as a large negative impact on performance. While fragmentation of 30 percent is a good starting point, each database and index should be reviewed and adjusted if performance shows more negative effects with less than 30 percent fragmentation.

The chief benefit of performing an index rebuild is that the resulting new index has contiguous pages. When an index is highly fragmented, sometimes the best way to resolve the fragmentation is to simply start over with the index and rebuild. Another benefit of rebuilding an index is that the index options can be modified during the rebuild. Lastly, for most indexes, the index can remain online while it is being rebuilt.

> **Note**   Since SQL Server 2012, clustered indexes with varchar(max),
> nvarchar(max), varbinary(max), and XML data types can be rebuilt online.
> Clustered indexes still cannot be rebuilt online when they contain the following
> data types: image, ntext, or text. Online rebuilds are limited to SQL Server
> Enterprise, Developer, and Evaluation Editions. Additionally, online rebuilds require
> double the space for the index since both the old and new versions of the index
> need to exist to complete the rebuild, which can be a problem with larger tables.

The first option for rebuilding an index is to use the CREATE INDEX statement, shown in Listing 11-24. This is accomplished using the DROP_EXISTING index option. There are a few reasons to choose the CREATE INDEX option instead of ALTER INDEX:

- The index definition needs to be changed, such as when the columns need to be added or removed or their order needs to change.

- The index needs to be moved from one filegroup to another.

- The index partitioning needs to be modified.

Listing 11-24. Index Rebuild with CREATE INDEX

```
CREATE [ UNIQUE ] [ CLUSTERED | NONCLUSTERED ] INDEX index_name
    ON <object> ( column [ ASC | DESC ] [ ,...n ] )
    [ INCLUDE ( column_name [ ,...n ] ) ]
    [ WHERE <filter_predicate> ]
    [ WITH ( <relational_index_option> [ ,...n ] ) ]
    [ ON { partition_scheme_name ( column_name )
        | filegroup_name
        | default
        }
    ]
    [ FILESTREAM_ON { filestream_filegroup_name | partition_scheme_name |
    "NULL" } ]
[ ; ]
<relational_index_option> ::=
    DROP_EXISTING = { ON | OFF }
    | ONLINE = { ON | OFF }
```

```
| RESUMABLE = {ON | OF }
| MAX_DURATION = <time> [MINUTES]
```

The other option is the ALTER INDEX statement, shown in Listing 11-25. This option utilizes the REBUILD option in the syntax. Conceptually, this accomplishes the same thing as the CREATE INDEX statement but with the following benefits:

- More than one index on a table can be rebuilt in a single statement.

- A single partition of an index can be rebuilt.

Listing 11-25. Index Rebuild with ALTER INDEX

```
ALTER INDEX { index_name | ALL }
  ON <object>
  { REBUILD
      [ [PARTITION = ALL]
        [ WITH ( <rebuild_index_option> [ ,...n ] ) ]
        | [ PARTITION = partition_number
            [ WITH ( <single_partition_rebuild_index_option>
                    [ ,...n ] )
            ]
        ]
      ]
  ]
```

The primary downside to index rebuilds is the amount of space that is required for the index during the rebuild operation. At a minimum, there should be 120 percent of the size of the current index available within the database for the rebuilt index. The reason for this is that the current index will not be dropped until after the rebuild is completed. For a short time, the index will exist twice in the database.

There are two ways to mitigate some of the space required for an index during a rebuild. First, the SORT_IN_TEMPDB index option can be used to reduce the amount of space needed for intermediate results. Space will still be needed in the database for two copies of the index, but the 20 percent buffer won't be necessary. The second way to mitigate space needs is to disable the index prior to the rebuild. Disabling an index drops the index and data pages from an index while retaining the index metadata. This will allow a rebuild of the index in the space that the index previously occupied. Be aware that the disabling option applies only to non-clustered indexes.

An option starting with SQL Server 2019 is the ability to resume index builds. When an index is being built online, the RESUMABLE option can be set to ON and the MAX_DURATION to the number of minutes the index build will run until it should stop. When the index rebuild stops, the old index remains available, and the completed portion of the rebuild is stored until the time when it is restarted. Additionally, if an index rebuild fails with the RESUMABLE option set to ON, this will allow the index rebuild to be restarted. This can be extremely useful if the transaction log runs out of space or the index rebuild is interrupted by maintenance or a service restart.

Always consider the size of an index prior to issuing a rebuild command as a larger index will require more time and resources to rebuild. Also determine if an index is naturally write-heavy and is destined to be fragmented heavily, regardless of how much maintenance is run against it. Queues, session data, or intermediary data storage tables will often be heavily fragmented due to frequent write operations. If these tables are limited in size, then rebuilds against them will provide little to no benefit. Tables that are identified as fitting this usage pattern may be excluded from index rebuild processes and conserve maintenance resources for other tables that would benefit more from a rebuild operation.

Index Reorganization

An alternative to an index rebuild is to reorganize an index. This type of defragmentation happens just as it sounds. Data pages in the index are reordered across the pages already allocated to the index. After the reorganization is complete, the physical order of pages in an index matches the logical order of pages. Indexes should be reorganized when they are not heavily fragmented. In general, indexes fragmented less than 30 percent are reorganization candidates. Like all best practices, 30 percent is a guideline that provides a solid starting point for maintenance. Real-world use cases will exist that require tweaking of this guideline based on the type of table, its usage, and size.

To reorganize an index, the ALTER INDEX syntax is used (see Listing 11-26) with the REORGANIZE option. The reorganization option allows for a single partition to be reorganized at a time, if needed.

Listing 11-26. Index Reorganization with ALTER INDEX

```
ALTER INDEX { index_name | ALL }
    ON <object>
    | REORGANIZE
        [ PARTITION =partition_number ]
        [ WITH ( LOB_COMPACTION = { ON | OFF } ) ]
```

There are a couple of benefits to using the REORGANIZE option. First, indexes are online or available for use by the optimizer in a new execution plan or in cached execution plans for the duration of the reorganization. Second, the process is designed around minimal resource usage, which significantly lowers the chance that locking and blocking issues will occur during the transaction.

The downside to index reorganizations is that the reorganization uses only the data pages already allocated to the index. With fragmentation, the extents allocated to one index can often be intertwined with the extents allocated to other indexes. Reordering the data pages won't make the data pages any more contiguous than they currently are, but it will make certain that the pages allocated are sorted in the same order as the data itself.

Drop and Create

The third way to defragment an index is to simply drop the index and recreate it. This option is included for completeness, but note that it is not widely practiced or advised. There are a few reasons that illustrate why dropping and creating an index can be a bad idea.

If the index is a clustered index, then all other indexes will need to be rebuilt when the clustered index is dropped. Clustered indexes and heaps use different structures for identifying rows and storing data. The non-clustered indexes on the table will need information on where the record is and will need to be recreated to obtain this information.

If the index is a primary key or unique, there are likely other dependencies on the index. For instance, the index may be referenced in a foreign key. The index could be tied to a business rule, such as uniqueness, that cannot be removed from the table, even in a maintenance window.

The third reason to avoid this method is that it requires knowledge of all properties on an index. With the other strategies, the index retains all the existing index properties. By having to recreate the index, there is a risk that a property may not be retained in the DDL for the index and important aspects of an index could be lost.

After an index is dropped from that table, it cannot be used. This should be an obvious issue, but it is often overlooked when considering this option. The purpose of an index is usually the performance improvements that it brings; removing it from the table takes those improvements along with it.

Defragmentation Strategies

This chapter has thus far been about how fragmentation occurs, why it is an issue, and how it can be removed from indexes. It is important to apply this knowledge to the indexes in any given database. In this section, two methods for defragmentation of indexes will be provided.

Maintenance Plans

The first automation option available is defragmentation through maintenance plans, which offer the opportunity to quickly create and schedule maintenance for indexes that will either be reorganized or rebuilt. For each of the types of index defragmentation, there is a task available in the maintenance plans.

There are a couple of ways in which maintenance plans can be created. For the purposes of brevity, it will be assumed that the user is familiar with maintenance plans in SQL Server, and thus this section will focus on the specific tasks related to defragmenting indexes.

Reorganize Index Task

The first task available is the Reorganize Index Task. This task provides a wrapper for the `ALTER INDEX REORGANIZE` syntax from the previous section. Once configured, this task will reorganize all indexes that match the criteria for the task.

There are a few properties that need to be configured when using the Reorganize Index Task (see Figure 11-22):

- *Connection*: The SQL Server instance the task will connect to when it executes.

- *Database(s)*: The databases the task will connect to for reorganizing. The options for this property are

  - All databases.

  - All system databases.

  - All user databases.

  - These specific databases (a list of available databases is included, and one must be selected).

  - Ignore databases where the state is not online.

- *Object*: Determines whether the reorganization will be against tables, views, or tables and views.

- *Selection*: Specifies the tables or indexes affected by this task. This is not available when Tables and Views is selected in the Object box.

- *Compact large objects*: Determines whether the reorganization uses the option `ALTER INDEX LOB_COMPACTION = ON`.

- *Scan type*: Indicates how you want SQL Server to gather the statistics for the remaining options. The available options are Fast, Sampled, or Detailed.

- *Optimize index only if*: Provides ability to limit reorganization by percent fragmentation, page count, and whether the index was used in the last 7 days.

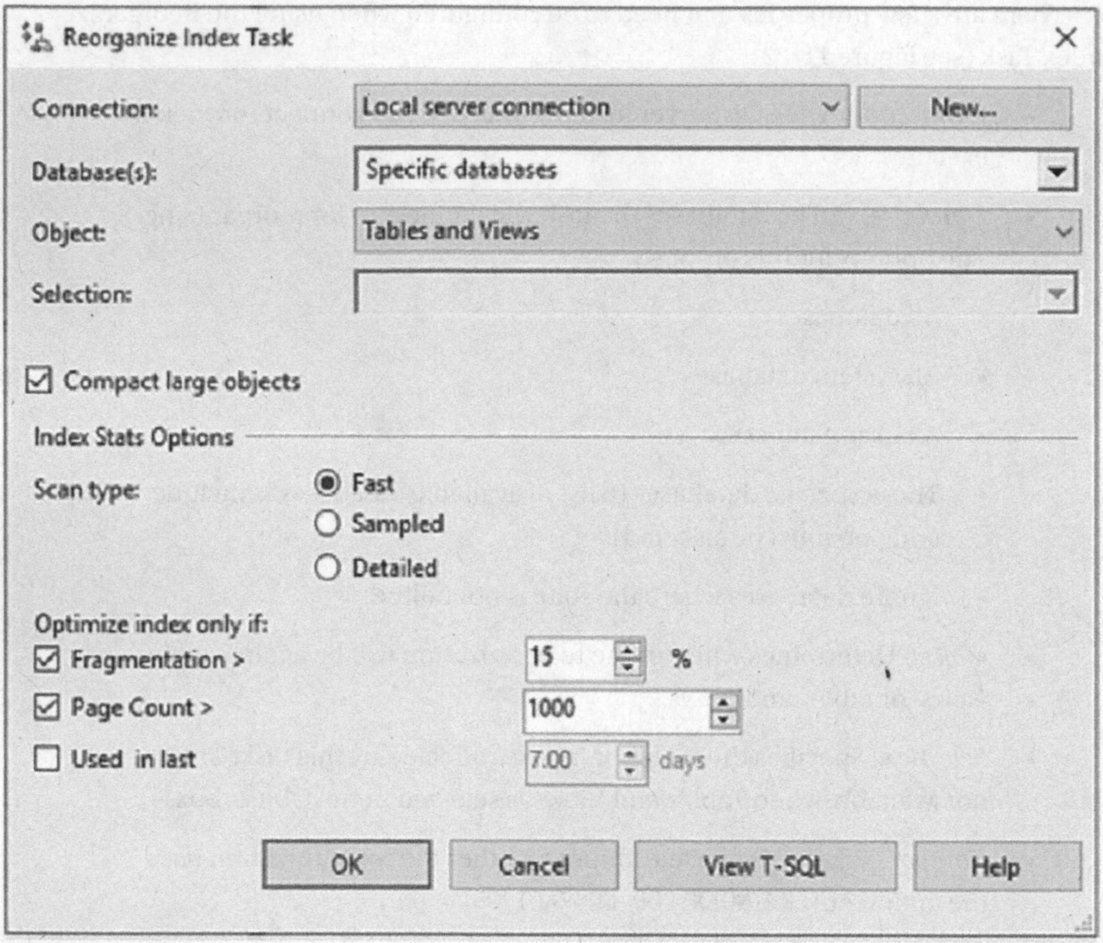

Figure 11-22. Properties window for Reorganize Index Task

The index stats options were introduced in SQL Server 2016 and are a helpful addition to this feature. In environments that do not have database administrators actively managing the indexes within a server, this is a great option for ensuring indexes are being maintained.

Rebuild Index Task

The other task available is the Rebuild Index Task. This provides a wrapper for the ALTER INDEX REBUILD syntax. Once configured, this task rebuilds all indexes that match the criteria for the task.

Similar to the Reorganize Index Task, the Rebuild Index Task has a number of properties that need to be configured before using it (see Figure 11-23):

- *Connection*: The SQL Server instance the task will connect to when it executes.

- *Database(s)*: The databases the task will connect to for rebuilding. The options for this property are

  - All databases.

  - All system databases.

  - All user databases.

  - These specific databases (a list of available databases is included, and one must be selected).

  - Ignore databases where the state is not online.

- *Object*: Determines whether the rebuild will be against tables, views, or tables and views.

- *Selection*: Specifies the tables or indexes affected by this task. This is not available when Tables and Views is selected in the Object box.

- *Default free space per page*: Specifies whether the rebuild should use the current fill factor on the index.

- *Change free space per page to*: Allows the rebuild to specify a new fill factor when the index is rebuilt.

- *Sort results in tempdb*: Determines whether the rebuild uses the option `ALTER INDEX SORT_IN_TEMPDB = ON`.

- *MAXDOP*: Determines the max degree of parallelism for the rebuild, which determines the max number of CPU threads SQL Server can use to rebuild the index.

- *Keep index online while re-indexing*: Determines whether the rebuild uses the option ALTER INDEX ONLINE = ON. For indexes that cannot be rebuilt online, there is an option to determine whether to skip or rebuild the index offline. Along with that, you can set Low Priority Used to determine if blocking will cancel an index rebuild and whether it cancels itself or blockers and after how much time.

- *Scan type*: Indicates how you want SQL Server to gather the statistics for the remaining options. The available options are Fast, Sampled, or Detailed.

- *Optimize index only if*: Provides ability to limit rebuild by percent fragmentation, page count, and whether the index was used in the last 7 days.

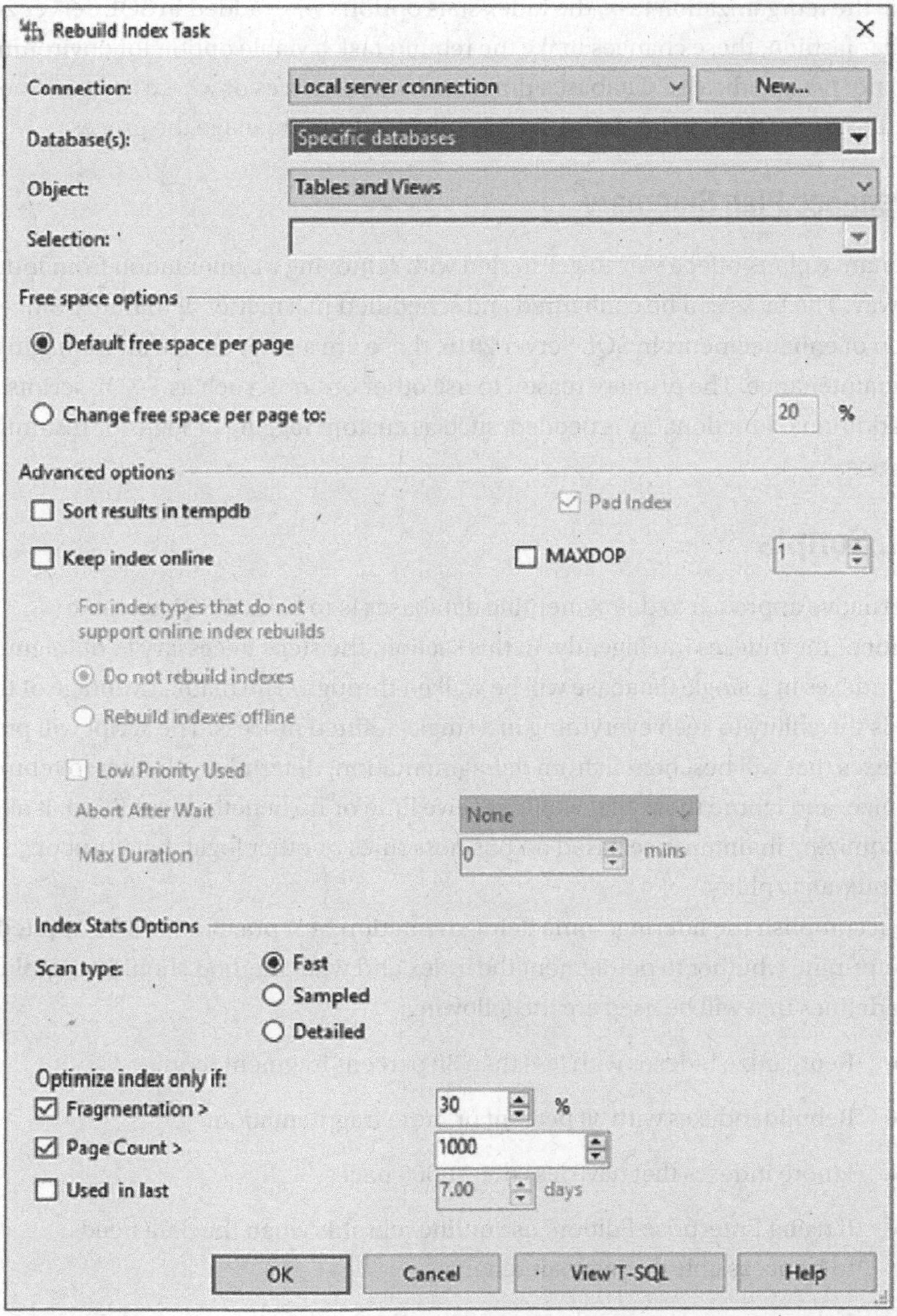

Figure 11-23. *Properties window for Rebuild Index Task*

Like the reorganization task, the index stats options were added in SQL Server 2016. In similar fashion, these changes make the rebuild task a viable option for environments that do not have dedicated database administration resources or where there is a need to keep index maintenance simple and avoid custom code to manage the process.

Maintenance Plan Summary

Maintenance plans offer a way to get started with removing fragmentation from indexes right away. The tasks can be configured and scheduled in a matter of minutes. Since the addition of enhancements in SQL Server 2016, these are a great choice for managing index maintenance. The primary reason to use other options, such as T-SQL scripts, is when additional functionality is needed, such as custom logging or logic for resuming operations.

T-SQL Scripts

An alternative approach to defragmenting databases is to use a T-SQL script to defragment the indexes intelligently. In this section, the steps necessary to defragment all the indexes in a single database will be walked through. The main advantage of this choice is the ability to keep everything in a single, refined process. The script will pick the indexes that will best benefit from defragmentation, determine whether to rebuild or reorganize, and ignore those that would receive little or no benefit. In addition, it allows for customizing maintenance based on business rules or other logic that is out of scope for maintenance plans.

To accomplish the filtering, some defragmentation best practices will be applied that help determine whether to defragment the index and what method should be applied. The guidelines that will be used are the following:

- Reorganize indexes with less than 30 percent fragmentation.

- Rebuild indexes with 30 percent or more fragmentation.

- Ignore indexes that have less than 1,000 pages.

- If using Enterprise Edition, use online rebuilds when the data needs to be accessible during maintenance.

- If the clustered index is being rebuilt, rebuild all indexes in the table.

Note   Just because an index is fragmented does not mean that it should always be defragmented. When dealing with indexes for small tables, there isn't a lot of benefit in defragmenting the index. For instance, an index having fewer than eight pages will fit into one extent, and thus there is no benefit in terms of reduced I/O from defragmenting that index. Some Microsoft documentation and SQL Server experts recommend not defragmenting tables with fewer than 1,000 pages. Whether that value is appropriate for your database is dependent on your database, but it is a starting point for building index maintenance strategies.

There are a few steps that a defragmentation script will perform to intelligently defragment the indexes:

1. Collect fragmentation data.

2. Determine what indexes to defragment.

3. Build the defragmentation statement.

Before starting on the fragmentation steps, a template is needed for the index maintenance script. The template, shown in Listing 11-27, declares several variables and utilizes a CURSOR to loop through each of the indexes and perform the necessary index maintenance. The variables are set at the DECLARE statement with the thresholds defined at the start of this section. Also in the template is a table variable that is used to store intermediate results on the state of fragmentation in the database.

Listing 11-27. Index Defragmentation Script Template

```
DECLARE @MaxFragmentation TINYINT=30
,@MinimumPages SMALLINT=1000
,@SQL nvarchar(max)
,@ObjectName NVARCHAR(300)
,@IndexName NVARCHAR(300)
,@CurrentFragmentation DECIMAL(9, 6)

DECLARE @FragmentationState TABLE
(
SchemaName SYSNAME
,TableName SYSNAME
```

```
,object_id INT
,IndexName SYSNAME
,index_id INT
,page_count BIGINT
,avg_fragmentation_in_percent FLOAT
,avg_page_space_used_in_percent FLOAT
,type_desc VARCHAR(255)
)
INSERT INTO @FragmentationState
<Script to Collect Fragmenation Data (Listing 9-28)>

DECLARE INDEX_CURSE CURSOR LOCAL FAST_FORWARD FOR
<Script to Identify Fragmented Indexes (Listing 9-29)>
OPEN INDEX_CURSE
WHILE 1=1
BEGIN
    FETCH NEXT FROM INDEX_CURSE INTO @ObjectName, @IndexName
        ,@CurrentFragmentation
    IF @@FETCH_STATUS <> 0
        BREAK
<Script to Build Index Defragmentation Statements(Listing 9-30)>
    EXEC sp_ExecuteSQL @SQL
 END

CLOSE INDEX_CURSE
DEALLOCATE INDEX_CURSE
```

To get started, fragmentation data needs to be collected about the indexes and populated into the `table` variable. In the script in Listing 11-28, the DMF `sys.dm_db_index_physical_stats` is used with the SAMPLED option. This option is used to minimize the impact that executing the DMF will have on the database. Included in the results are the schema, table, and index names to identify the index that is being reported on, along with the `object_id` and `index_id`. Statistical columns on the index fragmentation from the DMF are included in the columns `page_count`, `avg_fragmentation_in_percent`, and `avg_page_space_used_in_percent`. The last column in the results is `has_LOB_column`. This column is the result of a correlated subquery that determines whether any of the columns in the index are LOB types, which disallow online index rebuilds.

Listing 11-28. Script to Collect Fragmentation Data

```
SELECT
    s.name as SchemaName
    ,t.name as TableName
    ,t.object_id
    ,we.name as IndexName
    ,we.index_id
    ,x.page_count
    ,x.avg_fragmentation_in_percent
    ,x.avg_page_space_used_in_percent
    ,we.type_desc
FROM sys.dm_db_index_physical_stats(db_id(), NULL, NULL, NULL, 'SAMPLED') x
    INNER JOIN sys.tables t ON x.object_id = t.object_id
    INNER JOIN sys.schemas s ON t.schema_id = s.schema_id
    INNER JOIN sys.indexes we ON x.object_id = we.object_id AND x.index_id
    = we.index_id
WHERE x.index_id > 0
AND x.avg_fragmentation_in_percent > 0
AND alloc_unit_type_desc = 'IN_ROW_DATA'
```

The results of the query in Listing 11-28 will vary for every reader. In general,
the results should be similar to those in Figure 11-24, which include clustered, non-
clustered, and XML indexes from the AdventureWorks2017 database.

	SchemaName	TableName	object_id	IndexName	index_id	page_count	avg_fragmentation_in_percent	avg_page_space_used_in_percent	type_desc
1	HumanResources	EmployeePayHistory	2099048	PK_EmployeePayHistory_BusinessEntityID_RateChange...	1	2	50	74.1536940943909	CLUSTERED
2	Sales	SalesOrderHeaderSalesReason	30623152	PK_SalesOrderHeaderSalesReason_SalesOrderID_Sales...	1	86	0	90.2700642451198	CLUSTERED
3	Sales	SalesPerson	62623266	PK_SalesPerson_BusinessEntityID	1	1	0	16.3577950981962	CLUSTERED
4	Sales	SalesPerson	62623266	AK_SalesPerson_rowguid	2	1	0	5.43612552508031	NONCLUSTERED
5	Production	Illustration	66099276	PK_Illustration_IllustrationID	1	1	0	4.78131949592291	CLUSTERED

Figure 11-24. *Query results for table fragmentation data*

The next step in the defragmentation script is to build the list of indexes that
need to be defragmented. The list of indexes, created through Listing 11-29, is used
to populate the cursor. The cursor then loops through each of the indexes to perform
the defragmentation. One point of interest in the script is that for clustered indexes,
all underlying indexes will be rebuilt. This is not a requirement when defragmenting
indexes, but it is an option that should be considered. When there are only a few indexes

on a table, this may be a worthwhile way to manage them. As the count of indexes increases, this may become less appealing. The results from this query should look similar to those in Figure 11-25.

Listing 11-29. Script to Identify Fragmented Indexes

```
SELECT  QUOTENAME(x.SchemaName)+'.'+QUOTENAME(x.TableName)
    ,CASE WHEN x.type_desc = 'CLUSTERED' THEN 'ALL'
        ELSE QUOTENAME(x.IndexName) END
    ,x.avg_fragmentation_in_percent
FROM    @FragmentationState x
LEFT OUTER JOIN @FragmentationState y ON x.object_id = y.object_id AND
y.index_id = 1
WHERE   (
        x.type_desc = 'CLUSTERED'
        AND y.type_desc = 'CLUSTERED'
        )
        OR y.index_id IS NULL
ORDER BY x.object_id
        ,x.index_id
```

	(No column name)	(No column name)	avg_fragmentation_in_percent
1	[HumanResources].[EmployeePayHistory]	ALL	50
2	[HumanResources].[JobCandidate]	ALL	9.09090909090909
3	[dbo].[AllocationCycle]	ALL	30.8965377195654
4	[dbo].[PageCompression]	ALL	2
5	[Sales].[SalesPersonQuotaHistory]	ALL	50
6	[dbo].[LOBAccess]	ALL	25
7	[Person].[Person]	ALL	2.10498960498961

Figure 11-25. *Indexes for rebuild/reorganize operations*

The last part of the template is where the magic happens. The script in Listing 11-30 is used to construct the ALTER INDEX statement that is used to defragment the index. At this point, the level of fragmentation is checked to determine whether to issue a REBUILD or REORGANIZATION. For indexes that can support ONLINE index rebuilds, a CASE statement adds the appropriate syntax.

Listing 11-30. Script to Build Index Defragmentation Statements

```
SET @SQL = CONCAT('ALTER INDEX ', @IndexName,' ON ',@ObjectName,
  CASE WHEN @CurrentFragmentation <= 30 THEN ' REORGANIZE;'
  ELSE ' REBUILD' END,
  CASE WHEN CONVERT(VARCHAR(100), SERVERPROPERTY('Edition')) LIKE
  'Enterprise%'
  OR CONVERT(VARCHAR(100), SERVERPROPERTY('Edition')) LIKE 'Developer%'
  THEN ' WITH (ONLINE=ON, SORT_IN_TEMPDB=ON) ' END, ';');
```

Note   One of the improvements in SQL Server 2017 Enterprise Edition is the ability to perform online index rebuilds when the index contains columns with large object (LOB) data types.

Combining all of these pieces into the template from the beginning of this section to create an index defragmentation script provides similar functionality to that of the maintenance plan tasks. With the ability to set the size and fragmentation levels in which the defragmentation occurs, this script removes the fragmentation from indexes that really need the work done on them vs. defragmenting every index in the database. Using Extended Events on AdventureWorks2017 to trace the output of the script reveals that the ALTER INDEX syntax for the results of the previous queries is similar to that in Listing 11-31.

Listing 11-31. Index Defragmentation Statements

```
ALTER INDEX ALL ON [HumanResources].[EmployeePayHistory] REBUILD WITH
(ONLINE=ON, SORT_IN_TEMPDB=ON) ;
ALTER INDEX ALL ON [HumanResources].[JobCandidate] REORGANIZE; WITH
(ONLINE=ON, SORT_IN_TEMPDB=ON) ;
ALTER INDEX ALL ON [dbo].[AllocationCycle] REBUILD WITH (ONLINE=ON,
SORT_IN_TEMPDB=ON) ;
ALTER INDEX ALL ON [dbo].[PageCompression] REORGANIZE; WITH (ONLINE=ON,
SORT_IN_TEMPDB=ON) ;
ALTER INDEX ALL ON [Sales].[SalesPersonQuotaHistory] REBUILD WITH
(ONLINE=ON, SORT_IN_TEMPDB=ON) ;
```

As the code in this section demonstrated, using a T-SQL script can be much more complicated than using the maintenance plan tasks. The upside to the complexity is that once the script is complete, it can be wrapped in a stored procedure and used on any SQL Server instances. This script is meant as a first step in automating defragmentation with T-SQL scripts. It does not account for partitioned tables and does not check to see whether the index is being used before rebuilding or reorganizing the index. On the upside, rather than driving a truck through a set of databases and re-indexing everything, a scripted solution can intelligently decide how and when to defragment your indexes.

In addition, a custom T-SQL solution can allow for databases, tables, or indexes to be maintained or ignored on a customized basis. This is helpful when an administrator has intimate knowledge of how an application works and knows which indexes require special maintenance (or none).

Note   For a complete index defragmentation solution, check out Ola Hallengren's index maintenance scripts at `https://ola.hallengren.com`.

Preventing Fragmentation

Fragmentation within an index is not always a foregone conclusion. There are some methods that can be utilized to mitigate the rate at which fragmentation occurs. When there are indexes that are often affected by fragmentation, it is advisable to investigate why the fragmentation is occurring.

It is possible that this research may uncover application, server, or maintenance issues that can be solved via other means unrelated to index maintenance. For this reason, understanding how an application and its infrastructure operate can provide valuable insight into suboptimal query or usage patterns. For example, an application may be updating a table far more often than it needs to. These updates could manifest as unexpected fragmentation. For a problem such as this, resolving the application bug would also reduce fragmentation without the need to implement any additional indexing or maintenance options.

There are a few strategies that can help mitigate fragmentation; these are fill factor, data typing, and default values.

Fill Factor

Fill factor is an option that can be used when building or rebuilding indexes. This property is used to determine how much space per page should be left available in the index when it is first created or the next time it is rebuilt. For example, with a fill factor of 75, about 25 percent of every data page is left empty.

If an index encounters a significant or frequent amount of fragmentation, it is worthwhile to adjust the fill factor to mitigate the fragmentation. By doing this, the activities that are causing fragmentation should be less impactful, which should reduce the frequency that the index needs to be defragmented.

By default, SQL Server creates all indexes with a fill factor of 0. This is a recommended value for both the server and database levels. Not all indexes are created equal, and fill factor should be applied as it is needed, not as a blanket insurance policy. Also, a fill factor of 0 is the same as a fill factor of 100.

The one downside of fill factor is that leaving space available in data pages means that the index will require more data pages for all the records in the index. More pages mean more storage is used, more I/O, and possibly less utilization of the index if there are alternate indexes to select from.

Data Typing

Another way to avoid fragmentation is through appropriate data typing. This strategy applies to data types that can change length depending on the data that they contain. These are data types such as VARCHAR and NVARCHAR, which have lengths that can change over time.

In many cases, variable-length data types are a great fit for columns in a table. Issues arise when the volatility of the data is high and the length of the data is volatile as well. As the data changes length, there can be page splits, which lead to fragmentation. If the length volatility occurs across significant portions of the index, then there may also be significant numbers of page splits and thus fragmentation.

A great example of bad data typing comes from my experience with the first data warehouse that I worked with. The original design for many of the tables included a column with a data type of VARCHAR(10). The column was populated with dates in the format of yyyymmdd, with values similar to 20191011. As part of the import process, the date values were updated into a format of yyyy-mm-dd. When the import was moved to production and millions of rows were being processed at a time, the increase in the length of the column from eight to ten characters led to an astounding level of fragmentation because of page splits. Resolving the problem was as simple as changing the data type of the column from VARCHAR(10) to CHAR(10).

Such simple solutions can apply to many databases. It requires a bit of investigation into why the fragmentation is occurring, but by tracking write operations step-by-step, it is possible to establish when fragmentation occurs and be able to formulate a response to it.

Default Values

The proper application of default values may not seem to be something that can assist in preventing fragmentation, but there are some scenarios in which it can have a significant effect on fragmentation. The poster child for this type of mitigation is when databases utilize the uniqueidentifier data type.

In most cases, uniqueidentifier values are generated using the NEWID() function. This function creates a globally unique identifier (GUID) that should be unique across the entire planet. This is useful for generating unique identifiers for rows but is likely scoped larger than that of your database. In many cases, the unique value probably needs to be unique for the server or the table.

The main problem with the NEWID() function is that generating the GUID is not a sequential process. As demonstrated at the beginning of the chapter, using this function to generate values for the clustered index key can lead to severe levels of fragmentation.

An alternative to the NEWID() function is the NEWSEQUENTIALID() function. This function returns a GUID just like the other function but with a couple variations on how the values are generated. First, each GUID generated by the function on a server is sequential to the last value. The second variation is that the GUID value generated is unique only to the server that is generating it. If another SQL Server instance generates a GUID with this function for the same table, it is possible that duplicate values will be generated, and the values will not be sequential since these are scoped to the server level.

With these restrictions in mind, if a table must use the uniqueidentifier data type, the NEWSEQUENTIALID() function is an excellent alternative to the NEWID() function. The values will be sequential, and the amount of fragmentation encountered will be much lower and less frequent.

Index Statistics Maintenance

In Chapter 3, the statistics collected on indexes were discussed. These statistics provide crucial information that the query optimizer uses to compile execution plans for queries. When this information is out of date or inaccurate, the database will provide suboptimal or inaccurate query plans.

For the most part, index statistics do not require significant maintenance. In this section, the processes within SQL Server that can be used to create and update statistics will be reviewed. Maintaining statistics in situations where the automated processes cannot keep up with the rate of data change within an index will also be discussed.

It is important to note that statistics in SQL Server are estimates of the cardinality and frequency of values found in a table. They are not maintained real-time as to do so would be prohibitively expensive.

Automatically Maintaining Statistics

The easiest way to build and maintain statistics in SQL Server is to let SQL Server do it automatically. There are three database properties that control whether SQL Server will automatically build and maintain statistics:

- AUTO_CREATE_STATISTICS
- AUTO_UPDATE_STATISTICS
- AUTO_UPDATE_STATISTICS_ASYNC

By default, the first two properties are enabled in databases. The last option is disabled by default. In most scenarios, all three of these properties should be enabled.

Automatic Creation

The first database property is AUTO_CREATE_STATISTICS. This database property directs SQL Server to automatically create single-column statistics on columns that do not have statistics. From the perspective of indexes, this property does not have an impact. When an index is created, a statistics object is created for the index.

Automatic Updating

The next two properties are AUTO_UPDATE_STATISTICS and AUTO_UPDATE_STATISTICS_ ASYNC. At a high level, these two properties are quite similar. When an internal threshold is surpassed, SQL Server will initiate an update of the statistics object. The update occurs to keep the values within the statistics object current with the cardinality of values within the table.

The threshold for triggering a statistics update can change from table to table. The threshold is based on a couple of calculations relating to the number of rows that have changed. For an empty table, when more than 500 rows are added to the table, a statistics update will be triggered. If the table has more than 500 rows, then statistics will be updated when 500 rows plus at most 20 percent of the cardinality of rows have been modified. At this point, SQL Server will schedule an update to the statistics. As the number of rows in the table increases, then the 20 percent threshold decreases, which accommodates the need to update statistics more frequently when there are larger numbers of rows within a table. At about 500,000 rows, the percentage drops to about 5 percent and then less than 1 percent for over 1 billion rows. This is the behavior that was previously available through trace flag 2371, which is on by default since SQL Server 2016.

When the statistics update occurs, there are two modes in which it can be accomplished: synchronously and asynchronously. By default, statistics update synchronously. This means that when statistics are deemed out of date and require an update, the query optimizer will wait until after the statistics have been updated before it will compile an execution plan for the query. This is extremely useful for tables that have data that is volatile. For instance, the statistics for a table before and after a TRUNCATE TABLE would be quite different. Optionally, statistics can be built asynchronously through enabling the AUTO_UPDATE_STATISTICS_ASYNC property. This changes how the query optimizer reacts when an update statistics event is triggered. Instead of waiting for the statistics update to complete, the query optimizer will compile an execution plan based on the existing statistics and use the updated statistics for future queries after the update is completed. For databases with high volumes of queries and data being pushed through, this is often the preferred manner of updating statistics. Instead of occasional pauses in transactional throughput, the queries will flow through unencumbered, and plans will update as improved information is available.

For an environment where AUTO_UPDATE_STATISTICS had been disabled in previous SQL Server versions, it would be worthwhile to consider enabling it now with AUTO_UPDATE_ STATISTICS_ASYNC. The most common reason to disable AUTO_UPDATE_STATISTICS in the past was the delay caused by the update of statistics. With the option to enable AUTO_UPDATE_STATISTICS_ASYNC, those performance concerns can likely be mitigated. Automatic updating of statistics should not be disabled without a compelling use case to thoroughly justify that decision.

Preventing Auto-update

Depending on the indexes on a table, there will be times in which automatically updating the indexes will do more harm than good. For instance, an automatic statistics update on a large table may lead to performance issues while the statistics object is updated. In that situation, the existing statistics object may be good enough until the next maintenance window. Similarly, a table that is subject to heavy data updates via controlled data load processes may be better off having statistics updated at the end of the data load process, rather than automatically.

There are a number of ways in which AUTO_UPDATE_STATISTICS can be disabled on an individual statistics object rather than across the entire database:

- Executing an sp_autostats system store procedure on the statistics object

- Using the NORECOMPUTE option on the UPDATE STATISTICS or CREATE STATISTICS statement

- Using STATISTICS_NORECOMPUTE on the CREATE INDEX statement

Each of these options can be used to disable or enable the AUTO_UPDATE_STATISTICS option on indexes. Before disabling this feature, always be sure to validate that the statistics update is truly necessary.

Memory-Optimized Table Statistics

When considering statistics, one area where statistics are created and used a bit differently is with memory-optimized tables. It's important to understand that statistics cannot be generated automatically on memory-optimized tables and that they always require a full scan. In addition, natively compiled stored procedures on memory-optimized tables retrieve statistics only when the stored procedure is compiled or when SQL Server restarts. This means that when considering the impact of statistics on indexes, memory-optimized tables require additional care in timing the maintenance for statistics objects.

Manually Maintaining Statistics

There will be times when the automated processes for maintaining statistics will not be good enough. This is often tied to situations where the data is changing but not enough has changed to trigger a statistics update. One example of when this can happen is when update statements change the cardinality of the table without affecting a large number of rows. For instance, if 10 percent of a table was changed from many values to a single value, then the plan for querying the data could end up being suboptimal. In situations like this, there is value in being able to manually update statistics. As with index fragmentation, there are two methods for manually maintaining statistics:

- Maintenance plans

- T-SQL scripts

In the next sections, each of these methods will be explained alongside walkthroughs of how they can be implemented.

Maintenance Plans

Within maintenance plans, there is a task that allows statistics maintenance: the Update Statistics Task. When using this task, there are a number of properties that can be configured to control its behavior (see Figure 11-26):

- *Connection*: The SQL Server instance the task will connect to when it executes.

- *Database(s)*: The databases that the task will connect to for maintenance processes. The options for this property are

  - All databases.

  - All system databases.

  - All user databases.

  - These specific databases (a list of available databases is included, and one must be selected).

  - Ignore databases where the state is not online.

- *Object*: Determines whether the rebuild will be against tables, views, or tables and views.

318

- *Selection*: Specifies the tables or indexes affected by this task. This is not available when Tables and Views is selected in the Object box.

- *Update*: For each table, determines whether all existing statistics, column statistics only (using the WITH COLUMN clause), or index statistics only (using the WITH INDEX clause) are updated.

- *Scan type*: A choice between a full scan of all leaf-level pages of the indexes and "Sample by," which will scan a percentage or number of rows to build the statistics object.

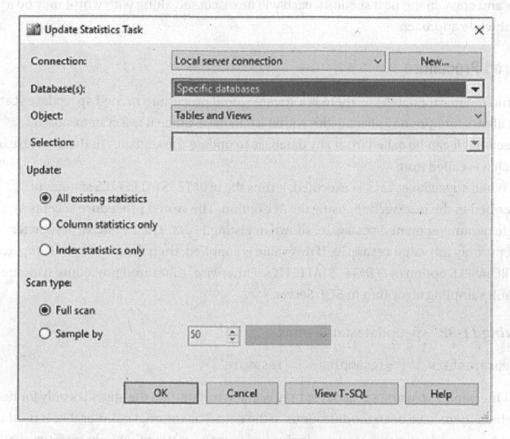

Figure 11-26. *Properties window for Update Statistics Task*

Unlike the maintenance plans previously discussed, the Update Statistics Task doesn't have deeper controls to help determine whether the statistics should be updated. A useful option would be to limit the statistics updates to a specified date range, which would reduce the number of statistics updated during each execution. For the most part, the lack of that option is not problematic. Statistics updates are not like indexes where each update requires enough space to rebuild the entire index. However, it would be good to be able to retain the current sample scan type since that can influence performance and may not result in desired performance with a one-size-fits-all approach.

T-SQL Scripts

Through T-SQL, there are a couple of alternative approaches for updating statistics: using a stored procedure or using DDL statements. Each of these approaches has pros and cons. In the next sections, each will be discussed along with why it may be a worthwhile approach.

Stored Procedure

Within the master database, there is a system stored procedure named `sp_updatestats` that allows for updating all statistics within a database. Since it is a system stored procedure, it can be called from any database to update the statistics in the database in which it is called from.

When `sp_updatestats` is executed, it runs the `UPDATE STATISTICS` statement, described in the next section, using the `ALL` option. The stored procedure accepts a single parameter named `resample`, shown in Listing 11-32. The `resample` parameter accepts only the value `resample`. If this value is supplied, then the stored procedure uses the `RESAMPLE` option of `UPDATE STATISTICS`. Otherwise, the stored procedure uses the default sampling algorithm in SQL Server.

Listing 11-32. sp_updatestats Syntax

```
sp_updatestats [ [ @resample = ] 'resample']
```

One benefit to using `sp_updatestats` is that it will update the statistics only for items in which there have been modifications to the data. The internal counter that is used to trigger automatic statistics updates is checked to make certain that only statistics that have been changed will be updated. Additionally, the resample option uses the most recently used sample rate for the statistics.

In situations where a statistics update is needed, the `sp_updatestats` is a great tool for updating statistics on just those that have the potential for being out of date since the last update. Where the Update Statistics Task is an oversized blanket that smothers the entire database, `sp_updatestats` is a comforter that covers just the right places.

DDL Command

The other option for updating statistics is through the DDL command UPDATE STATISTICS, shown in Listing 11-33. The UPDATE STATISTICS statement allows for finely tuned statistics updates on a per-statistics basis with a number of options for how to collect and build statistics information.

Listing 11-33. UPDATE STATISTICS Syntax

```
UPDATE STATISTICS table_or_indexed_view_name
    [
        {
            { index_or_statistics_name }
          | ( { index_or_statistics_name } [ ,...n ] )
            }
    ]
    [   WITH
        [
        FULLSCAN
          [ [ , ] PERSIST_SAMPLE_PERCENT = { ON | OFF } ]
        | SAMPLE number { PERCENT | ROWS }
          [ [ , ] PERSIST_SAMPLE_PERCENT = { ON | OFF } ]
        | RESAMPLE
          [ ON PARTITIONS ( { <partition_number> | <range> } [, ...n] ) ] ]
          [ [ , ] [ ALL | COLUMNS | INDEX ]
          [ [ , ] NORECOMPUTE ]
          [ [ , ] INCREMENTAL = { ON | OFF } ]
          [ [ , ] MAXDOP = max_degree_of_parallelism ]
    ] ;
```

The first parameter to set when using UPDATE STATISTICS is *table_or_indexed_ view_name*. This parameter references the table in which the statistics will be updated. With the UPDATE STATISTICS command, only one table or view can have its statistics updated at a time.

The next parameter is *index_or_statistics_name*. This parameter is used to determine whether a single statistic, list of statistics, or all statistics on a table will be updated. To update a single statistic, include the name of the statistics object after the name of the table or view. For a list of statistics objects, the names of the statistics are included in a comma-separated list within parentheses. If no statistics are named, then all statistics will be considered for updating.

After the parameters are set, the applicable options need to be added to the UPDATE STATISTICS command. This is where the power and flexibility of this syntax really shines. These parameters allow statistics to be finely tuned to the data available in them to get the right statistics for the right table and the right index:

- FULLSCAN: When the statistics object is built, all rows and pages in the table or view are scanned. For large tables, this will have an impact on performance while creating the statistics object. This is the same as performing a SAMPLE 100 PERCENT operation.

- SAMPLE: The statistics object is created using either a count or a percentage sample of the rows in the table or view. When the sample rate is not selected, SQL Server will determine an appropriate sample rate based on the number of rows in the table.

- RESAMPLE: Updates the statistics using the sample rate from the last time that the statistics were updated. For instance, if that last update used a FULLSCAN, then a RESAMPLE will result in a FULLSCAN as well.

- PERSIST_SAMPLE_PERCENT: Determines whether the defined sample rate should be persisted into the statistics as their future default value for when default values are not specified.

- ALL | COLUMNS | INDEX: Determines whether column statistics, index statistics, or both should be updated.

- NORECOMPUTE: Disables the option for the query optimizer to request an automatic update to the statistics. This is useful for locking in statistics that shouldn't change or are optimal with the current sample. Take caution when using this on tables that have frequent data modifications and make certain there are other mechanisms in place to update statistics if needed.

- INCREMENTAL: When enabled, statistics are created as per-partition statistics, which allows statistics to be updated per partition using the ON PARTITIONS clause.

- MAXDOP: Determines the max degree of parallelism for the statistics update operation and overrides the max degree of parallelism configuration for the server.

The first three options in this list are mutually exclusive. Only one of the options may be chosen. Selecting more than one of those options will generate an error.

Since UPDATE STATISTICS is a DDL command, it can easily be automated similar to how index defragmentation can be automated. For brevity, a sample script is not included, but the template for the index fragmentation maintenance could be used as a starting point. sp_updatestats uses UPDATE STATISTICS under the covers. This DDL command is a powerful way to update statistics as needed in your databases without doing more than is necessary. To continue the analogy from the previous section, using UPDATE STATISTICS replaces the blanket and comforter with a handmade, fitted sweater.

Summary

In this chapter, a variety of maintenance considerations were introduced that impact table indexing and are important to ensuring optimal query performance. These break down to managing the fragmentation of indexes and managing their statistics. For index fragmentation, the ways in which indexes can become fragmented were discussed, as well as why it is an issue and strategies to remove the fragmentation. These maintenance tasks are critical for making certain that SQL Server can use indexes to the best of its ability. Along with maintenance activity, statistics on indexes must also be maintained. Out-of-date or inaccurate statistics can lead to execution plans that do not match the data in the table. Without proper execution plans, performance will suffer regardless of the indexes in place.

CHAPTER 12

Indexing Tools

With respect to indexing, Microsoft has two tools built into SQL Server that can be used to help identify indexes that can improve database performance. These are the missing index dynamic management objects (DMOs) and the Database Engine Tuning Advisor (DTA). Both tools are useful to assist with indexing databases and can provide valuable input when working on tuning a database.

In addition, Azure SQL Database contains a feature called Automatic Index Management. This feature automatically creates and drops indexes based on usage and is intended for environments where there are no developers or administrators available to monitor and manage indexing.

This chapter delves into these tools, describing how to use them and the benefits of each. The chapter is divided into two sections that each describe the capabilities of each tool, as well as a brief discussion of Automatic Index Management.

Missing Indexes

The missing index DMOs are a set of management objects that provide indexing feedback from the query optimizer. When the query optimizer compiles an execution plan, it can identify when materializing statistics for a set of columns into a physical index would improve performance. In these situations, the query optimizer will compile the results and store the information in the missing index DMOs.

There are a couple of benefits that the missing index DMOs provide. First, the missing index information is collected from the query optimizer without any action required on your part. Unlike Extended Events and other performance monitoring tools, there is no need to configure and enable it for information to be collected. The other consideration is that the missing index information is based on actual activity occurring on the SQL Server instance. The index suggestions are not based on a test load you believe might happen in production but rather on the production load itself.

© Edward Pollack and Jason Strate 2023
E. Pollack and J. Strate, *Expert Performance Indexing in Azure SQL and SQL Server 2022*,
https://doi.org/10.1007/978-1-4842-9215-0_12

As the usage patterns of the data in a database change, so too will the missing index recommendations.

Despite the benefits provided by the missing index DMOs, it is important take into account a few considerations when using them. The limitations on the missing index DMOs can be summarized into the following categories:

- Size of queue

- Depth of analysis

- Accuracy

- Type of indexes

The size of the queue for missing indexes is one of the limitations that is easy to miss. Regardless of the number of databases on the SQL Server instance, there can be no more than 600 missing index groups. Once 600 missing index groups have been identified, the query optimizer will stop reporting new missing index suggestions. It will not make any determinations to decide whether a new possible missing index is of better quality than items already reported; the information is simply not collected. When this occurs, Microsoft recommends addressing existing index recommendations in order to help alleviate this limitation.

Note   As with other dynamic management objects, the information within the missing index DMOs resets when SQL Server restarts and gets dropped for a database whenever the database is brought offline.

When considering the information in missing indexes, the depth of the analysis is a limitation that needs to be considered whenever reviewing the suggestions. The query optimizer considers only the current plan and whether the missing index would benefit the execution plan. Sometimes, adding the missing index to the database will result in a new plan with a new missing index suggestion. These suggestions are only a first pass at improving performance on an execution plan. The other half of this limitation is that the missing index details don't include tests to determine whether the order of the columns in the missing index suggestion is optimal. When looking at missing index suggestions, it will be necessary to test to determine the proper column order.

The third limitation of the missing index suggestion is the accuracy of the information returned with the statistics. There are two things that need to be considered with this limitation. When queries use inequality predicates, the cost information is less effective than those returned with equality predicates. Also, it is possible to return the same missing index suggestion with multiple cost estimates. How and where the missing index would be leveraged may change the cost estimate that is calculated. For each cost estimate, a missing index suggestion will be logged.

Lastly, the missing index tool is limited in the types of indexes it can suggest. The main limitation is index types and the inability of missing indexes to suggest clustered, XML, spatial, or columnstore indexes. The suggestions also will not include information on when to make an index filtered. Along these same lines, suggestions may, at times, contain only INCLUDED columns. When this happens, one of the INCLUDED columns will need to be designated as the key column.

Note   Missing index information for a table will be dropped whenever there are metadata operations made on the table. For instance, when a column is added to a table, the missing index information will be dropped. A less obvious example is when an index on a table changes. In this case as well, the missing index information will be dropped.

As mentioned at other times in this book, it is always important to carefully weigh whether a new index is valuable enough to warrant its creation. Following every index recommendation in these DMOs would quickly result in over-indexed tables. Keep this in mind as these DMOs are introduced as it helps highlight the fact that not all indexes are created equal. Some can provide exceptional value, whereas others may incur more cost to maintain than the value they offer.

Explaining the DMOs

There are four DMOs that can be used to return information on missing indexes. Each DMO provides a portion of the information needed to build indexes that the query optimizer can use to improve the performance of a query. The DMOs for missing indexes are as follows:

- sys.dm_db_missing_index_details
- sys.dm_db_missing_index_columns
- sys.dm_db_missing_index_group_stats
- sys.dm_db_missing_index_groups

In the next four sections, each of the dynamic management objects will be reviewed alongside details to how each provides information on how to identify missing indexes.

sys.dm_db_missing_index_details

The DMO sys.dm_db_missing_index_details is a dynamic management view that returns a list of missing index suggestions. Each row in the dynamic management view (DMV) provides a single suggested missing index. The columns in Table 12-1 provide information on the database and the table to create the index on. It also includes the columns that should comprise the key and the included columns for the index.

Table 12-1. *Columns in sys.dm_db_missing_index_details*

Column Name	Data Type	Description
index_handle	int	Unique identifier for each missing index suggestion. This is the key value for this DMV.
database_id	smallint	Identifies the database where the table with the missing index resides.
object_id	int	Identifies the table where the index is missing.
equality_columns	nvarchar(4000)	Comma-separated list of columns that contribute to equality predicates.
inequality_columns	nvarchar(4000)	Comma-separated list of columns that contribute to inequality predicates.
included_columns	nvarchar(4000)	Comma-separated list of columns needed as covering columns for the query.
statement	nvarchar(4000)	Name of the table where the index is missing.

There are two columns in sys.dm_db_missing_index_details that are used to identify key columns on missing index suggestions. These are equality_columns and inequality_columns. The equality_columns are generated when there is a comparison within the query plan that makes a direct equality comparison. For instance, when the filter for a query is ColumnA = @Parameter, this is an equality predicate. The inequality_columns details are created when any nonequal filter is used in a query plan. Examples of this are when there are greater than, less than, or NOT IN comparisons being used.

With regard to the included_columns information, this is generated when there are columns that are not part of the filter but that would be used to allow the index to cover the query request using a single index. Included columns are covered in more depth in Chapter 10. The use of included columns will help prevent the query plan from having to use a key lookup in the execution plan if the missing index is created. That being said, it is valuable to test a new index without included columns first and measure the resulting performance improvement. Missing index suggestions often contain included columns, but those additional included columns (and their associated maintenance) may not be needed in order to realize sufficient performance gains.

sys.dm_db_missing_index_columns

The next DMO is sys.dm_db_missing_index_columns, which is a dynamic management function (DMF). This function returns a list of columns for each missing index listed in sys.dm_db_missing_index_details. To use the DMF, an index_handle is passed into the function as a parameter. Each row in the result set represents a column in the missing index suggestion from sys.dm_db_missing_index_details and repeats the information in equality_columns, inequality_columns, and included_columns. Table 12-2 lists the output for sys.dm_db_missing_index_columns.

Table 12-2. *Columns in sys.dm_db_missing_index_columns*

Column Name	Data Type	Description
column_id	int	ID of the column
column_name	sysname	Name of the table column
column_usage	varchar(20)	Description of how the column will be used in the index

The primary information in this DMF is the column_usage column. For every row, this column will return one of the following values: EQUALITY, INEQUALITY, or INCLUDE. These values map to equality_columns, inequality_columns, and included_columns in sys.dm_db_missing_index_details. Depending on the type of usage in the former DMV, the use will be the same for this DMF.

sys.dm_db_missing_index_groups

The DMV `sys.dm_db_missing_index_groups` is the next missing index DMO. The DMV returns a list of missing index groups paired with missing index suggestions. Table 12-3 lists the columns for `sys.dm_db_missing_index_groups`. Although this DMV supports the ability for many-to-many relationships within missing index suggestions, they are always made in a one-to-one relationship.

Table 12-3. *Columns in sys.dm_db_missing_index_groups*

Column Name	Data Type	Description
`index_group_handle`	`int`	Identifies a missing index group. This value joins to group_handle in `sys.dm_db_missing_index_group_stats`.
`index_handle`	`int`	Identifies a missing index handle. This value joins to index_handle in `sys.dm_db_missing_index_details`.

sys.dm_db_missing_index_group_stats

The last missing index DMO is the DMV `sys.dm_db_missing_index_group_stats`. The information in this DMV contains statistics on how the query optimizer would expect to use the missing index if it were built. From this, using the columns in Table 12-4, it can be determined which missing indexes would provide the greatest benefit and the scope to which the index will be used. This information is exceptionally useful and provides a wide variety of metrics that can help better understand why an index is being suggested and the potential impact it could have on performance if implemented.

Using the DMOs

Now that the missing index DMOs have been explained, it is time to look at how they can be used together to provide missing index suggestions. The results of the missing index DMOs have been referred to as suggestions instead of recommendations. This variation in wording is not only intentional but critically important. Typically, when someone receives an index recommendation from a colleague, it is fully thought through and ready to be implemented. This is not so with the missing index DMOs; thus, they are referred to as suggestions.

The suggestions from the missing index DMOs provide a starting point to begin looking at and building new indexes. There are two things that are important to consider when looking at missing index suggestions. First, variations of each missing index suggestion may appear multiple times in the results. It is not recommended that each of these variations be implemented. Common patterns within the suggestions should be found. An index that covers a few of the suggestions is usually ideal. Second, when more than one column is suggested, the order of the columns needs to be tested to determine which is optimal.

To help explain how the missing index DMOs work and are related to one another, an example will be provided that includes a few SQL statements. These statements, shown in Listing 12-1, execute queries against the SalesOrderHeader table in the AdventureWorks2017 database. For each of the queries, the filtering is on either the DueDate or OrderDate column or both.

Listing 12-1. SQL Statements to Generate Missing Index Suggestions

```
USE AdventureWorks2017
GO

SELECT DueDate FROM Sales.SalesOrderHeader
WHERE DueDate = '2014-07-01 00:00:00.000'
AND OrderDate = '2014-06-19 00:00:00.000'
GO
SELECT DueDate FROM Sales.SalesOrderHeader
WHERE OrderDate Between '20140601' AND '20140630'
AND DueDate Between '20140701' AND '20140731'
GO
SELECT DueDate, OrderDate FROM Sales.SalesOrderHeader
WHERE DueDate Between '20140701' AND '20140731'
GO
SELECT CustomerID, OrderDate FROM Sales.SalesOrderHeader
WHERE OrderDate Between '20140601' AND '20140630'
AND DueDate Between '20140701' AND '20140731'
GO
```

Table 12-4. *Columns in sys.dm_db_missing_index_group_stats*

Column Name	Data Type	Description
group_handle	int	Unique identifier for each missing index group. This is the key value for this DMV. All queries that would benefit from using the missing index group are included in this group.
unique_compiles	bigint	Count of the execution plan compilations and recompilations that would benefit from this missing index group.
user_seeks	bigint	Count of seeks in user queries that would have occurred if the missing index had been built.
user_scans	bigint	Count of scans in user queries that would have occurred if the missing index had been built.
last_user_seek	datetime	Date and time of last user seek from user queries that would have occurred if the missing index had been built.
last_user_scan	datetime	Date and time of last user scan from user queries that would have occurred if the missing index had been built.
avg_total_user_cost	float	Average cost of the user queries that could be reduced by the index in the group.
avg_user_impact	float	Average percentage benefit that user queries could experience if this missing index group had been implemented.
system_seeks	bigint	Count of seeks in system queries that would have occurred if the missing index had been built.
system_scans	bigint	Count of scans in system queries that would have occurred if the missing index had been built.
last_system_seek	datetime	Date and time of last system seek from system queries that would have occurred if the missing index had been built.
last_system_scan	datetime	Date and time of last system scan from system queries that would have occurred if the missing index had been built.
avg_total_system_cost	float	Average cost of the system queries that could be reduced by the index in the group.
avg_system_impact	float	Average percentage benefit that system queries could experience if this missing index group had been implemented.

Examining the execution plan for any of the example queries reveals that they each use a clustered index scan to satisfy the query. Figure 12-1 shows the execution plan for the first query. In this execution plan, there is an index scan across the table's clustered index and a missing index suggestion that may help eliminate the index scan.

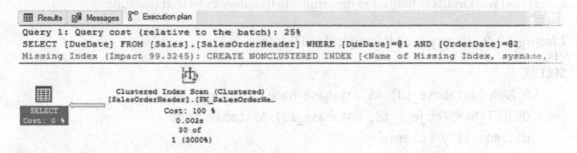

Figure 12-1. *Execution plan for the first query from Listing 12-1*

To see more details on this missing index suggestion, it can be double-clicked to generate the index creation statement. While helpful, this does not provide the details behind the suggestion. Those details allow for a better understanding of why this index suggestion was provided and the detailed metrics that describe its potential impact. For this detail, it is necessary to look at the missing index DMOs. A query against the missing index DMOs will look similar to Listing 12-2. The query includes the equality, inequality, and included column information that was described earlier. It also includes two calculations not previously described: Impact and Score.

The Impact calculation helps identify missing index suggestions that will have the highest overall impact across multiple query executions. This is calculated by adding the potential seeks and scans on the missing index based on the average impact; the resulting value represents the total improvement across all queries that might have used the index. The higher the value, the more improvement the index could provide.

The Score calculation also helps identify missing index suggestions that will improve query performance. The difference between Impact and Score is the inclusion of the average total user cost. For the Score calculation, the average total user cost is multiplied by the Impact score and divided by 100. The inclusion of the cost value helps differentiate between expensive and inexpensive queries when deciding whether to consider the missing index. For instance, a missing index suggestion that provides an 80 percent improvement on queries with an average cost value of 1,000 would likely provide a better return than a 90 percent improvement for a query with an average cost value of 1.

When reviewing an index suggestion, always consider both the frequency of the query that the index is addressing and its query cost. If a query runs once a month and can be improved by 100,000×, is it worth it? Similarly, if a query runs once a second and can be improved by 10 percent, is it worth it? An understanding of these queries' associated workloads is helpful in determining the answer to that question.

Listing 12-2. Query for Missing Index DMOs

```
SELECT
    DB_NAME(database_id) AS database_name
    ,OBJECT_NAME(object_id, database_id) AS table_name
    ,mid.equality_columns
    ,mid.inequality_columns
    ,mid.included_columns
    ,(migs.user_seeks + migs.user_scans) * migs.avg_user_impact AS Impact
    ,migs.avg_total_user_cost * (migs.avg_user_impact / 100.0) * (migs.user_
    seeks + migs.user_scans) AS Score
    ,migs.user_seeks
    ,migs.user_scans
FROM sys.dm_db_missing_index_details mid
        INNER JOIN sys.dm_db_missing_index_groups mig ON mid.index_handle =
        mig.index_handle
        INNER JOIN sys.dm_db_missing_index_group_stats migs ON mig.index_
        group_handle = migs.group_handle
WHERE DB_NAME(database_id) = 'AdventureWorks2017'
ORDER BY migs.avg_total_user_cost * (migs.avg_user_impact / 100.0) * (migs.
user_seeks + migs.user_scans) DESC
```

Figure 12-2 shows some results from executing this query.

	database_name	table_name	equality_columns	inequality_columns	included_columns	Impact	Score	user_seeks	user_scans
1	AdventureWorks2017	SalesOrderHeader	[OrderDate], [DueDate]	NULL	NULL	99.32	0.563358070973333	1	0
2	AdventureWorks2017	SalesOrderHeader	NULL	[OrderDate], [DueDate]	NULL	94.96	0.561335496986667	1	0
3	AdventureWorks2017	SalesOrderHeader	NULL	[OrderDate], [DueDate]	[CustomerID]	94.21	0.556902034236667	1	0
4	AdventureWorks2017	SalesOrderHeader	NULL	[DueDate]	[OrderDate]	94.79	0.542435174663333	1	0

Figure 12-2. *Results from the missing index query*

With the results from the missing index query, shown in Figure 12-2, there are a few items to consider from these suggestions. First, there are quite a few similarities between the suggestions. The predicate columns between each of the suggestions include the OrderDate and DueDate, except for one missing index. Since the column order has not been tested, the optimal column order is not clear. To satisfy the missing index suggestion, one possible index could have the key column DueDate followed by OrderDate. This configuration would create an index that would satisfy all four of the missing index items.

The next item to look at is included_columns. For two of the suggestions, there are included_columns values listed. On the fourth missing index suggestion, it suggests including the column OrderDate. Since it will be one of the key columns of the index, it doesn't need to be included. The other column, from the third missing index suggestion, is the CustomerID column. While only one index needs this column, as an included column, the addition of this column would likely be negligible since it is a narrow column. There would be value in adding this column to the index, though it may not be required to obtain desired performance on the query.

After looking at these results and considering four missing index suggestions, a single suggestion for one index that can cover all four of the missing index items was able to be proposed. If an index is built using a DDL statement similar to that in Listing 12-3, the result will be an index that solves each of these missing indexes. If the queries in Listing 12-1 are executed again, the execution plan output will show all of the queries are now using index seeks against the new index, shown in Figure 12-3.

Listing 12-3. Index from Missing Index DMOs

```
USE AdventureWorks2017
GO
CREATE NONCLUSTERED INDEX missing_index_SalesOrderHeader
ON Sales.SalesOrderHeader([DueDate], [OrderDate])
INCLUDE ([CustomerID])
```

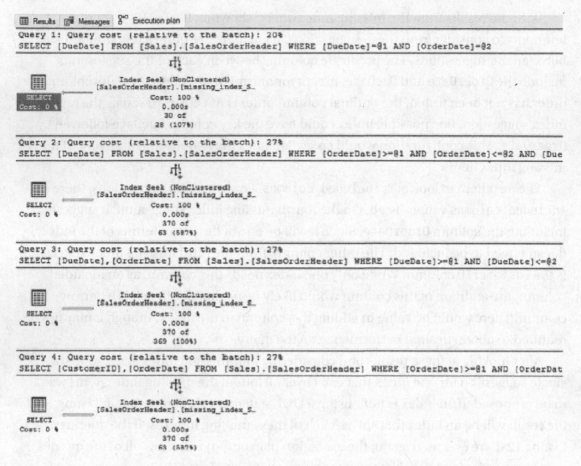

Figure 12-3. *Execution plans for queries after missing index creation*

Note   There are many negative opinions regarding the value of the Database
Engine Tuning Advisor. This is a tool that fills a role, and provided a sufficient
workload is used with the tool, it will return worthwhile recommendations. These
recommendations provide a better starting point for tuning a database than
starting with nothing.

Database Engine Tuning Advisor

The other indexing tool available in SQL Server is the Database Engine Tuning Advisor. This tool allows SQL Server to analyze a workload from a file, a table, the plan cache, or the Query Store. The output of the DTA can assist in providing recommendations for indexing and configuring partitions for the workload. The chief benefit of using the tool is that it does not require a deep understanding of the underlying databases to make the recommendations.

Whether working with a single query or a full day's workload, the DTA provides index recommendations for the following types of objects:

- Rowstore and columnstore tables for both clustered and non-clustered indexes

- Aligned or nonaligned partitions

- Views that could support indexing

With the sessions in the DTA, it is possible to really focus the recommendations on what is expected from a given environment. It is possible to leverage workload based on a specific environment, whether transactional or analytical, and set the focus on both reads and writes so that index recommendations are provided that align to those needs. It is also possible to modify the environment to look for indexing recommendations for changes in disk space.

Once the analysis is completed, the DTA provides a number of reports and outputs. This information allows the recommendations to be reviewed and to develop an understanding of how it will impact the database.

Although the DTA has quite a few capabilities, there are also some limitations on the tool. The following are some of these limitations:

- Not able to recommend indexes on system tables.

- Cannot add or drop unique indexes or indexes that enforce primary key or unique constraints.

- May provide variations in recommendations on some workloads. The DTA samples data while it executes, which will influence the recommendations.

- Unable to tune trace tables on remote servers.

- Constraints placed on tuning workloads can have a negative impact on suggestions if the tuning session exceeds the constraints.

Note   As an indexing tool, the DTA can easily be misused. This is often due to not providing a representative workload or to taking recommendations without proper testing. When using the tool, be sure to validate any change that is recommended and test those changes thoroughly before applying them to a production environment.

Explaining the DTA

There are two ways in which users can interact with the DTA. These are the graphical user interface (GUI) and the command-line utility. Both methods offer most of the same capabilities. Depending on comfort level, either can be used effectively.

The GUI tool, which will be used throughout most of this chapter, provides a wrapper for the DTA. It allows for the selection of the available options, and it enables the viewing of tuning sessions that were previously executed. For viewing tuning results, the GUI is well-suited to the task. Tuning sessions can be configured and executed through the GUI.

The command-line utility provides the same capabilities as the GUI when it comes to configuring and executing sessions. The command-line utility can be configured through either switches or an XML configuration file. Both options allow database administrators (DBAs) and developers to build processes to automate tune activities for reviewing and analyzing workloads and to build an index tuning process that allows the DBA to work directly with the results. Integrating the DTA utility into a performance tuning methodology will be discussed in Chapter 17.

With both tools, two general areas of configuration need to occur. The first determines how the tuning session will interact and makes suggestions with the physical design structures (PDSs). The second determines which type of partitioning strategy the DTA should employ when trying to tune the database.

There are two parts to the options on how physical design structure suggestions will be generated. The first option to configure is which type of PDS to utilize in the tuning.

The physical design structure can be augmented to include considering filtered and columnstore indexes. The options for physical design structure use are as follows:

- Indexes and indexed views.

- Indexes (default option).

- Evaluate utilization of existing PDSs only.

- Indexed views.

- Non-clustered indexes.

The next PDS option is the partitioning to consider in the index tuning. The DTA offers to use no partitioning, aligned partitioning, or full partitioning. With full partitioning, recommendations will consider whether a table should include indexes that are partitioned and nonpartitioned.

The last PDS option determines which objects to keep within the database. This option can help ensure that the recommendations provided do not adversely affect tuning that was previously tested and deployed. The following are the options for PDS items to retain in the database:

- Do not keep any existing PDSs.

- Keep all existing PDSs (default option).

- Keep aligned partitioning.

- Keep indexes only.

- Keep clustered indexes only.

Outside these options, there are a few other options that can be configured. These options determine how long the tuning session will run, which can be critically important if a lot of databases need to be analyzed. Similarly, for a large workload, there may be a desire to prevent it from running too long. Additionally, the max disk space for the recommendations and max columns for each index can be defined. The last setup option indicates whether index recommendations can or must be able to be deployed online.

Note Before following along in the next section, run the code in Listing 12-1. If the index in Listing 12-3 has been created, drop the index using the DROP INDEX statement provided in Listing 12-4.

Listing 12-4. DDL Statement to Drop Index missing_index_SalesOrderHeader

```
USE AdventureWorks2017
GO
DROP INDEX IF EXISTS Sales.SalesOrderHeader.missing_index_SalesOrderHeader;
```

Using the DTA GUI

As mentioned earlier in the chapter, one of the ways to interact with the DTA is through the GUI. In this section, a scenario will be provided that demonstrates how to use the DTA for index tuning. There are a few methods for launching the tool. The first option is within SQL Server Management Studio (SSMS). Within SSMS, navigate to Tools ➤ Database Engine Tuning Advisor from the menu bar. The other option is to open the Database Engine Tuning Advisor from Microsoft SQL Server Tools on the Start menu.

After launching the DTA, there will be a prompt to connect to a SQL Server instance. Once connected, the tool will open a new tuning session for configuration. Figure 12-4 shows a DTA session.

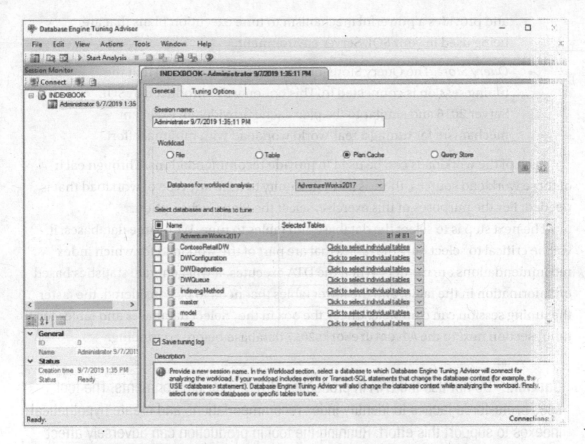

***Figure 12-4.** General configuration screen from the Database Engine Tuning Advisor*

In the session launch screen on the General options tab, there are a few things to configure initially. To start, there is the session name, which can be any value. The default value includes the username with the date and time. Next, select the type of workload that will be used. There are four options for the workload:

- *File*: A file containing SQL Trace output, an XML configuration, or SQL scripts.

- *Table*: SQL Server database table containing SQL Trace output. Before using the table, be sure the trace populating it has been completed.

- *Plan Cache*: The plan cache of the SQL Server that the tuning session is connected to. This capability was introduced in SQL Server 2012

and provides a powerful mechanism to tune execution plans that are
being used in your SQL Server environment.

- *Query Store*: The Query Store for the selected database(s) that the
  tuning session is connected to. This option was introduced in SQL
  Server 2016 and similar to the plan cache provides an excellent
  mechanism for tuning a real-world workload with minimal effort.

Each of the workloads can be used to provide recommendations. Through each
of these workload sources, there is an opportunity to tune any type of workload that is
needed. For the purposes of this exercise, select the Plan Cache option.

The next step is to select the database and tables to tune. With large databases, it
will be critical to select only the tables that are part of the workload for which index
recommendations are needed. When the DTA executes, it will generate statistics based
on information in the table, and the fewer tables that need to be considered, the faster
the tuning session can complete. Check the box in the "Select databases and tables to
tune" section next to the AdventureWorks2017 database before continuing.

Caution   Do not use the DTA in production SQL Server environments. The tool
uses brute-force tactics to identify index recommendations and create hypothetical
indexes to support this effort. Running the tool in production can adversely affect
the performance of other workloads on the server. Consider running the DTA from
a command line and on a remote SQL Server for analyzing production databases.
This technique will be demonstrated later in this chapter and discussed further in
Chapter 17.

With the General options configured, the next step is to configure the Tuning Options
settings. On the screen shown in Figure 12-5, deselect the "Limit tuning time" option.
For the other options, leave them as the default selections. These should be as follows:

- *Physical Design Structures (PDS) to use in database*: Indexes

- *Partitioning strategy to employ*: No partitioning

- *Physical Design Structures (PDS) to keep in database*: Keep all
  existing PDS

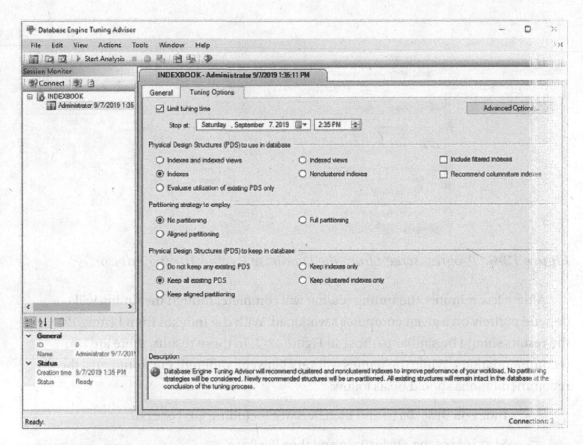

Figure 12-5. *Tuning Options configuration screen from the Database Engine Tuning Advisor*

The next step is to start the Database Engine Tuning Advisor. This can be accomplished through the toolbar or the menu, by selecting Actions ➤ Start Analysis. After starting the DTA, the Progress tab will open, as shown in Figure 12-6.

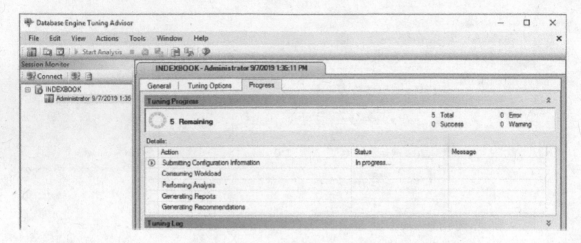

Figure 12-6. *Progress screen from the Database Engine Tuning Advisor*

After a few minutes, the tuning session will complete, though the timing will depend entirely on a given computer's workload. With the indexes from Listing 12-1, the results should be similar to those in Figure 12-7. In these results, there are two recommendations. While the names will vary between different environments, the recommendations should be as follows:

- Index on `OrderDate` and then `DueDate` including `CustomerID`

- `Statistics on OrderDate` and then `DueDate`

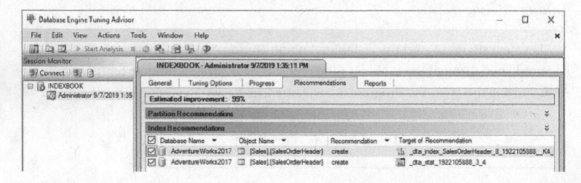

Figure 12-7. *Recommendations from the Database Engine Tuning Advisor*

This index is similar to the suggestion previously found with the missing index DMOs. In situations where there are multiple recommendations provided, it will be necessary to go through the same considerations that were part of reviewing the suggestions from the missing index DMOs, such as "Can the recommendations be consolidated?" Additionally, when statistics are recommended, do they match an index that will be created enough that the index can provide the statistics required for queries? To remove any item from the list of recommendations, deselect the check box, and it will not be included in any of the recommendation outputs.

At this point, there are a few options that can be used to apply the indexes:

- *Apply the indexes*: To apply the indexes, select Actions in the menu bar and select Apply Recommendations. In the Apply Recommendations window that comes up, leave the default, Apply Now, selected and click OK.

- *Apply the indexes in the future*: To apply the indexes in the future, select Actions in the menu bar and select Apply Recommendations. In the Apply Recommendations window that comes up, select "Schedule for later." Alter the scheduled date as desired and click OK. This will create the SQL Agent job. Ensure the SQL Agent is running and the agent service account has the required permissions to apply the indexes.

- *Save recommendations*: To save recommendations, click the Save Recommendations icon in the menu bar and press the key combination Ctrl+S or select Actions ➤ Save Recommendations in the menu bar.

If the recommendations are saved, they will create a script like the one in Listing 12-5. Before applying indexes from the DTA, it is recommended that the names of indexes be changed to match your organization's index naming standards. Also important is to consider whether to apply compression to the index. When it comes to statistics, it's not as important to add these for a couple of reasons. First, SQL Server will create statistics as needed behind the scenes, removing the need for customized statistics to be built. Second, indexes include statistics and usually provide what is required.

Listing 12-5. Database Engine Tuning Advisor Index Recommendations

```
use AdventureWorks2017;
go

CREATE NONCLUSTERED INDEX [_dta_index_SalesOrderHeader_8_1922105888__K4_
K3_11] ON [Sales].[SalesOrderHeader]
```

```
(
      [DueDate] ASC,
      [OrderDate] ASC
)
INCLUDE([CustomerID]) WITH (SORT_IN_TEMPDB = OFF, DROP_EXISTING = OFF,
ONLINE = OFF) ON [PRIMARY]
go
```

By using the DTA through its GUI, it is possible to quickly optimize a workload. The recommendations returned provide a level of index tuning above using the missing index DMOs. In essence, they provide a brute-force indexing exercise to improve performance without improving code. Instead of spending many hours on tuning that can be resolved with a few new indexes, time and energy can be focused on more complex performance tuning issues than simply adding an index.

Note   When the DTA is terminated while processing, it will sometimes leave behind hypothetical indexes that were used while it was investigating possible indexes that could improve an environment. A hypothetical index is an index that contains only statistics and no data. These indexes can be identified through the `is_hypothetical` column in `sys.indexes`. If they exist in your environment, they should always be dropped.

Using the DTA Utility

The GUI isn't the only way to use the DTA within a SQL Server environment. The other method is through the command line with the DTA utility. What the DTA utility lacks in an interactive interface, it makes up for with the flexibility to leverage the utility in scripts and automation.

The syntax for using the DTA utility, shown in Listing 12-6, includes a number of arguments. These arguments, defined in Table 12-5, allow the DTA utility to contain the same features and flexibility of the GUI. Instead of clicking through many screens, the configuration information is passed in through these arguments.

Table 12-5. *DTA Utility Arguments*

Argument	Description
-?	Returns help information, including a list of all arguments.
-A	Provides a time limit, in minutes, in which the DTA utility will spend tuning the workload. The default time limit is 8 hours, or 640 minutes. Setting the limit to 0 will result in an unlimited tuning session.
-a	After the workload is tuned, the recommendations are applied without further prompting.
-B	Specifies the maximum size, in megabytes, that recommended indexes can consume. By default, this value is set to either three times the current raw data size or the free space on attached disk drives plus raw data size, whichever is smaller.
-c	Maximum number of key columns that the DTA will recommend in an index. This value defaults to 16. The restriction does not include INCLUDED columns.
-C	Maximum number of columns that the DTA will recommend in an index. The value defaults to 16 but can be raised as high as 1024, the maximum columns allowed in an index.
-d	Identifies the database that the DTA session connects to when the session begins. Only a single database can be specified for this argument.
-D	Identifies the databases that the DTA session will tune the workload against. One or more databases can be specified for this argument. To add multiple databases to a session, either include all the database names in a comma-separated list in one argument or add one argument per database.
-e	Identifies the name of the logging table or file where the DTA session will output events that could not be tuned. When specifying a table name, use the three-part naming convention of [database_name].[schema_name].[table_name]. With an output file, the extension for the file should be .xml.
-E	Sets the database connection using a trusted connection. The required argument if -U is not used.
-F	Grants DTA permission to overwrite an output file if it already exists.

(continued)

Table 12-5. (*continued*)

Argument	Description
-fa	Identifies the types of physical design structures that the DTA session can include in the recommendations. The default value for this argument is IDX. The available values are as follows: • IDX_IV: Indexes and indexed views • IDX: Indexes only • IX: Indexed views only • NCL_IDX: Non-clustered indexes only
-fi	Allows the DTA session to include recommendations for filtered indexes.
-fc	Allows the DTA session to include recommendations for columnstore indexes.
-fk	Sets the limitations on the existing physical design structures that the DTA session can modify in the recommendations. The available values are as follows: • NONE: No existing structures • ALL: All existing structures • ALIGNED: All partition-aligned structures • CL_IDX: All clustered indexes on tables • IDX: All clustered and non-clustered indexes on tables
-fp	Determines whether partitioning recommendations can be included in the DTA session recommendations. The default value for this argument is NONE. The available values are as follows: • NONE: No partitioning • FULL: Full partitioning • ALIGNED: Aligned partitioning
-fx	Limits the DTA session to only including recommendations to drop existing physical design structures. Lightly used indexes in the session are evaluated, and recommendations for dropping them are provided. This argument cannot be used with the arguments -fa, -fp, and -fk ALL.
-ID	Sets a numerical identifier for the DTA session. Either this argument or -s must be specified.
-ip	Sets the source of the workload for the DTA session to the plan cache. The top –n plan cache events for the databases specified with argument –D are analyzed.

(*continued*)

Table 12-5. (*continued*)

Argument	Description
-ipf	Sets the source of the workload for the DTA session to the plan cache. The top -n plan cache events for all databases are analyzed.
-if	Sets the source of the workload for the DTA session to a file source. The path and file name are passed in through this argument. The file must be a SQL Server Profiler trace file (trc), SQL file (sql), or SQL Server trace file (log).
-it	Sets the source of the workload for the DTA session to a table. When specifying a table name, use the three-part naming convention of [database_name].dbo.[table_name]. The schema for the table must be dbo.
-ix	Identifies an XML file containing the configuration information for the DTA session. The XML file must conform to the DTASchema.xsd (which is located at http://schemas.microsoft.com/sqlserver/2004/07/dta/dtaschema.xsd).
-m	Sets the minimum percentage of improvement that a recommendation must provide.
-n	Sets the number of events in the workload that the DTA session should tune. When specified for a trace file, the order of the events selected is based on the decreasing order of duration.
-N	Determines whether the physical design structures are created online or offline. The available values are as follows: • OFF: No objects are created online. • ON: All objects are created online. • MIXED: Objects are created where possible.
-of	Configures the DTA session to output the recommendations in a T-SQL format in the path and file specified.
-or	Configures the DTA session to output the recommendations to a report in an XML format. When a file name is not provided, a file name based on the session (-s) name will be used.
-ox	Configures the DTA session to output the recommendations in an XML format in the path and file specified.
-P	Sets the password to be used for the SQL login in the database connection.
-q	Sets the DTA session to execute in quiet mode.

(*continued*)

Table 12-5. (*continued*)

Argument	Description
-rl	Configures the reports that will be generated by the DTA session. One or more reports can be selected in a comma-separated list. The available values are as follows: • ALL: All analysis reports • STMT_COST: Statement cost report • EVT_FREQ: Event frequency report • STMT_DET: Statement detail report • CUR_STMT_IDX: Statement-index relations report (current configuration) • REC_STMT_IDX: Statement-index relations report (recommended configuration) • STMT_COSTRANGE: Statement cost range report • CUR_IDX_USAGE: Index usage report (current configuration) • REC_IDX_USAGE: Index usage report (recommended configuration) • CUR_IDX_DET: Index detail report (current configuration) • REC_IDX_DET: Index detail report (recommended configuration) • VIW_TAB: View-table relations report • WKLD_ANL: Workload analysis report • DB_ACCESS: Database access report • TAB_ACCESS: Table access report • COL_ACCESS: Column access report
-S	Sets the instance of SQL Server to be used for the DTA session.
-s	Sets the name of the DTA session.
-Tf	Identifies the name of a path and file containing a list of tables to be used for tuning. The file should contain one table per line using the three-part naming convention. After each table name, the number of rows can be specified to tune the workload for a scaled version of the table. If -Tf and -Tl are omitted, the DTA session will default to using all tables.
-Tl	Sets a list of tables to be used for tuning. Each table should be listed using the three-part naming convention, with each table name separated by a comma. If -Tf and -Tl are omitted, the DTA session will default to using all tables.
-U	Sets the username to be used for the SQL login in the database connection. The required argument if -E is not used.

(continued)

Table 12-5. (*continued*)

Argument	Description
-u	Launches the GUI interface for the DTA with all of the configuration values specified to the DTA utility.
-x	Starts the DTA session and exists upon completion.

Listing 12-6. DTA Utility Syntax

```
dta
[ -? ] |
[
        [ -S server_name[ \instance ] ]
        { { -U login_id [-P password ] } | -E  }
        { -D database_name [ ,...n ] }
        [ -d database_name ]
        [ -Tl table_list | -Tf table_list_file ]
        { -if workload_file | -it workload_trace_table_name  | -ip | -ipf }
        { -ssession_name | -IDsession_ID }
        [ -F ]
        [ -of output_script_file_name ]
        [ -or output_xml_report_file_name ]
        [ -ox output_XML_file_name ]
        [ -rl analysis_report_list [ ,...n ] ]
        [ -ix input_XML_file_name ]
        [ -A time_for_tuning_in_minutes ]
        [ -n number_of_events ]
        [ -m minimum_improvement ]
        [ -fa physical_design_structures_to_add ]
        [ -fi filtered_indexes]
        [ -fc columnstore_indexes]
        [ -fp partitioning_strategy ]
        [ -fk keep_existing_option ]
        [ -fx drop_only_mode ]
        [ -B storage_size ]
        [ -c max_key_columns_in_index ]
```

```
    [ -C max_columns_in_index ]
    [ -e | -e tuning_log_name ]
    [ -N online_option]
    [ -q ]
    [ -u ]
    [ -x ]
    [ -a ]
]
```

Using the DTA utility is easy. Two scenarios for using this tool will be provided that result in different outcomes. In the first scenario, the DTA utility will be used to recommend indexing improvements by allowing only non-clustered indexing changes. For the second scenario, the DTA utility will be configured to recommend any change to indexing that would improve workload performance. In both scenarios, the SQL Server plan cache will be used as the workload source. To populate the plan cache, execute the script in Listing 12-7.

Listing 12-7. Scenario Setup

```
USE AdventureWorks2017
GO
IF OBJECT_ID('dbo.SalesOrderDetail') IS NOT NULL
        DROP TABLE dbo.SalesOrderDetail;
SELECT SalesOrderID, SalesOrderDetailID, CarrierTrackingNumber, OrderQty,
ProductID, SpecialOfferID, UnitPrice, UnitPriceDiscount, LineTotal,
rowguid, ModifiedDate
INTO dbo.SalesOrderDetail
FROM Sales.SalesOrderDetail;
CREATE CLUSTERED INDEX CL_SalesOrderDetail ON dbo.SalesOrderDetail(SalesOrd
erDetailID);
CREATE NONCLUSTERED INDEX IX_SalesOrderDetail ON dbo.SalesOrderDetail(Sale
sOrderID);
GO
SELECT SalesOrderID, CarrierTrackingNumber
INTO #temp
FROM dbo.SalesOrderDetail
WHERE SalesOrderID = 43660;
```

```
DROP TABLE #temp;
GO 1000
SELECT SalesOrderID, OrderQty
INTO #temp
FROM dbo.SalesOrderDetail
WHERE SalesOrderID = 43661;
DROP TABLE #temp;
GO 1000
```

For the first scenario, a command-line script will be built that is similar to the one shown in Listing 12-8. For your environment, the server name (-S) will be different. The rest, however, will be identical. The database (-D and –d arguments) will be AdventureWorks2017. The source of the workload will be the plan cache (-ip argument). The name of the session (-s argument) is "First Scenario."

Listing 12-8. First Scenario DTA Utility Syntax

```
"C:\Program Files (x86)\Microsoft SQL Server Management Studio 18\
Common7\dta"
-S localhost -E
-D AdventureWorks2017
-d AdventureWorks2017
-ip
-s "First Scenario"
-Tl AdventureWorks2017.dbo.SalesOrderDetail
-of "C:\Temp\First Scenario.sql"
-fa NCL_IDX
-fp NONE
-fk ALL
```

With the DTA utility syntax prepared, the next step is to execute the script through the Command Prompt window. Depending on your SQL Server instance and the amount of information in the plan cache, this execution may take a few minutes. When it completes, the output in the Command Prompt window will look similar to the output shown in Figure 12-8. This output indicates that the file C:\Temp\First Scenario.sql contains the recommendations for tuning the query in Listing 12-7.

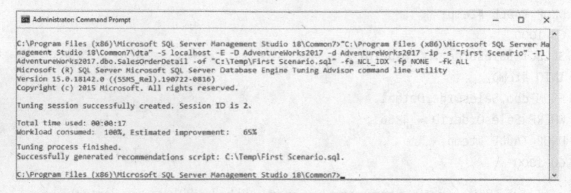

Figure 12-8. *Command Prompt window for the first scenario*

Based on the arguments passed into the DTA utility and the current workload, the recommendation from the first scenario tuning session includes the creation of two non-clustered indexes and statistics on two columns, shown in Listing 12-9. These indexes function as covering indexes for the queries in Listing 12-7; as a result, the key lookup is no longer required as part of the execution plan. The statistics provide information that SQL Server can use to build good plans for queries on the columns used in the query.

Note   Listing 12-9 creates the dbo.SalesOrderDetail table.

Listing 12-9. First Scenario DTA Utility Output

```
use [AdventureWorks2017]
go
CREATE NONCLUSTERED INDEX [_dta_index_SalesOrderDetail_8_2119678599__K1_
K2_3] ON [dbo].[SalesOrderDetail]
(
     [SalesOrderID] ASC,
     [SalesOrderDetailID] ASC
)
INCLUDE([CarrierTrackingNumber]) WITH (SORT_IN_TEMPDB = OFF, DROP_EXISTING
= OFF, ONLINE = OFF) ON [PRIMARY]
go
CREATE NONCLUSTERED INDEX [_dta_index_SalesOrderDetail_8_2119678599__K1_
K2_4] ON [dbo].[SalesOrderDetail]
```

```
(
     [SalesOrderID] ASC,
     [SalesOrderDetailID] ASC
)
INCLUDE([OrderQty]) WITH (SORT_IN_TEMPDB = OFF, DROP_EXISTING = OFF, ONLINE
= OFF) ON [PRIMARY]
go
CREATE STATISTICS [_dta_stat_2119678599_2_1] ON [dbo].[SalesOrderDetail]
([SalesOrderDetailID], [SalesOrderID])
go
```

The downside to the arguments that were selected in the first scenario is that there isn't any information included that helps determine the value in adding this index and the statistics. For the next scenario, that information will be obtained along with moving deeper into providing recommendations on the physical structure of your databases.

To begin the next scenario, the same database and query will be used. The arguments, though, will be modified slightly to accommodate the new goals, as shown in Listing 1210. First, you'll change the name of the session (-s) to "Second Scenario". Next, change the allowed physical structure changes (argument -fa) from non-clustered indexes only (NCL_IDX) to indexes and indexed views (IDX_IV). The final change, for the reporting output, is to add the report list (argument -rl) to the script with the all analysis reports (ALL) option.

Listing 12-10. Second Scenario DTA Utility Syntax

```
"C:\Program Files (x86)\Microsoft SQL Server Management Studio 18\
Common7\dta"
-S localhost
-D AdventureWorks2017
-d AdventureWorks2017
-ip
-s "Second Scenario"
-Tl AdventureWorks2017.dbo.SalesOrderDetail
-of "C:\Temp\Second Scenario.sql"
-fa IDX_IV
-fp NONE
-fk ALL
-rl ALL
```

Executing the DTA utility using the second scenario produces entirely different results from the first scenario. Instead of recommending non-clustered indexes, the second scenario recommends a change in the clustered key columns. With this solution, the DTA session identified the `SalesOrderID` column as the column frequently used to access data and recommended that as the clustered index. Listing 12-11 shows these recommendations.

Listing 12-11. Second Scenario DTA Utility Output

```
use [AdventureWorks2017]
go
CREATE NONCLUSTERED INDEX [_dta_index_SalesOrderDetail_8_2119678599__K1_
K2_3] ON [dbo].[SalesOrderDetail]
(
      [SalesOrderID] ASC,
      [SalesOrderDetailID] ASC
)
INCLUDE([CarrierTrackingNumber]) WITH (SORT_IN_TEMPDB = OFF, DROP_EXISTING
= OFF, ONLINE = OFF) ON [PRIMARY]
go
CREATE NONCLUSTERED INDEX [_dta_index_SalesOrderDetail_8_2119678599__K1_
K2_4] ON [dbo].[SalesOrderDetail]
(
      [SalesOrderID] ASC,
      [SalesOrderDetailID] ASC
)
INCLUDE([OrderQty]) WITH (SORT_IN_TEMPDB = OFF, DROP_EXISTING = OFF, ONLINE
= OFF) ON [PRIMARY]
go
CREATE STATISTICS [_dta_stat_2119678599_2_1] ON [dbo].[SalesOrderDetail]
([SalesOrderDetailID], [SalesOrderID])
go
```

The one other difference with the second scenario is the creation of an XML report file. The session used the ALL option for the `-rl` argument, which includes all the reports listed for the argument in Table 12-5. These reports provide information regarding the statements that were tuned, the costs associated with the statements, the amount of improvement the recommendations provide, and much more (Figure 12-9). Through these reports, all of the information needed to make decisions about which recommendations to apply to your databases is provided.

```xml
<?xml version="1.0" encoding="UTF-16"?>
<DTAXML>
  <DTAOutput>
    <AnalysisReport>
      <StatementCostReport>
      <EventWeightReport>
      <StatementDetailReport>
      <StatementIndexReport Current="true">
      <StatementIndexReport Current="false">
      <StatementCostRangeReport>
      <IndexUsageReport Current="true">
      <IndexUsageReport Current="false">
      <IndexDetailReport Current="true">
        <Database>
          <Name>AdventureWorks2017</Name>
          <Schema>
            <Name>dbo</Name>
            <Table>
              <Name>MythOne</Name>
              <Index FilterDefinition="" NumberOfRows="121317" IndexSizeInMB="11.70" FilteredIndex="false" Heap="true" Unique="false" Clustered="false">
                <Name>MythOne</Name>
              </Index>
            </Table>
            <Table>
              <Name>AllocationCycle</Name>
              <Index FilterDefinition="" NumberOfRows="100000" IndexSizeInMB="77.23" FilteredIndex="false" Heap="false" Unique="true" Clustered="true">
                <Name>PK_AllocationCycle</Name>
              </Index>
            </Table>
            <Table>
              <Name>ErrorLog</Name>
              <Index FilterDefinition="" NumberOfRows="0" IndexSizeInMB="0.01" FilteredIndex="false" Heap="false" Unique="true" Clustered="true">
                <Name>PK_ErrorLog_ErrorLogID</Name>
              </Index>
            </Table>
            <Table>
              <Name>tl_2017_us_county</Name>
              <Index FilterDefinition="" NumberOfRows="3233" IndexSizeInMB="136.32" FilteredIndex="false" Heap="true" Unique="false" Clustered="false">
                <Name>tl_2017_us_county</Name>
              </Index>
            </Table>
```

Figure 12-9. *Sample report output from the DTA utility*

One thing to remember with the last two scenarios is that the table and queries being tuned were tuned in a vacuum. There were no constraints or foreign key relationships on the table that needed to be considered. In the real world, this will not be the way a database is designed, and foreign key relationships will affect how recommendations are provided. Also, the load for these scenarios contained only two queries. When building test workloads, be sure to use a sample that is representative of the environment and its typical queries.

Through the DTA scenarios provided in this section, a foundation has been created for using tools for index tuning activities. Not only can the DTA identify missing indexes, but given a workload, it can also help identify where clustered indexes and partitioning can assist with performance. The physical changes that the DTA can provide can be extremely useful when performance issues need to be quickly addressed in a database:

Automatic tuning - SQL Server | Microsoft Learn

Enable automatic tuning - Azure SQL Database | Microsoft Learn

Summary

This chapter walked through using the built-in indexing tools available in SQL Server. Each of these tools can be a great addition to your SQL Server tool belt. They allow informed indexing decisions to be made quickly and efficiently without expending extensive time and resources to do so.

With regard to the missing index DMOs, the index suggestions are based on existing activity on the SQL Server instance. These are real-world applications that represent areas where performance improvements can be identified, tested, and implemented quickly and effectively in production environments.

The DTA, while not as readily available as the missing index DMOs, allows indexes to be tuned from a single query to a full workload with minimal effort. The option to tune the contents of the plan cache allows the work currently being done in an environment to be leveraged to build recommendations without the need to create a test workload.

CHAPTER 13

Indexing Strategies

Indexing databases is often thought of as an art where the database is the canvas and the indexes are the paints that come together to form a beautiful tapestry of storage and performance. A little color here, a little color there, and paintings will take shape. In much the same way, a clustered index on a table and then a few non-clustered indexes can result in blazingly fast performance as beautiful as any masterpiece. Going a little too abstract or minimalist with indexing might feel good, but the resulting performance will be a reminder that it may not be practical.

As colorful as this analogy is, there is more science behind designing and applying indexes than there is artistry. A few columns pulled together because they might work well together are often less beneficial than an index built upon well-established patterns. The indexes that are based on tried-and-true practices are often the best solutions. In this chapter, a number of common indexing patterns will be discussed to help identify potentially useful indexes.

Heaps

There are few valid cases for using heaps in databases. The general rule of thumb for most DBAs is that all tables in a database should be built with clustered indexes instead of heaps. While this practice rings true in most situations, there are isolated use cases when using a heap is acceptable and preferred. This section looks at one of these scenarios and discusses the others in generalities. The reason for being generic is that it is difficult to make blanket statements about when to use a heap instead of a clustered index (which will be explained more later in the section).

E. Pollack and J. Strate, *Expert Performance Indexing in Azure SQL and SQL Server 2022*, https://doi.org/10.1007/978-1-4842-9215-0_13

Temporary Objects

One of the situations in which heaps are most useful is with temporary objects, such as temporary tables and table variables. When these objects are used, they are often created without considering building a clustered index on them. The result is that heaps are often used for temporary tables.

Consider for a moment the last time you created a table variable or a temporary table. Did the syntax for the object specifically create a CLUSTERED index or a PRIMARY KEY with the default configuration? If not, then the temporary object was created as a heap. This is in no way a problem. It is common in most workloads, though not necessarily a reason to change coding practices. As will be demonstrated in the examples in this section, the performance difference between a temporary object with a heap and a clustered index can be immaterial.

For this example, a simple use case for a temporary table will be introduced. The example uses the table Sales.SalesOrderHeader from which a few rows will be retrieved based on a SalesPersonID. Those rows will then be inserted into a temporary table. The temporary table will be used to return all rows from Sales.SalesOrderDetail that match the results in the temporary table. Two versions of the example will be used to demonstrate how using a heap or a clustered index on the temporary table does not change the query execution.

In the first version of the example, shown in Listing 13-1, the temporary table is built using a heap. This is the method that is most often used to create temporary objects. As the execution plan in Figure 13-1 shows, when the temporary table is accessed, as identified by the arrow, a table scan is used to access the rows in the object. This behavior is expected with a heap. Since the rows aren't ordered, there is no way to access specific rows without checking all the rows first. To find all the rows in Sales.SalesOrderDetail that match those in the temporary table, the execution plan uses a nested loop with an index seek.

Listing 13-1. Temporary Object with a Heap

```
USE AdventureWorks2017
GO

IF OBJECT_ID('tempdb..##TempWithHeap') IS NOT NULL
    DROP TABLE ##TempWithHeap
CREATE TABLE ##TempWithHeap
```

```
    (
    SalesOrderID INT
    );
INSERT INTO ##TempWithHeap
SELECT SalesOrderID
FROM Sales.SalesOrderHeader
WHERE SalesPersonID = 283;

SELECT sod.* FROM Sales.SalesOrderDetail sod
    INNER JOIN ##TempWithHeap t ON t.SalesOrderID = sod.SalesOrderID;
GO
```

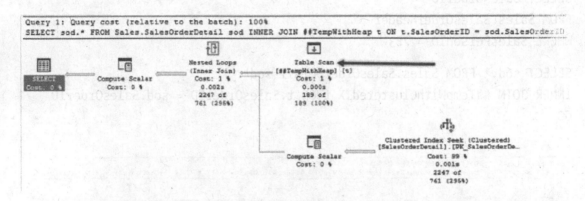

Figure 13-1. *Execution plan for a heap temporary object*

In the second version of the script, shown in Listing 13-2, the temporary table is created instead with a clustered index on the SalesOrderID column. The index is the only difference between the two scripts. This difference results in a slight change in the execution plan. Figure 13-2 shows the clustered index version of the execution plan. The difference between the two plans is that instead of a table scan, there is a clustered index scan against the temporary table. While these are different operations, the work done by both is essentially the same. During query execution, all rows in the temporary object are accessed while joining them to rows in Sales.SalesOrderDetail.

Listing 13-2. Temporary Object with a Clustered Index

```
USE AdventureWorks2017
GO
IF OBJECT_ID('tempdb..##TempWithClusteredIX') IS NOT NULL
    DROP TABLE ##TempWithClusteredIX
CREATE TABLE ##TempWithClusteredIX
    (
    SalesOrderID INT PRIMARY KEY CLUSTERED
    )
INSERT INTO ##TempWithClusteredIX
SELECT SalesOrderID
FROM Sales.SalesOrderHeader
WHERE SalesPersonID = 283

SELECT sod.* FROM Sales.SalesOrderDetail sod
INNER JOIN ##TempWithClusteredIX t ON t.SalesOrderID = sod.SalesOrderID
GO
```

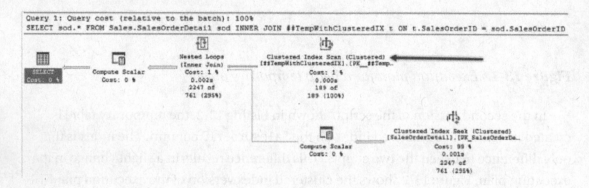

Figure 13-2. *Execution plan for a clustered temporary object*

Note   Since SQL Server 2014, table variables can have both clustered and non-clustered indexes on them. The requirement is that the indexes are created when the variable is declared. DDL operations are not allowed on table variables after they are defined.

In queries similar to the example in this section, the execution plans for temporary tables with heaps and clustered indexes are nearly the same. As with all rules, there may be exceptions where performance will differ. A good example of when using a heap can affect performance is any T-SQL syntax that leverages a sort in its execution. Listing 13-3 shows a specific example using EXISTS in the WHERE clause. Figure 13-3 shows the execution plan for the query. Before the nested loop joins to resolve the EXISTS predicate, the data must first be sorted. In this case, the use of a heap has hindered the performance of the query because the heap table forces a sort operation.

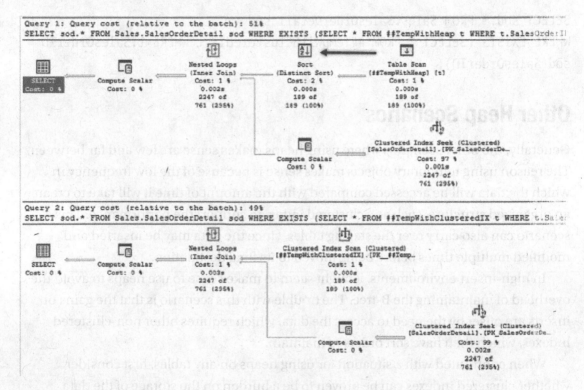

Figure 13-3. *EXISTS example execution plan*

With small datasets, the performance difference may be negligible. As the size of the dataset increases, seemingly minor changes such as the inclusion of a sort operation can reduce the performance of those queries.

Listing 13-3. EXISTS Example

```
USE AdventureWorks2017
GO

SELECT sod.* FROM Sales.SalesOrderDetail sod
WHERE EXISTS (SELECT * FROM ##TempWithHeap t WHERE t.SalesOrderID = sod.
SalesOrderID);
GO

SELECT sod.* FROM Sales.SalesOrderDetail sod
WHERE EXISTS (SELECT * FROM ##TempWithClusteredIX t WHERE t.SalesOrderID =
sod.SalesOrderID);
```

Other Heap Scenarios

Generally, the other scenarios where using heaps makes sense are few and far between. The reason using temporary objects makes sense is because of the low frequency in which the data will be accessed compared with the amount of time it will take to create an organized structure, such as a clustered index, to support the performance. This scenario can also carry over the staging tables, since the data may be inserted and modified multiple times before being moved to its final destination.

In high-insert environments, it might seem to make sense to use heaps to avoid the overhead of maintaining the B-tree. The trouble with this scenario is that the gains on inserts are offset by the need to access the data, which requires other non-clustered indexes, which then have sort orders to maintain.

When confronted with a situation for using heaps on any tables, first consider whether clustered indexes can be proven to be a burden on the storage of the data before using them. Before looking to the heap, also consider whether newer indexing structures such as clustered columnstore indexes or memory-optimized tables provide the performance required. Lastly, ensure that the performance gains of a given change are meaningful. Researching, testing, and implementing an indexing change that results in a 1 percent improvement will only on very rare occasions be worthwhile.

The main point of this section is to emphasize that heaps are used more often in the real world than is often realized. While most best practices rail against their use, there are some situations where they are a good fit and others where it does not matter whether they are there or not. As the discussion moves into clustered indexes, it will become clear why it is usually a good idea to default to clustered indexes and use heaps only in situations where either it won't matter, such as most use cases with temporary objects, or where they outperform clustered indexes.

Clustered Indexes

Throughout this book, the value of and preference for using a clustered index as the structure for organizing the data pages of a table has been discussed. Clustered indexes organize the data in their tables based on their key columns. All the data pages for the index are stored logically according to the key columns. The benefit of this is optimal access to the data through the key columns.

New tables should almost always be built with clustered indexes. The question, though, when building the tables is what should be selected for the key columns in the clustered index. There are a few characteristics that are most often attributed to well-defined clustered indexes. These characteristics are

- Static

- Narrow

- Unique

- Ever-increasing

There are a number of reasons that each of these attributes helps create effective clustered indexes.

First, a clustered index should be static. The key columns defined for the clustered index should be expected to be static for the lifetime of the row. By using a static value, the position of the row in the index will not change when the row is updated. When non-static key columns are used, the position of the row in the clustered index can change, which may require the row to be inserted on a different page. Also, all non-clustered indexes would need to be modified to change the key columns' values stored in those indexes, since clustered index key columns are included in non-clustered indexes. Together, these issues lead to the potential for extensive fragmentation in the clustered and non-clustered indexes on a table.

The next attribute that a clustered index should have is that it is narrow. Ideally, there should be only a single column for the clustered index key. This column should be defined with the smallest data type reasonable for the data being stored in that table.

Narrow clustered indexes are important because the clustered index key for every row is included in all non-clustered indexes associated with the table. The wider the clustered index key, the wider all non-clustered indexes will be, and the more pages they will require. As discussed in other sections, the more pages in an index, the more resources are required to use it. This can affect query performance on that table.

Clustered indexes should also be unique. Clustered indexes store a single row in a specific location in the index; for duplicate rows within the key columns of a clustered index, a uniquifier needs to provide the uniqueness required for the row. When the uniquifier is added to a row, it is extended by 4 bytes, which changes how narrow the clustered index is and results in the same concerns that are associated with a non-narrow clustered index. More information about the uniquifier can be found in Chapter 2.

Lastly, a well-defined clustered index will be based on an ever-increasing value. Using an ever-increasing clustered key causes new rows to be added to the end of the clustered index. Placing new rows at the end of the B-tree reduces the fragmentation that would likely occur if the rows were inserted in the middle of the clustered index.

One additional consideration when selecting the clustered index key columns is that they represent the columns that will frequently be used to access rows. Are there specific columns or values that will most often be used to retrieve rows from the table? If so, these columns are good candidates for the clustering index key. Ultimately, queries against the table will perform best when they can access data through the path of least resistance. Similarly, write operations will be most efficient and least intrusive when rows can be quickly written to the end of the index without the need to perform additional background tasks on the fly.

While considering the previous guidelines for selecting clustered index strategies, there are a number of patterns that can be used to identify and model clustered indexes. The clustered index patterns are

- Identity Sequence
- Natural Key
- Foreign Key
- Multiple Column
- Globally Unique Identifier

In the rest of this section, each of these patterns will be walked through, describing each and how to identify when to utilize the pattern.

Identity Sequence

The most frequent pattern for building a clustered index is to pair it with a column on a table that has been configured to be ever-increasing using either the IDENTITY property or the SEQUENCE object. In this pattern, the IDENTITY column is often also the PRIMARY KEY on the table. The data type is usually an integer, which includes tinyint, smallint, int, and bigint. The primary benefit of this pattern is that it achieves (and enforces) all of the attributes of a well-defined clustered index. It is static, narrow, unique, and ever-increasing. When considering how data in the table will be accessed, in most cases the key value will most often be used to access rows in the table.

One distinction of the Identity Sequence pattern is that the column used for the clustered index key has no relationship between the data in the row and the clustered index key. To implement the pattern, either a column is included in the table definition that has the IDENTITY property or a column is added to the table that uses SEQUENCE values. This column is then set as the clustered index key and often the PRIMARY KEY as well.

Examples of this pattern can be found in nearly all databases. Creating a table with this pattern would look similar to the CREATE TABLE statements in Listing 13-4. Both tables are built to contain fruit: two apple rows, a banana row, and a grape row are inserted. The Color column would not have been a good clustering key since it does not identify the rows in the table. The FruitName column could have identified the rows in the table, except it is not unique across the table, which would have required the uniquifier and lead to a larger clustering key. Indexing the table to the Identity Sequence pattern, a FruitID column is created.

Listing 13-4. Creating and Populating Tables for the Identity Sequence Pattern

```
USE AdventureWorks2017
GO

IF OBJECT_ID('IndexStrategiesFruit_Identity') IS NOT NULL
    DROP TABLE IndexStrategiesFruit_Identity
CREATE TABLE dbo.IndexStrategiesFruit_Identity
(
FruitID int IDENTITY(1,1)
,FruitName varchar(25)
,Color varchar(10)
```

```
,CONSTRAINT PK_Fruit_FruitID_Idnt PRIMARY KEY CLUSTERED (FruitID)
);
INSERT INTO dbo.IndexStrategiesFruit_Identity(FruitName, Color)
VALUES('Apple','Red'),('Banana','Yellow'),('Apple','Green'),('Grape',
'Green');
SELECT FruitID, FruitName, Color
FROM dbo.IndexStrategiesFruit_Identity;
IF OBJECT_ID('IndexStrategiesFruit_Sequence') IS NOT NULL
    DROP TABLE IndexStrategiesFruit_Sequence
IF OBJECT_ID('FruitSequence') IS NOT NULL
    DROP SEQUENCE FruitSequence
CREATE SEQUENCE FruitSequence AS INTEGER
    START WITH 1;
CREATE TABLE dbo.IndexStrategiesFruit_Sequence
(
FruitID int DEFAULT NEXT VALUE FOR FruitSequence
,FruitName varchar(25)
,Color varchar(10)
,CONSTRAINT PK_Fruit_FruitID_Seq PRIMARY KEY CLUSTERED (FruitID)
);
INSERT INTO dbo.IndexStrategiesFruit_Sequence(FruitName, Color)
VALUES('Apple','Red'),('Banana','Yellow'),('Apple','Green'),('Grape',
'Green');
SELECT FruitID, FruitName, Color
FROM dbo.IndexStrategiesFruit_Sequence;
```

One of the effects of using the Identity Sequence pattern is that the value for the clustering key column has no relationship to the information that it represents. In the query output from Listing 13-4, shown in Figure 13-4, the value of 1 is assigned to the first row inserted for both result sets. Then, a value of 2 is assigned for the next row and so on. As more rows are added, the FruitID column increments and does not require any single piece of information in the record in order to designate the instance of information.

	FruitID	FruitName	Color
1	1	Apple	Red
2	2	Banana	Yellow
3	3	Apple	Green
4	4	Grape	Green

	FruitID	FruitName	Color
1	1	Apple	Red
2	2	Banana	Yellow
3	3	Apple	Green
4	4	Grape	Green

Figure 13-4. *Results for the Identity Sequence pattern*

Note SEQUENCE was introduced in SQL Server 2012. Through sequences, ranges of numeric values can be generated, which are either ascending or descending. A sequence is not associated with any specific table. Sequences provide distinct benefits when a numeric primary key needs to be scoped across multiple tables or when customization is required. A detailed discussion of sequences is outside the context of this book.

Natural Key

In some cases, using a natural key in the data for the clustering key is as valid as adding an identity column to the table to use for the Identity Sequence pattern. A natural key is a column within the dataset that can uniquely identify one row from all the other rows. The cases where using a natural key is valid can be identified when there is a natural key in the data that meets the attributes of a well-defined clustering key. When using natural keys for clustering keys, they are less likely to be ever-increasing, but they should still be unique, narrow, and static.

A common example of when a natural key may be used instead of an identity column is when looking at tables that contain one- or two-character abbreviations for the information they represent. These abbreviations may be for the status of an order, the size of a product, or a list of states or provinces. Compared with using an `int`, which is 4 bytes, in the Identity Column pattern, using a `char(1)` or `char(2)` data type with the Natural Key pattern will result in a clustering key that is narrower than the former.

Another example is using dates in the yyyymmdd or timestamp format on date tables. Similarly, a dataset may already include an identifying column, such as an invoice ID, purchase order number, or account number. Columns such as these that are unique and already generated by an application can be used effectively as clustered index columns, assuming they are unique, narrow, static, and (maybe) ever-increasing.

The Natural Key pattern also has the added benefit of providing an easier-todecipher key value. When using the Identity Sequence pattern, there is no inherent meaning when the clustering key has a value of 1 or 7. These values are (intentionally) meaningless. With the Natural Key pattern, for example, the abbreviations of *O* and *C* represent real information (Opened and Closed, respectively).

As a simple example of the Natural Key pattern, consider a table that contains states and their abbreviations. Also included is the name of the country for the states. Listing 13-5 shows the SQL to create and populate the table. The table has a `StateAbbreviation` column, which is a `char(2)`. Since this is a narrow, unique, and static value for each state, the clustered index is created on the column. Next, a few rows are added to the table for the four states that the fictitious database requires.

Listing 13-5. Creating and Populating a Table for the Natural Key Pattern

```
USE AdventureWorks2017
GO

CREATE TABLE dbo.IndexStrategiesNatural
(
StateAbbreviation char(2)
,StateName varchar(25)
,Country varchar(25)
,CONSTRAINT PK_State_StateAbbreviation PRIMARY KEY CLUSTERED
(StateAbbreviation)
);
INSERT INTO dbo.IndexStrategiesNatural(StateAbbreviation, StateName,
Country)
VALUES('MN','Minnesota','United States')
,('FL','Florida','United States')
,('WI','Wisconsin','United States')
,('NH','New Hampshire','United States');
```

```
SELECT StateAbbreviation, StateName, Country
FROM dbo.IndexStrategiesNatural;
```

In situations where the natural key matches the Natural Key pattern, the technique in Listing 13-5 can be a useful way of selecting the clustering key column. Reviewing the contents of dbo.IndexStrategiesNatural (shown in Figure 13-5), the four rows are in the table, and using StateAbbreviation in another table as a foreign key value can be useful since the value MN has some inherent meaning.

	StateAbbreviation	StateName	Country
1	FL	Florida	United States
2	MN	Minnesota	United States
3	NH	New Hampshire	United States
4	WI	Wisconsin	United States

Figure 13-5. *Results for the Natural Key pattern*

This pattern may seem ideal and more worthwhile than the Identity Column pattern—especially since the value of the clustering key helps describe the data. However, there are a few downsides to using this pattern, which relate to the attributes that can make it a well-defined clustering key.

First, consider the uniqueness of the clustering key. Provided that the use cases for the database and table never change, there can be trust that the values will remain unique. What happens, though, when the database needs to be used in an international context? If states in other countries such as the Netherlands need to be included, there is a great potential for data issues. In the Netherlands, FL is the abbreviation for Flevopolder, and NH is the abbreviation for Noord-Holland. Sending an order to Florida that should go to Flevopolder can have serious business consequences. To retain the uniqueness, something outside of the two-character abbreviation would need to be added to the natural key and clustering key.

Changing the natural key would then affect the narrowness of the clustering key. There are two approaches that could be taken to address this problem. The first option is to add another column to the natural key, such as the country or some other location identifier. The second option is to increase the size of the state abbreviation to include a country abbreviation in the same column. With either of the solutions, the size of the clustering key will exceed the 4 bytes used to maintain a narrow clustering key through the use of an int data type and the Identity Column pattern.

Additionally, always consider whether natural keys are truly static. State abbreviations can change. While this doesn't happen often, it has historically occurred. The last change in the United States happened in 1987 when state abbreviations were all standardized. Similar changes will happen occasionally with nearly all types of natural keys. One example is the country of Yugoslavia with its six republics, each of which became its own country. Another is the Soviet Union, which evolved into the Russian Federation, resulting in the formation of numerous other countries. As static as values such as state and country abbreviations may seem, on a grander scale there is variance. Also, looking to applications, status codes that represent the states of a workflow may be accurate today but could have new and different meanings in the future.

Lastly, sometimes apparent natural keys can be made of data that shouldn't be widely distributed. For years, government identifiers, like Social Security Number, were often used for natural keys in databases, especially in healthcare and educational systems. While this did an adequate job of identifying an individual, it definitely isn't information that should be easily available to database users. In most modern databases, government identifiers now need to be encrypted, which can cause immense problems when these types of natural keys are used for clustered indexes and potentially as primary keys.

The Natural Key pattern for selecting what an index does is a valid pattern for designing clustered indexes. As the example showed, it can be unique, narrow, and static. Carefully examine the current and future applications of the table before using a natural key for the clustered index to ensure that it will not be impacted by future change.

Foreign Key

One of the most often overlooked patterns for creating clustered indexes is to use a foreign key column in the clustering keys for the table. The Foreign Key pattern is not appropriate for all foreign keys but does have its use in designs where there is a one-to-many relationship between information in a header table and the related detail information. The Foreign Key pattern contains all the attributes that are part of a well-defined clustering key. There are, though, a few caveats with a few of the attributes.

Implementing this pattern is similar to the way the Identity Column pattern is implemented. The pattern contains two tables that have columns with the IDENTITY property set on them. Listing 13-6 shows an example. In the example, there are three tables created. The first is the header table, named dbo.IndexStrategiesHeader, with a clustered index built on the HeaderID column. The next table is the first version of the detail table, named dbo.IndexStrategiesDetail_ICP. The table is designed as a child to the header table, the clustered index is built using the Identity Column pattern, and an index on the HeaderID column is used to improve performance. The third table is also a detail table, named dbo.IndexStrategiesDetail_FKP; this table is designed using the Foreign Key pattern. Instead of clustering the table on the column with the IDENTITY property, the clustered index includes two columns. The first column is the column from the parent table, HeaderID, and the second is the primary key for this table, DetailID. To provide sample data, sys.indexes and sys.index_columns are used to populate all the tables.

Listing 13-6. Creating and Populating Tables for the Foreign Key Pattern

```
USE AdventureWorks2017
GO
CREATE TABLE dbo.IndexStrategiesHeader
(
HeaderID int IDENTITY(1,1)
,FillerData char(250)
,CONSTRAINT PK_Header_HeaderID PRIMARY KEY CLUSTERED (HeaderID)
);
CREATE TABLE dbo.IndexStrategiesDetail_ICP
(
DetailID int IDENTITY(1,1)
,HeaderID int
,FillerData char(500)
,CONSTRAINT PK_Detail_ICP_DetailID PRIMARY KEY CLUSTERED (DetailID)
,CONSTRAINT FK_Detail_ICP_HeaderID FOREIGN KEY (HeaderID) REFERENCES IndexS
trategiesHeader(HeaderID)
);
CREATE INDEX IX_Detail_ICP_HeaderID ON dbo.IndexStrategiesDetail_ICP
(HeaderID)
```

```
CREATE TABLE dbo.IndexStrategiesDetail_FKP
(
DetailID int IDENTITY(1,1)
,HeaderID int
,FillerData char(500)
,CONSTRAINT PK_Detail_FKP_DetailID PRIMARY KEY NONCLUSTERED (DetailID)
,CONSTRAINT CLUS_Detail_FKP_HeaderIDDetailID UNIQUE CLUSTERED (HeaderID,
DetailID)
,CONSTRAINT FK_Detail_FKP_HeaderID FOREIGN KEY (HeaderID) REFERENCES
IndexStrategiesHeader(HeaderID)
);
GO
INSERT INTO dbo.IndexStrategiesHeader(FillerData)
SELECT CONVERT(varchar,object_id)+name
FROM sys.indexes
INSERT INTO dbo.IndexStrategiesDetail_ICP
SELECT ish.HeaderID, CONVERT(varchar,ic.index_column_id)+'-'+FillerData
FROM dbo.IndexStrategiesHeader ish
        INNER JOIN sys.indexes i ON ish.FillerData = CONVERT(varchar,i.
        object_id)+i.name
        INNER JOIN sys.index_columns ic ON i.object_id = ic.object_id AND
        i.index_id = ic.index_id
INSERT INTO dbo.IndexStrategiesDetail_FKP
SELECT ish.HeaderID, CONVERT(varchar,ic.index_column_id)+'-'+FillerData
FROM dbo.IndexStrategiesHeader ish
        INNER JOIN sys.indexes i ON ish.FillerData = CONVERT(varchar,i.
        object_id)+i.name
        INNER JOIN sys.index_columns ic ON i.object_id = ic.object_id AND
        i.index_id = ic.index_id
```

At this point, there are three tables designed using the two clustered index patterns, Identity Sequence and Foreign Key. The key to this pattern is to design the table so that in their common usage patterns the data will be returned as efficiently as possible. There are two use cases that are common in this type of scenario. The first is returning the header and all the detail rows for one row in the header table. The second is to return multiple rows from the header table and all the related rows from the detail table.

First, the difference in performance for returning one row from the header table and all the related detail rows will be examined. The code in Listing 13-7 implements this use case using both clustered indexing patterns. As expected, the dataset returned by both queries is the same. The difference lies in the statistics and query plan for the two queries. Examine the statistics output when STATISTICS IO is used during the first use case, as shown in Figure 13-6. The reads for the Identity Column pattern show that there were four reads as opposed to two reads by the Foreign Key pattern. While these numbers are low, this is a twofold difference that could impact a database significantly if these are highly utilized queries. The big difference in execution, though, can be seen when reviewing the execution plans for the two queries (Figure 13-7). For the first query, to retrieve the results, an index seek, key lookup, and nested loop are required against the detail table. Compare this with the second query, which obtains the same information using a clustered index seek. This example clearly indicates that the Foreign Key pattern is able to perform better than the Identity Column pattern.

Listing 13-7. Single Header Row on the Foreign Key Pattern

```
Use AdventureWorks2017
GO

SET STATISTICS IO ON

SELECT  ish.HeaderID, ish.FillerData, isd.DetailID, isd.FillerData
FROM dbo.IndexStrategiesHeader ish
        INNER JOIN dbo.IndexStrategiesDetail_ICP isd ON ish.HeaderID = isd.
        HeaderID
WHERE ish.HeaderID = 10

SELECT  ish.HeaderID, ish.FillerData, isd.DetailID, isd.FillerData
FROM dbo.IndexStrategiesHeader ish
        INNER JOIN dbo.IndexStrategiesDetail_FKP isd ON ish.HeaderID = isd.
        HeaderID
WHERE ish.HeaderID = 10
```

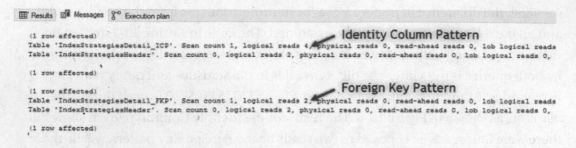

Figure 13-6.   *Results for a single header row on the Foreign Key pattern*

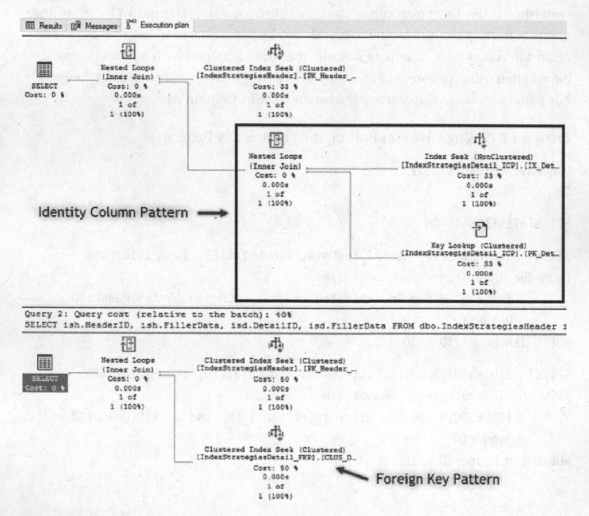

Figure 13-7.   *Execution plans for a single header row on the Foreign Key pattern*

With the success of the first use case, the second one can now be examined. In this example, shown in Listing 13-8, the queries will retrieve multiple rows from the header table and the data from the detail table that matches the HeaderID from the header rows. Again, the data returned by the queries using both of the clustered index patterns is the same, and there are performance differences between the two executions. The first difference is in the STATISTICS IO output, shown in Figure 13-8. In the first execution, there are 158 reads on the header table and 44 reads on the detail table. Comparing those with the four reads on the header and eight reads on the detail for the Foreign Key pattern, it's clear that the Foreign Key pattern performs better. The reads are a magnitude lower for the Foreign Key over the Identity Column pattern! The reason for the performance difference can be explained through the execution plan shown in Figure 13-9. In the execution plan, the first query requires a clustered index scan on the detail table to return the rows from the detail table. The second query, using the Foreign Key pattern, does not require this and uses a clustered index seek.

Listing 13-8. Multiple Header Rows on the Foreign Key Pattern

```
Use AdventureWorks2017
GO

SET STATISTICS IO ON

SELECT ish.HeaderID, ish.FillerData, isd.DetailID, isd.FillerData
FROM dbo.IndexStrategiesHeader ish
      INNER JOIN dbo.IndexStrategiesDetail_ICP isd ON ish.HeaderID = isd.
      HeaderID
WHERE ish.HeaderID BETWEEN 10 AND 50;

SELECT ish.HeaderID, ish.FillerData, isd.DetailID, isd.FillerData
FROM dbo.IndexStrategiesHeader ish
      INNER JOIN dbo.IndexStrategiesDetail_FKP isd ON ish.HeaderID = isd.
      HeaderID
WHERE ish.HeaderID BETWEEN 10 AND 50;
```

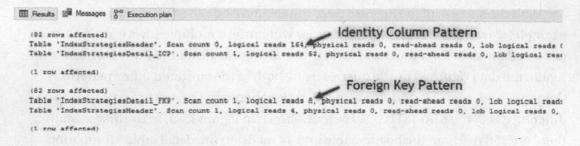

Figure 13-8. *Results for multiple header rows on the Foreign Key pattern*

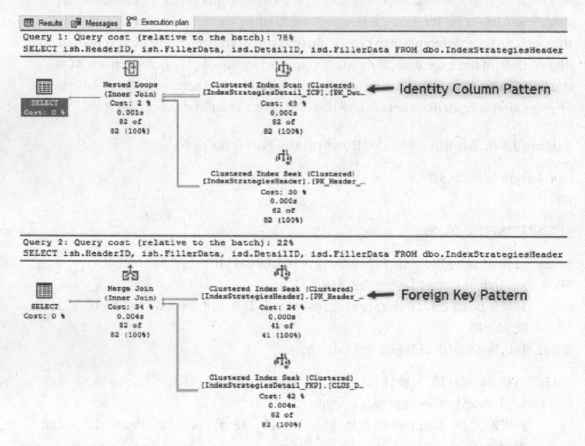

Figure 13-9. *Execution plans for multiple header rows on the Foreign Key pattern*

Through the two use cases in this section, we can see how the Foreign Key pattern can outperform the Identity Column pattern. However, there are things that need to be considered in databases before implementing this pattern. The chief question that needs to be answered is whether rows will most often be retrieved going through the primary key of the detail table or its foreign key relationship to the header table. Not all foreign keys are suited for this clustered index pattern; it is valid only when there is a header-to-detail relationship between tables.

There are a few caveats regarding the attributes of a well-defined clustered index when using the Foreign Key pattern. In regard to being narrow, the pattern is not as narrow as the Identity Column pattern. Instead of a single integer-based column, two of them make up the clustering keys. When using the int data type, this will increase the size of the clustering key from 4 bytes to 8 bytes. While not an overly large value, it will impact the size of all non-clustered indexes on the table. In most cases, the clustering keys under the Foreign Key pattern will be static. There is a chance that the header row for some detail rows will need to change from time to time, maybe when two orders are logged and need to be merged for shipping. For this reason, the Foreign Key pattern isn't entirely static. The key can change, but it shouldn't change frequently. If there are frequent changes, then reconsider using this clustered index pattern. The last attribute that has a caveat is whether the clustering keys are ever-increasing. In general, this should be the case. The typical insert pattern is to create a header and the detail records. In this situation, the header rows are created and inserted sequentially, followed by their detail records. If there is a delay in writing the detail records or more detail records are added to a header row at a later date, the key won't be ever-increasing. As a result, there could be additional fragmentation and maintenance associated with this clustered index pattern.

The Foreign Key pattern is not a clustered index pattern that will be applicable in most tables. When it is, though, it is quite beneficial and can alleviate performance issues that may not be as obvious as other issues. It is important to consider using this pattern when designing clustered indexes and to review the caveats associated with it to determine whether it is the right fit.

Multiple Column

The next pattern that can be used to design clustered indexes is the Multiple Column pattern. In this pattern, two or more tables have a relationship to another table that allows for many-to-many relationships to exist between the information. For instance, there might be a table that stores employee information and another that contains job roles. To represent the relationship, a third table is used. Through the Multiple Column pattern, instead of using a new column with the IDENTITY property on it, the columns used for the relationship serve as the clustering keys.

The Multiple Column pattern is similar to the Foreign Key pattern and provides many of the same performance enhancements as the previous pattern. There is often one column or another in the many-to-many relationship table that is the best candidate for the clustering key. Like the other patterns, this one also adheres to most of the attributes for a well-defined clustered index. The pattern is unique and mostly narrow and static; these properties will be apparent as an example of the Multiple Column pattern is illustrated.

To demonstrate the Multiple Column pattern, begin by defining a few tables and their relationships. To start, there are tables that will store information about employees and job roles, named dbo.Employee and dbo.JobRole, respectively. Two tables named dbo.EmployeeJobRole_ICP and dbo.EmployeeJobRole_MCP are used to represent the Identity Column and Multiple Column patterns in the example relationships (see Listing 13-9). The example script includes insert statements to provide some sample data to use. Also, non-clustered indexes are created on the tables to provide a real-world scenario.

Listing 13-9. Multiple Column Pattern Script

```
USE AdventureWorks2017
GO
CREATE TABLE dbo.Employee (
EmployeeID int IDENTITY(1,1)
,EmployeeName varchar(100)
,FillerData varchar(1000)
,CONSTRAINT PK_Employee PRIMARY KEY CLUSTERED (EmployeeID));

CREATE INDEX IX_Employee_EmployeeName ON dbo.Employee(EmployeeName);

CREATE TABLE dbo.JobRole (
JobRoleID int IDENTITY(1,1)
,RoleName varchar(25)
,FillerData varchar(200)
,CONSTRAINT PK_JobRole PRIMARY KEY CLUSTERED (JobRoleID));

CREATE INDEX IX_JobRole_RoleName ON dbo.JobRole(RoleName);
CREATE TABLE dbo.EmployeeJobRole_ICP (
EmployeeJobRoleID int IDENTITY(1,1)
,EmployeeID int
,JobRoleID int
```

```
,CONSTRAINT PK_EmployeeJobRole_ICP PRIMARY KEY CLUSTERED
(EmployeeJobRoleID)
,CONSTRAINT UIX_EmployeeJobRole_ICP UNIQUE (EmployeeID, JobRoleID))

CREATE INDEX IX_EmployeeJobRole_ICP_EmployeeID ON dbo.EmployeeJobRole_
ICP(EmployeeID);
CREATE INDEX IX_EmployeeJobRole_ICP_JobRoleID ON dbo.EmployeeJobRole_
ICP(JobRoleID);

CREATE TABLE dbo.EmployeeJobRole_MCP (
EmployeeJobRoleID int IDENTITY(1,1)
,EmployeeID int
,JobRoleID int
,CONSTRAINT PK_EmployeeJobRoleID PRIMARY KEY NONCLUSTERED
(EmployeeJobRoleID)
,CONSTRAINT CUIX_EmployeeJobRole_ICP UNIQUE CLUSTERED (EmployeeID,
JobRoleID));

CREATE INDEX IX_EmployeeJobRole_MCP_JobRoleID ON dbo.EmployeeJobRole_
MCP(JobRoleID);
INSERT INTO dbo.Employee (EmployeeName)
SELECT OBJECT_SCHEMA_NAME(object_id)+'|'+name
FROM sys.tables;

INSERT INTO dbo.JobRole (RoleName)
VALUES ('Cook'),('Butcher'),('Candlestick Maker');
INSERT INTO dbo.EmployeeJobRole_ICP (EmployeeID, JobRoleID)
SELECT EmployeeID, 1 FROM dbo.Employee
UNION ALL SELECT EmployeeID, 2 FROM dbo.Employee WHERE EmployeeID / 4 = 1
UNION ALL SELECT EmployeeID, 3 FROM dbo.Employee WHERE EmployeeID / 8 = 1;

INSERT INTO dbo.EmployeeJobRole_MCP (EmployeeID, JobRoleID)
SELECT EmployeeID, 1 FROM dbo.Employee
UNION ALL SELECT EmployeeID, 2 FROM dbo.Employee WHERE EmployeeID / 4 = 1
UNION ALL SELECT EmployeeID, 3 FROM dbo.Employee WHERE EmployeeID / 8 = 1;
```

The first test against the example tables will look at querying against all three tables to retrieve information on employee names and job roles. These queries, shown in

Listing 13-10, retrieve information based on the RoleName from dbo.JobRole. In the code, the two versions of the EmployeeJobRole table are created with different clustering keys. This results in a drastic difference in the execution plans, shown in Figures 13-10 and 13-11, from the test queries. The first execution plan using the table with the Identity Column pattern applied to it is more complex than the execution plan for the second query and has 61 percent of the cost compared with the other plan. The second plan, which has its clustering keys based on the Multiple Column pattern, has fewer operations and accounts for 39 percent of the execution. The main difference between the two plans is that using the Multiple Column pattern allows the clustered index to cover table access based on a column that is likely to be used to frequently access rows in the table, in this case the JobRoleID column. Using the other pattern does not provide this benefit and represents a data access path that will not likely be used, except potentially when needing to delete the row.

Listing 13-10. Script for the Identity Column Pattern

```
USE AdventureWorks2017
GO

SELECT e.EmployeeName, jr.RoleName
FROM dbo.Employee e
INNER JOIN dbo.EmployeeJobRole_ICP ejr ON e.EmployeeID = ejr.EmployeeID
INNER JOIN dbo.JobRole jr ON ejr.JobRoleID = jr.JobRoleID
WHERE RoleName = 'Candlestick Maker'

SELECT e.EmployeeName, jr.RoleName
FROM dbo.Employee e
INNER JOIN dbo.EmployeeJobRole_MCP ejr ON e.EmployeeID = ejr.EmployeeID
INNER JOIN dbo.JobRole jr ON ejr.JobRoleID = jr.JobRoleID
WHERE RoleName = 'Candlestick Maker'
```

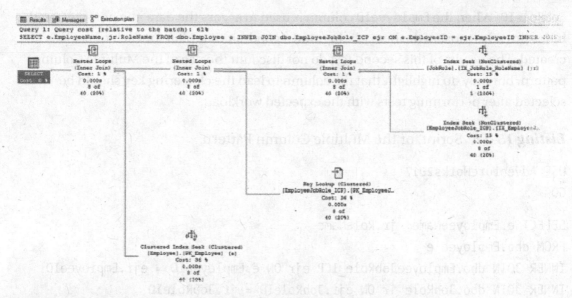

Figure 13-10. *Execution plan for the Identity Column pattern*

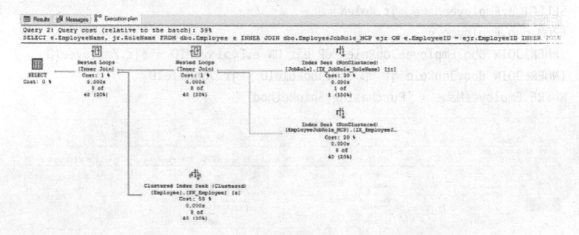

Figure 13-11. *Execution plan for the Multiple Column pattern*

While the benefits are significant with the first set of test results, they are less impressive when looking at some other methods that can be used. For instance, what if instead of using RoleName as the predicate, EmployeeName was used as the predicate? The script in Listing 13-11 demonstrates this scenario. Contrary to the last test script, the results this time are no different than the others for either clustered index design (see Figures 13-12 and 13-13). The cause of the identical plans is based on the decision to optimize the clustering index keys in the Multiple Column pattern to favor the

JobRoleID. When the EmployeeID column is used to access the data, the non-clustered index provides most of the heavy lifting, and a good, similar plan for each query is created. The results of this second test do not discount the use of the Multiple Column pattern, but they do highlight that the column to lead the clustering key should be selected after performing tests with the expected workload.

Listing 13-11. Script for the Multiple Column Pattern

```
USE AdventureWorks2017
GO

SELECT e.EmployeeName, jr.RoleName
FROM dbo.Employee e
INNER JOIN dbo.EmployeeJobRole_ICP ejr ON e.EmployeeID = ejr.EmployeeID
INNER JOIN dbo.JobRole jr ON ejr.JobRoleID = jr.JobRoleID
WHERE EmployeeName = 'Purchasing|ShipMethod'

SELECT e.EmployeeName, jr.RoleName
FROM dbo.Employee e
INNER JOIN dbo.EmployeeJobRole_MCP ejr ON e.EmployeeID = ejr.EmployeeID
INNER JOIN dbo.JobRole jr ON ejr.JobRoleID = jr.JobRoleID
WHERE EmployeeName = 'Purchasing|ShipMethod'
```

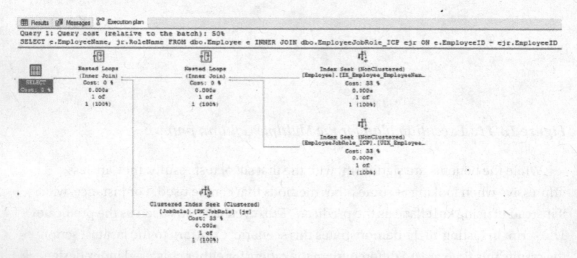

Figure 13-12. *Execution plan for the Identity Column pattern*

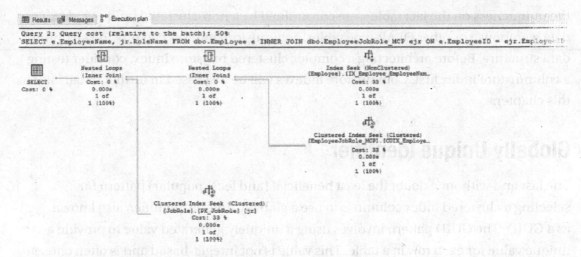

Figure 13-13. *Execution plan for the Multiple Column pattern*

There are various ways in which the Multiple Column pattern can be implemented. The key columns in the clustered index can be reversed, which would change the execution plans generated for the test scripts. While this pattern can be beneficial, be cautious when using it and fully understand the workload expected before using it.

To wrap up the Multiple Column pattern, the attributes of a well-defined clustered index will be reviewed. First, the values are static. If there were to be a change, it would likely be deleting a record and inserting a new one. This is still effectively an update. To mitigate this risk, attempt to lead the clustered index with the value least likely to change or have variations in population. The second is whether the clustering key is narrow. In this example, the key was mostly narrow. It was comprised of two 4-byte columns. If using larger columns or more than two columns, carefully consider if this is the right approach. The next attribute is whether the values are unique. They are in this scenario and should be in any scenario in the real world. If not, then this pattern is naturally disqualified. Like with the other non–Identity Column patterns, this pattern does not provide an ever-increasing clustering key.

As a final note, fact tables in data warehouses often succumb to the temptation to use the Multiple Column pattern. In these cases, all the dimension keys in the fact table are placed in the clustered index. The aim in doing this is to enforce uniqueness on the fact rows. The effect is the creation of an extremely wide clustering key, which is then added to all the non-clustered indexes on the table. Most likely, each of the dimension columns in the clustered key will have a separate index on the fact table. As a result, these indexes waste a lot of space and, because of their size, perform much worse than if the uniqueness on the fact table were constrained by a non-clustered unique index. For data warehouse or other OLAP-type tables, columnstore indexes can provide an optimal data structure. Before architecting a complex clustered rowstore index, consider testing a columnstore index first. Columnstore indexes will be discussed in further detail later in this chapter.

Globally Unique Identifier

The last and without a doubt the least beneficial (and least popular) pattern for selecting a clustered index column is to use a globally unique identifier, also known as a GUID. The GUID pattern involves using a uniquely generated value to provide a unique value for each row in a table. This value is not integer-based and is often chosen because it can be generated at any location (within the topology of an application) and has a guarantee that it will be unique. The problem this pattern solves is the need to be able to generate new unique values while disconnecting from the source that typically controls the list of unique values. Unfortunately, the GUID pattern often creates as many challenges as it solves.

There are two main methods for generating GUID values. The first is through the NEWID() function. This function generates a 16-byte hexadecimal value that is partially based on the MAC address of the computer creating it at the time. Each value generated is unique and can start with any value from 0 to 9 or a to f. The next value created can be either ahead of or after the previous value in a sort. There is no guarantee that the next value is ever-increasing. The second option for generating a GUID is through NEWSEQUENTIALID(). This function also creates a 16-byte hexadecimal value. Unlike the other function, NEWSEQUENTIALID() creates new values that are greater than the previous value generated since the computer was last started. The last point is important in that when the server restarts, it is possible that new values with NEWSEQUENTIALID() will be less than the value created before the restart. The logic for NEWSEQUENTIALID() ensures sequential values only from the time in which the server is started.

As discussed, using the GUID pattern does not provide for an ever-increasing value. With either NEWID() or NEWSEQUENTIALID(), there is no guarantee that the next value will always be greater than the last value. Along with that, it does not provide a narrow index. When storing a GUID as a uniqueidentifier, it requires 16 bytes of storage. This is the size of four ints or two bigints. Comparatively, the GUID is quite large, and that value will be used in all non-clustered indexes on the table. The space used for the

GUID pattern can sometimes be worse than this, though. In some cases, when the GUID pattern is poorly implemented, the GUID value is stored as characters that require 36 bytes to store or 72 bytes if using a Unicode data type.

Even with the failings of the GUID pattern, it does achieve some of the other attributes of a well-defined clustering key. First, the value is unique. With both the NEWID() and NEWSEQUENTIALID() functions, the values generated for the GUID value are unique. The value is also static since the GUID value generated has no business meaning and therefore has no reason to change.

To demonstrate the impact of using the GUID pattern, its use on a table with a comparison with other implementations will be examined. In this scenario, shown in Listing 13-12, there are three tables. Table dbo.IndexStrategiesGUID_ICP is designed using the Identity Column pattern. Table dbo.IndexStrategiesGUID_UniqueID is built with the GUID pattern using a uniqueidentifier, as best practices dictate. The last script contains table dbo.IndexStrategiesGUID_String, which uses a varchar(36) to store the GUID value. The last method is not the proper way to implement the GUID pattern, and the analysis will help highlight that. With all three tables built, insert statements will populate 250,000 rows to each table. The final statement in the scenario retrieves the number of pages used by each of the tables.

Listing 13-12. Script for the GUID Pattern Scenario

```
USE AdventureWorks2017
GO

CREATE TABLE dbo.IndexStrategiesGUID_ICP (
RowID int IDENTITY(1,1)
,FillerData varchar(1000)
,CONSTRAINT PK_IndexStrategiesGUID_ICP PRIMARY KEY CLUSTERED (RowID)
);
CREATE TABLE dbo.IndexStrategiesGUID_UniqueID (
RowID uniqueidentifier DEFAULT(NEWSEQUENTIALID())
,FillerData varchar(1000)
,CONSTRAINT PK_IndexStrategiesGUID_UniqueID PRIMARY KEY CLUSTERED (RowID)
);
CREATE TABLE dbo.IndexStrategiesGUID_String (
RowID varchar(36) DEFAULT(NEWID())
,FillerData varchar(1000)
```

```
,CONSTRAINT PK_IndexStrategiesGUID_String PRIMARY KEY CLUSTERED (RowID)
);
INSERT INTO dbo.IndexStrategiesGUID_ICP (FillerData)
SELECT TOP (250000) a1.name+a2.name
FROM sys.all_objects a1 CROSS JOIN sys.all_objects a2
INSERT INTO dbo.IndexStrategiesGUID_UniqueID (FillerData)
SELECT TOP (250000) a1.name+a2.name
FROM sys.all_objects a1 CROSS JOIN sys.all_objects a2
INSERT INTO dbo.IndexStrategiesGUID_String (FillerData)
SELECT TOP (250000) a1.name+a2.name
FROM sys.all_objects a1 CROSS JOIN sys.all_objects a2
SELECT OBJECT_NAME(object_ID) as table_name, in_row_used_page_count,
in_row_reserved_page_count
FROM sys.dm_db_partition_stats
WHERE object_id IN (OBJECT_ID('dbo.IndexStrategiesGUID_ICP')
        ,OBJECT_ID('dbo.IndexStrategiesGUID_UniqueID')
        ,OBJECT_ID('dbo.IndexStrategiesGUID_String'))
ORDER BY 1
```

Figure 13-14 shows some output from this query.

	table_name	in_row_used_page_count	in_row_reserved_page_count
1	IndexStrategiesGUID_ICP	1869	1889
2	IndexStrategiesGUID_String	2959	2977
3	IndexStrategiesGUID_UniqueID	2250	2273

Figure 13-14. *Page counts for the GUID pattern*

Unlike the other scenarios, the use of the GUID pattern is similar to the Identity Column pattern. There are two primary differences. First, the GUID pattern does not provide a narrow clustering key. For the clustering key with the uniqueidentifier data type, the change in size of the clustering key requires about 400 more pages to store the same information (see Figure 13-14). Even worse, when improperly storing the GUID in a varchar data type, the table requires about 1,100 more pages. Without a doubt, using the GUID pattern amounts to a lot of wasted space in the clustered index, which would also be included in any non-clustered indexes on the table. The second challenge with the GUID pattern is tied with the ever-increasing attribute of clustered indexes. GUIDs are not presented in an ordered fashion. The next value can be greater or less than the previous value, and this leads to a random placement of rows within a table, which results in fragmentation. For more information on index fragmentation as a result of GUIDs, read Chapter 10.

In regard to the last two attributes of a well-defined clustering key, the GUID pattern does well with those. The value is static and should not be expected to change over time. The value is also unique. It should, in fact, be unique throughout the entire database. Even though the GUID pattern does achieve the two attributes of a well-defined clustered index, they do not mitigate the aforementioned issues with this pattern. The GUID pattern should be a pattern of last resort when determining how to build the clustered index for a table.

Note Using the new `sp_sequence_get_range` stored procedure in conjunction with SEQUENCEs can be a valid replacement in applications using the `uniqueidentifier` pattern that would like to migrate to using an Identity Column pattern for clustered index design.

Non-clustered Indexes

In the previous two sections, the discussion focused on heaps and clustered indexes, which are used to determine the primary method for storing data. With heaps, the data is stored unsorted. With clustered indexes, data is sorted based on one set of columns. In nearly all databases, there will need to be other ways of accessing the data in the table that do not align with the sort order in which the data is stored. This is where non-clustered indexes come in. Non-clustered indexes provide another method for accessing data in addition to the heap or clustered index to locate data in a table.

In this section, a number of patterns that are associated with non-clustered indexes will be reviewed. These patterns will help identify when and where to consider building non-clustered indexes. For each pattern, the chief components and situations where it may be leveraged will be discussed. Similar to the clustered index patterns, each non-clustered index pattern will include scenarios to demonstrate the benefit of the pattern. The non-clustered index patterns that will be discussed are

- Search Columns
- Index Intersection

- Multiple Column

- Covering Index

- Included Columns

- Filtered Indexes

- Foreign Keys

Before reviewing the patterns, there are a number of guidelines that will apply to all non-clustered indexes. These guidelines differ from the attributes of well-defined clustered indexes. With those attributes, one of the key goals was to adhere to them as much as possible. The non-clustered indexing guidelines form considerations that will help strengthen the case for an index but may not disqualify the use of the index. Some of the most common considerations to think of when designing indexes are the following:

- *What is the frequency of change for the non-clustered index key columns?* The more frequent the data changes, the more often the row in the non-clustered index may need to change its position in the index.

- *What frequent queries will the index improve?* The more queries an index can cover and the more often they execute, the better the database platform will operate as a whole.

- *What business needs does the index support?* Infrequently used indexes that support critical business operations can sometimes be more important than frequently used indexes.

- *What is the cost in time to maintain the index vs. the cost in time to query the data?* There can be a point where the performance gain from an index is outweighed by the time spent creating and defragmenting an index and the space that it requires.

As mentioned in the introduction, indexing can often feel like art. Fortunately, science or statistics can be used to demonstrate the value of indexes. As each of these patterns is reviewed, we'll look at scenarios where they can be applied and use some science, or metrics in this case, to determine whether the index provides value. The two things that will be used to judge indexes will be reads during the execution and complexity of the execution plan.

Search Columns

The most basic and common pattern for designing non-clustered indexes is to build them based on defined or expected search patterns. The Search Columns pattern should be the most widely known pattern but also happens to be easily, and often, overlooked.

If queries will be searching tables with contacts in them by first name, then index the first name column. If the address table will have searches against it by city or state, then index those columns. The primary goal of the Search Columns pattern is to reduce scans against the clustered index and move those operations to a non-clustered index that can provide a more direct route to the data.

To demonstrate the Search Columns pattern, the first scenario mentioned in this section will be used, a contact table. For simplicity, the examples will use a table named dbo.Contacts that contains data from the AdventureWorks2017 table Person.Person (see Listing 13-13). There should be 19,972 rows inserted into dbo.Contacts, though this will vary depending on the freshness of your AdventureWorks2017 database.

Listing 13-13. Setup for the Search Columns Pattern

```
USE AdventureWorks2017;
GO
CREATE TABLE dbo.Contacts (
    ContactID INT IDENTITY(1, 1),
    FirstName NVARCHAR(50),
    LastName NVARCHAR(50),
    IsActive BIT,
    EmailAddress NVARCHAR(50),
    CertificationDate DATETIME,
    FillerData CHAR(1000),
    CONSTRAINT PK_Contacts PRIMARY KEY CLUSTERED (ContactID));
INSERT INTO dbo.Contacts (
    FirstName,
    LastName,
    IsActive,
    EmailAddress,
    CertificationDate )
SELECT pp.FirstName,
```

```
      pp.LastName,
      IIF(pp.BusinessEntityID / 10 = 1, 1, 0),
      pea.EmailAddress,
      IIF(pp.BusinessEntityID / 10 = 1, pp.ModifiedDate, NULL)
FROM Person.Person pp
   INNER JOIN Person.EmailAddress pea
      ON pp.BusinessEntityID = pea.BusinessEntityID;
```

With the table dbo.Contacts in place, the first test against it is to query the table with no non-clustered indexes built on it. In the example, shown in Listing 13-14, the query is searching for rows with the first name of Catherine. Executing the query shows that there are 22 rows in dbo.Contacts that match the criteria (see Figure 13-15). To retrieve the 22 rows, SQL Server ended up reading 2,866 pages, which are all the pages in the table. And as Figure 13-16 indicates, the page reads were the result of an index scan against PK_ Contacts on dbo.Contacts. The aim of the query is to retrieve 22 out of the more than 19,000 rows, so checking every page in the table for rows with Catherine for FirstName is not an optimal approach and is one that should be avoided.

Listing 13-14. Search Columns Pattern with no Non-clustered Index

```
USE AdventureWorks2017;
GO
SET STATISTICS IO ON;
SELECT ContactID,
       FirstName
FROM dbo.Contacts
WHERE FirstName = 'Catherine';
```

⊞ Results	🗐 Messages	℘ Execution plan

```
(22 rows affected)
Table 'Contacts'. Scan count 1, logical reads 2866, physical reads 0, read-ahead reads 0, lob logical reads 0,

(1 row affected)
```

Figure 13-15. *Statistics I/O results for the Search Columns pattern without a non-clustered index*

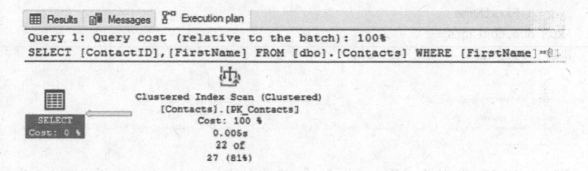

Figure 13-16. *Execution plan for the Search Columns pattern without a non-clustered index*

Achieving the aim of retrieving all the rows for Catherine optimally is relatively simple by adding a non-clustered index to dbo.Contacts. In the next script (Listing 13-15), a non-clustered index is created on the FirstName column. Besides the filter on FirstName, the query needs to also return ContactID. Since non-clustered indexes include the clustering index key, the value in ContactID is included in the index by default.

Executing the script in Listing 13-15 leads to substantially different performance than before the non-clustered index was added to the table. Instead of reading every page in the table, the non-clustered index reduces the number of pages used for the query to two pages (Figure 13-17). The reduction here is significant and highlights the power and value in using non-clustered indexes to provide more direct access to information in your tables on columns other than those in the clustered index keys. There is one other change in the execution: instead of a scan against PK_Index, the execution plan now uses an index seek against IC_Contacts_FirstName, shown in Figure 13-18. The change in the operator is further proof that the non-clustered index helped improve the performance of the query.

Listing 13-15. Search Columns Pattern with a Non-clustered Index

```
USE AdventureWorks2017;
GO

CREATE INDEX IX_Contacts_FirstName ON dbo.Contacts (FirstName);

SET STATISTICS IO ON;
SELECT ContactID,
```

```
        FirstName
FROM dbo.Contacts
WHERE FirstName = 'Catherine';
```

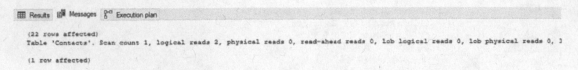

Figure 13-17. *Statistics I/O results for the Search Columns pattern with a non-clustered index*

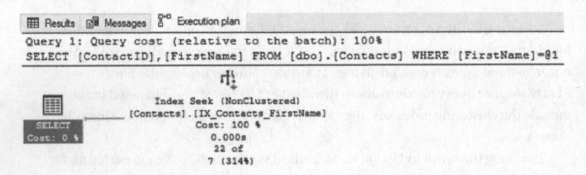

Figure 13-18. *Execution plan for the Search Columns pattern with a non-clustered index*

Using the Search Columns pattern is probably the most important first step in applying non-clustered indexing patterns to databases. It provides alternative paths for accessing data that can be the difference between getting data from a couple of pages vs. thousands of pages. The Search Columns example in this section shows building an index on a single column. The next few patterns will expand on this foundation.

Index Intersection

The aim of the Search Columns pattern is to create an index that will minimize the page reads for a query and improve the performance of it. Sometimes, though, the queries go beyond the single column example that was demonstrated. Additional columns may be part of the predicate or returned in the SELECT statement. One of the ways to address this is to create non-clustered indexes that include the additional columns. When there are indexes that can satisfy each of the predicates in the WHERE clause, SQL Server can use multiple non-clustered indexes to find the rows between both that match on the clustering key. This operation is called Index Intersection.

To demonstrate the Index Intersection pattern, a review will be made of what happens when the filtering is expanded to cover multiple columns. The code in Listing 13-16 includes the expanded SELECT statement and WHERE clause, expanding the predicate to include rows where LastName is Cox.

The change in the query results in a significant change in performance over the previous section's results. With the additional column in the query, there are 68 pages read to satisfy the query vs. the 2 pages when LastName was not included (Figure 13-19). The increase in pages read is because of the change in the execution plan (Figure 13-20). In this execution plan, an additional two operations are added to the execution of the query: a key lookup and a nested loop. These operators are added because the index IX_Contacts_FirstName cannot provide all of the information needed to satisfy the query. SQL Server determines that it is still cheaper to use IX_Contacts_FirstName and look up the missing information from the clustered index than to scan the clustered index. The problem is that for every row that matches on the non-clustered index, a lookup has to be done on the clustered index. While key lookups are not always a problem, they can potentially drive up the CPU and I/O costs for a query.

Listing 13-16. Query that Does Not Take Advantage of the Index Intersection Pattern

```
USE AdventureWorks2017;
GO
SET STATISTICS IO ON;
SELECT ContactID,
       FirstName,
       LastName
FROM dbo.Contacts
WHERE FirstName = 'Catherine'
     AND LastName = 'Cox';
```

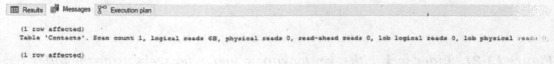

```
(1 row affected)
Table 'Contacts'. Scan count 1, logical reads 68, physical reads 0, read-ahead reads 0, lob logical reads 0, lob physical reads 0.

(1 row affected)
```

Figure 13-19. *Statistics I/O results when not taking advantage of the Index Intersection pattern*

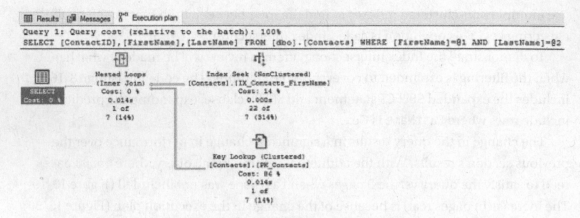

Figure 13-20. *Execution plan when not taking advantage of the Index Intersection pattern*

Leveraging the Index Intersection pattern is one of a few ways that the performance of the query in Listing 13-16 can be improved. An index intersection occurs when SQL Server can use multiple non-clustered indexes on the same table to satisfy the requirements for a query. In the case of the query in Listing 13-16, the most direct path for finding FirstNames was through the index IX_Contacts_FirstName. At that point, though, to filter and return the LastName column, SQL Server used the clustered index and performed a lookup on each row, similar to the image on the left side of Figure 13-21. Alternatively, if there had been an index for the LastName column, SQL Server could have used that index with IX_Contacts_FirstName. In essence, through the Index Intersection pattern, SQL Server is able to perform operations similar to joins between indexes on the same table to find rows that overlap between the two, as shown on the right of Figure 13-21.

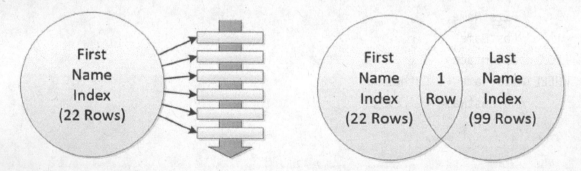

Figure 13-21. *Index seek with a key lookup vs. two index seeks using the Index Intersection pattern*

To demonstrate the Index Intersection pattern and have SQL Server use index intersection, the next example creates an index on the LastName column (Listing 13-17). With the index IX_Contacts_LastName created, the results change significantly from when the index had not been created. The first change is in the number of reads. Instead of the 68 reads that occurred in the previous execution, there are now only 5 reads (Figure 13-22). The cause of the reduction in reads is from SQL Server leveraging index intersection in the query plan (Figure 13-23). The indexes IX_Contacts_FirstName and IX_Contacts_LastName were used to satisfy the query without returning to the clustered index to retrieve data for the query. This happened because the two indexes together can satisfy the query completely.

Listing 13-17. Index Intersection Pattern

```
USE AdventureWorks2017;
GO
CREATE INDEX IX_Contacts_LastName ON dbo.Contacts (LastName);
SET STATISTICS IO ON;
SELECT ContactID,
       FirstName,
       LastName
FROM dbo.Contacts
WHERE FirstName = 'Catherine'
     AND LastName = 'Cox';
```

⊞ Results	📰 Messages	ℛ Execution plan

```
(1 row affected)
Table 'Contacts'. Scan count 2, logical reads 5, physical reads 0, read-ahead reads 0, lob logical reads 0,

(1 row affected)
```

Figure 13-22. *Statistics I/O results for the Index Intersection pattern*

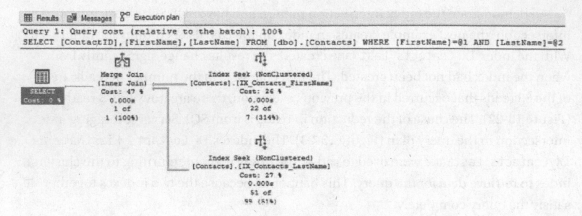

Figure 13-23. *Execution plan for the Index Intersection pattern*

Index intersection is a feature of SQL Server that is used to better satisfy queries when more than one non-clustered index from the same table can provide the results for the queries. When indexing for index intersection, the aim is to have multiple indexes based on the Search Columns pattern that can be used together in numerous combinations to allow for a variety of filters. One key thing to remember with the Index Intersection pattern is that SQL Server cannot be instructed as to when to use index intersection; it will opt to use it when it is appropriate for each request, the underlying indexes, and their associated data.

Multiple Column

The examples in the previous two sections focused on indexes that included a single key column in the index. Non-clustered indexes, though, can have up to 16 columns. While being narrow was an attribute of a well-defined clustered index, the same does not always apply to non-clustered indexes. Instead, non-clustered indexes should contain as many columns as necessary to be used by the most queries possible. If many queries use the same columns as predicates, it is often a good idea to include them all in a single index.

It is worth noting that just because an index can have many columns in, it does not mean it should. If one or two columns are highly selective, then those few columns may be sufficient to ensure a reasonably fast index seek, even if a key lookup is also required. Query duration should generally be the primary benchmark as to index effectiveness, followed by resource consumption.

A simple method for demonstrating an index using the Multiple Column pattern is to use the same query from the previous section and apply this pattern to it. In that query, two indexes were built, one each on the FirstName and LastName columns. For the Multiple Column pattern, the new index will include both the columns together (Listing 13-18).

As the statistics indicate (Figure 13-24), by using the Multiple Column pattern, there is a reduction in the number of reads necessary to return the request results. Instead of five reads from the Index Intersection pattern, there are only two reads with the Multiple Column pattern. Additionally, the execution plan (shown in Figure 13-25) has been simplified. There is only an index seek on the index IX_Contacts_FirstNameLastName.

Listing 13-18. Multiple Column Pattern

```
USE AdventureWorks2017;
GO

CREATE INDEX IX_Contacts_FirstNameLastName
  ON dbo.Contacts (FirstName, LastName);
SET STATISTICS IO ON;

SELECT ContactID,
       FirstName,
        LastName
FROM dbo.Contacts
WHERE FirstName = 'Catherine'
      AND LastName = 'Cox';
```

▦ Results   ▦ Messages   ৪ᵃ Execution plan

```
(1 row affected)
Table 'Contacts'. Scan count 1, logical reads 2, physical reads 0, read-ahead reads 0, lob logical reads 0, lob physical reads 0.

(1 row affected)
```

Figure 13-24. *Statistics I/O results for the Multiple Column pattern*

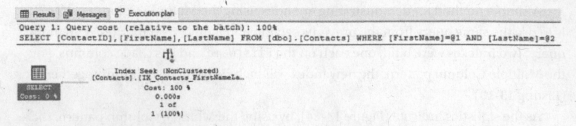

Figure 13-25. Execution plan for the Multiple Column pattern

The Multiple Column pattern is as important to implement as the Search Columns pattern when indexing a database. This pattern can help reduce the number of indexes used by putting the columns together that are most often used in predicates. While this pattern does contradict some of the value of the Index Intersection pattern, the key between them is balance. In some cases, relying on index intersection on single-column indexes will provide the best performance for a table with many variations on the query predicates. In other times, wider indexes with specific orders to the columns will be beneficial. Also consider if candidate indexes will be useful elsewhere in an application. If so, then use that information to make an informed decision between a multicolumn index or multiple single-column indexes.

Try both patterns and apply them in the manner that provides the best overall performance. Remember that indexes can always be removed if they don't work out.

Covering Index

The next indexing pattern is the Covering Index pattern. With the Covering Index pattern, columns outside the predicates are added to an index's key columns to allow those values to be returned as part of the SELECT clauses of queries. This pattern has been a standard indexing practice for a while with SQL Server. Enhancements in how indexes can be created, though, make this pattern less useful than it was in the past. It is a worthwhile pattern to discuss as it is familiar to many people who work with SQL Server.

To begin looking at the Covering Index pattern, an example will be provided that defines the problem that the index solves. To show the issue, the next test query will include the IsActive column in the SELECT list (Listing 13-19). With this column added, the I/O statistics increase again from two reads to five reads, shown in Figure 13-26. The change in performance is directly related to the change in the execution plan (see Figure 13-27) that includes a key lookup and a nested loop. As with the previous examples, as items not included in the non-clustered index are added to the query, they need to be retrieved from the clustered index, which contains all data for the table.

Listing 13-19. Query that does not take advantage of the Covering Index Pattern

```
USE AdventureWorks2017;
GO

SET STATISTICS IO ON;

SELECT ContactID,
       FirstName,
       LastName,
       IsActive
FROM dbo.Contacts
WHERE FirstName = 'Catherine'
      AND LastName = 'Cox';
```

Results   Messages   Execution plan

```
(1 row affected)
Table 'Contacts'. Scan count 1, logical reads 5, physical reads 0, read-ahead reads 0, lob logical reads 0.

(1 row affected)
```

Figure 13-26. *Statistics I/O results for a query that does not take advantage of the Covering Index pattern*

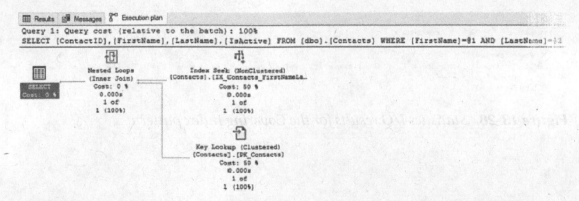

Figure 13-27. *Execution plan for a query that does not take advantage of the Covering Index pattern*

An ideal index would be able to accommodate the filters on the query and also return the columns requested in the SELECT list. The Covering Index pattern can fulfill these requirements. Even though IsActive is not one of the predicates for the query, it can be added to the index, and SQL Server can use that key column to return the column values with the query. To demonstrate the Covering Index pattern, an index will be created that has FirstName, LastName, and IsActive as the key columns (see Listing 13-20). With the index IX_Contacts_FirstNameLastName in place, the reads return to two per execution (see Figure 13-28). The execution plan is also now using only an index seek (see Figure 13-29).

Listing 13-20. Covering Index Pattern

```
USE AdventureWorks2017
GO

CREATE INDEX IX_Contacts_FirstNameLastNameIsActive ON dbo.
Contacts(FirstName, LastName, IsActive);
SET STATISTICS IO ON;

SELECT ContactID,
       FirstName,
       LastName,
       IsActive
FROM dbo.Contacts
WHERE FirstName = 'Catherine'
      AND LastName = 'Cox';
```

```
▦ Results  ▦ Messages  ♂ Execution plan

    (1 row affected)
    Table 'Contacts'. Scan count 1, logical reads 2, physical reads 0, read-ahead reads 0, lob logical reads 0,

    (1 row affected)
```

Figure 13-28. *Statistics I/O results for the Covering Index pattern*

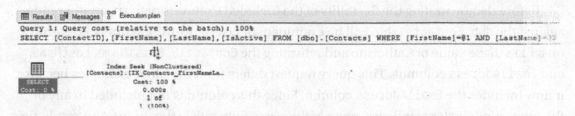

Figure 13-29. Execution plan for the Covering Index pattern

The Covering Index pattern can be useful and has the potential to improve performance in many areas. The downside to this approach is that each column included in the key columns of an index needs to be sorted. If a column needs to be returned by a query, but will not be sorted on, then it is better off as an included column rather than a key column.

Note   Some consider covering indexes and indexes with included columns the same thing. While very similar, the key difference between the two is the location of the columns as part of the key or data included in the index.

Included Columns

The Included Columns pattern is a close cousin to the Covering Index pattern. The Included Columns pattern leverages the INCLUDE clause of the CREATE and ALTER INDEX syntax. The clause allows non-key columns to be added to non-clustered indexes, similar to how non-key data is stored in clustered indexes. This is the primary difference between the Included Columns and Covering Index patterns, where the additional columns in the Covering Index are key columns on the index. Like clustered indexes, the non-key columns that are part of the INCLUDE clause are not sorted, although they can be used as predicates in some queries.

The use case for the Included Columns pattern comes from the flexibility that it provides. It is generally the same as the Covering Index pattern, and sometimes the names are used interchangeably. The key difference, which is demonstrated in this section, is that the Covering Index pattern is limited by the sort order of all columns in the index. The Included Columns pattern can avoid this potential issue by including non-key data, thereby increasing its flexibility of use.

Before demonstrating the flexibility of the Included Columns pattern, another index against the dbo.Contacts table will be examined. In Listing 13-21, the query is filtering on a FirstName value of Catherine and returning the ContactID, FirstName, LastName, and EmailAddress columns. This query request differs from the other examples because it now includes the EmailAddress column. Since this column is not included in any of the other non-clustered indexes, none of them can fully satisfy the query. As a result, the execution plan uses IX_Contacts_FirstName to identify the Catherine rows and then looks up the rest of the data from the clustered index, shown in Figure 13-30. With the key lookup, the I/O for the query increases to 68 reads (see Figure 13-31), as they have in previous examples.

Listing 13-21. Included Columns Pattern with the Existing Index

```
USE AdventureWorks2017;
GO

SET STATISTICS IO ON;

SELECT ContactID,
       FirstName,
       LastName,
       EmailAddress
FROM dbo.Contacts
WHERE FirstName = 'Catherine';
```

```
⊞ Results  🗐 Messages  ⚙ Execution plan

(22 rows affected)
Table 'Contacts'. Scan count 1, logical reads 68, physical reads 0, read-ahead reads 0, lob logical reads 0,
Table 'Worktable'. Scan count 0, logical reads 0, physical reads 0, read-ahead reads 0, lob logical reads 0,

(1 row affected)
```

Figure 13-30. *Statistics I/O results for the Included Columns pattern with the Existing index*

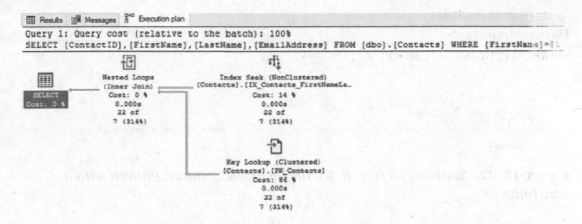

Figure 13-31. *Execution plan for the Included Columns pattern with the Existing index*

To improve the performance of this query, another index based on either the Multiple Column pattern or the Covering Index pattern could be created. The trouble with these options, though, is that the resulting index would have the same limitations as the queries that it could improve. Instead, a new index based on the Included Columns pattern will be created. This new index, shown in Listing 13-22, has FirstName as the key column and includes LastName, IsActive, and EmailAddress as the non-key columns. Even though the IsActive column is not used in the index, it is being included to allow additional flexibility for the index, which a later example in this section will use. With the index in place, the performance of the query in Listing 13-21 improves significantly. In this example, the reads drop from the previous 68 per execution to 3 reads (see Figure 13-32). In the execution plan, the key lookup and nested loop are no longer needed; instead, there is just the index seek, which is now using the index IX_Contacts_FirstNameINC (see Figure 13-33).

Listing 13-22. Included Columns Pattern with a New Index

```
USE AdventureWorks2017
GO
CREATE INDEX IX_Contacts_FirstNameINC ON dbo.Contacts(FirstName)
        INCLUDE (LastName, IsActive, EmailAddress);
SET STATISTICS IO ON;
SELECT ContactID,
        FirstName,
        LastName,
```

```
        EmailAddress
FROM dbo.Contacts
WHERE FirstName = 'Catherine';
```

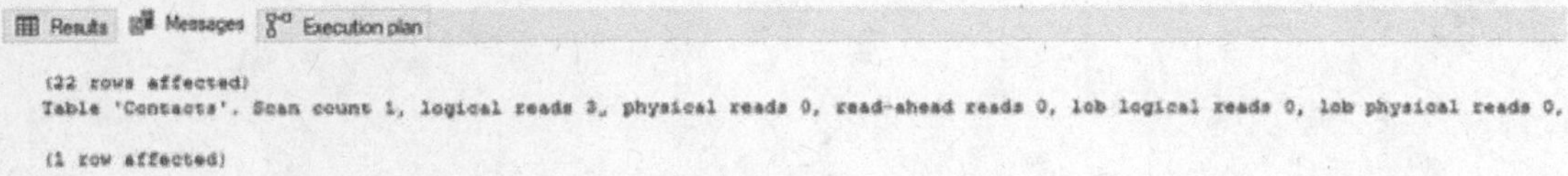

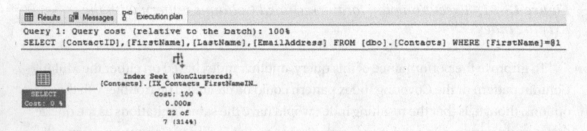

Figure 13-32. *Statistics I/O results for the Included Columns pattern with a new index*

Figure 13-33. *Execution plan for the Included Columns pattern with a new index*

While the number of reads is slightly higher with an index created with the Included Columns pattern, there is flexibility with the index that offsets that difference. With each of the examples in this chapter, a new index has been added to the table dbo.Contacts. At this point, there are six indexes on the table, each serving a different purpose and four leading with the same column, FirstName. Each of these indexes takes up space and requires maintenance when the data in dbo.Contacts is modified. In active tables, over-indexing can have a negative impact on all activity on the table.

The Included Columns pattern can assist with this issue. In scenarios where there are multiple indexes with the same leading key column, it is possible to consolidate those indexes into a single index using the Included Columns pattern with some of the key columns added to the index instead as non-key columns. To demonstrate, first remove all the indexes that start with FirstName, except for the one created using the Included Columns pattern (script provided in Listing 13-23).

Listing 13-23. Dropping Indexes in the Included Columns Pattern

```
USE AdventureWorks2017
GO

DROP INDEX IF EXISTS IX_Contacts_FirstNameLastName ON dbo.Contacts
GO

DROP INDEX IF EXISTS IX_Contacts_FirstNameLastNameIsActive ON dbo.Contacts
GO

DROP INDEX IF EXISTS IX_Contacts_FirstName ON dbo.Contacts
GO
```

The dbo.Contact table now has only three indexes on it. There is the clustered index on the ContactID column, a non-clustered index on LastName, and an index on FirstName with the columns LastName, IsActive, and EmailAddress included as data on the index. With these indexes in place, the queries from the previous patterns, shown in Listing 13-24, need to be tested against the table.

There are two key points to pay attention to regarding how the queries perform with the Included Columns pattern vs. with the other patterns. First, all execution plans for the queries, shown in Figure 13-35, are using index seek operations. The seek operation is expected for the query that is just filtering on FirstName, but it can also be used when there is an additional filter on LastName. SQL Server can do this because underneath the index seek, it is performing a range scan of the rows that match the first predicate and then removing the LastName results that don't have the value of Cox. The second item to note is the number of reads for each of the queries, as shown in Figure 13-34. The reads increased from two to three. While this constitutes a 50 percent increase in reads, the performance change is not significant enough to justify creating four indexes when one index can adequately provide the needed performance.

Listing 13-24. Other Queries Against the Included Columns Pattern

```
USE AdventureWorks2017;
GO

SET STATISTICS IO ON;

SELECT ContactID,
```

```
        FirstName
FROM dbo.Contacts
WHERE FirstName = 'Catherine';

SELECT ContactID,
        FirstName,
        LastName
FROM dbo.Contacts
WHERE FirstName = 'Catherine'
     AND LastName = 'Cox';

SELECT ContactID,
        FirstName,
        LastName,
        IsActive
FROM dbo.Contacts
WHERE FirstName = 'Catherine'
     AND LastName = 'Cox';
```

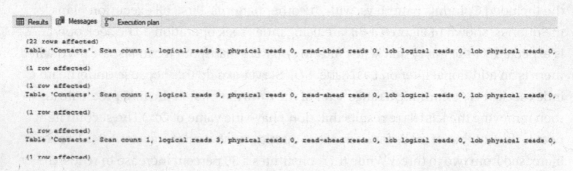

Figure 13-34. *Statistics I/O results for the Included Columns pattern*

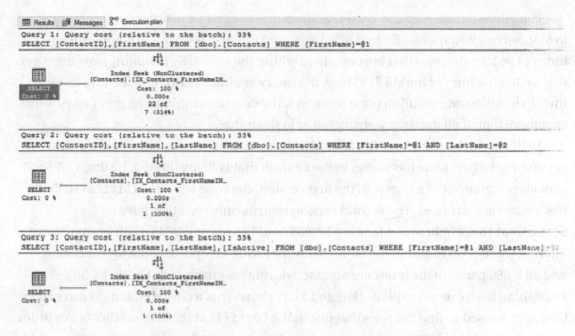

Figure 13-35. *Execution plans for the Included Columns pattern*

The Included Columns pattern for building non-clustered indexes is an important pattern to use when creating indexes. When used with specific queries that result in lookup operations, it provides improved read and execution performance. It also provides opportunities to consolidate similar indexes to reduce the overall number of indexes on the table while still providing performance improvements over situations where the indexes do not exist.

Filtered Indexes

In some tables, there are rows with certain values that will rarely, or never, be returned in the result set as part of the applications using the databases. In these scenarios, it may be beneficial to remove the rows as an option to be returned by the result set. In some other situations, it may be useful to identify a subset of data in a table and create indexes based on it. Instead of querying across millions or billions of records in the table, indexes can be used that cover the hundreds or thousands of rows that the query needs to return results. Both of these situations identify scenarios where using the Filtered Indexes pattern can help improve performance.

The Filtered Indexes pattern uses, as the name suggests, the filtered index feature in SQL Server. When using filtered indexes, a `WHERE` clause is added to a non-clustered index to reduce the rows that are contained within the index. By including only the rows that match the filter of the `WHERE` clause, the query engine has to consider only those rows in building an execution plan; moreover, the cost of scanning a range of rows is less expensive than if all the rows were included in the index.

To illustrate the value in using filtered indexes, consider a scenario where only a small subset of the table has values in the column that is being filtered. Listing 13-25 considers variations of a query. In the first version, the rows where `CertificationDate` has a value are returned. The second version returns only rows that have a `CertificationDate` between January 1, 2005, and February 1, 2005. With both of these queries, there is no index on the table that will provide an optimal plan for execution, and all 2,866 pages of the index are accessed during execution (see Figure 13-36). Examining both execution plans (Figure 13-37) shows that a clustered index scan of `dbo.Contacts` is used to find the rows that match the `CertificationDate` predicate. An index on the `CertificationDate` column could, as the missing index hint suggests, improve the performance of the query.

Listing 13-25. Query that does not use the Filtered Indexes Pattern

```
USE AdventureWorks2017;
GO

SET STATISTICS IO ON;

SELECT ContactID,
       FirstName,
       LastName,
       CertificationDate
FROM dbo.Contacts
WHERE CertificationDate IS NOT NULL
ORDER BY CertificationDate;

SELECT ContactID,
       FirstName,
       LastName,
       CertificationDate
```

```
FROM dbo.Contacts
WHERE CertificationDate
BETWEEN '20110101' AND '20110201'
ORDER BY CertificationDate;
```

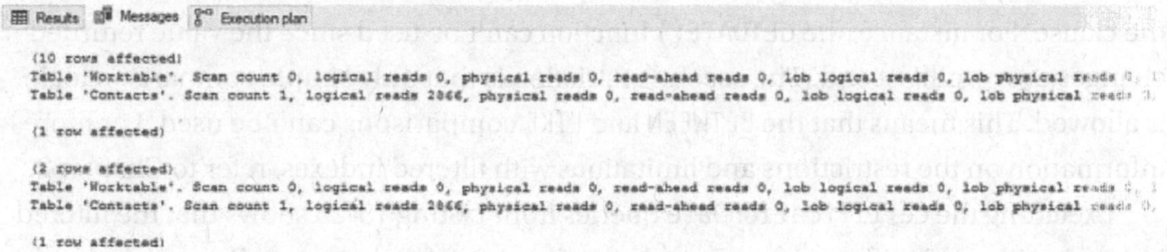

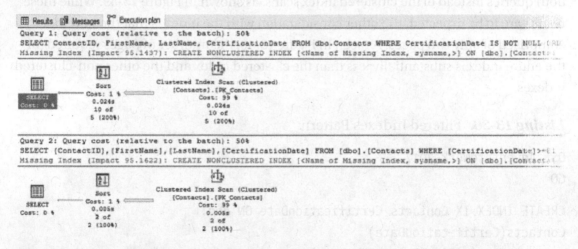

Figure 13-36. *Statistics I/O results for a query that does not use the Filtered Indexes pattern*

Figure 13-37. *Execution plans for a query that does not use the Filtered Indexes pattern*

Before applying the missing index suggestion, consider how the index will be used in this and future queries. In this scenario, assume that there will never be a query that uses CertificationDate when the value is NULL. Does it make sense then to store the empty values for all the NULL rows in the index? Given the stated assumption, it doesn't make sense; doing so would waste space in the database and potentially lead to execution plans that were not optimal if the index on CertificationDate was skipped because the reads for a scan were high enough that other indexes were selected.

In this scenario, it makes sense to filter the rows in the index. To do so, the index is created like any other index, except that a WHERE clause is added to its index creation statement (see Listing 13-26). When creating filtered indexes, there are a few things to keep in mind about the WHERE clause. To start with, the WHERE clause must be deterministic. It cannot change over time depending on the results of functions within the clause. For instance, the GETDATE() function can't be used since the value returned changes every millisecond. The second restriction is that only simple comparison logic is allowed. This means that the BETWEEN and LIKE comparisons can't be used. For more information on the restrictions and limitations with filtered indexes, refer to Chapter 2.

Executing the CertificationDate queries from Listing 13-26 shows that the filtered index provides a significant impact on the performance for the query. Regarding the reads incurred, there are now only 2 reads as opposed to the 2,866 reads before the index was applied (see Figure 13-38). Also, the execution plans now use index seeks for both queries instead of the clustered index scans, as shown in Figure 13-39. While these results are to be expected, the other consideration with the index is that the new index is comprised of only two pages. As seen in Figure 13-40, the number of pages required for the entire index is substantially less than the clustered index and the other non-clustered indexes.

Listing 13-26. Filtered Indexes Pattern

```
USE AdventureWorks2017
GO

CREATE INDEX IX_Contacts_CertificationDate ON dbo.
Contacts(CertificationDate)
     INCLUDE (FirstName, LastName)
     WHERE CertificationDate IS NOT NULL;
SET STATISTICS IO ON;

SELECT ContactID,
     FirstName,
     LastName,
     CertificationDate
FROM dbo.Contacts
WHERE CertificationDate IS NOT NULL
ORDER BY CertificationDate;
```

```
SELECT ContactID,
        FirstName,
        LastName,
        CertificationDate
FROM dbo.Contacts
WHERE CertificationDate
BETWEEN '20110101' AND '20110201'
ORDER BY CertificationDate;
SET STATISTICS IO OFF;
SELECT OBJECT_NAME(object_id) as table_name
     ,CASE index_id
       WHEN INDEXPROPERTY(object_id , 'IX_Contacts_CertificationDate',
       'IndexID') THEN 'Filtered Index'
     WHEN 1 THEN 'Clustered Index'
     ELSE 'Other Indexes' END As index_type
     ,index_id
     ,in_row_data_page_count
     ,in_row_reserved_page_count
     ,in_row_used_page_count
FROM sys.dm_db_partition_stats
WHERE object_id = OBJECT_ID('dbo.Contacts');
```

```
Results   Messages   Execution plan

(10 rows affected)
Table 'Contacts'. Scan count 1, logical reads 2, physical reads 0, read-ahead reads 0, lob logical reads 0, lob physical reads 0.

(1 row affected)

(2 rows affected)
Table 'Contacts'. Scan count 1, logical reads 2, physical reads 0, read-ahead reads 0, lob logical reads 0, lob physical reads 0.

(1 row affected)

(4 rows affected)

(1 row affected)
```

Figure 13-38. *Statistics I/O results for the Filtered Indexes pattern*

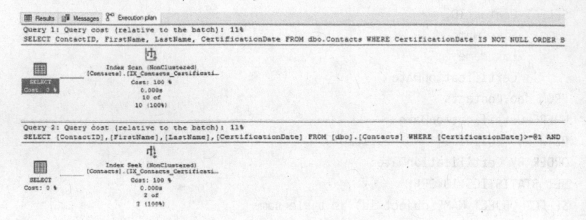

Figure 13-39. *Execution plans for the Filtered Indexes pattern*

	table_name	index_type	index_id	in_row_data_page_count	in_row_reserved_page_count	in_row_used_page_count
1	Contacts	Clustered Index	1	2854	2889	2866
2	Contacts	Other Indexes	5	63	73	65
3	Contacts	Filtered Index	6	1	9	2
4	Contacts	Other Indexes	8	242	267	246

Figure 13-40. *Page count comparison for the filtered index*

Including only a subset of the rows in a table within an index has a number of advantages. One advantage is that since the index is smaller, there are fewer pages in the index, which translates directly to lower storage requirements for the database. Similarly, if there are fewer pages in the index, there are fewer opportunities for index fragmentation and less effort required to maintain the index. The final advantage of filtered indexes relates to performance and plan quality. Since the values in the filtered index are limited, the statistics for the index are limited as well. Since there are fewer pages to traverse in the filtered index, a scan against a filtered index is almost always less of a performance issue than a scan on a clustered index or heap.

There are a few situations where using the Filtered Indexes pattern can and should be used when creating indexes. The first situation is when an index is needed on a column that is configured as sparse. In this case, the expected number of rows that will have the value will be small compared with the total number of rows. One of the benefits of using sparse columns is avoiding the storage costs associated with storing NULL values in these columns. Make certain that the indexes on these columns don't store the NULL values by using filtered indexes. The second situation is when uniqueness needs to be enforced on a column that can have multiple NULL values in it. Creating the filtered index as unique where the key columns are not NULL will bypass the restrictions on uniqueness that allow only a single NULL value in the columns. If a column contained Social Security Numbers that can sometimes contain NULL, but should always be unique when NOT NULL, a unique filtered index could enforce uniqueness on the non-NULL values.

The last situation that is a good fit for filtered indexes is when queries need to be run that don't fit the normal index profile for a table. In this case, there might be a query for a one-off report that needs to retrieve a few thousand rows from the database. Instead of running the report and dealing with the potential scan of the clustered index or heap, create filtered indexes that mimic the predicates of the query. This will allow the query to be quickly executed, without having to spend the time building indexes that contain values the query would never have considered.

Use caution when implementing filtered indexes on columns where their values change often. SQL Server will need to re-evaluate changed values each time they change to determine if they should be added to the filtered index, removed, or no change made. Performance and load testing of common write operations is a reliable way to offset this risk.

As this section has detailed, the Filtered Indexes pattern is one that can be useful in a variety of situations. Be sure to consider it when indexing a large table where only a small subset of data is routinely needed. Often, when the first use for a filtered index is found, there are others that start appearing, and these situations will be identified with selecting and modifying data, as earlier, that can benefit from its use.

Foreign Keys

The last non-clustered index pattern is the Foreign Keys pattern. This is the only pattern that relates directly to objects in the database design. Foreign keys provide a mechanism to constrain values in one table to the values in rows in another table. This relationship provides referential integrity that is critical in most database deployments. However, foreign keys can sometimes be the cause of performance issues in databases without anyone realizing that they are interfering with performance.

Since foreign keys provide a constraint on the values that are possible for a column, there is a check that is done when the values need to be validated. There are two types of validations that can occur with a foreign key. The first happens on the parent table, dbo.ParentTable, and the second happens on the child table, dbo.ChildTable (see

Figure 13-41). Validations occur on dbo.ParentTable whenever rows are modified in dbo.ChildTable. In these cases, the ParentID value from dbo.ChildTable is validated with a lookup of the value in dbo.ParentTable. Usually, this does not result in a performance issue since ParentID in dbo.ParentTable will be the primary key in the table and also usually the column upon which the table is clustered. The other validations occur on dbo.ChildTable when there are modifications to dbo.ParentTable. For instance, if one of the rows in dbo.ParentTable were to be deleted, then dbo.ChildTable would need to be checked to see whether the ParentID value is being used in that table. This validation is where the Foreign Keys pattern needs to be applied.

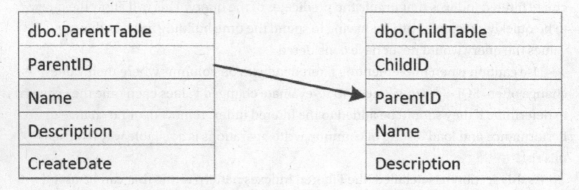

Figure 13-41. *Foreign key relationship*

To demonstrate the Foreign Keys pattern, a couple of tables will be needed for the examples. The code in Listing 13-27 builds two tables, dbo.Customer and dbo.SalesOrderHeader. For these tables, a foreign key relationship exists between them on the CustomerID columns. For every dbo.SalesOrderHeader row, there is a customer associated with the row. Conversely, every row in dbo.Customer may relate to one or more rows in dbo.SalesOrderHeader.

Listing 13-27. Setup for the Foreign Keys Pattern

```
USE AdventureWorks2017
GO

CREATE TABLE dbo.Customer(
        CustomerID int
        ,FillterData char(1000)
```

```
        ,CONSTRAINT PK_Customer_CustomerID PRIMARY KEY CLUSTERED
        (CustomerID)
        );
CREATE TABLE dbo.SalesOrderHeader(
        SalesOrderID int
        ,OrderDate datetime
        ,DueDate datetime
        ,CustomerID int
        ,FillterData char(1000)
        ,CONSTRAINT PK_SalesOrderHeader_SalesOrderID
            PRIMARY KEY CLUSTERED (SalesOrderID)
        ,CONSTRAINT GK_SalesOrderHeader_CustomerID_FROM_Customer
            FOREIGN KEY (CustomerID) REFERENCES dbo.Customer(CustomerID)
        );
INSERT INTO dbo.Customer (CustomerID)
SELECT CustomerID
FROM Sales.Customer;
INSERT INTO dbo.SalesOrderHeader
  (SalesOrderID, OrderDate, DueDate, CustomerID)
SELECT SalesOrderID, OrderDate, DueDate, CustomerID
FROM Sales.SalesOrderHeader;
```

In this example, what happens in dbo.SalesOrderHeader when a row in dbo.
Customer is modified? To demonstrate activity on dbo.Customer, the script in
Listing 13-28 executes a DELETE on the row where CustomerID equals 701. This row
should have no rows in dbo.SalesOrderHeader. Even though this is the case, the
foreign key does require that a check be made to determine whether there are rows
in dbo.SalesOrderHeader for that CustomerID. If so, then SQL Server would throw
an error on the delete, and the deletion would fail. Since there are no rows in dbo.
SalesOrderHeader, the row in dbo.Customer can be deleted.

The execution identifies a couple of potential performance problems with the
delete. First, with only one row being deleted, there are a total of 4,516 reads (see
Figure 13-42). Of the reads, 3 occur on dbo.Customer, while 4,513 occur on dbo.
SalesOrderHeader. The reason for this is the clustered index scan that had to occur
on dbo.SalesOrderHeader (shown in Figure 13-43). The scan occurred because the only
way to check which rows were using Customer equal to 701 was to scan all the rows in the

table. There is no index that can provide a faster path to verifying whether the value was being used.

Listing 13-28. Foreign Keys Pattern with No Index

```
USE AdventureWorks2017
GO

SELECT MAX(c.CustomerID)
    FROM dbo.Customer c
    LEFT OUTER JOIN dbo.SalesOrderHeader soh ON c.CustomerID = soh.
    CustomerID
    WHERE soh.CustomerID IS NULL;

SET STATISTICS IO ON;

DELETE FROM dbo.Customer
WHERE CustomerID = 701;
```

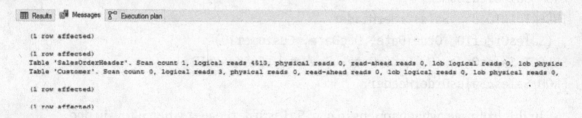

Figure 13-42. *Statistics I/O results for the Foreign Keys pattern with no index*

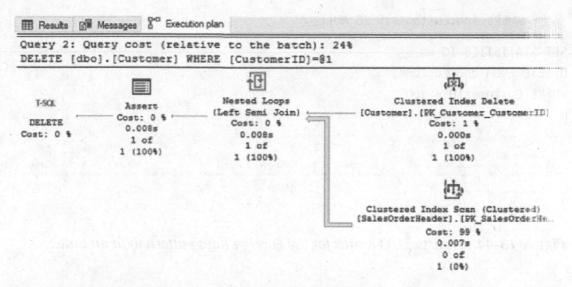

Figure 13-43. *Execution plan for the Foreign Keys pattern with no index*

Improving the performance of the DELETE on dbo.Customer can be done simply through the Foreign Keys pattern. An index built on dbo.SalesOrderHeader on the CustomerID column will provide a reference point for validation with the next delete operation (see Listing 13-29). Reviewing the execution with the index in place yields quite different results. Instead of 4,513 reads on dbo.SalesOrderHeader, there are now only two reads against that table (see Figure 13-44). This change is, of course, because of the index that was created on the CustomerID column (see Figure 13-45). Instead of a clustered index scan, the delete operation can utilize an index seek on dbo. SalesOrderHeader.

Listing 13-29. Foreign Keys Pattern with an Index

```
USE AdventureWorks2017
GO

CREATE INDEX IX_SalesOrderHeader_CustomerID ON dbo.
SalesOrderHeader(CustomerID);

SELECT MAX(c.CustomerID)
    FROM dbo.Customer c
    LEFT OUTER JOIN dbo.SalesOrderHeader soh ON c.CustomerID = soh.
    CustomerID
```

```
    WHERE soh.CustomerID IS NULL;

SET STATISTICS IO ON
DELETE FROM dbo.Customer
WHERE CustomerID = 700
```

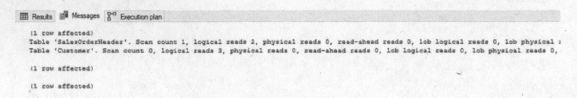

Figure 13-44. *Statistics I/O results for the Foreign Keys pattern with an index*

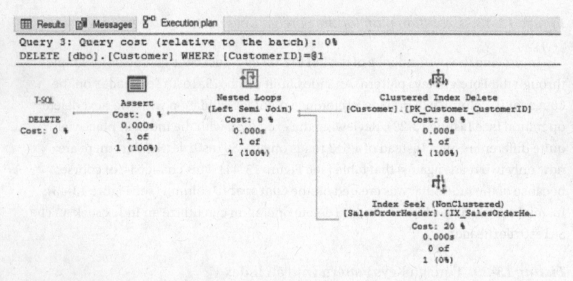

Figure 13-45. *Execution plan for the Foreign Keys pattern with an index*

The Foreign Keys pattern is important to keep in mind with building foreign key relationships between tables. The purpose of those relationships is to validate data, and it is important to be certain that the indexes to support that activity are in place. Do not use this pattern as an excuse to remove validation from a database; instead, use it as an opportunity to properly index busy tables. If the column needs to be queried to validate and constrain the data, it will likely be accessed by applications when the data needs to be used for other purposes.

Columnstore Index

As the sizes of databases have grown, there are more and more situations where traditional clustered and non-clustered indexes do not adequately provide the performance needed for calculating results. This presents the greatest challenge with large data warehouses, and for this problem, the columnstore index was introduced in SQL Server 2012. Previous chapters discussed how the columnstore utilizes column-based storage vs. row-based storage. This section looks at some guidelines with both clustered and non-clustered versions of columnstore indexes and how to recognize when to build a columnstore index. After the guidelines, an example implementing a columnstore index will be provided.

Note   The columnstore examples in this section utilize the Microsoft Contoso BI Demo Dataset for Retail Industry. This database has a fact table with more than 8 million records. It is available for download at `www.microsoft.com/download/en/details.aspx?displaylang=en&id=18279`.

The key to using columnstore indexes is to be able to properly identify the situations where they should be applied. While it could be useful with some OLTP databases to use the columnstore index, that is not the target scenario. While the performance of the columnstore index could be useful in an OLTP database, the restrictions associated with this index type prevent using it in a meaningful way for transactional workloads. The columnstore index is primarily useful for data warehouses, where aggregations across numerous rows are required and few columns will be returned. With the column-wise storage and built-in compression, this index type provides a way to get to the data requested as fast as possible without having to load columns that are not part of the query. Within a data warehouse, columnstore indexes are geared toward fact tables vs. dimension tables. Columnstore indexes prove their worth when they are used on large tables. The larger the table, the more a columnstore index will be able to improve performance over traditional indexes. Additionally, when considering data warehouse queries, one common quality that they share is aggregations and subsets of the available columns. Through the aggregations, the batch mode processing of columnstore indexes provides greater performance improvements. Fewer columns in the queries means less data is loaded into memory, as only the columns being accessed are used in the context of the query.

When a scenario for using a columnstore index is discovered, there are a couple of things to first consider. Since columnstore indexes can be both clustered and non-clustered, the first decision is which type to use. With clustered columnstore indexes, all the data in the table is stored with the index, meaning that only one copy of the data appears in the database. Since it is all the data, the results in all the columns from the table appear in the columnstore index. For a workload that is mostly or entirely analytic in nature, this is likely to be the ideal choice.

Alternatively, a columnstore index can be non-clustered. This provides the ability to limit the number of columns that are part of the index. The non-clustered columnstore index will rely on a clustered rowstore index being part of the table, which means that non-clustered columnstore indexes will increase the overall storage footprint of the table.

Non-clustered columnstore indexes have more considerations when creating them, so there are a number of guidelines to consider when building them. First, the order of the columns in the non-clustered columnstore index does not matter. Each column is stored separately from the other columns, and there are no relationships. The next thing to remember is that all columns in the table that will be leveraged by the columnstore index must appear in the columnstore index. If a column from a query does not appear in the non-clustered columnstore index, then the index cannot be used in its execution.

If using SQL Server versions prior to SQL Server 2017, it is important to remember that non-clustered columnstore indexes are read-only, and any table or partition that has a non-clustered columnstore index built upon it will be placed in a read-only state. To modify the table, the non-clustered columnstore index will need to be disabled or dropped and then rebuilt or created after the updates are completed. This limitation does not affect clustered columnstore indexes and was lifted from non-clustered columnstore indexes beginning with SQL Server 2017.

Non-clustered columnstore indexes are ideal for tables that are primarily transactional in nature, but that also support critical analytic queries. As a bonus, the column list can be specified for a non-clustered columnstore index, allowing for the index to target columns that are to be used for important analytic queries.

A limitation that affects both types of columnstore indexes is the length of time that it takes to create the index. In many cases, it can take four to five times longer to create a columnstore index than it does to build a clustered or non-clustered index. Therefore, index creation should be scheduled for times when sufficient resources are available for their completion. For more information on columnstore indexes, see Chapter 2.

Before demonstrating the value in columnstore indexes, it is worth reviewing a demonstration of a query against a data warehouse with traditional indexing. In Listing 13-30, the query is summarizing SalesQuantity values by CalendarQuarter and ProductCategoryName. Executing the query does not take a substantial amount of time; Figure 13-46 shows an elapsed time of 4,293 ms (or 4.2 seconds), with a little less than 20,000 reads on dbo.FactSales. The results are reasonable for the current volume of records, but consider if the table had 10 or 100 times as many rows. At what point would the 4.2 seconds of execution grow outside the acceptable execution time?

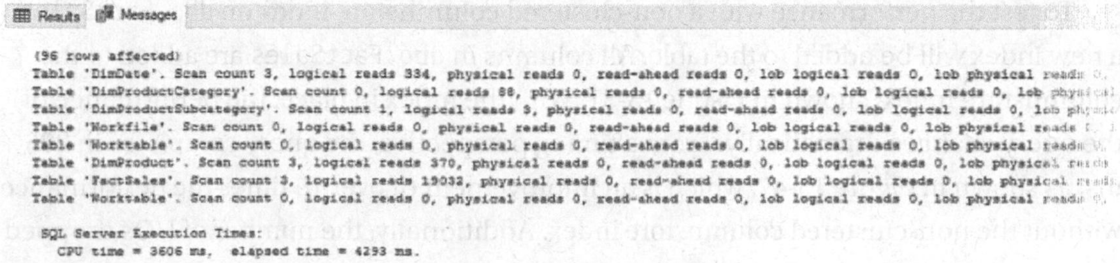

Figure 13-46. Statistics I/O results for a clustered index on a fact table

---

Note Because of the size of the execution plans, they are not being included in the columnstore index examples. And since this section is relying on CPU time to demonstrate performance, they are run multiple times to ensure that disk-to-memory performance is not a factor.

Listing 13-30. Analytic query that makes use of Traditional Indexing

```
USE ContosoRetailDW
GO

SET STATISTICS IO ON
SET STATISTICS TIME ON

SELECT dd.CalendarQuarter
    ,dpc.ProductCategoryName
    ,COUNT(*) As TotalRows
    ,SUM(SalesQuantity) AS TotalSales
FROM dbo.FactSales fs
```

```
        INNER JOIN dbo.DimDate dd ON fs.DateKey = dd.Datekey
        INNER JOIN dbo.DimProduct dp ON fs.ProductKey = dp.ProductKey
        INNER JOIN dbo.DimProductSubcategory dps ON dp.ProductSubcategoryKey
        = dps.ProductSubcategoryKey
        INNER JOIN dbo.DimProductCategory dpc ON dps.ProductCategoryKey =
        dpc.ProductCategoryKey
GROUP BY dd.CalendarQuarter
        ,dpc.ProductCategoryName;
```

To test the performance with a non-clustered columnstore index on dbo.FactSales, a new index will be added to the table. All columns in dbo.FactSales are added to the columnstore index, shown in Listing 13-31. With the index in place, the performance of the query changes dramatically. From a timing perspective, the query completes in 286 ms, as shown in Figure 13-47, which is an improvement of over 15 times the performance without the non-clustered columnstore index. Additionally, the number of I/Os dropped from nearly 20,000 to 2,608.

Listing 13-31. Adding a Non-clustered Columnstore Index

```
USE ContosoRetailDW
GO

CREATE NONCLUSTERED COLUMNSTORE INDEX IX_FactSales_CStore ON dbo.
FactSales (
    SalesKey, DateKey, channelKey, StoreKey, ProductKey, PromotionKey,
    CurrencyKey, UnitCost, UnitPrice,
    SalesQuantity, ReturnQuantity, ReturnAmount, DiscountQuantity,
    DiscountAmount, TotalCost, SalesAmount,
    ETLLoadID, LoadDate, UpdateDate);

SET STATISTICS IO ON;
SET STATISTICS TIME ON;

SELECT dd.CalendarQuarter
    ,dpc.ProductCategoryName
    , COUNT(*) As TotalRows
    ,SUM(SalesQuantity) AS TotalSales
FROM dbo.FactSales fs
```

```
    INNER JOIN dbo.DimDate dd ON fs.DateKey = dd.Datekey
    INNER JOIN dbo.DimProduct dp ON fs.ProductKey = dp.ProductKey
    INNER JOIN dbo.DimProductSubcategory dps ON dp.ProductSubcategoryKey
    = dps.ProductSubcategoryKey
    INNER JOIN dbo.DimProductCategory dpc ON dps.ProductCategoryKey =
    dpc.ProductCategoryKey
GROUP BY dd.CalendarQuarter
    ,dpc.ProductCategoryName;
```

```
⊞ Results   📄 Messages

(96 rows affected)
Table 'DimProductSubcategory'. Scan count 1, logical reads 3, physical reads 0, read-ahead reads 0, lob logical reads 0, lob phys
Table 'FactSales'. Scan count 4, logical reads 0, physical reads 0, read-ahead reads 0, lob logical reads 2608, lob physical reads
Table 'FactSales'. Segment reads 5, segment skipped 0.
Table 'DimProduct'. Scan count 3, logical reads 370, physical reads 0, read-ahead reads 0, lob logical reads 0, lob physical reads
Table 'DimProductCategory'. Scan count 0, logical reads 88, physical reads 0, read-ahead reads 0, lob logical reads 0, lob physica
Table 'DimDate'. Scan count 3, logical reads 334, physical reads 0, read-ahead reads 0, lob logical reads 0, lob physical reads 0,
Table 'Worktable'. Scan count 0, logical reads 0, physical reads 0, read-ahead reads 0, lob logical reads 0, lob physical reads 0,
Table 'Worktable'. Scan count 0, logical reads 0, physical reads 0, read-ahead reads 0, lob logical reads 0, lob physical reads 0,

SQL Server Execution Times:
    CPU time = 186 ms,  elapsed time = 286 ms.
```

Figure 13-47. *Statistics I/O results for a non-clustered columnstore index*

As workloads are tested, analyzed, and optimized, it is important to consider which columns belong in the non-clustered columnstore index. Columns that are not the target of analytic queries can be omitted. This saves storage, reduces the time spent performing index maintenance, and reduces write times as there are less segments and rowgroups that require updating when data is inserted, updated, or deleted.

Next, consider the impact of using a clustered columnstore index on dbo.FactSales. Since a clustered index was created on the table, the script in Listing 13-32 will be used to create a new table called dbo.FactSales_CCI, populate it with the same data in dbo.FactSales, and add the clustered columnstore index to it.

When using the same aggregate query from the previous examples, the performance value of the clustered columnstore is evident. Considering the execution time (shown in Figure 13-48), it drops further to 164 ms, which is more than 26 times faster than the fact table with the clustered index. The I/Os are reduced as well with only 1,309 I/Os for the execution. While the I/O footprint is similar to the non-clustered columnstore, remember that the clustered columnstore is stored only a single time and the values in it can be modified.

Listing 13-32. Create a Fact Table with a Clustered Columnstore Index

```
USE ContosoRetailDW
GO
IF OBJECT_ID('dbo.FactSales_CCI') IS NOT NULL
    DROP TABLE FactSales_CCI

CREATE TABLE dbo.FactSales_CCI(
    SalesKey int NOT NULL,
    DateKey datetime NOT NULL,
    channelKey int NOT NULL,
    StoreKey int NOT NULL,
    ProductKey int NOT NULL,
    PromotionKey int NOT NULL,
    CurrencyKey int NOT NULL,
    UnitCost money NOT NULL,
    UnitPrice money NOT NULL,
    SalesQuantity int NOT NULL,
    ReturnQuantity int NOT NULL,
    ReturnAmount money NULL,
    DiscountQuantity int NULL,
    DiscountAmount money NULL,
    TotalCost money NOT NULL,
    SalesAmount money NOT NULL,
    ETLLoadID int NULL,
    LoadDate datetime NULL,
    UpdateDate datetime NULL
    )

INSERT INTO dbo.FactSales_CCI
SELECT * FROM dbo.FactSales

CREATE CLUSTERED COLUMNSTORE INDEX FactSales_CStore ON dbo.FactSales_CCI

SET STATISTICS IO ON;
SET STATISTICS TIME ON;

SELECT dd.CalendarQuarter
```

```
    ,dpc.ProductCategoryName
    , COUNT(*) As TotalRows
    ,SUM(SalesQuantity) AS TotalSales
FROM dbo.FactSales_CCI fs
    INNER JOIN dbo.DimDate dd ON fs.DateKey = dd.Datekey
    INNER JOIN dbo.DimProduct dp ON fs.ProductKey = dp.ProductKey
    INNER JOIN dbo.DimProductSubcategory dps ON dp.ProductSubcategoryKey
    = dps.ProductSubcategoryKey
    INNER JOIN dbo.DimProductCategory dpc ON dps.ProductCategoryKey =
    dpc.ProductCategoryKey
GROUP BY dd.CalendarQuarter
    ,dpc.ProductCategoryName;
```

```
 Results   Messages

(96 rows affected)
Table 'DimProductSubcategory'. Scan count 1, logical reads 3, physical reads 0, read-ahead reads 0, lob logical reads 0, lob physica
Table 'FactSales_CCI'. Scan count 2, logical reads 0, physical reads 0, read-ahead reads 0, lob logical reads 1309, lob physical re
Table 'FactSales_CCI'. Segment reads 5, segment skipped 0.
Table 'DimProduct'. Scan count 3, logical reads 370, physical reads 0, read-ahead reads 0, lob logical reads 0, lob physical reads
Table 'DimProductCategory'. Scan count 0, logical reads 88, physical reads 0, read-ahead reads 0, lob logical reads 0, lob physical
Table 'DimDate'. Scan count 3, logical reads 334, physical reads 0, read-ahead reads 0, lob logical reads 0, lob physical reads 0,
Table 'Worktable'. Scan count 0, logical reads 0, physical reads 0, read-ahead reads 0, lob logical reads 0, lob physical reads 0,
Table 'Worktable'. Scan count 0, logical reads 0, physical reads 0, read-ahead reads 0, lob logical reads 0, lob physical reads 0,

SQL Server Execution Times:
   CPU time = 187 ms,  elapsed time = 164 ms.
```

Figure 13-48. *Statistics I/O results for a clustered columnstore index*

While a clustered columnstore index is optimal for analytic workloads, it will not perform well for transactional queries. If a table services OLTP queries, then a clustered columnstore index is likely the wrong solution. A mixed workload that contains both OLAP and OLTP queries can be challenging to optimize. If indexing those workloads proves difficult, consider ways to separate transactional and analytic queries and data from each other. The intermingling of transactional and analytic workloads is one of the more complex challenges that database administrators and developers face, and therefore an effective solution to that problem may require additional optimization tactics beyond indexing alone.

Non-clustered rowstore indexes may be built on clustered columnstore indexed tables. These can support alternate search paths that do not match the natural data order of the table. Before implementing a non-clustered rowstore index on a clustered columnstore table, be sure to test query performance without the additional indexes.

Oftentimes the speed provided by compression, rowgroup elimination, and other columnstore features may be enough to provide adequate performance without the need for additional indexes.

Columnstore indexes may also be created on memory-optimized tables. Memory-optimized tables are intended for highly contentious, heavy OLTP workloads. This makes them poor candidates for columnstore indexes. A columnstore index on a memory-optimized table should be tested carefully to ensure that it not only performs well but also does not consume excessive memory or impede OLTP performance.

Ordered columnstore indexes were introduced in SQL Server 2022 and allow for data to be pre-sorted as it is inserted. This is an offline operation (by partition) that uses TempDB to sort the newly inserted data. If a table has a dedicated offline period where a data load can be performed unimpeded, then this can be a useful way to improve data order, therefore improving rowgroup elimination. For more information on this feature, review the following documentation from Microsoft:

`https://docs.microsoft.com/en-us/azure/synapse-analytics/sql-data-warehouse/performance-tuning-ordered-cci`

Note that because sorting of the data is required in TempDB, a large INSERT operation may cause extensive I/O on TempDB, as well as consume space within the system database. Ensure that TempDB has sufficient space available to support this option, if used.

The following is a brief list of best practices for columnstore indexes that can help in knowing when to use them and how to ensure optimal performance:

- Columnstore indexes should target tables that have (or will grow to) at least tens of millions of rows per partition.

- Insert rows into clustered columnstore indexes in batches of at least 102,400 rows or more to allow for the minimally logged bulk load process to be used.

- Ordered data allows for effective rowgroup elimination. Ensure that data is inserted into columnstore indexes ordered by a column that will be the most common target of filters.

- Partition large tables that have columnstore indexes on them. This allows for partition elimination and the ability to target maintenance tasks at individual partitions (backup, rebuild, reorganization, truncation, partition swapping)

- Avoid UPDATE operations against a columnstore index. They manifest as a DELETE plus an INSERT and will create fragmentation due to deleted data bloat. UPDATE operations also result in out-of-order data, reducing the effectiveness of rowgroup elimination.

- When using a columnstore index, only query columns that are needed. This reduces the segments that must be read, reducing I/O and memory usage and improving query speed.

- Only use non-clustered columnstore indexes on tables that meet many or all of the preceding criteria. A heavily fragmented non-clustered columnstore index may not provide much (if any) more value than a classic rowstore covering index.

Columnstore indexes are a significant improvement in the way that data warehouses can be indexed. With each version of SQL Server, columnstore indexes improve and become more efficient ways of indexing large analytic data. These performance improvements open opportunities to scale databases even further than is possible with traditional indexing solutions. Columnstore indexes allow OLAP tables to be scaled into tens or hundreds of billions of rows (or more) with ease.

Note   The next section utilizes the WorldWideImporters databases, which can be downloaded from `https://github.com/Microsoft/sql-server-samples/releases/tag/wide-world-importers-v1.0`.

JSON Indexing

SQL Server 2016 introduced the ability to process JSON (JavaScript Object Notation) data within SQL Server. JSON defines methods of structuring data that are easy for both applications and people to read and write. Due to this ease, it has become very popular within application development.

Instead of tags and attributes that are used in XML, JSON leverages brackets, colons, and quotes to define entity-attribute relationships. As an example, Listing 13-33 contains an XML document that defines extra information regarding an employee of WideWorldImporters. That same information represented by JSON is shown in Listing 13-34.

Comparing the two, the JSON is quite a bit easier to read and understand than the same data represented as XML.

Listing 13-33. XML Example

```
<CustomFields>
  <OtherLanguages>
    <Language>Polish</Language>
    <Language>Chines</Language>
    <Language>Japanese</Language>
  </OtherLanguages>
  <HireDate>2008-04-19T00:00:00</HireDate>
  <Title>Team Member</Title>
  <PrimarySalesTerritory>Plains</PrimarySalesTerritory>
  <CommissionRate>0.98</CommissionRate>
</CustomFields>
```

Listing 13-34. JSON Example

```
{
"OtherLanguages": ["Polish","Chinese","Japanese"] ,
"HireDate":"2008-04-19T00:00:00",
"Title":"Team Member",
"PrimarySalesTerritory":"Plains",
"CommissionRate":"0.98"
}
```

While SQL Server can process JSON data, Microsoft implemented JSON a bit differently than how XML and spatial were implemented. Instead of a dedicated data type, JSON data is stored in columns defined with the data types varchar(max) or nvarchar(max). The information within the data can then be retrieved using the function JSON_VALUE or JSON_QUERY. The advantage of this implementation is that there are no special indexing types associated with JSON data, which is why there is not a chapter dedicated to JSON indexing. Instead, JSON data takes advantage of existing indexing capabilities by using computed columns persisted through indexes.

Before diving into how to index JSON data, an example will be shown of how the JSON functions work and their effect on performance. To begin, create the table dbo.

People from Application.People in WideWorldImporters, provided in Listing 13-35. In that table, a column will be included for HireDate that retrieves the HireDate from the JSON document in CustomFields.

Listing 13-35. JSON Example Setup

```
USE WideWorldImporters;
GO

DROP TABLE IF EXISTS dbo.People;

CREATE TABLE [dbo].[People]
(
    [PersonID] [INT] NOT NULL,
    [FullName] [NVARCHAR](50) NOT NULL,
    [CustomFields] [NVARCHAR](MAX) NULL,
    [HireDate] AS JSON_VALUE([CustomFields], N'$.HireDate'),
    [Junk] [VARCHAR](4000) NULL,
    CONSTRAINT [PK_People]
        PRIMARY KEY CLUSTERED ([PersonID])
);
GO
INSERT INTO dbo.People
(
    PersonID,
    FullName,
    CustomFields,
    Junk
)
SELECT PersonID,
       FullName,
       CustomFields,
       REPLICATE('x', 4000) AS Junk
FROM Application.People;
GO
```

When dbo.People is queried using the code in Listing 13-36, the desired results will
be returned from the JSON data using the computed column. Unfortunately, to retrieve
these results, SQL Server needed to scan the clustered index, as shown in Figure 13-50.
The impact of this scan is that all 1,111 rows in the table are accessed, which the statistics
output in Figure 13-49 indicates and leads to 762 reads for the query.

Listing 13-36. Query Computed JSON Column

```
USE WideWorldImporters;
GO

SET STATISTICS IO ON;

SELECT PersonID,
       HireDate
FROM dbo.People
WHERE HireDate IS NOT NULL;
```

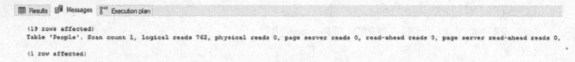

Figure 13-49. *Statistics I/O results for the computed JSON column*

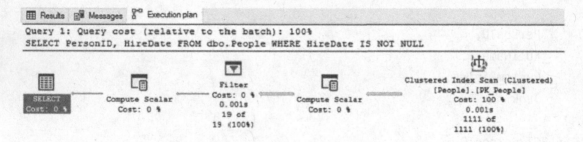

Figure 13-50. *Execution plan for the computed JSON column*

To alleviate the performance impact of the computed JSON column, an index can
be added to the computed column, as shown in Listing 13-37, and the query executed
against dbo.People again. This time the performance is greatly improved. Instead of 762
reads, Figure 13-51 shows that there are only 3 reads. Additionally, the execution plan in
Figure 13-52 indicates that an index seek on the index added was used.

Listing 13-37. Index and Query JSON Computed Column

```
USE WideWorldImporters;
GO

CREATE INDEX IX_People_HireDate ON dbo.People (HireDate);
GO

SET STATISTICS IO ON;

SELECT PersonID,
        HireDate
FROM dbo.People
WHERE HireDate IS NOT NULL
```

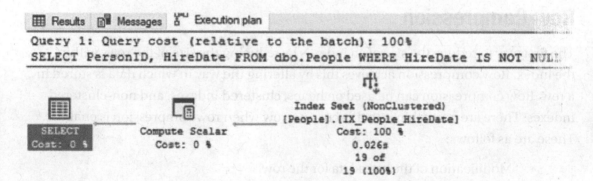

Figure 13-51. *Statistics I/O results for the computed and indexed JSON column*

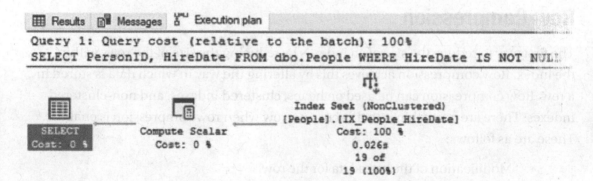

Figure 13-52. *Execution plan for the computed and indexed JSON column*

By leveraging computed columns, JSON data can be easily and efficiently accessed within a table. Rather than needing to learn about new indexing technologies to gain that efficiency, it is possible to leverage existing features. This makes it easier to both adopt and support JSON and efficiently query JSON data.

Index Storage Strategies

The strategies in the chapter have thus far primarily focused on improving the performance of queries using indexes through the key and non-key column design of the index. There are other options that can be used in conjunction to column selection that can be considered in the design of indexes. These alternative strategies all relate to the way in which indexes are stored in the database.

There are two options available for addressing how an index stores its data. The basic premise for both of these options is that the smaller the index, the fewer pages that it will contain, and the fewer reads and writes will be required when querying the data. The first option available is row compression, and the second is page compression. Both of these options provide the potential for substantial storage savings and performance improvement.

Note   The use of row and page compressions is limited to SQL Server Enterprise Edition until SQL Server 2016 SP1, when it was made available to all SQL Server editions.

Row Compression

The first way to reduce the size of an index is by reducing the size of the rows within the index. Row compression achieves this by altering the way in which data is stored in a row. Row compression can be used on heaps, clustered indexes, and non-clustered indexes. There are a few things that occur on a row when row compression is enabled. These are as follows:

- Modification of the metadata for the row.

- Fixed-length character data is stored in a variable-length format.

- Numeric-based data types are stored in variable-length format.

With the metadata changes, the information stored for each column is generally reduced compared with a non–row compression record. Excessive bits in the row overhead are removed, and the information is streamlined to reduce waste. There is an exception to this change, though: some of the changes to fixed-length data types may result in a larger row overhead to accommodate for the additional information required for data length and offset values.

For fixed-length character data, white space is removed from the end of values in the column. This information is not lost, and the behavior of fixed-length data types, such as char and nchar, is unaffected. The difference is only in the manner in which the data is stored. For binary data, trailing zeros on the value are removed, similar to white space. Information on the characters removed from a column is stored in the row overhead.

Numeric data types are the data types that are manipulated the most with row compression. These data types are stored in the smallest form possible for the data type. This means a column with the bigint data type, which typically requires 8 bytes, would require only 1 byte if the value stored is between 0 and 255. At the value 256, the column would then store it in 2 bytes. This progression continues until the need to store the value in 8 bytes is reached. This applies to all numeric-based data types, including smallint, int, bigint, decimal, numeric, smallmoney, money, float, real, datetime, datetime2, datetimeoffset, and timestamp.

To demonstrate, a table is needed to implement compression, which is provided in Listing 13-38. This script creates two tables, dbo.NoCompression and dbo. RowCompression. These tables are used to demonstrate the effect of row compression on the size of the table via the clustered index and on query performance.

Listing 13-38. Setup for Row Compression

```
USE AdventureWorks2017
GO

IF OBJECT_ID('dbo.NoCompression') IS NOT NULL
    DROP TABLE dbo.NoCompression;

IF OBJECT_ID('dbo.RowCompression') IS NOT NULL
    DROP TABLE dbo.RowCompression;

SELECT SalesOrderID
    ,SalesOrderDetailID
    ,CarrierTrackingNumber
    ,OrderQty
    ,ProductID
    ,SpecialOfferID
    ,UnitPrice
    ,UnitPriceDiscount
```

```
    ,LineTotal
    ,rowguid
    ,ModifiedDate
INTO dbo.NoCompression
FROM Sales.SalesOrderDetail;
SELECT SalesOrderID
    ,SalesOrderDetailID
    ,CarrierTrackingNumber
    ,OrderQty
    ,ProductID
    ,SpecialOfferID
    ,UnitPrice
    ,UnitPriceDiscount
    ,LineTotal
    ,rowguid
    ,ModifiedDate
INTO dbo.RowCompression
FROM Sales.SalesOrderDetail;
```

Implementation of row compression relies on the use of DATA_COMPRESSION index options on the CREATE or ALTER INDEX statement. Compression can be used on either clustered or non-clustered indexes. For row compression, the ROW option is shown in Listing 13-39. In this example, a clustered index is added to both of the example tables. The impact of using row compression on this table is impressive; there is a reduction of more than 35 percent in the number of pages required for the clustered index (see Figure 13-53).

Listing 13-39. Implementing Row Compression

```
USE AdventureWorks2017
GO

CREATE CLUSTERED INDEX CLIX_NoCompression ON dbo.NoCompression
    (SalesOrderID, SalesOrderDetailID);

CREATE CLUSTERED INDEX CLIX_RowCompression ON dbo.RowCompression
    (SalesOrderID, SalesOrderDetailID)
```

```
    WITH (DATA_COMPRESSION = ROW);
SELECT OBJECT_NAME(object_id) AS table_name
    ,in_row_reserved_page_count
FROM sys.dm_db_partition_stats
WHERE object_id IN (OBJECT_ID('dbo.NoCompression'),OBJECT_ID('dbo.
RowCompression'));
```

	table_name	in_row_reserved_page_count
1	NoCompression	1531
2	RowCompression	971

Figure 13-53. *Row compression output*

Storage is not the only place where there is an improvement by using row compression; there is also an improvement in query performance. To demonstrate this benefit, execute the code in Listing 13-40. In this script, two queries are executed against the tables from the previous example. While the business rules for the queries are identical, there is more than a 36 percent reduction in page reads for the table with row compression. Storing an index on less pages means that less pages need to be read into memory when retrieving rows to execute queries. By adding compression to the index, the resources required for the query are reduced, and performance is improved without a change to the query design, as seen in Figure 13-54.

Listing 13-40. Row Compression Query

```
USE AdventureWorks2017
GO

SET STATISTICS IO, TIME ON

SELECT SalesOrderID, SalesOrderDetailID, CarrierTrackingNumber
FROM dbo.NoCompression
WHERE SalesOrderID BETWEEN 51500 AND 52000;

SELECT SalesOrderID, SalesOrderDetailID, CarrierTrackingNumber
FROM dbo.RowCompression
WHERE SalesOrderID BETWEEN 51500 AND 52000;
```

```
▦ Results  ⊞ Messages
  SQL Server parse and compile time:
     CPU time = 0 ms, elapsed time = 0 ms.

  (4569 rows affected)
  Table 'NoCompression'. Scan count 1, logical reads 66, physical reads 0, read-ahead reads 0, lob logical reads 0, lob physical reads 0, :

   SQL Server Execution Times:
     CPU time = 0 ms,  elapsed time = 169 ms.
  SQL Server parse and compile time:
     CPU time = 0 ms, elapsed time = 0 ms.

  (4569 rows affected)
  Table 'RowCompression'. Scan count 1, logical reads 42, physical reads 0, read-ahead reads 0, lob logical reads 0, lob physical reads 0,

   SQL Server Execution Times:
     CPU time = 0 ms,  elapsed time = 93 ms.
```

Figure 13-54. *Row compression query statistics*

There are a number of things that need to be considered when implementing row compression on an index. First, the amount of compression achieved by any use of compression will vary depending on the data types used and the data being stored. The improvement will, and should be expected to, vary per table and over time. Compression cannot be enabled if the maximum possible size of the row exceeds 8,060 bytes (including the size of the data and the row overhead). Non-clustered indexes will not inherit the compression settings of the clustered index or heap; this must be specified when the index is created. However, clustered indexes will inherit the compression settings of the heap they are being created on if none is specified.

Row compression is a useful mechanism for altering how indexes are stored. It reduces the size of rows, which has the dual benefit of improving query performance and reducing storage requirements for indexes. The primary concern when implementing row compression is the additional overhead associated with its use; this overhead manifests as a slight increase in CPU utilization. This is usually offset by the reduced I/O required to process the query, as shown in Figure 13-54.

Row compression is an effective way to index OLTP workloads that have many numeric data types, as well as string/binary data that tends to contain white space within it. Because each row is compressed individually, UPDATE operations do not become significantly more expensive as only the data for a single row needs to be updated for each row updated by an UPDATE query.

Page Compression

The other method to reduce the size of an index is by using variable-length data types and removing repeating values on a page. SQL Server accomplishes this through the page compression option on indexes. Like row compression, this compression type can be applied to heaps or clustered and non-clustered indexes. There are three components of page compression:

- Row compression

- Prefix compression

- Dictionary compression

The row compression component of page compression is identical to the row compression option. Before compressing a page, each row on the page is first compressed.

The next step in page compression is accomplished through prefix compression. Prefix compression scans through each column and removes similar values and groups them into the page header. For example, if multiple values in one column start with "abc," this value is placed in the page header, and the value is replaced in the column with a pointer to the prefix. If another row contains the value "abcd," a reference to the abc value in the page header is included, changing the column value to 0d. This is continued for all values to remove the most prevalent patterns and reduce the information stored per row of the column. Prefix compression is evaluated separately for each column. Therefore, similar values in different columns will not be able to share prefixes.

The last step in page compression is dictionary compression. Through dictionary compression, the values in all columns are checked for repeating values. Continuing the previous example, if there are values in two columns across multiple rows that match the 0d value, then that value is placed in the page header, and a reference to the value is stored in those columns. This is done across the entire page, reducing the repeated prefix-compressed values.

For a demonstration of the benefits of page compression, the example from the row compression section will be expanded upon. To begin, execute the script in Listing 13-41. This creates the dbo.PageCompression table similar to the tables from the previous example.

Listing 13-41. Setup for Page Compression

```
USE AdventureWorks2017
GO

IF OBJECT_ID('dbo.PageCompression') IS NOT NULL
    DROP TABLE dbo.PageCompression;
SELECT SalesOrderID
    ,SalesOrderDetailID
    ,CarrierTrackingNumber
    ,OrderQty
    ,ProductID
    ,SpecialOfferID
    ,UnitPrice
    ,UnitPriceDiscount
    ,LineTotal
    ,rowguid
    ,ModifiedDate
INTO dbo.PageCompression
FROM Sales.SalesOrderDetail;
```

Implementing page compression is very similar to row compression. Both use the DATA_COMPRESSION option, but page compression uses the PAGE option. To observe the effect of page compression on the tables, execute the code in Listing 13-42. In this example, page compression has significantly more impact on the table than was observed with row compression. This time, the number of pages used by the table decreases by 55 percent, as shown in Figure 13-55.

Listing 13-42. Implementing Page Compression

```
USE AdventureWorks2017
GO

CREATE CLUSTERED INDEX CLIX_PageCompression ON dbo.PageCompression
    (SalesOrderID, SalesOrderDetailID)
    WITH (DATA_COMPRESSION = PAGE);

SELECT OBJECT_NAME(object_id) AS table_name
    ,in_row_reserved_page_count
```

```
FROM sys.dm_db_partition_stats
WHERE object_id IN (OBJECT_ID('dbo.NoCompression'),OBJECT_ID('dbo.
PageCompression'));
```

	table_name	in_row_reserved_page_count
1	NoCompression	1531
2	PageCompression	683

Figure 13-55. *Page compression output*

The improvements from page compression are not limited to index storage. These improvements carry over to querying the table. Comparing the previous results against dbo.NoCompression with those against dbo.PageCompression (Listing 13-43) shows that the savings in reads continues with page compression. In this case, the reads decreased to 29 (see Figure 13-56), which is more than a 55 percent decrease in I/O cost.

Listing 13-43. Page Compression Query

```
USE AdventureWorks2017
GO

SET STATISTICS IO, TIME ON

SELECT SalesOrderID, SalesOrderDetailID, CarrierTrackingNumber
FROM dbo.PageCompression
WHERE SalesOrderID BETWEEN 51500 AND 52000;
```

```
▦ Results  ▥ Messages

(4569 rows affected)
Table 'PageCompression'. Scan count 1, logical reads 29, physical reads 0, read-ahead reads 0, lob logical reads 0, lob physical reads 0.

SQL Server Execution Times:
   CPU time = 0 ms,  elapsed time = 187 ms.
```

Figure 13-56. *Page compression query statistics*

The considerations for page compression are similar in nature to those for row compression with the addition of a few items. First, because of the nature in which page compression is implemented, there are times when SQL Server will decide that the rate of compression for a page is not sufficient to justify the cost of compressing the page. In these cases, SQL Server will attempt to compress the page but will record a failure of page compression and store the page without the benefit of page compression over row compression. It is important to monitor the rate at which page compression attempts do not succeed since they can indicate when there is low value in using page compression on an index. This is discussed further in Chapter 3.

Next, the CPU cost for page compression is much higher than with row compression or without compression. If there are not sufficient CPU resources available, this can lead to other performance challenges. Lastly, page compression is not ideal for tables and indexes that expect frequent data modifications. Compressing and uncompressing a page to modify a single row can have a significant impact on CPU. Therefore, tables that are ideal candidates for page compression should not be the target of frequent UPDATE operations.

Both row and page compressions can provide substantial cost savings to indexing solutions. Consider both when architecting indexing solutions. Doing so will provide performance improvements in situations where other options may not have yielded the desired results.

Note   Additional considerations related to compression can be found in the Books Online topic "Data Compression" at `https://docs.microsoft.com/en-us/sql/relational-databases/data-compression/data-compression`.

Indexed Views

In many cases, the way in which data is stored in the database does not fully represent the information that the users need to retrieve. To solve this, queries can be built to pull the data that users need together into result sets that can be more easily consumed. In the process of performing these activities, data can be aggregated to provide the results at the level of detail that the users require.

As an example, users may want to see the total amount sold for a product across all orders in a database but without including information on the detail items. In most situations, retrieving this information is not an issue. However, in some cases, performing that aggregation on the fly can create bottlenecks in the database. While indexes can assist in streamlining the aggregations, they sometimes do not provide the needed cost improvement to achieve the required performance.

One possible solution for this issue is to create indexes on a view in the database. The view can be created to provide the summary and aggregations that are required, and an index can be used to materialize the information in the view into an aggregated form. When indexing a view, the results of the query are stored in the database in much the same way as any table is stored. By storing this information ahead of time, queries that use the aggregations in the view can obtain improved response time.

Before looking at how to implement an indexed view, let's first walk through the problem outlined earlier with retrieving summary information for products. In this example, suppose that there is a need for summary information for all products at the product subcategory level. The query for this, provided in Listing 13-44, would need to provide a sum aggregation of the LineTotal and OrderQty values and then an average of UnitPrice. While the number of reads for the query does not seem substantially high (see Figure 13-57), it may be considered too significant for a query to be released into some production environments. This is especially true if the query is to be executed very frequently. Examining the execution plan, provided in Figure 13-58, shows that while it is not overly complicated, the plan includes a number of steps and would not be considered a trivial plan.

Listing 13-44. Expensive Aggregation Query

```
USE AdventureWorks2017
GO

IF OBJECT_ID('dbo.ProductSubcategorySummary') IS NOT NULL
    DROP VIEW dbo.ProductSubcategorySummary;

SET STATISTICS IO ON;

SELECT psc.Name
    ,SUM(sod.LineTotal) AS SumLineTotal
    ,SUM(sod.OrderQty) AS SumOrderQty
    ,AVG(sod.UnitPrice) AS AvgUnitPrice
FROM Sales.SalesOrderDetail sod
    INNER JOIN Production.Product p ON sod.ProductID = p.ProductID
    INNER JOIN Production.ProductSubcategory psc ON p.ProductSubcategoryID
= psc.ProductSubcategoryID
GROUP BY psc.Name
ORDER BY psc.Name;
```

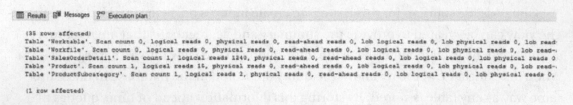

(35 rows affected)
Table 'Worktable'. Scan count 0, logical reads 0, physical reads 0, read-ahead reads 0, lob logical reads 0, lob physical reads 0, lob read-
Table 'Workfile'. Scan count 0, logical reads 0, physical reads 0, read-ahead reads 0, lob logical reads 0, lob physical reads 0, lob read-
Table 'SalesOrderDetail'. Scan count 1, logical reads 1240, physical reads 0, read-ahead reads 0, lob logical reads 0, lob physical reads 0
Table 'Product'. Scan count 1, logical reads 15, physical reads 0, read-ahead reads 0, lob logical reads 0, lob physical reads 0, lob read-
Table 'ProductSubcategory'. Scan count 1, logical reads 2, physical reads 0, read-ahead reads 0, lob logical reads 0, lob physical reads 0,

(1 row affected)

Figure 13-57. *Statistics I/O results for the expensive aggregation*

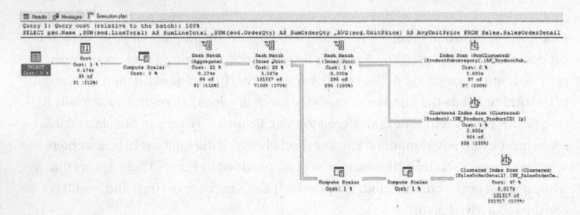

Figure 13-58. *Execution plan for the expensive aggregation*

A solution for this performance problem can be found through creating a view for the query in Listing 13-44 and adding an index to the view. There are a number of things to consider when adding indexes to views, such as the following:

- All columns in the view must be deterministic.

- The view must be created using the SCHEMA_BINDING view option.

- The clustered index must be created as unique.

- Tables referenced in the view must use two-part naming.

- If aggregating values, the COUNT_BIG() function must be included.

- Some aggregations, such as AVG(), are disallowed in indexed views.

Additional consideration when creating indexed views is included in the Books Online topic "Create Indexed Views" (https://docs.microsoft.com/en-us/sql/relational-databases/views/create-indexed-views?).

The first step in creating an indexed view is to create the underlying view. Given the considerations listed, the query in Listing 13-44 cannot be directly turned into a view.

The query must be changed to remove the AVG function and include the COUNT_BIG function. While this change removes one of the required data elements from the output, that value can be calculated after indexing the view. In addition, the view definition must include the WITH SCHEMABINDING option. The result is the view definition in Listing 13-45. The last step is to create a unique clustered index on the table using the Name column from the Production.ProductSubcategory table.

Listing 13-45. Indexed View Definition

```
USE AdventureWorks2017
GO

CREATE VIEW dbo.ProductSubcategorySummary
WITH SCHEMABINDING
AS
SELECT psc.Name
    ,SUM(sod.LineTotal) AS SumLineTotal
    ,SUM(sod.OrderQty) AS SumOrderQty
    ,SUM(sod.UnitPrice) AS TotalUnitPrice
    ,COUNT_BIG(*) AS Occurrences
FROM Sales.SalesOrderDetail sod
    INNER JOIN Production.Product p ON sod.ProductID = p.ProductID
    INNER JOIN Production.ProductSubcategory psc ON p.ProductSubcategoryID
= psc.ProductSubcategoryID
GROUP BY psc.Name;
GO

CREATE UNIQUE CLUSTERED INDEX CLIX_ProductSubcategorySummary
    ON dbo.ProductSubcategorySummary(Name)
```

With the indexed view in place, the next step is to test how the view performs compared with the original query. Before executing the code in Listing 13-46, first look at the second query that is using the TotalUnitPrice and Occurrences columns to generate AvgUnitPrice. While the AVG function cannot be included in the definitions for indexed views, the same results can be achieved with minimal effort.

After executing the queries in Listing 13-46, it can be observed that the queries performed substantially better than in the example in Listing 13-44. Instead of more than 1,200 reads, there are only 2 reads required (see Figure 13-59), and the execution plan (Figure 13-60) is quite a bit simpler. Instead of many operators, the plan was simplified to three.

Listing 13-46.   Query that uses an Indexed View

```
USE AdventureWorks2017;
GO

SET STATISTICS IO ON;
SELECT psc.Name,
       SUM(sod.LineTotal) AS SumLineTotal,
       SUM(sod.OrderQty) AS SumOrderQty,
       AVG(sod.UnitPrice) AS AvgUnitPrice
FROM Sales.SalesOrderDetail sod
    INNER JOIN Production.Product p
        ON sod.ProductID = p.ProductID
    INNER JOIN Production.ProductSubcategory psc
        ON p.ProductSubcategoryID = psc.ProductSubcategoryID
GROUP BY psc.Name
ORDER BY psc.Name;
SELECT Name,
       SumLineTotal,
       SumOrderQty,
       TotalUnitPrice / Occurrences AS AvgUnitPrice
FROM dbo.ProductSubcategorySummary
ORDER BY Name;
```

Results | Messages | Execution plan

```
(35 rows affected)
Table 'ProductSubcategorySummary'. Scan count 1, logical reads 2, physical reads 0, read-ahead reads 0, lob logical reads 0, lob physical reads 0,

(1 row affected)

(35 rows affected)
Table 'ProductSubcategorySummary'. Scan count 1, logical reads 2, physical reads 0, read-ahead reads 0, lob logical reads 0, lob physical reads 0,

(1 row affected)
```

Figure 13-59.   *Statistics I/O results for the Indexed View pattern*

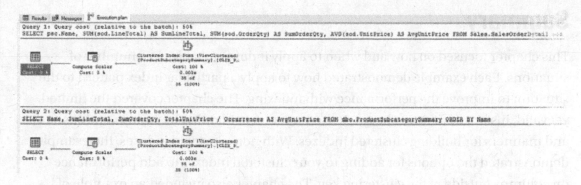

Figure 13-60. *Execution plan for the Indexed View pattern*

Another peculiar thing occurred in the execution that can be observed. Both the query against the base tables and the query against the view performed identically after implementing the indexed view. This is one of the added benefits of indexed views. When SQL Server is determining the execution plan for the first query, it can deduce that there is an indexed view that can cover the same logic as the query, even though the calculation for the average column is not the same.

Note that the cost of indexed views is in maintaining their indexes. Whenever any underlying value changes in its source tables, the index needs to also be updated. The ideal indexed views are targeted toward specific use cases and do not attempt to re-index an entire table. When indexed views become excessively complex or begin to contain many different indexes, it is worth considering ways to rearchitect the underlying tables to reduce the complexity of the business logic that requires them.

Indexed views are an extremely useful tool when multiple tables need to be joined together in a single unit to reduce the I/O required to join the data at runtime. While there are restrictions associated with indexed views, there are numerous benefits, including the ability to use indexed views in situations like the one in Listing 13-46. When there are views and queries with the same shape that are used frequently, consider whether an inclusion of the view can provide the benefit that indexes on the base tables do not provide.

Summary

This chapter focused on how and when to apply indexes to tables in a number of situations. Each example demonstrated how to apply a particular index pattern to the situation to improve the performance with indexing. The chapter covered the limited, yet valid, instances for using heaps. It then went on to identify the various options and manners for building clustered indexes. With non-clustered indexes, the example demonstrated the options for adding to your clustered indexes to add performance on columns outside of the clustering key. The chapter also included an example of implementing columnstore indexes and discussed when to apply this type of index. Overall, these patterns provide the groundwork for identifying the types of indexes that are most useful for different types of columns and workloads, and they provide the ability to meaningfully compare one indexing solution with another.

CHAPTER 14

Query Strategies

In the previous chapter, strategies were discussed to identify potential indexes for a wide variety of tables. That is often only half of the story, though. Once indexes have been created, performance is expected to improve within a database, leading then to the next bottleneck. Unfortunately, coding practices and selectivity can negatively influence the application of indexes to queries. Sometimes how the database and tables are being accessed will prevent the use of some of the most beneficial indexes available.

Proper indexing provides an efficient set of paths to critical data. Effective querying is needed to ensure that data is written and read in ways that follow those paths and provides good performance.

This chapter covers querying strategies where indexes may not be used as expected. These scenarios are

- LIKE comparison
- Concatenation
- Computed columns
- Scalar functions
- Data conversions

In each scenario, the circumstances around them will be discussed along with why they don't perform as expected. For each scenario, mitigation strategies will be provided along with some tips on how to use the right index in the right place. This chapter will provide the tools needed to recognize situations that will hamper the ability to index the database for performance, as well as strategies to resolve these challenges.

© Edward Pollack and Jason Strate 2023
E. Pollack and J. Strate, *Expert Performance Indexing in Azure SQL and SQL Server 2022*,
https://doi.org/10.1007/978-1-4842-9215-0_14

LIKE Comparison

When looking at the impact of queries on the use of indexes, the first and simplest place to start is with the LIKE comparison. The LIKE comparison allows searches in columns on any characters or pattern. If there is a need to identify all values in a table that start with the letters *AAA* or *BBB*, the LIKE comparison would provide this functionality. In these searches, the query can read through the index and find the values that match to the characters or pattern. Problems can arise when using this comparison in queries to find values that contain or end with a character or pattern.

In this situation, the index becomes immaterial because statistics are collected only on the leftmost side of character values. Assuming a random distribution, the likelihood that the letter *B* appears in the first value in the index is equal to it appearing in the last value in the index. To determine which records in the table have a *B* anywhere in the column, all rows must be checked. There are no statistics available to identify whether a letter is contained within a character string. Without reliable statistics to use, SQL Server will not know what index to use to satisfy a query and will likely end up scanning the clustered index to return the matching values.

To understand the problems that can occur with the LIKE comparison, a few demonstrations will be provided that show both scenarios and their related statistics. To start, consider a scenario querying the Person.Address table for records where AddressLine1 starts with "710%" (see Listing 14-1). A review of the STATISTICS IO output in Figure 14-1 shows the query required three logical reads. Examining the execution plan in Figure 14-2 shows an index seek on the non-clustered index.

Listing 14-1. Query for Addresses Beginning with 710

```
USE AdventureWorks2017
GO

SET STATISTICS IO ON;

SELECT AddressID, AddressLine1, AddressLine2, City, StateProvinceID,
PostalCode
FROM Person.Address
WHERE AddressLine1 LIKE '710%';
```

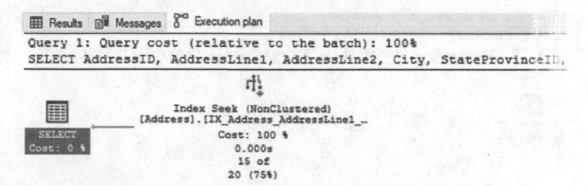

```
⊞ Results  ⊡ Messages  ⎕ Execution plan

(15 rows affected)
Table 'Address'. Scan count 1, logical reads 3, physical reads 0, read-ahead reads 0, lob logical reads 0.

(1 row affected)
```

Figure 14-1. *STATISTICS I/O for addresses beginning with 710*

```
⊞ Results  ⊡ Messages  ⎕ Execution plan

Query 1: Query cost (relative to the batch): 100%
SELECT AddressID, AddressLine1, AddressLine2, City, StateProvinceID,
```

```
                              Index Seek (NonClustered)
                           [Address].[IX_Address_AddressLine1_...
 SELECT                              Cost: 100 %
 Cost: 0 %                             0.000s
                                       15 of
                                     20 (75%)
```

Figure 14-2. *Execution plan for addresses beginning with 710*

In this situation, the LIKE comparison worked well, and the execution plan, statistics, and I/O were all appropriate for the request. Because the filter checked the leftmost characters in *AddressLine1*, SQL Server was able to use an index on that column to effectively filter that column and return the expected results.

Unfortunately, this is not the only way LIKE comparisons can be used. It can be used to find values within a column. Consider a scenario where there is a need to find all addresses that match a specific street name, such as "Longbrook" (see Listing 14-2). With this query, the execution plan uses a scan on the non-clustered index and requires 216 logical reads, as shown in Figure 14-3. Figure 14-4 shows the execution plan.

Listing 14-2. Query for Addresses Containing "Longbrook"

```
USE AdventureWorks2017
GO

SET STATISTICS IO ON;

SELECT AddressID, AddressLine1, AddressLine2, City, StateProvinceID,
PostalCode
FROM Person.Address
WHERE AddressLine1 LIKE '%Longbrook%';
```

Results   Messages   Execution plan

```
(6 rows affected)
Table 'Address'. Scan count 1, logical reads 216, physical reads 0, read-ahead reads 0, lob logical reads 0,

(1 row affected)
```

Figure 14-3. *STATISTICS I/O for addresses containing "Longbrook"*

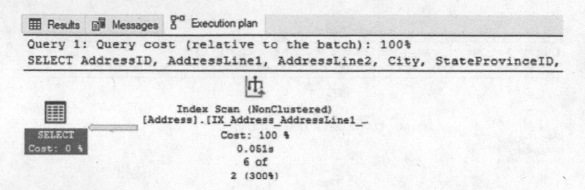

Results   Messages   Execution plan

```
Query 1: Query cost (relative to the batch): 100%
SELECT AddressID, AddressLine1, AddressLine2, City, StateProvinceID,
```

```
                         Index Scan (NonClustered)
                         [Address].[IX_Address_AddressLine1_
  SELECT                        Cost: 100 %
 Cost: 0 %                         0.051s
                                    6 of
                                  2 (300%)
```

Figure 14-4. *Execution plan for addresses containing "Longbrook"*

Because the filter on *AddressLine1* had a leading wildcard, SQL Server was unable to use an index on the column to satisfy the filter. Instead, it was forced to scan the index in its entirety to determine which values met the filter criteria.

In this scenario, the table and index were both small. The difference between an index seek and a scan was not extreme. Consider if this scenario was happening in a production system with a much larger table. Instead of being able to quickly filter out records that match the search values, SQL Server is required to look through all rows using brute force. Even when that time may be just tens of seconds to complete, it opens the opportunity for blocking, locking, and deadlocking, which will further slow down queries in an environment. When queries execute, they lock resources as rows are written or read, and the longer locks are held, the greater the probability that those locked resources will impact other queries that are trying to access the same data.

A popular method of avoiding this situation is to declare that wildcards are never allowed on the left edge of searches. In some applications, this is reasonable and can be implemented without any changes to SQL Server.

Unfortunately, this can be an unrealistic expectation. There are few business managers in the world who would agree to require their users to enter all possible street number combinations in an attempt to find every address that matches the street name search. Just reading that explanation here makes it sound silly.

A much more appropriate and useful solution (though less popular) for this scenario is to create a full-text index on the table. A contributing factor to full-text indexes being less popular than non-clustered indexes is because of the difference in building and creating them, which has made them less familiar to most people. With a full-text index, words within one or more columns are cataloged, along with their position in the table. This enables the query to search quickly for the discrete values within a column without having to check all the records in an index.

To use a full-text index on the `Person.Address` table, a full-text catalog must first be built, as shown in Listing 14-3. After that, the full-text index is created and includes the column that will be searched in the queries. Lastly, the query needs to be modified to use one of the full-text predicate functions. In this example, the `CONTAINS` function will be used.

Listing 14-3. Query for Addresses Using CONTAINS

```
USE AdventureWorks2017
GO

SET STATISTICS IO ON;

CREATE FULLTEXT CATALOG ftQueryStrategies AS DEFAULT;

CREATE FULLTEXT INDEX ON Person.Address(AddressLine1)
KEY INDEX PK_Address_AddressID;
GO

SELECT AddressID, AddressLine1, AddressLine2, City, StateProvinceID,
PostalCode
FROM Person.Address
WHERE CONTAINS (AddressLine1,'Longbrook');
```

With the full-text index in place, the performance of the search for streets named Longbrook is similar to the first search where the query was looking for addresses starting with 710. In the execution plan in Figure 14-6, instead of a scan of the non-clustered index, the query is using a seek operation on the clustered index with a table-valued function lookup against the full-text index. As a result, instead of the 216 logical reads when using the `LIKE` comparison, using the full-text index requires only 12 logical reads (shown in Figure 14-5). The difference in reads provides a substantial improvement in performance over the first search attempt.

For more information on full-text indexes, read Chapter 9.

Results   Messages   Execution plan

```
(6 rows affected)
Table 'Address'. Scan count 0, logical reads 12, physical reads 0, read-ahead reads 0, lob logical reads 0,

(1 row affected)
```

Figure 14-5. *STATISTICS I/O for addresses using CONTAINS*

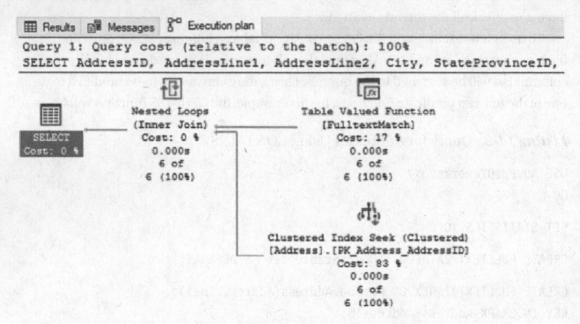

Figure 14-6. *Execution plan for addresses using CONTAINS*

There are other potential solutions to this problem, such as the manual creation of N-gram tables to manage discrete keywords within a string column. This can be an effective way to customize a string search solution when the set of search terms is limited and can be maintained in some automated fashion. Demonstrating this is out of scope for this book, but it is worth mentioning for scenarios where standard indexing and full-text indexing are inadequate to solve a string searching challenge.

Concatenation

Another scenario that can wreak havoc on indexing strategies is the use of concatenation. *Concatenation* is when two or more values are appended to one another. When this happens in a WHERE clause, it can often lead to poor performance that isn't expected.

To demonstrate this scenario, consider a query for someone with the name Gustavo Achong. Searching for this value requires using the FirstName and LastName columns, which are concatenated together with a space between the columns. Listing 14-4 shows the query. A script to build an index on these columns is also included in the code listing. The execution plan generated for this query, shown in Figure 14-8, shows that the new index is used but the operation is a scan instead of a seek, which would be more desirable. Even though the leading left edge of the index matches the left-side values of the concatenated values, the index is not able to determine where to find the values in the index. This results in the index using 99 logical reads to return the query results, shown in Figure 14-7.

Listing 14-4. Query with Concatenation

```
USE AdventureWorks2017
GO

SET STATISTICS IO ON;

CREATE INDEX IX_PersonContact_FirstNameLastName ON Person.Person
(FirstName, LastName)
GO

SELECT BusinessEntityID, FirstName, LastName
FROM Person.Person
WHERE CONCAT(FirstName,' ',LastName) = 'Gustavo Achong'
```

```
⊞ Results  ▥ Messages  ▦ Execution plan
   Table 'Worktable'. Scan count 0, logical reads 0, physical reads 0, read-ahead reads 0, lob logical reads
   Table 'Person'. Scan count 1, logical reads 106, physical reads 0, read-ahead reads 0, lob logical reads 0

   (1 row affected)
   Table 'Person'. Scan count 1, logical reads 99, physical reads 0, read-ahead reads 0, lob logical reads 0.

   (1 row affected)
```

Figure 14-7. *STATISTICS I/O for concatenation*

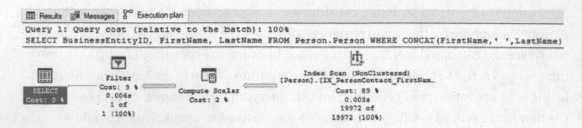

Figure 14-8. *Execution plan for concatenation*

As mentioned, using a scan on the index is not necessarily a bad thing. However, using a scan when there are a lot of concurrent users or data modifications occurring could lead to contention and latency. When it comes to larger tables with millions or more records, this can possibly lead to a lack of scalability for the database.

It may seem reasonable at first glance to remove the space between the first and last names (see Listing 14-5), since then it's using the two columns from the index we created. The issue with this solution is that it doesn't work. As the execution plan in Figure 14-10 shows, it is nearly identical to the one with the space in the concatenated value with the same 99 reads as well (shown in Figure 14-9).

Listing 14-5. Concatenation Without Spaces

```
USE AdventureWorks2017
GO

SET STATISTICS IO ON;

SELECT BusinessEntityID, FirstName, LastName
FROM Person.Person
WHERE CONCAT(FirstName, LastName)= 'GustavoAchong';
```

🔲 Results 📊 Messages 📊 Execution plan

```
(1 row affected)
Table 'Person'. Scan count 1, logical reads 99, physical reads 0, read-ahead reads 0, lob logical reads 0,

(1 row affected)
```

Figure 14-9. *STATISTICS I/O for concatenation without spaces*

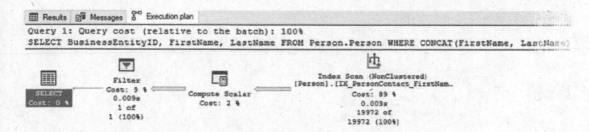

Figure 14-10. *Execution plan for concatenation without spaces*

Probably the best way to fix issues with concatenated values is to remove the need to concatenate. Instead of searching for the value `Gustavo Achong`, search for the first name `Gustavo` and the last name `Achong` (see Listing 14-6). When this change is made, the query is then able to use a seek operation on the non-clustered index and return the results with only two logical reads (see Figure 14-11). These results are a significant improvement over when the values were concatenated together. See Figure 14-12 for the execution plan.

Listing 14-6. Query with Concatenation Removed

```
USE AdventureWorks2017
GO

SET STATISTICS IO ON;

SELECT BusinessEntityID, FirstName, LastName
FROM Person.Person
WHERE FirstName = 'Gustavo'
AND LastName = 'Achong';
```

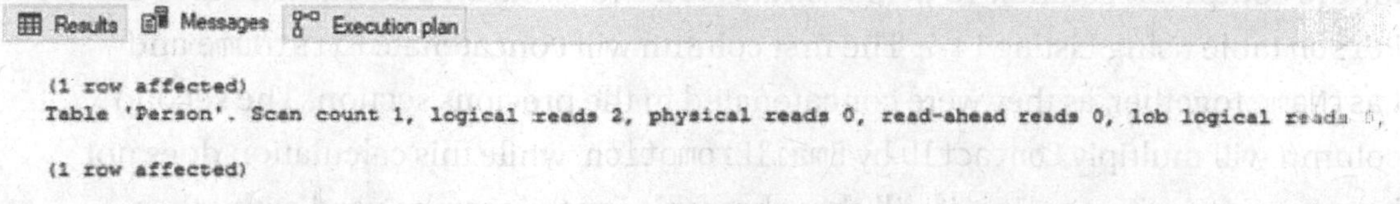

```
(1 row affected)
Table 'Person'. Scan count 1, logical reads 2, physical reads 0, read-ahead reads 0, lob logical reads 0,

(1 row affected)
```

Figure 14-11. *STATISTICS I/O for concatenation removed*

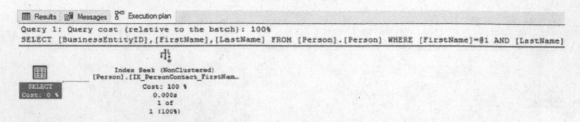

Figure 14-12. *Execution plan with concatenation removed*

The ideal WHERE clause is composed of simple predicates that can be easily resolved. Functions, transformations, combinations, and other attempts to alter data on the fly while trying to filter data are more likely to lead to unexpected index scans, unwanted contention, and longer-running queries.

At times, you won't have the option to remove concatenation from a query. In these scenarios, there is another way to resolve index performance issues: the concatenated values can be added to the table as a computed column. This solution, along with some of its challenges, is discussed in the next section.

Computed Columns

Sometimes one or more columns in a table are defined as an expression. These types of columns are referred to as *computed columns*. Computed columns can be useful when a column is needed to hold the result of a function or calculation that will change over time based on the other columns in the table. Rather than spending the CPU cycles to make certain that all modifications to a table always include changes to all the related columns, the components can be changed and the results computed when queried.

Note that computed columns cannot leverage the indexes on the source columns for the computed column. To demonstrate, add two computed columns to the Person. Person table using Listing 14-7. The first column will concatenate FirstName and LastName together, as they were concatenated in the previous section. The second column will multiply ContactID by EmailPromotion; while this calculation does not have any intrinsic meaning, it will show how this strategy can be used with other calculation types.

Listing 14-7. Add Computed Columns to Person.Person

```
USE AdventureWorks2017
GO
ALTER TABLE Person.Person
ADD FirstLastName AS (FirstName + ' ' + LastName)
,CalculateValue AS (BusinessEntityID * EmailPromotion);
```

With the columns in place, the next step is to test querying the table. Execute two queries against the table using Listing 14-8. The first query is similar to the first and last name query from the previous section (when searching for Gustavo Achong). The second query will return all records with the `CalculatedValue` of 198.

Listing 14-8. Computed Column Queries

```
USE AdventureWorks2017
GO

SET STATISTICS IO ON

SELECT BusinessEntityID, FirstName, LastName, FirstLastName
FROM Person.Person
WHERE FirstLastName = 'Gustavo Achong';

SELECT BusinessEntityID, CalculateValue
FROM Person.Person
WHERE CalculateValue = 198;
```

After executing both queries, the execution plans in Figure 14-14 show that both used scan operations to return the query results. These results are less than ideal for the same reasons mentioned earlier in this chapter since they can lead to blocking and utilize more I/O than should be necessary for the query requests. By more I/O, the query results for both require read I/Os from scanning the entire table, shown in Figure 14-13.

```
⊞ Results  🗊 Messages  ⅗⊟ Execution plan

  (1 row affected)
  Table 'Person'. Scan count 1, logical reads 99, physical reads 0, read-ahead reads 0, lob logical reads 0, 1

  (1 row affected)

  (1 row affected)
  Table 'Person'. Scan count 1, logical reads 3858, physical reads 0, read-ahead reads 0, lob logical reads 0,

  (1 row affected)
```

Figure 14-13. *STATISTICS I/O for computed columns*

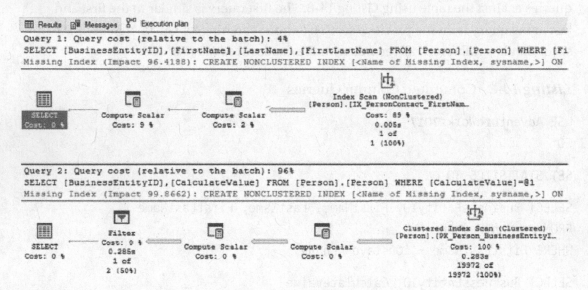

Figure 14-14. *Computed column execution plans*

An indexing option available for computed columns is to index the computed columns themselves, which SQL Server will suggest as missing indexes, as shown in Figure 14-14. As the query for FirstLastName shows, the query can use any of the indexes on the table. The restriction is that it cannot use them any better than if the expression for the computed column was in the query itself. Indexing the computed columns, as shown in Listing 14-9, provides the necessary distribution and record information to allow queries, such as those in Listing 14-8, to use seeks instead of scans. The index materializes the values in the computed column, allowing quick access to the data, which results in a significant reduction in I/O from 99 to 5 reads and 3,878 to 2 reads, shown in Figure 14-15. Figure 14-16 shows the execution plans.

Note   When indexing a computed column, the expression for the column must be deterministic. Every time the expression executes with the same variables, it will always return the same results. As an example, using GETDATE() in a computed column expression would not be deterministic.

Listing 14-9. Computed Column Indexes

```
USE AdventureWorks2017
GO

CREATE INDEX IX_PersonPerson_FirstLastName ON Person.Person(FirstLastName);
CREATE INDEX IX_PersonPerson_CalculateValue ON Person.
Person(CalculateValue);
```

Figure 14-15. *STATISTICS I/O for indexed computed column*

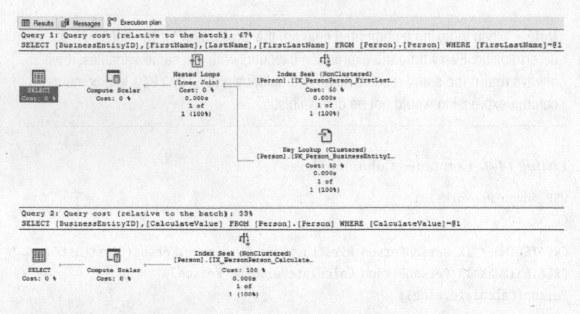

Figure 14-16. *Indexed computed column execution plans*

Note that the cost of indexing a computed column is the additional I/O required to update the index when any of the underlying columns used in the computed column change. Therefore, indexing a computed column should be reserved for scenarios where frequently executed (or critically important) queries are benefiting from the index.

As this section demonstrates, computed columns can be extremely useful when expressions are needed to define values as part of a table. For example, if an application can only send in searches where the first and last names were combined, computed columns can provide the data in the format that the application is sending. The columns can use underlying indexes to return results but usually can't fully use the statistics and underlying sort of the data in those indexes because of the expression in the column definition. By indexing computed columns, data can be provided in the exact format needed by an application, allowing for optimal performance, even when multiple columns or complex calculations are involved.

Scalar Functions

The previous few sections discussed filtering query results by searching within column values or by combining values across columns. This section looks at the effect of scalar functions used in the WHERE clauses of queries. Scalar functions provide the ability to transform values to other values that can be more useful when querying the database.

User-defined scalar functions can also be created and used in the WHERE clause. The trouble with both system and user-defined scalar functions is that if they transform a column where an index exists, then SQL Server is no longer able to use the index efficiently. Because the values of the calculations are not known until runtime, the query optimizer does not have statistics to determine the frequency of values in the index or information on where the calculated values are located in the index or table.

To demonstrate the effect of scalar functions on queries, consider the two queries in Listing 14-10 that return information from Person.Person. Both queries will return all rows that have the value Gustavo in the FirstName column. The difference between the two queries is that the second query will use the RTRIM function in the WHERE clause on the FirstName column.

Listing 14-10. Queries on FirstName Gustavo

```
USE AdventureWorks2017
GO

SET STATISTICS IO ON

SELECT BusinessEntityID, FirstName, LastName
FROM Person.Person
WHERE FirstName = 'Gustavo';

SELECT BusinessEntityID, FirstName, LastName
FROM Person.Person
WHERE RTRIM(FirstName) = 'Gustavo';
```

As the second execution plan in Figure 14-18 shows, when the scalar function is added to the WHERE clause, the execution plan continues to use the same index that the first plan did, but leverages an index scan instead of an index seek. This change increases the I/Os from 2 to 99 (shown in Figure 14-17), which is similar to other examples. In this scenario, excluding the scalar function, as in the first query, can provide the same results as with the function in place. That will not be the case for all queries, but the way to allow indexes to be best used is to move the scalar function from the key columns to the parameters of a query.

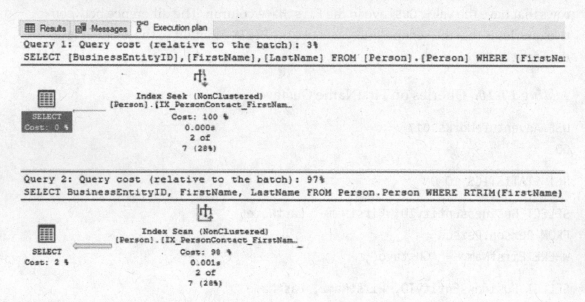

Figure 14-17. *STATISTICS I/O when a scalar function is used in the WHERE clause*

```
Results    Messages    Execution plan
Query 1: Query cost (relative to the batch): 3%
SELECT [BusinessEntityID],[FirstName],[LastName] FROM [Person].[Person] WHERE [FirstNa

                                  Index Seek (NonClustered)
                                [Person].[IX_PersonContact_FirstNam…
       SELECT                         Cost: 100 %
       Cost: 0 %                         0.000s
                                           2 of
                                         7 (28%)


Query 2: Query cost (relative to the batch): 97%
SELECT BusinessEntityID, FirstName, LastName FROM Person.Person WHERE RTRIM(FirstName)

                                   Index Scan (NonClustered)
                                 [Person].[IX_PersonContact_FirstNam…
       SELECT                          Cost: 98 %
       Cost: 2 %                          0.001s
                                            2 of
                                          7 (28%)
```

Figure 14-18. *Execution plans for Gustavo queries*

A good example of how scalar functions can be moved off key columns and into parameters is when the functions MONTH and YEAR are used. Suppose a query needs to return all sales orders for the month of December in the year 2001. This could be accomplished with the first SELECT query in Listing 14-11. Using the MONTH and YEAR functions changes the value of OrderDate, though, and the index on that column is still used, but with a scan instead of a seek (see the first execution plan in Figure 14-20). This issue can be avoided by changing the query in such a way that, instead of using the functions, the filter is applied to a range of values, such as in the second SELECT statement in Listing 14-11. As the second execution shows, the query can return the results with a seek instead of a scan, providing a significant reduction in reads, from 73 to 3, as shown in Figure 14-19. The beauty of a fix like this is that performance can be greatly improved without any tangible cost.

Listing 14-11. Queries using a value range instead of functions in the
WHERE clause

```
USE AdventureWorks2017
GO

CREATE INDEX IX_SalesSalesOrderHeader_OrderDate ON Sales.
SalesOrderHeader(OrderDate);

SET STATISTICS IO ON;

SELECT SalesOrderID, OrderDate
FROM Sales.SalesOrderHeader
WHERE MONTH(OrderDate) = 12
AND YEAR(OrderDate) = 2012;

SELECT SalesOrderID, OrderDate
FROM Sales.SalesOrderHeader
WHERE OrderDate BETWEEN '20121201' AND '20121231';
SET STATISTICS IO OFF;
```

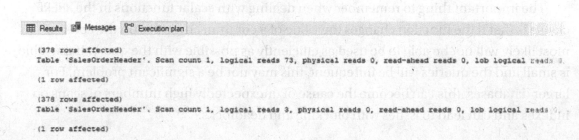

Figure 14-19. *STATISTICS I/O when using a value range instead of functions in the WHERE clause*

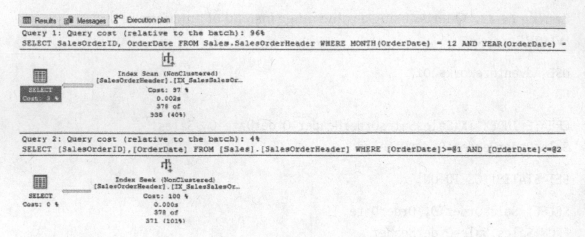

Figure 14-20. *Execution plans for date queries*

It will not always be possible to remove scalar functions from the WHERE clause of queries. One good example of this is if leading spaces were added to a column that should not be included when comparing the column values to parameters. In such a situation, more creativity will be required to resolve the problem. One possible solution is to use a computed column with an index on it, as introduced in the previous section.

The important thing to remember when dealing with scalar functions in the WHERE clause is that if the function changes the value of a column, any index on the column most likely will not be able to be used as efficiently as possible with the query. If the table is small and the queries will be infrequent, this may not be a significant problem. For larger databases, this can become the cause of unexpectedly high numbers of scans on indexes and can lead to issues with blocking and deadlocks.

Data Conversion

One last area where queries can negatively affect how indexes are used is when the data types of columns change within a JOIN operation or WHERE clause. When data types do not match in either of those conditions, SQL Server will need to convert the values in one column to match the other column. If the data conversion is not included in the syntax of the query, SQL Server will attempt the data conversion behind the scenes.

The reason that data conversions can have a negative effect on query performance is similar to the issues related to scalar functions. If a column in an index needs to be converted from varchar to int, the statistics for this index will not be useful in determining the frequency and location of values. For instance, the number 10 and the string "10" would be sorted into entirely different positions in the same index. To illustrate the effect that data conversions can have on a query, start by executing the code in Listing 14-12.

Listing 14-12. Data Conversion Setup

```
USE AdventureWorks2017
GO

SELECT BusinessEntityID
    ,CAST(FirstName as varchar(50)) as FirstName
    ,CAST(MiddleName as varchar(50)) as MiddleName
    ,CAST(LastName as varchar(50)) as LastName
INTO PersonPerson
FROM Person.Person;
CREATE CLUSTERED INDEX IX_PersonPerson_ContactID ON PersonPerson
(BusinessEntityID);

CREATE INDEX IX_PersonContact_FirstName ON PersonPerson(FirstName);
```

Listing 14-12 will create a table with varchar data in it. It will then add two indexes to the table that will be used in the demonstration queries. The two sample queries, shown in Listing 14-13, will be used to show how data conversions can affect the performance and utilization of an index. For both queries, the RECOMPILE option is being used to prevent inadvertent parameter sniffing.

Note   For more information on parameter sniffing, read Paul White's "Parameter Sniffing, Embedding, and the RECOMPILE Options" article on SQLPerformance.com at http://sqlperformance.com/2013/08/t-sql-queries/parameter-sniffing-embedding-and-the-recompile-options.

The first SELECT query uses the @FirstName variable with the nvarchar data type. This data type does not match the data type for the column in the table PersonContact, so the column in the table must be converted from varchar to nvarchar. The execution plan for the query (Figure 14-21) shows that the query is using an index seek on the non-clustered index to satisfy the query, and the predicate is converting the data in the column to nvarchar, with a key lookup on the clustered index for the columns not in the non-clustered index. Also note that the cost for the first query is 40 percent of the total batch, which is just the two queries.

Listing 14-13. Implicit Conversion Queries

```
USE AdventureWorks2017
GO

SET STATISTICS IO ON
DECLARE @FirstName nvarchar(100)
SET @FirstName = 'Gail';

SELECT FirstName, LastName FROM PersonPerson
WHERE FirstName = @FirstName
OPTION (RECOMPILE);

GO
DECLARE @FirstName varchar(100)
SET @FirstName = 'Gail';

SELECT FirstName, LastName FROM PersonPerson
WHERE FirstName = @FirstName
OPTION (RECOMPILE);
```

Note   The additional information shown for the operators in the execution plans is available in the Properties window in SQL Server Management Studio. The Properties window is full of useful information about the operations from the columns that are used for estimated and actual row counts.

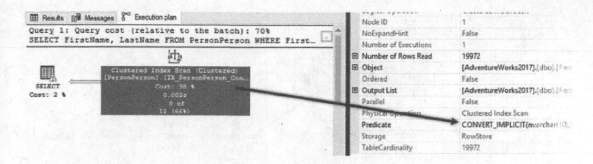

Figure 14-21. *Execution plan with implicit data conversion*

One other item to note in the execution plan in Figure 14-22 is the warning included on the SELECT operation for the first query. SQL Server 2012 and above include detailed warning messages in execution plans that contain implicit conversions. The warning message appears as a yellow triangle with an exclamation mark in it. Checking the properties for the operator will include details of the operator and for the warning message. These messages include information about what column is being converted and the issue associated with the problem. In this example, the issue is SeekPlan ConvertIssue. In other words, SQL Server does not have statistics on the converted data to build an execution plan that knows the frequency of the values in the predicate.

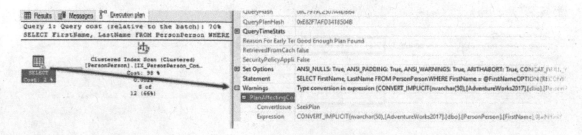

Figure 14-22. *Warning included with implicit conversion*

The second SELECT query in Listing 14-13 uses a variable with a varchar data type. Since this data type already matches the data type of the column in the table, the non-clustered index can be used. As the execution plan in Figure 14-23 shows, with matching data types, the query optimizer can build a plan that knows where the rows in the index are and can perform a seek to obtain them.

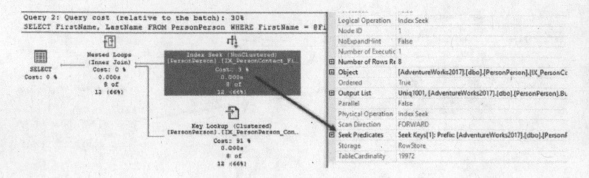

Figure 14-23. *Execution plan without data conversion*

At first glance, the second execution plan may appear less efficient due to there being more operations, higher complexity, and a key lookup, but this is not the case. Reviewing the logical reads from STATISTICS IO, shown in Figure 14-24, allows for a clearer understanding of performance. For the first query, there were 89 logical reads with an index scan on the clustered index. The second query had only 18 reads while accessing two indexes. The difference in I/O is attributed to the high number of reads required to scan the clustered index, which ends up being greater than the cost of both an index seek and a key lookup.

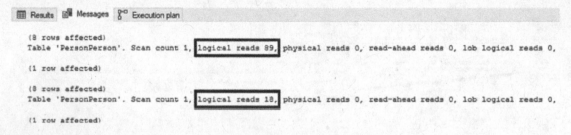

Figure 14-24. *STATISTICS I/O for implicit conversion queries*

In this section, the discussion focused on implicit data conversions and the negative impact they can have on query performance. While these can be more silent than explicit data conversions, the same concepts and mitigations apply. Since they are more intentional, they should be less frequent. Even so, when performing data conversions, pay close attention to the data types involved because how they are changed will impact query performance and index utilization.

Summary

In this chapter, the structure of queries was examined to understand when they can effectively use indexes and when index use is impeded, negatively affecting performance. There are times when a specific type of index may not be appropriate for a situation, such as searching for values within character strings in large tables. In other situations, applying the right type of index or function in the right place can have a significant impact on whether the query can use an index or not.

In many of the examples in this chapter, problematic index usage was made clear via the use of index scans rather than seeks. In these scenarios, index seeks were the ideal index operation. This will not always be the case, and there are situations where scans against an index are the optimal operator, such as when an entire table (or most of it) needs to be read. It is important to understand what type of transactions the environment is geared for and the size of the tables that are being accessed.

The main takeaway from this chapter is that query structure is often as important as index structure. The choices made when developing database code can completely unravel the work done to properly index a database. Be sure to complement indexing strategies with efficient code that leverages them to their maximum potential.

CHAPTER 15

Monitoring Indexes

Throughout this book, many topics have been discussed, such as what indexes are, what they do, patterns for building them, and many other aspects for determining how a SQL Server database should be indexed. All of that information is necessary for the final piece in indexing your databases: analyzing databases to determine which indexes are required. The final three chapters in this book will pull together the information needed to implement an indexing methodology.

To start, in this chapter, a general practice will be discussed that can be used for monitoring indexes. It will include steps that can be taken to observe the behavior of indexes and understand how they impact an environment. This methodology can be applied to a single database, to a server, or as an entire SQL Server environment. Regardless of the type of operations or business that the database supports, similar monitoring processes can be used.

The main goal behind monitoring indexes is creating the ability to collect, store, and report on information about indexes. This information will come from a variety of sources. The sources for monitoring should be familiar because they are often used with tasks similar to indexing, such as performance tuning. For some sources, the information will be collected over time to provide an idea of general trends. For other sources, a snapshot at a specific point in time is sufficient. It is important to collect some information over time to provide a baseline against which to compare performance. This will help in understanding when changes in index usage and effectiveness have occurred.

There are a number of sources from which information will be collected to monitor indexes. The sources that will be discussed in this chapter are as follows:

- Performance counters
- Dynamic management objects
- Event tracing

© Edward Pollack and Jason Strate 2023
E. Pollack and J. Strate, *Expert Performance Indexing in Azure SQL and SQL Server 2022*,
https://doi.org/10.1007/978-1-4842-9215-0_15

For each of these sources, the subsequent sections will describe what is to be collected and will provide guidance on how to collect this information. By the end of the chapter, there will be a framework that is capable of providing the information necessary to start the Analyze phase.

Note   All monitoring information from this chapter will be collected in a database named `IndexingMethod`. The scripts can be run in that database or in another performance monitoring database.

Performance Counters

The first source of monitoring information for indexes is SQL Server performance counters. Performance counters are metrics provided by Microsoft to measure the rate of events or state of resources within applications and hardware on the server. With some of the performance counters, there are general guidelines that can be used to indicate when a problem with indexing may exist. For others, changes in the rate or level of the performance counter may indicate a need to adjust the indexing on a server.

The primary challenge with using performance counters is that they represent the server-level, or SQL Server instance–level, state of the counters. They do not indicate at a database or table level where possible indexing issues are occurring. This level of detail, though, is acceptable and useful when considering the other tools available for monitoring indexes and identifying potential indexing needs. One advantage to collecting counter information at this level is that we are forced to consider the whole picture and the effect of all the indexes on performance. In an isolated situation, a couple of poorly performing indexes on a table might be acceptable. However, in conjunction with other tables with poor indexing, the aggregate performance may reach a tipping point where index performance needs to be addressed. With the server-level statistics provided by performance counters, we will be able to identify when this point has been reached.

There are many performance counters available for both SQL Server and Windows Server. From the perspective of indexing, though, many of the performance counters can be ignored. The performance counters that are most useful are those that map to operations related to how indexes operate or are accessed, such as forwarded records and index searches. For a definition of the performance counters that are most useful with indexing, see Table 15-1. The reasons for collecting each of the counters and how they impact indexing decisions will be discussed in the next chapter.

Table 15-1. *Index-Related Performance Counters*

Option name	Description
Access Methods\Forwarded Records/sec	Number of records per second fetched through forwarded record pointers
Access Methods\FreeSpace Page Fetches/sec	Number of pages fetched per second within allocated pages to an object to insert or modify a record
Access Methods\FreeSpace Scans/sec	Number of scans per second initiated to search for free space within allocated pages to an object to insert or modify a record
Access Methods\Full Scans/ sec	Number of unrestricted full scans per second. These can be either base-table or full-index scans
Access Methods\Index Searches/sec	Number of index searches per second. These are used to start range scans and single index record fetches and to reposition an index
Access Methods\Page compression attempts/sec	Number of page compression attempts per second using PAGE compression; this will include failed page compressions
Access Methods\Pages compressed/sec	Number of pages compressed per second using PAGE compression
Access Methods\Page Splits/ sec	Number of page splits per second that occur as the result of overflowing index pages
Buffer Manager\Page Lookups/sec	Number of requests to find a page in the buffer pool
Locks(*)\Lock Wait Time (ms)	Total wait time (in milliseconds) for locks in the last second
Locks(*)\Lock Waits/sec	Number of lock requests per second that required the caller to wait
Locks(*)\Number of Deadlocks/sec	Number of lock requests per second that resulted in a deadlock
SQL Statistics\Batch Requests/sec	Number of Transact SQL command batches received per second

There are a number of ways to collect performance counters. For the monitoring in this chapter, the DMV sys.dm_os_performance_counters will be used. This DMV returns a row for all SQL Server counters for an instance. The values returned are the raw values for the counters. Depending on the type of counter, the value can be a point in time state value or an ever-accumulating aggregate.

To begin collecting performance counter information for monitoring, a table will need to be created for storing this information. The table definition in Listing 15-1 provides for this need. When collecting the performance counters, a table will be used that stores the counter name with the value and then date-stamps each row to identify when the information was collected.

Listing 15-1. Performance Counter Snapshot Table

```
USE IndexingMethod;
GO
CREATE TABLE dbo.IndexingCounters
    (
    counter_id INT IDENTITY(1, 1),
    create_date DATETIME2(0),
    server_name VARCHAR(128) NOT NULL,
    object_name VARCHAR(128) NOT NULL,
    counter_name VARCHAR(128) NOT NULL,
    instance_name VARCHAR(128) NULL,
    Calculated_Counter_value FLOAT NULL,
    CONSTRAINT PK_IndexingCounters
        PRIMARY KEY CLUSTERED (counter_id)
    );
GO
CREATE NONCLUSTERED INDEX IX_IndexingCounters_CounterName
ON dbo.IndexingCounters (counter_name)
INCLUDE (create_date, server_name, object_name, Calculated_Counter_value);
```

For the purposes of collecting information for monitoring indexing, the information from sys.dm_os_performance_counters will be collected and used to calculate the appropriate values from the DMV. These would be the same values that are available when viewing performance counter information from other tools, such as Performance Monitor. There are a few steps required to populate dbo.IndexingCounters. The DMV contains raw counter values. To calculate these values properly, it is necessary to take multiple snapshots of the values in the DMV, separated by a number of seconds before calculating the difference in values. In Listing 15-2, the counter value is calculated after 10 seconds. Once the time has expired, the counters are calculated and inserted into the dbo.IndexingCounters tables. This script should be scheduled and executed frequently.

Ideally, this information should be collected every 1–5 minutes, though frequency can be adjusted based on the level of index activity in a given environment. Feel free to customize the timing of this process to meet the indexing needs of a given database.

Note   Performance counter information can be collected more frequently. For instance, Performance Monitor defaults to every 15 seconds. For the purposes of index monitoring, that frequency is not necessary.

Listing 15-2. Performance Counter Snapshot Script

```
USE IndexingMethod;
GO
DROP TABLE IF EXISTS #Counters;
SELECT pc.object_name,
    pc.counter_name
INTO #Counters
FROM sys.dm_os_performance_counters pc
WHERE pc.cntr_type IN ( 272696576, 1073874176 )
  AND (
      pc.object_name LIKE '%:Access Methods%'
    AND (
       pc.counter_name LIKE 'Forwarded Records/sec%'
     OR pc.counter_name LIKE 'FreeSpace Scans/sec%'
     OR pc.counter_name LIKE 'FreeSpace Page Fetches/sec%'
     OR pc.counter_name LIKE 'Full Scans/sec%'
     OR pc.counter_name LIKE 'Index Searches/sec%'
     OR pc.counter_name LIKE 'Page Splits/sec%'
     OR pc.counter_name LIKE 'Page compression attempts/sec%'
     OR pc.counter_name LIKE 'Pages compressed/sec%'
    )
  )
   OR (
       pc.object_name LIKE '%:Buffer Manager%'
```

```
    AND (
        pc.counter_name LIKE 'Page life expectancy%'
      OR pc.counter_name LIKE 'Page lookups/sec%'
    )
  )
  OR (
      pc.object_name LIKE '%:Locks%'
    AND (
        pc.counter_name LIKE 'Lock Wait Time (ms)%'
      OR pc.counter_name LIKE 'Lock Waits/sec%'
      OR pc.counter_name LIKE 'Number of Deadlocks/sec%'
    )
  )
  OR (
      pc.object_name LIKE '%:SQL Statistics%'
    AND pc.counter_name LIKE 'Batch Requests/sec%'
  )
GROUP BY pc.object_name,
    pc.counter_name;
DROP TABLE IF EXISTS #Baseline;
SELECT GETDATE() AS sample_time,
    pc1.object_name,
    pc1.counter_name,
    pc1.instance_name,
    pc1.cntr_value,
    pc1.cntr_type,
    x.cntr_value AS base_cntr_value
INTO #Baseline
FROM sys.dm_os_performance_counters pc1
INNER JOIN #Counters c ON c.object_name = pc1.object_name
                   AND c.counter_name = pc1.counter_name
OUTER APPLY (
    SELECT cntr_value
    FROM sys.dm_os_performance_counters pc2
    WHERE pc2.cntr_type          = 1073939712
```

```
        AND UPPER(pc1.counter_name) = UPPER(pc2.counter_name)
        AND pc1.object_name        = pc2.object_name
        AND pc1.instance_name      = pc2.instance_name
) x;
WAITFOR DELAY '00:00:15';
INSERT INTO dbo.IndexingCounters (
    create_date,
    server_name,
    object_name,
    counter_name,
    instance_name,
    Calculated_Counter_value
)
SELECT GETDATE(),
    LEFT(pc1.object_name, CHARINDEX(':', pc1.object_name) - 1),
    SUBSTRING(pc1.object_name, 1 + CHARINDEX(':', pc1.object_name),
    LEN(pc1.object_name)),
    pc1.counter_name,
    pc1.instance_name,
    CASE
        WHEN pc1.cntr_type = 65792 THEN pc1.cntr_value
        WHEN pc1.cntr_type = 272696576 THEN
            COALESCE((1. * pc1.cntr_value - x.cntr_value) /
            NULLIF(DATEDIFF(s, sample_time, GETDATE()), 0), 0)
        WHEN pc1.cntr_type = 537003264 THEN COALESCE((1. * pc1.cntr_value)
        / NULLIF(base.cntr_value, 0), 0)
        WHEN pc1.cntr_type = 1073874176 THEN
            COALESCE(
                (1. * pc1.cntr_value - x.cntr_value) /
                NULLIF(base.cntr_value - x.base_cntr_value, 0)
                / NULLIF(DATEDIFF(s, sample_time, GETDATE()), 0),
                0
            ) END AS real_cntr_value
FROM sys.dm_os_performance_counters pc1
INNER JOIN #Counters c ON c.object_name = pc1.object_name
                    AND c.counter_name = pc1.counter_name
```

```
OUTER APPLY (
    SELECT cntr_value,
        base_cntr_value,
        sample_time
    FROM #Baseline b
    WHERE b.object_name   = pc1.object_name
      AND b.counter_name  = pc1.counter_name
      AND b.instance_name = pc1.instance_name
) x
OUTER APPLY (
    SELECT cntr_value
    FROM sys.dm_os_performance_counters pc2
    WHERE pc2.cntr_type              = 1073939712
      AND UPPER(pc1.counter_name) = UPPER(pc2.counter_name)
      AND pc1.object_name         = pc2.object_name
      AND pc1.instance_name       = pc2.instance_name
) base;
```

The first time performance counters are collected for indexes, it will not be possible to compare the counters to other reasonable values for a SQL Server database instance. As time goes on, though, previous performance counter samples can be retained to make comparisons. As part of monitoring, it is important to identify periods in which values for the performance counters represent the typical activity for your environment. Using that data, it is possible to identify anomalies or periods when usage is atypical and requires attention.

To store these values, insert them into a table similar to the one in Listing 15-3. This table has start and end dates to indicate the range that the baseline represents. Also, there are minimum, maximum, average, and standard deviation columns to store values from the collected counters. The minimum and maximum values will allow for an understanding of how the performance counters vary. The average value provides an idea of what the counter value will be when it is "good." The standard deviation allows us to understand the variability of the counter values. The lower the number, the more frequently the counter values cluster around the average value. Higher values indicate that the counter values vary more frequently and are often nearer to the minimum and maximum values.

Listing 15-3. Performance Counter Baseline Table

```
USE IndexingMethod;
GO
CREATE TABLE dbo.IndexingCountersBaseline
    (
    counter_baseline_id INT IDENTITY(1, 1),
    start_date DATETIME2(0),
    end_date DATETIME2(0),
    server_name VARCHAR(128) NOT NULL,
    object_name VARCHAR(128) NOT NULL,
    counter_name VARCHAR(128) NOT NULL,
    instance_name VARCHAR(128) NULL,
    minimum_counter_value FLOAT NULL,
    maximum_counter_value FLOAT NULL,
    average_counter_value FLOAT NULL,
    standard_deviation_counter_value FLOAT NULL,
    CONSTRAINT PK_IndexingCountersBaseline
        PRIMARY KEY CLUSTERED (counter_baseline_id)
    );
GO
```

When populating the values into dbo.IndexingCountersBaseline, there are two steps to the process. First, a sample needs to be collected from the performance counters that represent a typical week. If there are no typical weeks, pick this week and collect samples for it. Once data is collected for a typical week, the next step is to aggregate the information into the baseline table. This is a matter of summarizing the information in the table dbo.IndexingCounters for a range of days. In Listing 15-4, the data is from August 1 to August 15, 2019. The next step is to validate the baseline. Just because the average for the past week states that the Forwarded Records/sec value is at 100 does not mean that value represents a good baseline. Experience with servers and databases should be used to influence the values in the baseline. Adjust the baseline as needed if there is a recent trend below or above what is normal.

Listing 15-4. Populate Counter Baseline Table

```
USE IndexingMethod;
GO

DECLARE @StartDate DATETIME = '20190911',
    @EndDate        DATETIME = '20190918';
INSERT INTO dbo.IndexingCountersBaseline (
    start_date,
    end_date,
    server_name,
    object_name,
    counter_name,
    instance_name,
    minimum_counter_value,
    maximum_counter_value,
    average_counter_value,
    standard_deviation_counter_value
)
SELECT MIN(create_date),
    MAX(create_date),
    server_name,
    object_name,
    counter_name,
    instance_name,
    MIN(Calculated_Counter_value),
    MAX(Calculated_Counter_value),
    AVG(Calculated_Counter_value),
    STDEV(Calculated_Counter_value)
FROM dbo.IndexingCounters
WHERE create_date BETWEEN @StartDate AND @EndDate
GROUP BY server_name,
    object_name,
    counter_name,
    instance_name;
```

There are other ways to collect and view performance counters for SQL Server instances. Windows application Performance Monitor can be used to view performance counters in real time. It can also be used to log performance counters to a binary or text file. The command-line utility Logman can be used to interact with Performance Monitor to create data collectors and start and stop them as needed. Also, PowerShell can assist in the collection of performance counters.

These alternatives are all valid options for collecting performance counters on databases and indexes. The key is that if we want to monitor your indexes, we must collect the information necessary to know when potential indexing issues may arise. Pick a tool that is most comfortable to use and start collecting these counters today.

Dynamic Management Objects

Some of the best index performance information for monitoring is included in dynamic management objects (DMOs). The DMOs contain information on logical and physical uses for the indexes and overall physical structure. For monitoring, there are four DMOs that provide information on the usage of the indexes: sys.dm_db_index_usage_stats, sys.dm_db_index_operational_stats, sys.dm_db_index_physical_stats, and sys.dm_os_wait_stats. In this section, a process will be introduced to monitor indexes using each of these DMOs.

The first three following sections will discuss the sys.dm_db_index_* DMOs. Chapter 5 defined and demonstrated the contents of the DMOs. One thing to remember with these DMOs is that they can be flushed through various operations on the server, such as restarting the service or recreating the index. The fourth DMO, sys.dm_os_wait_stats, relates to index monitoring and provides information that can help during index analysis.

Warning   The indexing DMOs do not have information at the row level to precisely indicate when the information collected for the index has been reset. Because of this, there can be situations where the statistics reported can be slightly higher or lower than they actually are. While this should not greatly affect the outcome during analysis, it is something to keep in mind.

Index Usage Stats

The DMO `sys.dm_db_index_usage_stats` provides information on how indexes are being used and when an index was last used. This can be useful when we want to track whether indexes are being used and which operations are being executed against them.

The monitoring process for this DMO, which is similar to the other DMOs, consists of the following steps:

1. Create a table to hold snapshot information.

2. Insert the current state of the DMO into the snapshot table.

3. Compare the most recent snapshot to the previous snapshot, and insert the delta between the rows in the output into a history table.

To build the process, we'll first need to create the snapshot and history tables. The schema for these tables will be identical and will contain all columns from the DMO and a `create_date` column (see Listing 15-5). For consistency with the source DMO, the columns for the table will match the schema of the DMO.

Listing 15-5. Index Usage Stats Snapshot Tables Stats

```
USE IndexingMethod;
GO

CREATE TABLE dbo.index_usage_stats_snapshot
    (
    snapshot_id INT IDENTITY(1, 1),
    create_date DATETIME2(0),
    database_id SMALLINT NOT NULL,
    object_id INT NOT NULL,
    index_id INT NOT NULL,
    user_seeks BIGINT NOT NULL,
    user_scans BIGINT NOT NULL,
    user_lookups BIGINT NOT NULL,
    user_updates BIGINT NOT NULL,
    last_user_seek DATETIME,
    last_user_scan DATETIME,
    last_user_lookup DATETIME,
```

```
        last_user_update DATETIME,
        system_seeks BIGINT NOT NULL,
        system_scans BIGINT NOT NULL,
        system_lookups BIGINT NOT NULL,
        system_updates BIGINT NOT NULL,
        last_system_seek DATETIME,
        last_system_scan DATETIME,
        last_system_lookup DATETIME,
        last_system_update DATETIME,
        CONSTRAINT PK_IndexUsageStatsSnapshot
            PRIMARY KEY CLUSTERED (snapshot_id),
        CONSTRAINT UQ_IndexUsageStatsSnapshot
            UNIQUE (create_date, database_id, object_id, index_id)
    );
CREATE TABLE dbo.index_usage_stats_history
    (
    history_id INT IDENTITY(1, 1),
    create_date DATETIME2(0),
    database_id SMALLINT NOT NULL,
    object_id INT NOT NULL,
    index_id INT NOT NULL,
    user_seeks BIGINT NOT NULL,
    user_scans BIGINT NOT NULL,
    user_lookups BIGINT NOT NULL,
    user_updates BIGINT NOT NULL,
    last_user_seek DATETIME,
    last_user_scan DATETIME,
    last_user_lookup DATETIME,
    last_user_update DATETIME,
    system_seeks BIGINT NOT NULL,
    system_scans BIGINT NOT NULL,
    system_lookups BIGINT NOT NULL,
    system_updates BIGINT NOT NULL,
    last_system_seek DATETIME,
    last_system_scan DATETIME,
```

```
last_system_lookup DATETIME,
last_system_update DATETIME,
CONSTRAINT PK_IndexUsageStatsHistory
    PRIMARY KEY CLUSTERED (history_id),
CONSTRAINT UQ_IndexUsageStatsHistory
    UNIQUE (create_date, database_id, object_id, index_id)
);
```

The next component of capturing index usage history stats is collecting the current values in sys.dm_db_index_usage_stats. Similar to the performance monitor script, the collection query, shown in Listing 15-6, needs to be scheduled to run about every 4 hours. The activity in a database environment and rate in which indexes are modified should help determine the frequency in which the information is captured. Be certain to schedule a snapshot prior to any index defragmentation processes to capture information that might be lost when indexes are rebuilt.

Listing 15-6. Index Usage Stats Snapshot Population

```
USE IndexingMethod;
GO
INSERT INTO dbo.index_usage_stats_snapshot
SELECT GETDATE(),
    database_id,
    object_id,
    index_id,
    user_seeks,
    user_scans,
    user_lookups,
    user_updates,
    last_user_seek,
    last_user_scan,
    last_user_lookup,
    last_user_update,
    system_seeks,
    system_scans,
    system_lookups,
    system_updates,
```

```
    last_system_seek,
    last_system_scan,
    last_system_lookup,
    last_system_update
FROM sys.dm_db_index_usage_stats;
```

After populating the snapshot for the index usage stats, the delta between the most recent and the previous snapshot needs to be inserted into the index_usage_stats_history table. Since there is no indicator within the rows from sys.dm_db_index_usage_stats to identify when the stats for the index have been reset, the process for identifying when a delta between two entries for an index exists is to remove the row if any of the statistics on the index return a negative value. The resulting query, shown in Listing 15-7, implements this logic along with removing any rows where no new activity has happened.

Listing 15-7. Index Usage Stats Snapshot Population

```
USE IndexingMethod;
GO
WITH IndexUsageCTE
  AS (SELECT DENSE_RANK() OVER (ORDER BY create_date DESC) AS HistoryID,
          create_date,
          database_id,
          object_id,
          index_id,
          user_seeks,
          user_scans,
          user_lookups,
          user_updates,
          last_user_seek,
          last_user_scan,
          last_user_lookup,
          last_user_update,
          system_seeks,
          system_scans,
          system_lookups,
          system_updates,
```

```
            last_system_seek,
            last_system_scan,
            last_system_lookup,
            last_system_update
        FROM dbo.index_usage_stats_snapshot)
INSERT INTO dbo.index_usage_stats_history
SELECT i1.create_date,
    i1.database_id,
    i1.object_id,
    i1.index_id,
    i1.user_seeks - COALESCE(i2.user_seeks, 0),
    i1.user_scans - COALESCE(i2.user_scans, 0),
    i1.user_lookups - COALESCE(i2.user_lookups, 0),
    i1.user_updates - COALESCE(i2.user_updates, 0),
    i1.last_user_seek,
    i1.last_user_scan,
    i1.last_user_lookup,
    i1.last_user_update,
    i1.system_seeks - COALESCE(i2.system_seeks, 0),
    i1.system_scans - COALESCE(i2.system_scans, 0),
    i1.system_lookups - COALESCE(i2.system_lookups, 0),
    i1.system_updates - COALESCE(i2.system_updates, 0),
    i1.last_system_seek,
    i1.last_system_scan,
    i1.last_system_lookup,
    i1.last_system_update
FROM IndexUsageCTE i1
LEFT OUTER JOIN IndexUsageCTE i2 ON i1.database_id = i2.database_id
    AND i1.object_id   = i2.object_id
    AND i1.index_id    = i2.index_id
    AND i2.HistoryID   = 2
    --Verify no rows are less than 0
    AND NOT (
            i1.system_seeks - COALESCE(i2.system_seeks, 0) < 0
            AND i1.system_scans - COALESCE(i2.system_scans, 0) < 0
```

```
            AND i1.system_lookups - COALESCE(i2.system_lookups, 0) < 0
            AND i1.system_updates - COALESCE(i2.system_updates, 0) < 0
            AND i1.user_seeks - COALESCE(i2.user_seeks, 0) < 0
            AND i1.user_scans - COALESCE(i2.user_scans, 0) < 0
            AND i1.user_lookups - COALESCE(i2.user_lookups, 0) < 0
            AND i1.user_updates - COALESCE(i2.user_updates, 0) < 0
        )
WHERE i1.HistoryID                                              = 1
    --Only include rows are greater than 0
    AND (
        i1.system_seeks - COALESCE(i2.system_seeks, 0)          > 0
    OR i1.system_scans - COALESCE(i2.system_scans, 0)           > 0
    OR i1.system_lookups - COALESCE(i2.system_lookups, 0)       > 0
    OR i1.system_updates - COALESCE(i2.system_updates, 0)       > 0
    OR i1.user_seeks - COALESCE(i2.user_seeks, 0)               > 0
    OR i1.user_scans - COALESCE(i2.user_scans, 0)               > 0
    OR i1.user_lookups - COALESCE(i2.user_lookups, 0)           > 0
    OR i1.user_updates - COALESCE(i2.user_updates, 0)           > 0
    );
    GO
```

Index Operational Stats

The DMO sys.dm_db_index_operational_stats provides information on the physical operations that happen on indexes during plan execution. This information can be useful for tracking the physical plan operations that occur when indexes are used and the rates for those operations. One of the other things this DMO monitors is the success rate for compression.

The process for monitoring this DMO involves a few simple steps. First, tables will be created to store snapshot and history information on the DMO output. Then, periodic snapshots of the DMO output are inserted into the snapshot table. After the snapshot is retrieved, the delta between the current and previous snapshot is inserted into the history table.

The process utilizes a snapshot and history table that is nearly identical to the schema of `sys.dm_db_index_operational_stats`. The chief variance in the schema is the addition of a `create_date` column, used to identify when the snapshot occurred. The code in Listing 15-8 provides the schema required for the snapshot and history tables.

Note   The columns version_generated_inrow, version_generated_offrow, ghost_version_inrow, ghost_version_offrow, insert_over_ghost_version_inrow, and insert_over_ghost_version_offrow are new as of SQL Server 2019. If using this code in previous versions of SQL Server, these columns should be removed.

Listing 15-8. Index Operational Stats Snapshot Tables Stats

```
USE IndexingMethod;
GO
CREATE TABLE dbo.index_operational_stats_snapshot
    (
    snapshot_id INT IDENTITY(1, 1),
    create_date DATETIME2(0),
    database_id SMALLINT NOT NULL,
    object_id INT NOT NULL,
    index_id INT NOT NULL,
    partition_number INT NOT NULL,
    hobt_id BIGINT NOT NULL,
    leaf_insert_count BIGINT NOT NULL,
    leaf_delete_count BIGINT NOT NULL,
    leaf_update_count BIGINT NOT NULL,
    leaf_ghost_count BIGINT NOT NULL,
    nonleaf_insert_count BIGINT NOT NULL,
    nonleaf_delete_count BIGINT NOT NULL,
    nonleaf_update_count BIGINT NOT NULL,
    leaf_allocation_count BIGINT NOT NULL,
    nonleaf_allocation_count BIGINT NOT NULL,
    leaf_page_merge_count BIGINT NOT NULL,
    nonleaf_page_merge_count BIGINT NOT NULL,
```

```
range_scan_count BIGINT NOT NULL,
singleton_lookup_count BIGINT NOT NULL,
forwarded_fetch_count BIGINT NOT NULL,
lob_fetch_in_pages BIGINT NOT NULL,
lob_fetch_in_bytes BIGINT NOT NULL,
lob_orphan_create_count BIGINT NOT NULL,
lob_orphan_insert_count BIGINT NOT NULL,
row_overflow_fetch_in_pages BIGINT NOT NULL,
row_overflow_fetch_in_bytes BIGINT NOT NULL,
column_value_push_off_row_count BIGINT NOT NULL,
column_value_pull_in_row_count BIGINT NOT NULL,
row_lock_count BIGINT NOT NULL,
row_lock_wait_count BIGINT NOT NULL,
row_lock_wait_in_ms BIGINT NOT NULL,
page_lock_count BIGINT NOT NULL,
page_lock_wait_count BIGINT NOT NULL,
page_lock_wait_in_ms BIGINT NOT NULL,
index_lock_promotion_attempt_count BIGINT NOT NULL,
index_lock_promotion_count BIGINT NOT NULL,
page_latch_wait_count BIGINT NOT NULL,
page_latch_wait_in_ms BIGINT NOT NULL,
page_io_latch_wait_count BIGINT NOT NULL,
page_io_latch_wait_in_ms BIGINT NOT NULL,
tree_page_latch_wait_count BIGINT NOT NULL,
tree_page_latch_wait_in_ms BIGINT NOT NULL,
tree_page_io_latch_wait_count BIGINT NOT NULL,
tree_page_io_latch_wait_in_ms BIGINT NOT NULL,
page_compression_attempt_count BIGINT NOT NULL,
page_compression_success_count BIGINT NOT NULL,
version_generated_inrow BIGINT NOT NULL,
version_generated_offrow BIGINT NOT NULL,
ghost_version_inrow BIGINT NOT NULL,
ghost_version_offrow BIGINT NOT NULL,
insert_over_ghost_version_inrow BIGINT NOT NULL,
insert_over_ghost_version_offrow BIGINT NOT NULL,
```

```
    CONSTRAINT PK_IndexOperationalStatsSnapshot
        PRIMARY KEY CLUSTERED (snapshot_id),
    CONSTRAINT UQ_IndexOperationalStatsSnapshot
        UNIQUE (create_date, database_id, object_id, index_id,
        partition_number)
    );
CREATE TABLE dbo.index_operational_stats_history
    (
    history_id INT IDENTITY(1, 1),
    create_date DATETIME2(0),
    database_id SMALLINT NOT NULL,
    object_id INT NOT NULL,
    index_id INT NOT NULL,
    partition_number INT NOT NULL,
    hobt_id BIGINT NOT NULL,
    leaf_insert_count BIGINT NOT NULL,
    leaf_delete_count BIGINT NOT NULL,
    leaf_update_count BIGINT NOT NULL,
    leaf_ghost_count BIGINT NOT NULL,
    nonleaf_insert_count BIGINT NOT NULL,
    nonleaf_delete_count BIGINT NOT NULL,
    nonleaf_update_count BIGINT NOT NULL,
    leaf_allocation_count BIGINT NOT NULL,
    nonleaf_allocation_count BIGINT NOT NULL,
    leaf_page_merge_count BIGINT NOT NULL,
    nonleaf_page_merge_count BIGINT NOT NULL,
    range_scan_count BIGINT NOT NULL,
    singleton_lookup_count BIGINT NOT NULL,
    forwarded_fetch_count BIGINT NOT NULL,
    lob_fetch_in_pages BIGINT NOT NULL,
    lob_fetch_in_bytes BIGINT NOT NULL,
    lob_orphan_create_count BIGINT NOT NULL,
    lob_orphan_insert_count BIGINT NOT NULL,
    row_overflow_fetch_in_pages BIGINT NOT NULL,
    row_overflow_fetch_in_bytes BIGINT NOT NULL,
```

```
column_value_push_off_row_count BIGINT NOT NULL,
column_value_pull_in_row_count BIGINT NOT NULL,
row_lock_count BIGINT NOT NULL,
row_lock_wait_count BIGINT NOT NULL,
row_lock_wait_in_ms BIGINT NOT NULL,
page_lock_count BIGINT NOT NULL,
page_lock_wait_count BIGINT NOT NULL,
page_lock_wait_in_ms BIGINT NOT NULL,
index_lock_promotion_attempt_count BIGINT NOT NULL,
index_lock_promotion_count BIGINT NOT NULL,
page_latch_wait_count BIGINT NOT NULL,
page_latch_wait_in_ms BIGINT NOT NULL,
page_io_latch_wait_count BIGINT NOT NULL,
page_io_latch_wait_in_ms BIGINT NOT NULL,
tree_page_latch_wait_count BIGINT NOT NULL,
tree_page_latch_wait_in_ms BIGINT NOT NULL,
tree_page_io_latch_wait_count BIGINT NOT NULL,
tree_page_io_latch_wait_in_ms BIGINT NOT NULL,
page_compression_attempt_count BIGINT NOT NULL,
page_compression_success_count BIGINT NOT NULL,
version_generated_inrow BIGINT NOT NULL,
version_generated_offrow BIGINT NOT NULL,
ghost_version_inrow BIGINT NOT NULL,
ghost_version_offrow BIGINT NOT NULL,
insert_over_ghost_version_inrow BIGINT NOT NULL,
insert_over_ghost_version_offrow BIGINT NOT NULL,
CONSTRAINT PK_IndexOperationalStatsHistory
    PRIMARY KEY CLUSTERED (history_id),
CONSTRAINT UQ_IndexOperationalStatsHistory
    UNIQUE (create_date, database_id, object_id, index_id,
    partition_number)
);
```

With the tables in place, the next step is to capture a current snapshot of the information in sys.dm_db_index_operational_stats. The information can be populated using the script in Listing 15-9. Since the Indexing Method is geared toward capturing information on indexing for all databases on the server, the values for the parameters for sys.dm_db_index_operational_stats are set to NULL. This will return results for all partitions of all indexes on all tables in all databases on the server. If there is a need to limit the list of databases, tables, or indexes, then filters may be added to reduce the amount of index metrics to collect.

Like the index usage stats, this information should be captured about every 4 hours, with one of the scheduled points being before the index maintenance on the server.

Listing 15-9. Index Operational Stats Snapshot Population

```
USE IndexingMethod;
GO
TRUNCATE TABLE dbo.index_operational_stats_snapshot
INSERT INTO dbo.index_operational_stats_snapshot
SELECT GETDATE(),
    database_id,
    object_id,
    index_id,
    partition_number,
    hobt_id,
    leaf_insert_count,
    leaf_delete_count,
    leaf_update_count,
    leaf_ghost_count,
    nonleaf_insert_count,
    nonleaf_delete_count,
    nonleaf_update_count,
    leaf_allocation_count,
    nonleaf_allocation_count,
    leaf_page_merge_count,
    nonleaf_page_merge_count,
    range_scan_count,
    singleton_lookup_count,
    forwarded_fetch_count,
    lob_fetch_in_pages,
    lob_fetch_in_bytes,
```

```
            lob_orphan_create_count,
            lob_orphan_insert_count,
            row_overflow_fetch_in_pages,
            row_overflow_fetch_in_bytes,
            column_value_push_off_row_count,
            column_value_pull_in_row_count,
            row_lock_count,
            row_lock_wait_count,
            row_lock_wait_in_ms,
            page_lock_count,
            page_lock_wait_count,
            page_lock_wait_in_ms,
            index_lock_promotion_attempt_count,
            index_lock_promotion_count,
            page_latch_wait_count,
            page_latch_wait_in_ms,
            page_io_latch_wait_count,
            page_io_latch_wait_in_ms,
            tree_page_latch_wait_count,
            tree_page_latch_wait_in_ms,
            tree_page_io_latch_wait_count,
            tree_page_io_latch_wait_in_ms,
            page_compression_attempt_count,
            page_compression_success_count,
            version_generated_inrow,
            version_generated_offrow,
            ghost_version_inrow,
            ghost_version_offrow,
            insert_over_ghost_version_inrow,
            insert_over_ghost_version_offrow
FROM sys.dm_db_index_operational_stats(NULL, NULL, NULL, NULL)
WHERE database_id > 4;
```

The next step after populating the snapshot is populating the history table. As before, the purpose of the history table is to store statistics on the deltas between two snapshots. The deltas provide information on which operations occurred, and they also help to timebox those operations so that, if needed, more focus can be placed on those during core vs. noncore hours. The business rule identifying when the statistics have been reset is similar to index usage stats: if any of the statistics on the index return a negative value, the row from the previous snapshot will be ignored. Also, any rows that return all zero values will not be included. Listing 15-10 shows the code used to generate the history delta.

Listing 15-10. Index Operational Stats Snapshot Population

```
USE IndexingMethod;
GO
WITH IndexOperationalCTE
  AS (SELECT DENSE_RANK() OVER (ORDER BY create_date DESC) AS HistoryID,
         create_date,
         database_id,
         object_id,
         index_id,
         partition_number,
         hobt_id,
         leaf_insert_count,
         leaf_delete_count,
         leaf_update_count,
         leaf_ghost_count,
         nonleaf_insert_count,
         nonleaf_delete_count,
         nonleaf_update_count,
         leaf_allocation_count,
         nonleaf_allocation_count,
         leaf_page_merge_count,
         nonleaf_page_merge_count,
         range_scan_count,
         singleton_lookup_count,
         forwarded_fetch_count,
         lob_fetch_in_pages,
         lob_fetch_in_bytes,
         lob_orphan_create_count,
```

```
            lob_orphan_insert_count,
            row_overflow_fetch_in_pages,
            row_overflow_fetch_in_bytes,
            column_value_push_off_row_count,
            column_value_pull_in_row_count,
            row_lock_count,
            row_lock_wait_count,
            row_lock_wait_in_ms,
            page_lock_count,
            page_lock_wait_count,
            page_lock_wait_in_ms,
            index_lock_promotion_attempt_count,
            index_lock_promotion_count,
            page_latch_wait_count,
            page_latch_wait_in_ms,
            page_io_latch_wait_count,
            page_io_latch_wait_in_ms,
            tree_page_latch_wait_count,
            tree_page_latch_wait_in_ms,
            tree_page_io_latch_wait_count,
            tree_page_io_latch_wait_in_ms,
            page_compression_attempt_count,
            page_compression_success_count,
            version_generated_inrow,
            version_generated_offrow,
            ghost_version_inrow,
            ghost_version_offrow,
            insert_over_ghost_version_inrow,
            insert_over_ghost_version_offrow
        FROM dbo.index_operational_stats_snapshot)
INSERT INTO dbo.index_operational_stats_history
SELECT i1.create_date,
    i1.database_id,
    i1.object_id,
    i1.index_id,
```

```
    i1.partition_number,
        i1.hobt_id,
    i1.leaf_insert_count - COALESCE(i2.leaf_insert_count, 0),
    i1.leaf_delete_count - COALESCE(i2.leaf_delete_count, 0),
    i1.leaf_update_count - COALESCE(i2.leaf_update_count, 0),
    i1.leaf_ghost_count - COALESCE(i2.leaf_ghost_count, 0),
    i1.nonleaf_insert_count - COALESCE(i2.nonleaf_insert_count, 0),
    i1.nonleaf_delete_count - COALESCE(i2.nonleaf_delete_count, 0),
    i1.nonleaf_update_count - COALESCE(i2.nonleaf_update_count, 0),
    i1.leaf_allocation_count - COALESCE(i2.leaf_allocation_count, 0),
    i1.nonleaf_allocation_count - COALESCE(i2.nonleaf_allocation_count, 0),
    i1.leaf_page_merge_count - COALESCE(i2.leaf_page_merge_count, 0),
    i1.nonleaf_page_merge_count - COALESCE(i2.nonleaf_page_merge_count, 0),
    i1.range_scan_count - COALESCE(i2.range_scan_count, 0),
    i1.singleton_lookup_count - COALESCE(i2.singleton_lookup_count, 0),
    i1.forwarded_fetch_count - COALESCE(i2.forwarded_fetch_count, 0),
    i1.lob_fetch_in_pages - COALESCE(i2.lob_fetch_in_pages, 0),
    i1.lob_fetch_in_bytes - COALESCE(i2.lob_fetch_in_bytes, 0),
    i1.lob_orphan_create_count - COALESCE(i2.lob_orphan_create_count, 0),
    i1.lob_orphan_insert_count - COALESCE(i2.lob_orphan_insert_count, 0),
    i1.row_overflow_fetch_in_pages - COALESCE(i2.row_overflow_fetch_in_
    pages, 0),
    i1.row_overflow_fetch_in_bytes - COALESCE(i2.row_overflow_fetch_in_
    bytes, 0),
    i1.column_value_push_off_row_count - COALESCE(i2.column_value_push_off_
    row_count, 0),
    i1.column_value_pull_in_row_count - COALESCE(i2.column_value_pull_in_
    row_count, 0),
    i1.row_lock_count - COALESCE(i2.row_lock_count, 0),
    i1.row_lock_wait_count - COALESCE(i2.row_lock_wait_count, 0),
    i1.row_lock_wait_in_ms - COALESCE(i2.row_lock_wait_in_ms, 0),
    i1.page_lock_count - COALESCE(i2.page_lock_count, 0),
    i1.page_lock_wait_count - COALESCE(i2.page_lock_wait_count, 0),
    i1.page_lock_wait_in_ms - COALESCE(i2.page_lock_wait_in_ms, 0),
```

```
    i1.index_lock_promotion_attempt_count - COALESCE(i2.index_lock_
    promotion_attempt_count, 0),
    i1.index_lock_promotion_count - COALESCE(i2.index_lock_promotion_
    count, 0),
    i1.page_latch_wait_count - COALESCE(i2.page_latch_wait_count, 0),
    i1.page_latch_wait_in_ms - COALESCE(i2.page_latch_wait_in_ms, 0),
    i1.page_io_latch_wait_count - COALESCE(i2.page_io_latch_wait_count, 0),
    i1.page_io_latch_wait_in_ms - COALESCE(i2.page_io_latch_wait_in_ms, 0),
    i1.tree_page_latch_wait_count - COALESCE(i2.tree_page_latch_wait_
    count, 0),
    i1.tree_page_latch_wait_in_ms - COALESCE(i2.tree_page_latch_wait_
    in_ms, 0),
    i1.tree_page_io_latch_wait_count - COALESCE(i2.tree_page_io_latch_wait_
    count, 0),
    i1.tree_page_io_latch_wait_in_ms - COALESCE(i2.tree_page_io_latch_wait_
    in_ms, 0),
    i1.page_compression_attempt_count - COALESCE(i2.page_compression_
    attempt_count, 0),
    i1.page_compression_success_count - COALESCE(i2.page_compression_
    success_count, 0),
    i1.version_generated_inrow - COALESCE(i2.version_generated_inrow, 0),
    i1.version_generated_offrow - COALESCE(i2.version_generated_offrow, 0),
    i1.ghost_version_inrow - COALESCE(i2.ghost_version_inrow, 0),
    i1.ghost_version_offrow - COALESCE(i2.ghost_version_offrow, 0),
    i1.insert_over_ghost_version_inrow - COALESCE(i2.insert_over_ghost_
    version_inrow, 0),
    i1.insert_over_ghost_version_offrow - COALESCE(i2.insert_over_ghost_
    version_offrow, 0)
FROM IndexOperationalCTE i1
LEFT OUTER JOIN IndexOperationalCTE i2 ON i1.database_id = i2.database_id
AND i1.object_id = i2.object_id
AND i1.index_id = i2.index_id
AND i1.partition_number = i2.partition_number
AND i2.HistoryID = 2
--Verify no rows are less than 0
```

```
AND NOT (i1.leaf_insert_count - COALESCE(i2.leaf_insert_count, 0) < 0
     AND i1.leaf_delete_count - COALESCE(i2.leaf_delete_count, 0) < 0
     AND i1.leaf_update_count - COALESCE(i2.leaf_update_count, 0) < 0
     AND i1.leaf_ghost_count - COALESCE(i2.leaf_ghost_count, 0) < 0
     AND i1.nonleaf_insert_count - COALESCE(i2.nonleaf_insert_count, 0) < 0
     AND i1.nonleaf_delete_count - COALESCE(i2.nonleaf_delete_count, 0) < 0
     AND i1.nonleaf_update_count - COALESCE(i2.nonleaf_update_count, 0) < 0
     AND i1.leaf_allocation_count - COALESCE(i2.leaf_allocation_count, 0) < 0
     AND i1.nonleaf_allocation_count - COALESCE(i2.nonleaf_allocation_
     count, 0) < 0
     AND i1.leaf_page_merge_count - COALESCE(i2.leaf_page_merge_count, 0) < 0
     AND i1.nonleaf_page_merge_count - COALESCE(i2.nonleaf_page_merge_
     count, 0) < 0
     AND i1.range_scan_count - COALESCE(i2.range_scan_count, 0) < 0
     AND i1.singleton_lookup_count - COALESCE(i2.singleton_lookup_
     count, 0) < 0
     AND i1.forwarded_fetch_count - COALESCE(i2.forwarded_fetch_
     count, 0) < 0
     AND i1.lob_fetch_in_pages - COALESCE(i2.lob_fetch_in_pages, 0) < 0
     AND i1.lob_fetch_in_bytes - COALESCE(i2.lob_fetch_in_bytes, 0) < 0
     AND i1.lob_orphan_create_count - COALESCE(i2.lob_orphan_create_
     count, 0) < 0
     AND i1.lob_orphan_insert_count - COALESCE(i2.lob_orphan_insert_
     count, 0) < 0
     AND i1.row_overflow_fetch_in_pages - COALESCE(i2.row_overflow_fetch_
     in_pages, 0) < 0
     AND i1.row_overflow_fetch_in_bytes - COALESCE(i2.row_overflow_fetch_
     in_bytes, 0) < 0
     AND i1.column_value_push_off_row_count - COALESCE(i2.column_value_
     push_off_row_count, 0) < 0
     AND i1.column_value_pull_in_row_count - COALESCE(i2.column_value_
     pull_in_row_count, 0) < 0
     AND i1.row_lock_count - COALESCE(i2.row_lock_count, 0) < 0
     AND i1.row_lock_wait_count - COALESCE(i2.row_lock_wait_count, 0) < 0
     AND i1.row_lock_wait_in_ms - COALESCE(i2.row_lock_wait_in_ms, 0) < 0
```

```
AND i1.page_lock_count - COALESCE(i2.page_lock_count, 0) < 0
AND i1.page_lock_wait_count - COALESCE(i2.page_lock_wait_
count, 0) < 0
AND i1.page_lock_wait_in_ms - COALESCE(i2.page_lock_wait_in_
ms, 0) < 0
AND i1.index_lock_promotion_attempt_count - COALESCE(i2.index_lock_
promotion_attempt_count, 0) < 0
AND i1.index_lock_promotion_count - COALESCE(i2.index_lock_promotion_
count, 0) < 0
AND i1.page_latch_wait_count - COALESCE(i2.page_latch_wait_
count, 0) < 0
AND i1.page_latch_wait_in_ms - COALESCE(i2.page_latch_wait_in_
ms, 0) < 0
AND i1.page_io_latch_wait_count - COALESCE(i2.page_io_latch_wait_
count, 0) < 0
AND i1.page_io_latch_wait_in_ms - COALESCE(i2.page_io_latch_wait_in_
ms, 0) < 0
AND i1.tree_page_latch_wait_count - COALESCE(i2.tree_page_latch_wait_
count, 0) < 0
AND i1.tree_page_latch_wait_in_ms - COALESCE(i2.tree_page_latch_wait_
in_ms, 0) < 0
AND i1.tree_page_io_latch_wait_count - COALESCE(i2.tree_page_io_
latch_wait_count, 0) < 0
AND i1.tree_page_io_latch_wait_in_ms - COALESCE(i2.tree_page_io_
latch_wait_in_ms, 0) < 0
AND i1.page_compression_attempt_count - COALESCE(i2.page_compression_
attempt_count, 0) < 0
AND i1.page_compression_success_count - COALESCE(i2.page_compression_
success_count, 0) < 0
AND i1.version_generated_inrow - COALESCE(i2.version_generated_
inrow, 0) < 0
AND i1.version_generated_offrow  - COALESCE(i2.version_generated_
offrow, 0) < 0
AND i1.ghost_version_inrow - COALESCE(i2.ghost_version_inrow, 0) < 0
```

```
        AND i1.ghost_version_offrow - COALESCE(i2.ghost_version_
        offrow, 0) < 0
        AND i1.insert_over_ghost_version_inrow   - COALESCE(i2.insert_over_
        ghost_version_inrow, 0) < 0
        AND i1.insert_over_ghost_version_offrow - COALESCE(i2.insert_over_
        ghost_version_offrow, 0) < 0
)
WHERE i1.HistoryID = 1
--Only include rows are greater than 0
AND (
    i1.leaf_insert_count - COALESCE(i2.leaf_insert_count, 0) > 0
    OR i1.leaf_delete_count - COALESCE(i2.leaf_delete_count, 0) > 0
    OR i1.leaf_update_count - COALESCE(i2.leaf_update_count, 0) > 0
    OR i1.leaf_ghost_count - COALESCE(i2.leaf_ghost_count, 0) > 0
    OR i1.nonleaf_insert_count - COALESCE(i2.nonleaf_insert_count, 0) > 0
    OR i1.nonleaf_delete_count - COALESCE(i2.nonleaf_delete_count, 0) > 0
    OR i1.nonleaf_update_count - COALESCE(i2.nonleaf_update_count, 0) > 0
    OR i1.leaf_allocation_count - COALESCE(i2.leaf_allocation_count, 0) > 0
    OR i1.nonleaf_allocation_count - COALESCE(i2.nonleaf_allocation_
    count, 0) > 0
    OR i1.leaf_page_merge_count - COALESCE(i2.leaf_page_merge_count, 0) > 0
    OR i1.nonleaf_page_merge_count - COALESCE(i2.nonleaf_page_merge_
    count, 0) > 0
    OR i1.range_scan_count - COALESCE(i2.range_scan_count, 0) > 0
    OR i1.singleton_lookup_count - COALESCE(i2.singleton_lookup_
    count, 0) > 0
    OR i1.forwarded_fetch_count - COALESCE(i2.forwarded_fetch_count, 0) > 0
    OR i1.lob_fetch_in_pages - COALESCE(i2.lob_fetch_in_pages, 0) > 0
    OR i1.lob_fetch_in_bytes - COALESCE(i2.lob_fetch_in_bytes, 0) > 0
    OR i1.lob_orphan_create_count - COALESCE(i2.lob_orphan_create_
    count, 0) > 0
    OR i1.lob_orphan_insert_count - COALESCE(i2.lob_orphan_insert_
    count, 0) > 0
    OR i1.row_overflow_fetch_in_pages - COALESCE(i2.row_overflow_fetch_in_
    pages, 0) > 0
```

```
OR i1.row_overflow_fetch_in_bytes - COALESCE(i2.row_overflow_fetch_in_
bytes, 0) > 0
OR i1.column_value_push_off_row_count - COALESCE(i2.column_value_push_
off_row_count, 0) > 0
OR i1.column_value_pull_in_row_count - COALESCE(i2.column_value_pull_
in_row_count, 0) > 0
OR i1.row_lock_count - COALESCE(i2.row_lock_count, 0) > 0
OR i1.row_lock_wait_count - COALESCE(i2.row_lock_wait_count, 0) > 0
OR i1.row_lock_wait_in_ms - COALESCE(i2.row_lock_wait_in_ms, 0) > 0
OR i1.page_lock_count - COALESCE(i2.page_lock_count, 0) > 0
OR i1.page_lock_wait_count - COALESCE(i2.page_lock_wait_count, 0) > 0
OR i1.page_lock_wait_in_ms - COALESCE(i2.page_lock_wait_in_ms, 0) > 0
OR i1.index_lock_promotion_attempt_count - COALESCE(i2.index_lock_
promotion_attempt_count, 0) > 0
OR i1.index_lock_promotion_count - COALESCE(i2.index_lock_promotion_
count, 0) > 0
OR i1.page_latch_wait_count - COALESCE(i2.page_latch_wait_count, 0) > 0
OR i1.page_latch_wait_in_ms - COALESCE(i2.page_latch_wait_in_ms, 0) > 0
OR i1.page_io_latch_wait_count - COALESCE(i2.page_io_latch_wait_
count, 0) > 0
OR i1.page_io_latch_wait_in_ms - COALESCE(i2.page_io_latch_wait_in_
ms, 0) > 0
OR i1.tree_page_latch_wait_count - COALESCE(i2.tree_page_latch_wait_
count, 0) > 0
OR i1.tree_page_latch_wait_in_ms - COALESCE(i2.tree_page_latch_wait_in_
ms, 0) > 0
OR i1.tree_page_io_latch_wait_count - COALESCE(i2.tree_page_io_latch_
wait_count, 0) > 0
OR i1.tree_page_io_latch_wait_in_ms - COALESCE(i2.tree_page_io_latch_
wait_in_ms, 0) > 0
OR i1.page_compression_attempt_count - COALESCE(i2.page_compression_
attempt_count, 0) > 0
OR i1.page_compression_success_count - COALESCE(i2.page_compression_
success_count, 0) > 0
```

```
    OR i1.version_generated_inrow - COALESCE(i2.version_generated_
    inrow, 0) > 0
    OR i1.version_generated_offrow - COALESCE(i2.version_generated_
    offrow, 0) > 0
    OR i1.ghost_version_inrow - COALESCE(i2.ghost_version_inrow, 0) > 0
    OR i1.ghost_version_offrow - COALESCE(i2.ghost_version_offrow, 0) > 0
    OR i1.insert_over_ghost_version_inrow - COALESCE(i2.insert_over_ghost_
    version_inrow, 0) > 0
    OR i1.insert_over_ghost_version_offrow - COALESCE(i2.insert_over_ghost_
    version_offrow, 0) > 0
);
```

Index Physical Stats

The last indexing DMO for monitoring indexes is sys.dm_db_index_physical_stats. This DMO provides statistics on the current physical structure of the indexes in a database. The value of this information is in determining the fragmentation of the index, which is discussed more in Chapter 8. From a monitoring perspective, physical statistics are being collected to aid with later analysis. The goal is to identify potential issues that may be affecting the efficiency in how the index is stored, or vice versa, thus impacting query performance.

With the physical stats DMO, the statistics are collected a bit differently than with the other DMOs. The main difference between this DMO and the others is the impact that can be placed on the database while collecting the information. With the other two reference in-memory tables, index_physical_stats reads the pages in the index to determine the actual fragmentation and physical layout of the indexes. Chapter 5 can be referenced for more about the impact of using sys.dm_db_index_physical_stats. To accommodate this difference, the statistics are stored only in a history table; the deltas between the points in which the history is retrieved are not determined. Also, because of the nature of the statistics contained in the DMO, there would be little value in calculating delta values.

The first piece needed to begin collecting statistics on index physical stats is the previously mentioned history table. This table, shown in Listing 15-11, uses the same schema as the DMO, with the addition of the create_date column.

Tip   When generating the table schema needed for the DMOs, a table-valued function introduced in SQL Server 2012 is used. The function `sys.dm_exec_describe_first_result_set` can be used to identify the column names and data types for a query.

Listing 15-11. Index Physical Stats History Table

```
USE IndexingMethod;
GO
CREATE TABLE dbo.index_physical_stats_history
    (
    history_id INT IDENTITY(1, 1),
    create_date DATETIME2(0),
    database_id SMALLINT,
    object_id INT,
    index_id INT,
    partition_number INT,
    index_type_desc NVARCHAR(60),
    alloc_unit_type_desc NVARCHAR(60),
    index_depth TINYINT,
    index_level TINYINT,
    avg_fragmentation_in_percent FLOAT,
    fragment_count BIGINT,
    avg_fragment_size_in_pages FLOAT,
    page_count BIGINT,
    avg_page_space_used_in_percent FLOAT,
    record_count BIGINT,
    ghost_record_count BIGINT,
    version_ghost_record_count BIGINT,
    min_record_size_in_bytes INT,
    max_record_size_in_bytes INT,
    avg_record_size_in_bytes FLOAT,
    forwarded_record_count BIGINT,
    compressed_page_count BIGINT,
```

```
hobt_id BIGINT NULL,
columnstore_delete_buffer_state TINYINT NULL,
columnstore_delete_buffer_state_desc NVARCHAR(60) NULL,
version_record_count BIGINT NULL,
inrow_version_record_count BIGINT NULL,
inrow_diff_version_record_count BIGINT NULL,
total_inrow_version_payload_size_in_bytes BIGINT NULL,
offrow_regular_version_record_count BIGINT NULL,
offrow_long_term_version_record_count BIGINT NULL,
CONSTRAINT PK_IndexPhysicalStatsHistory
    PRIMARY KEY CLUSTERED (history_id),
CONSTRAINT UQ_IndexPhysicalStatsHistory
    UNIQUE
    (
        create_date,
        database_id,
        object_id,
        index_id,
        partition_number,
        alloc_unit_type_desc,
        index_depth,
        index_level
    )
);
```

The collection of the history for index_physical_stats differs from the previous
two DMOs. Since it is only history, there is no need to capture the snapshot information
to build the delta between the two snapshots for the history. Instead, the current
statistics are inserted directly into the history table, as shown in Listing 15-12. Also, since
index_physical_stats performs physical operations on the index while collecting
the statistics, there are a few things to keep in mind when generating the history
information. First, the script will collect information from each database independently
from the other databases through a CURSOR-drive loop. This provides a batched
separation between the collections of statistics for each database and limits the impact
of the DMO. Second, the query should be executed during noncore hours. The start of
the daily maintenance window would be ideal. It is important that this information is

collected prior to defragmentation or re-indexing since these operations will change the information provided by the DMO. Usually, this information is collected as a step in the defragmentation process, which is discussed in Chapter 8. If so, there's no need to collect the information twice. Collect it for defragmentation and store it for later use in monitoring indexes.

Listing 15-12. Index Physical Stats History Population

```
USE IndexingMethod;
GO

DECLARE @DatabaseID INT;

DECLARE DatabaseList CURSOR FAST_FORWARD FOR
SELECT database_id
FROM sys.databases
WHERE state_desc = 'ONLINE'
AND database_id > 4;

OPEN DatabaseList;
FETCH NEXT FROM DatabaseList
INTO @DatabaseID;
WHILE @@FETCH_STATUS = 0
BEGIN
    INSERT INTO dbo.index_physical_stats_history (
        create_date,
        database_id,
        object_id,
        index_id,
        partition_number,
        index_type_desc,
        alloc_unit_type_desc,
        index_depth,
        index_level,
        avg_fragmentation_in_percent,
        fragment_count,
        avg_fragment_size_in_pages,
        page_count,
```

```
        avg_page_space_used_in_percent,
        record_count,
        ghost_record_count,
        version_ghost_record_count,
        min_record_size_in_bytes,
        max_record_size_in_bytes,
        avg_record_size_in_bytes,
        forwarded_record_count,
        compressed_page_count,
        hobt_id,
        columnstore_delete_buffer_state,
        columnstore_delete_buffer_state_desc,
        version_record_count,
        inrow_version_record_count,
        inrow_diff_version_record_count,
        total_inrow_version_payload_size_in_bytes,
        offrow_regular_version_record_count,
        offrow_long_term_version_record_count
    )
    SELECT GETDATE(),
        database_id,
        object_id,
        index_id,
        partition_number,
        index_type_desc,
        alloc_unit_type_desc,
        index_depth,
        index_level,
        avg_fragmentation_in_percent,
        fragment_count,
        avg_fragment_size_in_pages,
        page_count,
        avg_page_space_used_in_percent,
        record_count,
        ghost_record_count,
```

```
        version_ghost_record_count,
        min_record_size_in_bytes,
        max_record_size_in_bytes,
        avg_record_size_in_bytes,
        forwarded_record_count,
        compressed_page_count,
        hobt_id,
        columnstore_delete_buffer_state,
        columnstore_delete_buffer_state_desc,
        version_record_count,
        inrow_version_record_count,
        inrow_diff_version_record_count,
        total_inrow_version_payload_size_in_bytes,
        offrow_regular_version_record_count,
        offrow_long_term_version_record_count
    FROM sys.dm_db_index_physical_stats(@DatabaseID, NULL, NULL, NULL,
    'SAMPLED');
    FETCH NEXT FROM DatabaseList
    INTO @DatabaseID;
END;

CLOSE DatabaseList;
DEALLOCATE DatabaseList;
```

Wait Statistics

One other DMO that provides information related to indexing is sys.dm_os_wait_stats.
This DMO collects information related to resources that SQL Server is waiting on in
order to start or continue executing a query or other request. Most performance tuning
methodologies include a process for collecting and analyzing wait statistics. From an
indexing perspective, there are a number of wait resources that can indicate that there
may be indexing issues on the SQL Server instance. By monitoring these statistics, we
can be informed when these issues may exist. Table 15-2 provides a short list of wait
types that most often indicate that indexing issues may exist.

Table 15-2. *Index-Related Wait Statistics*

Option name	Description
CXPACKET	Synchronizes threads involved in a parallel query. This wait type means a parallel query is attempting to synchronize data within a parallel query between operators and can indicate an unbalanced workload or a worker is blocked by a preceding request
IO_COMPLETION	Indicates a wait for I/O for operation (typically synchronous) like sorts and various situations where the engine needs to do a synchronous I/O. This wait type represents nondata page I/O
LCK_M_*	Occurs when a task is waiting to acquire a lock on an index or table
PAGEIOLATCH_*	Occurs when a task is waiting on a latch for a buffer that is in an I/O request. Long waits may indicate problems with the disk subsystem

Similar to performance counters, wait statistics are general indicators of health that reflect information about the SQL Server instance as a whole. They do not point directly to resources; instead, they collect information on when there was a wait for a specific resource on the SQL Server instance.

Note   Many performance monitoring tools from third-party vendors collect wait statistics as a part of their monitoring. If there is a tool already installed in your environment, check to see whether wait statistics information can be retrieved from that tool.

The process for collecting wait statistics follows the pattern of using snapshot and history tables. To do this, the data will be collected first in a snapshot table with the deltas between snapshots stored in a history table. The snapshot and history tables, shown in Listing 15-13, contain the columns needed to support the snapshot and history patterns.

Listing 15-13. Wait Statistics Snapshot and History Table

```
USE IndexingMethod;
GO

CREATE TABLE dbo.wait_stats_snapshot
    (
    wait_stats_snapshot_id INT IDENTITY(1, 1),
    create_date DATETIME2(0),
    wait_type NVARCHAR(60) NOT NULL,
    waiting_tasks_count BIGINT NOT NULL,
    wait_time_ms BIGINT NOT NULL,
    max_wait_time_ms BIGINT NOT NULL,
    signal_wait_time_ms BIGINT NOT NULL,
    CONSTRAINT PK_wait_stats_snapshot
        PRIMARY KEY CLUSTERED (wait_stats_snapshot_id)
    );
CREATE TABLE dbo.wait_stats_history
    (
    wait_stats_history_id INT IDENTITY(1, 1),
    create_date DATETIME2(0),
    wait_type NVARCHAR(60) NOT NULL,
    waiting_tasks_count BIGINT NOT NULL,
    wait_time_ms BIGINT NOT NULL,
    max_wait_time_ms BIGINT NOT NULL,
    signal_wait_time_ms BIGINT NOT NULL,
    CONSTRAINT PK_wait_stats_history
        PRIMARY KEY CLUSTERED (wait_stats_history_id)
    );
```

To collect the wait statistics information, the output from sys.dm_os_wait_stats is queried. Unlike the other DMOs discussed in this chapter, there is some summarization of the information that needs to occur prior to inserting the data. In a previous version of SQL Server, the wait_stats DMO contains two rows for the wait type MISCELLANEOUS. To accommodate for this variance, the sample script in Listing 15-14 uses aggregations to get around the issue. Another difference between wait_stats_snapshot and the other snapshots is the frequency in which the information should be collected. Wait_stats reports information on when requested resources were not available. Being able to tie this information to specific times of the day can be critical. As such, wait_stats information should be collected about once every hour. It can be collected more frequently in busier environments to increase granularity as to when significant events have occurred.

Listing 15-14. Wait Statistics Snapshot Population

```
USE IndexingMethod;
GO

TRUNCATE TABLE dbo.wait_stats_snapshot
INSERT INTO dbo.wait_stats_snapshot (
    create_date,
    wait_type,
    waiting_tasks_count,
    wait_time_ms,
    max_wait_time_ms,
    signal_wait_time_ms
)
SELECT GETDATE(),
    wait_type,
    waiting_tasks_count,
    wait_time_ms,
    max_wait_time_ms,
    signal_wait_time_ms
FROM sys.dm_os_wait_stats;
```

With each snapshot collected, the delta between it and the previous snapshot needs to be added in the wait_stats_history table. For determining when the information in sys.dm_os_wait_stats has been reset, the column waiting_tasks_count is used. If the value in the column is lower than the previous snapshot, the information in the DMO is reset. Listing 15-15 provides the code for populating the history table.

While there are only a few wait types that point toward indexing issues, the history table will show results for all wait types that are encountered. The reason is that waits on resources need to be compared to the total number of other waits that occur. For instance, if CXPACKET is the lowest relative wait on the server, there isn't much value in researching the queries and determining the indexing that could reduce the occurrence of this wait type since other issues would likely impact performance more significantly.

Listing 15-15. Wait Statistics History Population

```
USE IndexingMethod;
GO

WITH WaitStatCTE
  AS (SELECT create_date,
          DENSE_RANK() OVER (ORDER BY create_date DESC) AS HistoryID,
          wait_type,
          waiting_tasks_count,
          wait_time_ms,
          max_wait_time_ms,
          signal_wait_time_ms
      FROM dbo.wait_stats_snapshot)
INSERT INTO dbo.wait_stats_history
SELECT w1.create_date,
    w1.wait_type,
    w1.waiting_tasks_count - COALESCE(w2.waiting_tasks_count, 0),
    w1.wait_time_ms - COALESCE(w2.wait_time_ms, 0),
    w1.max_wait_time_ms - COALESCE(w2.max_wait_time_ms, 0),
    w1.signal_wait_time_ms - COALESCE(w2.signal_wait_time_ms, 0)
FROM WaitStatCTE w1
LEFT OUTER JOIN WaitStatCTE w2 ON w1.wait_type = w2.wait_type
                        AND w1.waiting_tasks_count >= COALESCE(w2.
                        waiting_tasks_count, 0)
                        AND w2.HistoryID = 2
WHERE w1.HistoryID = 1
AND w1.waiting_tasks_count - COALESCE(w2.waiting_tasks_count, 0) > 0;
```

Data Cleanup

While all the information for monitoring is needed for the index analysis, this information is not needed indefinitely. The process for monitoring would not be complete without tasks in place to clean up the information collected after a reasonable amount of time. A generally acceptable schedule for cleaning up information is to purge snapshots after 3 days and history information after 90 days. This may be adjusted as needed if there is a desire to maintain history data for longer periods of time.

The snapshot information is used simply to prepare the history information and is not needed once the delta is created. Since SQL Agent jobs can error and collection points may be a day apart from the previous, a 3-day window generally provides the leeway needed to support the process and accommodate any issues that may arise.

The data in the history tables is more crucial than the snapshot information and needs to be kept longer. This information feeds the activities during index analysis. The window for retaining this information should match the amount of time that it generally takes to go through the Indexing Method three or more times. This way, the information retained can be used for reference in a few cycles of the process.

When scheduling the cleanup process, it should be at least daily and during noncore processing hours. This will minimize the amount of information deleted in each execution and reduce the possible contention of the delete with other activity on the server. The delete script, shown in Listing 15-16, covers each of the tables discussed throughout this section.

Listing 15-16. Index Monitoring Snapshot and History Cleanup

```
USE IndexingMethod
GO

DECLARE @SnapshotDays INT = 3
    ,@HistoryDays INT = 90

DELETE FROM dbo.index_usage_stats_snapshot
WHERE create_date < DATEADD(d, -@SnapshotDays, GETDATE())

DELETE FROM dbo.index_usage_stats_history
WHERE create_date < DATEADD(d, -@HistoryDays, GETDATE())

DELETE FROM dbo.index_operational_stats_snapshot
```

```
WHERE create_date < DATEADD(d, -@SnapshotDays, GETDATE())

DELETE FROM dbo.index_operational_stats_history
WHERE create_date < DATEADD(d, -@HistoryDays, GETDATE())

DELETE FROM dbo.index_physical_stats_history
WHERE create_date < DATEADD(d, -@HistoryDays, GETDATE())

DELETE FROM dbo.wait_stats_snapshot
WHERE create_date < DATEADD(d, -@SnapshotDays, GETDATE())

DELETE FROM dbo.wait_stats_history
WHERE create_date < DATEADD(d, -@HistoryDays, GETDATE())
```

Event Tracing

The last set of information that can be collected for monitoring indexes is event tracing. The trace information collects SQL statements that represent production activity that can be used during index analysis to identify indexes that could be useful based on the query activity in a production environment and on the data that is being stored there. While the statistics collected so far provide information on the effect of activity on indexes and other resource use on the SQL Server instance, event tracing collects the activity that is causing those statistics. With SQL Server, there are two methods that can be used to collect event tracing data:

- SQL Trace

- Extended Events

For the purposes of completeness, both methods will be discussed. In my opinion, only Extended Events should be used to collect event tracing data in SQL Server. This is due to how well Extended Events are incorporated into SQL Server to help prevent it from causing performance issues while monitoring. And the level of detail that it can retrieve goes far beyond the capabilities of SQL Trace.

SQL Trace

SQL Trace, and by extension SQL Profiler, is the original tracing tool for SQL Server. It is one of the most common tools that DBAs have available to them and can easily collect events in SQL Server. With SQL Trace, there are a number of areas to be careful of when collecting information. First, SQL Trace will likely collect a lot of information, and this will need to be accommodated. In other words, the more active the server and the databases, the larger the trace (.trc) files will be. Filtering events can help ensure that only relevant details are returned. Along these same lines, do not collect the trace information on drives that are already heavily used or dedicated to data or transaction log files. Doing this can, and likely will, impact the performance of I/O on those drives. The end goal for monitoring is to improve the performance of the system; care needs to be taken to minimize the impact of monitoring.

Finally, SQL Trace and SQL Profiler were deprecated in SQL Server 2012. This does not mean that these tools no longer function, but they are slated for removal in a future SQL Server release. While SQL Trace is deprecated, it is still the most convenient tool in some scenarios for collecting trace information, such as for building workloads for the Database Engine Tuning Advisor.

Note   It is always advisable to keep apprised of deprecated features within SQL Server. For more information on deprecated features, see SQL Docs at `https://learn.microsoft.com/en-us/sql/database-engine/deprecated-database-engine-features-in-sql-server-2022`.

There are four basic steps to creating a SQL Trace session:

1.   Build the trace session.

2.   Assign the events and columns to the session.

3.   Add filters to the session.

4.   Start the SQL Trace session.

The next few pages will cover these steps and describe the components used in creating the SQL Trace session in SQL Server 2022. The script will also work in earlier versions of SQL Server.

To begin monitoring with SQL Trace, a trace session must first be created. Sessions are created using the sp_trace_create stored procedure. This procedure accepts a number of parameters that configure how the session will collect information. In the example session, shown in Listing 15-17, the SQL Trace session will create files that automatically rollover when they reach the 50 MB file size limit. The file size is limited to allow for better file management. In most environments, it's easier to copy many 50 MB files compared to files that are 1 GB or more. This size may be adjusted if larger files are preferred over a large number of them. The trace files are being created in c:\temp with the file name IndexingMethod. Be sure to create this folder if it doesn't exist. Note that this name can be changed to anything that suits the needs of the server and databases where the monitoring is being set up.

Listing 15-17. Create SQL Trace Session

```
USE master;
GO
DECLARE @rc INT,
    @TraceID INT,
    --Maximum .trc file size in MB
    @maxfilesize BIGINT = 50,
    --File name and path, minus the extension
    @FileName NVARCHAR(256) = N'c:\temp\IndexingMethod';
EXEC @rc = sp_trace_create @TraceID OUTPUT, 0, @FileName,
@maxfilesize, NULL;
IF (@rc <> 0)
    RAISERROR('Error creating trace file', 16, 1);
SELECT *
FROM sys.traces
WHERE id = @TraceID;
```

After creating the SQL Trace session, the next step is to add events to the session. There are two events that will collect the information that is of most value to index monitoring: RPC:Completed and SQL:BatchCompleted. RPC:Completed returns results whenever a remote procedure call completes; the best example of this is the completion of a stored procedure. The other event, SQL:BatchCompleted, occurs when ad hoc and prepared batches are completed. Between these two events, all the completed SQL statements on the server will be collected.

To add events to the SQL Trace session, the sp_trace_set event stored procedure is used. The stored procedure adds events and the column requested from the event to the trace with each execution of the stored procedure. For two events with 15 columns each, the stored procedure will need to be executed 30 times. For the example session, shown in Listing 15-18, the following columns are being collected for each of the sessions:

- ApplicationName
- ClientProcessID
- CPU
- DatabaseID
- DatabaseName
- Duration
- EndTime
- HostName
- LoginName
- NTUserName
- Reads
- SPID
- StartTime
- TextData
- Writes

The codes for the events and columns can be found in system catalog views. Events are listed in view sys.trace_events. The columns available are listed in sys.trace_columns. The columns view also includes an indicator to identify whether the values from the column can be filtered, which is useful in the next step in creating SQL Trace sessions.

Listing 15-18. Add Events and Columns to SQL Trace Session

```
USE master;
GO
DECLARE @on INT = 1,
    @FileName NVARCHAR(256) = N'c:\temp\IndexingMethod',
    @TraceID INT;
SET @TraceID = (
    SELECT id FROM sys.traces WHERE path LIKE @FileName + '%'
);
-- RPC:Completed
EXEC sp_trace_setevent @TraceID, 10, 1, @on;
EXEC sp_trace_setevent @TraceID, 10, 10, @on;
EXEC sp_trace_setevent @TraceID, 10, 11, @on;
EXEC sp_trace_setevent @TraceID, 10, 12, @on;
EXEC sp_trace_setevent @TraceID, 10, 13, @on;
EXEC sp_trace_setevent @TraceID, 10, 14, @on;
EXEC sp_trace_setevent @TraceID, 10, 15, @on;
EXEC sp_trace_setevent @TraceID, 10, 16, @on;
EXEC sp_trace_setevent @TraceID, 10, 17, @on;
EXEC sp_trace_setevent @TraceID, 10, 18, @on;
EXEC sp_trace_setevent @TraceID, 10, 3, @on;
EXEC sp_trace_setevent @TraceID, 10, 35, @on;
EXEC sp_trace_setevent @TraceID, 10, 6, @on;
EXEC sp_trace_setevent @TraceID, 10, 8, @on;
EXEC sp_trace_setevent @TraceID, 10, 9, @on;

--SQL:BatchCompleted
EXEC sp_trace_setevent @TraceID, 12, 1, @on;
EXEC sp_trace_setevent @TraceID, 12, 10, @on;
EXEC sp_trace_setevent @TraceID, 12, 11, @on;
EXEC sp_trace_setevent @TraceID, 12, 12, @on;
EXEC sp_trace_setevent @TraceID, 12, 13, @on;
EXEC sp_trace_setevent @TraceID, 12, 14, @on;
EXEC sp_trace_setevent @TraceID, 12, 15, @on;
EXEC sp_trace_setevent @TraceID, 12, 16, @on;
```

```
EXEC sp_trace_setevent @TraceID, 12, 17, @on;
EXEC sp_trace_setevent @TraceID, 12, 18, @on;
EXEC sp_trace_setevent @TraceID, 12, 3, @on;
EXEC sp_trace_setevent @TraceID, 12, 35, @on;
EXEC sp_trace_setevent @TraceID, 12, 6, @on;
EXEC sp_trace_setevent @TraceID, 12, 8, @on;
EXEC sp_trace_setevent @TraceID, 12, 9, @on;
```

The next step is to filter out unneeded events from the SQL Trace session. There is no need to collect all statements all the time for all databases and all applications with every SQL Trace session. In fact, in Listing 15-19, events from the system databases, those with a database ID less than 5, are removed from the session. The stored procedure for filtering SQL Trace sessions is sp_trace_setfilter. The stored procedure accepts the ID for columns from sys.trace_columns. Columns not included in the events can be filtered, and filters apply to all events.

Listing 15-19. Add Filters to SQL Trace Session

```
USE master;
GO
DECLARE @intfilter INT = 5,
    @FileName NVARCHAR(256) = N'c:\temp\IndexingMethod',
    @TraceID INT;
SET @TraceID = (
    SELECT id FROM sys.traces WHERE path LIKE @FileName + '%'
);
--Remove system databases from output
EXEC sp_trace_setfilter @TraceID, 3, 0, 4, @intfilter;
```

The last step in setting up the monitoring for SQL Trace is to start the trace. This task is accomplished using the sp_trace_setstatus stored procedure, shown in Listing 15-20. Through this procedure, SQL Trace sessions can be started, paused, and stopped. Once the trace is started, it will start to create .trc files in the file location provided, and the configuration for SQL Trace monitoring will be complete. When the collection period for the SQL Trace session completes, this script will be used with the status code 2 instead of 1 to terminate the session. Listing 15-21 provides this script.

Listing 15-20. Start SQL Trace Session

```
USE master;
GO

DECLARE @FileName NVARCHAR(256) = N'c:\temp\IndexingMethod',
    @TraceID INT;

SET @TraceID = (
    SELECT id FROM sys.traces WHERE path LIKE @FileName + '%'
);

-- Set the trace status to start
EXEC sp_trace_setstatus @TraceID, 1;
```

Note   Some SQL Server experts prefer to not use the Database Engine Tuning Advisor due to the chance of receiving invalid advice, preferring instead to manually analyze the database and determine the indexes needed. This bias misses the opportunity to uncover low-hanging fruit or situations where changing the location of the clustered index can improve performance.

Listing 15-21. Stop SQL Trace Session

```
USE master;
GO

DECLARE @FileName NVARCHAR(256) = N'c:\temp\IndexingMethod',
    @TraceID INT;

SET @TraceID = (
    SELECT id FROM sys.traces WHERE path LIKE @FileName + '%'
);

-- Set the trace status to stop
EXEC sp_trace_setstatus @TraceID, 0;
```

The SQL Trace session example in this section is fairly basic. In any given production environment, a more intelligent process may need to be crafted that collects information in each trace file for a specified amount of time instead of using a file size to control the file rollover rate. These types of changes to collecting information from SQL Trace for monitoring indexes should have no impact on the ability to use the SQL Trace information for the purposes intended later in this chapter. There is one last item to consider when using a SQL Trace. Trace information does not need to constantly be gathered, like performance counter and DMO information. Instead, the SQL Trace information is often better suited to being collected for a 4–8-hour period that represents a regular day of activity on your database platform. If there is a known time period when poor performance is experienced, then that specific period can be targeted.

With SQL Trace, it is possible to collect too much information, which can overwhelm the analyze phase and delay indexing recommendations. Therefore, filtering and targeting key times and events can make uncovering useful information significantly easier to accomplish.

Extended Events

Extended Events is the preferred tracing tool in SQL Server. It contains far more functionality than SQL Trace but lacks its straightforward simplicity. Given the opportunity to choose between these solutions, creating traces with Extended Events is the preferable option. There are two ways to create Extended Events sessions. The first is through T-SQL, which will be demonstrated in this chapter. The second uses a GUI in SQL Server Management Studio that includes wizards for building a new session. The best practices in session creation are the same as SQL Trace for the most part. For example, be sure to collect session logs on drives other than those in which data and log files are stored.

The trace that will be created in Extended Events will collect the same general information as SQL Trace. The main differences will be how the session is created and some of the names of events and columns. Instead of RPC:Completed and SQL:BatchCompleted, the events to capture in Extended Events are `rpc_completed` and `sql_batch_completed`, respectively. Each of these events captures their own set of columns, or data elements, which are listed in Table 15-3.

Table 15-3. *Extended Events Columns*

Event	Columns
rpc_completed	• connection_reset_option • cpu_time • data_stream • duration • logical_reads • object_name • output_parameters • physical_reads • result • row_count • statement • writes
sql_batch_completed	• batch_text • cpu_time • duration • logical_reads • physical_reads • result • row_count • writes

Some additional data will be included in the Extended Events session that is available as global fields, or actions, which can be used to extend the default information included in each event. These are similar to the elements included in the SQL Trace session from the previous session. The global fields to be included are as follows:

- client_app_name
- client_hostname
- database_id
- database_name
- nt_username
- process_id

- session_id

- sql_text

- username

With the session defined, the next step is to create the sessions. Extended Events leverages the T-SQL data definition language (DDL) instead of stored procedures to create sessions. The code in Listing 15-22 provides the DDL for the session and starts the session. For each event added, the ADD EVENT syntax is used, and the ACTION clause is used to include the global fields. For convenience, the session is designed to store the output in the default log folder for SQL Server in the file EventTracingforIndexTuning.

Listing 15-22. Create and Start Extended Events Session

```
USE master;
GO
IF EXISTS (
    SELECT *
    FROM sys.server_event_sessions
    WHERE name = 'EventTracingforIndexTuning'
)
    DROP EVENT SESSION [EventTracingforIndexTuning] ON SERVER;
CREATE EVENT SESSION [EventTracingforIndexTuning]
ON SERVER
    ADD EVENT sqlserver.rpc_completed
    (ACTION (
        package0.process_id,
        sqlserver.client_app_name,
        sqlserver.client_hostname,
        sqlserver.database_id,
        sqlserver.database_name,
        sqlserver.nt_username,
        sqlserver.session_id,
        sqlserver.sql_text,
        sqlserver.username
    )
    ),
```

```
ADD EVENT sqlserver.sql_batch_completed
(ACTION (
    package0.process_id,
    sqlserver.client_app_name,
    sqlserver.client_hostname,
    sqlserver.database_id,
    sqlserver.database_name,
    sqlserver.nt_username,
    sqlserver.session_id,
    sqlserver.sql_text,
    sqlserver.username
)
)
ADD TARGET package0.event_file
(SET filename = N'EventTracingforIndexTuning')
WITH (
    STARTUP_STATE = ON
);
GO
ALTER EVENT SESSION [EventTracingforIndexTuning] ON SERVER STATE = START;
GO
```

Similar to SQL Trace sessions, Extended Events sessions can be started and stopped. There is no need to pause them since the metadata for a session exists independent from whether the session is running. Listing 15-22 includes the syntax for starting the trace. Listing 15-23 shows the code to stop the trace. Additionally, if SQL Server restarts, the Extended Events tracing session will be retained and can be configured to restart, unlike SQL Trace which disappears on restart.

Listing 15-23. Create and Start Extended Events Session

```
USE master;
GO
ALTER EVENT SESSION [EventTracingforIndexTuning] ON SERVER STATE = STOP;
GO
```

This Extended Events session represents a relatively simple use case. The benefit of Extended Events is its ability to easily capture workloads from SQL Server instances. Using the workloads from tracing, common queries can be located, analyzed, and targeted with appropriate indexing changes, if needed. This allows performance in an environment to be improved using that information and then those improvements monitored and tested using additional tracing.

Query Store

Introduced in SQL Server 2016, Query Store is a per-database data store that contains execution plan information and related execution statistics. While it doesn't necessarily provide direct index tuning information, advances in this feature allow for automated indexing capabilities. This is based on the existing changes available to SQL Server in Azure SQL Database, which is detailed at `https://docs.microsoft.com/en-us/sql/relational-databases/automatic-tuning/automatic-tuning?view=sql-server-ver15#automatic-index-management`. Automated index management is not available in SQL Server 2022 or earlier, as of the time of this writing.

Query Store provides direct insight into the queries executed in a database, their resource consumption, execution plans, and more. This provides a clean interface to understand what is in the plan cache, without the need for complex system view queries that may be challenging on a larger SQL Server.

An additional benefit to using Query Store is that in situations where execution plans are being replaced by other execution plans for improved performance, this can sometimes be index-related. This could be due to poor statistics available for the indexes or a lack of the best indexes to provide desired performance without replaced plans. For either scenario, identifying these performance issues by monitoring Query Store activity can provide insight into indexes needed in an environment.

For the purposes of monitoring indexes, those reasons provide an additional reason to leverage Query Store. To enable Query Store on a database, execute the code in Listing 15-24. Note that Query Store is enabled by default starting in SQL Server 2022.

While a deep dive into Query Store is itself outside the scope of this book, there is a lot of flexibility that can be leveraged around how frequently data is collected, how much data is stored, what the rate of dropping data is, and whether the Query Store is currently writable. Further reading on Query Store is recommended; a great start is *Query Store for SQL Server 2019* by Apress.

Listing 15-24. Enable Query Store on AdventureWorks2017

```
USE [master]
GO
ALTER DATABASE [AdventureWorks2017] SET QUERY_STORE = ON
GO
ALTER DATABASE [AdventureWoListing 15-24. Enable Query Store on
AdventureWorks2017
USE [master]
GO
ALTER DATABASE [AdventureWorks2017] SET QUERY_STORE = ON
GO
ALTER DATABASE [AdventureWoListing 15-24. Enable Query Store on
AdventureWorks2017
USE [master]
GO
ALTER DATABASE [AdventureWorks2017] SET QUERY_STORE = ON
GO
ALTER DATABASE [AdventureWorks2017] SET QUERY_STORE (OPERATION_MODE =
READ_WRITE)
GO
```

Summary

In this chapter, we walked through the steps to monitor indexes using a variety of tools. Monitoring indexes is an extension of general platform monitoring but an important part of providing the foundation for determining whether indexes are adequate or if further tuning would be beneficial. Through monitoring and index analysis, we reviewed how to gather dynamic management data and performance counters. In the next chapter, this information will be applied to analyze whether the right indexes are present or not.

CHAPTER 16

Index Analysis

In the previous chapter, we discussed what information should be collected when monitoring indexes. All of that information is necessary for the next process of indexing databases, which is determining which indexes to apply. In this chapter, we will take all the information gathered while monitoring and use it to analyze the state of performance and the value of the existing indexes. The end goal of the index analysis is to build a list of indexes to create, modify, and, potentially, drop from the databases. In some cases, the index analysis will appear to border on art. There are many decisions in which previous performance will be used to anticipate future indexing needs. Ultimately, though, with every change proposed, there will be supporting evidence before and after the indexing solutions to statistically confirm or disprove the value of the index. This helps to ensure that regardless of the complexity of an indexing challenge, it will and always should be more science than art.

The general process of index analysis is broken down into several components. Each component contains a process in which the analysis will start from high levels to identify the needed focus and then zoom into existing issues. The analysis components are as follows:

- Review of server state
- Schema discovery
- Database Engine Tuning Advisor
- Unused indexes
- Index plan usage

Before any exercise in analyzing the indexes of a database can take place, it is first necessary to know the current deployment state. The tactics that can be used for a database in deployment vs. a database already deployed to the production environment will be roughly the same. There is a significant difference between the two, though, when it comes to where and how the statistics are gathered.

E. Pollack and J. Strate, *Expert Performance Indexing in Azure SQL and SQL Server 2022*,
https://doi.org/10.1007/978-1-4842-9215-0_16

For a database that has not been developed, the focus will be on how users are expected to interact with the data and application after it is deployed. Tests and workloads against the database will focus on validating that the indexing in the database supports those activities. The activity that is chosen for the testing will likely be the result of estimations and projections of what users will do with the application. Determining the activity will be the responsibility of the business analysts who develop the requirements for the application.

Once the database has been deployed, the monitoring shifts from what the activity could be to what the activity is. The rate at which users adopt features and what the distribution of the data is with that activity will be known. At this point, the indexes developed during testing and planning may not be correct for the workload. The first round of using the Indexing Method on the database after deployment may lead to significant indexing changes. The key to indexing databases that have been deployed is that the analysis needs to be against the statistics of the workload in production. Doing so will provide the necessary guidance for implementing indexes that provide the best benefit to the database and pair them with the features that users are using and the frequency in which they use them.

Going through the index analysis with databases in either deployment state will provide a set of indexes that are optimal for what is currently known and understood about the database. When the indexes are applied, their effectiveness can and will vary. An index may provide the perfect access path for data for an activity in the database last month, but with a new release, new clients, or changes in user behavior, it may not continue to be optimal. As is often heard with regard to the stock market, past performance does not predict future results.

Fortunately, with a well-practiced use of the Indexing Method, we will be able to provide the indexing that an environment needs. In this chapter, the focus is on databases that are already deployed to production. As mentioned, these tactics will work with databases and servers in both states—development and production—but for simplicity, a production environment will be the default perspective and approach.

As we move through each of the areas in the index analysis, a list of indexes will be developed to either create, modify, delete, or investigate further. For the indexes that require further investigation, subsequent portions of the index analysis process will be used to determine how to progress and handle the index.

> **Note**   In this chapter, it will be important to run the monitoring scripts from
> Chapter 15 between the scripts that create the workload and the queries to review
> the statistics. Depending on the schedule used for collecting the statistics, it could
> be hours before the statistics are collected that prevent the queries from providing
> the anticipated results.

Review of Server State

The first step in index analysis is to review the state of the server. Review both the host
server environment and the SQL Server instance environment to identify whether there
are conditions indicating that there may be indexing issues. By starting at a high level
and not looking directly at tables and individual indexes, we can avoid getting blinded by
the trees in the forest. Often, when there are hundreds (or thousands) of indexes in many
databases, it is easy to get overly focused on an index or table that looks poorly indexed,
only to later discover that the table has fewer than a hundred rows in a database with
billions of rows in other tables.

When analyzing the server state, the following three areas will be considered:

- Performance counters

- Wait statistics

- Buffer allocation

Each of these areas provides an idea of where to start focusing the index analysis
process. They let the database platform determine where the performance issues related
to indexing may reside.

Performance Counters

The first set of information collected for index monitoring included the performance
counters. Naturally, we want to look at these performance counters first when
performing index analysis. Tracking performance counters over a monitoring period and
over time will not provide prescriptive guidance on what to do about indexing issues, but
it will provide a point for discovering performance issues and thus where to begin.

For each of the counters, some general guidelines will be discussed. These guidelines are generalities that should be taken with a grain of salt. Use them to initially guide whether the counter is outside of what might be considered normal. If there is a reason that counters on your platform trend higher than typical, then maintaining the baseline tables ensures that the norm is identified prior to highlighting outliers. Work with the counter values that are valid for an environment as opposed to those that work best for others.

There are two ways in which performance counters should be analyzed. The first is to use Excel and/or Power BI to view graphs and trend lines based on the performance counters. The second is to review the performance counters with a query that takes a snapshot of the information in the performance counter table. The second approach is the one used in this chapter due to its ease in setup and demonstration. The guidelines for the snapshot queries apply to both approaches.

Note   For simplicity, the snapshot analysis queries in this section will be scoped to the database level. In most cases, they will need to be executed against every database on the SQL Server instance. Options for accomplishing this are using sp_MSForEachDB or a process that loops through a given set of databases one-at-a-time.

Forwarded Records per Second

As discussed in Chapter 2, forwarded records occur when heap records are updated and no longer fit on the page in which they were originally stored. In these situations, a pointer is placed in the original record to the new record location. The performance counter Forwarded Records/sec measures the rate at which forwarded rows are accessed on the server. Generally, the ratio of Forwarded Records/sec should not exceed 10 percent of Batch Requests/sec. This ratio can be a misnomer since Forwarded Records represents the access of data at the row level and Batch Requests represents a higher-scoped operation. The ratio, though, provides an indicator of when the balance of Forwarded Records/sec may be exceeding an advisable level.

The snapshot query for forwarded records, shown in Listing 16-1, provides columns for the Forwarded Records/sec counter and the ratio calculation. In this query, the values are aggregated into minimum, average, and maximum values. The ratio is calculated on each set of collected counters and aggregated after that calculation. The final column, PctViolation, shows the percentage of time in which the Forward Records to Batch Requests ratio exceeds the 10 percent guideline.

Listing 16-1. Forwarded Records Counter Analysis

```
USE IndexingMethod;
GO
WITH CounterSummary
  AS (SELECT create_date,
          server_name,
          MAX(IIF(counter_name = 'Forwarded Records/sec', Calculated_
          Counter_value, NULL)) AS ForwardedRecords,
          MAX(IIF(counter_name = 'Forwarded Records/sec', Calculated_
          Counter_value, NULL))
          / (NULLIF(MAX(IIF(counter_name = 'Batch Requests/
          sec', Calculated_Counter_value, NULL)), 0) * 10) AS
          ForwardedRecordRatio
      FROM dbo.IndexingCounters
      WHERE counter_name IN ( 'Forwarded Records/sec', 'Batch
      Requests/sec' )
      GROUP BY create_date,
          server_name)
SELECT server_name,
    MIN(ForwardedRecords) AS MinForwardedRecords,
    AVG(ForwardedRecords) AS AvgForwardedRecords,
    MAX(ForwardedRecords) AS MaxForwardedRecords,
    MIN(ForwardedRecordRatio) AS MinForwardedRecordRatio,
    AVG(ForwardedRecordRatio) AS AvgForwardedRecordRatio,
    MAX(ForwardedRecordRatio) AS MaxForwardedRecordRatio,
    FORMAT(1. * SUM(IIF(ForwardedRecordRatio > 1, 1, NULL)) / COUNT(*),
'0.00%') AS PctViolation
FROM CounterSummary
GROUP BY server_name;
```

When reviewing the output from the snapshot query, there are a few things to ask about the information returned. First, review the minimum and maximum values for the counter and ratio. Is the minimum value close to or at zero? How high is the maximum? How does it compare to previous values collected during monitoring? Is the average value for the counter and ratio closer to the minimum or maximum value? If the volume and peaks of forwarded records is increasing, then further analysis is warranted. Next, consider the PctViolation column. Is the percentage greater than 1 percent? If so, further analysis of forwarded records is warranted. If there is a need to dig deeper into Forward Records, the next step is to move the analysis from the server level to individual databases.

To provide an example of some forwarded record activity, execute the script in Listing 16-2. This script will create a table with a heap, insert records into it, and update those records, causing some to be expanded and leading to record forwarding. Finally, a query will access the forwarded records, causing forwarded record access operations.

Listing 16-2. Forwarded Records Example

```
USE AdventureWorks2017
GO
DROP TABLE IF EXISTS dbo.HeapExample;
GO
CREATE TABLE dbo.HeapExample (
    ID INT IDENTITY,
    FillerData VARCHAR(2000)
    );
INSERT INTO dbo.HeapExample (FillerData)
SELECT REPLICATE('X',100)
FROM sys.all_objects
UPDATE dbo.HeapExample
SET FillerData = REPLICATE('X',2000)
WHERE ID % 5 = 1
GO
SELECT *
FROM dbo.HeapExample
WHERE ID % 3 = 1
GO 2
```

Note that Forwarded Records/sec analysis is only necessary when heaps are used in a database or if there is a desire to identify when heaps have been used inappropriately.

Once determining that Forwarded Records/sec analysis needs to go into the database, the process will leverage information available in DMOs. There are two DMOs that will help to determine the scope and extent of forwarded record issues. These are sys.dm_db_index_physical_stats and sys.dm_db_index_operational_stats. For the analysis, the sys.dm_db_index_operational_stats information will come from the monitoring table dbo.index_operational_stats_history. The analysis process, shown in Listing 16-3, involves identifying all heaps in a database and then checking the physical structure of the heap. This information is then joined to what is collected in dbo.index_operational_stats_history. The physical stature of the index is retrieved from sys.dm_db_index_operational_stats because the DETAILED option for the DMO is required to get the forwarded record information.

Listing 16-3. Forwarded Records Snapshot Query

```
USE AdventureWorks2017
GO
IF OBJECT_ID('tempdb..#HeapList') IS NOT NULL
    DROP TABLE #HeapList
CREATE TABLE #HeapList
    (
     database_id int
    ,object_id int
    ,page_count INT
    ,avg_page_space_used_in_percent DECIMAL(6,3)
    ,record_count INT
    ,forwarded_record_count INT
    )
DECLARE HEAP_CURS CURSOR FORWARD_ONLY FOR
    SELECT object_id
    FROM sys.indexes i
    WHERE index_id = 0
DECLARE @IndexID INT
OPEN HEAP_CURS
FETCH NEXT FROM HEAP_CURS INTO @IndexID
```

```
WHILE @@FETCH_STATUS = 0
BEGIN
    INSERT INTO #HeapList
    SELECT
        DB_ID()
        ,object_id
        ,page_count
        ,CAST(avg_page_space_used_in_percent AS DECIMAL(6,3))
        ,record_count
        ,forwarded_record_count
    FROM
        sys.dm_db_index_physical_stats(DB_ID(), @IndexID, 0,
NULL,'DETAILED') ;
    FETCH NEXT FROM HEAP_CURS INTO @IndexID
END
CLOSE HEAP_CURS
DEALLOCATE HEAP_CURS
SELECT
    QUOTENAME(DB_NAME(database_id))
    ,QUOTENAME(OBJECT_SCHEMA_NAME(object_id)) + '.'
        + QUOTENAME(OBJECT_NAME(object_id)) AS ObjectName
    ,page_count
    ,avg_page_space_used_in_percent
    ,record_count
    ,forwarded_record_count
    ,x.forwarded_fetch_count
    ,CAST(100.*forwarded_record_count/record_count AS DECIMAL(6,3)) AS
forwarded_record_pct
    ,CAST(1.*x.forwarded_fetch_count/forwarded_record_count AS
DECIMAL(12,3)) AS forwarded_row_ratio
FROM #HeapList h
    CROSS APPLY(
        SELECT SUM(forwarded_fetch_count) AS forwarded_fetch_count
        FROM IndexingMethod.dbo.index_operational_stats_history i
        WHERE h.database_id = i.database_id
```

```
        AND h.object_id = i.OBJECT_ID
        AND i.index_id = 0) x
WHERE forwarded_record_count > 0
ORDER BY page_count DESC
```

The results of the snapshot query, shown in Figure 16-1, provide information on all the heaps in a database that have any forwarded records. Through these results, the heaps that have issues with forwarding and forwarded records can be identified. The first columns to pay attention to are `page_count` and `record_count`. Heaps with many records with forwarded record issues will be more important than those with few rows. It is worthwhile to focus on those tables that will provide the greatest relief to forwarded records when investigating this counter. The columns `forwarded_record_count` and `forwarded_fetch_count` provide a count of the number of records in a table that have been forwarded and the number of times those forwarded records have been accessed, respectively. These columns provide a scope to the size of the problem. The last columns to look at are `forwarded_record_pct` and `forwarded_row_ratio`. These columns detail the percentage of columns that are forwarded and how many times each of the forwarded rows has been accessed.

In the example table, the statistics indicate that there is an issue with forwarded records. The table has more than 16 percent of its rows forwarded. Each of these rows has been accessed three times, based on the forwarded_fetch_count. From the code sample, there have been only three queries executed on the table, meaning that every time there has been data access, all forwarded rows are being accessed. When analyzing the indexes in this database, mitigating the forwarded records for this table would be worthwhile. Do pay special attention to whether forwarded records are being accessed. Mitigating forwarded records on a table that has very high forwarded records but no forwarded record access would not be worth the effort and would have no impact on the Forwarded Records/sec counter.

	(No column name)	ObjectName	page_count	avg_page_space_used_in_percent	record_count	forwarded_record_count	forwarded_fetch_count	forwarded_record_pct	forwarded_row_ratio
1	[AdventureWorks2017]	[dbo].[HeapExample]	239	76.314	3530	589	1767	16.686	3.000

Figure 16-1. *Forwarded record snapshot query results*

When heaps that have forwarded record issues have been identified, there are generally two ways in which the forwarded record can be mitigated. The first approach is to change the data types for the columns that are variable to fixed-length data types. For instance, the varchar data type would be changed to char. This approach is not always ideal since it can result in more space being required by the table, and some queries may not accommodate the extra space at the end of character fields and could return incorrect results. The second option is to add a clustered index to the table, which would remove the heap as the organizational method for storing data in the table. The downside to this approach is in identifying the appropriate key column to cluster the table on. If there is a primary key on the table, it can usually suffice as the clustered index key. There is a third option available: the heap can be rebuilt, which will rewrite the heap back to the database file and remove all forwarded records (using the script in Listing 16-4). This is generally considered a poor approach to resolving forwarded records in heaps since it does not provide a meaningful permanent fix to the issue. It is important to consider that forwarded records are not necessarily bad. They do, though, provide a potential performance challenge when the ratio of operations for forwarded records starts to increase when compared to batch requests.

Listing 16-4. Rebuild Heap Script

```
USE AdventureWorks2017
GO

ALTER TABLE dbo.HeapExample REBUILD
```

FreeSpace Scans and Page Fetches per Second

The performance counter FreeSpace Scans/sec is another counter related to heaps. This counter represents the activity that happens when records are being inserted into a table with a heap. During inserts into heaps, there can be activity on the GAM, SGAM, and PFS pages. If the rate of inserts is high enough, contention can occur on these pages. Analyzing the values of the FreeSpace Scans/sec and FreeSpace Page Fetches/sec counters provides an opportunity to keep track of this activity and determine when the volume of activity is increasing and when heaps may need to be analyzed further. Used in conjunction, FreeSpace Scans/sec and FreeSpace Page Fetches/sec counters indicate the frequency and volume of scan activity on heaps, respectively.

As with forwarded records, this metric only applies to heaps and will not provide useful insight in environments that do not use heaps for data storage.

Listing 16-5 provides the query to analyze the FreeSpace Scans/sec counter. It provides a snapshot of FreeSpace Scans activity on the SQL Server instance. The query provides aggregations of the counter with minimum, average, and maximum values. Similar to the previous counter, this counter also follows recommended guidelines of one FreeSpace Scans/sec for every ten Batch Requests. The PctViolation column measures the percentage of time that the counter exceeds the guideline.

Listing 16-5. FreeSpace Scans Counter Analysis

```
USE IndexingMethod;
GO

WITH CounterSummary
  AS (SELECT create_date,
        server_name,
        MAX(IIF(counter_name = 'FreeSpace Scans/sec', Calculated_Counter_
        value, NULL)) FreeSpaceScans,
        MAX(IIF(counter_name = 'FreeSpace Page Fetches/sec', Calculated_
        Counter_value, NULL)) FreeSpacePageFetches,
        MAX(IIF(counter_name = 'FreeSpace Scans/sec', Calculated_Counter_
        value, NULL))
        / (NULLIF(MAX(IIF(counter_name = 'Batch Requests/
        sec', Calculated_Counter_value, NULL)), 0) * 10) AS
        ForwardedRecordRatio
      FROM dbo.IndexingCounters
      WHERE counter_name IN ( 'FreeSpace Scans/sec', 'FreeSpace Page
      Fetches/sec', 'Batch Requests/sec' )
      GROUP BY create_date,
        server_name)
SELECT server_name,
    MIN(FreeSpaceScans) AS MinFreeSpaceScans,
    AVG(FreeSpaceScans) AS AvgFreeSpaceScans,
    MAX(FreeSpaceScans) AS MaxFreeSpaceScans,
    MIN(FreeSpacePageFetches) AS MinFreeSpacePageFetches,
    AVG(FreeSpacePageFetches) AS AvgFreeSpacePageFetches,
    MAX(FreeSpacePageFetches) AS MaxFreeSpacePageFetches,
```

```
    MIN(ForwardedRecordRatio) AS MinForwardedRecordRatio,
    AVG(ForwardedRecordRatio) AS AvgForwardedRecordRatio,
    MAX(ForwardedRecordRatio) AS MaxForwardedRecordRatio,
    FORMAT(1. * SUM(IIF(ForwardedRecordRatio > 1, 1, NULL)) / COUNT(*),
    '0.00%') AS PctViolation
FROM CounterSummary
GROUP BY server_name;
```

When the FreeSpace Scans/sec number is high, the analysis will focus on determining which heaps in the databases have the highest rate of inserts. To identify the tables with the highest inserts on heaps, use the information in the monitoring tables from sys.dm_db_index_operational_stats. The column with the information on inserts is leaf_insert_count. The query in Listing 16-6 provides a list of the heaps in the monitoring table dbo.index_operational_stats_history with the most indexes.

Listing 16-6. FreeSpace Scans Snapshot Query

```
USE IndexingMethod
GO

SELECT
    QUOTENAME(DB_NAME(database_id)) AS database_name
    ,QUOTENAME(OBJECT_SCHEMA_NAME(object_id, database_id)) + '.'
        + QUOTENAME(OBJECT_NAME(object_id, database_id)) AS ObjectName
    , SUM(leaf_insert_count) AS leaf_insert_count
    , SUM(leaf_allocation_count) AS leaf_allocation_count
FROM dbo.index_operational_stats_history
WHERE index_id = 0
AND database_id > 4
and QUOTENAME(OBJECT_NAME(object_id, database_id)) IS NOT NULL
GROUP BY object_id, database_id
ORDER BY leaf_insert_count DESC
```

Reviewing the table in the demonstration script in Listing 16-3 with the FreeSpace Scans snapshot query yields the results in Figure 16-2. As this example shows, there were thousands of inserts into the heap. While only a single table is shown in the results, the tables that appear at the top of this list are going to be the ones most often contributing to FreeSpace Scans/sec.

	database_name	ObjectName	leaf_insert_count	leaf_allocation_count
1	[AdventureWorks2017]	[dbo].[HeapExample]	2941	197
2	[AdventureWorks2017]	[sys].[sysfiles1]	0	0

Figure 16-2. *FreeSpace Scans per second snapshot query results*

Once the contributing heaps are identified, the best method for mitigating this issue is to create a clustered index on the tables with the most inserts. Since the counter is based on scans of free space on the GAM, SGAM, and PFS pages, building clustered indexes on the heap tables will move the allocation of pages to IAM pages, which are dedicated to each clustered index, as compared to heaps where they will compete for page allocations with other heaps.

Full Scans per Second

Through the performance counter Full Scans/sec, the number of full scans on clustered and nonclustered indexes and heaps is measured. Within execution plans, this counter is triggered during index scans and table scans. The higher the rate in which full scans are performed, the more likely that there can be performance issues related to full scans. From a performance perspective, this can impact the Page Life Expectancy value as data is churned in memory, and there may be I/O contention as queries need to wait for data to be brought into memory.

Using the query in Listing 16-7, the current state of Full Scans/sec can be analyzed for the current monitoring window. As with the previous counters, it is important to consider the relationship between this counter and the Batch Requests/sec counter. When the ratio of Full Scans/sec to Batch Requests/sec exceeds one for every thousand, there may be an issue with Full Scans/sec that merits further review.

Listing 16-7. Full Scans Counter Analysis

```
USE IndexingMethod;
GO
WITH CounterSummary
  AS (SELECT create_date,
         server_name,
```

```
        MAX(IIF(counter_name = 'Full Scans/sec', Calculated_Counter_
        value, NULL)) FullScans,
        MAX(IIF(counter_name = 'Full Scans/sec', Calculated_Counter_
        value, NULL))
        / (NULLIF(MAX(IIF(counter_name = 'Batch Requests/sec',
        Calculated_Counter_value, NULL)), 0) * 1000) AS FullRatio
    FROM dbo.IndexingCounters
    WHERE counter_name IN ( 'Full Scans/sec', 'Batch Requests/sec' )
    GROUP BY create_date,
        server_name)
SELECT server_name,
    MIN(FullScans) AS MinFullScans,
    AVG(FullScans) AS AvgFullScans,
    MAX(FullScans) AS MaxFullScans,
    MIN(FullRatio) AS MinFullRatio,
    AVG(FullRatio) AS AvgFullRatio,
    MAX(FullRatio) AS MaxFullRatio,
    FORMAT(1. * SUM(IIF(FullRatio > 1, 1, 0)) / COUNT(*), '0.00%') AS
PctViolation
FROM CounterSummary
GROUP BY server_name;
```

Before demonstrating how to examine the underlying causes for high Full Scans/sec counter values, some example statistics will be set up. Listing 16-8 will provide plenty of full scans that can be collected through the monitoring process detailed in the previous section. Be certain to execute the scripts that collect the monitoring information after executing the example script.

Listing 16-8. Full Scans Example Query

```
USE AdventureWorks2017
GO

SET NOCOUNT ON

EXEC ('SELECT * INTO #temp FROM Sales.SalesOrderHeader')
GO 1000
```

The primary goal is to identify which indexes the Full Scans/sec counter is being affected by. Once the indexes are identified, they need to be analyzed to determine whether they are the proper indexes for that operation or whether there are other performance tuning tactics required to reduce the use of the index in a full-scan operation. The DMO to use for investigating full scans is sys.dm_db_index_usage_stats from the monitoring tables; from the monitoring, this is stored in the dbo.index_usage_stats_history table.

The indexes can be identified using the query shown in Listing 16-9. The snapshot results exclude any indexes with no rows in them. Those indexes are still being used for full scans, but mitigating the scans on those indexes would not greatly impact performance. To sort the results, the number of scans on the indexes is multiplied by the number of rows in the table. Sorting in this manner weighs the output to put focus on those indexes that might not have a high impact on reducing the Full Scans/sec value but will provide the greatest improvement to index performance.

Listing 16-9. Full Scans Snapshot Query

```
USE IndexingMethod;
GO

SELECT QUOTENAME(DB_NAME(uh.database_id)) AS database_name,
    QUOTENAME(OBJECT_SCHEMA_NAME(uh.object_id, uh.database_id)) + '.'
    + QUOTENAME(OBJECT_NAME(uh.object_id, uh.database_id)) AS ObjectName,
    uh.index_id,
    SUM(uh.user_scans) AS user_scans,
    SUM(uh.user_seeks) AS user_seeks,
    x.record_count
FROM dbo.index_usage_stats_history uh
CROSS APPLY (
    SELECT DENSE_RANK() OVER (ORDER BY ph.create_date DESC) AS RankID,
        ph.record_count
    FROM dbo.index_physical_stats_history ph
    WHERE ph.database_id = uh.database_id
    AND ph.object_id = uh.object_id
    AND ph.index_id = uh.index_id
) x
```

```
WHERE uh.database_id > 4
AND uh.database_id <> DB_ID()
AND OBJECT_NAME(uh.object_id, uh.database_id) IS NOT NULL
AND x.RankID = 1
GROUP BY uh.database_id,
    uh.object_id,
    uh.index_id,
    x.record_count
ORDER BY SUM(uh.user_scans) * x.record_count DESC;
GO
```

The results of the Full Scans snapshot query will look similar to the output in
Figure 16-3. With this output, the next step is to identify which indexes require further
analysis. The purpose of the current analysis is to identify problem indexes for later
analysis. Once identified, the next step is to determine where they are being used and
how to mitigate full scans in those places, which is demonstrated later in this chapter in
the "Index Plan Usage" section.

	database_name	ObjectName	index_id	user_scans	user_seeks	record_count
1	[AdventureWorks2017]	[Sales].[SalesOrderHeader]	1	1000	0	31465
2	[AdventureWorks2017]	[dbo].[HeapExample]	0	3	0	2941
3	[AdventureWorks2017]	[Production].[Document]	1	0	1	13
4	[AdventureWorks2017]	[Production].[Document]	1	0	1	40
5	[AdventureWorks2017]	[HumanResources].[JobCandidate]	1	0	1	4
6	[AdventureWorks2017]	[HumanResources].[JobCandidate]	1	0	1	13
7	[AdventureWorks2017]	[Production].[ProductReview]	1	0	1	4

Figure 16-3. *Full Scans snapshot query results*

Index Searches per Second

The alternative to scanning indexes is to perform seeks against them. The performance
counter Index Searches/sec provides reporting on the rate of index seeks on a SQL
Server instance. This can include operations such as range scans and key lookups. In
most environments, it is preferable to see high Index Searches/sec counter values. Along
those lines, the higher this performance counter is in relationship to Full Scans/sec,
the better.

The analysis of Index Searches/sec will begin with reviewing the performance counter information collected over time (shown in Listing 16-10). The ratio of Index Searches/sec to Full Scans/sec is one of the metrics that can be used to evaluate whether Index Searches/sec is indicating a potential indexing issue. The guideline for evaluating the ratio between the two counters is to look for 1,000 Index Searches/sec for every 1 Full Scans/sec. The analysis query provides this calculation, along with determining the amount of time in which the counter values exceeded this ratio, through the column PctViolation.

Listing 16-10. Index Searches Counter Analysis

```
USE IndexingMethod;
GO
WITH CounterSummary
  AS (SELECT create_date,
          server_name,
          MAX(IIF(counter_name = 'Index Searches/sec', Calculated_Counter_
          value, NULL)) IndexSearches,
          MAX(IIF(counter_name = 'Index Searches/sec', Calculated_Counter_
          value, NULL))
          / (NULLIF(MAX(IIF(counter_name = 'Full Scans/sec', Calculated_
          Counter_value, NULL)), 0) * 1000) AS SearchToScanRatio
      FROM dbo.IndexingCounters
      WHERE counter_name IN ( 'Index Searches/sec', 'Full Scans/sec' )
      GROUP BY create_date,
          server_name)
SELECT server_name,
    MIN(IndexSearches) AS MinIndexSearches,
    AVG(IndexSearches) AS AvgIndexSearches,
    MAX(IndexSearches) AS MaxIndexSearches,
    MIN(SearchToScanRatio) AS MinSearchToScanRatio,
    AVG(SearchToScanRatio) AS AvgSearchToScanRatio,
    MAX(SearchToScanRatio) AS MaxSearchToScanRatio,
    FORMAT(1. * SUM(IIF(SearchToScanRatio > 1, 1, NULL)) / COUNT(*),
    '0.00%') AS PctViolation
FROM CounterSummary
GROUP BY server_name;
```

If the analysis indicates an issue with index searches, the next step is to verify that the analysis for Full Scans/sec in the previous section was completed. That analysis will provide the most insight into which indexes have many full scans, which would contribute to high ratios for Index Searches/sec.

To help demonstrate how to examine the Index Searches/sec counter values, the query in Listing 16-11 will be executed. This query will provide some full scans that can be collected through the monitoring process detailed in the previous section. Be certain to execute the scripts that collect the monitoring information after running the example script.

Listing 16-11. Full Scans Example Query

```
USE AdventureWorks2017
GO

SET NOCOUNT ON

EXEC('SELECT SOH.SalesOrderID, SOD.SalesOrderDetailID
INTO #temp
FROM Sales.SalesOrderHeader SOH
INNER JOIN Sales.SalesOrderDetail SOD ON SOH.SalesOrderID = SOD.
SalesOrderID
WHERE SOH.SalesOrderID = 43659')
GO 1000
```

Once that analysis is complete, we can begin to identify where there are issues with the ratios of scans to seeks at the index level. Using the query in Listing 16-12, indexes with a high ratio of scans to seeks can be identified. Similar to the performance counter guideline of 1,000 seeks to every 1 scan, the query returns results for those indexes with fewer than 1,000 seeks for every scan. Since full-scan issues should have been identified in the previous section, the analysis also removes any indexes that do not have seeks against them.

Listing 16-12. Index Searches Snapshot Query

```
USE IndexingMethod;
GO

SELECT QUOTENAME(DB_NAME(uh.database_id)) AS database_name,
    QUOTENAME(OBJECT_SCHEMA_NAME(uh.object_id, uh.database_id)) + '.'
```

```
    + QUOTENAME(OBJECT_NAME(uh.object_id, uh.database_id)) AS ObjectName,
    uh.index_id,
    SUM(uh.user_scans) AS user_scans,
    SUM(uh.user_seeks) AS user_seeks,
    1. * SUM(uh.user_seeks) / NULLIF(SUM(uh.user_scans), 0) AS
    SeekScanRatio,
    x.record_count
FROM dbo.index_usage_stats_history uh
CROSS APPLY (
    SELECT DENSE_RANK() OVER (ORDER BY ph.create_date DESC) AS RankID,
        ph.record_count
    FROM dbo.index_physical_stats_history ph
    WHERE ph.database_id = uh.database_id
    AND ph.object_id = uh.object_id
    AND ph.index_id = uh.index_id
) x
WHERE uh.database_id > 4
AND uh.database_id <> DB_ID()
AND x.RankID = 1
AND x.record_count > 0
GROUP BY uh.database_id,
    uh.object_id,
    uh.index_id,
    x.record_count
HAVING 1. * SUM(uh.user_seeks) / NULLIF(SUM(uh.user_scans), 0) < 1000
AND SUM(uh.user_seeks) > 0
ORDER BY 1. * SUM(uh.user_seeks) / NULLIF(SUM(uh.user_scans), 0) DESC,
    SUM(uh.user_scans) DESC;
GO
```

Viewing the results of the snapshot query, shown in Figure 16-4, there is just a single index identified where the seek-to-scan ratio is close to 1. This is the case since in the previous section about 1,000 scans were executed against Sales.SalesOrderHeader, but none against Sales.SalesOrderDetail, even though both of these tables and their indexes were accessed in Listing 16-11. The advantage of considering Index Searches in conjunction with Full Scans is they help to offset the severity by identifying the frequency in which more desirable activity is occurring.

	database_name	ObjectName	index_id	user_scans	user_seeks	SeekScanRatio	record_count
1	[AdventureWorks2017]	[Sales].[SalesOrderHeader]	1	1005	1002	0.99701492537313432	31465

Figure 16-4. *Index search snapshot query sample results*

When delving into further analysis, there are a few things to consider that might indicate an issue with the indexes identified. First is the current seek vs. scan behavior new to the index; in other words, has the variance been on a common trend that has slowly been getting worse? If the change is sudden, there could be a plan that is no longer using the index as it once did, maybe because of a coding change or bad parameter sniffing. Second is when the change has been gradual; look at increased data volumes and whether a query or feature within the database is being used more than it was previously. This can also hint at changes in how people are using the database and its applications, which is sometimes gradual until it reaches the point where indexing, and the performance the indexes support, suffers.

Page Splits per Second

Similar to how clustered indexes are the "opposite" of heaps, page splits are the opposite of forwarded records. An in-depth discussion of page splits is included in Chapter 2. For the purposes of this chapter, though, page splits occur when a clustered or nonclustered index needs to make room in the ordering of the pages of the index to place data into its proper position. Page splits can be resource-intensive because the single page is divided into two or more pages and involves locking and, potentially, blocking. The more frequent the page splits, the more likely that indexes will incur blocking and performance will suffer. Also, the fragmentation caused by page splits reduces the size of reads that can be performed in single operations.

To begin analyzing the performance counters for page splits, the counter Page Splits/ sec is utilized. The query in Listing 16-13 provides a method for summarizing page split activity. The query includes the minimum, maximum, and average levels of the performance counter. A ratio of Page Splits/sec to Batch Requests/sec is also included. When identifying whether there are issues with page splits on a SQL Server instance, the general rule of thumb is to look for times in which there is more than one page split/sec for every 20 batch requests/sec. As with the other counters, pay attention to the amount of time, through PctViolation, that the counter exceeded the threshold.

Listing 16-13. Page Splits Counter Analysis

```
USE IndexingMethod;
GO
WITH CounterSummary
  AS (SELECT create_date,
          server_name,
          MAX(IIF(counter_name = 'Page Splits/sec', Calculated_Counter_
          value, NULL)) PageSplits,
          MAX(IIF(counter_name = 'Page Splits/sec', Calculated_Counter_
          value, NULL))
          / (NULLIF(MAX(IIF(counter_name = 'Batch Requests/sec',
          Calculated_Counter_value, NULL)), 0) * 20) AS FullRatio
      FROM dbo.IndexingCounters
      WHERE counter_name IN ( 'Page Splits/sec', 'Batch Requests/sec' )
      GROUP BY create_date,
          server_name)
SELECT server_name,
    MIN(PageSplits) AS MinPageSplits,
    AVG(PageSplits) AS AvgPageSplits,
    MAX(PageSplits) AS MaxPageSplits,
    MIN(FullRatio) AS MinFullRatio,
    AVG(FullRatio) AS AvgFullRatio,
    MAX(FullRatio) AS MaxFullRatio,
    FORMAT(1. * SUM(IIF(FullRatio > 1, 1, 0)) / COUNT(*), '0.00%') AS
PctViolation
FROM CounterSummary
GROUP BY server_name;
```

To determine the indexes that are being affected by page splits, a few values should be considered. A couple of the values come from sys.dm_db_index_operational_stats or dbo.index_operational_stats_history from the index monitoring process. These columns report each page allocation that occurs on an index, whether from inserts at the end of the B-tree or page splits in the middle of it. Since for this analysis, we care only about operations that are part of page splits, the next two columns provide information on whether fragmentation from page splits is occurring. To determine fragmentation, the column `avg_fragmentation_in_percent` from `sys.dm_db_index_physical_stats` is included in the monitoring table `dbo.index_physical_stats_history`. For the average fragmentation, there are two values returned. The first is the last fragmentation value reported for the index; the second is the average of all the fragmentation values collected. See Listing 16-14.

Listing 16-14. Page Splits Snapshot Query

```
USE IndexingMethod;
GO
SELECT QUOTENAME(DB_NAME(database_id)) AS database_name,
    QUOTENAME(OBJECT_SCHEMA_NAME(object_id, database_id)) + '.' +
    QUOTENAME(OBJECT_NAME(object_id, database_id)) AS ObjectName,
    SUM(leaf_allocation_count) AS leaf_insert_count,
    SUM(nonleaf_allocation_count) AS nonleaf_allocation_count,
    MAX(IIF(RankID = 1, x.avg_fragmentation_in_percent, NULL)) AS last_
    fragmenation,
    AVG(x.avg_fragmentation_in_percent) AS average_fragmenation
FROM dbo.index_operational_stats_history oh
CROSS APPLY (
    SELECT DENSE_RANK() OVER (ORDER BY ph.create_date DESC) AS RankID,
        CAST(ph.avg_fragmentation_in_percent AS DECIMAL(6, 3)) AS avg_
        fragmentation_in_percent
    FROM dbo.index_physical_stats_history ph
    WHERE ph.database_id = oh.database_id
    AND ph.object_id = oh.object_id
    AND ph.index_id = oh.index_id
) x
WHERE database_id > 4
AND database_id <> DB_ID()
AND oh.index_id <> 0
AND (
```

```
        leaf_allocation_count > 0
        OR nonleaf_allocation_count > 0
)
GROUP BY object_id,
        database_id
ORDER BY leaf_insert_count DESC;
```

Investigating page splits in this manner provides a way to see the number of allocations and pairs that information with fragmentation. A table with low fragmentation and a high `leaf_insert_count`, such as the table `dbo.IndexingCounters` shown in Figure 16-5, is not a concern from a page split perspective. On the other hand, `dbo.index_operational_stats_history` does show a high amount of fragmentation and `leaf_insert_count`. It would be worthwhile to investigate that index further. While the scripting in Listing 16-14 doesn't typically show index results for the IndexingMethod database, the script was modified from what is in the listing to provide some results to examine.

	database_name	ObjectName	leaf_insert_count	nonleaf_allocation_count	last_fragmenation	average_fragmenation
1	[IndexingMethod]	[dbo].[IndexingCounters]	11660	160	99.671	74.399480
2	[IndexingMethod]	[dbo].[index_operational_stats_snapshot]	7300	100	75.000	32.422925
3	[IndexingMethod]	[dbo].[wait_stats_snapshot]	4465	0	7.631	13.039000
4	[IndexingMethod]	[dbo].[index_physical_stats_history]	3640	0	36.842	33.724625
5	[IndexingMethod]	[dbo].[index_operational_stats_history]	1620	80	60.000	21.307964
6	[IndexingMethod]	[dbo].[index_usage_stats_snapshot]	600	40	42.857	16.722300
7	[IndexingMethod]	[dbo].[index_usage_stats_history]	300	40	75.000	20.938920
8	[IndexingMethod]	[dbo].[wait_stats_history]	171	19	36.364	43.639947

Figure 16-5. *Page Split snapshot query sample results*

With the indexes requiring further analysis identified, the next step is mitigation. There are a number of ways to mitigate page splits on indexes. The first is to review the fragmentation history for the index. If the index needs to be rebuilt on a regular basis, one of the first things that can be done is to decrease the fill factor on the index. Reducing the fill factor will increase the space remaining on pages after rebuilding indexes, which will reduce the likelihood for page splits. The second strategy for reducing fragmentation is to consider the columns in the index. Are the columns highly volatile and do the values change dramatically? For instance, an index on `create_date` would likely not incur frequent page splits. But one on `update_date` would be prone to fragmentation. If the usage rates for the index do not justify the index, it might be worthwhile to remove it altogether. Or, in multicolumn indexes, move the volatile columns to the right side of the index or add them as included columns. A third approach to mitigating page splits can be to identify where the index is being used. One final approach to mitigating page splits on indexes is to review the data types being used by the index. In some cases, a variable data type might be better suited to being a fixed-length data type.

Page Lookups per Second

The performance counter Page Lookups/sec measures the number of requests made in the SQL Server instance to retrieve individual pages from the buffer pool. When this counter is high, it often means that there is inefficiency in query plans, which can often be addressed through execution plan analysis. Often, high levels of Page Lookups/sec are attributed to plans with large numbers of page lookups and row lookups per execution. Generally speaking, in terms of performance issues, the value of Page Lookups/sec should not exceed a ratio of 100 operations for each Batch Request/sec.

The initial analysis of Page Lookups/sec involves looking at both Page Lookups/sec and Batch Request/sec. To start, use the query shown in Listing 16-15; the analysis will include the minimum, maximum, and average Page Lookups/sec values over the data from the monitoring period. Next, the minimum, maximum, and average values of the ratio are included, with the PctViolation column, for the ratio of Page Lookups/sec to Batch Request/sec for each time period. The violation calculation verifies whether the ratio of operations exceeds 100 to 1.

Listing 16-15. Page Lookups Counter Analysis

```
USE IndexingMethod;
GO
WITH CounterSummary
  AS (SELECT create_date,
          server_name,
          MAX(IIF(counter_name = 'Page Lookups/sec', Calculated_Counter_
          value, NULL)) PageLookups,
          MAX(IIF(counter_name = 'Page Lookups/sec', Calculated_Counter_
          value, NULL))
          / (NULLIF(MAX(IIF(counter_name = 'Batch Requests/sec',
          Calculated_Counter_value, NULL)), 0) * 100) AS PageLookupRatio
      FROM dbo.IndexingCounters
```

```
        WHERE counter_name IN ( 'Page Lookups/sec', 'Batch Requests/sec' )
        GROUP BY create_date,
            server_name)
SELECT server_name,
    MIN(PageLookups) AS MinPageLookups,
    AVG(PageLookups) AS AvgPageLookups,
    MAX(PageLookups) AS MaxPageLookups,
    MIN(PageLookupRatio) AS MinPageLookupRatio,
    AVG(PageLookupRatio) AS AvgPageLookupRatio,
    MAX(PageLookupRatio) AS MaxPageLookupRatio,
    FORMAT(1. * SUM(IIF(PageLookupRatio > 1, 1, 0)) / COUNT(*), '0.00%') AS
    PctViolation
FROM CounterSummary
GROUP BY server_name;
```

As with the other counters, when the analysis dictates that there are potential problems with the counter, the next step is to dig deeper. There are three approaches that can be taken to address high Page Lookups/sec values. The first is to query sys. dm_exec_query_stats to identify queries that are frequently executed and have high I/O; more information on this DMV can be found at http://msdn.microsoft.com/en-us/library/ms189741.aspx. Those queries need to be reviewed and a determination made as to whether the queries are utilizing an excessive amount of I/O. Another approach is to review the database in the SQL Server instance for missing indexes. The third approach, which will be detailed in this section, is to review the occurrences of lookups on clustered indexes and heaps.

To investigate lookups on clustered indexes and heaps, the primary source for this information is the DMO sys.dm_db_index_usage_stats. Thanks to the monitoring implemented in the previous chapter, this information is available in the table dbo. index_usage_stats_history. To perform the analysis, use the query in Listing 16-16; we'll review lookups, seeks, and scans that have occurred from a user perspective. With these values, the query calculates the ratio of user lookups to user seeks and returns all that have a ratio higher than 100 to 1.

Listing 16-16. Page Lookups Snapshot Query

```
USE IndexingMethod;
GO

SELECT QUOTENAME(DB_NAME(uh.database_id)) AS database_name,
    QUOTENAME(OBJECT_SCHEMA_NAME(uh.object_id, uh.database_id)) + '.'
    + QUOTENAME(OBJECT_NAME(uh.object_id, uh.database_id)) AS ObjectName,
    uh.index_id,
    SUM(uh.user_lookups) AS user_lookups,
    SUM(uh.user_seeks) AS user_seeks,
    SUM(uh.user_scans) AS user_scans,
    x.record_count,
    CAST(1. * SUM(uh.user_lookups) / IIF(SUM(uh.user_seeks) = 0, 1, SUM(uh.
    user_seeks)) AS DECIMAL(18, 2)) AS LookupSeekRatio
FROM dbo.index_usage_stats_history uh
CROSS APPLY (
    SELECT DENSE_RANK() OVER (ORDER BY ph.create_date DESC) AS RankID,
        ph.record_count
    FROM dbo.index_physical_stats_history ph
    WHERE ph.database_id = uh.database_id
    AND ph.object_id = uh.object_id
    AND ph.index_id = uh.index_id) x
WHERE uh.database_id > 4
AND x.RankID = 1
AND x.record_count > 0
GROUP BY uh.database_id,
    uh.object_id,
    uh.index_id,
    x.record_count
HAVING CAST(1. * SUM(uh.user_lookups) / IIF(SUM(uh.user_seeks) = 0, 1,
SUM(uh.user_seeks)) AS DECIMAL(18, 2)) > 100
ORDER BY 1. * SUM(uh.user_lookups) / IIF(SUM(uh.user_seeks) = 0, 1, SUM(uh.
user_seeks)) DESC;
GO
```

Once indexes with issues are identified, the next step is to determine how and where the indexes are being used, the process for which is described later in this chapter.

Page Compression

The performance counters Page compression attempts/sec and Pages compressed/sec measure the number of pages compressed and attempted to be compressed. When the rate of Pages Compressed/sec decreases in comparison with the Page Compressions/sec, it indicates failures in the SQL Server compression algorithm to save data pages in a compressed state. While there is data that is more efficiently stored uncompressed, scenarios where the CPU cost to decompress pages exceeds the point where there is value in compressing the data, then reviewing whether compression is ideal or not for a table or index may be worthwhile. This often happens on data that appears random, such as the raw output of an image file. The challenge with compression failures is that SQL Server already spent time, specifically CPU resources, attempting to compress the page. Generally, when more than 5 percent of page compression attempts fail, it is worthwhile identifying and reviewing indexes that failures are occurring on.

To analyze if there is an issue with page compression, the counters for page compression should first be reviewed. Using the query shown in Listing 16-17, we can review the minimum, maximum, and average Page compression attempts/sec and Pages compressed/sec values from the monitoring period. Additionally, the ratio of Pages compressed/sec to Page compression attempts/sec is included with the minimum, maximum, and average values. The PctViolation column lets us know the percentage of time the 5 percent threshold is violated.

Listing 16-17. Page Compression Counter Analysis

```
USE IndexingMethod;
GO
WITH CounterSummary
  AS (SELECT create_date,
          server_name,
          MAX(IIF(counter_name = 'Page compression attempts/sec',
          Calculated_Counter_value, NULL)) PageCompressionAttempts,
          MAX(IIF(counter_name = 'Pages compressed/sec', Calculated_
          Counter_value, NULL)) PagesCompressed,
```

```
            MAX(IIF(counter_name = 'Page compression attempts/sec',
            Calculated_Counter_value, NULL))
            / (NULLIF(MAX(IIF(counter_name = 'Pages compressed/sec',
            Calculated_Counter_value, NULL)), 0) * 100.) AS CompressionRate
    FROM dbo.IndexingCounters
    WHERE counter_name IN ( 'Page compression attempts/sec', 'Pages
    compressed/sec')
    GROUP BY create_date,
        server_name)
SELECT server_name,
    MIN(PageCompressionAttempts) AS MinPageCompressionAttempts,
    AVG(PageCompressionAttempts) AS AvgPageCompressionAttempts,
    MAX(PageCompressionAttempts) AS MaxPageCompressionAttempts,
    MIN(PagesCompressed) AS MinPagesCompressed,
    AVG(PagesCompressed) AS AvgPagesCompressed,
    MAX(PagesCompressed) AS MaxPagesCompressed,
    MIN(CompressionRate) AS MinCompressionRate,
    AVG(CompressionRate) AS AvgCompressionRate,
    MAX(CompressionRate) AS MaxCompressionRate,
    FORMAT(1. * SUM(IIF(CompressionRate < 95, 1, 0)) / COUNT(*), '0.00%')
AS PctViolation
FROM CounterSummary
GROUP BY server_name;
```

If there is an indication that page compression failures are high or gaining in frequency, it's worth investigating within the databases to determine which tables and indexes are failing to page compress. Using the data that has been stored for the indexes, it can be determined which specific index has page compression failures, or the lowest page compression success rate, using the query in Listing 16-18. The results would look similar to those in Figure 16-6. That index was created with all the columns from Person. Person, which included some XML and varchar(max) columns. The success rate for page compressions for this index is just over 50 percent which is a suboptimal result.

Listing 16-18. Page Compression Snapshot Query

```
USE IndexingMethod;
GO

SELECT QUOTENAME(DB_NAME(database_id)) AS database_name,
    QUOTENAME(OBJECT_SCHEMA_NAME(object_id, database_id)) + '.' +
    QUOTENAME(OBJECT_NAME(object_id, database_id)) AS ObjectName,
    oh.index_id,
    SUM(oh.page_compression_attempt_count) AS page_compression_
    attempt_count,
    SUM(oh.page_compression_success_count) AS page_compression_
    success_count,
    SUM(1. * oh.page_compression_success_count / NULLIF(oh.page_
    compression_attempt_count, 0)) AS page_compression_success_rate
FROM dbo.index_operational_stats_history oh
WHERE database_id > 4
AND database_id <> DB_ID()
AND oh.page_compression_attempt_count > 0
GROUP BY object_id,
    database_id,
    index_id;
```

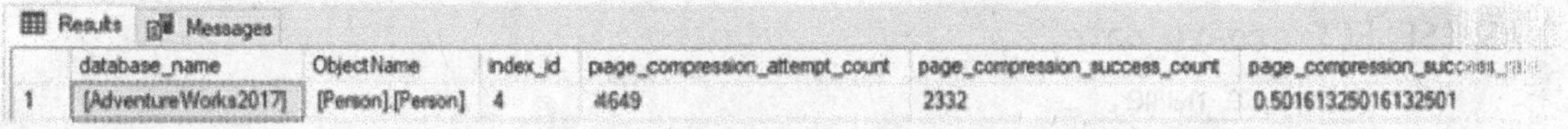

database_name	ObjectName	index_id	page_compression_attempt_count	page_compression_success_count	page_compression_succe...
1	[AdventureWorks2017]	[Person].[Person]	4	4649	2332	0.50161325016132501

Figure 16-6. *Page Compression snapshot query sample results*

Once indexes with suboptimal compression are identified, the next step is to determine whether page compression is appropriate for the index. Indexes that contain data types such as XML or varchar(max) are poor candidates for page compression, as seen in Figure 16-6.

Lock Wait Time

Some performance counters can be used to determine whether there is pressure on the indexes based on their usage. One such counter is Lock Wait Time (ms). This counter measures the amount of time, in milliseconds, that SQL Server spends waiting to implement a lock on a table, index, or page. There are not any specific "good" guidance values for this counter. Generally, the lower this value, the better, but what "low" means is entirely dependent on the database platform and the applications that are accessing it.

Since there are no guidelines for the level at which the values from Lock Wait Time (ms) are acceptable or not, the best method for evaluating the counter is to compare it to baseline values. In this case, collecting a baseline becomes incredibly important in terms of being able to monitor when index performance regressions related to Lock Wait Time occur. Using the query in Listing 16-19, the Lock Wait Time (ms) value is compared to the available baseline values. For both the baseline and the values from the monitoring period, an aggregate of the counter values is provided for the minimum, maximum, average, and standard deviation. These aggregations assist in providing a profile of the state of the counter and whether it has increased or decreased compared to the baseline.

Listing 16-19. Lock Wait Time Counter Analysis

```
USE IndexingMethod;
GO

WITH CounterSummary
  AS (SELECT create_date,
          server_name,
          instance_name,
          MAX(IIF(counter_name = 'Lock Wait Time (ms)', Calculated_Counter_
          value, NULL)) / 1000 LockWaitTime
      FROM dbo.IndexingCounters
      WHERE counter_name = 'Lock Wait Time (ms)'
      GROUP BY create_date,
          server_name,
          instance_name)
```

```
SELECT CONVERT(VARCHAR(50), MAX(create_date), 101) AS CounterDate,
    server_name,
    instance_name,
    MIN(LockWaitTime) AS MinLockWaitTime,
    AVG(LockWaitTime) AS AvgLockWaitTime,
    MAX(LockWaitTime) AS MaxLockWaitTime,
    STDEV(LockWaitTime) AS StdDevLockWaitTime
FROM CounterSummary
GROUP BY server_name,
    instance_name
UNION ALL
SELECT 'Baseline: ' + CONVERT(VARCHAR(50), start_date, 101) + ' --> ' +
CONVERT(VARCHAR(50), end_date, 101),
    server_name,
    instance_name,
    minimum_counter_value / 1000,
    maximum_counter_value / 1000,
    average_counter_value / 1000,
    standard_deviation_counter_value / 1000
FROM dbo.IndexingCountersBaseline
WHERE counter_name = 'Lock Wait Time (ms)'
ORDER BY instance_name,
    CounterDate DESC;
```

As an example, in Figure 16-7, the average and maximum Lock Wait Times have decreased from the baseline values which is what would be desired. In the case where there was an increase in the average lock wait over the baseline, there could be a cause for concern, especially if that increase is in tens of milliseconds. Also, if there were an increase in the range to the maximum value, it would be something else to investigate. The more that the time spent waiting to acquire locks increases, the more it is going to directly impact users.

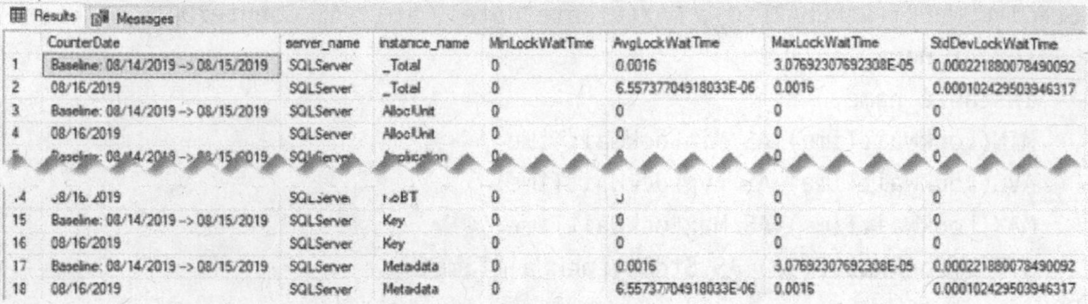

	CounterDate	server_name	instance_name	MinLockWaitTime	AvgLockWaitTime	MaxLockWaitTime	StdDevLockWaitTime
1	Baseline: 08/14/2019 -> 08/15/2019	SQLServer	_Total	0	0.0016	3.07692307692308E-05	0.000221880078490092
2	08/16/2019	SQLServer	_Total	0	6.55737704918033E-06	0.0016	0.000102429503946317
3	Baseline: 08/14/2019 -> 08/15/2019	SQLServer	AllocUnit	0	0	0	0
4	08/16/2019	SQLServer	AllocUnit	0	0	0	0
5	Baseline: 08/14/2019 -> 08/15/2019	SQLServer	Application	0	0	0	0
14	08/16/2019	SQLServer	HoBT	0	0	0	0
15	Baseline: 08/14/2019 -> 08/15/2019	SQLServer	Key	0	0	0	0
16	08/16/2019	SQLServer	Key	0	0	0	0
17	Baseline: 08/14/2019 -> 08/15/2019	SQLServer	Metadata	0	0.0016	3.07692307692308E-05	0.000221880078490092
18	08/16/2019	SQLServer	Metadata	0	6.55737704918033E-06	0.0016	0.000102429503946317

Figure 16-7. *Lock Wait Time counter analysis sample results*

When investigating Lock Wait Time, it is important to identify which indexes are generating the most Lock Wait Time by using the query in Listing 16-20. This information is found in the DMO `sys.dm_db_index_operational_stats` or the monitoring table `dbo.index_operational_stats_history`. The columns reviewed for Lock Wait Time are `row_lock_wait_count`, `row_lock_wait_count`, `row_lock_wait_count`, and `page_lock_wait_in_ms`. These columns report the number of waits per index and the time for those waits. As the columns indicate, there are locks at both the row and page levels; most often the variations between the lock types correlate with seek and scan operations on the index.

Listing 16-20. Lock Wait Time Snapshot Query

```
USE IndexingMethod;
GO

SELECT QUOTENAME(DB_NAME(database_id)) AS database_name,
    QUOTENAME(OBJECT_SCHEMA_NAME(object_id, database_id)) + '.' +
QUOTENAME(OBJECT_NAME(object_id, database_id)) AS ObjectName,
    index_id,
    SUM(row_lock_wait_count) AS row_lock_wait_count,
    SUM(row_lock_wait_in_ms) / 1000. AS row_lock_wait_in_sec,
    ISNULL(SUM(row_lock_wait_in_ms) / NULLIF(SUM(row_lock_wait_count), 0) /
    1000., 0) AS avg_row_lock_wait_in_sec,
    SUM(page_lock_wait_count) AS page_lock_wait_count,
    SUM(page_lock_wait_in_ms) / 1000. AS page_lock_wait_in_sec,
    ISNULL(SUM(page_lock_wait_in_ms) / NULLIF(SUM(page_lock_wait_count), 0) /
    1000., 0) AS avg_page_lock_wait_in_sec
```

```
FROM dbo.index_operational_stats_history oh
WHERE database_id > 4
AND database_id <> DB_ID()
AND (
    row_lock_wait_in_ms > 0
    OR page_lock_wait_in_ms > 0
)
GROUP BY database_id,
    object_id,
    index_id;
```

Looking at the results of the snapshot query, shown in Figure 16-8, there are several things to point out. First, all locks are occurring across the pages of the table, not at the row level. This can result in larger-scale blocking since more than the rows being accessed will be locked. Also, the average page lock is about 7 seconds. For most environments, this is an excessive amount of time for locking. Based on this information, the clustered index (`index_id=1`) on the table `Sales.SalesOrderDetail` should be investigated.

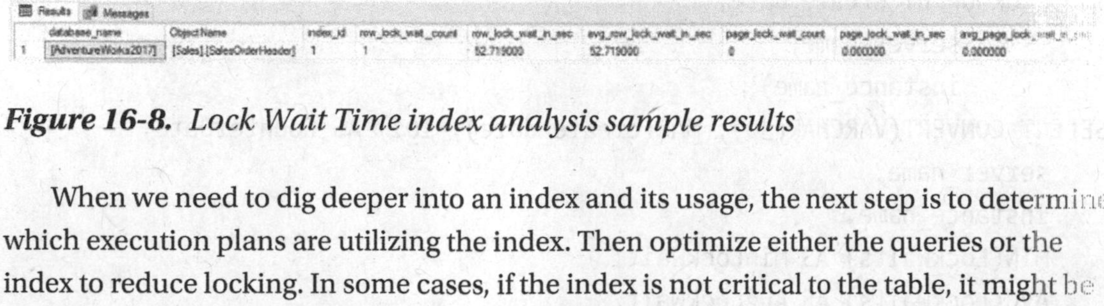

	database_name	ObjectName	index_id	row_lock_wait_count	row_lock_wait_in_sec	avg_row_lock_wait_in_sec	page_lock_wait_count	page_lock_wait_in_sec	avg_page_lock_wait_in_sec
1	[AdventureWorks2017]	[Sales].[SalesOrderHeader]	1	1	52.719000	52.719000	0	0.000000	0.000000

Figure 16-8. Lock Wait Time index analysis sample results

When we need to dig deeper into an index and its usage, the next step is to determine which execution plans are utilizing the index. Then optimize either the queries or the index to reduce locking. In some cases, if the index is not critical to the table, it might be better to remove the index and allow other indexes to satisfy the queries instead.

Lock Waits per Second

The next counter, Lock Waits/sec, has a similar approach for analysis to that of Lock Wait Time (ms). With Lock Waits/sec, the counter measures the number of lock requests that could not be satisfied immediately. For these requests, SQL Server waited until the row or page was available for the lock before granting the lock. As with the previous counter, this one does not have any specific guidelines on what "good" values are. For these, we should turn to the baseline and compare against it to determine when this counter is outside of normal operational boundaries.

The analysis of Lock Waits/sec includes the same minimum, maximum, average, and standard deviation aggregations as used for Lock Wait Time (ms). These values are aggregated for both the per-counter table dbo.IndexingCounters and the baseline table dbo.IndexingCountersBaseline, shown in Listing 16-21. Figure 16-9 displays the results from the query.

Listing 16-21. Lock Waits Counter Analysis

```
USE IndexingMethod;
GO

WITH CounterSummary
  AS (SELECT create_date,
             server_name,
             instance_name,
             MAX(IIF(counter_name = 'Lock Waits/sec', Calculated_Counter_
             value, NULL)) LockWaits
      FROM dbo.IndexingCounters
      WHERE counter_name = 'Lock Waits/sec'
      GROUP BY create_date,
             server_name,
             instance_name)
SELECT CONVERT(VARCHAR(50), MAX(create_date), 101) AS CounterDate,
    server_name,
    instance_name,
    MIN(LockWaits) AS MinLockWait,
    AVG(LockWaits) AS AvgLockWait,
    MAX(LockWaits) AS MaxLockWait,
    STDEV(LockWaits) AS StdDevLockWait
FROM CounterSummary
GROUP BY server_name,
    instance_name
UNION ALL
SELECT 'Baseline: ' + CONVERT(VARCHAR(50), start_date, 101) + ' --> ' +
CONVERT(VARCHAR(50), end_date, 101),
    server_name,
    instance_name,
```

```
     minimum_counter_value / 1000,
     maximum_counter_value / 1000,
     average_counter_value / 1000,
     standard_deviation_counter_value / 1000
FROM dbo.IndexingCountersBaseline
WHERE counter_name = 'Lock Waits/sec'
ORDER BY instance_name,
     CounterDate DESC;
```

There will be times, such as those included in Figure 16-9, when Lock Wait/
sec is not problematic, but there were issues with Lock Wait Time(ms). Those cases
point to long duration blocking situations. Conversely, Lock Wait/sec is important to
monitor since it will indicate when there is widespread blocking. The blocking may
not be long in duration, but it is widespread; a single long block can cause significant
performance issues.

	CounterDate	server_name	instance_name	MinLockWait	AvgLockWait	MaxLockWait	StdDevLockWait
1	Baseline: 08/14/2019 -> 08/15/2019	SQLServer	_Total	0	8E-05	1.53846153846154E-06	1.10940039245046E-05
2	08/16/2019	SQLServer	_Total	0	0.0003715170278863777	0.08	0.00497053990489004
3	Baseline: 08/14/2019 -> 08/15/2019	SQLServer	AllocUnit	0	0	0	0
4	08/16/2019	SQLServer	AllocUnit	0	0	0	0
5	Baseline: 08/14/2019 -> 08/15/2019	SQLServer	Application	0	0	0	0
14	08/16/2019	SQLServer	HoBt	0	0	0	0
15	Baseline: 08/14/2019 -> 08/15/2019	SQLServer	Key	0	0	0	0
16	08/16/2019	SQLServer	Key	0	0	0	0
17	Baseline: 08/14/2019 -> 08/15/2019	SQLServer	Metadata	0	8E-05	1.53846153846154E-06	1.10940039245046E-05
18	08/16/2019	SQLServer	Metadata	0	0.000247678018575851	0.08	0.00445131907259726

Figure 16-9. *Lock Waits counter analysis sample results*

In a situation with widespread blocking, as indicated by high values for Lock Wait/
sec, the analysis will require investigating the statistics of indexes using the DMO sys.
dm_db_index_operational stats. With the monitoring process, this information will
be available in the table dbo.index_operational_stats_history. Using the query
in Listing 16-22, the count and percentage of locks that wait can be determined. As
with Lock Wait Time (ms), this counter analysis also looks at statistics at the row and
page levels.

Listing 16-22. Lock Waits Snapshot Query

```
USE IndexingMethod;
GO

SELECT QUOTENAME(DB_NAME(database_id)) AS database_name,
    QUOTENAME(OBJECT_SCHEMA_NAME(object_id, database_id)) + '.' +
    QUOTENAME(OBJECT_NAME(object_id, database_id)) AS ObjectName,
    index_id,
    SUM(row_lock_count) AS row_lock_count,
    SUM(row_lock_wait_count) AS row_lock_wait_count,
    ISNULL(SUM(row_lock_wait_count) / NULLIF(SUM(row_lock_count), 0), 0) AS
    pct_row_lock_wait,
    SUM(page_lock_count) AS page_lock_count,
    SUM(page_lock_wait_count) AS page_lock_wait_count,
    ISNULL(SUM(page_lock_wait_count) / NULLIF(SUM(page_lock_count), 0), 0)
AS pct_page_lock_wait
FROM dbo.index_operational_stats_history oh
WHERE database_id > 4
AND (
    row_lock_wait_in_ms > 0
    OR page_lock_wait_in_ms > 0
)
GROUP BY database_id,
    object_id,
    index_id;
```

Indexes that have a high percentage of lock waits to locks are prime for index tuning. Often, when there are excessive lock waits on a database, the end users will see slowness in their applications and, in the worst cases, application timeouts. The aim of analyzing this counter is to identify indexes that can be optimized and then to investigate where the indexes are being used. Once this is done, address the causes for the locks, and tune the indexes and queries to reduce the locking on the index.

Number of Deadlocks per Second

In extreme cases, poor indexing and excessive locking/blocking can lead to deadlocks. Deadlocks occur in situations where locks have been placed by two or more transactions in which the locking order of one of the transactions is prevented from acquiring and/ or releasing its locks because of the locks of the other transactions. If an application does not explicitly retry queries that deadlock, then the result can be important transactions never getting executed. This can have profoundly negative consequences for an application that manages important user data. There are a number of ways to address deadlocking, one of which is to improve indexing.

To determine whether deadlocks are occurring on the SQL Server instance, review the performance counters collected during the monitoring process. The query in Listing 16-23 provides an overview of the deadlock rate during the monitoring window. The query returns aggregate values for the minimum, average, maximum, and standard deviation for the deadlocks on the server.

Listing 16-23. Number of Deadlocks Counter Analysis

```
USE IndexingMethod;
GO

WITH CounterSummary
  AS (SELECT create_date,
          server_name,
          Calculated_Counter_value AS NumberDeadlocks
      FROM dbo.IndexingCounters
      WHERE counter_name = 'Number of Deadlocks/sec')
SELECT server_name,
    MIN(NumberDeadlocks) AS MinNumberDeadlocks,
    AVG(NumberDeadlocks) AS AvgNumberDeadlocks,
    MAX(NumberDeadlocks) AS MaxNumberDeadlocks,
    STDEV(NumberDeadlocks) AS StdDevNumberDeadlocks
FROM CounterSummary
GROUP BY server_name;
```

In general, a well-tuned database platform should not have deadlocks occurring. When they occur, each should be investigated to determine the root cause for the deadlock. Before a deadlock can be examined, though, the deadlock first needs to be retrieved. There are a number of ways in which deadlock information can be collected from SQL Server. These include trace flags, SQL Profiler, and event notifications. Another method is through Extended Events, using the built-in system_health session. The query in Listing 16-24 returns a list of all the deadlocks that are currently in the ring_buffer for that session.

Listing 16-24. System-Health Deadlock Query

```
USE IndexingMethod;
GO

WITH deadlock
  AS (SELECT CAST(target_data AS XML) AS target_data
      FROM sys.dm_xe_session_targets st
      INNER JOIN sys.dm_xe_sessions s ON s.address = st.event_
session_address
      WHERE name = 'system_health'
      AND target_name = 'ring_buffer')
SELECT c.value('(@timestamp)[1]', 'datetime') AS event_timestamp,
    c.query('data/value/deadlock')
FROM deadlock d
CROSS APPLY target_data.nodes('//RingBufferTarget/event') AS t(c)
WHERE c.exist('.[@name = "xml_deadlock_report"]') = 1;
```

When deadlocks have been identified, they are returned in an XML document. For most, reading the XML documents is not a natural way to examine a deadlock. Instead, it is often preferable to review the deadlock graph that is associated with the deadlock, such as the one shown in Figure 16-10. To obtain a deadlock graph for any of the deadlocks returned by Listing 16-22, open the deadlock XML document in SQL Server Management Studio, and then save the file with an .xdl extension. When the file is reopened, it will open with the deadlock graph instead of as an XML document.

Figure 16-10. *Deadlock graph in SQL Server Management Studio*

Once deadlocks are identified, it is important to determine why they occur to prevent them from recurring. A common issue that causes deadlocks is the order of operations between numerous transactions. This cause is often difficult to resolve since it may require rewriting parts of applications. To address deadlocks, one of the easiest approaches is to decrease the amount of time in which the transaction occurs. Indexing the tables that are accessed is a typical approach that can resolve deadlocks in many cases by shrinking the window in which deadlocks can be created.

Wait Statistics

The analysis process for wait statistics is similar to that of performance counters. For both sets of data, the information points to areas where resources are potentially being taxed, identifying the resources and indicating next steps. A lot of the same processes for performance counters apply to wait statistics. One main difference between the two sets of information is that wait statistics are looked at as a whole, and their value is determined by comparing them to other wait statistics on the SQL Server instance.

Because of this difference, when reviewing wait statistics, there is only a single query required for analysis. Before using the wait statistics analysis query, provided in Listing 16-25, there are a few aspects to wait statistics analysis that should be discussed. First, as the list of ignore wait stats shows, there are some wait states that accumulate regardless of the activity on the server. For these, there is not any value in investigating behavior related to them, either because they are just the ticking of CPU time on the server or they are related to internal operations that cannot be affected. As such, they are out-of-scope for a discussion of indexing. Second, the value in wait statistics is in looking at them in relationship to the time that has transpired on the server. While one wait state being higher than another is important, without knowing the amount of time that has transpired, there is no scale by which to measure the pressure the wait state is having on the server. To accommodate for this, the waits from the first set of results in the monitoring table are ignored, and the date between them and the last collection point is used to calculate the time that has transpired. The length of time that a wait state occurred compared to the total time provides the values needed to determine the pressure of the wait state on the SQL Server instance.

Note   The pct columns in the results for Listing 16-25 will be null if there is only a single sample in the table dbo.wait_stats_history.

Listing 16-25. Wait Statistics Analysis Query

```
USE IndexingMethod;
GO
WITH WaitStats
  AS (SELECT DENSE_RANK() OVER (ORDER BY w.create_date ASC) AS RankID,
          create_date,
          wait_type,
          waiting_tasks_count,
          wait_time_ms,
          max_wait_time_ms,
          signal_wait_time_ms,
          MIN(create_date) OVER () AS min_create_date,
          MAX(create_date) OVER () AS max_create_date
      FROM dbo.wait_stats_history w
      WHERE wait_type NOT IN ( 'BROKER_EVENTHANDLER', 'BROKER_RECEIVE_
      WAITFOR', 'BROKER_TASK_STOP', 'BROKER_TO_FLUSH', 'BROKER_
      TRANSMITTER', 'CHECKPOINT_QUEUE', 'CHKPT', 'CLR_AUTO_EVENT',
      'CLR_MANUAL_EVENT', 'CLR_SEMAPHORE', 'CXCONSUMER', 'DBMIRROR_
      DBM_EVENT', 'DBMIRROR_EVENTS_QUEUE', 'DBMIRROR_WORKER_QUEUE',
      'DBMIRRORING_CMD', 'DIRTY_PAGE_POLL', 'DISPATCHER_QUEUE_SEMAPHORE',
      'EXECSYNC', 'FSAGENT', 'FT_IFTS_SCHEDULER_IDLE_WAIT', 'FT_IFTSHC_
      MUTEX', 'HADR_CLUSAPI_CALL', 'HADR_FILESTREAM_IOMGR_IOCOMPLETIO,',
      'HADR_LOGCAPTURE_WAIT', 'HADR_NOTIFICATION_DEQUEUE', 'HADR_TIMER_
      TASK', 'HADR_WORK_QUEUE', 'KSOURCE_WAKEUP', 'LAZYWRITER_SLEEP',
      'LOGMGR_QUEUE', 'MEMORY_ALLOCATION_EXT', 'ONDEMAND_TASK_QUEUE',
      'PARALLEL_REDO_DRAIN_WORKER', 'PARALLEL_REDO_LOG_CACHE', 'PARALLEL_
```

```
REDO_TRAN_LIST', 'PARALLEL_REDO_WORKER_SYNC', 'PARALLEL_REDO_WORKER_
WAIT_WORK', 'PREEMPTIVE_HADR_LEASE_MECHANISM', 'PREEMPTIVE_SP_SERVER_
DIAGNOSTICS', 'PREEMPTIVE_OS_LIBRARYOPS', 'PREEMPTIVE_OS_COMOPS',
'PREEMPTIVE_OS_CRYPTOPS', 'PREEMPTIVE_OS_PIPEOPS', 'PREEMPTIVE_OS_
AUTHENTICATIONOPS', 'PREEMPTIVE_OS_GENERICOPS', 'PREEMPTIVE_OS_
VERIFYTRUST', 'PREEMPTIVE_OS_FILEOPS', 'PREEMPTIVE_OS_DEVICEOPS',
'PREEMPTIVE_OS_QUERYREGISTRY', 'PREEMPTIVE_OS_WRITEFILE',
'PREEMPTIVE_XE_CALLBACKEXECUTE', 'PREEMPTIVE_XE_DISPATCHER',
'PREEMPTIVE_XE_GETTARGETSTATE', 'PREEMPTIVE_XE_SESSIONCOMMIT',
'PREEMPTIVE_XE_TARGETINIT', 'PREEMPTIVE_XE_TARGETFINALIZE', 'PWAIT_
ALL_COMPONENTS_INITIALIZED', 'PWAIT_DIRECTLOGCONSUMER_GETNEXT',
'PWAIT_EXTENSIBILITY_CLEANUP_TASK', 'QDS_PERSIST_TASK_MAIN_LOOP_
SLEEP', 'QDS_ASYNC_QUEUE', 'QDS_CLEANUP_STALE_QUERIES_TASK_MAIN_
LOOP_SLEEP', 'REQUEST_FOR_DEADLOCK_SEARCH', 'RESOURCE_QUEUE',
'SERVER_IDLE_CHECK', 'SLEEP_BPOOL_FLUSH', 'SLEEP_DBSTARTUP',
'SLEEP_DCOMSTARTUP', 'SLEEP_MASTERDBREADY', 'SLEEP_MASTERMDREADY',
'SLEEP_MASTERUPGRADED', 'SLEEP_MSDBSTARTUP', 'SLEEP_SYSTEMTASK',
'SLEEP_TASK', 'SLEEP_TEMPDBSTARTUP', 'SNI_HTTP_ACCEPT', 'SOS_WORK_
DISPATCHER', 'SP_SERVER_DIAGNOSTICS_SLEEP', 'SQLTRACE_BUFFER_FLUSH',
'SQLTRACE_INCREMENTAL_FLUSH_SLEEP', 'SQLTRACE_WAIT_ENTRIES',
'STARTUP_DEPENDENCY_MANAGER', 'WAIT_FOR_RESULTS', 'WAITFOR',
'WAITFOR_TASKSHUTDOW', 'WAIT_XTP_HOST_WAIT', 'WAIT_XTP_OFFLINE_CKPT_
NEW_LOG', 'WAIT_XTP_CKPT_CLOSE', 'WAIT_XTP_RECOVERY', 'XE_BUFFERMGR_
ALLPROCESSED_EVENT', 'XE_DISPATCHER_JOI,', 'XE_DISPATCHER_WAIT',
'XE_LIVE_TARGET_TVF', 'XE_TIMER_EVENT'))
SELECT wait_type,
    DATEDIFF(ms, min_create_date, max_create_date) AS total_time_ms,
    SUM(waiting_tasks_count) AS waiting_tasks_count,
    SUM(wait_time_ms) AS wait_time_ms,
    CAST(1. * SUM(wait_time_ms) / NULLIF(SUM(waiting_tasks_count),0) AS
    DECIMAL(18, 3)) AS avg_wait_time_ms,
    CAST(100. * SUM(wait_time_ms) / NULLIF(DATEDIFF(ms, min_create_date,
    max_create_date),0) AS DECIMAL(18, 3)) AS pct_time_in_wait,
    SUM(signal_wait_time_ms) AS signal_wait_time_ms,
    CAST(100. * SUM(signal_wait_time_ms) / NULLIF(SUM(wait_time_ms), 0) AS
    DECIMAL(18, 3)) AS pct_time_runnable
```

```
FROM WaitStats
GROUP BY wait_type,
    min_create_date,
    max_create_date
ORDER BY SUM(wait_time_ms) DESC;
```

The query includes a number of calculations to help identify when there are issues with specific wait types. To best understand the information provided, see the definitions provided in Table 16-1. These calculations and their definitions will help focus the performance issues related to wait statistics.

When reviewing the results of the wait statistics query, shown in Figure 16-11, there are two thresholds to watch. First, if any of the waits exceed 5 percent of the total wait time, there is likely a bottleneck related to that wait type, and further investigation into the wait should happen. Similarly, if any of the waits exceed 1 percent of the time, they should be considered for further analysis, but not before reviewing the items with higher waits. One thing to consider when reviewing wait statistics is that if the time spent on the wait is mostly because of signal wait time, then the resource contention can be better resolved by first focusing on CPU pressure on the server.

Table 16-1. *Wait Statistics Query Column Definitions*

Option name	Description
wait_type	Wait statistics that incurred the wait
total_time_ms	Total amount of time measured by the query in milliseconds
waiting_tasks_count	Count of the number of waits for this wait type
wait_time_ms	Time in milliseconds accumulated for this wait type. This includes the time spent on signal_wait_time_ms
avg_wait_time_ms	Average time per wait type in milliseconds
pct_time_in_wait	Percent of total time spent for this wait type
signal_wait_time_ms	Time in milliseconds accumulated after the wait type was available and no longer waiting before it was running. This is the time spent in the RUNNABLE state
pct_time_runnable	Percentage of time spent for this wait type in the RUNNABLE state

	wait_type	total_time_ms	waiting_tasks_count	wait_time_ms	avg_wait_time_ms	pct_time_in_wait	signal_wait_time_ms	pct_time_running
1	HADR_FILESTREAM_IOMGR_IOCOMPLETION	611513000	560610	281775535	502.623	46.078	45293	0.016
2	PAGEIOLATCH_SH	611513000	174404	1474528	8.455	0.241	26994	1.831
3	PAGEIOLATCH_EX	611513000	61824	160722	2.600	0.026	1005	0.625
4	RESOURCE_SEMAPHORE	611513000	2	122020	61010.000	0.020	0	0.000
5	SOS_SCHEDULER_YIELD	611513000	794601	120025	0.151	0.020	117740	98.096
6	SLEEP_BUFFERPOOL_HELPLW	611513000	3704	58742	15.859	0.010	1116	1.900
7	WRITELOG	611513000	60691	52737	0.869	0.009	7270	13.785
8	LCK_M_IX	611513000	1	48706	48706.000	0.008	81	0.166
9	BACKUPTHREAD	611513000	27	46966	1739.481	0.008	6	0.013
10	BACKUPIO	611513000	2567	45905	17.883	0.008	1543	3.361

Figure 16-11. *Wait statistics analysis output*

Once wait states with issues have been identified, the next step is to review the wait and the recommended courses of actions for the wait. Since this chapter focuses on more index-centric wait types, we'll focus on those definitions only. To learn more about the other wait types, review the Books Online topic for sys.dm_os_wait_stats (Transact SQL).

CXPACKET

The CXPACKET wait type occurs when there are waits due to parallel query execution, otherwise known as *parallelism*. There are two main scenarios where parallel queries can experience CXPACKET waits. The first is when an operator in a parallel query is unable to execute due to other threads already running on the scheduler. The second is when a thread from an operator in a parallel thread takes longer to execute than the rest of the threads and the rest need to wait for the slower thread to complete. The first cause is the more common cause for parallel waits, but it is outside the scope of this book and generally tied to configuration settings and query tuning. The second cause, though, can be addressed through indexing. Often, by addressing the second reason for CXPACKET waits, the first cause of parallel waits can be mitigated as well.

Note   There is a second parallelism wait named CXCONSUMER that identifies waits associated with parallel operators waiting for threads to send rows to the operator. This is generally not an actionable wait and is outside the context of this book.

Two approaches that are common for addressing CXPACKET waits are to adjust the max degree of parallelism and cost threshold for parallelism server properties. As with the first cause of parallelism waits, addressing parallelism with these server properties is outside the context of the book. There are valid approaches for utilizing these two properties, but the focus here is on indexing rather than constraining the degree and cost of parallelism. For a simple explanation, the max degree of parallelism limits the total number of cores that any single query can use during parallel processing. Alternatively, the cost threshold for parallelism increases the threshold in which SQL Server determines that a query can use parallelism, without limiting the scope of parallelism.

What is within the context here is mitigating CXPACKET waits through indexing, which can be paired with query tuning. To address the indexing for queries running in parallel, we need to first identify the queries that are using parallelism. There are a number of ways that queries and indexes participating in parallel operations can be identified.

The first method is to examine execution plans that have used parallelism in previous executions. For this approach, the plan cache can be queried to identify the execution plans that were created that contain parallel operators. This provides an ideal list of queries that may be tuned to reduce the I/O consumed or remove the need for parallelism. The need for the parallel query can sometimes be attributed to improper indexing on the underlying tables. For example, a parallel operation on a table that leverages a scan may be alleviated with an index that supports the predicates or sorts within the query. The query in Listing 16-26 provides a list of execution plans in the plan cache that utilize parallelism.

Listing 16-26. Execution Plans in the Plan Cache That Utilize Parallelism

```
SET TRANSACTION ISOLATION LEVEL READ UNCOMMITTED;
WITH XMLNAMESPACES (
    DEFAULT 'http://schemas.microsoft.com/sqlserver/2004/07/showplan'
)
SELECT COALESCE(
        DB_NAME([p].[dbid]),
        [p].[query_plan].[value]('(//RelOp/OutputList/ColumnReference/@
        Database)[1]', 'nvarchar(128)')
    ) AS [database_name],
    IIF([p].[objectid] <> 0,
        CONCAT(
            QUOTENAME(DB_NAME([p].[dbid])),
            '.',
```

```
        QUOTENAME(OBJECT_SCHEMA_NAME([p].[objectid], [p].[dbid])),
        '.',
        QUOTENAME(OBJECT_NAME([p].[objectid], [p].[dbid]))
    ),
    NULL) AS [object_name],
    [cp].[objtype],
    [p].[query_plan],
    [cp].[usecounts] AS [use_counts],
    [cp].[plan_handle],
    CAST('<?query --' + CHAR(13) + [q].[text] + CHAR(13) + '--?>' AS XML)
    AS [sql_text]
FROM [sys].[dm_exec_cached_plans] AS [cp]
CROSS APPLY [sys].[dm_exec_query_plan]([cp].[plan_handle]) AS [p]
CROSS APPLY [sys].[dm_exec_sql_text]([cp].[plan_handle]) AS [q]
WHERE [cp].[cacheobjtype] = 'Compiled Plan'
AND [p].[query_plan].[exist]('//RelOp[@Parallel = "1"]') = 1
ORDER BY COALESCE(
        DB_NAME([p].[dbid]),
        [p].[query_plan].[value]('(//RelOp/OutputList/
        ColumnReference/@Database)[1]', 'nvarchar(128)')
    ),
    [cp].[usecounts] DESC;
```

Warning   This chapter features a number of queries that are executed against
the plan cache and Query Store. These are accessed through DMOs that provide
access to the execution plans in SQL Server, which allows for investigations
into current and recent execution activity on the server. While this information
is extremely useful, take care when executing this code on production systems.
An overly expensive query against these views can impact the performance
of your SQL Server. Be sure to monitor these types of queries and test them in
nonproduction environments before using them in a production environment.

The next method is similar to using the plan cache, but instead uses the Query Store. Provided this is running on the database, there is a column in sys.query_store_plan that identifies parallel plans. Using this with a few other DMOs provides a list of T-SQL statements that have parallel operators. A query that returns parallel queries from the Query Store is provided in Listing 16-27, which includes a count of the number of executions for the T-SQL statement. One advantage to using the Query Store is that it limits the results down to a single database.

Listing 16-27. Execution Plans in the Query Store That Utilize Parallelism

```
SET TRANSACTION ISOLATION LEVEL READ UNCOMMITTED;
SELECT IIF([qsq].[object_id] <> 0,
         CONCAT(
             QUOTENAME(DB_NAME()),
             '.',
             QUOTENAME(OBJECT_SCHEMA_NAME([qsq].[object_id])),
             '.',
             QUOTENAME(OBJECT_NAME([qsq].[object_id]))
         ),
         NULL) AS [object_name],
    CAST([qsp].[query_plan] AS XML) AS [query_plan],
    [deqs].[execution_count],
    CAST('<?query --' + CHAR(13) + [qsqt].[query_sql_text] + CHAR(13) + '--
?>' AS XML) AS [sql_text],
    [qsp].[engine_version],
    [qsp].[compatibility_level],
    [qsq].[query_parameterization_type_desc],
    [qsp].[is_forced_plan],
    [deqs].[total_worker_time]
FROM [sys].[query_store_plan] AS [qsp]
INNER JOIN [sys].[query_store_query] AS [qsq] ON [qsp].[query_id] = [qsq].
[query_id]
INNER JOIN [sys].[query_store_query_text] AS [qsqt] ON [qsq].[query_text_
id] = [qsqt].[query_text_id]
INNER JOIN sys.[dm_exec_query_stats] AS deqs ON [last_compile_batch_sql_
handle] = [deqs].[sql_handle]
```

```
WHERE [qsp].[is_parallel_plan] = 1
ORDER BY [deqs].[execution_count] DESC,
    [deqs].[total_worker_time] DESC;
```

Another way to research parallelism waits is to investigate plans that are currently executing. This information is available in the DMO sys.dm_os_tasks which returns waits that are currently using multiple workers; a sample query to retrieve this information is provided in Listing 16-28. This query provides a list of currently executing parallel plans.

Listing 16-28. Parallel Queries Currently Executing

```
WITH executing
  AS (SELECT er.session_id,
        er.request_id,
        MAX(ISNULL(exec_context_id, 0)) AS number_of_workers,
        er.sql_handle,
        er.statement_start_offset,
        er.statement_end_offset,
        er.plan_handle
    FROM sys.dm_exec_requests er
    INNER JOIN sys.dm_os_tasks t ON er.session_id = t.session_id
    INNER JOIN sys.dm_exec_sessions es ON er.session_id = es.session_id
    WHERE es.is_user_process = 0x1
    GROUP BY er.session_id,
        er.request_id,
        er.sql_handle,
        er.statement_start_offset,
        er.statement_end_offset,
        er.plan_handle)
SELECT QUOTENAME(DB_NAME(st.dbid)) AS database_name,
    QUOTENAME(OBJECT_SCHEMA_NAME(st.objectid, st.dbid)) + '.' +
QUOTENAME(OBJECT_NAME(st.objectid, st.dbid)) AS object_name,
    e.session_id,
    e.request_id,
    e.number_of_workers,
    SUBSTRING(
        st.text,
```

```
        e.statement_start_offset / 2,
        (CASE
                WHEN e.statement_end_offset = -1 THEN
                LEN(CONVERT(NVARCHAR(MAX), st.text)) * 2
                ELSE e.statement_end_offset END - e.statement_start_offset
        ) / 2
    ) AS query_text,
    qp.query_plan
FROM executing e
CROSS APPLY sys.dm_exec_sql_text(e.plan_handle) st
CROSS APPLY sys.dm_exec_query_plan(e.plan_handle) qp
WHERE number_of_workers > 0;
```

The second way is to start an Extended Events session, capture transaction information, and then group that information on the available call stack. The session, defined in Listing 16-29, retrieves all parallel waits as they occur and groups them by their T-SQL stack. Before running the script, ensure that the value for the CXPACKET wait type matches the value in the query; for SQL Server 2019, the value is 265. The T-SQL stack contains all SQL statements that contribute to a final execution point. For example, drilling through an execution stack can provide information on a stored procedure that is executing a function that executes a single T-SQL statement. This provides details that can be used to track where the parallel wait is occurring. These statements are grouped using the histogram target, which allows us to minimize the size of the collection and focus on the items causing the most CXPACKET waits on the system.

Listing 16-29. Extended Events Session for CXPACKET

```
USE master;
GO
SELECT name,
    map_key,
    map_value
FROM sys.dm_xe_map_values
WHERE name = 'wait_types'
AND map_value = 'CXPACKET';
GO
```

```
IF EXISTS (
    SELECT *
    FROM sys.server_event_sessions
    WHERE name = 'ex_cxpacket'
)
    DROP EVENT SESSION ex_cxpacket ON SERVER;
GO
CREATE EVENT SESSION [ex_cxpacket]
ON SERVER
    ADD EVENT sqlos.wait_info
    (ACTION (
        sqlserver.plan_handle,
        sqlserver.tsql_stack)
     WHERE ([wait_type] = (265)
        AND [sqlserver].[is_system] = (0)))
    ADD TARGET package0.histogram
    (SET filtering_event_name = N'sqlos.wait_info', slots = (2048), source
= N'sqlserver.tsql_stack', source_type = (1))
WITH (STARTUP_STATE = ON);
GO
ALTER EVENT SESSION ex_cxpacket ON SERVER STATE = START;
GO
```

Once the Extended Events session has collected data for a while, the sessions with the most waits can be looked at more closely. Listing 16-30 provides a list of all the CXPACKET waits that have been collected and the statements and query plans associated with them. Once we know these, investigate the indexes being used to determine which are resulting in low selectivity or unexpected scans.

Listing 16-30. Query to View CXPACKET Extended Events Session

```
WITH XData
  AS (SELECT CAST(target_data AS XML) AS TargetData
      FROM sys.dm_xe_session_targets st
      INNER JOIN sys.dm_xe_sessions s ON s.address = st.event_
session_address
      WHERE name = 'ex_cxpacket'
```

```
        AND target_name = 'histogram'),
ParsedEvent
  AS (SELECT c.value('(@count)[1]', 'bigint') AS event_count,
          c.value('xs:hexBinary(substring((value/frames/frame/@handle)
          [1],3))', 'varbinary(255)') AS sql_handle,
          c.value('(value/frames/frame/@offsetStart)[1]', 'int') AS
          statement_start_offset,
          c.value('(value/frames/frame/@offsetEnd)[1]', 'int') AS
          statement_end_offset
      FROM XData d
      CROSS APPLY TargetData.nodes('//Slot') t(c) )
SELECT QUOTENAME(DB_NAME(st.dbid)) AS database_name,
    QUOTENAME(OBJECT_SCHEMA_NAME(st.objectid, st.dbid)) + '.' +
QUOTENAME(OBJECT_NAME(st.objectid, st.dbid)) AS object_name,
    e.event_count,
    SUBSTRING(
        st.text,
        e.statement_start_offset / 2,
        (IIF(e.statement_end_offset = -1, LEN(CONVERT(NVARCHAR(MAX),
st.text)) * 2, e.statement_end_offset)
          - e.statement_start_offset
        ) / 2
    ) AS query_text,
    qp.query_plan
FROM ParsedEvent e
CROSS APPLY sys.dm_exec_sql_text(e.sql_handle) st
CROSS APPLY (
    SELECT plan_handle
    FROM sys.dm_exec_query_stats qs
    WHERE e.sql_handle = qs.sql_handle
    GROUP BY plan_handle
) x
CROSS APPLY sys.dm_exec_query_plan(x.plan_handle) qp
ORDER BY e.event_count DESC;
```

SQL Server 2022 adds a new feature to Intelligent Query Processing (IQP) that greatly improves how parallelism is used in execution plans: Degree of Parallelism Feedback. This is a database-scoped configuration change that allows SQL Server to automatically adjust the degree of parallelism for individual queries when the query optimizer considers the current DOP to be suboptimal for a recurring query. This is a powerful enhancement that can automatically tune parallelism and is especially useful on servers that make heavy use of parallel execution plans. The T-SQL in Listing 16-31 provides the syntax for enabling DOP Feedback in SQL Server 2022+.

Listing 16-31. Query to View CXPACKET Extended Events Session

```
ALTER DATABASE SCOPED CONFIGURATION SET DOP_FEEDBACK = ON;
```

To validate the current (and default) setting for this feature, the T-SQL in Listing 16-32 may be used.

Listing 16-32. Query to View the Current DOP Feedback Setting

```
SELECT
        *
FROM sys.database_scoped_configurations
WHERE database_scoped_configurations.name = 'DOP_FEEDBACK';
```

The results in Figure 16-12 validate that DOP Feedback is now enabled and that the SQL Server default for this feature is disabled.

	configuration_id	name	value	value_for_secondary	is_value_default
1	37	DOP_FEEDBACK	1	NULL	0

Figure 16-12. *DOP_Feedback configuration details.*

While Degree of Parallelism Feedback cannot solve all issues related to parallelism, it can help to automatically correct problems that otherwise would consume valuable time and resources. This is especially valuable in scenarios where there is no clear indexing or query tuning solution available for a parallelism challenge.

IO_COMPLETION

The IO_COMPLETION wait type happens when SQL Server is waiting for I/O operations to complete for nondata page I/Os, such as index pages. Even though this wait is related to nondata operations, there are still some indexing-related actions that can be taken when this wait is high for the SQL Server instance.

First, review the state of Full Scans/sec on the server. If there is an issue with that performance counter, the operations under that counter could bleed through to nondata pages that are being used to manage the indexes. In cases where the two of these are high, place additional emphasis on analyzing Full Scans/sec issues first.

The second action that we can take is to review the missing index information within the SQL Server instance. That information is discussed in Chapter 9. Adding missing indexes can shift the pressure of the data being consumed to new structures where the query may no longer need to wait for the nondata I/Os to complete since the query now leverages a different index.

Next, consider the volume of page splits occurring on the index; page splits affect nondata pages when they reallocate the pages to new pages. Heavy page split activity will result in high nondata page I/Os which can be the source of or related to these waits.

Finally, if the cause of the IO_COMPLETION issues is not apparent, investigate them with an Extended Events session. This type of analysis is outside the scope of this book since these causes would likely be nonindex-related. The method used for investigating CXPACKET could apply and would be a place to start the investigation.

LCK_M_*

The LCK_M_* collection of wait types refers to waits that are occurring on the SQL Server instance. These are not just the use of locks but also the times when locks have waits associated with them. Each wait type in LCK_M_* references a distinct type of lock, such as exclusive or shared locks. To decipher the different wait types, use Table 16-2. When the LCK_M_* wait types increase, they will always be in conjunction with increases in Lock Wait Time (ms) and Lock Waits/sec, allowing these counters to help investigate this wait type.

When investigating increases in either the performance counters or the different lock types, see Table 16-2. Use the combination of the wait types and the performance counters to home in on specific issues. For instance, when the performance counters are pointing to Lock Wait Time (ms) issues, look for long-running waits on LCK_M_*. Use the wizard in SQL Server Management Studio to create the Count Query Lock session and determine which lock and which queries, through the query_hash, are causing the issue. Similarly, if the issue is with Lock Waits/sec, look for those with the most numerous locks.

Table 16-2. *LCK_M_* Wait Types*

Wait type	Lock type
LCK_M_BU	Bulk Update
LCK_M_IS	Intent Shared
LCK_M_IU	Intent Update
LCK_M_IX	Intent Exclusive
LCK_M_RIn_NL	Insert Range lock between the current and previous key with NULL lock on the current key value
LCK_M_RIn_S	Insert Range lock between the current and previous key with shared lock on the current key value
LCK_M_RIn_U	Insert Range lock between the current and previous key with Update lock on the current key value
LCK_M_RIn_X	Insert Range lock between the current and previous key with Exclusive lock on the current key value
LCK_M_RS_S	Shared Range lock between the current and previous key with shared lock on the current key value
LCK_M_RS_U	Shared Range lock between the current and previous key with Update lock on the current key value
LCK_M_RX_S	Exclusive Range lock between the current and previous key with shared lock on the current key value
LCK_M_RX_U	Exclusive Range lock between the current and previous key with Update lock on the current key value
LCK_M_RX_X	Exclusive Range lock between the current and previous key with Exclusive lock on the current key value
LCK_M_S	Shared

(*continued*)

Table 16-2. (*continued*)

Wait type	Lock type
LCK_M_SCH_M	Schema Modify
LCK_M_SCH_S	Schema Share
LCK_M_SIU	Shared with Intent Update
LCK_M_SIX	Shared with Intent Exclusive
LCK_M_U	Update
LCK_M_UIX	Update with Intent Exclusive
LCK_M_X	Exclusive

All the locks in Table 16-2 can appear with the suffixes _ABORT_BLOCKERS and _LOW_PRIORITY which are related to the low priority options added to online index and partition switching operations. This capability has been available since SQL Server 2014. If locks are seen with these suffixes, review the index maintenance operations that are occurring. When the waits are excessive, the maintenance schedule will likely need to be adjusted.

PAGEIOLATCH_*

The final index-related wait is PAGEIOLATCH_* wait types. This wait refers to the waits that occur when SQL Server is retrieving data pages from indexes and placing them into memory. The time in which the query is ready to retrieve the data pages and when they are available in memory is tracked by SQL Server with these counters. As with LCK_M_* waits, there are a number of different PAGEIOLATCH_* types, each of which are defined in Table 16-3.

First, monitor the indexes that are currently in the buffer cache to identify which indexes are available. Also, review the Page Life Expectancy/sec (PLE) counter, which is not currently collected in the monitoring section. Reviewing the allocation of pages to indexes in the buffer before and after changes in the PLE can help identify which indexes are pushing information out of memory. Then investigate query plans, and tune the queries or indexes to reduce the amount of data needed to satisfy the queries.

Table 16-3. *PAGEIOLATCH_* Wait Types*

Wait type	Lock type
PAGEIOLATCH_DT	IO Latch in Destroy mode
PAGEIOLATCH_EX	IO Latch in Exclusive mode
PAGEIOLATCH_KP	IO Latch in Keep mode
PAGEIOLATCH_SH	IO Latch in Shared mode
PAGEIOLATCH_UP	IO Latch in Update mode

The second tactic to addressing PAGEIOLATCH_* is to put more emphasis on the Full Scans/sec analysis. Often, indexes that lead to increases in this wait type are related to full scans that are in use by the database. By placing more emphasis on reducing the need for full scans in execution plans, less data will need to be pulled into memory, leading to a decrease in this wait type.

In some cases, the issues related to PAGEIOLATCH_* are unrelated to indexing. The issue can simply be a matter of slow disk performance. To verify whether this is the case, monitor the performance of the server counters for Physical disk: disk seconds/read and Physical disk: disk seconds/write and the virtual file stats for SQL Server. If these statistics are continually high, expand the investigation outside of indexing to hardware and the I/O storage level. Besides improving disk performance, this wait statistic can be reduced by increasing the available memory, which can decrease the likelihood that the data page will be pushed out of memory.

Note that high PAGEIOLATCH waits may be indicative of memory pressure and a need to increase memory allocation to SQL Server. This should be seen as a last resort when other research and tuning options have already been exhausted.

Buffer Allocation

The final area to look at when determining the server state with indexing is to look at the data pages that are in the buffer cache. This is not a typical area that is usually looked at when considering indexing, but it provides a wealth of information regarding what SQL Server is putting into memory. The basic question that this can answer for the SQL Server instance is: does the data in the buffer represent the data most important to the applications using the SQL Server?

The first part of answering this question is to review how many pages are in memory for each database. This might not seem important, but the amount of memory being used by the different databases can sometimes be surprising. Before indexes were added to the backup tables in the MSDB database, it wouldn't be uncommon for those tables to push all the data in the backup tables into memory. If the data in the tables wasn't trimmed often, this could be a lot of information not critical to the business applications consuming an unnecessary amount of data.

For the second part of the question, we will need to engage the owners and subject matter experts for the applications using the SQL Server instance. If the answers from these individuals do not match the information that is in the buffer, this provides a list of databases for which we can focus the index tuning effort.

Similarly, many applications have logging databases where error and processing events are stored for troubleshooting at a later date. When issues arise, instead of going to log files, the developers can simply query the database and extract the events they need to perform their troubleshooting. But what if these tables aren't properly indexed or the queries aren't SARGable? Log tables with millions or billions of rows may be pushed into memory, pushing the data from the line-of-business applications out of memory and harming overall SQL Server performance. If the data in the buffer is not being checked, there is no way to know what is in memory and if it is valuable or not.

Checking the data in memory is a relatively simple task that utilizes the DMO `sys.dm_os_buffer_descriptors`. This DMO lists each data page that is in memory and describes the information on the page. By counting each page for each database, the total number of pages and the size of memory allocated to the database can be determined. Using the query in Listing 16-33, we can see in Figure 16-13 that the `ContsoRetailDW` database occupies the most memory on the server with the `IndexingMethod` database currently using 8.84 MB of space.

Listing 16-33. Buffer Allocation for Each Database

```
SELECT LEFT(CASE database_id
                WHEN 32767 THEN 'ResourceDb'
                ELSE DB_NAME(database_id) END, 20) AS Database_Name,
    COUNT(*) AS Buffered_Page_Count,
    CAST(COUNT(*) * 8 / 1024.0 AS NUMERIC(10, 2)) AS Buffer_Pool_MB
FROM sys.dm_os_buffer_descriptors
```

```
GROUP BY DB_NAME(database_id),
    database_id
ORDER BY Buffered_Page_Count DESC;
```

	Database_Name	Buffered_Page_Count	Buffer_Pool_MB
1	ContosoRetailDW	8115	63.40
2	AdventureWorks2017	2006	15.67
3	IndexingMethod	1132	8.84
4	tempdb	784	6.13
5	master	226	1.77
6	ResourceDb	136	1.06
7	msdb	94	0.73

Figure 16-13. *Results for buffer allocation for each database query*

Once the databases in memory have been identified, it is also useful to determine what objects in the database are in memory. For the same reason as looking to see what databases are in memory, identifying the objects in memory helps with identifying the tables and indexes to focus on when indexing. Retrieving the memory use per table and index also utilizes sys.dm_os_buffer_descriptors but includes mapping the rows to allocation_unit_id values in the catalog views sys.allocation_units and sys. partitions.

Through the query in Listing 16-34, the memory used by each of the user tables and indexes is returned. In the results in Figure 16-14, it is shown that the tables FactSales and FactOnlineSales are taking up a substantial amount of memory. If this was unexpected and it was not obvious these were fact tables, we would definitely want to understand more about why they were taking up so much memory. This can lead us to other questions, such as: What is this data? Why is it so large? Is the space used by the table impacting the ability of other databases to use memory optimally with their indexes? In these cases, we need to investigate the indexes on these tables because the tables that consume the most memory ought to have the best-honed indexing profiles.

Listing 16-34. Buffer Allocation by Table/Index

```
WITH BufferAllocation
  AS (SELECT object_id,
          index_id,
          allocation_unit_id
```

```
        FROM sys.allocation_units AS au
        INNER JOIN sys.partitions AS p ON au.container_id = p.hobt_id
                                    AND (au.type = 1 OR au.type = 3)
        UNION ALL
        SELECT object_id,
            index_id,
            allocation_unit_id
        FROM sys.allocation_units AS au
        INNER JOIN sys.partitions AS p ON au.container_id = p.hobt_id
                                    AND au.type = 2)
SELECT t.name,
    we.name,
    we.type_desc,
    COUNT(*) AS Buffered_Page_Count,
    CAST(COUNT(*) * 8 / 1024.0 AS NUMERIC(10, 2)) AS Buffer_MB
FROM sys.tables t
INNER JOIN BufferAllocation ba ON t.object_id = ba.object_id
LEFT JOIN sys.indexes we ON ba.object_id = we.object_id
                    AND ba.index_id = we.index_id
INNER JOIN sys.dm_os_buffer_descriptors bd ON ba.allocation_unit_id =
bd.allocation_unit_id
WHERE bd.database_id = DB_ID()
GROUP BY t.name,
    we.index_id,
    we.name,
    we.type_desc
ORDER BY Buffered_Page_Count DESC;
```

	name	name	type_desc	Buffered_Page_Count	Buffer_MB
1	FactSales	PK_FactSales_SalesKey	CLUSTERED	18918	147.80
2	FactOnlineSales	PK_FactOnlineSales_SalesKey	CLUSTERED	17208	134.44
3	FactITSLA	PK_FactITSLA_ITSLAKey	CLUSTERED	9	0.07
4	FactStrategyPlan	PK_FactStrategyPlan_StrategyPlanKey	CLUSTERED	7	0.05
5	DimMachine	PK_DimMachine_MachineKey	CLUSTERED	5	0.04
6	FactITMachine	PK_FactITMachine	CLUSTERED	3	0.02
7	FactInventory	PK_FactInventory_InventoryKey	CLUSTERED	2	0.02
8	DimAccount	PK_DimAccount_AccountKey	CLUSTERED	2	0.02
9	DimGeography	PK_DimGeography_GeographyKey	CLUSTERED	1	0.01
10	DimSalesTerritory	PK_DimSalesTerritory_SalesTerritoryKey	CLUSTERED	1	0.01
11	FactSalesQuota	PK_FactSalesQuota_SalesQuotaKey	CLUSTERED	1	0.01

Figure 16-14. *Results for buffer allocation for each table/index query*

Schema Discovery

After investigating the state of the server and its indexing needs, the next step in the index analysis process is to investigate the schema of the databases to determine whether there are schema-related indexing issues that can be addressed. For these issues, the primary focus will be on a few key details that can be discovered through catalog views.

Identify Heaps

It is often more ideal to utilize clustered indexes on tables as opposed to storing tables as heaps. When heaps are preferred, it should be when the use of a clustered index has been shown to negatively impact performance as opposed to a heap. When investigating heaps, it is best to consider the number of rows and the utilization of the heap. When a heap has a low number of rows or is not being used, taking the effort to cluster its table will likely have little to no impact on performance.

To identify heaps, use the catalog views sys.indexes and sys.partitions. The performance information is available in the table dbo.index_usage_stats_history. It can be used in conjunction to form the query in Listing 16-35, which provides the output in Figure 16-15.

The results show that dbo.DatabaseLog has many rows. The next step is to review the schema of the table. If there is a primary key already on the table, it's a good candidate for the clustered index key. If not, check for another key column, such as a business key. If there is no key column, it may be worthwhile to add a surrogate key to the table.

Listing 16-35. Query to Identify Heaps

```
SELECT QUOTENAME(DB_NAME()) AS database_name,
    QUOTENAME(OBJECT_SCHEMA_NAME(we.object_id)) + '.' + QUOTENAME(OBJECT_
NAME(we.object_id)) AS object_name,
    we.index_id,
    p.rows,
    SUM(h.user_seeks) AS user_seeks,
    SUM(h.user_scans) AS user_scans,
    SUM(h.user_lookups) AS user_lookups,
    SUM(h.user_updates) AS user_updates
FROM sys.indexes we
INNER JOIN sys.partitions p ON we.index_id = p.index_id
                            AND we.object_id = p.object_id
LEFT OUTER JOIN IndexingMethod.dbo.index_usage_stats_history h ON p.object_
id = h.object_id
                                            AND p.index_id = h.index_id
WHERE type_desc = 'HEAP'
GROUP BY we.index_id,
    p.rows,
    we.object_id
ORDER BY p.rows DESC;
```

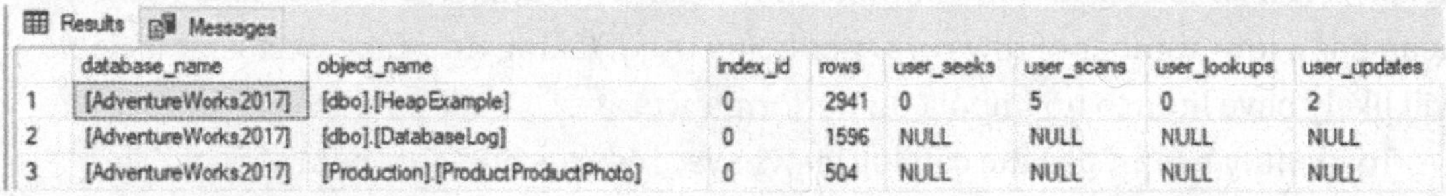

	database_name	object_name	index_id	rows	user_seeks	user_scans	user_lookups	user_updates
1	[AdventureWorks2017]	[dbo].[HeapExample]	0	2941	0	5	0	2
2	[AdventureWorks2017]	[dbo].[DatabaseLog]	0	1596	NULL	NULL	NULL	NULL
3	[AdventureWorks2017]	[Production].[ProductProductPhoto]	0	504	NULL	NULL	NULL	NULL

Figure 16-15. *Output for query identifying heaps*

Duplicate Indexes

The next schema issue to review is duplicate indexes. Except for very rare edge cases, there is no need to have duplicate indexes in a database. They waste space and cost resources to maintain without providing any benefit. To determine that an index is a duplicate of another, review the key columns and included columns of the index. If these values match, the index is considered a duplicate.

To uncover duplicate indexes, the sys.indexes view is used in conjunction with the sys.index_columns catalog view. Comparing these views to each other using the code in Listing 16-36 will provide a list of the indexes that are duplicates. The results from the query, displayed in Figure 16-16, show that in the AdventureWorks2017 database, the indexes AK_Document_rowguid and UQ__Document__F73921F7C5112C2E are duplicates.

When duplicates are found, one of the two indexes should be removed from the database. While one of the indexes will have index activity, removing either will shift the activity from one to the other. Before removing either index, review the non-column properties of the index to make sure important aspects of the index are not lost. For instance, if one of the indexes is designated as unique, be sure that the index retained still has that property.

Listing 16-36. Query to Identify Duplicate Indexes

```
USE AdventureWorks2017;
GO
WITH IndexSchema
  AS (SELECT we.object_id,
        we.index_id,
        we.name,
        ISNULL(we.filter_definition, '') AS filter_definition,
        we.is_unique,
        (
            SELECT QUOTENAME(CAST(ic.column_id AS VARCHAR(10)) + CASE
                                  WHEN ic.is_descending_key = 1 THEN '-'
                                            ELSE '+' END,
                  '('
            )
```

```
        FROM sys.index_columns ic
        INNER JOIN sys.columns c ON ic.object_id = c.object_id
                            AND ic.column_id = c.column_id
        WHERE we.object_id = ic.object_id
        AND we.index_id = ic.index_id
        AND is_included_column = 0
        ORDER BY key_ordinal ASC
        FOR XML PATH('')
    ) + COALESCE((
            SELECT QUOTENAME(CAST(ic.column_id AS VARCHAR(10)) + CASE
                            WHEN ic.is_descending_key = 1 THEN '-'
                            ELSE '+' END,
                    '('
                )
            FROM sys.index_columns ic
            INNER JOIN sys.columns c ON ic.object_id = c.object_id
                                AND ic.column_id = c.column_id
            LEFT OUTER JOIN sys.index_columns ic_key ON c.object_id =
            ic_key.object_id
                                                AND c.column_id =
                                                ic_key.column_id
                                                AND we.index_id =
                                                ic_key.index_id
                                                AND ic_key.is_
                                                included_column = 0
        WHERE we.object_id = ic.object_id
        AND ic.index_id = 1
        AND ic.is_included_column = 0
        AND ic_key.index_id IS NULL
        ORDER BY ic.key_ordinal ASC
        FOR XML PATH('')
    ),
        ''
    ) + CASE
            WHEN we.is_unique = 1 THEN 'U'
            ELSE '' END AS index_columns_keys_ids,
```

```
      CASE
          WHEN we.index_id IN ( 0, 1 ) THEN 'ALL-COLUMNS'
          ELSE COALESCE((
                  SELECT QUOTENAME(ic.column_id, '(')
                  FROM sys.index_columns ic
                  INNER JOIN sys.columns c ON ic.object_id =
                  c.object_id
                                              AND ic.column_id =
                                              c.column_id
                  LEFT OUTER JOIN sys.index_columns ic_key ON
                  c.object_id = ic_key.object_id
                                          AND c.column_id = ic_key.
                                          column_id
                                          AND ic_key.index_id = 1
                  WHERE we.object_id = ic.object_id
                  AND we.index_id = ic.index_id
                  AND ic.is_included_column = 1
                  AND ic_key.index_id IS NULL
                  ORDER BY ic.key_ordinal ASC
                  FOR XML PATH('')
              ),
                  SPACE(0)
              ) END AS included_columns_ids
    FROM sys.tables t
    INNER JOIN sys.indexes we ON t.object_id = we.object_id
    INNER JOIN sys.data_spaces ds ON we.data_space_id = ds.data_space_id
    INNER JOIN sys.dm_db_partition_stats ps ON we.object_id =
    ps.object_id
                                          AND we.index_id =
                                          ps.index_id)
SELECT QUOTENAME(DB_NAME()) AS database_name,
    QUOTENAME(OBJECT_SCHEMA_NAME(is1.object_id)) + '.' + QUOTENAME(OBJECT
    NAME(is1.object_id)) AS object_name,
    is1.name AS index_name,
    is2.name AS duplicate_index_name
FROM IndexSchema is1
```

```
INNER JOIN IndexSchema is2 ON is1.object_id = is2.object_id
                             AND is1.index_id <> is2.index_id
                             AND is1.index_columns_keys_ids = is2.index_
                             columns_keys_ids
                             AND is1.included_columns_ids = is2.included_
                             columns_ids
                             AND is1.filter_definition = is2.filter_
                             definition
                             AND is1.is_unique = is2.is_unique;
```

	database_name	object_name	index_name	duplicate_index_name
1	[AdventureWorks2017]	[Production].[Document]	UQ__Document__F73921F7C5112C2E	AK_Document_rowguid
2	[AdventureWorks2017]	[Production].[Document]	AK_Document_rowguid	UQ__Document__F73921F7C5112C2E

Figure 16-16. *Output for query identifying duplicate indexes*

Note   The original inspiration for the overlapping index query is from the blog post at `http://sqlblog.com/blogs/paul_nielsen/archive/2008/06/25/ find-duplicate-indexes.aspx` by Paul Nielsen.

Overlapping Indexes

After identifying duplicate indexes, the next step is to look for overlapping indexes. An index is considered to be overlapping another index when its key columns make up all or part of another index's key columns. Included columns are not considered when looking at overlapping columns; the focus for this evaluation is only on the key columns.

To identify overlapping indexes, the same catalog views, sys.indexes and sys. index_columns, are used. For each index, its key columns will be compared using the LIKE operator and a wildcard to the key columns of the other indexes on the table. When there is a match, it will be flagged as an overlapping index. The query for this check is provided in Listing 16-37, with the results from executing against the AdventureWorks2017 database shown in Figure 16-17.

Decisions on handling overlapping indexes are not as simple as with duplicate indexes. To help illustrate overlapping indexes, the index IX_SameAsPK was created on the column DocumentNode. This is the same column that is used as the clustering key for the table Production.Document. What this example shows, though, is that a nonclustered index can be considered an overlapping index of a clustered index. In some cases, it might be advisable to remove the overlapping nonclustered index. In reality, the clustered index has the same key, and the pages are sorted in the same manner. We can find the same values in both. The gray area comes in when considering the size of the rows in the clustered index. If the rows are wide enough and if just querying for the clustering key, it will at times be more beneficial to use the nonclustered index instead. In this manner, more time will need to be spent analyzing indexes to determine if an overlapping index has any utility or not. This same gray area will apply to comparisons between two nonclustered indexes as well.

When reviewing overlapping indexes, there are a few other things to note. Be sure to retain the index properties, such as whether the index is unique. Also, pay close attention to the included columns. The included columns are not considered in the overlapping comparison. There may be unique sets of included columns between the two indexes. Watch for this and merge the included columns as appropriate. Similarly, check for filters or other index properties that may provide more context to why specific indexes exist and how to optimize them.

Listing 16-37. Query to Identify Overlapping Indexes

```
WITH IndexSchema
  AS (SELECT we.object_id,
          we.index_id,
          we.name,
          (
              SELECT CASE key_ordinal
                      WHEN 0 THEN NULL
                      ELSE QUOTENAME(column_id, '(') END
              FROM sys.index_columns ic
              WHERE ic.object_id = we.object_id
              AND ic.index_id = we.index_id
              ORDER BY key_ordinal,
                  column_id
              FOR XML PATH('')
          ) AS index_columns_keys
```

```
        FROM sys.tables t
        INNER JOIN sys.indexes we ON t.object_id = we.object_id
        WHERE we.type_desc IN ( 'CLUSTERED', 'NONCLUSTERED', 'HEAP' ))
SELECT QUOTENAME(DB_NAME()) AS database_name,
    QUOTENAME(OBJECT_SCHEMA_NAME(is1.object_id)) + '.' + QUOTENAME(OBJECT_
    NAME(is1.object_id)) AS object_name,
    STUFF((
                SELECT ', ' + c.name
                FROM sys.index_columns ic
                INNER JOIN sys.columns c ON ic.object_id = c.object_id
                                    AND ic.column_id = c.column_id
                WHERE ic.object_id = is1.object_id
                AND ic.index_id = is1.index_id
                ORDER BY ic.key_ordinal,
                    ic.column_id
                FOR XML PATH('')
            ),
        1,
        2,
        ''

    ) AS index_columns,
    STUFF((
                SELECT ', ' + c.name
                FROM sys.index_columns ic
                INNER JOIN sys.columns c ON ic.object_id = c.object_id
                                    AND ic.column_id = c.column_id
                WHERE ic.object_id = is1.object_id
                AND ic.index_id = is1.index_id
                AND ic.is_included_column = 1
                ORDER BY ic.column_id
                FOR XML PATH('')
            ),
        1,
        2,
        ''
```

```
          ) AS included_columns,
          is1.name AS index_name,
          SUM(CASE
                  WHEN is1.index_id = h.index_id THEN
                          ISNULL(h.user_seeks, 0) + ISNULL(h.user_scans, 0) +
                          ISNULL(h.user_lookups, 0)
                          + ISNULL(h.user_updates, 0) END
          ) index_activity,
          is2.name AS duplicate_index_name,
          SUM(CASE
                  WHEN is2.index_id = h.index_id THEN
                          ISNULL(h.user_seeks, 0) + ISNULL(h.user_scans, 0) +
                          ISNULL(h.user_lookups, 0)
                          + ISNULL(h.user_updates, 0) END
          ) duplicate_index_activity
FROM IndexSchema is1
INNER JOIN IndexSchema is2 ON is1.object_id = is2.object_id
                          AND is1.index_id > is2.index_id
                          AND (
                              is1.index_columns_keys LIKE is2.index_
                              columns_keys + '%'
                              AND is2.index_columns_keys LIKE is2.index_
                              columns_keys + '%'
                          )
LEFT OUTER JOIN IndexingMethod.dbo.index_usage_stats_history h ON is1.
object_id = h.object_id
GROUP BY is1.object_id,
    is1.name,
    is2.name,
    is1.index_id;
```

	database_name	object_name	index_columns	included_columns	index_name	index_activity	duplicate_index_name	duplicate_index_activity
1	[AdventureWorks2017]	[Production].[Document]	rowguid	NULL	AK_Document_rowguid	NULL	UQ__Document__F73921F7C5112C2E	209
2	[AdventureWorks2017]	[Production].[Document]	DocumentNode	NULL	IX_SameAsPK	NULL	PK_Document_DocumentNode	28493

Figure 16-17. *Output for query identifying overlapping indexes*

Unindexed Foreign Keys

Foreign keys are useful for enforcing constraints within a database. When there are parent and child relationships between tables, foreign keys provide the mechanism to verify that child tables are not referencing parent values that do not exist. Likewise, the foreign key makes certain that a parent value cannot be removed while child values are still in use (assuming no ON DELETE properties). To support these validations, the columns for the parent and child values between the tables need to be indexed. If one or the other is not indexed, SQL Server can't optimize the operation with a seek and is forced to use a scan to verify that the values are not in the related table. Similarly, if a parent row is deleted, then all rows in the child table need to be checked to determine if there are rows that depend on that value.

Verifying that foreign keys are indexed involves a process similar to the duplicate and overlapping indexes process. Along with the `sys.indexes` and `sys.index_columns` catalog views, the `sys.foreign_key_columns` view is used to provide an index template that the foreign key would rely upon. This is pulled together in the query in Listing 16-38 with results from the AdventureWorks2017 database shown in Figure 16-18.

The common best practice is that every foreign key should be indexed. This will not always be the case for every foreign key, though. There are a few things to consider before adding the index. First, how many rows are in the child table? If the row count is low, adding the index may not provide a performance gain. If the uniqueness of the column is fairly low, statistics may justify a scan of every row regardless of the index. In these cases, it could be argued that if the size of the table is small, the cost of the index is also small, and there is nothing to lose from adding the index. The other consideration is whether data will be deleted from the table and when activities that require validation of the foreign key will occur. With large tables with many columns and foreign keys, performance may suffer from having yet another index to maintain on the table. The index would probably be of value, but is it of enough value to justify creating it?

While those are good considerations when indexing foreign keys, the majority of the time, we will want to index your foreign keys by default. Similar to the recommendation for clustering tables, index your foreign keys unless we have performance documentation showing that indexing the foreign keys negatively impacts performance.

Listing 16-38. Query to Identify Unindexed Foreign Keys

```
WITH cIndexes
  AS (SELECT we.object_id,
         we.name,
         (
             SELECT QUOTENAME(ic.column_id, '(')
             FROM sys.index_columns ic
             WHERE we.object_id = ic.object_id
             AND we.index_id = ic.index_id
             AND is_included_column = 0
             ORDER BY key_ordinal ASC
             FOR XML PATH('')
         ) AS indexed_compare
     FROM sys.indexes we),
cForeignKeys
  AS (SELECT fk.name AS foreign_key_name,
         'PARENT' AS foreign_key_type,
         fkc.parent_object_id AS object_id,
         STUFF((
                 SELECT ', ' + QUOTENAME(c.name)
                 FROM sys.foreign_key_columns ifkc
                 INNER JOIN sys.columns c ON ifkc.parent_object_id =
                 c.object_id
                                     AND ifkc.parent_column_id =
                                     c.column_id
                 WHERE fk.object_id = ifkc.constraint_object_id
                 ORDER BY ifkc.constraint_column_id
                 FOR XML PATH('')
             ),
             1,
             2,
             ''
         ) AS fk_columns,
```

```
            (
                SELECT QUOTENAME(ifkc.parent_column_id, '(')
                FROM sys.foreign_key_columns ifkc
                WHERE fk.object_id = ifkc.constraint_object_id
                ORDER BY ifkc.constraint_column_id
                FOR XML PATH('')
            ) AS fk_columns_compare
        FROM sys.foreign_keys fk
        INNER JOIN sys.foreign_key_columns fkc ON fk.object_id = fkc.
constraint_object_id
        WHERE fkc.constraint_column_id = 1),
cRowCount
    AS (SELECT object_id,
            SUM(row_count) AS row_count
        FROM sys.dm_db_partition_stats ps
        WHERE index_id IN ( 1, 0 )
        GROUP BY object_id)
SELECT QUOTENAME(DB_NAME()),
    QUOTENAME(OBJECT_SCHEMA_NAME(fk.object_id)) + '.' + QUOTENAME(OBJECT_
NAME(fk.object_id)) AS ObjectName,
    fk.foreign_key_name,
    fk_columns,
    row_count
FROM cForeignKeys fk
INNER JOIN cRowCount rc ON fk.object_id = rc.object_id
LEFT OUTER JOIN cIndexes we ON fk.object_id = we.object_id
                            AND we.indexed_compare LIKE fk.fk_columns_
compare + '%'
WHERE we.name IS NULL
ORDER BY row_count DESC,
    OBJECT_NAME(fk.object_id),
    fk.fk_columns;
```

	(No column name)	ObjectName	foreign_key_name	fk_columns	row_count
1	[AdventureWorks2017]	[Sales].[SalesOrderDetail]	FK_SalesOrderDetail_SpecialOfferProduct_SpecialOfferIDP...	[SpecialOfferID], [ProductID]	121317
2	[AdventureWorks2017]	[Production].[WorkOrderRouting]	FK_WorkOrderRouting_Location_LocationID	[LocationID]	67131
3	[AdventureWorks2017]	[Sales].[SalesOrderHeader]	FK_SalesOrderHeader_Address_BillToAddressID	[BillToAddressID]	31465
4	[AdventureWorks2017]	[Sales].[SalesOrderHeader]	FK_SalesOrderHeader_CreditCard_CreditCardID	[CreditCardID]	31465
5	[AdventureWorks2017]	[Sales].[SalesOrderHeader]	FK_SalesOrderHeader_CurrencyRate_CurrencyRateID	[CurrencyRateID]	31465
6	[AdventureWorks2017]	[Sales].[SalesOrderHeader]	FK_SalesOrderHeader_ShipMethod_ShipMethodID	[ShipMethodID]	31465
7	[AdventureWorks2017]	[Sales].[SalesOrderHeader]	FK_SalesOrderHeader_Address_ShipToAddressID	[ShipToAddressID]	31465
8	[AdventureWorks2017]	[Sales].[SalesOrderHeader]	FK_SalesOrderHeader_SalesTerritory_TerritoryID	[TerritoryID]	31465
9	[AdventureWorks2017]	[Sales].[SalesOrderHeaderSalesReason]	FK_SalesOrderHeaderSalesReason_SalesReason_SalesR...	[SalesReasonID]	27647
10	[AdventureWorks2017]	[Person].[PersonPhone]	FK_PersonPhone_PhoneNumberType_PhoneNumberTypeID	[PhoneNumberTypeID]	19972

Figure 16-18. *Output for query identifying missing foreign key indexes*

Uncompressed Indexes

As discussed earlier in this chapter and in other parts of the book, it is usually beneficial to use some level of compression on indexes. With row compression, the indexes generally store fixed-length data as variable length, while page compression examines data and reduces duplication to compress further. In many cases, databases can be reduced to 25–75 percent of their current size through compression. That size reduction increases the amount of data SQL Server can process through the CPU. Oftentimes, the additional CPU cost to compress data is more than offset by the decrease in CPU effort to process the uncompressed data volume.

When examining databases for uncompressed indexes, the query in Listing 16-39 provides a list per database with the filegroup, partition boundary, row count, and size for each index. This information is especially useful because it can help identify the largest indexes where compression could provide the greatest gain. Review the list and determine which indexes to consider compressing, keeping in mind whether there are data types, such as varchar(max), that will compress poorly and may lead to compression failures, as discussed earlier in this chapter.

Listing 16-39. Query to Identify Uncompressed Indexes

```
WITH partitioning
  AS (SELECT dds.data_space_id,
          dds.partition_scheme_id,
          ds.name,
          dds.destination_id AS partition_number,
          CASE
```

```
            WHEN prv.value IS NOT NULL THEN
                CONCAT(
                    IIF(pf.boundary_value_on_right = 1, 'Less than ',
                    'Greater than or equal to '),
                    CAST(prv.value AS VARCHAR(MAX))
                )
            WHEN pf.boundary_value_on_right = 1 THEN 'Greater than MAX
            boundary'
            ELSE 'Less than MIN boundary' END AS Boundary
    FROM sys.destination_data_spaces AS dds
    INNER JOIN sys.partition_schemes AS ps ON ps.data_space_id = dds.
    partition_scheme_id
    INNER JOIN sys.partition_functions AS pf ON pf.function_id =
    ps.function_id
    INNER JOIN sys.data_spaces AS ds ON dds.data_space_id = ds.data_
    space_id
    LEFT OUTER JOIN sys.partition_range_values AS prv ON pf.function_id =
    prv.function_id
                                            AND prv.boundary_id =
                                            dds.destination_id)
SELECT S.name AS schema_name,
    T.name AS table_name,
    I.name AS index_name,
    I.index_id,
    P.partition_number,
    P.data_compression_desc,
    I.type_desc,
    IIF(DS.type_desc = 'PARTITION_SCHEME', PS.name, DS.name) AS file_group,
    PS.Boundary AS partition_boundary,
    DS.type_desc AS data_space_type,
    P.rows,
    CAST(dps.reserved_page_count * CAST(8 AS FLOAT) / 1024. AS DECIMAL(20,
    3)) AS mb_size
FROM sys.tables AS T
INNER JOIN sys.schemas AS S ON S.schema_id = T.schema_id
```

```
INNER JOIN sys.indexes AS I ON T.object_id = I.object_id
INNER JOIN sys.partitions AS P ON I.object_id = P.object_id
                           AND I.index_id = P.index_id
INNER JOIN sys.dm_db_partition_stats AS dps ON P.object_id = dps.object_id
                                        AND P.index_id = dps.index_id
                                        AND P.partition_number = dps.
                                        partition_number
LEFT OUTER JOIN partitioning AS PS ON I.data_space_id = PS.partition_
scheme_id
                                 AND P.partition_number =
                                 PS.partition_number
INNER JOIN sys.data_spaces AS DS ON DS.data_space_id = I.data_space_id
WHERE P.data_compression_desc = 'NONE';
GO
```

Note   The DTA is a good tool for determining useful indexes to add to a database. While there may be more pride in designing indexes for a database by hand without using a tool, it is not practical to ignore useful recommendations. Use the DTA as a starting point to discover indexing suggestions that would have taken hours to determine without the tool in place.

Database Engine Tuning Advisor

The Database Engine Tuning Advisor (DTA) was discussed in Chapter 9. In that chapter, the two modes for using the DTA were discussed: the GUI interface and the command-line utility. While tuning queries is often a process of reviewing statistics and evaluating execution plans, the DTA provides a means to accelerate this analysis by using the trace files from the monitoring process in the previous chapter to identify potentially useful indexing recommendations. This process can accomplish the tuning with minimal impact on the production environment since all recommendations are derived from analysis on a nonproduction environment.

The basic process for using the DTA index analysis can be broken out into five different steps, shown in Figure 16-19:

1. Collect a workload.

2. Gather the metadata.

3. Perform the tuning.

4. Consider recommendations and review.

5. Deploy changes.

Through this process, we can get a jump start on indexing and begin working with recommendations that relate to existing performance issues.

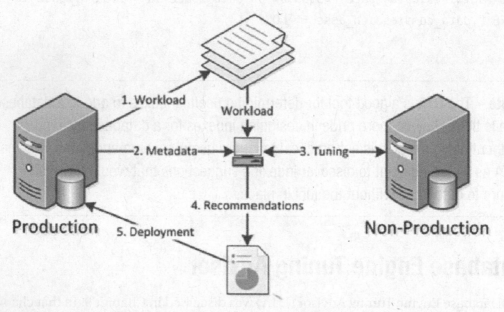

Figure 16-19. *Steps for using the DTA index analysis*

The first step in the process is to collect a workload. If we followed the process in the index monitoring process from the previous chapter, this information should already have been collected. There are two standard scenarios that workloads should represent. To begin, collect a workload that represents a typical day, because even a normal day can have underlying performance issues that tuning can help alleviate. Second, gather a workload during times where performance problems are known to exist. This will be useful for providing recommendations that may be able to be achieved through manual tuning.

After the workload is collected, the next step is to gather the necessary metadata to start the tuning sessions. There are two components to gathering metadata. The first is to create an XML input file for the DTA session. The XML input file contains the production and nonproduction server names and information on where the workload is and what type of tuning options to utilize (Listing 16-40 shows a sample). For more information on tuning options, see Chapter 9. The second part of this step is the effect on tuning from the first piece. When the tuning occurs, SQL Server will gather the schema and statistics for the database from the production database(s) and move that information to the nonproduction server. While the database won't have the production data, it will have the information necessary to make indexing recommendations.

Listing 16-40. Sample XML Input File for DTA

```xml
<?xml version="1.0" encoding="utf-16" ?>
<DTAXML xmlns:xsi="http://www.w3.org/2001/XMLSchema-instance"
xmlns="http://schemas.microsoft.com/sqlserver/2004/07/dta">
  <DTAInput>
    <Server>
      <Name>STR8-SQL-PRD</Name>
      <Database>
        <Name>AdventureWorks2017</Name>
      </Database>
    </Server>
    <Workload>
      <File>c:\temp\IndexingMethod.trc</File>
    </Workload>
    <TuningOptions>
      <TestServer>STR8-SQL-TEST </TestServer>
      <FeatureSet>IDX</FeatureSet>
      <Partitioning>NONE</Partitioning>
      <KeepExisting>NONE</KeepExisting>
    </TuningOptions>
  </DTAInput>
</DTAXML>
```

> **Note**   We can find more information on the XML input file configuration in Books Online at `https://learn.microsoft.com/en-us/sql/tools/dta/simple-xml-input-file-sample-dta?view=sql-server-ver16`.

The next step is the actual execution of the DTA tuning session. To run the session, execute the DTA command using the `-ix` command-line option, shown in Listing 16-41. Since all the configuration information for the session is located in the XML file, there is no need to add any additional parameters.

Listing 16-41.   DTA Command with XML Input File

```
dta -ix "c:\temp\SessionConfig.xml"
```

After the tuning session completes, a list of index recommendations will be received. This is not the last step in this portion of the process. Before any recommendations from the DTA can be implemented, they must be reviewed. While using this tool will accelerate the index analysis process, all recommendations need to be reviewed and vetted to verify that they make sense and do not overload a table with more indexes than SQL Server can support for the workload.

The last step is to deploy the indexing recommendations. This step is technically outside the scope of this phase of the Indexing Method. At this time, though, we should be familiar with the indexing changes that will be implemented. Add these changes to the existing list of indexing changes from other analysis, and prepare them for implementation, which is discussed in the next chapter.

Unused Indexes

One of the necessary and potentially dangerous steps during index analysis is determining which indexes to remove. Some indexes will be removed because of consolidation or because they are duplicates. Often these have less risk than when indexes are dropped. The indexes in this other category are those that are unused.

The easiest manner for identifying indexes that are not used is to check the list of indexes in each database against the `dbo.index_usage_stats_history` table in the `IndexingMethod` database. If there are any unused indexes in the database, the query in Listing 16-42 will identify them. One word of caution with unused indexes: In this analysis, heaps and clustered indexes are ignored, along with any unique indexes and primary keys. Indexes with these properties are often related to other business rules, and their removal should be based on other factors. Figure 16-20 shows an example of unused indexes in the AdventureWorks2017 database.

Listing 16-42. Query for Unused Indexes

```
SELECT OBJECT_NAME(we.object_id) AS table_name,
    COALESCE(we.name, SPACE(0)) AS index_name,
    ps.partition_number,
    ps.row_count,
    CAST((ps.reserved_page_count * 8) / 1024. AS DECIMAL(12, 2)) AS
size_in_mb,
    COALESCE(ius.user_seeks, 0) AS user_seeks,
    COALESCE(ius.user_scans, 0) AS user_scans,
    COALESCE(ius.user_lookups, 0) AS user_lookups,
    we.type_desc
FROM sys.all_objects t
INNER JOIN sys.indexes we ON t.object_id = we.object_id
INNER JOIN sys.dm_db_partition_stats ps ON we.object_id = ps.object_id
                                AND we.index_id = ps.index_id
LEFT OUTER JOIN sys.dm_db_index_usage_stats ius ON ius.database_id
= DB_ID()
                                        AND we.object_id = ius.
object_id
                                        AND we.index_id = ius.
index_id
WHERE we.type_desc NOT IN ( 'HEAP', 'CLUSTERED' )
AND we.is_unique = 0
AND we.is_primary_key = 0
AND we.is_unique_constraint = 0
AND COALESCE(ius.user_seeks, 0) <= 0
AND COALESCE(ius.user_scans, 0) <= 0
AND COALESCE(ius.user_lookups, 0) <= 0
ORDER BY OBJECT_NAME(we.object_id),
    we.name;
```

	table_name	index_name	partition_number	row_count	size_in_mb	user_seeks	user_scans	user_lookups	type_desc
1	Address	IX_Address_StateProvinceID	1	19614	0.38	0	0	0	NONCLUSTERED
2	BillOfMaterials	IX_BillOfMaterials_UnitMeasureCode	1	2679	0.26	0	0	0	NONCLUSTERED
3	BusinessEntityAddress	IX_BusinessEntityAddress_AddressID	1	19614	0.45	0	0	0	NONCLUSTERED
4	BusinessEntityAddress	IX_BusinessEntityAddress_AddressTypeID	1	19614	0.45	0	0	0	NONCLUSTERED
5	BusinessEntityContact	IX_BusinessEntityContact_ContactTypeID	1	909	0.20	0	0	0	NONCLUSTERED
6	BusinessEntityContact	IX_BusinessEntityContact_PersonID	1	909	0.20	0	0	0	NONCLUSTERED
7	CountryRegionCurrency	IX_CountryRegionCurrency_CurrencyCode	1	109	0.07	0	0	0	NONCLUSTERED
8	Customer	IX_Customer_TerritoryID	1	19820	0.38	0	0	0	NONCLUSTERED
9	Document	IX_Document_FileName_Revision	1	13	0.07	0	0	0	NONCLUSTERED
10	Document	IX_SameAsPK	1	13	0.07	0	0	0	NONCLUSTERED

Figure 16-20. *Output for query identifying missing foreign key indexes*

While this section did not discuss it, there are two additional scenarios for identifying unused indexes. These are lightly used indexes or no longer used indexes. A similar process can be used for these situations: instead of looking for indexes that have never been used, filter for low usage rates or no use in a period of weeks or months. But do not remove these indexes automatically without further research and consideration. If the index is lightly used, verify how the index is being used before dropping it. It may be used once a day, but that one use might be tied to critical processes. Also, with unused indexes, verify that the index is not part of a seasonal process. Removing indexes tied to seasonal activity can create more of a burden than maintaining them in off-peak times. For example, a large or complex monthly report may rely on an index to be able to complete in a reasonable amount of time, or using an acceptable amount of computing resources (or both).

Index Plan Usage

In previous sections of this chapter, the concept of checking the plan cache to analyze and investigate index usages was discussed. While statistics can show that there was a seek or a scan against an index, it does not provide enough detail to indicate which columns to add or what caused the index to use a scan rather than a seek. To gather this information, the execution plan needs to be consulted. And the place where execution plans for your databases are found is the plan cache. In this section, for index analysis, we'll be reviewing two queries that can be used to retrieve execution plans from the plan cache.

The first query is one that will be used when there is a need to retrieve all the plans for a specific index. Suppose we need to determine what processes, or T-SQL statements, are using one of the indexes on a table that is used once or twice a day. For this, we can turn to the plan cache with the query in Listing 16-43 and check whether the plan for that query is still in the cache. To use the query, replace the index name in the variable @ IndexName, and execute it to return a list of plans that use the index. Be cautious if with a database where there are many indexes with the same name, since index names need to be unique only on a per-table basis. If all indexes are named IX_1 and IX_2, we will need to verify the table name in the search to be certain the correct index is identified.

Listing 16-43. Query Plan Cache for Index Usage

```
SET TRANSACTION ISOLATION LEVEL READ UNCOMMITTED;
GO
DECLARE @IndexName sysname = 'PK_SalesOrderHeader_SalesOrderID';
SET @IndexName = QUOTENAME(@IndexName, '[');
WITH XMLNAMESPACES (
    DEFAULT 'http://schemas.microsoft.com/sqlserver/2004/07/showplan'
)
, IndexSearch
  AS (SELECT qp.query_plan,
            cp.usecounts,
            ix.query('.') AS StmtSimple
     FROM sys.dm_exec_cached_plans cp
     OUTER APPLY sys.dm_exec_query_plan(cp.plan_handle) qp
     CROSS APPLY qp.query_plan.nodes('//StmtSimple') AS p(ix)
     WHERE query_plan.exist('//Object[@Index = sql:variable ("@
     IndexName")]') = 1)
SELECT StmtSimple.value('StmtSimple[1]/@StatementText', 'VARCHAR(4000)') AS
sql_text,
    obj.value('@Database', 'sysname') AS database_name,
    obj.value('@Schema', 'sysname') AS schema_name,
    obj.value('@Table', 'sysname') AS table_name,
    obj.value('@Index', 'sysname') AS index_name,
    ixs.query_plan
FROM IndexSearch ixs
CROSS APPLY StmtSimple.nodes('//Object') AS o(obj)
WHERE obj.exist('//Object[@Index = sql:variable("@IndexName")]') = 1;
```

At other times, searching for just the name of an index will be too broad of a search of the plan cache. In these cases, the query in Listing 16-44 can be used. This query adds in the name of a physical operator to the plan cache search. For instance, suppose we are investigating Full Scans/sec and we know what index is causing the spike in the performance counter. Searching for just the index may return dozens of execution plans. Alternatively, we could add a search for a particular operator, such as an index scan, using the @op variable in the query provided.

Listing 16-44. Query Plan Cache for Index Usage and Physical Operation

```
DECLARE @IndexName sysname = 'IX_SalesOrderHeader_SalesPersonID';
DECLARE @op sysname = 'Index Scan';
;WITH XMLNAMESPACES (
    DEFAULT N'http://schemas.microsoft.com/sqlserver/2004/07/showplan'
 )
SELECT cp.plan_handle,
    DB_NAME(dbid) + '.' + OBJECT_SCHEMA_NAME(objectid, dbid) + '.' +
    OBJECT_NAME(objectid, dbid) AS database_object,
    qp.query_plan,
    c1.value('@PhysicalOp', 'nvarchar(50)'),
    c2.value('@Index', 'nvarchar(max)')
FROM sys.dm_exec_cached_plans cp
CROSS APPLY sys.dm_exec_query_plan(cp.plan_handle) qp
CROSS APPLY query_plan.nodes('//RelOp') r(c1)
OUTER APPLY c1.nodes('IndexScan/Object') AS o(c2)
WHERE c2.value('@Index', 'nvarchar(max)') = QUOTENAME(@IndexName, '[')
AND c1.exist('@PhysicalOp[. = sql:variable("@op")]') = 1;
```

Both of these queries provide mechanisms for investigating indexes in their environment and seeing exactly how SQL Server is using them. This information can be easily leveraged to identify when problems are occurring and why and then provide a path to resolving indexing issues without a lot of the guesswork that many use today.

Summary

As this chapter showed, the information collected from monitoring indexes can be used to analyze indexes and identify which require further research. The results from this analysis help to determine what types of indexes to modify and where. Indexing tools such as the Database Engine Tuning Advisor and missing index DMOs can be leveraged to discover "the low-hanging fruit," providing a head start on analysis that may not have been discovered otherwise. By following the processes laid out in this index analysis, we can build a stable, repeatable indexing process that can help improve the performance of your database platform and achieve stable performance over time.

If specific indexing changes are recommended by multiple types of analysis in this chapter, then prioritize those changes as they are more likely to be beneficial and have a greater positive impact on performance.

CHAPTER 17

Indexing Methodology

Throughout this book, we've discussed what indexes are, what they do, patterns for building them, and many other aspects for determining how a SQL Server database should be indexed. All that information is necessary for the last puzzle piece in database indexing, which is a methodology for managing indexes. To do this, a process is needed for applying that knowledge to determine the indexes that are best for an environment and provide the greatest performance gains.

In this last chapter, a general practice will be discussed that can be used to build an indexing methodology. A list of steps necessary to manage indexes will be provided. This methodology can be applied to a single database, a server, or an entire SQL Server environment. Regardless of the type of operations or business the database supports, the same methodology for building indexes can be used.

The Indexing Method

Before you can begin creating and dropping indexes, a process is first needed to analyze current and potential indexes. This process needs to provide a way to observe your databases and determine the indexes that are appropriate for them. As mentioned in previous chapters, indexing should be more science than an art. The information needed to properly index a database is available; through some research, potential indexes can be identified. Similar to how scientists use the scientific method to prove theories, database administrators and developers can use the Indexing Method to prove what indexes a database requires.

The Indexing Method used in this book is comprised of three phases: Monitor, Analyze, and Implement (see Figure 17-1). Within each component are a number of steps that, when completed, help to provide the appropriate indexing for the database. At the completion of the Implement phase, the Indexing Method restarts the first phase, making indexing a continuous and iterative process.

© Edward Pollack and Jason Strate 2023
E. Pollack and J. Strate, *Expert Performance Indexing in Azure SQL and SQL Server 2022*,
https://doi.org/10.1007/978-1-4842-9215-0_17

When starting with the Monitor phase, the primary activity is to observe the indexes. The observations entail reviewing both the performance and the behavior of the indexes (i.e., the indexing concepts described in Chapter 15). SQL Server will use the indexes that it finds most beneficial from those available. By observing this behavior, you can identify the indexes that are most often used and how they are used.

After the observations, the Analyze phase of the Indexing Method begins. In the Analyze phase, detailed in Chapter 16, the statistics collected in the previous phase are used to determine what indexes are best suited for the database. The goal is to identify what indexes need to be created, dropped, and modified. Along with this, the impacts of any indexing changes are also identified.

The last phase of the Indexing Method is the Implementation phase. In this phase, the indexes from the last phase are applied (or deployed) to the databases. For every database and environment, the deployment process may be different. For instance, the process for deploying indexes on third-party databases differs from applications owned by your company. Within this phase, though, there are core concepts that apply to all environments; outside of physically building the indexes, you will need to communicate the change plan and possible effects of the change. Then, you need to track the changes over time. There is more to implementing indexes than executing a CREATE INDEX statement.

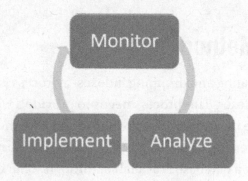

Figure 17-1. *The indexing life cycle*

After the last phase completes, the Indexing Method begins again with the first phase. In this way, indexing is a continuous and circular process. The indexes that provide the best performance today may not be the ideal indexes for tomorrow. Two events primarily contribute to the need for changing indexes over time. The first is data usage, where the functions and features of applications can change over time, so the purpose of the application can also change. Second, the data population and distribution can, and usually will, change over time. With these changes, indexes may shift out of usage, and other data access paths may be required. Data changes are not the only things that can cause index usage to change; changes to the query optimizer in a future SQL Server version or service pack may adjust how indexes are used by it.

Now that the basics of the Indexing Method are covered, the remainder of this chapter will focus on the Implement portion. The concepts for the Monitor and Analyze phases are covered in Chapters 15 and 16, respectively. It is important that as you learn more about indexes, new patterns will be discovered that can be used to identify indexes. As you learn more about indexing and your databases, you will find other ways to look at performance and usage statistics that provide more, or better informed, guidance. Use this book and the information you learn to continue to expand your indexing methodology.

Implement

The final phase of the Indexing Method is the Implement phase. This phase does as the name implies: it implements the indexing changes that were determined as necessary through the Analyze phase. While this phase is less complex, there are some important steps that need to be completed during the Implement phase that will help build out a successful process. The aim of the entire process is to improve the performance of a database environment. With this aim, there are three key points to consider during implementation:

- Communication
- Source code control (e.g., via deployment scripts)
- Execution

While the last step is the only one where the database is modified, the other two help ensure that the changes will be noticed and that the Indexing Method can continue to be used in the future.

Communication

The first hurdle in modifying the indexes on any database is the need to communicate with management and users of the database your intent to change the database. Modifications to the database can often raise red flags, especially when they are being prescribed by nonowners of the application the database supports. Preparing for and implementing open lines of communication between the owners of applications and the database administration and development teams will help not only in the indexing process but in other areas of mutual interest. Without this communication, teams can be blindsided by the indexing changes, which may impact something that the analysis did not uncover or a feature that is planned but not yet released.

When it comes to communication, there are basically two items that need to be prepared for the owners of the databases: an impact analysis of the indexing changes and a status report of the changes after implementation. This is analogous to the quality assurance processes that are followed when new features are architected, released, and tested.

Impact Analysis

When preparing for changes to indexing on a database, it is important to highlight the intended changes to application performance. Historically, this may have sometimes been a guessing game. There was not a lot of easily accessed information that would indicate where an index is being used, how it is being used, and the frequency of use.

With the processes laid out in the Monitor phase, you gain the ability to confidently understand index usage. You can determine when it was last used and what operations were included. There is information that can also be used to identify the trend in which an index will no longer be used or is being used more frequently.

Through the Analyze phase, steps were laid out that allow the identification of execution plans that are using different indexes. Use these steps to identify where an index change will have an impact, and then perform sample executions of the T-SQL statements before and after the indexing changes are made.

Ultimately, the impact analysis will impact two important roles within the Implement phase. First, it will communicate to managers and peers the intent of the indexing changes, informing them of the changes to validate what is being done and allowing them the chance for feedback. Second, the impact analysis provides an insurance policy in case an index change has an unexpected negative impact. This is not to say that there will not be negative repercussions to poor indexing recommendations, but with others involved and the impact documented, it is more likely that a negative impact can be mitigated quickly, possibly even before that impact is realized in a production environment.

Note   In one environment that I worked in, some lightly used indexes were removed from the database. They were generally used once per day. That one time was for a business-critical import process that could not perform without them. Had an impact analysis been done prior to removing those indexes, a lot of tough questions could have been avoided.

Status Report

On the opposite end of the Implement phase is the status report. As the name implies, the status report is a document that provides feedback to managers and peers about the actual impact of indexes. This document does not need to be extensive, but it does need to cover some key points. The status report should cover the following information:

- All index changes made

- Status on deployment of changes

- Brief performance review

- Information on any regressions noted

- What was learned in the deployment process

- Summary of issues encountered

Do not get too mired in the details while writing the status report. A successful indexing deployment will lead to additional Monitor and Analyze phases in the future. In the end, the status report needs to communicate two things. First, it provides an honest assessment of the successes and failures of the indexing deployment. Second, and most importantly, it lists what benefits are now being realized by the indexing changes. This is most important because it is the return on investment (ROI) that managers need to see to be able to justify the time and effort spent on indexing.

> **Note**   One of the most successful things I did as a consultant was constantly
> updating customers about the impact of indexing changes I'd make. A graph
> with before and after performance often looked like a "self-pat on the back"
> with some of the teams I was assisting, but the management that brought me in
> found it incredibly useful in identifying the ROI of bringing in consultants but also
> communicating further up the line the effort being placed in resolving business
> concerns with performance.

Deployment Scripts

The primary deliverable from the Analyze phase is a list of index changes that are
planned for the databases in your environment. During the Implement phase, those
indexes need to be reviewed and prepared for deployment. As part of preparing the
indexes for deployment, three steps need to occur:

1. Prepare the deployment and rollback of the schema.

2. Save index changes to source code control.

3. Share results of peer review with impact analysis.

Prepare Deployment and Rollback of Schema

Usually, at the completion of the Analyze phase, you will have a list of the index
changes that are being proposed. This list typically is not in a state that can be used
for deployment at the end of the phase. Between that point and the execution of the
changes, the indexing changes need to be put into a state that can be used for their
deployment.

When building the deployment scripts, be sure to observe the idea of "doing no
harm" to the database. In other words, scripts should be built that are intelligent enough
that they can be executed multiple times with the identical results. Also, this means that
scripts should be available to reverse any indexing changes being made. Never assume
that the previous indexing state of a table is being stored in source code control. Check
to be certain that the existing state is known, and develop scripts to revert to that state
if needed.

The deployment scripts also need to be aware of the edition of SQL Server that is being used. For instance, if you are using Enterprise Edition, leverage online index rebuilds for indexes that are being rebuilt with new characteristics. If appropriate for the index, Enterprise Edition also allows for compression on the index, which can save space and improve performance in many cases.

Similarly, ensure that deployment scripts are written to minimize disruption to production systems. If offline operations are required, ensure that they occur at times when such disruptions are acceptable to the affected application. Similar guidance should be considered for operations that will lock tables or cause blocking. Deployments that are less disruptive will not only impact software applications less, but they are less likely to cause operational problems for the database servers that are being targeted with the deployment script.

Save Index Changes to Source Code Repository

The current state of the indexes on tables should be in a source code repository. If they are not, then this iteration through the Implement phase provides the perfect opportunity to do so. Source code repositories offer a place to store the code, or schema, for a database to allow an organization to determine what the index, table, or store procedure schema was at a specific date and time. Source code is often well managed from an application perspective. Developers are usually quick to choose a tool and leverage it for their applications.

Source code repositories allow for point in time recovery for the database schema. If there are any development teams within an organization, they likely already have a desired repository in place. This may be an internal repository like Perforce or an externally available solution like GitHub.

Peer Review with Impact Analysis

The last thing to do before the Execution step is to seek a peer review of the indexing changes. There is nothing worse than working in a vacuum and not understanding the entirety of the impact of the changes that are being proposed against the applications that use the databases. It is easy to succumb to tunnel vision by focusing on the indexing goal and miss the business goals of the current deployment or overlook something that was not apparent in the index analysis. This peer review is analogous to code review processes that are used by software development teams. If your team already has processes in place to peer-review database scripts, then this need is already met.

The best way to avoid these pitfalls is to find a peer to review the indexing changes. Bring to the peer the index deployment scripts and the impact analysis, and go over the changes. Your peer does not necessarily need to know everything about the environment, just a basic understanding of indexing. The aim of the peer review is to explain each change. In this dialog, your peer serves as a sounding board as you explain the indexing need. This serves a dual role. First, your peer will be able to provide feedback on the indexing change. Second, by discussing the changes, you may hear yourself describe an indexing change that does not sound correct when it is explained.

In some environments, you may not have a peer that you can turn to review the indexes. In these cases, consider going to your manager for the peer review. If that is not possible, talk to your manager about leveraging others in your technical network. Leverage the forums and social networks to find either a peer or group of peers that will be willing to review your changes with you. Using social networks, such as Twitter, to connect with a technical peer and review some indexing changes is much better than not having a peer review at all.

With the peer review complete, the indexes are ready for the next step in the Implement phase: the step where the indexes are applied to the databases.

Note   Within the SQL Server community, Twitter is one of the more active social networking tools. Use hashtags `#sql` and `#sqlserver` to find general information on SQL Server. When looking for answers to questions specifically about SQL Server, you can use the hashtag `#sqlhelp`. Twitter also allows you to add people to your conversation by including their Twitter handle in the tweet. For instance, the authors of this book are available through the twitter handles `@stratesql` and `@edwardpollack`.

Execution

The last piece of the Implement phase is the execution of the T-SQL scripts that will apply the indexing changes to the database. These scripts should already be prepared through the Deploy Scripts step, and the scope of the changes should be well known from the Communication step. Thus, the Execution step should be relatively painless as the preparation work is already completed.

From an execution standpoint, the manner of execution is completely dependent on your organization's change control process. In some environments, there are automated processes where scripts can be loaded to a deployment mechanism and executed on a schedule. In others, an administrator will simply open SQL Server Management Studio and execute each script until all the changes are completed. Whatever the mechanism, the key is that the indexes get deployed.

As the deployment progresses, be sure to catalog the changes made and any issues that arise during execution. Pay attention to unintended blocking on the databases. If indexes are being deployed in an offline state, be sure to select an execution window that is during the database maintenance window. Remember even online index operations can cause short-lived blocking.

Repeat

At the beginning of this chapter, the discussion started by looking at the three phases of the Indexing Method. The diagram for the process (Figure 17-1) shows the three phases in a loop, with each phase leading to the next. This choice in layout was intentional. Indexing is not a fixed-point activity. Once the first round of the Indexing Method is completed, it is important to start the next round of indexing.

It can be tempting, when databases are properly tuned, to let the practice of indexing slip and to focus on other priorities. Unfortunately, new features are often added to applications as frequently as new data is added to the database. Both of these events will change the way in which indexes are used by the database and the effectiveness of the current state of "good" indexes.

To maintain the desired performance of a database platform, indexes must be continuously reviewed. This is not to say that a full-time resource always needs to be assigned to monitoring, analyzing, and implementing indexes. There does, though, need to be an acceptance that at some interval an evaluation of the state of indexing will be completed.

Summary

As this chapter showed, the Indexing Method is quite similar to the scientific method. Within a database platform, statistics can be collected on indexes in order to identify where indexing issues may exist. These statistics can then be further used to determine the types of indexes to modify and where. Indexing tools such as the Database Engine Tuning Advisor and missing index DMOs can be leveraged to discover "the low-hanging fruit," providing a head start on analysis that may not have been found otherwise. By following the phases laid out in the Indexing Method, you can build a stable, repeatable indexing process that can help improve the performance of your database platform and achieve stable performance over time.

Index

A

Accent sensitivity, 220, 221, 229
AdventureWorks2017 database, 97, 115,
    133, 137, 309, 331, 589, 592,
    596, 605
ALTER INDEX statement, 22, 294, 297,
    310, 436
Authorization, 220
Automatic Index Management, 325
AVG_RANGE_ROWS column, 102

B

Back pointer, 88
Balancing index count, 263, 264
Books, 2–14, 53, 218
Boot page, 32, 34, 70
B-trees, 40, 42–44, 46–49, 58, 60, 72, 90,
    158, 162, 182, 202, 212, 366
Bulk Changed Map page, 37
Bulk-loading, 46–47
BULK_LOGGED recovery model, 37
Bw-tree, 212

C

Cardinality, 96, 98, 100, 206, 218, 219, 315,
    316, 318
Cause Forwarded Records, 90
Cells-per-object rule, 183, 184, 186
Cleanup process, 35, 276, 514

Clustered indexes, 4, 48, 49
    characteristics, 365
    data, 389
    ever-increasing, 366
    foreign key pattern
        attributes, 372
        considerations, 379
        execution plans, 375–378
        header-to-detail relationship, 379
        implementation, 373
        multiple header rows, 377
        one-to-many relationship, 372
        queries, 375
        results, 375–378
        single header row, 375
        tables, 373, 374
        use cases, 374
    GUID pattern
        attributes, 389
        ever-increasing value, 386
        functions, 386
        vs. identity column pattern, 388
        methods, 386
        output, 388
        script, 387, 388
        space, 386
        sp_sequence_get_range, 389
        storage, 386
        tables, 387
        values, 387
    identity column pattern, 383, 384

J, K

L

X, Y

Z

Printed in the United States
by Baker & Taylor Publisher Services.

Printed in the United States
by Baker & Taylor Publisher Services